THE
Good Skiing
& Snowboarding
Guide 1999

The 500 best ski and snowboard resorts
around the world

Edited by Peter Hardy
and Felice Eyston

in association with the
Ski Club of Great Britain

CONSUMERS' ASSOCIATION

Which? Books are commissioned by
Consumers' Association and published by
Which? Ltd, 2 Marylebone Road, London NW1 4DF
Email address: guidereports@which.net

Distributed by The Penguin Group:
Penguin Books Ltd, 27 Wrights Lane, London W8 5TZ

First edition of *The Good Skiing Guide*: 1985
This edition September 1998

The views expressed herein are those of the Editors, and not necessarily those
of the Ski Club of Great Britain.

Editors	Peter Hardy and Felice Eyston
Sub-editor	Caroline Ellerby
Researchers	Jane Blount, Fiona Foote, Clare Thompson
Contributors	David Allsop, Minty Clinch, Doug Sager, Arnie Wilson
Design	Editorial Design Partnership
Cover design	Kyzen Creative Consultants
Cover photos	Don Cole Harvey for Skishoot
Maps	Holmes Linnette

British Library Cataloguing-in-Publication Data:
A catalogue record for this book is available from the British Library

ISBN 0 85202 734 6

For a full list of Which? books, please write to:
Which? Books, Castlemead, Gascoyne Way, Hertford X, SG14 1LH
or access our web site at: www.which.net

Typeset by	Editorial Design Partnership, London
Printed and bound in Spain by	Bookprint, Barcelona (The Hanway Press Ltd)

Contents

Email address
You can now send your resort reports by email to:
guide.reports@which.net

Introduction

European ski resorts are no longer trailing their slicker and fitter North American rivals in the annual bid to attract British skiers. They have lost the race. A lack of vision combined with a consequent lack of investment has seen all but a handful of the major European resorts sitting back on a beach of complacency, watching the sands of their former success slip through their fingers. Dozens of Alpine destinations have failed to grasp the needs of the average skier and snowboarder in the closing seasons of the century.In the course of a decade, the number of British skiers annually crossing the Atlantic has risen tenfold, from a trickle to a flood that shows no sign of abating.

Favourable exchange rates for the Canadian and, to a lesser extent, the US dollar during the post-recession years have contributed to but are not the causal factor of the popularity of US resorts. What skiers appreciate in North America are the superior lift systems, lack of over-crowding and fair prices combined with spacious, high-quality accommodation as well as the key ingredient which European resorts consistently fail to produce – courtesy towards customers. The simple truth is that North America offers better value for money. In addition, the investment currently being made in resorts is so enormous that it will take your breath away – that is if the shockingly refrigerated air of the northern Rockies in mid-winter has not already done so.

Big money

Take the case of Mont Tremblant in Canada. Intrawest, the world's largest ski resort developer, which already owns Whistler in British Columbia and 51 per cent of Mammoth in California – not to mention Panorama in British Columbia, Mont Sainte-Marie in Quebec, Copper Mountain in Colorado, Stratton in Vermont, and Snowshoe/Silver Creek in West Virginia – is in the process of investing CDN$1 billion over eight years to transform the sleepy Quebec village of Mont Tremblant, with its handful of antiquated lifts, into an international winter sports destination. By the year 2002 Intrawest expects that a total of two million visitors will be skiing here each winter and playing its three championship golf courses during the summer months. A recent addition to the Intrawest portfolio is Vernon Valley/Great Gorge in New Jersey, where a reported US$20 to $40 million has been allotted for renovations.

Paupers by comparison

Verbier, a Swiss resort of world renown, is a pauper by comparison. It proudly announced in 1998 that by the turn of the century it would – after a decade of prudent investment and frugal expenditure – be in a position to replace the antiquated Tortin cable-car, at a cost of £5 million.

In the 1996–7 season Kitzbühel, Austria's supreme alpine showcase, finally found the £13 million needed to replace the 70-year-old

Hahnenkamm cable-car with a new high-capacity gondola – but only after ten years of heated discussion.

In Italy, Cervinia, one of the most popular Italian resorts, still cannot find the funds to replace the ancient Furggen cable-car five years after its closure for safety reasons.

Yet in the past year the American Skiing Company, owner of a clutch of East Coast resorts, has snapped up Heavenly in California, Steamboat in Colorado and is in the process of pumping US$200 million into The Canyons in Utah in time for the next Winter Olympics. Meanwhile, in the four months leading up to the start of last season, Vail Resorts sunk US$75 million into improving lifts and mountain facilities at Vail, Beaver Creek, Breckenridge and Keystone. And they have even more ambitious plans for this season.

Buck up or shut up

If they want to compete against this level of dollar investment, the major European resorts have got to face the fact that the time is coming when they will have to 'buck' up or shut up. Skiers form a particularly discerning segment of the holiday market, one that is no longer prepared to accept high prices in return for second-rate standards of both facilities and service. Would you rather have lunch in a seedy self-service in the Trois Vallées, where a surly waiter slams down a £5 bowl of cold chips on the counter, or do you want a sumptuous and limitless hot buffet for the same money in Banff/Lake Louise served with a genuine smile of welcome?

The replacement of ancient cable-cars with jumbo gondolas, the changing of fixed double chair-lifts to high-speed detachable quads and the slow eradication of the T-bar seem to be the main preoccupations of the few European resorts that are susceptible to the tide of progress. But these changes alone are not solutions. Moving the crowd from the lift station to unaltered pistes is nothing short of dangerous. However, resort directors argue that in most cases the necessary complementary development of the mountainside is severely restricted by environmental issues.

While every effort must be made to conserve the heritage of the Alps in its natural format, growing evidence suggests a clash of interests between mountain users and central government. It may not be long before we see the equivalent of Britain's Countryside Alliance, in its fight to maintain rural rights, in the mountains of France, Switzerland and Austria.

What is needed is a fundamental rethink by the top dozen European ski destinations on what they are actually trying to achieve. This needs to be done with the participation of their clients, the skiers, whose interests appear to be secondary to overt commercial goals. The overriding need for improvement is not just in lifts but also in service. The first step in halting the defection of European skiers to Canada is for key resort employees at every level to take a look at the opposition. A spanking new six-seater chair-lift with magnificent views of the snow-clad Alps is not a solution unless you have six skiers or snowboarders to sit on it.

Both cool and warm

Sadly, it has taken the deaths of two well-known public figures to focus on the controversial subject of safety helmets for skiers and snowboarders. On New Year's Eve 1997 Michael Kennedy, son of the late Senator Robert F. Kennedy, was killed when he crashed into a tree while skiing on piste in Aspen. One week later Sonny Bono, the former husband of singer and actress Cher, died in a similar tragedy at Heavenly in California. Neither man was wearing any form of head protection. For the past five years *The Good Skiing and Snowboarding Guide* has campaigned for all children under the age of 14 to wear safety helmets, but now this clearly needs to be extended to include adults in certain conditions: off-piste skiing through trees, skiing rocky couloirs, and for those who ski particularly fast on the piste.

Ten years ago it was inconceivable that cyclists should wear helmets, but today it is unusual to see anyone cycling the streets of London without one. We are confident that skiing and snowboarding will follow a similar pattern. Last season in the United States helmet manufacturers used the publicity surrounding the two tragedies to increase sales. On-piste test centres allowed snow-users to try out different styles of helmet free of charge, and already about ten per cent of all recreational skiers and snowboarders in the US are wearing helmets.

In resorts such as Smuggler's Notch in Vermont, ski and snowboard school instructors are encouraged to do the same – and most of them do. As one teacher, Don Foote, put it: 'Everyone knows that they ought to wear a helmet but it is going to take a little more time before everyone wants to wear one. Not only does it give protection but it is comfortable and warm. At Smuggler's Notch, too, where most of our clients are children, we're extremely conscious that, as instructors, we are role models. If we wear them, then it shows that helmets are cool'.

A new range of helmets with ventilation and ear grilles has been developed to meet the demands of snow-users, but as yet the safety movement is confined to the United States. The only helmeted skiers we saw in Canada last season were Americans, while in Europe the practice is still strictly confined to racers. However, just as carving skis made their début in the US before conquering the world, safety helmets will surely follow the same path.

The 1997–8 season

The season began in Europe with adequate snow for Christmas, augmented by a general top-up over New Year, and all seemed set for a classic season. What followed were two months of almost unbroken sunshine with no further serious snowfalls until March. It is a tribute to the efficiency of modern snowmaking that the quality of skiing remained so remarkably high throughout January and most of February. The March snow came too late to last in most lowland resorts, where the ground had already warmed with the onset of an early spring. The great exception was a large part of Austria, where substantial falls produced Utah-style powder conditions in mid-March in Salzburgerland.

On the other side of the Atlantic, the East Coast had a season of poor cover, saved again by snowmaking on such a grand and successful scale that the real thing has become almost an optional extra.

SnowBlades

Salomon's on-snow answer to in-line skates has taken both the US and Europe by storm. For those still unfamiliar with the latest sliding sport, SnowBlades (used without poles) are short skis that bring yet another new dimension to the business of going down mountains as fast and with as much fun as you can. The mini-ski starts from the level of technology that its forerunner, BigFoot, aspired to; accomplished skiers can tackle any piste at the same speed or often considerably more quickly than a companion on conventional skis. One size of ski and an easily adjustable binding that fits all boots make it simple for anyone to have a go, and we think that SnowBlades are an important innovation that adds to the fun of a ski holiday.

Where and when to ski this winter

Most European ski resorts open in mid-December but will not necessarily run their entire lift system until the weekend before Christmas. American ski resorts traditionally open for Thanksgiving in the second half of November. At the start of the season, it is essential to choose a resort with a high top-station where at least some skiing is guaranteed. 'Safe' resorts in Europe include Val d'Isère/Tignes, Val Thorens, Les Deux Alpes, Alpe d'Huez, Saas-Fee, Zermatt and Obergurgl.

Prices and crowds peak over Christmas and New Year, the second week being the busier of the two – and the one to be avoided if you mind queuing.

The French February and April school holidays are staggered by geographical zones to avoid the gross overcrowding that used to be a feature of the main French ski resorts. Nevertheless, it is prudent to avoid the entire period if you can. The dates for winter 1998–9 are: 3 February to 3 March and 3 April to 3 May. At the very least, you should try to avoid the Paris holidays (17 February to 3 March and 17 April to 3 May). Visitors to the French Pyrenees and Andorra should note the holiday dates for Toulouse (10–24 February and 10–26 April).

How you can help

In order to update the Guide accurately each year, we need your help. Together with our team of researchers we try to visit as many resorts as possible, but it is not feasible to visit them all in a 20-week season. Lifts are constantly being upgraded, the standards of hotels and restaurants rise and fall. We need you to relate your ski holiday experiences – both the good and the bad – in as much detail as possible. Readers who send the best letters will receive a free copy of the Guide. Further details on how you can help can be found in 'Reporting on the resorts'. Remember too that you can email your report to us at guide.reports@which.net

The Ski Club of Great Britain and *The Good Skiing and Snowboarding Guide*

The Ski Club of Great Britain has enjoyed a strong association with *The Good Skiing Guide*, now *The Good Skiing and Snowboarding Guide*, for many years. Founded in 1903, it is the largest and most active club for British skiers and snowboarders in the UK. Catering for skiers and snowboarders of all ages, it offers members services and benefits unavailable elsewhere.

Information and web site

The Club's information department provides members with impartial details and recommendations for over 300 resorts around the world. The Club's award-winning web site (www.skiclub.co.uk) contains information on Club matters as well as regular snow reports.

Reps in resorts

The Ski Club's reps – unpaid volunteers, trained and experienced in leading groups of skiers and snowboarders in search of the best snow – now operate in approximately 40 resorts in Europe and North America.

Holidays

The Ski Club's holiday programme covers 30 resorts in 8 countries. Holidays are organised by skiing standard and run by Ski Club reps/leaders. A wide range of ski instruction trips is offered, together with off-piste and advanced tours.

Events and other member benefits

The Ski Club keeps its members informed about their sports and enables them to meet at social events. Members receive five free copies per year of the Club magazine *Ski and Board* (retailing at £2.75), and discounts from ski shops, tour and ferry operators, and artificial ski slopes.

INTRODUCTORY HALF-PRICE MEMBERSHIP OFFER
Only £22.50 – Individual, £33 – Family

This introductory offer, covering one year, is subject to production of the **corner flash** from the first page of this book, as proof of purchase, and signing a direct debit for your second and subsequent subscriptions. The offer expires on 30 April 1999 and may not be used in conjunction with any other offers.

To take advantage of this offer and for further information, call the Club's membership department on **0181-410 2015**

Family skiing

S kiing as a family can be one of life's great experiences. Few sensations match the thrill of seeing your child make his or her first wobbly turns down the mountain. Despite what you may hear from other families, it is possible to have a successful family skiing holiday. Not being a complete beginner yourself is an asset, but the most important requirements are an endless supply of energy and patience, and careful preparation. But, first you have to find your way through an avalanche of brochures to choose your resort and accommodation.

Which country?

Austria is the standard beginner territory, with its traditional villages, undemanding pistes and family-run hotels. Italy does not cater for families as well as you would expect – childcare for pre-school children is extremely limited. Switzerland is a more expensive option. France features in nearly all of the specialist family tour operator brochures; the prices and food are desirable, and parents will find enough skiing to keep themselves amused. Scandinavia is still relatively undiscovered by British families, but Norway and Sweden are fast becoming the most child-friendly of European ski countries. The instructors speak fluent English, safety on the slopes is paramount and queues are a rarity.

North America is recommended for a near-perfect family skiing holiday with all the right ingredients. Each resort, large or small, has unparalleled facilities for children. Ski lessons are fun and flexible, and the staff are dedicated to making your child happy. However, the comparatively higher cost and a long transatlantic flight may deter a lot of people.

Where to stay

Choosing the right accommodation is one of the vital ingredients of a successful family skiing holiday. Whichever country you choose, the hotels, chalets and apartments will all have their good and bad points. Remember that proximity to the nursery slopes, the lifts and ski school rendezvous place is a great energy-saver. Apartments are the cheapest option but are for dedicated shoppers and cooks, or for families with older children who are happy to eat out. All too easily what the parents hoped would be a week of relaxation becomes a working holiday.

A growing number of hotels are now embracing the family market. But hotels should be chosen with care: a combination of informality, other children, and tolerant staff will help. Remember to book the necessary extras such as cots and high-chairs, and check that some form of evening child-minding is available. An in-house crèche is a bonus, and a child-friendly dining-room essential, as are family-sized bedrooms.

Chalets offer a home-from-home experience and you will not have to worry about disturbing other guests. The chalet staff cook a separate children's supper, and babysitting can also be arranged. All the specialist family operators listed here should provide cots and other necessities.

A handful of resorts stand out as having the interests of the family at heart. France's best family resorts include Les Arcs, Avoriaz, La Clusaz, Courchevel, Les Deux Alpes, Les Gets and Valmorel. In Austria Kitzbühel, Mayrhofen, Obergurgl, Obertauern, Saalbach-Hinterglemm and Schladming all have good facilities. In Switzerland, Zermatt is trying hard to improve with a new non-ski kindergarten, while Wengen on the other hand has made its ski school hours less family-friendly. Selva Gardena is the best bet in Italy.

All the North American resorts are superb, with well-run ski schools and state-of-the-art facilities. There is no language barrier, and the teachers really do make the whole business of learning enjoyable. Almost every North American resort is recommended, but the outright winner must be Smuggler's Notch in Vermont, which is purpose-built for children. It would be prudent for those responsible for managing the major resorts in Europe to discover for themselves exactly what makes this village so outstanding for families. Other particularly family-friendly North American resorts are Beaver Creek, Keystone, Mammoth and Snowmass in the USA, as well as Lake Louise, Mont Tremblant and Whistler in Canada.

In 1992 the French Ministry of Tourism created a 'Label Kid' seal of approval. The aim is to help the public to identify the resorts that offer child-friendly facilities, activities and security, and which are adapted to children's needs. Les Arcs and La Clusaz both have a three-kids grading –which is the highest level – and all the resorts mentioned above have received a Label Kid stamp.

This season 21 tour operators offer specialist family skiing holidays.The large operators give you the widest choice, but the advantage of a small operator with only a couple of resorts is that the person on the other end of the phone may actually have been there. Check that your tour operator employs NNEB (Nursery Nurse Examination Board) or equivalently qualified British nannies.

Clothing and equipment

Borrow or hire appropriate ski clothing for your children whenever possible, and rent rather than buy equipment. A jacket and salopettes are more flexible than a one-piece suit, because the jacket can also be worn for the journey, for après-ski, and at home. Prices vary according to quality, and with ski wear, more than with any other garments, you get what you pay for. Modern 'breathable' fabrics such as Gore-Tex are more waterproof and hard-wearing than cheaper materials.

Ski tips

- Helmets are a vital safety measure
- Goggles are more practical than sunglasses, because they have a strap that fits around the helmet and are therefore less likely to break or get lost
- Mittens are warmer than gloves

- Do not send your child out skiing with sunscreen of less than Sun Protection Factor (SPF) 15, whatever the weather
- Forget about taking a pushchair – it will not work in a foot of snow. Take a baby backpack or hire a toboggan when you get to the resort
- Thermal underwear is essential in December and January, and at any time if you are going to North America
- Pack more nappies than you think you will need – the familiar brands may not be available in your resort

Specialist operators with childcare:
Club Med (0700 258 2633)
Collineige (01276 24262)
Crystal (0181 399 5144)
Inghams (0181 780 4444)
Mark Warner (0171 761 7002)
Meriski (01451 844788)
Neilson Ski (0990 994444)
Powder Byrne (0181 871 3300)
Silver Ski (01622 735544)
Simply Ski (0181 742 2541)
Ski Airtours (0541 504001)
Ski Club of Great Britain/Fresh Tracks (0181 410 2000)
Ski Esprit (01252 616789)
Ski Famille (01223 363777)
Ski Hillwood (0181 866 9993)
Ski Olympic (01709 579999)
Ski Peak (01252 794941)
Ski Scott Dunn (0181 767 0202)
Snowbizz Vacances (01778 341455)
Snowline Holidays (0181 870 4807)
Thomson Breakaway (0990 329329)

Using the Guide

The ratings (maximum three stars) at the start of each resort chapter show its suitability for different categories of skiers and for snowboarders. The tables on the following pages record our verdicts on the advantages and disadvantages of the resorts we have covered in detail in the Guide. Resorts are listed in alphabetical order by country to aid comparisons. Having selected one or more resorts from the tables, you should read the relevant section(s) in the following chapters. In the tables, we have focused on certain aspects of the resorts, which have been graded good or bad. This is indicated by a tick or a cross; where they are satisfactory the space is left blank.

A few headings need further clarification: **Snow probability** is based on the likelihood of skiing being possible in or around the resort, especially at the beginning of the season. **Tree-level** skiing denotes those resorts that offer sheltered skiing on bad-weather days, with the subsequent improvement in visibility. Ugly mountain scenery does not exist, so we have only used the affirmative tick for particularly **Outstanding scenery,** such as in the Dolomites. **Resort charm** applies to villages that either have beautiful architecture, like Kitzbühel, or are rich in atmosphere, like Alpbach or Jackson Hole. Aesthetically unpleasing resorts and busy towns with particularly heavy traffic receive a cross.

Big vertical drop applies to resorts that have a difference of at least 1300m in Europe and 1000m in North America from the top to the bottom of the ski area. In assessing how good or bad a resort is for **Tough runs**, we have concentrated on whether the resort as a whole is likely to appeal to skiers who relish a challenge. A tick for **Low prices** indicates the resort is cheaper than some others in the same country.

Après-ski receives a tick not only for a lively nightlife but also for a large choice of good restaurants, as in Aspen and Whistler. **Family skiing** refers to resorts suitable for a family with a mixture of ages. **Children's facilities** refers to whether or not a resort has ski - and non-ski kindergarten facilities. Resorts rated highly for easy **Resort access** are those that present no local difficulties for drivers, or are close to an airport, or have direct rail links.

The key on the right shows the types of lifts and grading of runs on the colour piste-maps.

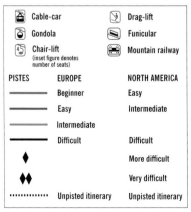

🚠	Cable-car	🚡	Drag-lift
🚟	Gondola	🚞	Funicular
🚡	Chair-lift (inset figure denotes number of seats)	🚃	Mountain railway

PISTES	EUROPE	NORTH AMERICA
	Beginner	Easy
	Easy	Intermediate
	Intermediate	
	Difficult	Difficult
◆		More difficult
◆◆		Very difficult
··············	Unpisted itinerary	Unpisted itinerary

15

AUSTRIA

	Beginners	Intermediates	Advanced	Snowboarders	Large ski area	Off-piste/ski-touring	Summer skiing	Cross-country	Lift queues
Alpbach	✔	✔	✗		✗				✔
Bad Gastein	✗	✔			✔			✔	
Innsbruck	✔	✔		✔			✔	✔	✗
Ischgl	✗	✔		✔	✔	✔			
Kitzbühel	✔	✔	✗		✔			✔	
Lech/Zürs	✔	✔		✔	✔	✔			✔
Mayrhofen	✔	✔	✗		✔		✔		
Niederau	✔		✗		✗				
Obergurgl	✔		✗			✔			
Obertauern	✔	✔	✗			✔			✔
Saalbach-Hinterglemm	✔	✔		✔	✔				✗
Schladming	✔	✔	✗		✔		✔	✔	
Söll and the Ski-Welt	✔	✔			✔				
St Anton	✗	✔	✔		✔	✔			
Zell am See/Kaprun	✔	✔		✔		✗	✔	✔	

	Long runs	Tree-level skiing	Big vertical drop	Skiing convenience	Snow probability	Non-skiing	Mountain restaurants	Outstanding scenery	Resort charm	Compact village	Traffic/car free	Resort access	Late holidays	Low prices	Après-ski	Family skiing
		✔		✘		✔	✔			✘	✘	✔		✔	✔	✘
					✔		✘	✔	✔				✔	✘	✔	
	✔			✔	✔		✘	✔	✔			✘		✘		✔
	✘	✔		✘								✔	✘	✔		✔
		✔		✔	✔	✘				✘	✔		✔		✘	✔
		✔	✘				✔					✔			✔	✔
	✔		✔	✔	✘					✘			✔		✔	✘

	Beginners	Intermediates	Advanced	Snowboarders	Large ski area	Off-piste/ski-touring	Summer skiing	Cross-country	Lift queues	
FRANCE										
Alpe d'Huez	✔	✔	✔	✔	✔	✔	✔		✔	
Les Arcs	✔	✔	✔	✔	✔	✔			✔	
Avoriaz	✔	✔	✔	✔	✔					
Barèges/La Mongie	✔	✔	✗						✗	
Chamonix	✗		✔	✔	✔	✔			✗	
Châtel	✔	✔		✔	✔					
Courchevel	✔	✔	✔	✔	✔	✔				
Les Deux Alpes		✔		✔	✔	✔	✔			
Flaine	✔	✔		✔	✔	✔			✔	
Megève	✔	✔	✗		✔			✔		
Les Menuires		✔	✔		✔	✔				
Méribel		✔	✔		✔	✔				
Montgenèvre	✔	✔			✔					
Morzine	✔	✔		✔	✔			✔		
La Plagne	✔	✔	✗	✔	✔	✔	✔	✔		
Risoul 1850	✔	✔	✗	✔	✔				✔	
La Rosière	✔	✔	✗						✔	

Long runs	Tree-level skiing	Big vertical drop	Skiing convenience	Snow probability	Non-skiing	Mountain restaurants	Outstanding scenery	Resort charm	Compact village	Traffic/car free	Resort access	Late holidays	Low prices	Après-ski	Family skiing
✔	✔	✔	✔	✔	✘		✔	✘		✔	✔	✔		✘	✔
				✘					✔		✔	✘	✔	✘	
✔				✘	✘				✘	✘	✔	✘		✘	✔
	✘	✔		✔	✘	✘	✔	✘	✘	✘		✔		✔	✔
✔	✔			✘	✔	✔		✔	✘	✘	✔	✘	✘	✔	✔
✔			✔						✘	✘					✔
✔	✔		✔	✘	✔				✘	✘	✔	✘			✔
	✔		✔	✔	✘	✘			✔	✔	✘	✔	✔	✘	✔

19

RESORT VERDICTS

	Beginners	Intermediates	Advanced	Snowboarders	Large ski area	Off-piste/ski-touring	Summer skiing	Cross-country	Lift queues
Serre Chevalier/Briançon	✔	✔		✔	✔	✔		✔	
Tignes	✗	✔	✔	✔	✔	✔	✔		✔
Val d'Isère	✗	✔	✔	✔	✔	✔	✔		✔
Valmorel	✔	✔			✔				
Val Thorens		✔	✔	✔	✔	✔	✔		✔
ITALY									
Bormio	✔	✔	✗		✗		✔		✔
Canazei	✔	✔			✔	✔		✔	✗
Cervinia	✔	✔	✗		✔		✔		✗
Cortina d'Ampezzo	✔	✔	✔		✔	✔		✔	✗
Courmayeur		✔				✔		✔	✗
Livigno	✔		✗						
Madonna di Campiglio	✔	✔			✔			✔	✔
Monte Rosa		✔			✔	✔			✔
Passo Tonale	✔	✔				✔			✔
Sauze d'Oulx	✔	✔			✔	✔		✔	✗
Selva Gardena	✔	✔			✔	✔		✔	✗
Sestriere	✔	✔			✔	✔			

Long runs	Tree-level skiing	Big vertical drop	Skiing convenience	Snow probability	Non-skiing	Mountain restaurants	Outstanding scenery	Resort charm	Compact village	Traffic/car free	Resort access	Late holidays	Low prices	Après-ski	Family skiing
✓	✗	✓	✓	✓	✗	✗		✗				✓		✗	✓
					✗			✓		✓	✓		✓		✓
✓			✗	✗		✓	✓		✗	✗		✗	✓	✓	✓
✓	✓		✗		✓	✓	✓	✓	✗	✗		✗	✗	✓	
			✓	✓	✗			✗	✗	✗	✗	✓	✓		✗
				✗	✗	✓		✓			✓	✓	✓	✓	✗
	✓	✓	✓		✗	✗		✗			✓		✓	✓	
✓				✓	✗			✗							

	Beginners	Intermediates	Advanced	Snowboarders	Large ski area	Off-piste/ski-touring	Summer skiing	Cross-country	Lift queues
La Thuile	✔	✔				✔			✔
SWITZERLAND									
Crans Montana	✔	✔		✔	✔		✔	✔	
Davos		✔	✔	✔	✔	✔		✔	
Grindelwald	✔	✔		✔	✔	✔			
Klosters		✔	✔	✔	✔	✔		✔	
Mürren	✗	✔	✔			✔		✗	
St Moritz		✔	✔		✔	✔	✔	✔	✗
Wengen	✔	✔		✔	✔	✔			
Verbier	✗	✔	✔	✔	✔	✔	✔		✗
Zermatt	✗	✔	✔		✔	✔	✔		
NORTH AMERICA									
Aspen	✔	✔	✔		✔	✔		✔	
Banff/Lake Louise	✔	✔	✔	✔		✔		✔	✔
Breckenridge	✔	✔		✔	✔				✗
Jackson Hole		✔	✔		✔				✗
Keystone	✔	✔	✔	✔		✔			✗
Killington	✔	✔		✔		✗			✔

	Long runs	Tree-level skiing	Big vertical drop	Skiing convenience	Snow probability	Non-skiing	Mountain restaurants	Outstanding scenery	Resort charm	Compact village	Traffic/car free	Resort access	Late holidays	Low prices	Après-ski	Family skiing
	✔	✔	✔	✗		✔	✔	✔	✗	✗	✗					
	✔	✔	✔	✗		✗	✔	✔	✔		✗				✗	✗
	✔		✔	✗	✔	✔	✔	✔	✗	✗		✗	✔	✗	✔	
	✔		✔	✗	✔	✗	✗	✔		✗	✗	✔	✔	✗	✔	✔
	✔	✔		✗	✔	✔		✔		✗		✔	✔	✔	✔	✔
	✔	✔	✔		✗	✔	✗	✔	✔			✗	✗		✔	✔
					✔	✗			✗	✗			✔	✔	✔	✔

	Beginners	Intermediates	Advanced	Snowboarders	Large ski area	Off-piste/ski-touring	Summer skiing	Cross-country	Lift queues
Lake Tahoe	✔	✔	✔	✔	✔	✔		✔	
Mammoth Mountain	✔	✔	✔	✔	✔	✔			✘
Mont Tremblant		✔	✔	✔					
Park City	✔	✔							
Smuggler's Notch/Stowe	✔	✔		✔		✘			✔
Snowbird		✔	✔	✔		✔			✔
Steamboat	✔	✔		✔	✘				✔
Vail/Beaver Creek	✔	✔		✔	✔	✔			
Whistler/Blackcomb	✔	✔	✔	✔	✔	✔	✔		✘
THE REST OF EUROPE									
Andorra	✔	✔	✘	✔	✘				✘
Eastern Europe	✔		✘		✘	✘			✘
Scandinavia	✔	✔	✘	✔	✘			✔	✔
Scotland	✔			✔	✘			✔	✘
Spain	✔	✔	✘		✘				✔

Long runs	Tree-level skiing	Big vertical drop	Skiing convenience	Snow probability	Non-skiing	Mountain restaurants	Outstanding scenery	Resort charm	Compact village	Traffic/car free	Resort access	Late holidays	Low prices	Après-ski	Family skiing
				✔		✘		✘	✘		✘	✔		✘	✔
	✔		✘	✔	✔			✔	✘		✔			✔	
			✔	✔	✘	✘	✔	✘			✔	✔		✘	
	✔		✔	✔	✘	✘					✔	✘			✔
✘	✔				✔	✘		✘				✘	✔		✔
✘			✘		✔	✘		✘				✔			

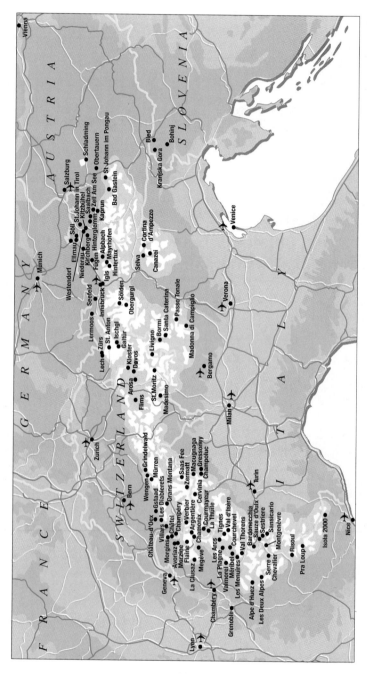

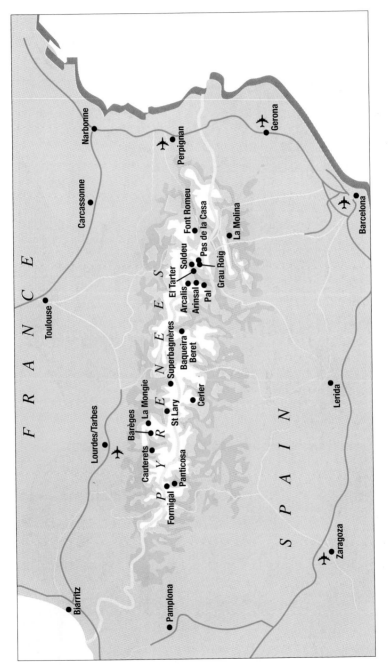

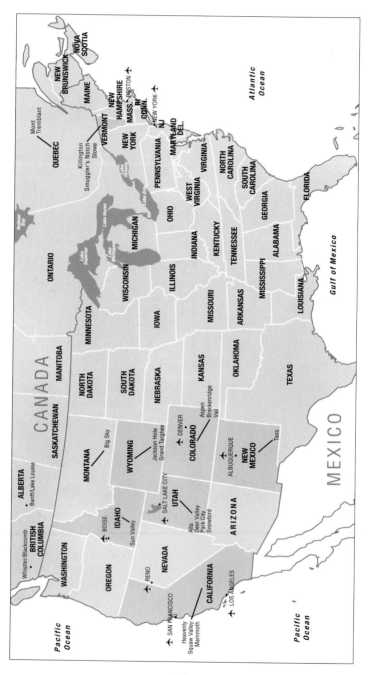

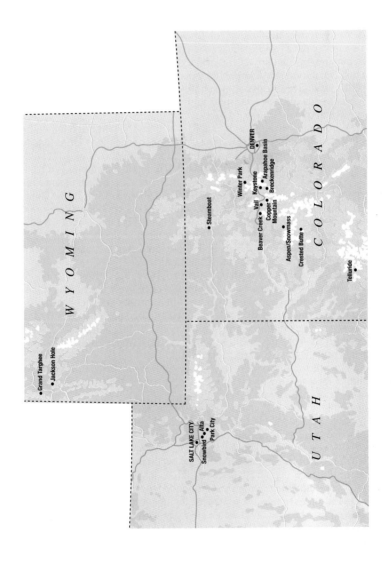

Austria

Only 15 years ago Austria held a seemingly impregnable position as the premier destination for British skiers. More chose the rolling pastures of the Tyrol, Salzburgerland and Styria, or the higher and more demanding mountains of the Arlberg for their holiday than anywhere else. The immutable Austrian formula was synonymous with snow fun: rolling, tree-lined slopes above chocolate-box villages, jolly inns, foaming tankards of beer, lively bars and discos, and liberal sound-bites of accordion music.

Within the space of just a couple of seasons, however, the twin evils of the tourist industry – currency and complacency – have cut a swathe of desolation from which the country is only just recovering.

Faced with an exchange rate against the pound which plunged from ATS24 to ATS15, tour operators and tourists alike looked around for alternative destinations. They were hastened upon their way by the blinkered mentality of far too many Austrian hoteliers who failed to see the wisdom of price maintenance. To them, the British market was merely the admittedly sweet icing on the solid German cake. But then the German economy crumbled and those unfortunate hoteliers found themselves up a mountain with a broken ski.

The Austrians have been quick to learn from their mistakes. A buoyant pound and a Euro-bound Germany once again make Austria an attractive ski destination – with prices often cheaper than in France. The problem it now faces is how to woo back those snow-users who have opted for France – which now attracts the largest amount of British snow-users – or the significant numbers who have tasted the forbidden fruits of Italy, the USA and Canada.

For as snow-users have now discovered, the downside of Austria is that, with a few major exceptions like St Anton, the skiing in general lacks both challenge and variety.

While the low and gentle pastures of the Tyrol are scenically beautiful and ideally suited to beginners and lower intermediates, more advanced skiers will quickly tire of this benign terrain in any but the best of powder conditions. The latter is by no means a rarity. In March 1998 when most of Europe was melting we experienced our best day of the season in thigh-deep Utah-style conditions in the Sportswelt Amadé.

The fact that the average resort altitude is much lower in Austria than in France does not necessarily mean that the former receives less snow. However, to be sure of adequate cover for early or late skiing, it is prudent to pick one of the higher or glacial resorts; these include Ischgl, Kaprun, Obergurgl, Obertauern, Sölden, St Anton and Zürs.

Skiers will find the standard of accommodation in Austria higher than anywhere else in Europe. Unfortunately, the same cannot always be said for the food.

Alpbach

ALTITUDE 1000m (3,280ft)

Beginners ✳✳ Intermediates ✳✳✳ Advanced ✳ Snowboarders ✳✳

If your Tyrolean holiday is incomplete without zither, harp and accordion music produced by rugged mountain lads in leather breeches, then Alpbach is the place for you. Tradition, combined with quality skiing and an intimate relationship with British skiers during the past 40 years, sets it apart from other Tyrolean destinations.

Alpbach has won successive awards as the most beautiful village in Austria. It is a secluded and strikingly attractive resort, far removed from the overt commercial influences of mainstream Tyrol, and all the better for it. It dates from about 1150, and in the Middle Ages was an important copper- and silver-mining community.

Summer and winter tourism started as far back as the 1930s, but unlike its brasher rivals, Alpbach has managed to reach the closing years of the century with its rural Austrian charm intact. Village life pivots around the sixteenth-century Böglerhof and Jakober hotels.

✔ Attractive village
✔ Alpine charm
✔ Lack of queues
✔ Ideal for non-skiers
✔ Long vertical drop
✘ Lack of challenging slopes
✘ Poor access to slopes
✘ Limited number of pistes
✘ Unexciting nightlife

Alpbach's long association with Britain begins at the quaint parish church that is mysteriously dedicated to St Oswald, a former king of Northumbria. More recently, the association can be attributed to the temporal enthusiasm of Major Billy Patterson, who arrived in Alpbach on leave from Germany in the 1950s and never left. In 1968 his wife, still a resident today, founded the Alpbach Visitors Ski Club, which acts as a private booking agency for about 1,500 guests a year and contributes strongly to the fact that as many as 23 per cent of Alpbach's skiers are British.

The ski area is limited in size but offers a variety of terrain. It is best suited to unadventurous intermediates. There is also considerable scope for off-piste. The inconvenience of having to take a five-minute bus ride from the village to the main mountain, the Wiedersberger Horn, and back again each day is a drawback, particularly for families with small children confined to the village-centre nursery slope. However, a number of reporters have commented on the efficiency of the service, and one said: 'Never have I done less walking in a ski resort. A car is useful for day-trips to other resorts but parking in the village can be a problem'.

Ski and board
top 2025m (6,643ft) bottom 830m (2,722ft)

Apart from the nursery slopes next to the village and the Böglerlift, with its south-facing red (intermediate) run, all of Alpbach's skiing is on the Wiedersberger Horn. One reporter comments: 'It is a great resort if you don't mind doing the same run over and over again'. Mountain access from Alpbach is via the two-stage, six-seater Achenwirt gondola across the wooded, north-facing slopes to Hornboden at 1850m. Queuing is not a problem, although the number of skiers increases at weekends.

Alpbach has a large vertical drop compared with other Austrian resorts of a similar village altitude, as well as some long runs. Although it has always had the reputation of being a beginners' resort, all but a couple of the runs on the mountain are marked red. Mountain access is also possible by chair-lift from **Inneralpbach** along the valley. Here the lifts join up with the skiing above Hornboden, and a long, easy red run takes you from Gmahkopf back down to Inneralpbach. The top lift here, Hornlift 2000, opens up some higher-altitude and more challenging intermediate skiing. Snowmaking on the lower, rocky meadows beneath the first stage of the gondola has made it possible to ski down to the bottom for most of the season.

The undulating terrain is a topographical dream for riders, and Alpbach regularly hosts international snowboarding events. However, the village authorities take a sadly blinkered view of the board. This is perhaps not surprising when you consider that their traditional values stand in direct opposition to the new sport and its exponents. However, the two snowparks prove that not even an Alpbacher can stand in the way of change.

Beginners

Complete novices need not stray from the village. Easy nursery runs are served by a drag-lift in the centre beside the Böglerhof. Once the basics have been mastered, or if poor snow conditions prevail at this low altitude, skiers progress to the *Familienabfahrt* on the Hornboden via the gondola. This is a long path from Gmahbahn to Kriegalm, which reporters claim is often icy.

Intermediates

With the exception of a couple of moderately challenging black (difficult) runs, the whole mountain is given over to intermediate skiing. The small number of pistes (ten) marked on the local lift map belies the actual size of the groomed area; the pistes are extremely wide, and an equivalent US resort would manage to triple the number and give them more interesting names. The standard of piste preparation is high.

Advanced

From Hornboden, a couple of wide pistes run back down to the Kriegalm mid-station, including an FIS (International Ski Federation) racecourse, which is one of the two black runs on the mountain; the

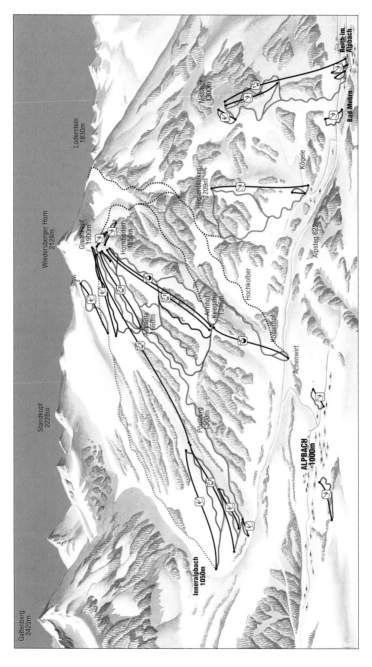

Galtenberg
2425m

Standkopf
2228m

Wiedersberger Horn
2128m

Loderstein
1850m

Gmahkopf
1900m

Hornboden
1850m

A-Hütte
1660m

Almhof
Kriegalm
1340m

Inneralpbach
1050m

Pöglberg
1300m

Hechenblaiken
1209m

Hochkolber

Hochkolber

Kohlerhof

Achenwirt

Kögele

Alpsteg 620m

Nißlhof
1300m

Reith im
Alpbach

Bad Mehrn

ALPBACH
1000m

Skiing facts: Alpbach

TOURIST OFFICE
Postfach 31, A–6236 Alpbach
Tel 43 5336 5211
Fax 43 5336 5012
Email alpbach@netway.at
Web site www.tiscover.com/
alpbach

THE RESORT
By road Calais 1080km
By rail Brixlegg 10km
By air Innsbruck 1hr, Munich 2 hrs
Visitor beds 2,400
Transport free ski bus between village
and gondola

THE SKIING
Linked or nearby resorts Reith (n),
Kramsach (n), Zillertal (n)
Longest run Kafner, 3km (red)
Number of lifts 21
Total of trails/pistes 45km (22% easy,
56% intermediate, 22% difficult)
Nursery slopes 7 lifts (5 at Alpbach,
others at Inneralpbach and Reith)
Summer skiing none
Snowmaking 15km covered

LIFT PASSES
Area pass (covers Alpbach and Reith)
ATS1,200–1,380 for 6 days
Day pass ATS300
Beginners no free lifts
Pensioners reduction for 65 yrs and over
Credit cards no

TUITION
Adults Alpbach Ski School and Alpbach

Aktiv Ski School, 10am–midday and
1.30–3.30pm, ATS1,300 for 6 days
Private lessons Both ski schools
ATS1,900 per day for 1–3 persons
Snowboarding Alpbach Snowboard
School, by appointment, details on
request, Alpbach Aktiv Ski School
ATS1,300 for 5 days (2½ hrs per day)
Cross-country Alpbach Ski School,
ATS1,100 for 6 half-days
Other courses ski-touring, off-piste,
monoski
Guiding through ski schools

CHILDREN
Lift pass (covers Alpbach and Reith),
6–14 yrs, ATS770–850 for 6 days,
free for 5 yrs and under if accompanied
by a parent
Ski kindergarten Alpbach Ski School
ATS1,900, and Alpbach Aktiv Ski
School ATS1,580, both for 5 days
including lunch
Ski school Alpbach Ski School and
Alpbach Aktiv Ski School both ATS1,300
for 6 days (4 hrs per day)
Non-ski kindergarten 3–5 yrs, 9.30am
–4.30pm, ATS350 per day including
lunch

OTHER SPORTS
Sleigh rides, parapente, tobogganing,
indoor tennis at Kramsach (12km away)

FOOD AND DRINK
Coffee ATS24, glass of wine ATS20,
small beer ATS23, dish of the day
ATS70–130

other is Brandegg. From here a red run goes to the bottom, creating a good, fast course of over 1000m vertical, which is used by British racing clubs for their competitions.

Off-piste

Alpbach is ideal for 'lazy powder skiers'. According to one reporter you can lie in bed after a night of new snow until 10.30am and still cut fresh tracks. 'Even four days after a big dump it is usually possible to find virgin corners of the mountain.' The long, red itinerary route from Gmahkopf down to Inneralpbach is not pisted, although it is usually well-skied. Some fairly challenging off-piste can be found around the Wiedersberger Horn, and the ski school runs special tours on Saturdays.

Tuition and guiding

Alpbach Ski School has 60 instructors and a sound reputation. One reporter commented: 'The standard of instruction was about the best I have had anywhere'. Another described it as 'friendly and traditional, absolutely not avant garde. In fact, the school mirrors the resort'. Guided powder tours can be arranged through the ski school. We have positive reports of the Alpbach Aktiv Snowboard School ('friendly teacher with reasonable English, but not exactly a cool dude').

Mountain restaurants

The Hornboden restaurant is situated 50m below the top stage of the gondola, which is fine for skiers but an inconvenience for the many non-skiers, who have to walk down a steep stretch of piste to reach it. The lower section is self-service with a pleasant sun terrace. The first-floor restaurant offers typical Tyrolean food of a reasonably high standard. The Gmahstuben is 'cheap and cheerful'. The Gasthof Wiedersberger Horn at Inneralpbach is said to be one of the best lunch – and evening – spots in the region.

The resort

Alpbach is a small, sunny village set on a steep hillside. The compact centre is dominated by a pretty green-and-white church surrounded by old wooden chalets and the buttressed walls of the two medieval inns. A 1953 building regulation ensured that all construction is in traditional Tyrolean style, with the obvious seasonal exception of a ubiquitous Siglu bar at the foot of the nursery slopes. Shopping is limited to just two sports shops, two boutiques and three souvenir shops.

Accommodation

Most of Alpbach's accommodation is in hotels and guest houses, ranging from basic bed-and-breakfasts to the very comfortable. Three of the most luxurious hotels are the Böglerhof, Alpbacherhof and the Alphof, the latter being a 15-minute uphill walk from the village. The Böglerhof is reported to have 'Superb facilities including a swimming-pool and a children's playroom'. The village takes considerable pride in the fact that many of its hotels have remained in the same families for centuries, which ensures a high standard of service. The Blatter is centrally placed, and several reporters found the food and service to be excellent.

Eating in and out

The restaurants do not offer much variety, although the recommended ones include the Gasthof Jakober, Alpbacher Taverne, the Reblaus for pizzas and the Gasthof Wiedersberger Horn. The restaurant in the Böglerhof is the most luxurious and also offers 'extensive vegetarian options'. The Rossmoos and Zottahof restaurants, both up the mountain, are popular in the evening.

Après-ski

If drinking and dancing until dawn are an integral component of your ski holiday, you should consider other, livelier resorts. Outside the main holiday weeks the resort is dead by 11pm, except at weekends when an influx of visitors gives it much needed cheer. Achenwirt, at the foot of the mountain, is 'good for a couple of beers on the way home'. The Siglu beside the nursery slopes attracts a busy crowd in the late afternoon. There is a long toboggan run at **Reith**, 7km away.

The recently extended Jakober Bar is an early-evening rendezvous point. The Hornbeisl bar next to the lifts in Inneralpbach is recommended. The Waschkuch'l is good for a quiet drink, and the Birdy Pub in the village centre is recommended for a noisier one. The Schneeloch disco in the Böglerhof, which was axed when the hotel was taken over by the Romantik group, has been reinstated with a Starship Enterprise bar. The Weinstadl is the alternative disco.

Childcare

Alpbach has a kindergarten that takes children from three years old. It is also possible to find baby-minders for younger children through the tourist board.

Bad Gastein

ALTITUDE 1100m (3,608ft)

Intermediates ✱✱✱   Advanced ✱✱   Snowboarders ✱✱

The Gasteinertal, a long closed valley flanked by the Hohe Tauern mountains, offers a higher class of skiing than the lowland pastures of the Tyrol and an altogether more cosmopolitan atmosphere. Bad Gastein, the main resort, is an important spa, which is more famous for the quality of its water than for the snow on the high slopes that surround it. However, problems with the German economy have led to a short-fall in visitors from its most important market, and the resort has experienced a depression in recent seasons.

✔ Large ski area
✔ Tree-level skiing
✔ Variety of après-ski
✔ Thermal baths
✔ Choice of mountain restaurants
✔ Easy rail access
✔ Reasonable prices
✘ Lack of skiing convenience
✘ Inefficient bus system
✘ Heavy traffic
✘ Poor piste-marking
✘ Awkward for families with small children

Five million gallons of hot water bubbles up from 17 natural springs and is piped into all the main hotels. The public indoor and outdoor pools at the Felsenbad by the Bahnhof (railway station) are a popular resort rendezvous where you can wallow in the waters and, through a haze of steam, watch snow-users in action just a few yards away. One million gallons of this surprisingly sulphur-free water is also piped down the road to Bad Gastein's sister spa of **Bad Hofgastein**. This is a spacious and comfortable resort in a more benign setting on the valley floor. It is more popular with families and better organised.

Dorf Gastein, at the entrance to the Gasteinertal, is a sleepy and unspoilt village with its own attractive ski area which extends over the 2027-m Kreuzkogel to **Grossarl** in a neighbouring valley. **Sport Gastein**, at the head of the valley, is a separate, high ski area based around an abandoned gold-mining village. In the Middle Ages the area was responsible for ten per cent of the world's gold and silver output.

Bad Gastein itself is a collection of once-grand hotels painted mostly in the imperial yellow of Vienna's Schönbrunn Palace and stacked dramatically up a steep hillside around a waterfall that plunges into the River Ache. The resort's elegant casino harks back to the days when this was one of the greatest watering resorts of Europe. Franz Schubert and Johann Strauss both composed here, and the guest list never failed to include at least a couple of crowned heads of state. However, the gold has long since been exhausted, and the year-round spa business is not what it was, although winter sports have given the region an injection of new life.

Ski and board
top 2686m (8,810ft) bottom 850m (2,788ft)

If you are accustomed to clicking into your bindings outside your hotel door and skiing home at the end of the day, then Bad Gastein is not for you. It was built on a steep hillside as a spa, not a ski resort, and the considerable amount of walking is unavoidable. Snow cover in the region has been variable in recent years, but a number of new snow-cannon were installed last season. The main Stubnerkogel ski area is situated on the western side of the valley and is reached by modern, two-stage gondola from the top of the town near the railway station. In theory, you can leave your equipment in the ski-and-boot store beside, which avoids the need to lug equipment up tough gradients from the town centre. However, you may not end up here again at the end of the day.

The east-facing runs back down to Bad Gastein provide good, tough skiing, with a mixture of open ground above and woods below. They are graded mostly red (intermediate) but can become difficult when conditions are poor. A blue (easy) run winds down the mountain and is usually crowded and often icy. The wide top-half of the slope gives plenty of opportunity for off-piste variations.

Stubnerkogel is the starting point for a series of lifts and runs that take you along the side of the valley and down to Bad Hofgastein. There are three other separate areas. Although the Graukogel runs above Bad Gastein on the far side of the valley are few in number they are long and satisfying descents for advanced snow-users. The friendly skiing shared by Dorf Gastein and Grossarl is a confidence-building but at times challenging, small area for beginners and intermediates.

Sport Gastein, at the head of the valley, is an icy place in which to find yourself when the weather closes in. However, on a fine day the piste-skiing is varied and the off-piste can be exceptional. If snow conditions are poor elsewhere, Sport Gastein can become crowded. Bad Gastein, Dorf Gastein, and Sport Gastein all have half-pipes, but riders congregate in the new funpark at Dorf Gastein.

Ski buses link the separate resorts and ski areas, but reporters consistently claim that the system is both oversubscribed and inefficient. 'Intervals of 90 minutes are not uncommon which is all you need when you are tired at the end of the day.' Taxis are plentiful but 'iniquitously expensive'. In order to explore the area fully a car is a necessity.

Beginners
The area has five nursery slopes served by drag-lifts, but overall it cannot be recommended for beginners or even second-week snow-users. From Bad Gastein, the main novice slopes are an inconvenient ten-minute bus-ride away at Angertal. Most blue (easy) runs are a

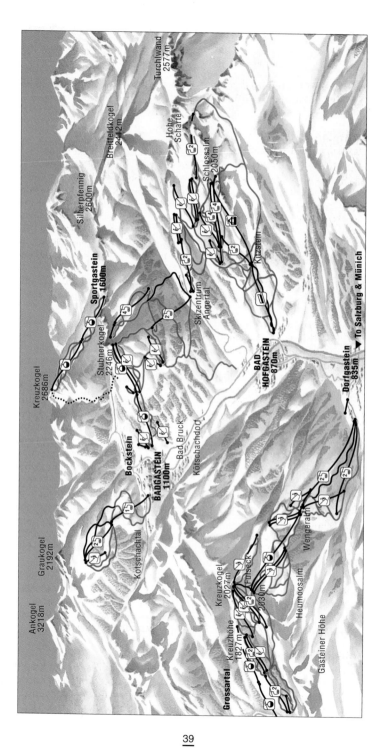

Ankogel
3218m

Graukogel
2192m

Kreuzkogel
2686m

Silberpfennig
2600m

Breitfeldkogel
2442m

Turchlwand
2577m

Hohe
Scharfe

Schlossalm
2050m

Kitzstein

Sportgastein 1600m

Stubnerkogel
2246m

Skizentrum
Angertal

Bockstein

**BADGASTEIN
1100m**

Bad Bruck

Kötschachdorf

Kötschachtal

**BAD
HOFGASTEIN
870m**

**Dorfgastein
835m**

▶ **To Salzburg & Münich**

Kreuzkogel
2027m

Fulseck
2030m

Wengeralm

Heumoosalm

Gasteiner Höhe

Grossartal

Kreuzhöhe
1827m

pinkish-red in comparison with similar-sized Austrian resorts, and the whole Gasteinertal is better geared towards more accomplished snow-users.

Intermediates

The entire valley is best suited to strong intermediates looking for a combination of mileage and challenge. Graukogel has superb tree-level skiing and is the place where the locals go on a snowy day. Confident snow-users will be interested mainly in the long run around the back of the mountain, which is reached either from Hohe Scharte at 2300m or from Kleine Scharte at 2050m. In good snow conditions it is possible to ski 1450m vertical over eight kilometres, all the way to the bottom of the railway. Skiing is possible with only a minimum of snow cover as most of it takes place on pastureland with few rocks and stones.

Advanced

The north-facing runs down into the Angertal area provide some of the best skiing in the region. From Jungeralm, a long, undulating black (difficult) run drops directly through the woods. Dorf Gastein's new funpark has a boardercross competition course.

Off-piste

Untracked opportunities abound above the Schlossalm next to Hohe Scharte. Both the north and south faces of Sport Gastein can provide excellent, long powder runs after a new snowfall.

Tuition and guiding

We have good reports of the Skischule Luigi in Bad Gastein. The size of classes seems to vary between 4 and 12 pupils. The standard of English is high ('the instructor even understood our jokes'). The Bad Hofgastein Ski and Racing School, run by Fritz Zettinig, has a fine reputation. We have no reports on the two alternatives, Robert's Ski School and the Ski School Schlossalm. Ski School Holleisn in Dorf Gastein is described as 'small and friendly with useful instruction by helpful locals'. Local high-mountain guide Hans Zlöbl takes groups and individuals off-piste.

Cross-country

Both Bad Gastein ski schools have a langlauf section, as does the Bad Hofgastein Ski and Racing School. Gerhard Gassner runs his Gasteiner Wander-Und Langlaufschule. Nearly 90km of prepared loipe are scattered around the valley. Routes are shown in detail in the *Gasteinertal Loipenbuch*, a booklet obtainable free of charge from the tourist offices.

Mountain restaurants

The area is plentifully served with pleasant huts on the slopes as well as with self-service cafeterias at the lift stations. Prices are no higher than in the valley, and there they are low by Austrian standards, which is surprising in a resort of this standing. Aeroplanstadl below Hohe Scharte has 'good, cheap, self-service food'. Reporters particularly recommend the Wengeralm above Dorf Gastein for its traditional fried potato pancakes. The top of the Stubnerkogel has both wait- and self-service sections and is recommended for local venison dishes. The Schlossalm has a warm atmosphere and is famed for its gulaschsuppe. The Hamburger Skiheim above Bad Hofgastein has a barbecue and ice-bar. The Panorama at Kreuzkogel has a children's slide between floors. Sport Gastein's restaurants are at the gondola mid-station and at the base; both are operated by the same family to an extremely high standard.

The resort

The main road and railway bypass the town centre, which is more easily negotiated on foot by the steep footpaths and stairways than by car. The main features of the resort are the casino, the waterfall and a modern conference centre beside it. The old hotels are flanked by smart boutiques and expensive jewellers, which set their sights at Bad Gastein's wealthy German health visitors rather than the snow-users. The resort's upper level, a steep but short climb away, is a collection of the less fashionable spa hotels which attract snow-users in winter because of their more convenient location. Bad Gastein has an annoyingly complicated one-way system; traffic is heavy, and parking can be difficult.

Accommodation

Most of the accommodation is in hotels, of which there are quite literally hundreds in the valley. The position of your accommodation in Bad Gastein is crucial because of the steep layout of the resort. The modern Elizabethpark beside the waterfall is said to be 'comfortable but a bit characterless and a long walk from the snow'. Villa Solitude, a magnificent town house next to the casino, has been lovingly restored as a designer hotel with six suites furnished in the style of the 1840s.

Among the hotels, within easy walking distance of the Stubnerkogel lifts, is the Bärenhof, which is one of the most comfortable and expensive. More charming and in a quieter position is the simple Fischerwirt. Hotel Mozart, named not after the maestro but after his mother, is recommended as comfortable and spacious and 'well-positioned for the skiing and the nightlife'. The Salzburgerhof is owned by a Swedish company, and readers warmly recommend it for 'exceptional attention to detail'. At the foot of the Graukogel lift is the Schillerhof, which has 'splendid views, clean and comfortable rooms'. Hotel Grüner Baum, built in 1831 by Archduke Johann as a hunting lodge, is 5km out of town in a beautiful rural setting and has a justified reputation as one of the great hotels of Austria.

Eating in and out

The choice of restaurants is limited mainly to the hotels, but the Bahnhof restaurant is particularly recommended as good value for money. The Mozart on Mozartplatz is praised for its fondue. The Restaurant am

Skiing facts: Bad Gastein

TOURIST OFFICE
Haus Austria, Kaiser-Franz-Josef-
Strasse 27, A-5640 Bad Gastein,
Salzburgerland
Tel 43 6434 2531
Fax 43 6434 2531 37
Email fvv.badgastein@aon.at
Web site www.badgastein.at

THE RESORT
By road Calais 1200km
By rail station in resort
Airport transfer Salzburg 1½ hrs
Visitor beds 6,500
Transport free ski bus with lift pass

THE SKIING
Linked or nearby resorts Bad
Hofgastein (l), Dorf Gastein (n), Sport
Gastein (n), Grossarl (n)
Longest run Angertal, 11km (red/blue)
Number of lifts 53
Total of trails/pistes 200km (30% easy,
59% intermediate, 11% difficult)
Nursery slopes 5 lifts and trails
Summer skiing none
Snowmaking 40km covered, 150km in
area

LIFT PASSES
Area pass Gastein Super Ski (covers
Schlossalm, Angertal-Stubnerkogel,
Graukogel, Grossarl and all Gastein
resorts), ATS1,990 for 6 days
Day pass ATS400
Beginners points tickets
Pensioners 10% reduction for women
60 yrs and over and men 65 yrs
and over

Credit cards yes

TUITION
Adults S-S Bad Gastein ATS1,550 for 6
days, Ski School Luigi ATS1,450 for
6 days
Private lessons S-S Bad Gastein
ATS470 per hr, full day ATS2,820 (5hrs)
Luigi ATS450 per hr, full day
ATS1,700 (4hrs)
Snowboarding S-S Bad Gastein
ATS1,500, S-S Luigi ATS1,050, both for
3 days (4 people for 2hrs per day)
Cross-country ATS470 per hr private
lesson. Loipe 37km in Bad Gastein,
90km in valley
Other courses off-piste
Guiding Hans Zlöbl

CHILDREN
Lift pass 6–15 yrs, ATS1,190 for 6 days,
ATS250 per day. Free for 5 yrs and under
Ski kindergarten 3–5 yrs, ATS550 per
day including lunch
Ski school Pflaum and Luigi, both 3 yrs
and over, ATS678 for 6 days including
lunch
Non-ski kindergarten at Hotel Gruner
Baum, 3–5 yrs, ATS200 per half-day,
ATS450 per day including lunch

OTHER SPORTS
Skating, curling, indoor golf and tennis,
squash, sleigh rides, rifle shooting,
parapente, shooting, snowshoeing

FOOD AND DRINK PRICES
Coffee ATS27, glass of wine ATS35, small
beer ATS24, dish of the day ATS130

Wasserfall is 'inexpensive and cheerful', as is the Felsenbad. The China-restaurant 'makes a pleasant change from Wienerschnitzel'.

The Villa Hiss offers 'outstanding gourmet fare at a price', and the Hotel Rader in Böckstein provides 'a great evening out for those who care about their food'. Villa Solitude Brasserie has the best gourmet fare in town, with the exception of the restaurant in the Grüner Baum. Both are owned by the Blumschein family.

Après-ski

The Felsenbad, opposite the Bahnhof, has thermal indoor and outdoor pools as well as a bar and attracts the crowds as they come off the slopes. The Austrians see nothing unhealthy in the marriage of beer and Bad, and a promotional video shows spa patients happily imbibing. No visitor should miss the chance to improve his or her health by taking a train ride to the Healing Galleries 2km inside the mountain near Dorf Gastein. The 90°C temperature, relative humidity and low doses of rare radon gas apparently cure respiratory and muscular ailments.

The Gatz Music Club and Hägblom's are the hot-spots at tea-time and again much later in the evening. Their late-night rival is the Visage near the Wasserfall. Eden's Pub is said to be usually crowded 'not least because a giant moose head takes up most of the

> **WHAT'S NEW**
> Funpark at Dorf Gastein

room'. Ritz in the Salzburgerhof Hotel has live music ('everything from UB40 to Glenn Miller') and is more sophisticated. The casino is worth a visit. Other late bars to check out include the Belmondo, Filou, Gasteiner Stamperl, Hexn-Häsl, Weinfassl, Pub am Wasserfall and the Zirbenstube. The bar at the British-owned Hotel Tannenburg has the cheapest drinks in town.

Childcare

Like all resorts with a disparate ski area it is difficult to recommend Bad Gastein for children. All the villages have ski kindergarten which take three-year-olds and upwards, but finding someone to care for younger ones is more difficult. Hotel Grüner Baum in Bad Gastein runs a crèche for its residents. The nursery slopes are 10 minutes' walk from the centre.

Linked or nearby resorts

Bad Hofgastein
top 2686m (8,810ft) bottom 870m (2,854ft)

Bad Hofgastein has neither the inconveniently steep and dark setting nor the faded grandeur of its neighbour. Although smaller, it is still a sizeable resort with 18 hotels spread along the broadest part of the valley. The Kitzstein funicular is a long walk or a bus-ride away. Bad Hofgastein is a good base for the valley's walks and cross-country trails, and busy skating and curling rinks complete the winter scene. There is an outdoor, naturally-heated swimming-pool as well as a modern sports centre with tennis and squash. Reporters complain that the funicular holds 100 people while the cable-car above it has a capacity of only 40; this leads to annoying 30-minute queues at peak times. Wise snow-users take the chair from the top of the train.

The resort has a strong conservation policy, and anyone who deliberately skis through sapling plantations is liable to forfeit his or her lift pass. Buses circle the northern part of the resort every 10 minutes and the southern section every 20 minutes. The kindergarten takes children from three years old. The thermal baths here are said to be a must, as are the evening sleigh rides.

Accommodation is mainly in hotels. The Gasthof zum Boten is described as an 'excellent old post house with big, clean comfortable rooms'. The most convenient hotels are the more recently built ones lining the road from the centre to the river. The Tennis Treff opposite the funicular attracts the main crowd as they come off the slopes with its 'good atmosphere, occasional live music and reasonably priced drinks'. Later on the action moves to Francky's Kneipe and Sonia's Pub. The one disco is not usually busy. The bowling alley is recommended as being 'great fun for a rowdy night out – the best excursion I've ever been on'.

TOURIST OFFICE
Tel 43 643 271100
Fax 43 643 2711031
Email bad.hofgastein@magnet.at
Web site www.badhofgastein.com

Dorf Gastein
top 2686m (8,810ft) bottom 835m (2,739ft)
Dorf Gastein is the first of the settlements you come to on entering the Gasteinertal. Too many visitors to the area drive through without stopping. What they miss is a delightful little village with a charming main street lined with arcades. It remains untouched by the slightly depressing health-conscious image of its bigger sisters. Horses and carts clatter along the narrow street past the old church, more often taking local folk about their business than taking tourists for joy rides. There are several well-kept, friendly and comfortable hotels in the centre. The skiing begins a good five-minute walk from the village. The Gasthof Schihäusl stands at the foot of the slopes. Evenings are said to be livelier than you might expect in a village of this size.

TOURIST OFFICE
Tel 43 6433 7277
Fax 43 6433 3737

Innsbruck

ALTITUDE 575m (1,886ft)

RESORTS COVERED Axamer Lizum, Fulpmes, Igls, Neustift, Seefeld

Beginners ✳✳ Intermediates ✳✳✳ Advanced ✳✳ Snowboarders ✳✳✳

Innsbruck enjoys a reputation as a minor ski resort in its own right but its true significance for the skier is as a jumping-off point for a host of big-name resorts in the Tyrol and even the Arlberg. These can be reached daily by bus, although a car adds both convenience and flexibility.

Austria's third most important city has twice hosted the Winter Olympics and has the advantage of having its own international airport, which is dramatically enclosed by towering mountain ranges on either side of the Inn Valley. Innsbruck is strategically positioned in western Austria and is well-served by a network of motorways. The Ötztal and the snow-sure skiing of **Obergurgl** and **Sölden** can be reached in under 90 minutes by car. The journey to **Kitzbühel** and the Ski-

✔ Attractive town
✔ Short airport transfer
✔ Variety of skiing in area
✔ Summer skiing on Stubai Glacier
✔ Extensive cross-country
✔ Activities for non-skiers
✘ Small, separate ski areas
✘ Weekend lift queues

Welt takes an hour. To add to the incentive of staying in the city, a single ski pass called the Innsbruck Glacier Skipass covers the main local areas of **Igls, Axamer Lizum, Neustift** and the **Stubai Glacier, Tulfes, Hungerberg and Mutters**; it gives access to a total of 53 lifts serving 112km of piste and is flexible, offering three days' skiing out of a total four or six days for people who do not want to ski every day.

The two permutations of the more expensive Innsbruck Super Skipass also allow you to ski Kitzbühel and/or the Arlberg for a day as well, thus providing 200 lifts and 500km of piste. It is as flexible as the Innsbruck Glacier Skipass, bus travel is included in the price, and anyone staying for more than three days is entitled to a Club Innsbruck discount card, giving a reduction on the passes.

The cost of staying in the city is lower than in a conventional ski resort. The choice of restaurants is wide, and nightlife is varied. The city's best hotel is the Europa, which is attractively wood-panelled and contains the well-respected Europastüberl restaurant.

Innsbruck's 'own' skiing is to be found just outside the city above **Hungerberg** on the south-facing slopes of the Hafelekar. The black (difficult) Karrine and the red (intermediate) Langes Tal runs are both challenging. The area above Tulfes on the other side of the valley consists of two blue (easy) runs and two reds.

Axamer Lizum
top 2343m (7,687ft) bottom 874m (2,867ft)

This is a somewhat characterless ski station comprising four hotels and a huge car park set in the heart of Austria's most appealing all-round ski area at 1553m beneath the peaks of the Hoadl and Pleisen mountains. Weekend lift queues, as in all the Innsbruck ski villages, can be a problem, but the ten lifts provide both extensive and varied pistes. The 6.5-km Axamer, graded black, but red by most resorts' standards, takes you all the way down to the quiet village of **Axams** at 874m. There is one mountain restaurant, the Hoadl-Gipfel at 2340m, which has panoramic views and home-cooking.

Across the narrow valley, a long chair-lift serves either a black run back to Axamer Lizum or gives access to the sunny, easy pistes above Mutters, the sixth and smallest of Innsbruck's own ski areas. Expectations of an improved link to form a ski circus here have not yet been met, and now seem likely to have evaporated in the light of the growing environmentalist lobby in the Tyrol.

Fulpmes
top 2200m (7,218ft) bottom 937m (3,074ft)

Slightly further away, but still within easy reach by post-bus, the Stubaital offers some of the best skiing in the area. **Mieders, Telfes, Fulpmes**, and Neustift all share a lift pass. Above Fulpmes, but not directly accessible from it, there is good skiing in a sheltered bowl now branded as Schlick 2000 Skizentrum. Lifts include a four-seater chair going up to 2200m. Some of the runs are tough and unpisted, but the majority are easy and confidence-building, and good for lower intermediates. The small, sunny nursery area receives favourable reports.

The Hotel Stubaierhof and the Hotel Alte Post are both recommended. Restaurants include the Leonardo Da Vinci ('popular and good value') and the Gasthaus Hofer, which serves 'simple, plain Austrian farmhouse fare'. The Café Corso, the Ossi-Keller, Platzwirt and Dorfalm discos make it a lively place by night.

Igls
top 2247m (7,372ft) bottom 893m (2,930ft)

Igls, 5km up towards the Europabrücke and the Italian border, has the best skiing in the immediate area and is a fine example of a traditional Tyrolean village. The skiing is served by a cable-car, a chair-lift, and four T-bars, and consists of four runs cut through the trees. The red Olympic downhill presents a challenge on the front face of the mountain. It was here in 1976 that Franz Klammer threw caution to the wind and hurled himself down the mountain to win the greatest Winter Olympics gold of all time. The blue *Familienabfahrt* follows a less direct route. There are off-piste opportunities from the top of the Gipfel lift. New snowmaking on the Patscherkofel should improve conditions for this season. There are four mountain restaurants, most of them criticised for their high prices, although the one at the top of the cable-car receives considerable praise.

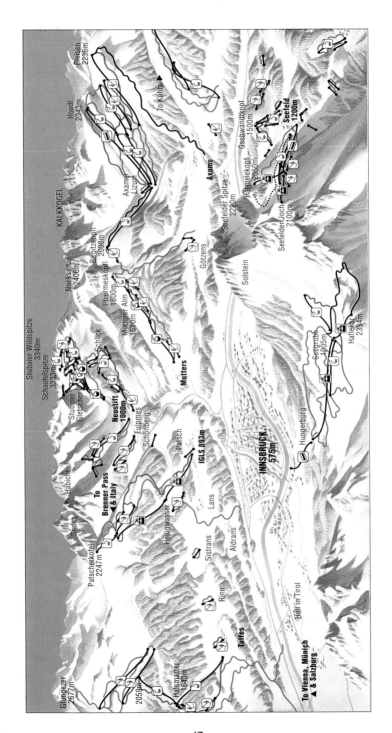

47

The resort supports two ski schools, both with instructors who speak good English. The two nursery slopes are covered by snow-cannon and are a five-minute walk from the village centre. There is a non-ski kindergarten, staffed by trained nursery nurses, and a children's ski school.

The village is small and uncommercialised, with sedate hotels and coffee houses, excellent winter walks, and the Olympic bob-run, which is open to the public. The Sporthotel Igls is recommended for its cuisine, while the Schlosshotel also rates five stars and is warmly praised. Après-ski is not the resort's strongest point, but the bars at the Bon Alpina and the Astoria are the livelier spots. The Sporthotel disco is open until late.

Neustift
top 3200m (10,499ft) bottom 1000m (3,281ft)

The main community of the broad and lush Stubaital, Neustift is a large, sprawling village that has expanded greatly in recent years. Nevertheless, it remains very much at heart the traditional Tyrolean village centred around a magnificent and ornately decorated church.

Recommended hotels include the Tirolerhof ('excellent food and a warm welcome') and the budget-priced and quaint Hotel Angelika in the centre of town. Nightlife is lively in the Romanastuben, and the Sumpflöchl in the Hotel Stubaierhof is popular. Neustift has its own gentle ski area on wooded north-facing slopes but it is also the main base for the Stubai Glacier, 20 minutes away at the end of the valley. A free ski bus operates regularly.

The Stubai Glacier is one of the most extensive summer ski areas in Europe. The old four-seater gondola from the base-station at Mutterbergalm has been supplemented by a six-person gondola running in parallel to the first stage at Fernau. From here you can either continue by gondola or chair-lift to a network of drags, which take you up to the top of the ski area. When snow is short elsewhere, the slopes can become unbelievably crowded, and German bank holidays are to be avoided. The Gamsgarten restaurant is singled out for its choice of reasonably-priced food ('amazing baked potatoes with a choice of fillings'.)

Keen skiers will stay in the comfortable Alpensporthotel Mutterberg at the base of the lifts. It has its own swimming-pool and disco. Separate ski schools operate in both Neustift and on the glacier and each has a kindergarten. The Stubai Superskipass also covers a small area at Milders and the assorted lifts in the valley.

Seefeld
top 2100m (6,890ft) bottom 1200m (3,937ft)

Seefeld is a tiny version of Innsbruck, Kitzbühel and the other beautiful towns of Austria, with its frescoed houses and medieval architecture. The village is stylish and sophisticated and has seven luxury hotels, a casino, an extensive health centre, horse-drawn sleighs and a pedestrianised centre. Seefeld's main winter activity is cross-country skiing. However, it also has three small, alpine ski-areas: Geigenbühel is for beginners, Gschwandtkopf is a low peak next to the cross-country loipe used mainly by the ski school, and Rosshütte is a more extensive area with steeper runs and a long, steep off-piste trail. All three areas are reached from the village centre by the free bus service.

The town boasts some exotic hotels, including the five-star Klosterbräu, a former sixteenth-century monastery complete with indoor and outdoor pools and a Roman sauna with steam grotto. Others include the Creativhotel Viktoria and the less pricey Hotel Bergland. The Kaltschmidt is 'very handy for the nursery slope with a nice pool on the fourth floor'. The luxury Gartenhotel Tümmlerhof is set in its own park and offers all-day childcare as well as a children's playground. The resort kindergarten is in the Olympia Sport and Congress Centre.

Gourmets can try the Alte Stube in the Hotel Karwendelhof. Café Nanni and Café Moccamühle are popular after-skiing places. The Big Ben bar is as English as you would expect, and the Brittania Inn is another popular pub. Monroe's disco-bar attracts the late-night crowd along with the Miramare and the popular Postbar in the Hotel Post. The Kanne in the Hotel Klosterbräu, the centre of the village's social life, has live music. Reporters recommend the Lammkeller in Hotel Lamm. The bar Fledermaus has live jazz in the evenings. Non-skiing activities include 'innertubing' down the bob-sleigh run, and grotto 'saunarium' and indoor-outdoor swimming-pool in the Olympia Sport and Congress Centre.

Snowboarding
Axamer Lizum is one of the top snowboarding resorts in Austria and is particularly popular with freestyle riders. The resort is busy at weekends because of its proximity to Innsbruck. The snowboard park is well maintained, with a half-pipe. Alpine riders are also well catered for, with a high proportion of wide pistes to the relatively small size of resort. The Stubai Glacier, Igls and Hungerberg all have funparks.

Cross-country
Seefeld is a year-round resort and in winter cross-country skiing is its *raison d'être*. Cross-country skiing started here as a recreational sport in 1964 when Seefeld hosted the Winter Olympics nordic events. The resort then went on to host the events in the 1976 Winter Olympics and in the 1985 Nordic World Championships.

The excellent facilities include a team of specialist cross-country instructors at the Nordic Ski School in the Olympia Sport and Congress Centre. The 200km of loipe are mechanically prepared here, and a special cross-country trail map is available from the tourist office.

TOURIST OFFICE
Innsbruck
Tel 43 512 59850
Fax 43 512 59850–7
Email info@innsbruck.tvb.co.at
Web site www.tiscover.com/innsbruck

Ischgl

ALTITUDE 1400m (4,529ft)

Beginners ✱ Intermediates ✱✱✱ Snowboarders ✱✱✱

Ischgl is the focus of the Silvretta ski area on the Austrian–Swiss border. It shares a lift pass with **Galtür** and **Kappl**, smaller neighbours in the Paznaun Valley, but for most visitors, duty-free **Samnaun** (also covered on the lift pass) on the Swiss side of the frontier is the greater attraction. Alcohol at competitive prices, rucksacks for sale to transport it back over the mountain and the allure of a Swiss lunch make it an irresistible day trip. The return journey involves a ride on the Pendelbahn, the world's first double-decker cable-car, which is handsomely engineered and fitted with escalators for easy access. This is the spearhead of a general upgrading of the lift system designed to reduce the bottlenecks that haunted Ischgl and Samnaun during the early 1990s. This season the Silvrettabahn gondola was replaced by a smart double-cable Funitel system, designed to allow operation even in high winds. Each car carries up to 24 people. The Höllenkar double drag-lift has been replaced by a quad-chair.

✔ Extensive intermediate cruising in large ski area
✔ Off-piste and ski-touring
✔ Largest funpark in Europe
✔ Reliable snow record
✔ Wide choice of nightlife
✔ Beautiful scenery
✘ Lack of easy runs
✘ Limited advanced skiing
✘ Crowded home pistes
✘ Poor mountain restaurants

Although Ischgl is only a few miles as the crow flies from its awesome neighbour St Anton it has remained largely unknown in Britain. Consequently the Paznaun Valley is altogether more peaceful. The first lift was not installed here until 1963. In the intervening 35 years, the resort developed from a small farming village into a bustling resort on a hillside to the south of the main road. Wealthy young Germans still dominate what has always been an expensive resort but the British are gradually discovering Ischgl. Many of the regulars consider it to be the second best resort in Austria (after St Anton) – an assessment that takes both the skiing and the nightlife into account.

Ski and board
top 2864m (9,394ft) bottom 1377m (4,517ft)

The spine of the ski area is the long ridge that forms the Austrian–Swiss border, with Ischgl's slopes facing north-west and west and Samnaun's facing south-east and east. The rapid Fimbabahn gondola, now connected by a tunnel to the centre of town, and the new Funitel

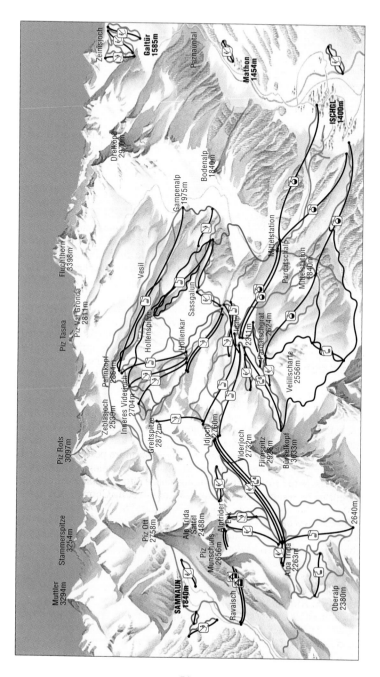

Silvrettabahn provide comfortable and rapid access to Idalp, an open, mid-mountain plateau, while a third lift – the Pardatschgratbahn – ends 300m higher. From this focal point the pistes fan out over the upper slopes, with extensive and well-linked opportunities for fast cruising.

Two chair-lifts provide a choice of routes to the run down to Samnaun, with the much longer, covered chair from Gampenalp as a third alternative. After eating and shopping, snow-users can take a short roadside descent below the village to Ravaisch, the departure point for the 180-person double cable-car, which arrives at Alpa Trida Sattel, a sun trap with spectacular views but no direct link back to Ischgl. Instead, snow-users must descend to Alp Trida, the starting point for parallel drag-lifts and a chair to Idjoch on the top of the ridge for the journey back to base.

The last link in the shortest possible circuit is a lift from Alpa Trida Sattel to Greitspitz. Unfortunately, it appears only as a dotted line on the piste map, and although planning permission has been negotiated, installation will not be completed until the year 2000. Once back in the Ischgl area snow-users have a choice of two long runs through woods to the resort; in high season, however, both are dangerously crowded.

The Silvretta area has established itself as a major snowboard centre, with the new Paradise Funpark at Idjoch, which is claimed to be the largest in Europe and has a vertical drop of 350m. It has a half-pipe and 30 obstacles.

Beginners

With only one resort-level lift and no blue (easy) runs leading back to the resort, Ischgl is neither cheap nor particularly user-friendly for first-timers, who have no sensible choice but to return to the village by gondola. Idalp's sunny nursery slopes are inviting, although frequently crowded with ski school classes. The next stage in the learning curve is also quite tricky as blue runs are interrupted on occasion by short sharp red (intermediate) stretches. This is true of the adventurous blue descent from Inneres Viderjoch back to Idalp, though advanced beginners should have the skills to tackle it. The six-person Velillbahn chair-lift from Idalp is a better option for the less confident.

Intermediates

Ischgl has a number of long, challenging red runs, which makes it ideal for aspirational intermediates. On the extreme edge of the skiing, the descent from Palinkopf (the highest point in the lift system) to Gampenalp attracts relatively few skiers. This is because the Fimbatal offers spectacular scenery. On the other side of the ridge the lovely valley run to Samnaun is a real thigh-burner, especially as conditions are often more icy on the south-facing side. Those who complete it without stopping will have earned their lunch. The Palinkopfbahn chair, another relatively new addition to the lift system, takes skiers to the start of an equally testing red run all the way down to Bodenalp.

Advanced

Ischgl is short of genuine black (difficult) runs. The best ones are found between the Inneres Viderjoch and the Paznauner Taya. From the top of the Pardatschgrat there is a mild black descent to the bottom of the Velilleckbahn chair, at which point it turns into a challenging itinerary back to the resort. This is marked as a red dotted line but, as it is narrow and popular with advanced snow-users, it provides a stern and bumpy workout. The new funpark at Idjoch is particularly recommended for advanced boarders.

Off-piste

Although the Paznaun Valley is famous for its spring ski-touring, Ischgl itself is not at the top of the list as far as off-piste specialists are concerned. In consequence, the powder is not skied out the moment the lifts open, as it would be in St Anton. The most favourable terrain is off the Gampenalp chair, an area that will be extended when the projected lift to Piz Val Gronda at the top of the Fimbatal is completed. Again, there is no great sense of urgency as the proposed opening date is the year 2000. Meanwhile, enthusiasts must climb on skins.

Tuition and guiding

The Silvretta Ski & Snowboard School offers tuition in German or English for groups of about 10 to 12 people. Carving is a new course offered for skiers. With 100 qualified instructors on the books, the school can arrange off-piste tours on demand.

Mountain restaurants

Why have an Austrian lunch when you can have a Swiss one? That is the question they trade on in Samnaun, but the reality is that it is quite difficult to find that great Swiss staple of rösti with bacon, cheese and fried egg among the pizzerias and yodel-led Austrian taverns that jostle for space among the duty-free shops. On the Swiss side the Samnaunerhof and the Schmuggler Alm are recommended. The best options on the Austrian side include the restaurant in the hotel at Bodenalp and the Restaurant Idalp.

The resort

Ischgl is a compact, if somewhat overgrown, village with some 8,600 beds. Its popularity with German skiers and snowboarders has resulted in quality hotels in each category, many of them with a degree of solid alpine charm. One reporter considered Ischgl to be: 'the quintessential Alpine ski town'. However, the recent building boom has produced ugly extensions and overcrowding as the demand for more beds tempts hoteliers to outgrow their sites. Negotiating the hilly terrain on foot can be hazardous, but progressive thinking has led to indoor public staircases linking the various resort levels. The international clientèle creates a real buzz when skiing finishes for the day, with the bars in the central area near the church overflowing into the streets when the weather is fine.

Ischgl is connected to Kappl and Galtür by free shuttle bus during the day but not in the evening. The Silvretta Centre has an adventure swimming-pool, bowling alley and pool tables. The farming museum in **Mathon** on the road to Galtür is also popular.

Accommodation

As you can walk through the village from end to end in 15 minutes, almost any hotel makes a convenient base for at least one of the three lifts up to the mid-station. The exception is the Hotel Anthony, which is isolated near the Madlein drag-lift on the hillside opposite the village but highly recommended in other respects. The curved bulk of the Hotel Elizabeth dominates the Pardatschgratbahn, while the Goldener Adler is close to the Silvrettabahn at the opposite end of the village. The family-run Hotel Solaria is central and comfortable, if somewhat quirky in its reception arrangements. Hotel Olympia is recommended for: 'Cost, location, accessible parking, as well as a small spa'.

WHAT'S NEW
Tunnel connecting centre with the Fimbabahn
New Funitel Silvrettabahn
Quad-chair replaces Höllenkar double drag-lift
Boarders' Paradise Funpark

Eating in and out

Hotel restaurants predominate, which means that there is a wide choice of typically Austrian meals that lack individuality or merit. One reporter complained: 'There appeared to be few restaurants that were not part of a hotel'. The Goldener Adler is praised for its ambience and its fresh trout, and the Trofana Alm bar-restaurant for its pizza. The Buffalo Western Saloon provides a limited American alternative; the menu in the cocktail bar is the most impressive, with chille con carne, hamburgers and chicken wings. The Heidelberger Hütte specialises in fondue evenings, with transport by snowcat or horse-drawn sleigh. Eating in is unusual in a resort that has little self-catering accommodation, but the basics are available in bakeries, delicatessen and grocery stores.

Après-ski

For many, the party starts at the end of the skiing day on the snow outside the Hotel Elizabeth, with beer drinking and piped rock music. In the early evening the crowds move on to the Kitzlock and Nicki's Stadl, which are *ancien régime* establishments that specialise in Austrian politesse and tea-dancing to the strains of Strauss. The Kuhstall by the Silvrettabahn attracts a young crowd in the early evening. A rowdier scene is on offer at the Trofana Alm, where high spirits lead to dancing on the tables but stop short of lager-loutishness, which is not welcome in this upscale resort. For clubbing, the best places are the Wunderbar in the Hotel Madelein and the bar in the Hotel Post. The Allegra Bar also has impromptu dancing and the Hotel Elizabeth has dancing girls.

Skiing facts: Ischgl

TOURIST OFFICE
Postfach 9, A–6561 Ischgl, Tyrol
Tel 43 5444 5266–0
Fax 43 5444 5636
Email tvb.ischgl@netway.at
Web site www.tiscover.com/ischgl\

THE RESORT
By road Calais 1017km
By rail Landeck 30km, frequent buses from station
Airport Transfer Innsbruck 1½ hrs
Visitor beds 8,600
Transport free bus service (with guest card) links Ischgl, Kappl and Galtür

THE SKIING
Linked or nearby resorts Samnaun (I), Galtür (n), Kappl (n)
Longest run Idjoch–Ischgl, 7km (red)
Number of lifts 42
Total of trails/pistes 200km (27% easy, 63% intermediate, 10% difficult)
Nursery slopes 3 lifts
Summer skiing none
Snowmaking 40 hectares covered

LIFT PASSES
Area pass Silvretta Ski Pass (covers Ischgl, Samnaun, Galtür, Kappl and See) ATS2,430 for 6 days, VIP pass ATS1,890 for 6 days
Day pass ATS385 (Ischgl/Samnaun)
Beginners book of tickets

Pensioners ATS1,380 for 60 yrs and over
Credit cards no

TUITION
Adults Silvretta S & S-S, 9am–midday and 1.30–3.30pm, ATS1430–1500 for 6 days
Private lessons ATS2,100 per day
Snowboarding ATS1,200 for 3 half-days
Cross-country as regular ski school. Loipe 48km
Other courses telemark, carving, Big Foot
Guiding Stefan Jungmann

CHILDREN
Lift pass ATS1,190 for 6 days
Ski kindergarten 3–5 yrs, ATS580 per day including lunch, or ATS1,980 for 6 days
Ski school 4 yrs and over, ATS1,910–1,980 for 6 days including lunch
Non-ski kindergarten Children's Room at the Idalp, 4 yrs and under, 10am–4pm, ATS170 per day, extra ATS80 per day for lunch

OTHER SPORTS
Indoor tennis, skating, sleigh rides, swimming, parapente, indoor climbing

FOOD AND DRINK PRICES
Coffee ATS25, glass of wine ATS25, small beer ATS30, dish of the day ATS110–120

Childcare
Three-year-olds can learn the basics in the ski kindergarten then graduate to the children's ski school from four years of age and upwards, according to ability. The meeting point is beside the adventure garden, and lunch is served in the youth centre. There is also a kindergarten in the Silvretta cableway building on Idalp.

Linked or nearby resorts

Galtür
top 2300m (7,546ft) bottom 1585m (5,200ft)

In comparison with Ischgl, Galtür is an oasis of calm tucked away round a bend in the valley near the head of the Paznaun Valley. Although it has more than 3,000 beds and a large modern sports centre, it has the genuine feel of an alpine village. It is easy to imagine Ernest Hemingway strolling into the local pub after climbing on skins from the neighbouring Montafon Valley in the spring of 1925.

Galtür's slopes are at **Wirl**, an outpost reached in five minutes by a free shuttle bus that runs frequently at peak times. There are several hotels here for those who prefer ski-in, ski-out arrangements, but the avalanche-prone slopes on both sides of the valley mean that the hamlet can be cut off after a major snowfall. The skiing is open, uncrowded and relaxing and well suited to beginners and families. Galtür is a notable centre for ski-touring.

Unlike Ischgl, Galtür is extremely quiet, particularly at night, but there are several bars where both locals and visitors meet. The most popular bar is La Tschuetta, just off the main square. The family-run Fluchthorn Hotel offers a warm welcome in a central location. The Post is also convenient. As in Ischgl, most dining takes place in hotel restaurants, with the Rossle and the Alpenrose recommended. Galtür's modern sports centre offers tennis, squash, swimming, bowling and pool. The village also has a hang-gliding and parapente school, and a natural ice rink with curling.

TOURIST OFFICE
Tel 43 5443 8521
Fax 43 5443 852176
Email galtuer@netway.at
Web site www.tiscover.com/galtuer

Samnaun
top 2864m (9,394ft) bottom 1840m (6,035ft)

Lost in an inaccessible pocket in the mountains on the Austrian–Swiss border, Samnaun lives off its duty-free status and its ski links with Ischgl. Although these are now very swift, thanks to the Ravaisch double cable-car, it is hard to imagine anyone choosing to spend a holiday in a place that is as lacking in atmosphere as this.

TOURIST OFFICE
Tel 41 81 8685858
Fax 41 81 8685652
Email info@samnaun.ch

Kitzbühel

ALTITUDE 760m (2,460ft)

Beginners ✱✱ Intermediates ✱✱✱ Advanced ✱ Snowboarders ✱✱

The smart six-person gondola that finally replaced the ancient 1926 Hahnenkamm cable-car has been instrumental in restoring Kitzbühel to its rightful place as one of the most attractive ski destinations in Europe. Two-hour queues at peak times for the old 'sardine tin' are now consigned to history, although one of the cabins still hangs like a sporting trophy from the gondola base-station as a remembrance of things past. The journey time has been cut from 20 to just 8 minutes. Uphill capacity has been nearly quadrupled to a potential 12,000 skiers per day, and queuing has been virtually eradicated.

Kitzbühel is a walled, medieval settlement of heavily buttressed buildings painted with delicate frescoes, which survives the relentless battering of a nine-month tourist season with measured aplomb. Only in April, May and November, when the snow has either just gone or is about to arrive, is Kitzbühel devoid of visitors. Its world renown as a ski centre is based largely around the annual Hahnenkamm downhill race, the blue riband event of the World Cup calendar. Racers who negotiate its tortuous twists and jumps, say that every survivor is a winner. The Hahnenkamm is the mountain, and the actual race course is called the Streif, which when not prepared for racing is the benign red (intermediate) *Familienabfahrt* piste. The notorious Mausfalle, the most technical section, is roped strictly out-of-bounds to holiday skiers. Contrary to the belief instilled by dramatic television images of gossamer-skinned racers each January, Kitzbühel's skiing is largely intermediate, with few pisted challenges for experts. Apart from Innsbruck, this is the one destination in the Tyrol which is really appropriate for skiers and non-skiers alike.

> ✔ Large ski area
> ✔ Beautiful architecture
> ✔ Alpine charm
> ✔ Lively après-ski
> ✔ Wide range of activities for non-skiers
> ✔ Short airport transfer
> ✘ Low altitude and poor snow record
> ✘ Heavy traffic outside pedestrian centre
> ✘ Lack of skiing convenience

Ski and board
top 2000m (6,562ft) bottom 760m (2,493ft)

The main skiing is divided between two mountains: the Kitzbüheler Horn and the more challenging Hahnenkamm, which is now easily accessed from near the centre of town by the new gondola. Skiers still have the option of taking a ski bus to the hamlet of **Klausen** (3km away on the road to **Kirchberg)** for the Fleckalm gondola, which takes you swiftly into the lift system. Alternatively, you can plod across the nursery slopes to the two-stage Streifalm chair, which deposits you at a slightly higher point than the top-station of the cable-car. From here an interesting network of mainly red and blue (easy) cruising runs spreads out down three faces of the mountain and surrounding 'peaklets' over undulating terrain to form the largest and most challenging of Kitzbühel's two main ski areas. Lift connections are not all that they should be, and a couple of notorious bottlenecks can result in annoying queues during high-season weeks. However, even though the area is confined, the variety of runs and scenery gives you the pleasant impression that you are going somewhere rather than skiing the same slopes over and over again.

Kitzbühel's second ski area, the Kitzbüheler Horn, is to the east of town, across the main road and the railway tracks. Towering above the resort, it is a distorted but beautiful pyramid of rock and ice. A cable-car takes you up to 1996m, the highest point in the area, where the views from the top of the rocky Wilder Kaiser peaks are spectacular. The skiing is pleasant and gentle, but experienced skiers will quickly find the Horn a disappointment, with pistes much easier than their grading suggests. When conditions are bad the runs become more difficult, which towards the bottom of the mountain happens frequently since they mostly face south-west. **Aurach,** a ten-minute ski bus ride away from Kitzbühel, is a third separate area served by a single-chair and a couple of drag-lifts, which provide access to three gentle blue runs and a marginally steeper reddish alternative. It is an area largely unknown to tourists and, if there has been a fresh snowfall, it is worthy of a morning's skiing.

Kitzbühel's insuperable problem is its lack of altitude. Outside the middle winter weeks you must be prepared to contend with slushy conditions as the norm – at least at lower levels – and be grateful if they are otherwise. At the insistence of the International Ski Federation, snow-making now covers the Streif, and the resort's fathers have finally woken up to the benefits of being able to make up for what nature does not always provide at these low altitudes. Cannons on the three Maierl lifts ensure adequate cover all the way down to Kirchberg.

The four cross-country trails total 36km. There are a further 120km of prepared tracks in Kirchberg, **Aschau, Reith, St Johann in Tirol, Pass Thurn** and around **Mittersill.** All are easily accessible by free ski bus.

Beginners

Kitzbühel has four good nursery slopes near the town and plenty of easy skiing for second-weekers. The blue Pengelstein run from the top of the chair of the same name all the way down to Kirchberg is one of the best in the resort. Over on the Kitzbüheler Horn, the long Hagstein blue run (number 3 on the piste map) is a gentle but interesting cruise all the way from top to bottom. However, nervous skiers should beware of the Pletzerwald variation through the trees, which turns into a choice between an awkward red and the steep black (difficult) Horn Standard.

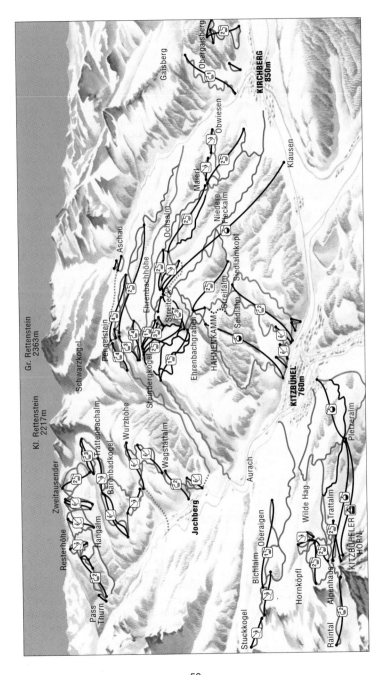

Intermediates

Kitzbühel is essentially for cruisers. Pengelstein-Süd is a long, flowing red that starts at the top of the Pengelstein double-chair and is the gateway into the Ski Safari (see below). It brings you down to the hamlet of **Trampelpfad**. The Hochsaukaser red at Pengelstein is a wide, fast piste with wonderful lips and rolls – one side is usually left unprepared and becomes a challenging mogul field.

The celebrated Ski Safari, marked by elephant signposts, is an enjoyable pisted itinerary that takes you from the Hahnenkamm up the Kitzbühel Valley to **Jochberg** and Pass Thurn. Anyone with a couple of weeks' ski experience can manage the outing, which consists of a series of blue and gentle red runs linked by lifts along the east-facing slopes of the valley. Some 18 of these are old-fashioned T-bars. The wooded skiing on the Wurzhöhe above Jochberg is always uncrowded, and it is worth spending some time here before moving on up the valley. Pass Thurn is an isolated ski area in its own right at the southern end of the valley. Wrap-up well in mid-winter as it can be extremely cold. However, the broad band of runs accessed by a sole double-chair from the roadside holds the best snow in the region. The downside is that the Safari is no circuit – it can only be fully skied in one direction. To return to Kitzbühel you have to queue for a bus for the 19-km road journey from Pass Thurn. You can ski back to Jochberg, which is only 9km from home, but you may wait much longer for a bus here because most seats will have already been filled by skiers joining at Pass Thurn. Plans to build the crucial link lift from Jochberg back up the Hahnenkamm are unlikely to be realised until well into the next century.

Advanced

The best of the steep skiing is reached via a network of lifts in the Ehrenbach sector of the Hahnenkamm. Try the Sedlboden and Ochsenboden. The black variation of Oxalm-Nord is part of the otherwise long intermediate run down to Kirchberg. Rettenstein at Pass Thurn is a short, sharp black, which ends up at the bottom of the Zweitausender double-chair. A new funpark on the Horn has a half-pipe and a boardercross course.

Off-piste

Those who are new to off-piste skiing can find plenty of easy powder skiing close to the pistes in the Hahnenkamm area after a fresh snowfall. Pass Thurn is particularly recommended. Bichlalm is another enjoyable area for powder. Kitzbühel has a specialist off-piste ski school called Ski Alpin-Kir.

Tuition and guiding

Kitzbühel has six separate ski schools including the famous Rote Teufel (Red Devils). All have a generally good reputation. However, we continue to receive mixed reports of the Rote Teufel. One reporter in a class of 13 notes that 'the instructor was a gloomy soul, older than usual, and his English was pretty basic'. Oversized classes and instruction that amounted to little more than guiding, with no individual tuition, are just some of the complaints.

Mountain restaurants

The Hoch Kitzbühel restaurant at the top of the Hahnenkamm gondola is a welcome addition. It has a sun terrace as well as wait- and self-service sections indoors. 'Wonderful Wienerschnitzel and a great atmosphere – don't miss the adjoining Hahnenkamm museum,' commented one reporter. The Alpenrose at the top of the Kitzbüheler Horn is noted for its *Germknödl*. The Hagstein, also on the Horn, is 'small, reasonably priced and overflowing with charm'. The Ochsalm on the Hahnenkamm is renowned for its Apfelstrudel. Trattenbergalm between Jochberg and Pass Thurn has some of the best simple food in the region. Panorama-Alm above Pass Thurn has a glass-walled bar outside to keep out the wind, and a roaring log fire within. The Pengelstein restaurant has been expensively extended but still tends to be crowded.

The resort

Kitzbühel attracts a diverse clientèle of skiers and non-skiers alike. Throughout the season it positively buzzes with excitement. Wealthy fur-clad Germans mix surprisingly well with younger and often more financially challenged skiers from Britain, Holland and Italy to form an alpine social melting-pot with few equals. The town centre is mercifully traffic-free, and a much improved ski-bus service ferries skiers to and from the Hahnenkamm and the Kitzbüheler Horn. However, the buses to surrounding villages are seriously over-subscribed at peak times. For skiing

WHAT'S NEW

Funpark on Kitzbüheler Horn
Increased snowmaking

convenience Kitzbühel gets a heavy minus mark, but the overwhelmingly elegant architectural beauty of the pedestrian Vorderstadt (centre), with its backdrop of snowy mountains, makes up for many of its detractions. However, serious shoppers will be disappointed. Apart from Louis Vuitton, the local Sportalm fashion outlet, and a scattering of ski shops and boutiques, Kitzbühel lacks the designer retailers you might expect in what is one of the most upmarket resorts in Austria.

Accommodation

For both comfort and service the Goldener Greif and the Jägerwirt head an impressive list of 16 four-star hotels. The Maria Theresia has undergone refurbishment as well as improving the standard of its restaurant. Sporthotel Bichlhof is centrally located and warmly recommended. The converted hunting lodge of Schloss Lebensberg, on the outskirts, offers a hedonistic level of pampering. This includes a health centre with swimming-pool and free babysitting on weekdays. The formerly gloomy Hotel zur Tenne in the town centre has been dramatically refurbished as a

Skiing facts: Kitzbühel

TOURIST OFFICE
Hinterstadt 18, Postfach 42
A-6370 Kitzbühel, Tyrol
Tel 43 5356 621550–0
Fax 43 5356 62307
Email office@tourist-kitzbuehel.co.at
Web site www.tiscover.com/kitzbuehel

THE RESORT
By road Calais 1130km
By rail station in resort
Airport transfer Salzburg 1½ hrs,
Munich 2½ hrs, Innsbruck 2hrs
Visitor beds 7,100
Transport free ski bus with lift pass

THE SKIING
Linked or nearby resorts Kirchberg (l),
Jochberg (l), Pass Thurn (l), St Johann in
Tirol (n), Aurach (n)
Longest run Pengelstein-Süd, 6.8km
(red)
Number of lifts 28 in Kitzbühel, 60 in
linked area
Total of trails/pistes 60km in Kitzbühel,
160km in linked area (39% easy, 46%
intermediate, 15% difficult)
Nursery slopes 5 lifts in Kitzbühel, 7 in
linked area
Summer skiing none
Snowmaking 15km in linked area

LIFT PASSES
Area pass (covers Kitzbühel, Kirchberg,
Jochberg, Pass Thurn, includes ski bus,
swimming-pool and reduction for sauna)
ATS1,820–1,980 for 6 days
Day pass ATS390–420
Beginners points cards
Pensioners ATS315–340 per day for

women 60yrs and over and men 65yrs
and over
Credit cards yes

TUITION
Adults Rote Teufel (Red Devils), Total ,
Kitzbüheler Horn, Hahnenkamm, Crystal,
Ski Alpin, all ATS1,500 for 6 days,
10am–12pm,2pm–4pm
Private lessons ATS2,200 per day
Snowboarding As ski schools, ATS600
for 2½hrs, ATS1,500 for 3 days
Cross-country ATS1,080 for 3 days.
Loipe 36km in Kitzbühel, 120km in area
Other courses telemark
Guiding Ski Alpin-Kir and through ski
schools

CHILDREN
Lift pass 6–15yrs, ATS990 for 6 days,
free for 5yrs and under
Ski kindergarten 3yrs and over,
10am–4pm, ATS1,800–2,000 for
6 days
Ski school all ski schools, 4yrs and over,
9am–4pm, ATS1,800 for 6 days
Non-ski kindergarten Anita Halder,
ATS80–120 per hr, ATS400 per day,
including meals

OTHER SPORTS
Curling, skating, indoor tennis and
squash, swimming, hot-air ballooning,
parapente, hang-gliding, shooting range,
horse-riding

FOOD AND DRINK PRICES
Coffee ATS28, glass of wine ATS23–28,
small beer ATS30, dish of the day
ATS80–100

designer hotel. The Weisses Rössl, once the town's prominent coaching inn, is a picture of faded splendour, slightly ragged around the edges but still enormously popular. Schloss Münichau, in the village of Reith on the far side of the Schwarzsee, is a 500-year-old castle, which is said to be 'delightfully quiet, with reasonable prices and superb food'.

Eating in and out

Austrian alpine food wins few gastronomic prizes, but you can eat better and with more variety in Kitzbühel than in most resorts. The Goldener Greif is renowned for its *Salzburger Nockerl*, a kind of hot meringue soufflé. The Hotel zur Tenne specialises in fresh trout and is said to be 'outstanding, but expensive'. The Landeshäusl and Huberbräu are both reasonably priced and cheerful. Landgasthof Oberaigen at the Bichlalm mid-station offers 'an enjoyable evening out, with wholesome cooking and a mountain ambience'. Chinarestaurant Peking in the Kirchplatz rings the culinary changes. The existence of a McDonald's seems a shame in such beautiful surroundings, but its presence is muted.

Après-ski

Life after skiing centres almost entirely around the pedestrian-only streets in the Vorderstadt. Two British-style pubs, The Londoner and Big Ben, attract the lion's share of business along with Highways, which offers live music. Seppi's is where Austria meets the Old Kent Road. The locals congregate in Stamperl and Fünferl while the Goldener Gams is a modest restaurant and bar with live music and a sophisticated Tyrolean atmosphere that attracts all ages. 'S Lichtl, also in the Vorderstadt, is a bar with a warm atmosphere, which draws a more sophisticated crowd. Late-night revellers head for Royal Dancing, the most popular disco. K und K and Take Five are more expensive nightclubs. Skiers and riders can now dance into the early hours, secure in the knowledge that no longer do they have to hit the Hahnenkamm by 8.30am to avoid the first two-hour queue. The Aquarena health centre is free with a ski pass.

Childcare

Five lifts make up the extensive nursery area on the golf course at the foot of the Hahnenkamm. There is a ski- and a non-ski kindergarten. The end-of-season Easter Bunny Package, promoted by the tourist board, is extremely good value: children up to 15 years of age are offered a free lift pass, ski or board rental, lessons and accommodation in a family room.

Linked or nearby resorts

Kirchberg
top 2000m (6,562ft) bottom 850m (2,788ft)

Once upon a time Kirchberg was the no-frills dormitory village that gave you a back door into Kitzbühel's skiing at knockdown prices, but without its medieval charm. This once poor relation, only 6km around the shoulder of the Hahnenkamm at the head of the Brixental, still gives alternative access to Kitzbühel's main ski area, but circumstances have changed and it now boasts 25 three- and four-star hotels. The resort has its own small beginner and intermediate lifts on the Gaisberg, as well as access to the Hahnenkamm by a two-stage chair and the Klausen gondola. It has a kindergarten and two ski schools.

The town's layout is not designed for ski convenience; distances are considerable, and the ski bus service is seriously over-subscribed. Choose where you stay with care in relation to both price and where you want to ski. The Tiroler Adler Schlössl is neither particularly convenient nor cheap, but is one of the best in town. The nightlife is just as busy as in Kitzbühel but less sophisticated. Charley's Club and Le Moustache are among the main centres of activity. A new 3.5km toboggan run on the Gaisberg is floodlit in the evenings.

TOURIST OFFICE
Tel 43 5357 2309
Fax 43 5357 3732
Email kirchberg.tvb@netway.at
Web site www.tiscover.com/kirchberg

Lech/Zürs

ALTITUDE Lech 1450m (4,756ft), Zürs 1720m (5,642ft)

Beginners ✱✱   Intermediates ✱✱✱   Advanced ✱✱   Snowboarders ✱✱

Lech and neighbouring Zürs, situated over the back of the Valluga from **St Anton**, are the most exclusive resorts in the Alps. Not only do they attract the rich and famous to their portfolio of five-star hotels but they quite literally exclude other skiers from the slopes when they consider these to be full. As soon as 14,000 tickets have been sold the tills are closed and electronic signs on approach motorways warn day-trippers to ski elsewhere. Priority is given to those skiers who are staying in the resort. The result is that even on the busiest weekends of the year queues are never longer than ten minutes.

Lech is by far the larger of the two resorts: a traditional Austrian village centred around the church and the river, which has changed surprisingly little over the past 40 years. The biggest expansion has been in **Oberlech**, a satellite 200m up the mountain that was once the summer home of herdsmen and shepherds. The collection of chalets and hotels here is ideally placed for the skiing and provides a safe and car-free centre for families with small children. The construction of a network of underground tunnels beneath the top cable-car station and the hotels means that visitors do not have to lug suitcases across the piste.

✔ Alpine charm
✔ Beautiful scenery
✔ Long runs
✔ Plenty of intermediate skiing
✔ Efficient lift system
✔ Varied off-piste skiing
✔ Good artificial snow cover
✔ High standard of hotels
✔ Lack of queues
✔ Facilities for families
✘ Difficult road and rail access
✘ Lack of mountain restaurants
✘ High prices

Zürs is little more than a collection of mainly four- and five-star hotels astride the Flexenpass, which gives the only access to Lech during the winter months. The first ski school in Austria opened here as long ago as 1906. In 1937 it was the site of Austria's first T-bar, although today the combined ski area is proudly T-bar free.

Zug, 3km through the woods from Lech up a pretty valley, also offers rural tranquillity. An evening journey from Lech through the star-lit woods by horse-drawn sleigh is delightful and romantic. Zug is fully integrated into the lift system that links Lech with Zürs.

The resorts share a varied and extensive ski area, although advanced skiers might be more interested in the abundant off-piste and ski-touring opportunities. St Anton (40 minutes' drive away), with its larger choice of expert piste terrain, is included in the lift pass, as is the bus service between the two. Parking in both villages is restricted and ruthlessly policed. Prices are high and as one reporter commented: 'Lech and Zürs are best suited to skiers who regard cost as secondary'.

Ski and board
top 2450m (8,036ft) bottom 1445m (4,741ft)

The Lech/Zürs circuit of 110km of prepared pistes, spread over three mountains and served by 34 lifts, provides mainly intermediate skiing of the highest quality. The circuit can be skied only in a clockwise direction, which results in crowds of people heading for the same lifts at the same time and used to mean high-season queues. However, the steady upgrading of the lifts and the limitation on the number of skiers have alleviated the problem; most of the chair-lifts have been speeded up and have 'moving carpets' (conveyor belts) to enable skiers to progress on to the lift more quickly.

> **WHAT'S NEW**
>
> Snowmaking on Trittkopf
> Zürsersee T-bar upgraded to chair-lift
> Schlegelkopfbahn and Seekopfbahn converted to covered chair-lifts

Mountain access to the circus is via the twin Rüfikopf cable-cars, which scale an impressive wall from the centre of Lech. Long and challenging itineraries lead down off the shoulder in either direction through the woods to the road by Zürs, or back to Lech via a scenic itinerary through the Wöstertäli. Alternatively, you can enjoy the lengthy and benignly beautiful pistes towards Zürs.

Lech's main skiing area, on the other side of the valley, is contrastingly open and mostly gentle, although the slopes immediately above the village are of a more challenging gradient. Mountain access on this side is via an assortment of four lifts – including a detachable quad-chair – from different points in or near the village. Above Oberlech, lifts and pistes spread throughout a wide, fragmented basin below the peaks of the Kriegerhorn and the Zuger Hochlicht. The two are linked by a cable-car with spectacular views.

Beginners
First-timers can use a beginner's ticket and should not buy the expensive Arlberg Ski Pass until advised to do so by their instructor. Lech has excellent nursery slopes behind the church as well as at Oberlech. Beginners should quickly progress to a whole range of blue (easy) runs on the Oberlech side of the valley. Second-week skiers should be able to negotiate the blue Rüfikopf run from the top of the cable-car, which in turn links into the *Familienabfahrt* to bring them all the way to Zürs with an ego-boosting sense of achievement.

Intermediates
Confident skiers head up the Rüfikopf cable-car for the choice of red (intermediate) pistes down the Hexenboden and Trittkopf. Follow the local lift map with care: appropriately coloured circles indicate pisted

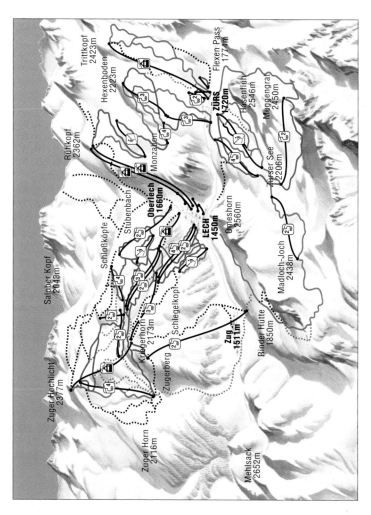

runs, while ski routes are marked by diamonds. It is easy to think that a red-diamond with a thin black border is a hard intermediate run. In fact it is an extreme itinerary that is neither patrolled nor pisted, although some are so well skied that they become pistes. From Zürs you can either take the scenic Zürsertäli or choose more direct routes down to the Zürsersee and on via the Madloch towards Lech.

Advanced

Zürs has the steeper skiing of the two main resorts, including a couple of short, sharp black (difficult) pistes, notably the Hexenboden Direkte. Langerzug and Tannegg are two challenging runs down the shoulder of the Rüfikopf, and Südhang is another recommended piste. The ski routes marked on the lift map offer a considerable challenge; number 33 from Zürs to Lech is a particularly satisfying one.

Lech's funpark on the Schlegelkopf is called the Swatch Boarderland. It is 300m long, with a half-pipe, a quarter-pipe and a series of obstacles. Zug has a natural half-pipe when snow conditions allow. A permanent carving course for skiers has been built on the Rüfikopf.

Off-piste
When fresh snow falls, both Lech and Zürs are a delight. Experts can try the various descents of the 2173-m Kriegerhorn and the Zuger Hochlicht beyond it. The long run down from the top to the village of Zug via the narrow Zuger Tobel can be spectacular in the powder snow conditions. Langerzug and Tannegg around the shoulder of the Rüfikopf are dramatic in the extreme. For environmental reasons, it is strictly forbidden to ski off-piste through the trees – anyone caught doing so risks having his or her lift pass confiscated. Ski-touring and heli-skiing are popular; some ski school instructors we spoke to spent most of their time taking private clients heli-skiing.

Tuition and guiding
The Austrian Ski School in Lech, Oberlech and Zürs has a particularly fine reputation, and we have received no adverse reports. At the ski school meeting area, instructors' names are nailed to the class boards – the same instructors teach the same level all season. This means that classes do not suffer from a change of instructor mid-week or even daily, as is the case in many resorts. On the whole good English is spoken, however, one reporter said that because the majority of guests are German, instructors have to be reminded to translate into English for their British pupils. Eighty per cent of ski teachers in Zürs and over 50 per cent in Lech are booked for private rather than group lessons each day – an indication of the spending power of the clientèle.

Skilifte Lech, headed by World Cup trainer Walter Hlebayna, offers racing courses for skiers, carvers and snowboarders.

Mountain restaurants
The choice of mountain restaurants is extremely limited, surprisingly so in an area that attracts so many discerning lunchers. This is because the hotels on the slopes in Oberlech and Zürs all serve lunch, so there is no need for other restaurants. Hotel Burg in Oberlech, which has recently expanded with a spa, has a gourmet restaurant that is consistently praised but needs to be booked in advance at weekends and during high season. The Mohnenfluh is criticised for its 'excruciatingly slow service'. The Rüfikopf restaurant (not to be confused with the burger bar) is also acclaimed ('serves mainly vegetarian food of a very high standard and is rarely crowded'). The Seekopf at Zürs is recommended. The Palmenalpe above Zug is one of the better self-service eating places, provided you avoid peak hours.

The resort

Every skiing nation has at least one ultra-smart resort that lures the 'beautiful people' to its manicured slopes. Sadly, Lech now has had to soldier on without its most famous annual visitor: Princess Diana was its popular patron who, by returning here with her children each year, did more than anyone else to enforce Lech's chic international image. The Dutch, Jordanian and Spanish royal families are also known to put in an appearance, while Princess Caroline of Monaco favours Zürs.

Lech was first inhabited by Swiss immigrants in the fourteenth century, and this corner still looks more towards Switzerland, its nearest neighbour, than to the main part of Austria. The modern expansion of the resort has been unobtrusive, and despite the presence of luxury hotels and designer boutiques Lech still has a real village feel to it.

Regular ski buses now connect Lech, Zug, Zürs, **Stuben** and St Anton. Post buses run to the railhead at Langen. However, public transport comes to a halt in the early evening. Taxis are expensive, but a late-night collection service called 'James' will return you to wherever you are staying in Lech, Zürs and Zug, as long as it is before 4am, for a reasonable set fee of ATS30 per person.

Zürs stands in an isolated position above the tree-line and lacks much of the charm of Lech, although resort-level snow is guaranteed for most of the season. It is little more than a collection of extremely smart hotels. While Zürs may completely lack the showy gaudiness of St Moritz or Gstaad, the clientèle's opulence is often even greater – it just wears wealth more discreetly.

Accommodation

Lodging is mostly in comfortable and expensive hotels, plus some apartments and the occasional tour operator's chalet. The village is fairly compact, and location is not particularly important (although we recommend that families with small children stay in Oberlech because of its traffic-free environment and skiing convenience). The smartest hotel, indeed one of the most celebrated five-stars in Austria, is the ornately frescoed Gasthof Post. It has only 38 rooms, and you need to book a year in advance. The Arlberg, Gotthard, Krone and the Almhof Schneider are all warmly recommended by regulars. The Tannbergerhof is popular with British people and is the centre of Lech's social life.

There are numerous less formal hotels and plenty of Fremdenzimmer (bed-and-breakfasts), but nothing is cheap. It is worth noting that even the smartest hotels do not generally accept credit cards.

In Oberlech, the Sporthotel Petersboden is known for its piste-side Red Umbrella bar, and Hotel Montana is owned by the family of ski racer Patrick Ortlieb. Zürs has three five-star hotels including Thurnhers Alpenhof where all rooms have superb mountain views. The four-star Arlberghaus receives glowing reports and has a curling-rink on its roof. Zug's original inn, the Rote Wand, is now a luxury four-star hotel.

Skiing facts: Lech/Zürs

TOURIST OFFICE
A-6764 Lech, A-6763 Zürs, Arlberg
Tel Lech: 43 5583 2161–0
Zürs: 43 5583 2245
Fax Lech: 43 5583 3155
Zürs: 43 5583 2982
Email Lech: lech-info@lech.at
Zürs: zuers-info@zuers.at
Web site www.lech.at/www.zuers.at

THE RESORT
By road Calais 1100km
By rail Langen 17km, frequent buses
Airport transfer Innsbruck 2hrs, Zurich 2½hrs
Visitor beds 8,250
Transport free ski buses between Lech, Zürs and St Anton

THE SKIING
Linked or nearby resorts St Anton (n), Stuben (n), St Christoph (n), Zug (l)
Longest run Madloch–Lech, 5.2km (red)
Number of lifts 34 in Lech/Zürs, 86 on the Arlberg Ski Pass, including St Anton
Total of trails/pistes 110km in Lech/Zürs (40% easy, 40% intermediate, 20% difficult). 260km on Arlberg Ski Pass, including St Anton
Nursery slopes 4 lifts
Summer skiing none
Snowmaking 75 hectares covered

LIFT PASSES
Area pass Arlberg Ski Pass (covers Lech, Oberlech, Zürs, Rauz, St Christoph, St Anton, Stuben, Sonnenkopf–Klösterle) ATS1,940–2,150 for 6 days
Day pass ATS425–470 (Arlberg)
Beginners some free lifts, points tickets
Pensioners Senior ticket for women 60yrs and over, and men 65yrs and over, for 6 days ATS1,690–1,850 for 6 days.

Seniors 75yrs and over, ATS100 for whole season
Credit cards Eurocheque

TUITION
Adults Lech and Oberlech, 9am–midday and 1–3pm, ATS1,750 for 6 days. Zürs, 2hrs am and pm, ATS1,980 for 6 days
Private lessons Lech and Oberlech, ATS2,170 per day. Zürs, ATS2,260 for 4hrs
Snowboarding times and prices as ski lessons
Cross-country private lessons only, same price. Loipe 19km
Other courses telemark, race training, snowshoeing, carving
Guiding through ski schools

CHILDREN
Lift pass (covers resorts and linked area) 6–15 yrs, ATS1,260–1,400 for 6 days. 6yrs and under, ATS100 for whole season
Ski kindergarten Oberlech, 2½ yrs and over, 9am–4pm, ATS1,600 for 6 days, extra ATS80 per day for lunch. Zürs, 4yrs and over, 9.30–3.30pm, ATS1,980 for 6 days, lunch ATS80
Ski school Lech, 4½–14yrs, 10am–3pm, ATS1,600 for 6 days. Zürs, 5–15yrs, 4hrs daily, ATS1,980 for 6 days
Non-ski kindergarten Lech 2½–3yrs, 9am–4pm. Zürs, 3–5yrs, ATS1,980 for 6 days, lunch ATS80

OTHER SPORTS
Skating, curling, helicopter rides, indoor tennis and squash, sleigh rides, swimming, paragliding, winter walks

FOOD AND DRINK PRICES
Coffee ATS27, glass of wine ATS20–35, small beer ATS33, dish of the day ATS150–250

Eating in and out

Good restaurants abound, as you might expect in resorts of this calibre, but most are in the hotels and none is cheap. In Lech, the Brunnenhof is strongly recommended, together with Bistro S'caserole, Rudi's Stamperl and the Dorf Stüberl. For a special evening, Gasthof Post and the Almhof Schneider are good bets. Pizzeria Charly is consistently popular with reporters for 'sound Italian fare served with a smile – not as Schilling-snatching as others'. The Käsknöpfle's food is described as 'a bit too Austrian, but nevertheless the restaurant is good fun and friendly'. In Oberlech, the Ilga Kellerstübli and the Goldener Berg are famous for fondues. In Zürs, the Chesa Verde is an award-winning restaurant, while in Zug the Klösterle is highly recommended.

Après-ski

The average age of the clientèle in Lech and Zürs is higher than that in other alpine resorts. Wherever you look you will see bronzed and fit 60-year-olds wearing the latest in designer ski suits, as well as 30-somethings who might, perhaps, aspire to look like this in the autumn of their lives. Consequently, après-skiers at these resorts prefer to put their hair up, rather than let it down.

The ice-bar outside the Tannbergerhof in Lech is where, weather permitting, the evening begins in earnest as the slopes close. Guests filter inside to join in the tea-dancing, which swings into action as night falls. The hotel also hosts a disco with a good atmosphere later on in the evening. The Sidestep Bar in the Hotel Krone attracts a rival crowd of over-25s for dancing, and the Klausur Bar in the Almhof Schneider is popular. After 5pm the Rüfikopf cable-car transforms into a 'flying bar' for a minimum of ten guests, who pay ATS170 each; a glass of champagne is included. Sleigh rides to Zug for dinner are a treat, and you can take the cable-car up to Oberlech and toboggan down afterwards (the cable-car closes at 1am). Skiers flock to Lech's s'Pfefferkörndl bar during the early evening. Die Vernissage in Zürs is recommended, and the Zürserl in the Hotel Edelweiss is the biggest disco in town, while the Rote Wand and the Sennkessel in Zug are both lively places.

Childcare

The area lends itself well to family skiing, particularly at Oberlech, site of the main nursery slopes. A number of hotels run their own crèches, and we have good reports of the ski kindergarten, which has mainly English-speaking staff and a sympathetic attitude. Children under six years old ski for ATS100 for the whole season. The ski school takes children all day and supervises lunch (parents must remember to provide lunch money each day). The new Lech Miniclub now fills the gap for non-skiing children aged from two-and-a-half years from 9am to 4pm each day. The Little Zürs kindergarten takes children from three years old and provides ski instruction for children from four years of age.

Mayrhofen

ALTITUDE 630m (2,066ft)

Beginners ✱✱✱   Intermediates ✱✱✱   Snowboarders ✱

Mayrhofen has taught generations of British skiers to love low-lying Tyrol. Many remain intensely loyal to a resort that does its best to take care of children, who ski for free under the age of six and receive a reduction up to the age of 19. The resort is only 75km from Innsbruck on fast, flat, snow-free roads; you arrive without having travelled perceptibly uphill. At the top of the broad Ziller Valley, Mayrhofen's own skiing on the Penken, Ahorn and **Finkenberg** slopes covers 99km of pistes with 30 lifts. Local passes are sold only for a maximum of three days; if you want to ski further, the regional Zillertal Superskipass allows access to a wider network of 154 lifts and 463km of piste – including the Hintertux Glacier as a supplementary option.

- ✔ Lively resort atmosphere
- ✔ Competent ski teaching
- ✔ High standard of accommodation
- ✔ Focus on children's activities
- ✔ Summer skiing on Hintertux Glacier
- ✔ Part of extensive ski pass region
- ✘ Low altitude skiing
- ✘ No skiing to village from main mountain
- ✘ Unconnected ski areas

Everybody loves to party in Mayrhofen, where clients are typically from the south of Germany or the north of England; British skiers total nine per cent of the market here. The resort has 'singles' weeks, and music events bring in bands such as the Four Tops and ELO. Regular live music takes place on the outdoor stage on Penken, and clowns perform in the village streets.

Mayrhofen claims the first-ever ski kindergarten in the Alps. It was started in 1954 by Riki Spiess-Mahringer, mother of downhiller Uli Spiess, the World Cup champion who used to beat Franz Klammer. Now in her 70s, Riki still spends every day with children on the mountain at Ahorn.

Ski and board
top 2250m (7,380ft) bottom 630m (2,066ft)

Mayrhofen's main mountain is the Penken, to which gondolas rise from the town centre as well as from the outlying hamlets of Finkenberg and **Schwendau**. There is no route whatsoever back down to Mayrhofen, and both the red (intermediate) piste to Finkenberg and black (difficult) ski route to Schwendau are usually bare of snow by March (although last

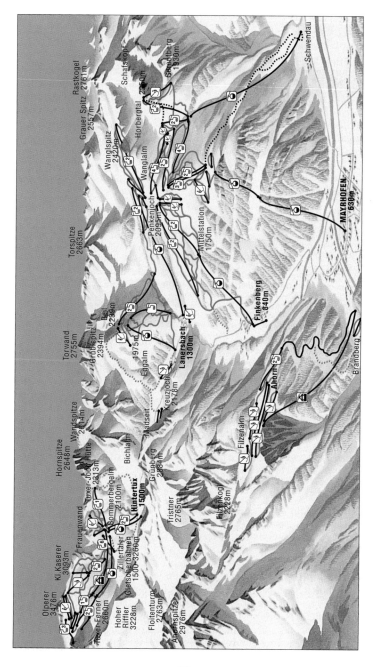

season was an exception). It is important to emphasise that whatever the charms of the Tyrol, with villages below 1000m and skiing not much over 2000m, good snow cover will always be ephemeral at best. Four live video cameras on the glacier enable weather views to be broadcast constantly on Penken and Ahorn. Mayrhofen's beginner mountain, the Ahorn, is accessed only by a limited-capacity cable-car, which is a 10-minute hike from town. The 4.5-km black Ebenwald piste on Ahorn – the only village run in Mayrhofen – now has snowmaking, but at this low altitude it is often too warm for the cannon to operate. Grooming is good, and electronic boards tell you which lifts have queues – always a problem on mountains with no skiing down to the village at the end of the day, no matter how modern the lifts. The funpark on Horberg/Tappenalm features two quarter-pipes and a range of obstacles for snowboarders.

Beginners

Children are better catered for than adult beginners. The former have their own play areas, whereas the latter are forced to ride awkward drag-lifts for all the blue (easy) runs on Ahorn and in most cases on Penken, which at least has one ultra-flat, long beginner itinerary – the 'Horberg Baby Tour'. The Ahorn is a good learning area for snowboarders.

Intermediates

Many Penken runs are graded red, not because they are steep but because they are narrow – often less than 20m wide. This creates difficulties for skiers and freeriders when descending together. Long fall-line cruises are conspicuous by their absence, and no red run deserves special comment.

Advanced

As one reader puts it: 'Experts are better off in another resort'. Their greatest challenge is avoiding collisions with aimlessly wandering schools of neophyte skiers and snowboarders. The Tappental and Schafskopf ski itineraries on Gerent offer the odd hour's amusement before you take the bus to the Hintertux Glacier.

Off-piste

The ingenious and the desperate will find short, steep descents through rocks and woods on Penken and Gerent. However, hiring a guide from Peter Habeler's mountaineering school for ski-touring is the only option for serious powderhounds.

Tuition and guiding

Mayrhofen has more than 150 instructors from four competing schools. Despite typical classes of 12, most students give the teaching high marks. Peter Habeler, who climbed Everest in 1978 without oxygen, has a school that also offers off-piste tours with overnight stops in a mountain hut. The ski school run by Uli Spiess is the only one to limit group lessons to 10 and to guarantee free lessons if you cannot ski a blue run within five days. Manfred Gager's school offers carving courses on parabolic skis. Max Rahm's SMT is the fourth school, offering video analysis and an F2 snowboard test centre. The Yeti Club for snowboarders is affiliated to the Uli Spiess ski school.

Mountain restaurants
Numerous 'umbrella bars', some open-air and others weatherised, serve quick snacks, schnapps and beer – generally to the accompaniment of raucous accordion music, but without the ear-splitting drinking games of Hilde's (priciest in region) and Vroni's (al fresco barbecue chicken). Josef's Bio Hütte under the Tappenalm chair is where an old farmer serves his own potato and cheese dishes and a popular home-made schnapps.

The resort
In Mayrhofen every house is a gasthaus, every home a gastheim, and 406 such inns and pensions account for the vast majority of the resort's 8,600 beds. Chalet and self-catering accommodation is considered inimical to local employment prospects. Large green areas are preserved; cows are kept (and slaughtered) right across the street from the Penken lift station. Mayrhofen is actually the third largest community in the Tyrol, although you can stroll across town in 15 minutes. Buses are free only when you are wearing ski clothes and are equipped with a ski pass. In the evenings the buses are neither available nor necessary. All lift stations in the Zillertal region have free parking, except for the Penkenbahn in the centre of Mayrhofen. There are no bargains along the winding high street, although the Spiess ski shop at Penken offers superb rental gear, and the Mikesch toy shop is a treasure. The Aqua Adventure Pool, with its 101-m chute, is unique in the Alps.

Accommodation
The general standard is superlative, with many hotels featuring swimming-pools, saunas or the Turkish baths beloved by Germans. Rooms are bigger and better than in Switzerland or France. The Strass Hotel is right next door to the Penken lift and home of both the Ice Bar and Sports Arena disco. Just up the road is the Waldheim, which has luxurious rooms with views. Most tour operators feature the Neuhaus ('excellent, with a high standard of food') along the main road, but the Elisabeth is more luxurious, and the impeccable Berghaus has its own indoor tennis courts. The Alpenhotel Kramerwirt is warmly recommended. Hotel Obermair is 'basic, but comfortable'.

Eating in and out
Most guests choose half-board arrangements, and several reporters complain that the portions are inadequate. Mayrhofen has fewer independent dining venues than one might expect. Among them is the Wirthaus zum Griena, which is a listed 400-year-old building and

includes a menu of 'poor people's food'. Singapore is an average Chinese restaurant, Mo's serves Cajun burgers, and Mamma Mia is a bright Italian. Grill Kuchl has a good, inexpensive menu, as does the Central Café. Café Dengg has the best pizza. The Sports Bar Grill in the Hotel Strass is the only Mexican.

Après-ski

The Ice Bar, with its dancing 'polar bear', claims to be Europe's biggest sales point for Grolsch beer and Mayrhofen's most popular meeting place. The glass marquee up from the Schlüssel Alm is less hip hop. Virtually every hotel has an après-ski entertainer. The Sports Arena is one of the most high-tech discos in the Alps. Rundum is a bar with green glass and a real tree upstairs. The Scotland Yard Pub is a popular hang-out for riders and has darts, a working red telephone box and British beer.

Childcare

If you register your child at the tourist office, he or she will receive a birthday gift in the post. In town, childcare includes Wuppy's Kinderland, which minds children from three months to seven years of age. SMT and Spiess also offer non-ski kindergarten. The choice of five ski kindergarten includes Bobo's, where kids ski with a 'penguin'.

Linked or nearby resorts

The Zillertal region covers 12 different local areas stretching down to the River Inn and the Germany–Innsbruck autobahn, and up the valley sides east as far as **Gerlos** and west as far as **Fügenberg. Hintertux, Lanersbach, Vorderlanersbach, Kramsach** and **Kaltenbach** are all included on the Zillertal ski pass. Few of these Zillertal resorts are linked together by piste. Individually none offers much more than a single day's interesting skiing. But bus transport is free and generally efficient, and a free train goes from Mayrhofen down the valley to **Zell am Ziller**, and on to **Fügen** and the mainline junction at **Jenbach**. Finkenberg is the closest village to Mayrhofen on the road up towards Hintertux. But its previous appeal, quicker access to Penken, was eliminated by construction of the Penken gondola from downtown Mayrhofen. Lanersbach is the best choice for price and nightlife, not to mention its own ski runs, for those focusing on daily skiing at Hintertux. With neighbouring Vorderlanersbach, Lanersbach boasts 13 lifts servicing the small areas of Eggalm and Rastkogel, with skiing up to 2300m on 33km of pistes.

After Mayrhofen, Zell am Ziller is the second most substantial valley resort. The name should not be confused with Kaprun's twin resort near Salzburg, Zell am See. In fact, Zell am Ziller is the antithesis of a ski resort. Sitting in the flatlands along the Ziller river at 570m, Zell is a bustling, commercialised market town. Counting the lift systems of its neighbours, **Ramsau-in-Zillertal** and **Hippach**, Zell am Ziller claims a regional area with 47km of pistes and 22 lifts. Neither of Zell's own two areas, Kreuzjoch or Gerlosstein, is within walking distance of the town.

Skiing facts: Mayrhofen

TOURIST OFFICE
Postfach 21, A-6290 Mayrhofen, Zillertal
Tel 43 5285 6760
Fax 43 5285 6760 33
Email mayrhofen@zillertal.tirol.at
Web site www.tiscover.com/mayrhofen

THE RESORT
By road Calais 1000km
By rail Jenbach station in resort
By air Innsbruck 1hr, Munich 2hrs
Visitor beds 8,600
Transport free day-time bus service around Zillertal included in lift pass

THE SKIING
Linked or nearby resorts Finkenberg (l), Fügen (n), Fugenberg (n), Gerlos (n), Hintertux (n), Kramsach (n), Lanersbach (n), Ramsau-in-Zillertal (n), Schwendau (n), Kaltenbach (n), Vorderlanersbach (n), Zell am Ziller (n)
Longest run Ahorn–Abfahrt, 5.5km (black)
Number of lifts 30 in Mayrhofen, 154 in Zillertal
Total of trails/pistes 99km in Mayrhofen (22% easy, 52% intermediate, 26% difficult), 463km in Zillertal
Nursery slopes 3 runs and lifts
Summer skiing 18km of runs and 7 lifts on Hintertux Glacier
Snowmaking 27.8 hectares in Mayrhofen

LIFT PASSES
Area pass Zillertal Superskipass (includes glacier), ATS2,010 for 6 days
Day pass ATS350
Beginners no free lifts
Pensioners no reduction
Credit cards no

TUITION
Adults Uli Spiess , Manfred Gager, SMT, Peter Habeler, all ATS1,450 for 6 days (4 hrs per day) or ATS600 per day
Private lessons all ski schools, ATS500 per hr, ATS2,000 per day
Snowboarding all ski schools, ATS380 for 2 hrs. Private as ski lessons
Cross-country all ski schools, ATS500 per day. Loipe 20km
Other courses ski-touring
Guiding Peter Habeler

CHILDREN
Lift pass Zillertal Superskipass, (includes glacier) ATS1,100–1,830 depending on age, for 6 days, free for 5yrs and under
Ski kindergarten Uli Spiess, Peter Habeler, SMT, Roten Profes and Bobo's, all 2–4 yrs, 10am–3pm, from ATS730 per day including lunch
Ski school all ski schools, 4–14 yrs, ATS600 per day (4 hrs) not including lunch
Non-ski kindergarten Wuppy's Kinderland, 3 mths–7 yrs, 9am–5pm, ATS370 per day including lunch or ATS1,750 for 5 days including lunch. SMT and Uli Spiess, prices and times on application

OTHER SPORTS
Parapente, skating, curling, indoor tennis, sleigh rides, winter walks and guided hikes, go-kart racing, indoor horse riding, squash, swimming, hot-air ballooning

FOOD AND DRINK PRICES
Coffee ATS24, glass of wine ATS30, small beer ATS25, dish of the day ATS80–200

Kreuzjoch's centrepiece is a swift eight-person gondola, and Gerlosstein has twin cable-cars – testimony to the crowds that flocks in from Germany each weekend.

Tuxer Glacier
top 3250m (10,663ft) bottom 1500m (4,920ft)

Hintertux, or the Tuxer Glacier as the locals insist on calling it, boasts the steepest glacier skiing in Austria and, snow permitting, is open 365 days a year (18km of the piste is open all summer). It also offers the most advanced skiing on the otherwise strictly low-altitude Zillertal ski pass. The glacier extends to 86km of piste served by 21 lifts carrying up to 30,000 skiers per hour. Even so, the run to the bottom from the glacier terminus at Sommerbergalm (2100m) is frequently closed. A piste map devoted solely to glacier runs would be helpful.

Hintertux consists of a handful of modern hotels, all four-star and little frequented by British skiers, who find more life at less cost down the valley in Lanersbach. The Tuxer Valley winds steeply south-west for 17km from Mayrhofen, requiring a 45-minute free shuttle transfer from Mayrhofen to Hintertux. Buses run every 20 minutes during the morning peak hours.

The glacier attracts such vast numbers that, as a result, two-metre-high metal cattle pens welcome skiers and snowboarders at the Hintertux base-station. Hotel residents in Hintertux with six-day lift passes enjoy their own separate entrance. Lower glacier lifts and pistes are very crowded. Higher lifts are antiquated, slow and less crowded, with the more testing top runs often empty in less than ideal weather.

From Hintertux a four-person gondola rises to the beginning of the glacier at Sommerbergalm, site of a comfortable self-service cafeteria and an outdoor umbrella bar blaring schmaltzy folk tunes. From here three drag-lifts and a covered chair branch to the right towards the Tuxerjoch. Branching to the left and up to the Tuxerfernerhaus restaurant complex is the recently installed Gletscherbus gondola, carrying up to 24 skiers in sit-down comfort. A succession of chair - and drag - lifts continue up to the famous Gefrorene Wand (the 'frozen wall') and Austria's highest privately owned mountain hut. Nowhere on the glacier is skiing overly challenging, with most runs groomed and free of bumps; the home run to Sommerbergalm is narrow and dangerously over-crowded in places. The only marked off-piste itinerary, the Schwarze Pfanne, goes all the way down to Hintertux, but is frequently closed. The ice-cave under the glacier is a popular free attraction.

Hintertux has its own ski and snowboard school. There is no snow-board park, but the soft snow and regular pitch of the glacier are ideal for boarder beginners.

TOURIST OFFICE
Tel 43 5287 8506
Fax 43 5287 8508
Email info@tux.at

Niederau

ALTITUDE 830m (2,722ft)

Beginners ✶✶　Intermediates ✶

The Wildschönau, a name dating from the twelfth century and roughly translated as 'wild beauty', is a quiet corner of the Tyrol within sight of the ski slopes of both **Alpbach** and **Söll**, about 70km from Innsbruck on the edge of the Kitzbüheler Alps. Niederau has neither the best skiing nor is it the biggest village in Wildschönau, but it is the most popular with the British skiers, who make up eight per cent of an otherwise predominantly German market (the border is only 20km away). The appeal of Wildschönau, with its 28 lifts and 42km of low-altitude pistes, seems to be the fact that the slopes are so benign. Skiing began here in 1947, with the first chair-lift built in the Tyrol. In 1995–6 a modern eight-person gon-

- ✔ High standard of accommodation
- ✔ Short airport transfer
- ✔ Low prices
- ✘ Exceptionally limited skiing network
- ✘ Low altitude
- ✘ Short ski season

dola was opened in Niederau. Nearby **Oberau** (3km from Niederau) and **Auffach** (7km) are linked by 13 free buses per day. The Wildschönau ski pass includes the old silver mining village of **Thierbach,** which has only two drag-lifts and 500 beds among a local population of 200, but boasts an elevation of 1150m.

Ski and board

top 1900m (6,232ft) bottom 830m (2,722ft)

From Niederau's gondola station, it is only seven minutes to the top at Markbachjoch (1500m), where traversing uphill left or right leads to a total of three pisted runs back to the bottom. Niederau has ten lifts, eight of which are drags, and Oberau has a further seven short drag-lifts. Both these skiing areas can suffer from a shortage of snow on the bottom runs from as early as February. Auffach's modern four-person gondola rises in two stages through woods to a series of five parallel drag-lifts, all high enough (between 1500 and 1900m) for good skiing when Niederau is green. Irritatingly for a beginner region, the Wildschönau's piste numbers and names do not appear on the lift map.

Beginners

Despite being touted by tour operators as a resort for beginners, the Wildschönau is exceptionally limited even in relatively snow-sure beginner terrain, and Niederau demands tiresome pushing with ski poles to get anywhere at all. It has three drag-lifts serving nursery slopes near the gondola and two more drags that are a 15- to 20-minute hike away. There is no blue (easy) route down to Niederau from the mountain top, and only three very short blues at the top for those who do commute up and down from the village.

Intermediates
An experienced intermediate who happens to find him- or herself in the Wildschönau will enjoy the fall-line Lanerköpfl International Ski Federation (FIS) downhill course. Auffach's four drag-lifts to the skier's left of the gondola serve exclusively red (intermediate) pistes, with some areas left unpisted. Auffach has the longest, most satisfying intermediate run in the region, with 1000 vertical metres of good cruising.

Advanced
Niederau has two ski routes down the fall-line to the skier's right of the gondola, and the black (difficult) racecourse Lanerköpfl, which would challenge any advanced skier if taken in a tuck from top to bottom. Auffach has a funpark.

Off-piste
Wildschönau's rounded, low-lying hills make for easy ski-tours when snow conditions allow for powder skiing.

Tuition and guiding
There are two Niederau schools, Activ and Wildschönau, with the former better prepared for ski-touring. Both have ample experience with beginners, and English is widely spoken. One experienced reporter points out that the lavish praise heaped on both schools in the past comes from readers who have not skied elsewhere in the Alps or North America to experience other teaching methods.

Mountain restaurants
At the top of Niederau, Rudi's Markbachjoch, with its blue curtains and sanded pine tables, is cosy and is celebrated for its plum pancakes. Auffach's Schatbergalm and Koglmoos are large self-service inns. The Anton Graf Hütte in Niederau is an authentic touring hut.

The resort
Niederau and its neighbouring villages sprawl for kilometres back and along the highway, although each has a small centre, mostly more serviceable than charming. Wildschönau has set itself the goal of becoming the cleanest valley in Europe and has won awards for its pure air. With only 2,600 guest beds and 1,300 local residents in the village, visitors do not get lost in the crowds. Indeed, some reporters remark on being recognised by name when returning a second year. Niederau has indoor horse-riding, a floodlit tobogganing run, two supermarkets and a quaint souvenir shop.

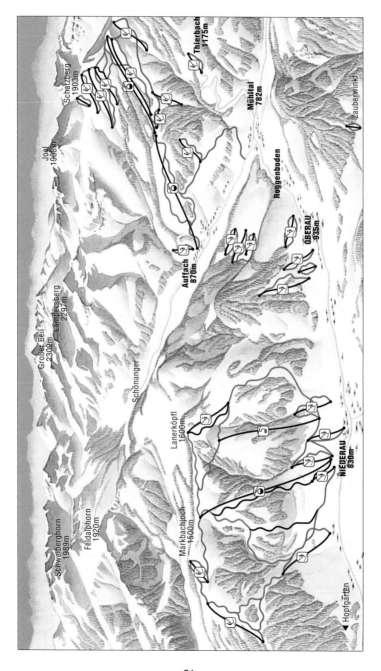

Thierbach 1175m

Mühltai 782m

Zauberwinkl

Roggenboden

Schatzberg 1903m

OBERAU 935m

Joel 1968m

Auffach 870m

Lämpersberg 2297m

Großer Beil 2309m

Schönanger

Lanerköpfl 1600m

NIEDERAU 830m

Schweiberghorn 1989m

Feldalphorn 1920m

Markbachjoch 1500m

▶ Hopfgarten

Skiing facts: Niederau

TOURIST OFFICE
A-6311 Niederau, Wildschönau
Tel 43 5339 8255
Fax 43 5339 2433

THE RESORT
By road Calais 1114km
By rail Wörgl 10km
Airport transfer Innsbruck 2hrs,
Salzburg 1½ hrs
Visitor beds 7,800 in Wildschönau
Transport ski bus to Oberau and
Auffach free with lift pass

THE SKIING
Linked or nearby resorts Oberau (n),
Auffach (n), Mühltal (n), Roggenboden
(n), Thierbach (n)
Longest run Schatzberg–Auffach,
7.5km (red)
Number of lifts 28 in area
Total of trails/pistes 42km
(6% beginner, 56% easy,
32% intermediate, 6% difficult)
Nursery slopes 3 lifts in Niederau,
2 in Oberau
Summer skiing none
Snowmaking 5 hectares covered

LIFT PASSES
Area pass Wildschönau (covers
Niederau, Oberau, Auffach,Thierbach)
ATS1,575 for 6 days, Kitzbüheler
Alpenskipass ATS1,990 for 6 days
Day pass ATS335
Beginners Package including lessons
Pensioners ATS1,110 for women 60yrs

and over, men 65yrs and over
Credit cards yes

TUITION
Adults Wildschönau and Aktiv, both
ATS1,150 for 6 days (2hrs per day)
Private lessons both ski schools,
ATS450 per hr, ATS1,700 for 4hrs
Snowboarding both ski schools,
ATS1,040 for 3 days
Cross-country both ski schools, ATS350
per day. Loipe 30km in the valley
Other courses ski-touring
Guiding Wildschönau or Aktiv
ski schools

CHILDREN
Lift pass 6–15yrs, ATS945 for 6 days,
free for 6yrs and under if accompanied by
an adult
Ski kindergarten Niederau and Auffach,
4–6yrs, 9.30am–4.30pm, ATS280 per
day including lunch
Ski school Wildschönau and Aktiv,
4yrs and over, ATS1,300 for 6 days
Non-ski kindergarten Wildschönau,
2–6yrs, 9.30am–4.30pm, ATS800 for
6 days not including lunch

OTHER SPORTS
Night-skiing, parapente, sleigh rides,
skating, curling, horse-riding, swimming

FOOD AND DRINK PRICES
Coffee ATS20–24, glass of wine
ATS21–20, small beer ATS24, dish of the
day ATS90–120

Accommodation
Hotel Sonnschein is 'in a class of its own: indoor pool, excellent half-
board meals and sumptuous rooms'. The older Hotel Austria also has an
indoor swimming-pool. The well-appointed Schneeberger houses a
popular disco.

Eating in and out

Most dining is done in hotels and guest houses. In Niederau, Café Lois has extremely filling pizzas. Sport Café-Pub has antique radios and TVs and serves cheap sausage and chips.

Après-ski

Zither and harp evenings, with Tyrolean costume, are regular hotel events. Sean plays the guitar at the Hotel Vicky, which now has a number of British and Irish brews on tap.

Serious drinking takes place at the Cave Bar. The Dorfstuben is more salubrious. Every Thursday there is Tyrolean Doughnut Making with Traudi at the Schwarzenauhof farmhouse.

Childcare

One reporter said she booked Niederau specifically because of a particular tour operator's childminding programme. Both ski schools give lessons to children from four years of age, and the Wildschönau school minds children from two years of age indoors.

Linked or nearby resorts

Auffach
top 1900m (6,232ft) bottom 875m (2,870ft)

Auffach has the region's best skiing but is not featured by any British tour operators. Aside from the kitsch woodcutter's chalet, the village of modern buildings is nondescript. The traditional town/barn house Weissbacher is popular, as is the three-star modern Schatzberghaus with its swimming-pool. The Avalanche Pub slides from afternoon to early morning (3pm to 3am) with old rock tunes prevailing.

TOURIST OFFICE
as Niederau

Oberau
top 1150m (3,773ft) bottom 935m (3,067ft)

Wildschönau's regional centre has an impressive Benedictine church and 1,850 locals. Oberau also accommodates 2,500 tourists in its central hotels, guesthouses and farms. The Tirolerhof Hotel has a swimming-pool. Gasthof Kellerwirt is an old monastery with elegant cuisine. The SnoBlau Pub is quite active. The skiing is extremely limited here, but a free ski bus links the resort with Niederau and Auffach.

TOURIST OFFICE
as Niederau

Obergurgl

ALTITUDE 1930m (6,330ft)

Beginners ✷ Intermediates ✷✷✷ Advanced ✷✷ Snowboarders ✷✷

Obergurgl has been transformed by the introduction of an ambitious on-mountain gondola, which connects directly to neighbouring Hochgurgl, thereby creating the sizeable linked ski area that it had sorely lacked. Situated at the head of the remote and beautiful Ötztal, which is a 90-minute drive from Innsbruck, Obergurgl has an entrenched reputation as Austria's leading skiing destination for families. Its high altitude means that snow is guaranteed from November until after even the latest of Easters, but in the past its limited piste skiing has acted as a deterrent for serious skiers who might otherwise have been drawn to this charming village.

✔ Ideal for families
✔ Extensive ski-touring
✔ Reliable snow record
✔ Late-season skiing
✔ Pleasant resort atmosphere
✗ Lack of tough runs
✗ Limited facilities for non-skiers
✗ High prices

Its wealth of four-star hotels attracts an upmarket, but by no means aloof, clientèle predominantly from Germany but traditionally bolstered by British families. The old village, centred around the church and the original hotel, the Edelweiss und Gurgl, manages to maintain its character despite the lashings of luxurious, modern accommodation that has sprung up around it.

Guests confess to being bowled over by the natural, unspoilt beauty of the resort, which instils unfailing loyalty. As one reader put it: 'I almost didn't want to send in this report in case too many others discover this lovely resort'.

Hochgurgl, formerly a free but annoying ski bus ride away, is now linked across the König and Verwall valleys by an eight-person gondola with an hourly capacity of 1,200 skiers. In the past the two have been seen as entirely separate destinations. While Obergurgl drew families like a moth to a searchlight, Hochgurgl had a more serious skiing image. Whether Obergurgl will lose some of its exclusivity as a result of the new link remains to be seen. Only limited **Vent** and mass-market **Sölden** are within easy reach for a day out from Obergurgl; lift passes are not compatible, and most Obergurgl visitors are more than content to remain in their elegant eyrie at the head of the valley.

Obergurgl made its mark on the European skiing map on 27 May 1931, when the Swiss aviation pioneer Professor Auguste Piccard force-landed his hot-air balloon on the Gurgler-Ferner Glacier. What he had just achieved was the world altitude record of 16203m, and what he was about to achieve was world recognition for one of Austria's most exclusive ski resorts. A local mountain guide, Hans Falkner, spotted the balloon landing in the last light of the day. The following morning he carried out a triumphant rescue of the explorers, leading them between the crevasses to Obergurgl and glory for the village and all concerned.

Ski and board
top 3080m (10,104ft) bottom 1793m (5,881ft)

The slopes of both Obergurgl and Hochgurgl occupy a north-west-facing area at the southern end of the Ötztal on the Italian border. These are now linked via the new 3.6-km gondola, which runs from the bottom of the Wurmkogel lift at Hochgurgl to the bottom of the blue Run 3, halfway up the Festkoglbahn. Most of the skiing is above the tree-line, and runs are intermediate. Not all of the handful of black (difficult) runs justify their gradings, and advanced snow-users – unless they are interested in ski-touring for which the area is outstanding – will soon tire of the limited pistes, despite the new link. However, there is plenty to keep less adventurous snow-users and families occupied in what are truly magnificent surroundings.

The skiing takes place over three small areas naturally divided by the contours of the terrain. Hochgurgl offers the greatest vertical drop off the glacier but also the most severe weather conditions: even on a sunny day in February, extreme cold can be the price you pay for high-quality snow. The wide, wooded hillside leads down to **Untergurgl**, which is little more than a roadside lift station and car park. Obergurgl's two sectors, properly linked in one direction only, generally comprise more interesting terrain, with the steeper runs at the top and some good off-piste alternatives. New and easy access to the Festkogl area is now provided via a four-seater enclosed chair, which starts from directly behind the Hotel Edelweiss and Gurgl in the centre of the village. Alternative access is via a gondola on the outskirts of Obergurgl, while Gaisberg is reached by a chair-lift, which rises lazily over gentle slopes from the village centre.

Beginners

Complete novices start on nursery slopes set well away from the village near the cross-country track. While Obergurgl has easy skiing in both its main sectors, Hochgurgl has a far more comprehensive selection of blue (easy) pistes. The top of the long glacier is served by two chairs – one a high-speed covered quad, which affords some protection against the often severe elements at this altitude.

Intermediates

The Festkogl gondola rises steeply to a sunny plateau with a restaurant and a couple of drag-lifts. The area of mainly red (but not difficult) intermediate runs is served by a modern quad-chair, which takes you up to the highest point of Obergurgl's skiing at 3035m. Less confident skiers and snowboarders will enjoy the blue run from the gondola station down to the bottom of the Rosskar double-chair.

While Hochgurgl's skiing is generally less challenging, the Schermer-Spitz chair, with conveyor-belt entry, gives access to a wide and easy red piste, which is the start of nearly 1500m vertical all the way down to Untergurgl. A two-stage covered quad-chair takes you up to the summit of the Wurmkogl, which offers an exciting descent for strong intermediates.

The drag-lift on the southern side of the ski area has a short, steep, second section. It serves a long and varied red run with moguls. One reporter described the bottom half as 'much more difficult than any other red run in the resort'.

Advanced

The pistes offer little serious challenge or scope. In the Gaisberg sector a long, antique single-chair goes up to the Hohe Mut at 2670m. The first part of the only official run down is a ski route, which in turn becomes a black piste, but the 1.8-km descent is not difficult when snow cover is deep, and one suspects that the grading is designed to reduce traffic and avoid bottlenecks at the outdated lift.

Accomplished snow-users will enjoy the black itinerary down the Ferwalltal from the top of the Festkogl gondola. However, the run is prone to avalanche danger, and great care should be taken. One reporter

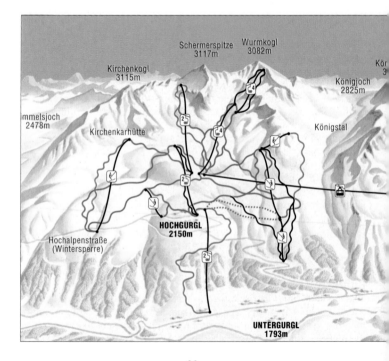

marvelled at 'the tricky, trappy, black No. 4 run under the Rosskar lift – anyone who says Obergurgl is all easy cruising should try this'. Wurmkogel has a half-pipe. There is a snowboard park with a small range of obstacles in the Festkogl ski area.

Off-piste

Obergurgl, with its 21 glaciers, is one of the great ski-touring centres of Europe. More limited opportunities also exist for those who prefer to take their powder by lift than on skins. An off-piste run in good powder conditions off the back of the Hohe Mut takes you on a glorious descent that ends up near the Schönwieshütte.

Tuition and guiding

Obergurgl is one of the homes of the Austrian Instructors' Ski School, and the standard of teaching and organisation here should therefore be among the highest in Austria. However, we have received considerable criticism of both the Obergurgl and Hochgurgl schools, with lack of motivation being the main complaint. One reporter was horrified to discover that his four-and-a-half-year-old twins were 'left in the care of a complete stranger when they became upset. It soon became clear that not only my own children but a large proportion of the class were in a state of almost permanent upset'. Other reporters complained of as

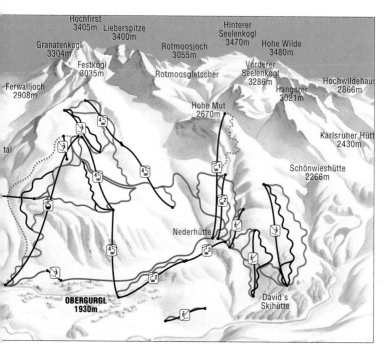

many as 15 pupils per class, and division into language groups is not always well organised ('the ski school seemed to allocate children mainly by size'). Gripes include a lack of English-speaking instructors, poor group selection and 'almost non-existent tuition skills'.

Mountain restaurants

The Hohe Mut Hütte, at the top of the single-chair at Gaisberg, provides magnificent views of the Ötztal and the Dolomites. Although you can make the return journey by chair-lift the alternative post-prandial prospect of the black ski route down acts as a deterrent to those wanting lunch and means that the old wooden chalet is the least crowded restaurant in the area. On fine days there is an ice-bar and barbecue on the terrace. The Schönwieshütte, a 15-minute walk from the Sattellift piste, is a touring refuge, which serves simple meals ('best gulaschsuppe and *Kaiserschmarren* ever'). David's Schihütte at the bottom of the Steinmannlift is recommended particularly for its *Tirolergröstl* (potato with bacon). The Festkogl mountain restaurant is described by a number of reporters as 'indifferent'. The Nederhütte is warmly recommended for 'good food and an excellent atmosphere'.

WHAT'S NEW

Gurgl Top Express gondola linking Obergurgl and Hochgurgl
Night-skiing on Festkogl
Rosskarbahn four-seater enclosed chair from Obergurgl to Festkogl area
Increased snowmaking

In Hochgurgl, the Wurmkogl by the top of the Wurmkogl quad-chair is the best of the three altitude restaurants. Reporters warn that restaurants in Hochgurgl itself are nearly all attached to the smart hotels and are expensive. Toni's Almhütte – a rustic wooden hut owned by the Sporthotel Olymp – is highly praised. The sun terrace of the Hotel Riml has 'the best views on the mountain'.

The resort

Building in Obergurgl has reached capacity within the avalanche-safe area, and despite the large number of luxury hotels Obergurgl remains a small village set on the lower level around the church and a handful of shops, and on the upper area around an open-air ice rink. At the heart of it all is the Edelweiss und Gurgl Hotel, once the local inn and now the focal four-star around which much of village life rotates. Post buses run to Sölden and beyond. Cars are banned from the village between 11pm and 6am, and parking is not easy. The handful of shops is strictly limited to sports and souvenirs.

Accommodation

Most of the accommodation is in smart hotels and, to a lesser extent, in gasthofs and pensions. It is also possible to rent attractive and spacious apartments by contacting the resort direct. Hotel Crystal is a monster of a building, completely out of keeping with resort character, but extremely comfortable inside. The Deutschmann takes its name from the old Obergurgl family that owns it. The Bergwelt ('art-deco furniture and a great pool') and the Austria are both highly recommended. Hotel Gotthard is also warmly praised, and 'the welcome matched the luxurious surroundings'.

In the centre, the Edelweiss und Gurgl is highly thought of, although its bedrooms are not as large or as well equipped as in the new four-stars. The Jenewein was praised for its friendly service and 'quite exceptional demi-pension food'. Hotel Alpina was described as 'outstanding, with wonderful hospitality from the owners'. The Schönblick has 'helpful owners, large rooms, and excellent buffet breakfasts'.

Eating in and out

Dining is largely confined to the main hotels, most of which have separate à la carte restaurants. Pizzeria Romantika in the Hotel Madeleine provides some respite from the ubiquitous rounds of Wienerschnitzel.

The Edelweiss has a comfortable candlelit stübli and offers 'relaxed elegance'. The Bergwelt is recommended for its nouvelle cuisine. Pizzeria Belmonte in Haus Gurgl has 'the best pizzas in town'. Restaurant Pic-Nic is also recommended. A reporter spoke warmly of fondue evenings organised at the Nederhütte. One small supermarket looks after the needs of self-caterers.

Après-ski

Obergurgl is surprisingly active in the evenings. The Nederhütte at the top of the Gaisberg lift becomes crowded as the lifts close for the day. Tea-dancing and copious measures of glühwein prepare you for the gentle run down to the village. The outdoor bar of the Edelweiss at the foot of the Gaisberg lift continues to attract customers until darkness falls.

The Joslkeller has a cosy atmosphere and good music, which gets louder with dancing as the evening progresses. You will find the odd person in ski suit and ski boots still here in the early hours. The Krump'n'Stadl is noisy, with yodelling on alternate nights. Hexenkuch'l has live music, as does Toni's Almhütte in Sporthotel Olymp in Hochgurgl. The Edelweiss cellar disco is said by most reporters to be the best in town.

Childcare

In a move to attract more families, children aged seven years and under can now ski for free – a higher age limit than in many other resorts in the Alps. The kindergarten takes non-skiing children aged between three and five years old. A number of hotels operate their own crèches, usually free of charge, and the minimum age accepted varies from hotel to hotel. These include the Alpina, Austria, Bellevue, Bergwelt, Crystal, Hochfirst, Hochgurgl and Olymp. Obergurgl Ski School takes children from five years old, and Hochgurgl accepts children as young as three years old for lessons.

Skiing facts: Obergurgl

TOURIST OFFICE
A–6456 Obergurgl, Ötztal
Tel 43 5256 466
Fax 43 5256 353
Email tvbgurgl@netway.at
Web site www.tis.co.at/tirol/gurgl

THE RESORT
By road Calais 1200km
By rail Ötztal 54km, regular buses
from station
By air Innsbruck 1½ hrs
Visitor beds 3,900
Transport free ski bus between
Obergurgl and Untergurgl

THE SKIING
Linked or nearby resorts Hochgurgl (n),
Sölden (n), Untergurgl (n), Vent (n)
Longest run Wurmkogl–Untergurgl,
8.5km (black/blue/red)
Number of lifts 24
Total of trails/pistes 110km (32% easy,
50% intermediate,18% difficult)
Nursery slopes 4 runs and lifts
Summer skiing none
Snowmaking 14km covered

LIFT PASSES
Area pass ATS2,060 for 6 days
Day pass ATS420
Beginners coupons ATS140
Pensioners 60yrs and over ATS1,280 for
6 days
Credit cards Eurocheque

TUITION
Adults Obergurgl ATS1,630 for 6 days,
Hochgurgl/Untergurgl ATS1,490 for 5

days, both 10am–midday and 2–4pm
Private lessons Obergurgl ATS2,360 and
Hochgurgl/Untergurgl ATS1,350 per
2-hr lesson
Snowboarding Obergurgl ATS1,850 for 6
half-days, private lessons through ski
schools
Cross-country Obergurgl, ATS360 per
half-day, private lessons through ski
schools. Loipe 12km
Other courses snowshoeing, telemark,
monoski
Guiding through Obergurgl Ski School

CHILDREN
Lift pass 8–15yrs, ATS1,280 for 6 days,
free for 7yrs and under if accompanied
by an adult
Ski kindergarten 3–5yrs,
9.30am–12.30pm and 1.30–4.30pm,
ATS1,530, for 6 days, ATS180 per day for
lunch
Ski school Obergurgl, 5–14yrs,
ATS1,530 for 6 days, ATS180 per day
including lunch. Hochgurgl/Untergurgl,
3 yrs and over, ATS1,490 for 5 days,
times as adults
Non-ski kindergarten Obergurgl, 3yrs
and over, ATS1,530 for 6 days, ATS180
per day for lunch

OTHER SPORTS
Skating, curling, squash, swimming,
shooting

FOOD AND DRINK PRICES
Coffee ATS24–30, glass of wine
ATS20–22, small beer ATS25–30, dish
of the day ATS80–150

Obertauern

ALTITUDE 1740m (5,707ft)

Beginners ✳✳ Intermediates ✳✳✳ Snowboarders ✳

Obertauern is one of Austria's top-five winter destinations, although it was only discovered by British skiers in the mid-1980s and its popularity has declined in recent years. Its renown is based largely on its reputation for guaranteed snow-cover. Indeed, if there is decent snow in Austria, you will find it here. What is Austria's best, or indeed only, shot at a purpose-built resort lies on a high pass in the Niedere Tauern mountains, 90km south of Salzburg. When other resorts are struggling to cope with a lack of cover during lean winters, Obertauern is usually rolling in metres of snow.

✔ Excellent snow record
✔ Reliable resort-level snow
✔ Superb piste-grooming
✔ Skiing convenience
✔ Interesting off-piste
✘ Late-season queues
✘ No bus system
✘ Lack of non-skiing activities
✘ Quiet après-ski
✘ Spread-out village

Thanks to a motorway tunnel, the Tauern Pass (once an important Roman trade route at the only point in the range where the altitude falls below 2000m) is a quiet backwater. The impressive peaks of the Niedere Tauern mountain range surround the road around the resort, allowing the construction of lifts from a central point to fan out into a natural ski circus. The ski area is not particularly extensive but provides an interesting variety of gradient and terrain.

Ski and board
top 2313m (7,587ft) bottom 1640m (5,379ft)

The circus can be skied in both directions, but the skiing is concentrated on the north side of the resort, spread around a broad, undulating and mainly treeless bowl ringed by rocky peaks. Four main lifts rise from around the bowl to points near the rim. Two of them ascend to approximately 2000m from almost the same point at Hochalm (1940m); the Seekareckbahn quad chair-lift takes you up over a steep, east-facing slope, and the Panorama triple-chair over a more varied south-facing one.

A clockwise circuit of this northern part of the area need not involve any of the higher, more difficult runs. However, the pistes of most interest to timid skiers are the easy, open runs across the middle of the bowl, served by drag-lifts including the long Zentral lift from just below the village. On the south side of the resort the mountains rise more dramatically, keeping the village in shade for much of the day in mid-winter. The local lift map fails to show either piste names or numbers, but the signposting of the clockwise and anticlockwise circuits is generally sufficient.

Beginners
The nursery slopes are excellent, with a short, gentle drag-lift in the heart of the village, just north of the main road, and another longer one on the lower slopes at the eastern end. Another runs parallel to and just south of the road. The high Gamskarlift, at the top of the steep Schaidberg chair, also affords gentle skiing.

Intermediates
The entire circuit is geared towards intermediates, with some truly excellent long, but not over-demanding, red (intermediate) descents from the lip of the bowl. Some of the best are accessed from the Panorama Sesselbahn and Hundskogel lifts. The top of the Plattenkarbahn quad-chair is the starting point for a challenging run of over 400m vertical.

Advanced
There is enough to keep advanced skiers happy here for a week, although the more adventurous will want to explore the other resorts in the region. Pistes can become heavily mogulled around the edge of the bowl.

Off-piste
In powder conditions the off-piste skiing is spectacular, with long runs both above and below the tree-line. To find the best and safest runs you need the services of a local guide.

Ski tuition and guiding
Obertauern has five ski schools including the Krallinger Obertauern-Süd, which has a higher than average number of female instructors and is much favoured by tour operators. The others are Schischule Koch Obertauern-Nord, CSA (known as Skischule Willi Grillitsch), Schischule Top, and Schischule Frau Holle. Christian and Werner Schmidt run their dedicated Snowwave Snowboardschule from the Hotel Solaria, and Gerfried Schuller runs the Obertauern Snowboardschule. The Frau Holle school and Blue Tomato also give snowboarding lessons.

Mountain restaurants
Because of the ski-in ski-out nature of Obertauern, it is quite easy to return to the village for lunch. Alternatively, the choice of mountain restaurants is more than adequate. The Seekarhaus at Kringsalm is a cosy spot with enjoyable food, but it can become crowded. Similarly, the Sonnhof is swarming with people at peak times. The Schaidberg Liftstube has an extensive menu.

The resort

Under its usual blanket of snow, the long straggle of roadside hotels and bars looks more like a Wild West town. It is by no means devoid of charm, but its growth in recent years has not always been absorbed with grace. It takes about 20 minutes to walk from one end to the other. The main cluster of buildings, which constitutes the centre, is around the village nursery slope and the tourist office.

Accommodation

Nearly all the accommodation is in hotels and guesthouses, few of them cheap. Location is not particularly critical unless you have small children (choose a hotel within easy walking distance of one of the kindergarten). Hotel Krallinger is recommended as a good ski-in ski-out base with satellite television in the rooms. Haus Kärntnerland is said to be 'clean, com-

> **WHAT'S NEW**
>
> Village crèche for children 6yrs and under

fortable and friendly, with exceptional food'. The Alpenrose apartments in the village centre are said to be 'cosy and well-appointed'. The lavish Sporthotel Marietta remains a favourite with reporters.

Eating in and out

Most of the restaurants are in hotels. The Stüberl restaurant in the Hotel Regina is reported to be extremely good value ('quiet, candlelit and serves enormous portions'). The Lurzeralm requires reservations and serves 'well-presented, good food'. The Latsch'n'Stüberl has friendly service and well-prepared food.

Après-ski

This is centred on the main hotel bars, of which more than 15 offer music and dancing. The Edelweisshütte is the place to go at the end of the skiing day, along with the Gamsmilch Bar. Later on the action moves to La Bar and Premillos, next to the Hotel Steiner. The Gasthof Taverne reportedly has the liveliest disco later in the evening.

Childcare

Non-skiing children of two to six years of age can be left all day in the Hotel Alpina crèche or in the new village crèche in the information centre (up to six years of age). All the ski schools run ski kindergarten with lunch provided on request.

TOURIST OFFICE
Tel 43 6456 7252
Fax 43 6456 7515
Email obertauern@magnet.at
Web site www.obertauern-info.co.at/obertauern

Saalbach-Hinterglemm

ALTITUDE 1000m (3,280ft)

Beginners ✱✱✱ Intermediates ✱✱✱ Advanced ✱✱ Snowboarders ✱✱✱

Saalbach-Hinterglemm is the collective marketing name of two once separate villages in the pretty Glemmtal near **Zell am See**. The narrow valley, with uniform 2000-m peaks on either side, lends itself to a natural ski circus, which can be skied as happily in one direction as in the other. It was justly chosen to host the 1991 Alpine World Skiing Championships, and it provides some of the best advanced intermediate skiing in Austria, second only to that in the Arlberg. Saalbach has devoted 13km of slopes for riders of all levels and is recognised as a major resort for snowboarders.

- ✔ Extensive ski area
- ✔ Short airport transfer
- ✔ Reliable snow cover
- ✔ Traffic-free village centres
- ✔ Large choice of accommodation
- ✔ Good child facilities
- ✘ Lift queues
- ✘ Sprawling village
- ✘ High prices
- ✘ Noisy at night

The two villages, a five-minute drive apart, have grown so much over the years that they now stretch along the valley and almost meet. Those looking for two cheap and cosy little Austrian villages will be disappointed; both are expensive. Saalbach is larger and brasher, while Hinterglemm is marginally more family-oriented. A third village, **Leogang**, provides a back door into the ski area and is a quieter, more attractive alternative.

Ski and board
top 2096m (6,877ft) bottom 1000m (3,280ft)

Both sides of the valley are lined with a network of 59 lifts, which is also linked to neighbouring Leogang. Much of the system has been upgraded to provide an easy traffic flow around the 200-km circuit of prepared pistes; this can be skied in either direction, although the anticlockwise route is longer. The resort was previously criticised for its annoying surfeit of T-bars; however, many of these have now been upgraded to chairs. A new gondola from Hinterglemm to Sportalm, halfway up Reiterkogel, is a major improvement.

From the bottom of Saalbach, the Schattberg-Ost cable-car gives direct and easy access – in good snow conditions – to the southern half of the circuit. The 100-person lift is prone to serious queues when the sunny side of the valley opposite has scarce snow cover. A triple-chair at the top end of the village is the starting point for the northern half of the

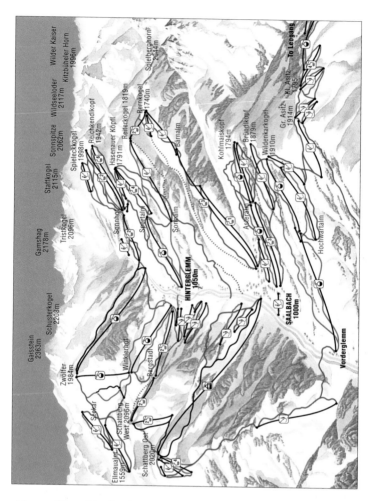

ski area. From **Vorderglemm**, which is a ski-bus ride down the valley towards Zell am See, the two-stage Schönleitenbahn gondola takes you up to Wildenkarkogel and into the Leogang ski area. You can also find your way here from Saalbach via a cluster-gondola, which feeds a network of gentle, south-facing runs. The picturesque Glemmtal offers considerable langlauf opportunities.

Beginners

Both villages have their own nursery slopes, and the north side of the valley is dotted with T-bars serving an unusual variety of beginner terrain. When you feel capable of graduating to the main circus, start on the gentler southern side, which offers a vast area of blue (easy) runs. When snow conditions are patchy, take either gondola to the 1984-m Zwölfer; the long *Familienabfahrt* back to the valley usually holds the snow well. From Schattberg-Ost the 7-km Jausernabfahrt is a gentle cruise down to Vorderglemm, from where you can take the Wildenkarkogel gondola up the other side of the valley for the easiest of cruises back to Saalbach.

Intermediates

Anyone who can ski parallel will enjoy the full circuit, although it is possible to shorten the outing by cutting across the valley at four separate points. Timid skiers seeking confidence-building slopes will have a field day here as most of the southern side of the valley is devoted to an easy blue playground. Challenging exceptions to this are the Schönleiten Talstation from beneath the Brundlkopf, the thigh-tingling women's downhill from Kohlmaiskopf, and a few shorter red (intermediate) runs above Hinterglemm. The Leogang sector has some usually uncrowded terrain that is well worth exploring at weekends when the main slopes are at their busiest.

Advanced

Schattberg-Ost, Schattberg-West and Zwölferkogel make up the more challenging north-facing slopes. The north face of the Zwölfer is a classic, harsh black (difficult) run, which can be heavily mogulled down its entire 3km. The home run from Schattberg-Ost can be extremely icy and crowded. A far more interesting route begins with the Westgipfel triple-chair to Schattberg-West, from where you can take a run down the steep black to the bottom and, after another chair ride, follow the challenging, unpisted itinerary down to Bergstadl. The snowboard park includes two half-pipes and a boardercross course.

WHAT'S NEW
Gondola from Hinterglemm to Sportalm
Après-ski bus service (8pm–3am)

Off-piste

The north side of the valley offers some outstanding powder runs, but a local guide is necessary to discover which slopes are safe, and when. Off-piste snowboarding opportunities are exceptional, with good riding down to the main valley road, which is served by a regular, free shuttle bus.

Tuition and guiding

Since deregulation permitted the establishment of alternative ski schools in Austria, no less than nine now compete for the resort's big business. Schischule Wolf ('wonderful off-piste guide'), based in Hinterglemm, attracts a disproportionate number of Anglo-Saxon guests. The smaller Mitterlengau, also in Hinterglemm, is praised for 'excellent instruction, with clear and precise analysis of bad habits and practical help in correcting them'. Schischule Fürstauer in Saalbach is particularly recommended for teaching children – 'all instructors were English-speaking, cheerful, professional and highly committed to teaching young people'. The other schools are Fritzenwallner, Heugenhauser, Hinterholzer, Zink, Gensbichler and Lechner.

Mountain restaurants

Saalbach-Hinterglemm has a wide selection of mountain eating establishments. As one reporter put it: 'There are almost as many restaurants and delightful huts as there are runs. The Pfefferalm above Hinterglemm is the most picturesque old farmhouse we have ever encountered. Don't be startled by the huge rabbits jumping about in the snow outside; you haven't had too much to drink – they live here'. The Goatssalm is equally rustic and is recommended for its glühwein. The good-value Rosswaldhütte, beside the Rosswald lift in the Hochalmspitze area, is an attractive chalet where the friendly staff wear traditional Austrian costumes. The rather twee Wildenkarkogel Hütte at the top of the Vorderglemm gondola is also accessible for non-skiers.

The resorts

The steep and thankfully pedestrianised main street of Saalbach, with its smart hotels and high-priced fashion boutiques, gives one the distinct feeling of having strayed on to the set of a Hollywood studio preparing to shoot a twenty-first-century sequel to *The Sound of Music*. The alpine charm is positively Disneyesque. Old it may appear, but most of the village dates from the 1980s. Hinterglemm is little more than a collection of stolid Austrian hotels, which act as an alternative base at the far end of the ski system. Both villages attract a predominantly German and Dutch clientèle. They are extremely lively places during the main winter weeks and contrastingly quiet at other times.

Accommodation

Alpen Hotel Hechenberg is a comfortable four-star. The Karlshof is praised for its buffet breakfast. Hotel Hasenauer in Hinterglemm is convenient for the lifts, but one reporter comments: 'Rooms, water and staff were all rather too cool for comfort'. Hotel Glemmtalerhof is described as 'pleasant enough, but German oriented'. Haus Wolf is said to be 'clean and very friendly'. The Hotel Ingonda in Saalbach is among the most luxurious. However, the resort also has some more reasonably priced establishments. Hotel Sonnblick at Hinterglemm has 'excellent food and a friendly bar – it is difficult to see the need to pay more for one of the posher hotels'.

Eating in and out

Bäckstättstall is the most exclusive restaurant in town. The Hotel Bauer is said to be 'good value, with a much more varied menu than you expect in Austria'. Hotel Hasenauer in Hinterglemm is 'cheaper than anywhere else'. The Bärenbachhof is 'not as expensive and better than most'. Two reporters spoke warmly of the Gollinger Hof.

Skiing facts: Saalbach-Hinterglemm

TOURIST OFFICE
Fremden Vertkehrs Verband
A-5753, Saalbach 550
Tel 43 6541 6800 68
Fax 43 6541 6800 69
Email contact@saalbach.com
Web site www.saalbach.com

THE RESORT
By road Calais 1193km
By rail Zell am See 19km
Airport transfer Salzburg 1½hrs
Visitor beds 20,000
Transport free ski bus with lift pass

THE SKIING
Linked or nearby resorts Bad Gastein (n), Bad Hofgastein (n), Grossarl (n), Kaprun (n), Leogang (l), Zell am See (n)
Longest run Jausernabfahrt, 7km (blue)
Number of lifts 59
Total of trails/pistes 200km (45% easy, 47% intermediate, 8% difficult)
Nursery slopes 5 lifts
Summer skiing none
Snowmaking 65 hectares covered

LIFT PASSES
Area pass (covers Saalbach-Hinterglemm and Leogang) ATS1,600–1,940
Day pass ATS380–400
Beginners points tickets
Pensioners reductions for women 60yrs and over, men 65yrs and over

Credit cards yes

SKI SCHOOLS
Adults all 9 schools, 10am–midday and 2–4pm, ATS1,590 for 6 days
Private lessons ATS1,800 per day
Snowboarding as regular ski schools
Cross-country as regular ski schools. Loipe 58km in linked area
Other courses telemark, competition
Guiding through ski schools

CHILDREN
Lift pass 6–10yrs ATS850, 11–15yrs ATS985–1,160, both for 6 days, free for 5yrs and under
Ski kindergarten Schischule Wolf, 4yrs and over, 10am–4pm, ATS1,550 for 6 days including lunch
Ski school as ski kindergarten
Non-ski kindergarten Gartenhotel Theresia, Hotel Lengauerhof, Hotel Egger, all 3yrs and over, and Partner hotels, 2½yrs and over, all 10am–4pm, ATS500 per day including lunch

OTHER SPORTS
Indoor tennis, swimming, skating, curling, hang-gliding, sleigh rides, ice hockey, squash, parapente, bowling

FOOD AND DRINK PRICES
Coffee ATS25, glass of wine ATS25–28, small beer ATS32, dish of the day ATS110

Après-ski

The endearing feature of Saalbach is the immutable, jolly Austrian formula. True, the folk dancers now save their thigh-slapping and yodels for the more appreciative lakes-and-mountains clientèle in the summer, but the waitresses still wear their *Dirndl* dresses and genuine smiles of welcome as they pocket your money. Après-ski starts with a drink at the Bäckstättstall Umbrella Bar with 'a disco/band and striking views over

Saalbach; they also do a potent glühwein to add some challenge to the very short run down to the street'. The Schirmbar is also recommended. Hinterhagalm has a huge copper pot of glühwein on the bar, and it is on draft at Bauer's Schialm by the church in Saalbach. The Classic bustles, and the snow-bar of the Glemmtalerhof Hotel is always crowded. Lumpi's Bla Bla in Hinterglemm has a good atmosphere. The Pfeiffenmuseum Café in the Glemmtalerhof houses a quite enormous collection of pipes and smoking paraphernalia. Later on, the village's 15 discos come to life: King's is popular with teenagers, and the Londoner is Hinterglemm's hot-spot for all ages. A regular bus service for night owls now runs up and down the valley from 8pm to 3am for a flat rate of ATS20.

Childcare

Schischule Wolf and Fürstauer both operate ski kindergartens every day except Sunday for children from four years of age. Hotels including Partners, Gartenhotel Theresia, Lengauerhof and Egger care for non-skiing children from two and a half or three years of age.

Linked or nearby resorts

Leogang
top 2096m (6,875ft) bottom 800m (2,625ft)

Leogang is a spread-out farming community, which claims the title of the longest village in Europe. A smart, modern gondola takes skiers and snowboarders up to Sitzhütte at 1758m. A short run down followed by a quad-chair and three subsequent T-bars brings you into the ski circus. Accommodation is in a mixture of hotels and chalets. We have excellent reports of the Chalet Thurnhaus, which is an eight-minute walk from the gondola. Readers recommend both the Gerhard Altenberger and Franz Deisenberger ski schools. Five cross-country trails total more than 40km, and snow-rafting is also available. The kindergarten in Hotel Krallerhof takes children from two years of age.

TOURIST OFFICE
Tel 43 6583 8234
Fax 43 6583 7302

Schladming

ALTITUDE 745m (2,224ft)

Beginners ✱✱✱   Intermediates ✱✱✱   Snowboarders ✱

This season Schladming – one of the most popular ski destinations in Austria for Austrians – is being transformed into a major linked ski area, which will give it the international credibility that it has previously lacked. Until now, 50 per cent of all visitors to the Tauern Alps have been nationals. In a country where the majority of the population likes to ski and has a huge choice of where to go, this must in itself say rather a lot.

✔ Large ski area
✔ Lively après-ski
✔ Tree-level skiing
✔ Excellent for cross-country
✔ Short airport transfer
✔ Summer skiing on Dachstein Glacier
✔ Variety of mountain restaurants
✘ Poor skiing convenience

Schladming is a small, medieval market town in the pretty Enns Valley in the province of Styria, a one-hour drive from Salzburg Airport and with good rail connections. The construction of a new gondola and a couple of high-speed detachable chair-lifts will now make it possible to ski – in both directions – almost the whole length of the valley from the villages of **Haus-im-Ennstal** to **Gleiming**, with Schladming strategically based in the middle. The building of the links coincides with the Nordic World Championships, which take place in 1999 at nearby **Ramsau**. Fifteen other small ski areas are included in the lift pass, giving the region an impressive total of 85 lifts. However, skiers and snowboarders in search of even greater variety can buy a larger regional lift pass (see *Advanced*).

Each year more snow falls on the Niedere Tauern mountain range than anywhere else in Austria. Over 75 per cent of the runs around Schladming are covered by snow-cannon, making it possible to ski down to the valley from as early as November. The skiing takes place in the foothills of the Tauern mountains and offers a series of long, broad runs through the woods from a top altitude of 2015m down to the valley floor. It also includes the snow-sure but limited alpine pistes of the **Dachstein Glacier**. One veteran reporter describes it as 'an intermediate paradise groomed to perfection'. The piste map is 'next to useless. So poorly printed and to such a small scale as to be barely legible'.

Ski and board
top 2015m (6,609ft) bottom 750m (2,460ft)
Schladming lies in the centre of a long and beautiful valley, with the main slopes spread disparately across the mountains on the southern side.

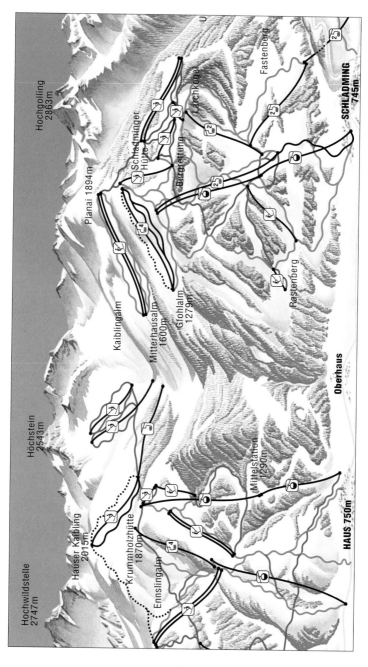

Planai at 1894m and Hochwurzen at 1850m are the mountains closest to Schladming. The easiest access to Planai is via a two-stage gondola from the edge of Schladming, which is a comfortable walk from the centre. The Kessleralm mid-station of the gondola can also be reached by car. Planai is somewhat precariously linked at valley level to the next mountain, Hochwurzen, by a series of chair-lifts. It offers several long red (intermediate) runs and a toboggan run, which are served by two steep drags, a jumbo gondola and a double-chair. A new gondola from the village of **Pichl** to the bottom of the Hochwurzenbahn now gives unbroken access to the Reiteralm, a previously separate mountain, which offers a variety of red and blue (easy) tree-lined runs served by a double chair-lift and a gondola

> **WHAT'S NEW**
>
> Gondola linking Hochwurzen and Reiteralm
> Chair-lifts linking Planai and Hauser Kaibling

Above Schladming, on the eastern side of Planai, two new chair-lifts link up with the Mitterhaus double drag-lift to give access to Hauser Kaibling, a 2015-m peak that towers over the pretty village of Haus-im-Ennstal. Mountain access from Haus is by a cable-car at either end of the village. Alternatively, motorists can drive up from Haus to Knappl on the eastern side of the mountain and work their way into the system via two drag-lifts.

Still further to the east along the valley, the Galsterbergalm at 1976m offers a few mainly gentle slopes reached by cable-car from the village of **Pruggern.** This in turn gives access to a couple of T-bars for some open skiing above the tree-line. The small, separate Fageralm ski area is now also included in the local lift pass.

On the other side of the valley from Schladming, the commune of **Ramsau Ort** at 1200m has no less than 19 lifts scattered around the hills on either side of the village. All are short beginner and easy slopes. **Turlwand,** outside Ramsau, is the starting point for the cable-car up to the Dachstein Glacier; the village has limited year-round skiing that is too gentle to be of much more than scenic interest for alpine skiers, and is served by a chair and three drag-lifts.

Beginners

At this altitude, the actual functioning of the 25 listed nursery slopes is heavily dependent on the weather. The gentle **Rohrmoos** meadows on the lower slopes of Hochwurzen provide the best arena for first turns when snow cover permits, with plenty of easy alternatives on the higher slopes of the main mountains.

Intermediates

Despite the lack of variety, the red and blue cruising terrain is plentiful enough to keep any skier busy for a week. The World Cup racecourses on both Planai and Hauser Kaibling should please fast intermediates, and the long downhill course on Hochwurzen is thigh burning. The usually uncrowded Reiteralm also gives plenty of opportunity for high-speed cruising. Less confident skiers will enjoy the remote area of gentle skiing at Kaiblingalm – served by two short drag-lifts – which has no crowds but benefits from good snow and a friendly restaurant.

Advanced

This is not a place for advanced piste-skiers, who will quickly tire of the limited terrain. However, Schladming is an attractive base from which to explore a huge range of skiing including **Obertauern** and the Sportwelt Amadé, which is centred on **St Johann im Pongau**. For a modest supplement you can buy the six-day Top-Tauern Skischeck lift pass, which gives access to 270 lifts serving 660km of prepared runs in this corner of Austria. All the resorts covered on the pass are within less than an hour's drive of Schladming.

Off-piste

Skiing outside the marked pistes is discouraged on the main mountains, except on the ski routes. In good snow conditions the north face of Hauser Kaibling offers great scope, and the runs through the trees from Bergstallalm on Planai are recommended. Opportunities for ski-touring in the region abound. In fresh snow conditions, a guide from the Alpinschule Schladming-Rohrmoos will help you find untracked powder.

Tuition and guiding

The WM-Planai ski school, owned by the veteran Austrian team-trainer Charly Kahr, has an outstanding reputation and counts Arnold Schwarzenegger among its annual pupils. The Franz Tritscher Ski School is also recommended ('good English, good teaching, good fun'). Hopl is the resort's third school. We have no reports of the Brandner or Ski Total schools in Haus-im-Ennstal.

Snowboarding has been a commercial success in Schladming, not least because it is the home of former European champion Gerfried Schuller, who runs his own school here, as well as the Blue Tomato snowboard shop. He also operates Kids On Board, Europe's first children's snowboard school, which takes *Jungen Shreddern* from five years of age. The school also organises various camps for riders throughout the season. Group and private lessons are offered by the local ski schools.

Cross-country

The Schladming area has some of the best langlauf in Austria, with 250km of trails against a dramatically scenic backdrop and plenty of small huts to call in at for refreshments.

Mountain restaurants

'Never,' said one reporter, 'have I been to a resort with so many mountain restaurants. Food and service vary, but at their best they are excellent'. However, first you have to find them – 'they are not marked on the inadequate piste map, and signs are nothing short of bemusing'. The Krümmelholze at Haus receives particular recommendation. On Planai the Mitterhausalm and Schladmingerhütte are praised, along with Onkel Willy's Hütte ('buzzing with atmosphere, and serves great ham and eggs in an individual frying pan') for live music and a sunny terrace. The Eiskarhütte on Reiteralm, and the Seiterhütte ('excellent food and service') on Hochwurzen are both praised.

The resort

Schladming is essentially an ordinary Austrian town that derives much of its income from outside skiing. Not much happens here. Indeed, during its entire 675-year history – unless you count a little bloodshed in the sixteenth century, the birth of Arnold Schwarzenegger and the staging of the 1982 Ski World Championships – you would be hard pushed to find any single event of international significance. Day-to-day life in this attractive provincial town, with its onion-domed church and magnificent eighteenth-century town square, the Hauptplatz, continues at a rhythm that is not dictated solely by tourism. The resort also has the smallest brewery and the largest lift pass in Austria.

All these contributory factors make Schladming an utterly charming and unspoilt base from which to explore huge tracts of intermediate skiing and snowboarding entirely unknown to the majority of British snow-users. As well as wooden chalets with painted shutters, Schladming has sober, old stone buildings, and the remains of the town walls, which date from 1629. The town is compact; most of its shops and a good many of its hotels, restaurants and bars are concentrated around the broad Hauptplatz. Anyone looking for *Lederhosen-und-oompah Gemütlichkeit* will discover that it still thrives here.

Accommodation

Most guests stay in hotels and guesthouses around the Enns Valley. Without a car, location is of crucial importance, and many of our reporters found themselves staying too far from the town centre or the lifts – or both. The Sporthotel Royer receives rave reviews. The Neue Post is criticised for its 'small, cramped rooms. The reception is not permanently manned, and the half-board food was disappointing, to say the least'. The nearby Alte Post ('small bedroom, but good food with Strauss, Mozart and Haydn in the background') is recommended. Haus Stangl, a simple bed-and-breakfast place, is also recommended.

Eating in and out

The restaurants are mainly in the hotels. We have good reports of the Rôtisserie Royer Grill in the Sporthotel Royer. The Alte Post is recommended for 'excellent trout and other dishes in a pretentious but friendly atmosphere. Its *Postreindl* (pork fillet with creamed mushrooms and gnocchi) is not to be missed'. The Neue Post has two recommended à la carte restaurants, the Jägerstüberl and the Poststüberl. Le Jardin is a

Skiing facts: Schladming

TOURIST OFFICE
Erzherzog-Johann-Str. 213, A-8970
Schladming
Tel 43 3687 22268–0
Fax 43 3687 24138
Email tourist.schladming@ppl.co.at
Web site www.planai.com

THE RESORT
By road Calais 1235km
By rail Station in resort
Airport transfer Salzburg 1hr,
Munich 2½ hrs
Visitor beds 3,600
Transport free ski bus with lift pass

THE SKIING
Linked or nearby resorts Haus-im-
Ennstal (l), Obertauern (n), Rohrmoos (l),
Ramsau/Dachstein (n), St Johann im
Pongau (n)
Longest run Hochwurzen 7.7km
Number of lifts 85
Total of trails/pistes 25 (27% easy,
63% intermediate, 10% difficult)
Nursery slopes 25 lifts in area
Summer skiing nearest on Dachstein
Glacier
Snowmaking 190 hectares covered

LIFT PASSES
Area pass Top-Tauern Skischeck (covers
Obertauern, Schladming, Dachstein,
Sportwelt Amadé and Lungau) ATS1,990
for 6 days
Day pass ATS365–385
Beginners reductions available
Pensioners day pass ATS340–365
for women 60yrs and over and men
65yrs and over

Credit cards Amex and Diners only

TUITION
Adults WM-Planai, Franz Tritscher,
and Hopl, ATS1,400 for 5 days,
10am–12.30pm, 2–4pm
Private lessons all ski schools, ATS500
per hr, ATS1,800 per day (4½hrs)
Snowboarding Dachstein Tauern
Snowboardschule,10am–12.30pm
and 13.30–4pm, ATS1,600 for 5 days
Cross-country ski school prices on
request. Loipe 20km, 250km in region
Other courses race-training, moguls
Guiding Alpinschule
Schladming-Rohrmoos

CHILDREN
Lift pass 16yrs and under ATS945 for
6 days, free for 3yrs and under.
Top-Tauern Skischeck ATS1,110
Ski kindergarten all ski schools, 4yrs
and over, 9am–5pm, ATS1,800 for 5
days including lunch
Ski school all ski schools, 4yrs and
over, 9am–5pm, ATS1,900 for 5 days
including lunch
Non-ski kindergarten Ma Petite Ecole,
3–6yrs, 7.30am–5pm, ATS2,100 for 5
days including lunch

OTHER SPORTS
Curling, skating, hot-air ballooning,
sleigh rides, parapente, indoor tennis and
squash, swimming

FOOD AND DRINK PRICES
Coffee ATS25, glass of wine ATS18,
small beer ATS27, dish of the day
ATS95–130

warmly commended French restaurant. The Gasthof Kirchenwirt is 'unmatched for quality of food, price, atmosphere and service'. Charly Kahr's Restaurant is also praised.

Après-ski

Après-ski starts early at Onkel Willy's Hütte on Planai before filtering down to the Siglu in the Hauptplatz. Later on the action moves to The Pub, La Porta, the Hanglbar and – still later – to the Sonderbar disco. The Schwalbenbraü brewery is worth a visit, although the deliberately cloudy beer it produces is not to everyone's taste and may explain why it is the smallest brewery in Austria. The Planaistub'n, also known as Charly's Treff, draws large crowds. Café-Konditorei Landgraf and Niederl are both praised. One reporter favoured Ferry's Pub in the Steirergasse, another the Hanglbar; the bowling alley behind the latter is said to offer a good night out. The Beisl bar is 'intimate and lively with good music'. La Porta is 'small, crowded, with a great atmosphere'. The toboggan run from the top to the bottom of Hochwurzen down the hair-pin road can be used only at night (when the road is closed) and is claimed to be the longest in Austria.

Childcare

Few resorts receive such resounding reviews for both their non-ski and ski kindergarten. 'Outstanding facilities for very young children,' commented one reader. 'There were 40 small children in the ski kindergarten, and the facilities were brilliant; this is definitely the area to bring small children to be looked after well and to learn to ski,' said another.

Linked or nearby resorts

Haus-im-Ennstal
top 2015m (6,611ft) bottom 750m (2,460ft)

Haus is a quiet village with its farming origins still in evidence, although it has a considerable amount of holiday accommodation in guesthouses and apartments. There are cafés, one of which has jazz nights, and a couple of shops. The upmarket Hauser Kaibling hotel has a swimming-pool and is recommended for its cuisine. Dorfhotel Kirchenwirt is a traditional hotel in the village centre, the Gasthof Reiter is a fine old chalet, which is much cheaper than most, and the Gürtl is a quiet family-run hotel well-situated for the cable-car. A gentle nursery slope lies between the village and the gondola station.

TOURIST OFFICE
Tel 43 3686 2234–0
Fax 43 3686 22344

Söll and the Ski-Welt

ALTITUDE 703m (2,306ft)

Beginners ✱✱✱ Intermediates ✱✱✱ Snowboarders ✱

Once the top package resort in Austria, and with a reputation in the 1980s for excessive drinking, Söll in the late 1990s is focusing on family values. Anyone unimpressed by purpose-built, ski-in ski-out tower blocks at 2000m, who wants a reasonable amount of easy skiing at modest cost, and who does not mind a bit of accordion music, should consider Söll as a destination. It is a small village with minimal claims to Tyrolean charm, and at the same time head-quarters to one of Austria's largest networks of interconnected pistes. Officially dubbed the Ski-Welt Wilder Kaiser-Brixental, the region counts 93 lifts and 250km of pistes spread around a 150-square-kilometre oval of nine resorts sandwiched between the Kitzbüheler Alps to the south and the craggy Wilder Kaiser peaks to the north. It is only 70km from Innsbruck and within easy reach of the German border.

✔ Short airport transfer
✔ Friendly, low-key atmosphere
✔ Value for money
✘ Low-altitude skiing
✘ Short season
✘ Bus-ride from town to lifts
✘ Runs to valley not snow-sure

Although skiing began here as early as 1948, when Europe's longest chair-lift was built in **Hopfgarten,** Söll's own lifts were not seriously developed until the 1960s, and links to the Ski-Welt were not finished before the 1970s.

All of the skiing in the region is well below 2000m. Despite snow-making on most of the essential links, the winter in sunny Tyrol is usually short – essentially January and February – and snow cover down to villages well below 1000m is never secure. An additional 45km of snow-cannon have now been added around the Ski-Welt, bringing the total to 238 hectares, including the main run down to Söll.

The British make up 20 per cent of what is a youngish clientèle, in which influxes of Scandinavians and Dutch outnumber the Germans. These groups like to party, and the main street resounds to shouts and the crashes of bottles on weekend nights until 3am. But with only one serious disco, Söll cannot begin to compare in this respect with **Kitzbühel,** a few kilometres down the road, or with **St Anton**.

Söll's own skiing, which now includes Hopfgarten, **Itter** and **Kelchsau** on its own local 30-lift ski pass covering 91km of pistes, is the best in the Ski-Welt. Children under seven ski free, and those 16 and under receive discounts of more than 40 per cent, as do women of any age on Wednesdays.

Ski and board
top 1892m (6,207ft) bottom 622m (2,040ft)

Söll's skiing starts with a free, 15-minute bus ride across the resort to a modern 8-person gondola. However, this is followed by an ancient single-chair, which is due to be replaced 'sometime soon', for the most direct access to Hohe Salve, which at 1829m is the highest point in the entire Ski-Welt.

Thanks to a lift capacity of over 100,000 skiers per hour, Ski-Welt queues seldom exceed 20 minutes, except when skiing links are closed due to lack of snow and the only way down the mountain is by lift. Grooming standards are ensured by 45 snowcats, which run all night long. *Pistenhilfe* security patrols were introduced with the aim of eliminating 'piste rowdies' and aiding lost tourists.

From Hohe Salve it is possible to ski to seven of the Ski-Welt resorts; **Westendorf** requires a short bus transfer from **Brixen,** and Kelchsau a less frequent and longer bus trip from Hopfgarten. Advanced terrain is often limited by lack of respectable snow depth. The Ski-Welt is primarily suited to beginners and undemanding intermediates who do not mind short runs and uphill traverses. Each Ski-Welt resort produces its own piste map, none of them showing sufficient detail and most not marking either the names or identifying numbers of ski pistes. However, these are clearly signposted on the mountain outside the lift stations. There is no ski bus itinerary connecting Ski-Welt resorts together, so care must be taken when skiing far afield. Brixen, Westendorf and Scheffau have official freestyle pistes.

Beginners
The Ski-Welt has more than 100km of blue (easy) runs. Most beginner areas are at the base of the ski area, where the snow often melts away. **Scheffau** is the only resort with a top-to-bottom blue piste. Söll has a simple, wooded run from mid-mountain. Zinsberg and Brandstadl offer ample easy terrain.

Intermediates
Almost half the pistes in the Ski-Welt are graded intermediate, but short runs down to lifts, rather than long itineraries from village to village, are the rule. The valley runs are not always open due to lack of snow; but when they are, the non-stop red (intermediate) trail in the sun down to Hopfgarten, and the less exposed run down to Söll from Hohe Salve, are good cruisers, as is the 7.5-km Kraftalm run to Itter.

Advanced
From Hohe Salve the Lärchenhang is one of the unmarked local runs on the north side, where a bowl region called Mulde (not marked on the piste map) presents some challenge and a reasonable pitch. Söll has a limited snowpark above Salvenmoos, with an amateur half-pipe and some jumps.

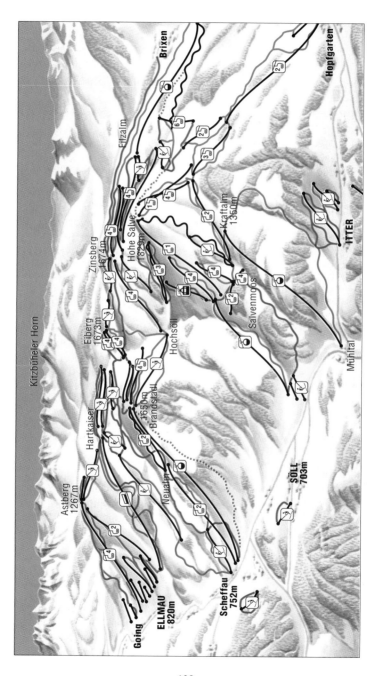

Off-piste

Short, steep sections that require ducking under warning ropes do appear in Westendorf and are regularly skied by locals. The Ski-Welt offers a wealth of guided ski-tours, for example Brechorn, which demands little uphill effort when there is enough snow to make powder skiing possible.

Tuition and guiding

More than 450 ski teachers in 16 Ski-Welt ski schools specialise in making skiing fun for beginners, with spoken English of a high standard and with reported success. Söll's two schools promise – but do not guarantee – that by the end of their first week, pupils will make it all the way from the very top to the very bottom of the area.

Mountain restaurants

The Ski-Welt lists a total of 63 mountain eateries, six of which are above Söll. Most suffer peak-season lunchtime crowds as everybody insists on eating at the same time. Self-service and simple meals abound. Stöcklalm, Kraftalm and Gründalm are typical, unexceptional inns, all with terraces and wide panoramas. The glass-walled Siglu Bar at Hochsöll is popular with children.

The resort

Söll is a quiet, modern town of family homes, which is set back off the highway in open fields. It was a summer resort for walkers until skiing offered its 3,000 inhabitants winter work, hosting some 4,300 guests per week. Söll's car-free main street runs for less than 100m and is largely devoid of the overly cute, wooden architecture that is typical of the Tyrol. Shopping is limited to supermarkets and ski and souvenir shops. A free bus runs every 30 minutes to the gondola station but not to other Ski-Welt resorts. Söll has its own indoor swimming-pool and sauna complex.

Accommodation

Most of Söll's 70 hotels and 150 guesthouses are reasonably priced. The main hotel is the four-star Postwirt with its distinctive stuccoed exterior. The Alpenschlössl is even more luxurious, with a swimming-pool and indoor waterfall, but it is situated a 30-minute walk from the centre. Tour-operator brochures feature the charming Tenne and the lively Christophorus, as well as the old-fashioned, out-of-town Agerhof.

Eating in and out

Most visitors are on hotel half-board packages. For Austrian coffee and cakes it is worth making the hike to Panorama for the view (and the eating), and the modest Söller Stube on the main street merits a visit. Al Dente and Venezia serve cheap pizza and pasta. The Hong Kong is the only Chinese restaurant. Hotel Austria claims an international cuisine.

Après-ski

Söll's tourist director claims that the resort's beer-swilling image was created entirely by British tour operators at a time when the latter wanted to build up the 'yoof' market; he has invited TV crews in to prove how dead Söll really is. However, it is not dead and buried yet; at the Whisky Mühle, scantily clad go-go girls (and boys) kick away each Friday night until 3am. The Dorfstadl in the Hotel Tyrol comes a poor second. Vis à Vis is a small, modern bar frequented by Swedes. Pub 15 has a DJ but no dance floor and a dearth of the promised age group. Buffaloes is a new venue with a Wild West theme.

WHAT'S NEW
3-km night-skiing piste to the village
Night-tobogganing
Additional snow-cannons

Childcare

Bobo's Kinder Club is part of the Söll-Hochsöll Ski School. Bobo the Penguin is the symbol of an Austrian association guaranteeing English-speaking, certified teachers with a training in psychology. The same school operates the Mini Club for non-skiers from three to five years old. Reporters commented that not all staff are English-speakers.

Linked or nearby resorts

Brixen im Thale
top 1892m (6,207ft) bottom 800m (2,624ft)

At the far end of the Ski-Welt, the last fully connected resort of Brixen accommodates no British package tourists in its 2,700 beds. A six-person gondola and covered high-speed chair lead up to Hohe Salve. The Parade Pub next to the lift station is unique in the Ski-Welt, if not in the Alps: a computer monitors demand for specific drinks, then raises or lowers prices to provide the ultimate in 'demand economy' drinking. Gustl's Treff is a favourite hangout for snowboarders.

TOURIST OFFICE
Tel 43 5334 8433
Fax 43 5334 8332
Email brixen.info@brixen.netwing.at
Web site www.netwing.at/tirol/brixen/rts

Ellmau
top 1892m (6,207ft) bottom 820m (2,690ft)

With 4,800 beds, Ellmau is the biggest Ski-Welt resort. Its 19 lifts include what is advertised as the fastest, most modern funicular in Austria. Toboggan runs are floodlit at night, and indoor tennis plus an adventure swimming complex keep non-skiers busy. Hotel Christoph, a five-minute walk from the funicular, is described as 'excellent, with helpful staff and good food'. Ellmau's nightlife rivals that of Söll, with Pub Memory,

Skiing facts: Söll

TOURIST OFFICE
Postfach 21, A-6306 Söll, Tyrol
Tel 43 5333 5216
Fax 43 5333 6180
Email tvb@fx.soell.netwing.at
Web site www.tvb-soell.com

THE RESORT
By road Calais 1114km
By rail Kufstein 12km, St Johann 25km, Wörgl 12km
Airport transfer Munich 2½hrs, Salzburg 1½hrs, Innsbruck 2hrs
Visitor beds 4,300
Transport free bus between village and ski area

THE SKIING
Linked or nearby resorts Brixen (l), Ellmau (l), Going (l), Hopfgarten (l), Itter (l), Kelchsau (n), Kirchberg (n), Kitzbühel (n), Scheffau (l), Westendorf (n)
Longest run Hohe Salve–Kraftalm–Söll, 8km (red)
Number of lifts 30 in Söll, 93 in Ski-Welt
Total of trails/pistes 91km in Söll, 250km in Ski-Welt (43% easy, 51% intermediate, 6% difficult)
Nursery slopes 8 lifts and runs
Summer skiing none
Snowmaking 238 hectares covered

LIFT PASSES
Area pass Ski-Welt (covers all lifts in area) ATS1,800, Kitzbüheler Alpen (covers 260 lifts) ATS2,200. Both for 6 days
Day pass Söll ATS350, Ski-Welt ATS370

Beginners points tickets
Pensioners reductions for 60yrs and over
Credit cards no

TUITION
Adults Söll-Hochsöll, Austria Söll, ATS1,315 for 5 x 4hrs
Private lessons both ski schools, ATS480 per hr
Snowboarding both ski schools, ATS370 per 2-hr session
Cross-country ATS370 per day. Loipe 30km in area
Other courses no
Guiding on request

CHILDREN
Lift pass 7–16yrs, Söll ATS850, Ski-Welt ATS1,000, Kitzbüheler Alpen ATS1,100. All for 6 days. Free for 6yrs and under if accompanied by an adult
Ski kindergarten Söll-Hochsöll Bobo's Kinder Club, 3–14yrs, ATS1,275 for 5 x 4hrs. Extra ATS100 per day for lunch
Non-ski kindergarten Mini Club, 3–5yrs, 9.30am–4.15pm, ATS1,500 for 5 days including lunch and snack

OTHER SPORTS
Parapente, skating, squash, swimming, winter walks

FOOD AND DRINK PRICES
Coffee ATS22–25, glass of wine ATS27, small beer ATS22–25, dish of the day ATS90–140

Ellmauer Alm, Heldenbar and the Tenne all lively destinations. For children there are the Kaiserbad water chutes and adventure swimming park.

TOURIST OFFICE
Tel 43 5358 2307
Fax 43 5358 3443
Email ellmau@netway.at
Web site www.tiscover.com/ellmau

Going
top 1892m (6,207ft) bottom 800m (2,624ft)

Fully linked into the Ski-Welt, with the best views of the Wilder Kaiser and a large nursery area, Going is beginning to be noticed by the British, not least because of the exceptional five-star Hotel Stanglewirt, which has indoor swimming, tennis and a Lippizaner riding school.

TOURIST OFFICE
Tel 43 5358 2438
Fax 43 5358 3501
Email going@netway.at
Web site www.tiscover.com/going

Hopfgarten
top 1892m (6,207ft) bottom 622m (2,040ft)

Few British skiers take advantage of the 2,000 beds in Hopfgarten, which has become an unlikely favourite with Australian package tourists. Access to the top of Hohe Salve requires three chair-lift rides. There is floodlit tobogganing, and the quiet village centre is dominated by the twin yellow towers of the impressive local church. Spirited nightlife and dancing can be found at the Ofenloch disco and the Cin-Cin.

TOURIST OFFICE
Tel 43 5335 2322
Fax 43 5335 2630
Email info@hopfgarten.tirol.at
Web site www.tiscover.com/hopfgarten-tirol

Itter
top 1892m (6,207ft) bottom 703m (2,306ft)

Itter has only 800 hotel beds, but a fast gondola with no queues for the uphill journey, plus the longest run in the Ski-Welt (8km) make it a quieter, cheaper alternative to Söll. The Schidisco in the Schusterhof Hotel and the Dorfpub are perhaps not up to the decibel level of Söll but sufficient for most.

TOURIST OFFICE
Tel 43 5335 2670
Fax 43 5335 3028

Kelchsau

top 1700m (5,576ft) bottom 800m (2,624ft)

Kelchsau is the odd man out of the Ski-Welt, not connected by piste in any way and served by infrequent buses from Hopfgarten. It is primarily a cross-country centre, despite its four ski lifts.

TOURIST OFFICE
Tel 43 5335 8105
Fax 43 5335 8156

Scheffau

top 1892m (6,207ft) bottom 752m (2,467ft)

Scheffau has only 2,200 beds and 15 lifts serving 23km of pistes, which begin at a gondola awkwardly situated across the main road from the sprawling village. Scheffau's hotel guests have their own queue-free VIP lift access. The Brandstadl bowl keeps its snow cover better than the sunnier slopes across in Söll, and Scheffau has more than its share of the Ski-Welt's snowmaking. CC-Pub, Conny's Corner and the Pub Royal are the only nightspots.

TOURIST OFFICE
Tel 43 5358 7373
Fax 43 5358 73737

Westendorf

top 1892m (6,207ft) bottom 800m (2,624ft)

Westendorf's broad shoulder of open pistes looks steep from the valley floor. It is more snowsure than elsewhere in the Ski-Welt, and skiing on the 40km of pistes can be more challenging. However, flat roads between lifts are an irritating feature, as is the 1-km distance between the modern gondola and the town. A bus is required to liaise with the Ski-Welt pistes at Brixen, and it is a good 20km back to Söll by car.

Westendorf is one of the most attractive of all the Ski-Welt villages and has a genuine Tyrolean atmosphere coupled with a vigour lacking in some of the others. The Brechhorn Haus mountain restaurant is warmly recommended. Westendorf's substantial accommodation base of 4,100 beds, almost equal to Söll's, makes for lively entertainment with acid house at Gerry's Inn, techno at the Wunderbar, and jello shots at the Mosquito Bar. Hotel Jakobwirt has 'friendly staff, good food, good facilities and a central location'. The Schermerhof apartments are 'modern, well-equipped, clean and fairly spacious'. Reporters recommend Ski School Top, the smallest of the three ski schools, for its more personal service.

TOURIST OFFICE
Tel 43 5334 6230
Fax 43 5334 2390
Email Westendorf@netway.at
Web site www.tiscover.com/westendorf

St Anton

ALTITUDE 1304m (4,278ft)

Intermediates ✳✳✳   Advanced ✳✳✳   Snowboarders ✳

St Anton is to skiing what St Andrew's is to golf. The Arlberg region, of which St Anton is the capital, is the birthplace of modern technique and in part responsible for the way in which we ski today. The awesome quality of the mountain here means that its star has never faded. Other resorts have since risen to dominate the world stage, but it still ranks among the top five for truly challenging skiing and high living. The percentage of snowboarders here is lower than in the majority of European resorts, largely because the steep and usually heavily mogulled main pistes are not ideal for any rider who is not extremely proficient. St Anton is twinned with Mount Buller in southern Australia, and the large number of Australians who work here may be either the cause or the result of this.

✔ Extensive off-piste
✔ Large ski area
✔ Ski–touring opportunities
✔ Efficient lift system
✔ Lively après-ski
✘ Not ideal for families
✘ Few activities for non-skiers
✘ Crowded pistes

Skiing came to the Arlberg in the late nineteenth century: the Pastor of Lech visited his parishioners on skis as early as 1895. In 1921, Hannes Schneider opened the Arlberg Ski School – a role model that underpinned subsequent advances worldwide. Generations of Europeans grew up with the distinctive Arlberg technique – skis clamped together, shoulders facing down the hill – a contrived yet elegant style that dominated the sport until the French and Jean-Claude Killy declared technical war in the 1960s.

St Anton is closer to Geneva than Vienna, and it is as easy to get to the resort from Switzerland as from Munich or Innsbruck. Austria's main east–west railway runs through the middle of town, and in March and April you can travel to the snow aboard the Orient Express.

Ski and board
top 2811m (9,222ft) bottom 1304m (4,278ft)

The Arlberg Ski Pass covers the linked area of St Anton, **St Christoph** and **Stuben**, as well as **Klösterle** and the more famous villages of **Lech** and **Zürs.** A free ski bus now operates between all the resorts.

St Anton's skiing takes place on both sides of the valley, but the most challenging area is on the northern slopes dominated by the 2811-m Valluga. The resort has been chosen to host the Alpine Skiing World

Championships in 2001 and, as a consequence, its somewhat antiquated lift system has been systematically upgraded. The old lifts on the Galzig and in St Christoph have been replaced by covered quad-chairs, which have done much to improve mountain access. The high-speed quad-chair to Gampen takes the morning strain off the Kandahar funicular and the Galzig cable-car. However, the inevitable result of this is that the volume of people has not been reduced but simply moved from the lift queue to the piste. The large number of snow-users on the piste – even in low-season January – can be frightening. In the afternoon on the home run skiers and boarders jostle for position like Parisian taxi drivers. Anyone lacking in courage or technique, or both, feels wholly intimidated.

At mid-mountain level, the ski area splits into two, separated by a valley. Gampen, at 1850m, has a restaurant and children's ski enclosure and is a sunny plateau with two chair-lifts rising to the higher slopes of Kapall at 2333m. Galzig is the focal point of the serious skiing.

From Galzig you can ski down to St Christoph at 1800m, a small hamlet crowned by the Hotel Arlberg-Hospiz. Above Galzig lie the more sublime challenges of the Valluga and the Schindlergrat at 2605m.

The Valluga is reached by a second and oversubscribed cable-car from Galzig, which is operated with a confusing and unsatisfactory numbered-ticket system. You take a ticket and ask the lift attendant to translate it into time so that you know when to return. The alternative is to ski down into the valley behind Galzig and take the quad up to the Schindlergrat. The skiing from here is some of the best in St Anton.

The Rendl at 2100m is a separate ski area on the other side of the St Anton valley and is reached by the Rendlbahn gondola, a short ski-bus ride from town. It offers interesting and often uncrowded skiing and catches so much sun its local nickname is Rendl Beach.

Beginners

St Anton is not a beginner's ski resort, and anyone less than a confident intermediate would be well advised to avoid it. The few blue (easy) slopes that exist would nearly all be classified as intermediate elsewhere. Even the crowded main run back into the village is seen as a challenging red (intermediate) by most skiers. There are three learner pistes with their own T-bars spread between Nasserein and the funicular railway. The Gampen has a children's ski area and the gentle Gampenlift T-bar. St Christoph has its own Maiensee beginner piste and lift. Those with a little experience may also find some of the runs on the Rendl negotiable.

Intermediates

Confident intermediates head for Galzig. The sunny slopes below are served by the Ostbahn high-speed quad, and the main runs are sufficiently self-contained to encourage confidence but vary dramatically in degree of difficulty. A delightful and easy blue run takes you down into St Christoph, and a quad-chair has been built to replace the old cable-car for the return journey. The Osthang, a fearsome bump run with a hostile

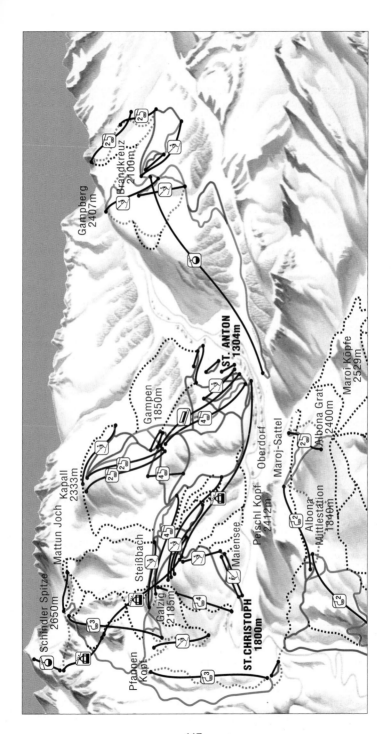

Schindler Spitze 2650m
Mattun Joch
Kapall 2333m
Gampberg 2407m
Brandkreuz 2100m
ST. ANTON 1304m
Gampen 1850m
Oberdorf
Maroj-Sattel
Maroi Köpfe 2529m
Albona Grat 2400m
Pepischl Kopf 2412m
Steißbach
Maiensee
Galzig 2185m
ST. CHRISTOPH 1800m
Albona Mittlestation 1840m
Pfannen Kopf

camber, takes you back down towards St Anton, but there are less extreme alternatives. Timid skiers should note with care that St Anton has dispensed with black (difficult) runs in favour of unpisted ski-routes in what some critics see as a negation of responsibility. These appear on the map as either plain red or black-bordered diamonds. For red read black, for black-border read double-black.

Advanced

Depending on the snow conditions almost all of St Anton's skiing can be considered advanced. From the Vallugagrat, three of St Anton's finest long runs lead back to the broad flat valley of the Steissbachtal, a corridor between the Valluga runs and those on the adjoining Kapall.

The toughest of the three is the Schindlerkar, a wide 30-degree mogul marathon that seems to go on forever. Strong skiers can repeat it continually by riding the Schindlergratbahn high-speed quad, but its south-facing aspect makes it vulnerable to early-morning ice and late-afternoon slush. The Mattun is a series of mogulled bowls linked by a traverse; it is less steep in pitch but more intriguing because of the variety of its challenges. The third, much easier, option – the long dog-leg via the Ulmerhütte – opens up the Valluga to confident intermediates. It is also the starting point for the run to the high, cold outpost of Stuben. The Rendl has a funpark with obstacle courses and a half-pipe.

Off-piste

The off-piste possibilities are limitless, and a guide can find fresh powder a week after the last fall. An experienced skier wanting to truly enjoy St Anton should view the services of a local guide along with accommodation and food as part of the basic cost of the holiday.

The patio-sized top of the Valluga is accessed by a final six-person cable-car confined to sightseers, or skiers accompanied by a qualified guide. From the top it is possible to ski down the Pazieltal into Zürs and Lech. The valley itself is not difficult to ski, but the first few metres of the north face of the Valluga are terrifying, with a cliff ready to take away anyone who falls. The Malfon Valley over the back of the Rendl is a wide, enjoyable off-piste run which, when there is sufficient snow, ends on a road at the base of the lift. Above Stuben, a 20-minute walk up the Maroi Kopfe gives entry to the Maroital Valley.

St Anton's mainly south-facing slopes have a good snow record but also harbour an extremely high avalanche risk, and the greatest care should be taken at all times.

Tuition and guiding

The Arlberg Ski School has 180 instructors, half of whom teach group ski-school classes at any one time while the other half are hired out as private guides. The rival St Anton Ski School run by Franz Klimmer has 30 instructors. Competition between the two is fierce, which helps to maintain standards, with class sizes usually restricted to ten. We now have excellent reports of both: 'our patient instructor spoke good English because he was English' (St Anton) and 'excellent instruction in private lesson' (Arlberg). Alpine Faszination is a small, off-piste guiding service, which is strongly recommended by readers. The rather pretentious-sounding St Anton am Arlberg Snowboard Academy is run under the banner of the Arlberg Ski School.

Mountain restaurants

According to reporters, most restaurants in the area offer reasonable fare at high-altitude prices. The Albonagrat seats only about 25 but is highly rated ('superb, great atmosphere, cheap food'). The bleak self-service at Galzig has panoramic views over the slopes and inevitably gets over-crowded, but it does have an adjoining wait-service restaurant. Stopp's at St Christoph is popular. The terrace of the Arlberg-Hospiz-Alm is particularly popular, with attentive service from traditionally dressed waiters. Lunchtime prices match those in other mountain restaurants but by night it is transformed into a centre for gourmet dining. The Hotel Post in Stuben and the Maiensee Stube in St Christoph are both praised for their 'warm, wood-panelled atmosphere and good food'.

The resort

St Anton's major drawback is that the village is bisected by the main railway line between Zurich and Vienna. To reach the main ski area you first have to cross over or underneath the tracks. For anyone staying on this side of town slumber is disturbed as much by night trains as by returning party-goers ('if the Swedes don't wake you, the shunting surely will'). However, all that is to change under an ambitious scheme to shift the railway line to the far side of the bypass, with the station to be situated near the present tennis courts.

The undistinguished village architecture is a blend of old and new that owes little to planning and a lot to those who recognised an opportunity and seized it before the current strict zoning regulations came into force. A fierce policy of no outside ownership, no holiday homes and no expansion in the number of guest beds has saved it from otherwise inevitable blight.

The opening of St Anton to the outside world began in 1884 when the railway tunnel under the Arlberg Pass was completed. What had been little more than a hamlet grew steadily into a

> **WHAT'S NEW**
>
> Covered chair-lift from Gampen to Kapall
> Additional snowmaking at Gampen/Kapall
> New blue run from Galzig to St Anton
> T-bar on Rendl replaced by double-chair-lift

village, with its narrow main street running parallel to the tracks. In the days before the road tunnel under the Arlberg Pass and the St Anton bypass were opened in 1977, the street was a traffic nightmare. Today it is a relatively peaceful pedestrian zone lined with shops, cafés and St Anton's most handsome, traditional hotels: the Post, the Alte Post and the Schwarzer Adler.

Skiing facts: St Anton

TOURIST OFFICE
A-6580 St Anton, Arlberg
Tel 43 5446 22690
Fax 43 5446 2532
Email st.anton@netway.at
Web site www.tiscover.com/st.anton

THE RESORT
By road Calais 1092km
By rail station in resort
Airport transfer Innsbruck 1hr,
Zurich 3–4 hrs, Munich 3–4 hrs
Visitor beds 8,500
Transport free ski bus

THE SKIING
Linked or nearby resorts St Christoph
(l), Lech (n), Pettneu (n), Stuben (l),
Zürs (n), Klösterle (n)
Longest run top of the Vallugagrat to
resort, 8km (black/blue)
Number of lifts 42 (86 on the Arlberg
Ski Pass, including Lech and Zürs)
Total of trails/pistes 260km of prepared
pistes (25% easy, 50% intermediate,
25% difficult)
Nursery slopes 8 lifts
Summer skiing none
Snowmaking 25km covered

LIFT PASSES
Area pass Arlberg Ski Pass (covers St
Anton, St Christoph, Stuben, Lech, Zürs,
Klösterle) ATS1,300–2,150 for 6 days
Day pass ATS425–470
Beginners no free lifts, ATS200 for 30
points per day
Pensioners ATS385–425 day pass for
women 60yrs and over and men 65yrs

and over
Credit cards no

TUITION
Adults Arlberg ATS1,580, St Anton
ATS1,520, both for 6 days (4½hrs
per day) 9.30am–3.30pm
Private lessons Arlberg ATS2,220,
St Anton ATS2,100, both per 4½hrs
Snowboarding St Anton am Arlberg
Snowboard Academy, St Anton, both
ATS1,950 for 6 days, or ATS500–
525 per day
Cross-country Arlberg and St Anton,
ATS715 per day. Loipe 40km
Other courses telemark, off-piste,
heli-skiing, ski-touring
Guiding Alpine Faszination, or through
ski schools

CHILDREN
Lift pass Arlberg Ski Pass, 7–15yrs,
ATS1,1701–1,300 for 6 days, 6yrs and
under, ATS100 for whole season
Ski kindergarten Children's World
(Arlberg Ski School), 2½yrs and over,
ATS1,580 for 6 days, 9am–4.30pm
including lunch
Ski school 4–14yrs, 9am–4.30pm,
ATS1,500–1,585
Non-ski kindergarten none

OTHER SPORTS
Curling, indoor tennis and squash,
paragliding, sleigh rides, skating, swimming

FOOD AND DRINK PRICES
Coffee ATS27, glass of wine ATS26, small
beer ATS32, dish of the day ATS80

The rest of the town straggles along the road in both directions, towards Mooserkreuz at the top of the resort to the west, and towards the satellite villages of **Nasserein** and **St Jakob** to the east. Nasserein is now to be wholly integrated into St Anton with the building of new lifts in time for the World Championships. The village is an important bed-base, but the shuttle bus does not run in the evening and the nightlife is limited to local bars unless you are prepared for a 20-minute walk.

Accommodation

The area has two five-star hotels: the historic and expensive Arlberg-Hospiz at St Christoph and the modern St Antoner Hof near the bypass. The four-star options are headed by the Post ('accommodation excellent, but staff snotty'), the Hotel Alte Post and the Schwarzer Adler ('comfortable and convenient'), all much richer in tradition and much closer to the lifts. St Anton has an abundance of chalets, as well as a large number of pensions and apartments.

One reporter strongly recommends Haus Lina ('fabulous breakfasts, en-suite bathrooms, Austrian décor and few Brits'). Hotel Arlberg has 'excellent food and rooms and friendly, helpful, English-speaking staff'. Those who find themselves uncomfortably far away from the slopes can leave their skis and boots overnight in the storage at the bottom of the Galzig lift.

Eating in and out

With the exception of the restaurant in the Arlberg-Hospiz and its sister restaurant, the Hospiz-Alm, where a magnum of Château Lafite Rothschild 1959 will set you back £1,875, dining out is not a strong feature of St Anton. Elsewhere the emphasis is on substantial rather than sophisticated fare. Austrian alpine food has dramatically improved in a generation, but boiled meats, dumplings and rich desserts still feature strongly. The restaurants in the Post and the Alte Post do these things rather better than the more contemporary rivals. The Brunnenhof in St Jakob has 'some of the best food in the region'.

Après-ski

St Anton's undeniably vibrant après-ski starts to warm up from lunch-time in the Sennehütte before sliding down to the Mooserwirt and the Australian-inspired Krazy Kanguruh just above the final descent to the resort where a 15-ft yellow inflatable marsupial perched on the roof beckons thirsty skiers as they make their way home. Long before the lifts close for the day the bar is packed tighter than a Boxing Day crowd on Bondi Beach.

In the après-ski world of *fin de siècle* St Anton, the sedate tea-dancing of old has become beer-dancing – with the intermittent bottle-to-mouth administration by a pretty waitress of Red-Bull-and-vodka at £1.50 a shot. Most guests, after dancing in their ski boots and consuming copious amounts of alcohol, still manage to negotiate on skis in the dark the final 800 metres home past a battery of active snow-cannon.

Down in the resort the action continues until sundown on the terrace of the Hotel Alte Post before switching to the Postkeller or to the Underground, which has good live music. The St Antoner Hof Bar is recommended for 'a quiet, sophisticated drink'. Scottie's Bar in the Hotel Rosanna is a rendezvous for Brits. Late-evening entertainment is centred on The Piccadilly, Drop-In, Amadeus and Kartouche.

Childcare

St Anton has done much to improve its previously inadequate facilities for small children. The Arlberg Ski School runs Children's World, a kindergarten with four 'campuses' at the ski school meeting place, on the Gampen, in Nassarein and in St Christoph. Small skiers are accepted from two-and-a-half years of age as long as they are out of nappies. The main kindergarten area is on the Gampen and is accessible either by chair-lift, or by the funicular railway. Children from five years of age (or four by arrangement) are welcome at the ski school.

Linked or nearby resorts

Stuben
top 2811m (9,222ft) bottom 1407m (4,616ft)

The village was named after the warm parlour – or Stube – of a solitary house on the Arlberg Pass where pilgrims used to shelter in the eighteenth century. Only 32 houses have been added since then, and Stuben has a mere 104 residents and 650 guest beds. The Post Inn, now a four-star hotel, was where mail-coach drivers changed horses for the steep journey up the pass. With its small collection of hotels and restaurants, Stuben is seen by some as an ideal way to enjoy the Arlberg.

TOURIST OFFICE
Tel 43 55 82 761
Fax 43 55 82 7626

St Christoph
top 2811m (9,222ft) bottom 1800m (5,906ft)

Further up the Arlberg Pass, St Christoph was the last resort for the pilgrim making his way between the mountains. In 1386 a shepherd called Heinrich Findelkind von Kempten built a hospice on the pass with his own savings and manned it in the winter with two servants. The Brotherhood of St Christoph (a charitable foundation of locals inspired by von Kempten) still exists, but the hospice burned down in 1957. The five-star Arlberg-Hospiz hotel was built on the site. St Christoph has five other hotels and the Bundessportheim Ski Academy, but very little else.

TOURIST OFFICE
Tel *as St Anton*
Fax *as St Anton*

Zell am See

ALTITUDE 750m (2,460ft)

Beginners ✳✳ Intermediates ✳✳✳ Advanced ✳ Snowboarders ✳✳

Zell am See, an attractive medieval town just one hour by road from Salzburg, used to suffer badly from traffic and pollution as a trans-Austrian arterial road ran slap through its centre. However, a 10-km tunnel now takes all the through-traffic underground from the satellite of **Schüttdorf** to the northern end of the lake, thereby restoring Zell to the peaceful backwater it used to be and adding to its attraction as a pleasant, unchallenging ski resort. Its summer trade, centred on water sports, is even larger than its winter trade, and the resort's huge international popularity rests on its hard-to-beat geographical setting at the foot of the 2000-m Schmittenhöhe. The mountain provides an ample amount of easy intermediate skiing, and the towering presence of the Kitzsteinhorn Glacier above neighbouring **Kaprun** means that snow is guaranteed. The Kitzsteinhorn is one of the best developed glaciers in Austria, with year-round skiing on the upper slopes. In times of poor snow cover it becomes a daily point of pilgrimage for thousands of tourists from other resorts in Salzburgerland, and overcrowding here can sometimes be unacceptable.

> ✔ Facilities for non-skiers
> ✔ Short airport transfer
> ✔ Extensive cross-country skiing
> ✔ Attractive pedestrian centre
> ✔ Lively nightlife
> ✔ Year-round skiing on Kitzsteinhorn Glacier
> ✘ Overcrowding at peak periods
> ✘ Skiing convenience

Kaprun and Zell am See have joined forces and market themselves under the unoriginal name of Europa Sport Region. The shared ski pass also includes a total of 130km of skiing and access to 60 lifts. Mountain facilities have improved, although Zell prides itself on its 'green' image and has vowed to replace old lifts but not to build any entirely new ones.

The focus on uphill transport to the Schmittenhöhe has switched from the slow and overcrowded Schmittenhöhe cable-car at Schmittental to Schüttdorf; the Areitbahn gondola from here has been extended by two further stages so that the summit of the mountain can be reached in just 20 minutes.

A long-standing legal tussle between the landowner and the lift company has finally been resolved and the old Hirschkogelbahn chair-lift, scene of the worst queues on the mountain, has been upgraded to a detachable quad chair-lift.

Ski and board
top 1965m (6,445ft) bottom 750m (2,460ft)

The Schmittenhöhe looks like a *Germknödl*, the rounded, sweet dumpling to be found in the nine mountain restaurants that are on it. Its moderate slopes provide long, gentle red (intermediate) runs both back down to the village and along the southern flank to the satellite of Schüttdorf. Steeper slopes drop from a bowl and provide the most challenging skiing (and off-piste if it were allowed) in the resort.

Until the tunnel opened, the main mountain access was on the 'wrong' side of the busy trunk road, where the Zeller Bergbahn gondola rises to the mid-station at 1320m. From Schmittental, 2km from the centre of Zell, the old Schmittenhöhe cable-car rises sedately to the summit, or a second cable-car takes you into the Sonnalm area on the sunny, south-facing side of the bowl, which is served by two more chairs and a drag-lift. A considerable number of skiers prefer to take the free bus and start the day on the Areitbahn gondola at Schüttdorf. A small area of blue (easy) and red runs behind the summit is served by a chair and a couple of drag-lifts. None of the skiing could be classified as difficult in good snow conditions, although a steepish pitch down the black (difficult) run below Sonnalm can present problems when it is worn and icy. The Ebernberglift, above the road between Zell and Schüttdorf, is used mainly for slalom practice. There is artificial snow on the black runs down into the pit of the bowl (without these, snow can become dangerously icy) as well as on the nursery slopes.

Thumersbach, on the other side of the lake, has a chair-lift and three short drags that provide a couple of gentle, uncrowded runs back down the wooded slopes with wonderful views of Zell am See.

The pretty village of Kaprun, a five-minute journey on the ski bus, also has its own ski area above the village comprising mainly blue runs. However, the best of its skiing is on the Kitzsteinhorn Glacier, 20 minutes by road from Zell. A gondola followed by quad-chair, or the original underground funicular, take you up to the Alpincenter at 2450m, where lifts whisk you on up to the top of the ski area at 3029m.

The Alpincenter includes a modest hotel, restaurants and a first-class ski shop. The glacier offers good but exposed blue and red runs, most of which are open nearly all year round. A cable-car takes you to the Aussichts restaurant at the top and gives access to the only difficult run: a short, steep mogul field. There is also a year-round cross-country circuit below the ridge at the top of the bowl. In winter, a long red takes you down to the mid-station of the funicular and ends in a push along the plastic floor of a long tunnel. The construction of a gondola up to the glacier has done much to reduce queuing, but when snow cover is poor in this part of Austria the extensive car parks fill up with coaches at first light.

Beginners

The main novice slopes are on the top of the mountain, and you will need to take the lift down again at the end of the day. There are also nursery slopes at the bottom of the cable-car and at Schüttdorf.

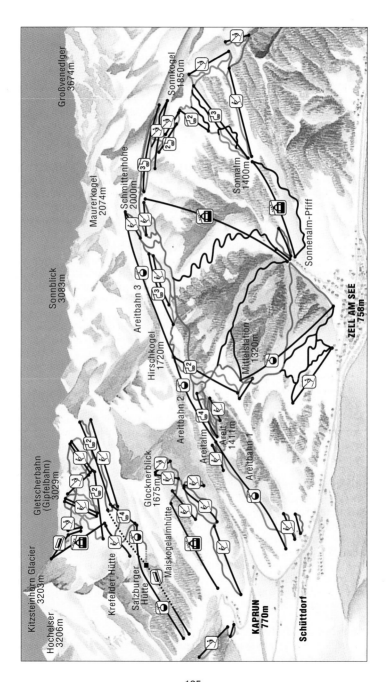

Intermediates

South of Schmittenhöhe, a succession of gentle, broad and sunny pistes descend along the ridge and on down to Schüttdorf. A right fork takes you to Areitalm, which is the arrival point for the first stage of the Schüttdorf gondola; the cruising piste down from here to the bottom does not keep its snow in warm weather. The left fork brings you down to the Zell am See mid-station. The Sonnalm area also provides plenty of easy cruising.

Advanced

The two black runs that branch off over the southern lip of the bowl provide the best advanced terrain. These soon steepen into testing, but not intimidating, long runs with the occasional pitch of almost 30 degrees. The other two runs to the base-stations are less severe but receive more sun.

Zell am See is committed to the development of snowboarding and has a boardercross park, which regularly hosts competitions; four riders simultaneously race down a challenging course, with the two fastest going through to the next round. Kaprun also has a funpark and half-pipe, which are in operation all year round.

WHAT'S NEW
Hirschkogelbahn upgraded to quad chair-lift
Two new chair-lifts on the Maiskogel at Kaprun
Snowmaking at Mittelstation
Half-pipe on the Glocknerwiese-Schmittenhöhe
Snowboard funpark on Kitzsteinhorn Glacier

Off-piste

Zell's strong environmental policy means that off-piste skiing is severely restricted to the point of being almost forbidden. After a fresh fall, a number of tree-line runs look particularly enticing, but protection of saplings is a priority, and you risk confiscation of your lift pass if you ski down them. Snowboarders should note that the small amount of off-piste that is available on the Schmittenhöhe is not open to them: snowboarding is forbidden outside the marked runs.

Tuition and guiding

Ski and snowboard schools in the valley seem to vary in quality, and we have mixed reports of the eight schools in the region. None of them has priority in the lift lines, so it is not worth taking lessons just to jump the queues. The Wallner Prenner in Zell am See is the most highly recommended, with 'excellent instructors, all of whom speak good English'. The Schmittenhöhe has a number of Australian teachers and also receives considerable praise. The Kitzsteinhorn Ski School at Kaprun operates year-round and has a high standard of instruction, particularly for advanced skiers.

Mountain restaurants

Zell am See has a good choice of mountain eating-places, although these are crowded during busy weeks; prices are reasonable. The black run down from Sonnalm has a pleasant hut for those who can get to it. The Sonnenalm-Pfiff is praised for its 'delicious hot chocolate'. Schmiedhofalm has amazing views from its sunny terrace. The mid-station restaurant serves 'huge and excellent *Kaiserschmarren*' (chopped pancake with stewed plums). Glocknerhaus, on the way down to Schüttdorf, is also popular. Hans' Schnapps Bar on the summit has a live rock band two days a week and attracts dancing in ski boots, even on the bar.

The resort

Zell am See, at the gateway to Austria's highest mountain, the Grossglockner, is an established town first settled by a monastic order in the eighth century. Its medieval guesthouses and shops cluster around a tenth-century tower, which houses an uninspiring museum of local history. In recent years the town has done much to smarten up its image. The whole of the centre has been pedestrianised and it has an upmarket look, resembling a mini Kitzbühel. Buses run every 15 minutes to the lifts and regularly to Kaprun and the Kitzsteinhorn. Reporters complain that the lifts tend to become very crowded, and if snow conditions confine skiing to the Kitzsteinhorn then a car is a necessity. There is a regular bus service to Thumersbach, but you can also walk across the lake in mid-winter.

Accommodation

Unfortunately, three large hotels have shut their doors, including the once popular Neue Post. The luxurious Grand Hotel, jutting out over the lake, narrowly missed a similar fate but was bought and relaunched by the owners of the five-star Salzburgerhof, which is the smartest hotel in town. The four-stars are the Alpin, Fischerwirt and the Alpenblick. Hotel Bellevue is a recommended three-star. Hotel St Georg is one of the best hotels, with its smart, pine-panelled rooms and views of the lake. The Tirolerhof has 'friendly staff with good English, and the four-course meals were excellent'. Hotel Berner is set above the town, has a heated outdoor swimming-pool and is popular with reporters ('decorated in a rather grand style, but the owners and staff are friendly').

Eating in and out

The Alpenkönig, Steinerwirt and Chataprunium are considered the best value for money along with the Kupferkessel and the Saustall. Hotel St Georg has a pleasant restaurant with good-quality food. The Ampere, Landhotel Erlhof and the Salzburgerhof are also recommended for their high standards of cuisine. Several reporters praise Zum Hirschen for its cosy atmosphere and tasty food. The Baum-Bar in Kaprun has a very un-Austrian-style restaurant in a large, modern conservatory.

Après-ski

Zell am See is lively by any standards. Once the lifts have closed for the day the first stop is a choice of the Kellerbar of the Hotel Schwebebahn

Skiing facts: Zell am See/Kaprun

TOURIST OFFICE
Brucker Bundesstrasse 3, A-5700
Zell am See, Salzburgerland
Tel 43 6542 770
Fax 43 6542 72032
Email zell@gold.at
Web site zell.gold.at

THE RESORT
By road Calais 1296km
By rail station in resort
Airport transfer Salzburg 1hr
Visitor beds 14,000
Transport free ski bus with lift pass

THE SKIING
Linked or nearby resorts Kaprun (l),
Saalbach-Hinterglemm (n) Maria Alm (n)
Longest run Schüttdorfabfahrt, 6.5km
(blue)
Number of lifts 33 in Zell am See, 60 in
Europa Sport Region
Total of trails/pistes 80km in Zell am
See (39% easy, 49% intermediate, 12%
difficult), 130km in Europa Sport Region
Nursery slopes 5 lifts
Summer skiing 15 lifts on glacier
Snowmaking 65 hectares covered

LIFT PASSES
Area pass Europa Sport Region
ATS1,820–1,970 for 6 days
Day pass Zell am See only or
Kitzsteinhorn only, ATS370–410
Beginners ATS10–20 per ride for lower
drag-lifts
Pensioners ATS1,640–1,775 for women
60yrs and over, men 65yrs and over
Credit cards yes

TUITION
Adults Wallner Prenner, Schmittenhöhe,
Areitbahn, Pro Alpin, Ski Magic, 10am–

12pm and 1pm–3pm, ATS1,600–1,850
for 6 days, ATS550 per day
Private lessons Wallner Prenner,
Schmittenhöhe, Areitbahn and
Thumersbach ATS500 per hr, full day
ATS2,200 (4hrs)
Snowboarding Wallner Prenner,
Schmittenhöhe, Areitbahn ATS1,050
for 3 half-days.
Private lessons ATS550 per hr,
ATS1,350 for 5 half-days
Cross-country Markus Werth/Schüttdorf
and Harald Nicka/Schüttdorf, ATS400 for
half day including tuition. Loipe 12km
Other courses telemark, monoski
Guiding Ludwig Kranabeller, Helmut
Göllner, Mont Alpin

CHILDREN
Lift pass 6–15yrs, ATS1,145–1,180
for 6 days, free for 6yrs and under
Ski kindergarten all ski schools,
9.30am–3pm, ATS1,750 for 6 days,
ATS580 per day including lunch
Ski school Wallner Prenner, 4yrs and
above, ATS1,750 for 6 days
Non-ski kindergarten Areitbahn, 3yrs
and over, ATS1,650 for 6 days. Feriendorf
Hagleitner, 12mths and over, ATS1,200
for 5 days. Ursula Zink, no age limit
ATS1,500 for 6 days

OTHER SPORTS
Parapente, hang-gliding, luge-ing,
hot-air ballooning, sleigh rides, skating,
curling, indoor tennis and squash,
swimming, shooting range, climbing wall,
snow rafting, ice-hockey, horse-riding

FOOD AND DRINK PRICES
Coffee ATS25–27, glass of wine ATS40,
small beer ATS32, dish of the day
ATS85–200

near the lifts, Café Feinschmeck with its vast variety of pastries, and the Mösshammer in the main square, which also has tasty coffee and cakes. Tea-dancing still exists in Zell, and a number of reporters have enjoyed watching major-league ice-hockey matches. The Crazy Daisy bar is a focal point for Anglo-Saxon visitors, but said by one reporter to be 'very expensive and unpleasantly crowded'. The Kellerbar of the Hotel zum Hirschen is lively, and the main bar of the Tirolerhof is a good place to relax and drink, and at the same time hear yourself think. Late-night action switches to the Viva nightclub, which swings on until dawn, Evergreens for the over 25s, and the Diele Bar, which attracts a young crowd until 2am.

Childcare
The children's facilities here are generally recommended, with a kindergarten taking children from 12 months old. Ski lessons are given from the age of three years. One parent described it as better than the adult ski school he attended: 'We have no complaints about the standard of tuition or care of the children'. The Grand Hotel and the Feriendorf Hagleitner both run crèches.

Linked or nearby resorts

Kaprun
top 3029m (9,938ft) bottom 770m (2,526ft)
This is a delightful, typical Austrian holiday village, a few kilometres back into the mountains from the lakeside. It has been expanded considerably in recent years and has developed into a year-round ski resort. But despite new hotel and apartment developments, Kaprun has managed to retain its essential village atmosphere. It has a handful of sports and gift shops, the odd tea-room, and a good attempt has been made at providing a nightlife for its visitors, who range from winter-holiday skiers to the professionals who use the glacier as their workbench during the summer months.

The four-star Orgler hotel has comfortable accommodation and one of the best restaurants. The Barbarahof and the Sportkristall are both recommended. The Sonnblick and the Kaprunserhof cater for families. We have favourable reports of the Pension Salzburgerhof ('pleasant, spacious bedrooms'), and Hotel Toni has good food, friendly staff and a self-catering annexe.

TOURIST OFFICE
Tel 43 6547 86430
Fax 43 6547 8192
Email kaprun@gold.at
Web site kaprun.gold.at

Round–up

RESORTS COVERED Bad Kleinkirchheim, Fieberbrunn, Lermoos, Maria Alm, Sölden, St Johann im Pongau, St Johann in Tirol, Waidring

Bad Kleinkirchheim
top 2000m (6,560ft) bottom 1080m (3,543ft)

Bad Kleinkirchheim – or BKK as it is usually known – is the home resort of Austrian super-hero Franz Klammer, and, as one reporter put it: 'What is good enough for Franz is good enough for me'. These days the greatest of all downhill champions spends more time in Colorado than in Carinthia, but the old spa town and thriving summer resort continues to develop its skiing in his absence. The ski area is linked to the neighbouring village of **St Oswald**, and together the two provide 85km of mainly intermediate pistes served by 33 lifts. BKK is quite spread out and has a wide choice of hotels, but après-ski is limited. There are a few bars, two discos and some good-value restaurants. The excellent spa facilities include indoor and outdoor thermal pools.

The ski area is low, with the top lifts reaching only 2000m; snow conditions are consequently unreliable both early and late in the season. The World Cup downhill course was designed by the master himself and includes a sequence of jumps which, even when prepared as a recreational run require considerable concentration. Most runs are wide and gentle, and queues are reported during high season. The lift pass also covers the neighbouring resorts of St Oswald and **Falkert**.

The BKK and St Oswald ski school gives group and private tuition in skiing, snowboarding and cross-country, the latter on its 42km of loipe. Three- to six-year-olds can attend the kindergarten, where a mixture of games and skiing is offered. BKK actively encourages snowboarders, with a floodlit funpark and the Crazy Carving Company snowboard school.

TOURIST OFFICE
Tel 43 4240 8212
Fax 43 4240 8537

Fieberbrunn
top 1870m (6,135ft) bottom 800m (2,625ft)

Ten kilometres up the road from St Johann in Tirol is the sprawling village of Fieberbrunn. Its small but attractive ski area is north-facing and is known as a *Schneewinkel*, or snowpocket. The main skiing is at tree level, with several long and easy runs and some varied off-piste skiing including treks over to **Kitzbühel**.

TOURIST OFFICE
Tel 43 5354 6304
Fax 43 5354 2606

Lermoos
top 2200m (7,216ft) bottom 1004m (3,293ft)

Lermoos and nearby Ehrwald, at the foot of the impressive Zugspitze, are typical Tirolean working villages. The two are linked by bus and lift and are in an attractive area to the north-west of **Innsbruck** near the German border. Both villages are unspoilt and boast plenty of bars and reasonably priced restaurants. The skiing is divided into four small sections all covered by one lift pass. Beginners can try the nursery slopes at the Lermoos base and graduate to a longer, gentle run by taking the gondola up Ehrwalder Alm. Intermediates will discover wide pistes and easy red (intermediate) runs in the Zugspitze Bowl, which lead over the border into Germany. Advanced skiers will find the area limited; there is one black (difficult) run on the Grubigstein above Lermoos. However, in good snow conditions you can ski down from the Zugspitze Glacier. This is an excellent area for cross-country skiing, with more than 100km of prepared tracks.

TOURIST OFFICE
Tel 43 5673 2401
Fax 43 5673 2694

Maria Alm
top 2000m (6,560ft) bottom 800m (2,624ft)

Maria Alm is a compact and largely unspoilt village close to Zell am See. It is dominated by a church boasting the highest spire in Salzburgerland. Maria Alm has twice won awards as the most beautiful village in this part of Austria. Many of its hotels are small, with good-value menus and cosy bars. The lift pass covers Maria Alm as well as the linked skiing of **Saalfelden**, **Hinterthal**, **Hintermoos**, **Dienten** and **Mühlbach**. The pistes are well groomed and ideal for intermediates who enjoy tree-lined runs that challenge rather than terrify.

TOURIST OFFICE
Tel 43 65 84 7816
Fax 43 65 84 7600

Sölden
top 3058m (10,030ft) bottom 1377m (4,517ft)

Sölden is a high-altitude, and therefore snow-sure, resort which sprawls along the main road in the upper reaches of the isolated Ötztal. The skiing is mainly suited to intermediates. Two developed glaciers – the Rettenbach and the Tiefenbach – which are separate from the main ski area, are useful when snow conditions on the main mountain are poor.

The vertical drop is substantial by Austrian standards and, at least in high season, the après-ski entertainment is lively to the point of being raucous. Sölden's ski area is in two sections linked by chairs up both walls of the narrow Rettenbachtal, which provides the toll road up to the glaciers. Both sectors are reached by gondolas from either end of the village, which are in turn linked by a ski bus that runs efficiently every nine minutes. Hochsölden is a collection of hotels set on a shelf with dramatic views of the Ötztal, 700m up the mountainside, which gives easy access to the slopes at the more mundane and busier side of the mountain.

The Rettenbach and Tiefenbach glaciers have a total of ten lifts that serve a selection of mainly blue runs, more enjoyable for their panoramic views than the actual challenge of their skiing. All three ski schools offer snowboarding lessons. The Giggijoch area has a funpark with a half-pipe and jumps. The choice of mountain restaurants is larger than usual: Gampe Alm, Eugen's Obstlerhütte and Löple Alm are all authentic huts with plenty of atmosphere.

The resort stretches over 2km on either side of the road and river along the valley floor. It is an unmemorable sprawl of hotels, restaurants and bars that lack charm. Position is important and a hotel near one of the two main lift stations is a must. The Hotel Regina, right by the Gaislachkoglbahn, is strongly recommended. Gästehaus Sonneheim, in the same area, is praised for being 'extremely cheap'. Hotel Stefan by the Giggijoch gondola station has a good restaurant. Gästehaus Paul Grüner continues to receive praise. Dominic is said to be the best eatery in the village. The Kupferpfanne in the Hotel Tirolerhof and the à la carte restaurants in the Alpina, Stefan and Hubertus hotels are also recommended. Hotel Sonne has a cosy stüberl bar.

Once the lifts close Sölden swings into life. Café Philip at Innerwald has a lively atmosphere and is a gathering point for young people. The single-chair down from here runs until 6pm. The Hinterer, Dominic and Café Heiner are always crowded. Later in the evening, Jakob's Weinfassl attracts a 30-something clientèle. The Piano Bar in the Hotel Central is a sophisticated disco. Apart from private babysitting, Sölden has no special facilities for non-skiing children. The Sölden/Hochsölden Ski School runs a ski kindergarten for skiers aged three and above.

TOURIST OFFICE
Tel 43 5254 22120
Fax 43 5254 3131

St Johann im Pongau
top 2188m (7,177ft) bottom 650m (2,132ft)

The four valleys of **St Johann**, **Wagrain**, **Flachau** and **Zauchensee** lie only 45 minutes from Salzburg and provide an intermediate playground offering some impressive statistics: a dozen resorts with 350km of linked (albeit not always on the mountain) skiing, served by 130 lifts all covered by one ski pass. St Johann itself (not to be confused with St Johann in Tirol) is a cathedral town that was all but devastated by a disastrous fire in 1852; consequently, it lacks the medieval charm of Austria's other county towns and larger resorts.

The ski area, which is known as the Sportwelt Amadé, has one of the best-value lift passes in Austria. It is popular with almost every nationality apart from the British; this is partly because few tour operators come here as they cannot contract enough hotel beds to make the area's inclusion in their brochures a commercial viability. Wagrain and Flachau are the most convenient and attractive bases from which to explore the circuit. St Johann has its own small, separate ski area, and the link into the Sportwelt Amadé is via the hamlet of **Alpendorf,** a 3-km ski-bus ride away. The pistes in the area are well serviced with eating places, from small huts to larger self-services.

Each of the resorts has at least one ski school, and St Johann has three. St Johann has a funpark. Vitamin B and Board Unlimited are two specialist boarding schools in Alpendorf. Langlaufers are well served by 160km of trails along the valleys.

Accommodation in St Johann includes the luxurious Sporthotel Alpenland, Hotel Brückenwirt-Tennerhof, and Gasthof-Pension Taxenbacher. Après-ski is limited to a few bars. The inconvenient bus journey to Alpendorf means that St Johann is not ideal for families.

The small village of Wagrain has fortunately been able to develop away from the minor road from St Johann to Flachau and Radstadt. Hotel Grafenwirt is discreetly upmarket, Hotel Enzian and the Wagrainerhof are both recommended. The ski kindergarten takes children from three years old.

Neighbouring Flachau has undergone considerable expansion in recent years. The main accommodation is in large chalet-style hotels and inns, as well as apartment blocks. Beginners learn to ski on a gentle piste in the village. There is a non-ski kindergarten, and the Griessenkar Ski School takes children from three years old. Hotel Reslwirt is central and medium-priced, along with Gasthof Salzburgerhof. There are two four-star hotels, Hotel Vierjahreszeiten and the luxurious Hotel Tauernhof.

The market town of **Altenmarkt** is a centre for the local sportswear and ski equipment industries where Atomic skis and Steffner sweaters among others are manufactured. A modest ski area is linked to neighbouring **Radstadt,** but the main skiing is a bus-ride away at Zauchensee (or Flachau). British-run Fun Ski is based in Zauchensee and offers specialist skiing courses. The kindergarten cares for children from three years old. The cross-country opportunities, as in the rest of the area, are extensive. The village has 22 hotels, including six of a luxury standard.

Filzmoos is another small village in the Sportwelt Amadé, which dates from Edwardian times, when it was a popular holiday spot for the wealthy Viennese. Today it has a ski area of 17 lifts, shared with neighbouring Neuberg. The Dachstein Glacier is only 18km away, and the Three Valleys are reached by bus via Flachau. The kindergarten takes children from three years old and has English-speaking staff. The choice of accommodation in 25 hotels and a selection of apartments is large in relation to the size of the village, which is known as the hot-air ballooning capital of Austria.

TOURIST OFFICE
Tel 43 6412 6036
Fax 43 6412 603674

St Johann in Tirol
top 1700m (5,576ft) bottom 680m (2,230ft)

St Johann in Tirol is a large, busy town with a small ski area. Its expansion from a pretty Tirolean village to a sprawling light-industrial centre has done little for its charm. Nevertheless, the centre, with its ornately frescoed buildings and fine old coaching inns, remains largely unspoilt, and the heavy traffic is confined to the outskirts. St Johann offers a pleasant setting for a lively and quite varied winter holiday at prices that are reasonable by Austrian standards. Queues are generally not a problem but are increased by weekend visitors from Innsbruck and Munich when conditions are good. However, the northward orientation of the slopes and competent grooming generally keep the slopes in fine condition.

The resort is particularly geared towards beginners, with six nursery-slope lifts scattered between the town and the hamlet of **Eichenhof,** which is served by ski bus. The rolling lower pastures are ideal novice terrain, with a choice of blue runs higher up to which beginners can progress after a few days. Practically all the skiing on the top-half of the mountain is graded red. The area is limited in size and lacks any real challenge. Another major drawback is the distance across town to the lifts. A choice of 18 mountain restaurants is way above average for a resort of this size. Practically every piste has a welcoming hut at the top, bottom or part-way down. The cross-country skiing is extensive and covers 75km of prepared tracks from St Johann to **Oberndorf**, **Going**, **Kirchdorf**, **Erpfendorf** and **Waidring**.

The central feature of St Johann is the three-star Hotel Gasthof Post, which dates from 1225 and is beautifully frescoed. Hotel Park, near the gondola, is recommended. Hotel Goldener Löwe is strongly endorsed for families. St Johann's après-ski is young and vibrant.

TOURIST OFFICE
Tel 43 5352 2218
Fax 43 5352 5200

Waidring
top 1860m (6,102ft) bottom 780m (2,558ft)

This unspoilt village is less than 20km from St Johann in Tirol and is situated in the same snowpocket as Fieberbrunn. The resort is known for its family skiing, with convenient nursery slopes in the village centre. The rest of the skiing is at Steinplatte, 4km from the village, and is suited to beginners and intermediates. There are five mountain restaurants on the slopes. The best hotel is the Waidringerhof, which has a swimming-pool and a pleasant dining-room. The central Hotel Tiroler Adler is also recommended. The nightlife in Waidring is relaxed and informal, with the Schniedermann Bar and the Alte Schmiede both popular venues.

TOURIST OFFICE
Tel 43 5353 5242
Fax 43 5353 52424

France

More British snow-users holiday in France than in any other country, and it is for the best of all possible reasons. The Savoie, Haute-Savoie and Dauphiné mountains offer more challenge than their counterparts in Austria, as well as a better chance of early- and late-season snow cover. The Pyrenees have less demanding, but nevertheless attractive, skiing and considerably lower prices. Myriad resorts – 319 to be exact – have been developed over the past 30 years and those with international pretensions are far better equipped than their equivalents in either Switzerland or Italy. France offers the largest and most sophisticated lift systems in the world. The size of some is truly staggering; Méribel alone has 16 gondolas, and the Trois Vallées has 200 lifts linking 600km of piste.

However, the down side is that even in these times of extraordinarily favourable currency exchange, prices in most of the big-name resorts are spiralling out of control. The price of drinks or lunch on the mountain in, for example, the Trois Vallées is unacceptably inflated by greedy locals, who are harvesting the tourist crop without thought for next year's seed.

Unlike their Alpine neighbours, the majority of French resorts are purpose-built *stations de ski*, which provide ski-in ski-out convenience often at a high cost to the ambience. The French have learned their lesson from the original architectural follies of the 1960s, such as Tignes, Flaine and the earlier villages of La Plagne. Valmorel, Risoul and other more recent developments have been constructed with more considera-tion for their natural mountain environment. In all the resorts there is more accommodation in apartments than in hotels, and the first concrete *résidences* were built with rooms that were far too small for the demands of today's tourist.

Many readers complain that French resorts lack the atmosphere of their Austrian cousins and that the staff and locals in France are not as welcoming as the North Americans. Skiers are no longer prepared to accept high prices in return for second-rate service.

With a few notable exceptions, such as Chamonix, Megève and Les Deux Alpes, après-ski struggles to survive in the country where the phrase originated. In the main purpose-built resorts, visitors find themselves forced to prop up the neighbourhood bar or make their own entertainment in their apartments. Discos are often grossly overpriced, underfrequented and play unrecognisable 'Euromusak'. However, none of these shortcomings seriously detracts from what the French Alps have to offer. The inescapable reason why more British now ski here than anywhere else is because, taking every factor into consideration, the skiing is the best in Europe.

Alpe d'Huez

ALTITUDE 1860m (6,100ft)

Beginners ✱✱✱ Intermediates ✱✱✱ Advanced ✱✱ Snowboarders ✱✱

Alpe d'Huez has two claims to international fame. The first originated back in 1936 when Jean Pomagalski, a young engineer of Polish extraction, watched members of the French national ski team in training as they plodded repeatedly up towards the Plat de Marmottes for a brief downhill run. He decided the team might improve more rapidly with the aid of a little uphill transport. With an ancient tractor engine and a rope borrowed from a farmer he promptly invented the drag-lift and donated his name to it. The Poma has since become to ski lifts what the Biro is to ballpoint pens.

✔ Extensive ski area
✔ Sunny position
✔ Beautiful scenery
✔ Variety of mountain restaurants
✔ Widespread artificial snow
✔ Ideal for families
✔ Varied off-piste
✔ Modern lift system
✘ Lack of alpine charm
✘ Weekend crowds
✘ Uninspiring nightlife

The second claim is that Alpe d'Huez is traditionally host to what is recognised as the toughest endurance test in sport, and one which has nothing whatsoever to do with skiing. Each July on what is unerringly a blisteringly hot day the riders of the Tour de France push their hearts, legs and bicycles through 1,130 vertical metres and 21 tortuous hairpin bends, from the valley town of **Bourg-d'Oisans** to this hotch-potch of a ski resort in the Dauphiné.

Winter visitors who make the same ascent at the end of the one-and-a-half- to two-hour coach journey from Grenoble or Lyon airports are mercifully allowed to make it in greater comfort. The sights of skiers are set considerably higher – on the 3330-m summit of Pic Blanc that dominates Les Grandes-Rousses, the fifth largest ski area in France and one of increasing importance to the British market. Alpe d'Huez, its capital and the hub of 220km of linked skiing served by 85 lifts, is not a purpose-built resort, but so great are the additions to the original village that it has all the convenience of one. The lower satellites of **Auris-en-Oisans**, **Oz Station**, **Vaujany** and **Villard-Reculas** have emerged as resorts in their own right and, to some extent, are in danger of eclipsing their grizzled old master.

Alpe d'Huez was chosen as one of the venues for the Killy Winter Olympics in 1968. In their enthusiasm, the village authorities plumbed new depths in Olympian disorganisation by building a sunny, south-facing bobsleigh run. For a while the village fathers toyed with the notion

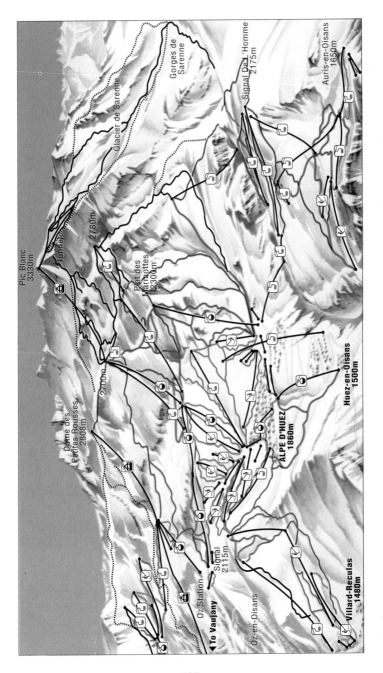

Pic Blanc
3330m

Tunnel

2780m

Glacier de Sarenne

Gorges de
Sarenne

Signal De l'Homme
2175m

Auris-en-Oisans
1650m

Plat des
Marmottes
2300m

Dôme des
Petites Rousses
2808m

2700m

Huez-en-Oisans
1500m

ALPE D'HUEZ
1860m

Oz Station

Signal
2115m

To Vaujany

Oz-en-Oisans

Villard-Reculas
1480m

of cultivating the *exclusif* tag, which is attached to Megève and Courchevel 1850. In the end, the need to pay for what is one of the most modern lift systems in the world pointed them in the direction of the mass-market. The clientèle remains predominantly French, but Alpe d'Huez is working hard at an international image that is not solely confined to that hot, hard day in July.

Ski and board
top 3330m (10,922ft) bottom 1100m (3,608ft)

Alpe d'Huez is a genuine all-round ski resort with excellent nursery slopes, good intermediate runs, long black (difficult) trails and extremely serious off-piste opportunities. Mountain access is multiple; two main modern gondolas feed traffic out of the village into the Pic Blanc sector, and there are alternative routes at peak times. Such is the efficiency of the lift system, capable of shifting 90,000 people per hour, that Alpe d'Huez claims to have dispensed with the lift queue. With the exception of the older cable-car up to the highest point of the ski area, this is largely true. However, a number of readers say that high-season queues for both the first and second stages of the DMC gondola can develop into a scrum. Feeding more skiers into any system has an obvious downside, and the pistes immediately above the village (Les Chamois, Le Signal and Le Lac Blanc) are prone to overcrowding.

> ## WHAT'S NEW
> Le Villarais quad-chair from La Bergerie to the top of Signal
> Rearrangement of drag-lifts in Villard-Reculas sector
> Additional shopping mall at Vaujany

First glances can be deceptive, and none more so than here. The skiing as seen from Les Bergers lift station looks disarmingly mild: an open mountainside served by an array of gondolas, chair- and drag-lifts. However, skiers who have cut their teeth on the gentle pastures of the Tyrol will be shocked by the hidden severity of the skiing. Much of the Pic Blanc is concealed from sight by the lie of the land – from its 3330-m summit it is possible to ski over 2000m vertical in good snow conditions down to well below Alpe d'Huez.

The area divides naturally into four main sectors: Pic Blanc, Signal de l'Homme/Auris, Signal/Villard-Reculas and Oz/Vaujany. The central part of the skiing takes place immediately north-east of the resort on sunny slopes and is reached via the two impressively efficient stages of the 25-person DMC gondola. Late in the season, some of the best skiing is in the Auris sector, which keeps its snow well.

Beginners
The first stage of the DMC gondola serves an enormous area of green (beginner) runs close to the resort. The Rif Nel piste is the gentlest of the long pistes from the base of the gondola back down to Les Bergers. All the satellites have nursery slopes, some of them more novice-friendly than others. Vaujany's ski area starts at Montfrais, a sunny balcony

above the resort that is reached by gondola. Two drag-lifts give access to green and blue (easy) runs, which are ideal debutant terrain. Oz Station and Villard-Reculas both have their own nursery slopes.

Intermediates
From the mid-station of the DMC gondola, the Lièvre Blanc chair provides access to a lot of challenging skiing. It serves its own red (intermediate) piste, which is more like a black run in places, but also leads to the satisfyingly secluded red Balme, which takes you all the way down to Alpe d'Huez. A reporter recommends Le Canyon, reached from the same chair, as 'a lot of fun'.

From the top of the DMC gondola try the long red Les Rousses (110 on the local piste map). Take the usually mogulled and crowded first 100m slowly so as not to miss the path that cuts north-west beneath the cableway into the Vaujany sector. From here you can ski all the way down to Oz or Vaujany. A wide and pleasant blue piste is L'Olympic from the top of Les Marmottes gondola.

Signal is a rounded, snow-covered peak adjacent to Alpe d'Huez. It is reached by a four-seater chair and some drag-lifts and provides some varied intermediate runs, which are easily accessible from the heart of the village. Behind Signal, longer runs drop down the open, west-facing slopes above the satellite village of Villard-Reculas. A new quad-chair now allows mountain access from the village, regardless of snow cover, and the drag-lifts have been rearranged.

Advanced
A new and still largely under-used piste takes you all the way down to the hamlet of **L'Enversin d'Oz**, which is linked to Vaujany by a cluster gondola. From the summit of Pic Blanc this represents a mighty vertical of 2330m, claimed to be the longest in the Alps (with lifts to take you back up again). The top of the Clocher de Mâcle chair-lift is the starting point for some interesting black runs. These include the beautiful Combe Charbonnière past Europe's highest disused coal mine; from here pistes lead either down into the Sarenne Gorge or back to the resort. The short run down from Clocher de Mâcle to Lac Blanc is steep, but the snow is usually good. From the top of Pic Blanc two black pistes, the Sarenne and the Château Noir, take you all the way down into the Sarenne Gorge and are claimed, at 16km, to be the longest black runs in the Alps. However, it should be pointed out that they accrue most of their length from the run-out along the bottom of the gorge. Only some pitches of the Sarenne are really difficult, but the run is long and tiring. Both pistes are narrow in places and can produce awkward bottlenecks.

The front face of Pic Blanc is accessed via a tunnel through the rock, 200m below the summit, with an awkward path at the end of it. The steep and usually icy Tunnel mogul field that awaits you can be extremely daunting when no snow has fallen for some weeks.

The funpark, accessed by the Lac Blanc drag-lift from Rond Point des Pistes, has a fairly dramatic half-pipe.

Off-piste

Opportunities for *ski sauvage* from the top of Pic Blanc are superb. Variations include the Grand Sablat, the Combe du Loup and a long and tricky descent via the Couloir de Fare. A 20-minute climb from the cable-car station takes you to the top of La Pyramide, the off-piste starting point for more than 2000m of vertical, bringing you down through a range of gulleys and open snowfields all the way to Vaujany or Oz. The top can be very icy, and ropes may be needed to negotiate the steeper couloirs in packed snow conditions. The off-piste variation from the ridge separating Oz from Alpe d'Huez is a gloriously steep powder field, which filters into the tree-studded gorge at the bottom. It is prone to avalanche and should only be attempted in the morning. There are seven itineraries in the area, all of which are marked on the piste map.

Tuition and guiding

The French Ski School (ESF) has 300 instructors based in Alpe d'Huez, Auris, Oz and Vaujany. Reports of the ESF are improving, with separate classes provided for English-speakers. One reporter remarked that although the initial impression of the ski school in Alpe d'Huez was one of 'total chaos, with hundreds of instructors and students jostling together,' the instructors were 'always cheerful and friendly with excellent English'. The International Ski School (ESI) offers classes restricted to eight (with tuition in English). BASI (British Association of Ski Instructors) instructor Stuart Adamson runs International Masterclass courses in Alpe d'Huez for English-speaking clients. Planète Surf is the major snowboarding school here. The ESI holds *nouvelles glisses* courses, which include snowboarding as one of the options, and the ESF offers snowboard tuition. Fun Evasion is said to be the best shop for hiring boards.

Mountain restaurants

Auberge de l'Alpette, a stone hut below the top of the Alpette gondola on the Oz piste, offers simple farmhouse fare at reasonable prices. Les Airelles is a restaurant built into the rock, with a sunny terrace, at the top of the nursery drag at Mont Frais above Vaujany. La Cabane du Poutat, above Alpe d'Huez, has the distinction for a mountain restaurant of being awarded a knife-and-fork in the *Guide Michelin*. Le Chardon Bleu at La Villette below Mont Frais is 'a wonderfully unexpected gastronomic surprise in the prettiest of farming hamlets'. La Bergerie, on the red run down to Villard-Reculas, is an alpine museum that doubles as a restaurant; the setting, complete with open fire and cow bells, is particularly attractive. The Chalet du Lac Besson, on the cross-country trail between the DMC gondola and Alpette, has a sunny terrace in a peaceful setting and specialises in grilled meats. Le Tetras in Auris serves fine pizzas and has a varied wine list. The Auberge Forêt de Maronne below Auris can usually only be reached in mid-winter via a choice of long blue or black runs through scenic alpine meadows; the reward is veal served in a creamy mélange of three types of local wild mushrooms, picked and preserved by the patron, but beware of the return drag-lift – it is as steep and difficult as the black run it serves. Combe Haute in the Sarenne Gorge has a welcoming atmosphere and is renowned for its salads.

The resort

Alpe d'Huez first opened as a resort in 1931 with a handful of tourist beds. At the time of the 1968 Olympics it was little more than a one-street alpine village dominated by a futuristic modern church. The massive, apparently uncontrolled building surge that followed led to the resort spreading out in all directions in a profusion of architectural styles. 'One of the worst blots on the landscape anywhere, but fortunately you only have to lift your eyes to the superb surroundings,' said one reporter. Traffic remains a problem, although it must be pointed out that as there is no through-road from the resort to anywhere else, it is more a question of overcrowded parking than busy main roads. A bucket lift acts as the primary people-mover. A shuttle bus takes skiers up to the slopes from the lower reaches of what is a steep resort for pedestrians, but several reporters say there was no sign of a bus during their entire stay. Shops are limited to a few boutiques and tacky T-shirt and souvenir establishments. Alpe d'Huez is one of the few resorts that can be reached directly by aircraft as it has its own altiport. **Les Deux Alpes** is several minutes away by helicopter or 45 minutes by road.

Accommodation

The higher up the hill you are, the easier it is to get to and from the skiing. The hardcore of one four-star (the Royal Ours Blanc) and eight three-star hotels is supported by numerous family-run hotels. Le Petit Prince is a small hotel that guests find relaxing but a little quiet ('an excellent standard of service'). The Christina is friendly and charming and one of the few attractive chalet-style buildings at the top of the resort. The Chamois d'Or is considered the best hotel, with a highly regarded restaurant. L'Ourson is a family-run hotel. The best apartments include those in the Rocher Soleil, which has its own outdoor heated swimming-pool and optional self-catering ('a little pokey but warm and comfortable'). Maeva's Les Bergers apartments are recommended by reporters.

Eating in and out

Dining is an important business in Alpe d'Huez, a legacy from its more exclusive days ('This is one of our favourite past-times, and Alpe d'Huez is an excellent place to indulge it'). There are more than 50 restaurants in the resort itself. Au P'tit Creux ('intimate atmosphere and wonderful, but avoid it at weekends') is one of the best restaurants here. One reporter praised it as being 'a restaurant to treasure'. Booking is essential. Le Chamois d'Or, Le Lyonnais ('stiffly formal atmosphere rather out of place in a ski resort') and L'Outa all vie with it as the principal centres for haute cuisine in town. Le Colporteur has a strong following.

La Pomme de Pin is praised for its 'enormous helpings – a meal like this would have cost quite a lot more in the Home Counties'. Another reporter commented: 'This restaurant certainly isn't cheap but the food is absolutely first class'. Le Génépi ('a fine restaurant that can be recommended with confidence'), La Crémaillère and Caribou all offer mountain specialities. La Taverne is praised: 'The atmosphere is lively without being rowdy and the food is both first-class and reasonably priced'. Pizza Origan is 'friendly with a good range of pizzas and pasta'. The restaurant in Vaujany's Hotel Rissiou is open to non-residents and has excellent cuisine and wines.

Supermarkets in Alpe d'Huez are adequate, and reporters recommend Les Bergers in the Centre Commercial as convenient and well stocked. Serious food shoppers can drive down to the Rallye supermarket in Bourg-d'Oisans.

Après-ski
Charley's Bar is popular and has pool and table football. The Cactus Bar offers a live band most nights and reasonably priced beer; Le Petit Bar has live blues every night. The Pacific Pub and the Avalanche Bar are said to be 'lacking in atmosphere' with 'music and loud holidaymakers'. Le Sporting, which overlooks the skating-rink, is 'a pleasant piano bar with an interesting and reasonably priced menu'. The Underground is 'noisy, crowded, and packed with Scandinavians'. Smithy's is 'more roomy than the Underground and also quieter'. Etoile des Neiges is a typical French café. Alpe d'Huez sports four discos, including the Igloo and Crystal.

Childcare
The ESF ski school guarantees class sizes of no more than 10. However, one reporter points out: 'We regularly saw classes of 13 or more small children during April high season'. The ESF Club des Oursons takes children from four years of age at Grandes-Rousses and at Bergers. Both have playgrounds and their own drag-lifts. The ESI runs Club des Mickeys et des Papotines, which takes children from three years, and the Club des Marmottes is for 4- to 13-year-olds. The Club des Eterlous, next to its Club Med building, takes children from three to 11 years of age. The crèche in Vaujany is one of the most flexible and best equipped we have come across in the Alps and, if you have small children, almost a reason in itself for choosing the resort. The age range here is from six months upwards. The crèche in Oz takes children from six months to six years.

Linked or nearby resorts
Auris-en-Oisans
top 3330m (10,922ft) bottom 1600m (5,249ft)
Auris consists mainly of apartment blocks and, though somewhat isolated from the bulk of the skiing in Les Grandes-Rousses, is well-positioned for

outings to Les Deux Alpes, **Briançon/Serre Chevalier** and **La Grave.**
The Beau Site hotel attracts predominantly French guests. Down the hill-
side in the old village is the more traditional Auberge de la Forêt de
Maronne with its fine cuisine, as well as chalets and *gîtes* to rent.

TOURIST OFFICE
Tel 33 4 76 80 13 52
Fax 33 4 76 80 20 16

Oz Station
top 3330m (10,922ft) bottom 1350m (4,429ft)

This small, purpose-built village lies above the old village of Oz-en-
Oisans. It is reached by a fast all-weather road from the valley in only 20
minutes and thereby provides an excellent back door into the lift system.
Two gondolas branch upwards in different directions, one to L'Alpette
above Vaujany and the other in two stages to the mid-station of the
DMC gondola above Alpe d'Huez. The resort, which was built in the late
1980s, has unfortunately never fulfilled its early promise, and many of
the spaces allocated for shops and restaurants are still boarded up. What
shopping and nightlife there is remains extremely limited.

TOURIST OFFICE
Tel 33 4 76 80 78 01
Fax 33 4 76 80 78 04

Vaujany
top 3330m (10,922ft) bottom 1250m (4,101ft)

Vaujany is a sleepy farming community that would have slowly crumbled into agronomic oblivion but for a quirk of fate. Its fortunes took a
turn for the better when compensation in the 1980s for a valley hydro-
electric scheme made the village rich beyond its residents' wildest
dreams. Oz benefited to a lesser extent from the scheme, and the two
villages plunged their millions into the winter sports industry. This
explains why Vaujany, an apparently impoverished mountain village,
manages to own a state-of-the-art 160-person cable-car that still ranks
among the top half-dozen in the world. No one has yet seen a queue
here.

Considerable, but considered, development is taking place, and a
number of new chalets and apartments have been built, as well as an
excellent crèche. In summer 1998 a central *place* was developed by the
cable-car station. However, the community retains its rural atmosphere. There are four simple hotels in the village centre, with
L'Etendard, closest to the lift station, the après-ski hub. The Rissiou is
under British management in winter and offers a good standard of
accommodation. Nightlife centres around the bars of L'Etendard and
the Rissiou in Vaujany itself, and Le Chardon Bleu in the sleepy neighbouring hamlet of **La Villette.** Two discos with an overridingly young
clientèle provide late-night entertainment.

Skiing facts: Alpe d'Huez

TOURIST OFFICE
BP 28, F-38750 Alpe d'Huez, Dauphiné
Tel 33 4 76 11 44 44
Fax 33 4 76 80 69 54
Email alpedhuez@laposte.fr

THE RESORT
By road Calais 934km
By rail Grenoble 63km
Airport transfer Lyon 2hrs,
Grenoble 1½ hrs
Visitor beds 32,000
Transport free ski bus

THE SKIING
Linked or nearby resorts Auris (I),
Oz-en-Oisans (I),Vaujany (I),La Grave (n)
Villard-Reculas (I), Les Deux Alpes (n)
Longest run Sarenne,16km (black)
Number of lifts 85
Total of trails/pistes 220km (36%
beginner, 28% easy,
25% intermediate,11% difficult)
Nursery slopes 11
Summer skiing on Sarenne Glacier
Snowmaking 100 hectares covered

LIFT PASSES
Area pass (covers whole
Grandes-Rousses area) 1,000FF for 6
days, including entry to sports centre
Day pass 189FF
Beginners 1 free lift at Alpe d'Huez and
Visalp Initiation Pass, 1,445FF for
6 morning lessons
Pensioners free for 70yrs and over
Credit cards yes

TUITION
Adults ESF, 920FF for 6 days, ESI,
1,050FF for 6 days, 672FFfor 6 mornings
or 525FF for 6 afternoons, International
Masterclass, details on request

Private lessons ESF and ESI,
180FF per hr
Snowboarding Planète Surf, 900FF for
6 days, private lessons 140FF per hr.
ESF and ESI, as regular ski school
Cross-country ESF, 920FF for 6 days
(5hrs per day). Loipe 50km
Other courses monoski, moguls,
freestyle, slalom, competition, ski
extreme
Guiding Bureau de Guides

CHILDREN
Lift pass 6–16yrs 700FF, free for 5yrs
and under. Visalp Initiation Pass,
1,445FF for 6 days including 6 morning
lessons
Ski kindergarten ESF Club des Oursons
at Bergers and at Grandes-Rousses, 4yrs
and over, 70FF per hr. ESI Club des
Mickeys et des Papotines, 3yrs and over,
672FF for 6 mornings. Les Eterlous,
3–11yrs, 1,290FF for 6 days
Ski school ESF, 4–13yrs, 800FF for 6
days. ESI Club des Marmottes, 4–13yrs,
580FF for 6 mornings, and 3–5pm,
460FF for 6 afternoons
Non-ski kindergarten Les Eterlous,
6mths–6yrs, 9am–5.45pm, 1,450FF for
6 days including lunch. Crèche Vaujany,
3mths–6yrs, 9am–5pm, 600FF for 6
days including lunch

OTHER SPORTS
Ice-driving, snowmobiling, snowshoeing,
aeroclub, parapente, hang-gliding, swimming, helicopter rides, skating, curling,
frozen-waterfall climbing, indoor tennis,
indoor climbing wall

FOOD AND DRINK
Coffee 10–16FF, glass of wine 15FF,
small beer 15FF, dish of the day 40–60FF

TOURIST OFFICE
Tel 33 4 76 80 72 37
Fax 33 4 76 80 82 49

Villard-Reculas
top 3330m (10,922ft) bottom 1500m (4,921ft)

This rustic old village is linked into the ski area by a new quad chair-lift. Much has been done in recent years to renovate the village; a number of apartments now supplement the single hotel and the converted cowsheds and barns. Sustenance is provided by one small supermarket and a couple of bars and restaurants, including the popular Bergerie. A blue piste from the bottom of the Petit Prince runs to the village, offering an alternative route to the steeper runs. The road to Allemont on the valley floor is wide and easily accessible in winter, but the one-track road to Huez is normally closed during the season.

TOURIST OFFICE
Tel 33 4 76 80 45 69
Fax 33 4 76 80 45 69

Les Arcs

ALTITUDE 1600−2000m (5,248-6,560ft)

Beginners ✱✱✱ Intermediates ✱✱✱ Advanced ✱✱✱ Snowboarders ✱✱✱

In the early 1960s, during the boom years of skiing, a mountain guide called Robert Blanc had a vision of a new type of ski resort to be built above his local market town of **Bourg-St-Maurice**. He managed to create not one but three ski villages at different altitudes, all of them sharing one ski area. Today Les Arcs has 200km of groomed runs served by 77 lifts. The first village, **Arc 1600**, opened in the winter of 1968. It consisted of one hotel and a few shops constructed on a plateau above Bourg. Subsequent altimeter readings proved it to be lower at 1450m, but the name stuck.

✔ Large ski area
✔ Modern lift system
✔ Excellent children's facilities
✔ Traffic-free villages
✔ Skiing convenience
✔ Extensive off-piste
✔ Beautiful scenery
✗ Lack of alpine charm
✗ Few activities for non-skiers
✗ Limited après-ski

Arc 1800, the largest and most cosmopolitan of the three, came on stream in 1974. Again it centred on one hotel and a collection of architecturally appealing apartment blocks.

Arc 2000 is the newest and bleakest village, with mountain accessibility and late-season skiing the sole reasons for staying here.

Throughout the first half of the 1980s, Les Arcs led the way with a range of snow sports known as *les nouvelles glisses* – alternative ways of sliding down a mountain. The monoski was first seen here, and the snowboard made its European debut in the resort. *Ski évolutif*, a revolutionary method of learning to ski, was introduced here when it crossed the Atlantic.

However, with worldwide recession in the late 1980s, Robert Blanc's dream began to fade. Skiers turned away from Les Arcs and the resort was forced to the financial wall; six years ago it looked as if it would be the first major ski resort in Europe to descend into receivership and it was saved from this fate by state intervention. Some of the properties that had fallen into disrepair were sold off to independent companies who were offered considerable incentives to refurbish.

Les Arcs is now looking towards a considerably brighter future and is continuing to try hard after its decade out in the cold. Both the resort and the lift system are steadily being upgraded.

The undulating contours of the slopes here make Les Arcs ideal for snowboarding, and ever since the sport was introduced to Europe from America the resort has played an important role in establishing its popularity.

Ski and board
top 3226m (10,581ft) bottom 850m (2,788ft)

According to visitor surveys, the snow-users of Les Arcs want bump-free pistes and that is what they now get. Considerable time and money is spent ironing out moguls and the result is a wealth of unusually long and smooth runs that start way above the tree-line and progress down through the woods to unspoilt villages like **Le Pré** and **Villaroger**, as well as extensive off-piste opportunities. Intermediates can cruise forever, and beginners are especially well looked after. The greatest concentration of lifts, slopes and therefore skiers is above Arc 1800, where sunny and gentle pistes attract intermediates and families. The skiing above Arc 1600 is steeper and more wooded, with some rewarding off-piste opportunities. Another claim to fame of Les Arcs is its Olympic speed-skiing track on the face of the Aiguille Rouge,

which can be tested by members of the public. With typical Les Arcs panache, the course has also been used to establish records for motorbikes and even mountain bikes.

Lift queues are not generally a problem, although there are a few exceptions. At Carreley 20 and Chantel 21 reporters came across 'huge queues until 10am and again at the end of the day'. Some found mid-afternoon crowds for the Vallandry 74 lift. The piste map is accurate but, according to one reporter: 'It was not always easy to find one's way around because the map goes across two pages'. One reporter noted that a small but vital lift link to Le Planay – Rhonaz 44 – is often closed, which means a hearty walk up the piste if you are unprepared.

Beginners

One of Robert Blanc's legacies was *ski évolutif*, an easy means of learning, that originated in America as GLM (Graduated Length Method). As the name implies, you start on skis as short as 100cm and progress to longer skis as your technique and confidence improve. The advantage is that by learning to ski parallel from day one, you can become a competent intermediate skier by day six. To reach that stage, skiers have a choice of 24 green (beginner) runs. Each of the three villages has user-friendly nursery slopes close by, with the most extensive just above Arc 1800 around the altiport and Le Chantel area, and in the bowl above Arc 2000. Above Arc 1600, strong beginners and timid intermediates can enjoy the long blue (easy) run from Les Deux Têtes.

Intermediates

As a rule, the bigger the ski area the more scope there is for intermediates, and Les Arcs is certainly no exception. Of the resort's 112 runs, 70 are divided equally between blue and red (intermediate) trails, and many of the reds are not difficult. The slopes above Arc 1800 are packed with relatively easy intermediate slopes. Good cruising runs are found between the Grand Col, Aiguille Grive and Arpette. Above **Peisey-Nancroix** and **Vallandry** there is much classic intermediate terrain. The Aigle and L'Ours reds are particularly recommended by reporters as 'nice, not too testing runs down through the trees'. Malgovert, down to Arc 1600, is described as 'quite narrow – it felt like an off-piste run but without the worry, and hazards were marked; it leads down to the wonderfully wide and flattering Mont Blanc blue run'.

Advanced

The black (difficult) run down Comborcières to **Pré-St-Esprit** is one of the places where those who want to can still find testing moguls. But the classic run in Les Arcs is the 7-km descent from the top of the Aiguille Rouge all the way down to Le Pré and Villaroger, with a vertical drop of more than 2000m. Of the total 18 black runs, the Piste de L'Ours from Arpette is one of the most exciting. Varet is a long, steep piste from the top of the Aiguille Rouge, which is a real challenge, especially in deep snow. The Robert Blanc piste is an excellent descent off the north face. Drosets, down to Pré-St-Esprit, is another testing run from the Aiguille Rouge. The Dou de l'Homme chair accesses several long black trails.

Arc 1600 has a dedicated snow park with seven jumps and a quarter-pipe. The park is served by a chair-lift and a shorter drag-lift. Freestylers favour the naturally wavy terrain of Les Deux Têtes black run and the red La Cachette. Hard-boot fans will enjoy Froides Fontaines, which is excellent for a carving work-out. The red Grand Renard is a natural downhill course, superb for big turns. The Peisey sector is also well-suited to snowboarders.

Off-piste

With so many off-piste opportunities in Les Arcs it really does pay, both in terms of safety and finding the best terrain, to hire a guide. In fresh snow conditions the most exhilarating and steepest powder skiing is below the Aiguille Rouge. Steep bowl-skiing is found beneath the Crête de L'Homme, accessed by a traverse to the right as you exit the Aiguille Rouge cable-car. Other good off-piste is behind the Aiguille Grive and the Aiguille Rouge at the south-western edge of Arc 1800's ski area. Exciting off-piste descents start from the Grand Col to **Villaroger**, with the route continuing behind the Aiguille Rouge, and from the Aiguille Grive down to Peisey-Nancroix. The Comborcières slopes offer a number of challenging opportunities. Serious off-piste experts can try a cluster of couloirs over the back of the Aiguille Rouge on the East Face, but special permission has to be given by the Vanoise Park authorities, who charge for access to these slopes.

Tuition and guiding

Les Arcs has the French Ski School (ESF) in all three villages, and the International Ski School (ESI)/Arc Aventures, Ecole de Ski Virages, and He'Enalu, which are all based in Arc 1800. All the ski schools run snowboarding courses. Tip Top is the small specialist snowboard school (just six instructors) based in Bourg-St-Maurice, and In Extremis and New School, both in Arc 1800, are also for riders.

Mountain restaurants

Mountain eating-places are not a particular strength of Les Arcs, but some excellent rustic-style establishments are in the lower hamlets. Pré-St-Esprit, below Arc 2000, has two popular lunch spots. Of these, the rustic Bélliou La Fumée, a 500-year-old hunting lodge, is the more attractive and is recommended by reporters for its wild mushroom omelettes. The cosy Solliet restaurant on the way down to Villaroger receives good reports, and in nearby Le Pré the Aiguille Rouge and La Ferme attract lunchtime skiers when the long run down is open. In nearby **Le Planay**, Chez Léa is highly recommended for its wholesome food and attractive farmhouse setting; booking is recommended. L'Ancolie at Nancroix, reached by bus from the bottom of the lift system at Peisey-Nancroix, 'serves outstanding food in an intimate atmosphere'.

The resort

Of the three distinct villages that make up Les Arcs, Arc 1600 is the lowest and, according to enthusiastic reporters, the most compact and friendly. Arc 1800 has grown dramatically from when it was built in the mid-1970s and is now divided into three sub-villages of **Charvet**, **Villards** and **Charmettoger**. It is the heart of the three villages with most of the accommodation, shops and après-ski. The highest village is Arc 2000, which sits in its own secluded bowl at the foot of the main mountain, l'Aiguille Rouge (3226m), and is close to some of the best skiing. One reporter said: 'It is to be avoided unless you want snow-sure skiing at the end of the season'. All three villages are served by a road from Bourg-St-Maurice; however, the Arc en Ciel (rainbow) funicular takes just seven minutes to reach Arc 1600. Although Les Arcs is largely car-free and the resorts are linked by bus, a car is useful to reach the other resorts available on the same lift pass.

Accommodation

About two-thirds of the skiers visiting Les Arcs stay in apartments, and of these the majority find themselves in Arc 1800. The Golf is the largest and most central hotel in Arc 1800 and, along with Hotel Charmettoger, is part of Les Latitudes chain. La Cachette at Arc 1600 has nurtured a reputation as one of the best family hotels in the Alps. It has been refurbished to a standard above its official three stars. The old Winston Hotel at 1600 has been modernised and renamed L'Explorer's. The Trois Arcs, also in 1600, is a small and friendly hotel now owned by the resort. At Arc 2000, the two-star Aiguille Rouge remains popular. We have no reports on the Mélèzes, formerly the Eldorador, which has been elevated to three stars. There is a Club Med and a Club Aquarius at Arc 2000. Les Lauziers apartments in 1800 are convenient for the slopes but have their drawbacks ('a functional building with strange sloping floors; we didn't like the cramped and spartan interiors'). For those preferring to stay in the valley town of Bourg-St-Maurice, which is linked directly into the lift system and convenient for visiting other resorts such as Val d'Isère, the Hostellerie du Petit-St-Bernard is good value, welcoming to families, and serves appetising food.

Eating in and out

Self-catering rules in Les Arcs, but no one wants to cook every night of the week. The best choice of restaurants is at Arc 1800; L'Equipe is the biggest but not necessarily the best ('excellent for a posh meal, with Savoyard dishes and a fixed-price menu'). Casa Mia specialises in Italian food ('basically a pasta and pizza place, décor rustic – after a fashion – and the service was friendly and informal'). L'Onglet and Le Coq Hardy are also recommended. For value-for-money family fare the Laurus is worth visiting.

At Arc 2000, Le Red Rock is popular and informal with live music, and Le St Jacques is more intimate with higher prices. Les Chabottes at Pont Baudin near Peisey-Nancroix serves 'excellent local specialities at prices lower than at Les Arcs'.

Self-caterers will find a wider selection and lower prices in Bourg-St-Maurice, with its two hypermarkets on the outskirts of town. In Arc 1800 there are 'some fine bakeries, an expensive butcher and a small supermarket with limited fresh supplies'.

Visitors considering an outing to the traditional restaurants in outlying villages between Les Arcs and Bourg-St-Maurice should try the rustic Bois de Lune at Montvenix. Booking is recommended, and the restaurant will collect you and take you back. Chez Mimi at Vallandry and Chez Léa at Le Planay are other options.

Après-ski

When the lifts close in Arc 1800, skiers and instructors tend to divide themselves between two bars at Le Charvet (Le Gabotte and Le Thuria). At nearby Les Villards, much of the action is at the Pub Russel and the Saloon Bar, which features live music. At 2000 the Red Rock is the 'in' place for a *vin chaud*. The Hotel du Golf has live jazz and Le Fairway disco in the basement. All three resorts have discos, including the Arcelle in 1600 and Rock Hill in Le Charvet, while snowboarders prefer the Carré Blanc in Les Villards. Apocalypse at 1800 is 'wildly expensive'. The music at KL 92 in Arc 2000 is said to be sufficiently sympa to allow conversation.

Childcare

Les Arcs has a three-kids grading, the highest of the Label Kid stamp of approval from the Ministry of Tourism, denoting that the resort offers children a safe environment with plenty of entertainment, toys and equipment. Babies aged four months and over are welcome in the day nurseries at La Cachette in Arc 1600 and at the Pomme d'Api in Bourg-St-Maurice. The nursery at Arc 1800 takes children from one year of

Skiing facts: Les Arcs

TOURIST OFFICE
BP 45, 73706 Les Arcs,
Bourg-St-Maurice
Tel 33 4 79 07 12 57
Fax 33 4 79 07 45 96
Email wlesarcs@lesarcs.com
Web site www.lesarcs.com
UK Agent Erna Low
(see *Which tour operator?*)

THE RESORT
By road Calais 937km
By rail Bourg-St-Maurice 15km, buses
and funicular to Arc 1600
Airport transfer Lyon 2½hrs, Chambéry
2hrs, Geneva 2½hrs
Visitor beds 29,399
Transport free shuttle bus

THE SKIING
Linked or nearby resorts Bourg-
St-Maurice (l), Peisey-Nancroix (l),
La Plagne (n), Le Pré (l), Vallandry (l),
Villaroger (l)
Longest run Aiguille Rouge,
7km (black)
Number of lifts 77
Total of trails/pistes 200km
(10% easy, 76% intermediate, 14%
difficult)
Nursery slopes 11 runs
Summer skiing with guides
Snowmaking 20 hectares covered

LIFT PASSES
Area pass 995FF for 6 days (covers Les
Arcs, Villaroger, Peisey and Vallandry,
La Plagne, and 1 day in La Rosière/Trois
Vallées/Tignes and Val d'Isère)
Day pass 212FF
Beginners 8 free lifts
Pensioners 65–70yrs, 180FF per day
Credit cards yes

TUITION
Adults ESF1600/1800/2000, Arc
Aventures, He'Enalu in 1800, all
580–700FF for 6 days
Private lessons 180–200FF per hr,
700FF for half-day, 1,350FF for full day
Snowboarding ESF 1600/1800/2000,
Arc Aventures, He'Enalu, Virages, In
Extremis, Tip Top, New School, all about
630–730FF for 6 half-days
Cross-country ESF, 600FF for 6 x 3hrs.
Loipe 15km in Les Arcs
Other courses monoski, speed skiing,
ski évolutif
Guiding ESF/ESI/Arc Aventures

CHILDREN
Lift pass 8–14yrs, 840FF for 6 days,
free for 7yrs and under
Ski kindergarten ESF Pommes de Pin
(1800), 3yrs and over, 990FF for 6 days.
Arc 1600, 3–6yrs 1,880FF, 7–12yrs
2,150FF, both for 6 days
Ski school ESF/Arc Aventures, 3–13yrs,
890FF for 6 days, Virages and He'Enalu
details on request
Non-ski kindergarten La Cachette
(1600), 4mths–3yrs, 1,415FF. ESF
Pommes de Pin (1800), 1–3yrs, 795FF,
3–6yrs, 805FF. Les Marmottons (2000),
2–6yrs 880FF. All for 6 days. Garderie
Pomme d'Api (Bourg-St-Maurice), 4mths
and over, details on request

OTHER SPORTS
Aeroclub, dog-sledding, ice-driving,
snowmobiling, snowshoeing, parapente,
microlight, hang-gliding, skating, winter
walks, squash

FOOD AND DRINK PRICES
Coffee 7FF, glass of wine 10FF, small
beer 13–18FF, dish of the day 80–90FF

age, Les Marmottons at Arc 2000 accepts children from two. The ESF organises courses for children aged three years and over in Les Pommes de Pin club. Older children can enrol in Ski Nature courses to explore the mountain environment and study animal tracks in the snow.

Linked or nearby resorts

Peisey-Nancroix/Vallandry
top 3226m (10,581ft) bottom 1350–1600m (4,428–5,248ft)

Snow-users in Les Arcs tend to regard this cluster of villages at the south-western end of the ski area as a useful tree-level bolt hole in bad weather. French families, who have been coming here since the Second World War, prefer to think of it as a peaceful, undemanding ski area that is occasionally invaded by Johnny-come-latelys from Les Arcs. These villages offer a more rural setting and a cheaper accommodation base for the region. Peisey is a traditional farming community and Nancroix is the starting point for 39km of cross-country trails. The small ski resorts of Plan Peisey and Vallandry are linked by gondola to Peisey in the valley below. Three lifts serve the nursery slopes.

TOURIST OFFICE
Tel 33 4 79 07 94 28
Fax 33 4 79 07 95 34

Barèges/La Mongie

ALTITUDE 1250–1800m (4,092–5,904ft)

Beginners ✱✱ Intermediates ✱✱✱ Snowboarders ✱

Barèges is one of the great skiing secrets of Europe. This unspoilt village in the Pyrenees forms the gateway to an unexpected network of 120km of pistes far superior in quality to most 'alternative' European resorts. Skiers who have tired of the characterless and overcrowded ski circuses of the French Alps, with their ever-rising prices, should look westwards to the Pyrenees. Here you will find that elusive combination of a timeless French country village with reasonable prices, a short transfer time from Lourdes Airport and the varied runs of a large ski area. The major attraction of the resort (and indeed of the rest of the French Pyrenees) is the people, who seem to be genuinely friendly and welcoming – a rare occurrence in some of the more popular resorts in the Alps. The locals have managed to retain their traditional way of life and at the same time to adapt to the needs of tourism without the compulsion to milk their visitors for every centime.

✔ Short airport transfer
✔ Sunny slopes
✔ Low prices
✔ Small and unspoilt village (Barèges)
✘ Weekend lift queues
✘ Lack of resort-level snow
✘ Unsuitable for late-season holidays
✘ Few activities for non-skiers
✘ Bleak village (La Mongie)

Barèges was one of the original ski resorts of the Pyrenees. The village also comes under the spotlight in July when it becomes part of the Tour de France route. Its lift system follows the course of the road, which (in summer only) leads over the Col du Tourmalet to the more modern resort of **La Mongie**. This is the larger, higher, but considerably less charming of the two resorts. It offers no more facilities than Barèges and is set in the blander half of the ski area. The lifts linking the two resorts sometimes close in bad weather.

Ski and board
top 2350m (7,708ft) bottom 1250m (4,100ft)

Snowfall in the Pyrenees is a subject that always causes disagreement. There is little to support the belief that the mountains receive less precipitation in winter than the Alps; the trouble is that it does not always fall as snow. Because the Pyrenees are further west and closer to the warm Atlantic, the winter is shorter, but the advantage is the high number of sunny days. Barèges and La Mongie form the largest ski area in the

Pyrenees, sharing 100km of wide, mainly easy-to-intermediate pistes served by 53 lifts. The area's upper slopes are open and sunny, while the lower ones above Barèges offer sheltered tree-level skiing. The slopes are reached from Barèges by two mountain access lifts. The track of the rebuilt Ayré funicular climbs steeply from the village centre through the woods to serve red (intermediate) and black (difficult) runs down to a clearing at Lienz – this is some of the best skiing in the area when conditions are favourable.

The alternative access lift from the resort is La Laquette gondola, which provides the direct route towards La Mongie, as well as the way up to the ski-school meeting place. At Tournaboup, from the top of the lift, an easy link-run leads on to **Super Barèges**, actually little more than a restaurant. A development to the north of Super Barèges, below the Lac d'Oncet, recently added to the size of the whole ski area. Queues can be a serious problem at weekends, especially on Sundays; as Barèges cannot cope with many cars, the lifts from the top of the village and from Tournaboup become crowded, and the Col du Tourmalet can turn into a bottleneck in both directions.

Beginners

La Mongie is the better base for complete beginners or nervous second-weekers, with easy slopes immediately around the resort that keep their snow relatively well. Barèges itself has no nursery slope; the main slope is at the top of La Laquette gondola. Tournaboup, just outside Barèges, has a small nursery slope beside the car park, and there is also a baby lift at **La Mongie-Tourmalet**. At Barèges, second- and third-week skiers can make their way across to Lienz from the mid-station of the Ayré funicular. Of the two runs from there down to the resort, the green (beginner) run is the path that begins with an uphill section.

Intermediates

A variety of short intermediate pistes cover the sides of the hill at the top of La Laquette gondola to Lienz on one side and to Tournaboup on the other. Above La Mongie the runs are mainly wide and easy. A gondola is the main lift on the north-facing side, serving a long and shaded blue (easy) gully. The slopes beneath the Sud chair-lift are not particularly gentle, and the blue run contains a narrow section. On this sunny side of the mountain, the most interesting trails are reached from the top of the Coume Lounque drag- and chair-lift, where there are a couple of reds. One trail follows a valley down to La Mongie, the other leads down to Super Barèges; part of this run is steep enough to be graded black and can be icy in the morning.

Advanced

Ayré at 2020m boasts some of the area's steepest skiing, and there is no easy way down from the top of the funicular. Some fairly sheer, west-facing slopes lie below the Col du Tourmalet, including a selection of short mogul fields. The rocky slopes bordering La Mongie and the road are steep and although there are lifts, the terrain does not give much scope for pistes. The most challenging run around La Mongie is the black under the Prade Berde chair-lift. La Mongie has a boardercross course and three other dedicated snowboard spots at different points around the ski area.

Off-piste

The itinerary round to the Lac d'Oncet is a good place for spring snow even in mid-winter. At Tournaboup there is a long chair-lift over a wide and fairly steep, west-facing mountainside which is left unpisted although it is much skied in good conditions. At the top of the Coume de Pourteilh gondola above La Mongie, the Quatre Termes chair-lift has added to the overall length of the run. It gives access to an off-piste itinerary down the Aygues Cluses Valley, ending at Tournaboup.

Tuition and guiding

French Pyrenean resorts have made considerable efforts to improve ski school standards in recent years, and the number of fluent English-speaking instructors has risen. Ecoloski in Barèges offers, among other classes, tuition in off-piste skiing, moguls and telemark. However, we have disappointing reports of this ski school: 'I was in much too difficult a group and when I asked to change I was told to "have courage" '. The

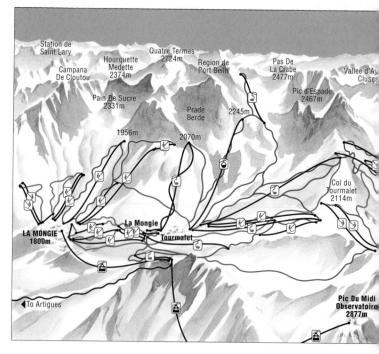

French Ski School (ESF) in Barèges is said to be well-organised: 'our instructor was patient, professional, and spoke good English'. Both La Mongie and La Mongie-Tourmalet have their own ski schools. Henri Nogué is a high-mountain guide who organises off-piste courses and ski-touring in the area.

Mountain restaurants

The mountain eating-places are inexpensive in comparison with alpine prices but are few and far between. Chez Louisette is popular, and Auberge La Couquelle is small and friendly with the highlight 'a delicious warm goat's cheese salad with honey dressing'. Le Bastan is 'both cheerful and cheap'. There is a restaurant at the Col du Tourmalet, and Le Yeti in La Mongie is recommended.

The resorts

At first sight, the little spa village of Barèges is down-at-heel and grey in its position near the head of a narrow valley. However, its lack of size engenders a friendly atmosphere. Prices are low by French standards, but there is little to do after skiing except soak up the sulphur waters of the thermal spa. The village consists of little more than a single street climbing steeply beside a river, surrounded by tree-lined mountainside. This is

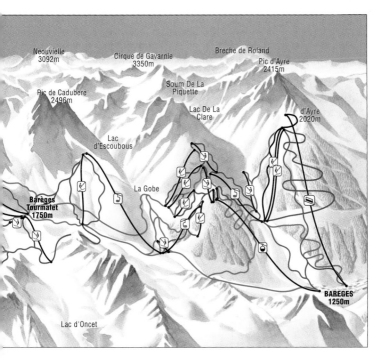

not a natural site for a village, and none would have appeared had it not been for the sulphur springs that became famous in the seventeenth century. Parking is restricted, and the ski bus cannot cope when runs to the village are closed and too many skiers have ended up at Tournaboup.

La Mongie is divided into two parts. The lower village is the centre, a bleak and charmless place with a crescent of restaurants, shops and hotels, with a car park in the middle. The upper village of La Mongie-Tourmalet is a long and jagged complex with a single hotel, a restaurant and apartments. The two sections are linked by bus and a new chair-lift to the Coume de Pourteilh gondola.

Accommodation

Those in search of luxury will be disappointed as Barèges has nothing more superior than simple two-star hotels. The family-run Richelieu is friendly and is located just below the funicular station. L'Igloo is run by a former ski champion and is close to La Laquette gondola. Some reporters found the Hotel Central unfriendly. The one-star Poste and Modern hotels both offer basic but clean bedrooms. The British-run Les Sorbiers is a popular, small hotel. One reporter summed up its attractions: 'simple, attractively furnished, clean accommodation. The bedrooms were warm but the public areas rather chilly. The vegetarian options were superb'.

Hotel Igloo has 'overfurnished rooms but excellent four-course dinners'. Shops are confined to a good chemist and the most simplistic of ski-hire and souvenir shops. There is a single supermarket for self-caterers. La Mongie has a three-star hotel, Le Pourteilh, plus four two-stars and two other smaller hotels. The Lamandia, which has ski-in ski-out access, is the only three-star hotel in La Mongie-Tourmalet.

Eating in and out

La Rozeli is good for fondues and pizzas and The Toscane is a pizzeria-takeaway. Le Pichounet serves a delicious *fondue au chocolat noir*. La Couquelle, with its welcoming fireplace, is close to Tournaboup and opens in the evenings as well as at lunch-time. The main event of the week is an evening at Chez Louisette, organised by the ESF, which culminates in a torch-light descent. You can also reach the restaurant by snowmobile, snowcat or on foot. The staple diet of the region is *magret de canard*, *confit de canard*, and *foie gras*. La Bohème pizzeria in Barèges is warmly praised.

Après-ski

Barèges is such a quiet resort that, as one reader put it 'even the church was closed on Sunday'. After-skiing entertainment centres on a few bars, a handful of restaurants and two discos. The liveliest places are Pub l'Oncet, L'Isba and the Café Richelieu. The discos open at 11pm and do not fill up until 1am; Le Club Jonathan is the most popular. Many visitors come to Barèges for the spa. Today, visitors are treated in an austere building at the top of the high street. Facilities include whirlpools, saunas, thermal baths and showers, an aqua-gym and aqua massage, all of which use the special healing waters – great for relaxing after a hard day on the slopes. La Mongie has a few restaurants and bars. Other activities in the resort include snowmobiling, swimming, ice-climbing, snowshoeing, parapente and attractive winter walks.

Childcare

The ESF and Ecoloski both have a ski kindergarten for children from three to eight years of age. The two non-ski kindergartens take children from two to six years of age and lunch can be provided. There is a kindergarten at La Mongie.

TOURIST OFFICES
Tel Barèges: 33 5 62 92 68 19 La Mongie: 33 5 62 91 94 15
Fax Barèges: 33 5 62 92 69 13 La Mongie: 33 5 62 95 33 13

Linked or nearby resorts

Cauterets
top 2350m (7,710ft) bottom 1000m (3,280ft)

This attractive thermal resort became a ski station in 1962 and today it has more than 22,000 visitor beds in a large selection of hotels. The nearest airport is Lourdes, which is 40km away. The skiing is in the exposed Cirque du Lys bowl, accessed by a two-stage cable-car which also brings skiers back to the resort at the end of the day. The terrain is best suited to beginners and intermediates. There are 20 runs, including one black, with the rest equally divided between red, blue and green. The 35km of pistes are served by 14 lifts. Another small but developing ski area is nearby at **Pont d'Espagne**, which is renowned for its cross-country trails. Tuition is offered in freestyle and off-piste skiing, snowboarding, parapente, as well as ordinary group and private lessons. Les Marmottes non-ski kindergarten takes children from three months to six years of age. Children from four to ten years old are taught in the ski school.

The extensive choice of accommodation includes *gîtes*, chalets and hotels, some of which date from the Belle Epoque. Hotel Bordeaux is recommended as a comfortable three-star with a good restaurant. The three-star Hotel Club Aladin has a fitness centre with a swimming-pool, squash courts and sauna among its facilities. The Astérides is the other three-star, and Etche-Ona is a two-star near the scenic Pont d'Espagne. The Royalty pub is popular, as is the St Trop video bar. Other resort facilities include a casino, a couple of discos, an indoor skating-rink and the thermal spa.

TOURIST OFFICE
Tel 33 5 62 92 50 27
Fax 33 5 62 92 59 12

Font-Romeu
top 2204m (7,229ft) bottom 1800m (5,906ft)

The resort, 19km from Perpignan and 200km from Toulouse, is set on a sunny plateau known for its mild climate, making it unreliable for snow at the beginning and end of the season. The skiing is 4km from the village, and is linked by a bus service. The 52km of piste and 32 lifts suit beginners to intermediates as well as families. Weekend queues are a problem as the resort is popular with both French and Spanish skiers. Fifty per cent of the total skiing terrain is covered by snow-cannon. There are two dozen hotels and pensions, over a dozen youth hostels and various self-catering apartments. Après-ski activities include a wide choice of restaurants, a casino, cinemas, three discos and ten bars. Cross-country skiing is very important here, with two specialist schools: Pyrénées Ski Nordique and ANCEF. The resort also boasts a snowpark.

TOURIST OFFICE
Tel 33 4 68 30 68 30
Fax 33 4 68 30 29 70
Web site www.skifrance.fr/-font-romeu

St-Lary
top 2450m (8,038ft) bottom 830m (2,722ft)

St-Lary-Soulan, 80km from Lourdes, is a typically Pyrenean village of stone-built houses and one main, rather narrow street. The skiing is suitable for beginners to intermediates and it begins a four-minute walk from the village centre at the cable-car to **St-Lary Pla d'Adret** (1680m), a small but dull modern ski station with some accommodation. From here a bus runs to two other small centres, **St-Lary La Cabane** and **St-Lary Espiaube**. The ski area is served by a chain of 32 lifts, including a new quad-chair, but is mainly treeless and lacks variety. It has a snowpark in the Vallon du Portet sector. There are six nursery slopes and three ski schools. Two mountain guiding companies arrange popular ski-tours. Grand Hotel Mir is recommended, as well as the Mercure Cristal Parc and Hotel La Terrasse Fleurie. The Andrédéna is in a quiet position. At Espiaube, Hotel La Sapinière provides reasonable accommodation at the bottom of the pistes.

TOURIST OFFICE
Tel 33 5 62 39 50 81
Fax 33 5 62 39 50 06

Superbagnères
top 2260m (7,415ft) bottom 1800m (5,904ft)

Luchon is a thermal spa town with shops and three nightclubs, Superbagnères is the quieter ski station 17km away by road and a few minutes by cable-car. Spain is just half-an-hour from Luchon, and Toulouse is the nearest airport. Superbagnères is one of the highest resorts in the Pyrenees, with nine drag-lifts, five chairs and one cable-car serving the area's 27km of pistes. The resort has a snowpark. There are two mountain restaurants, Céciré and La Hount, and two nursery slopes. The ESF runs a comprehensive ski kindergarten, with its own slope and ski lift, and cares for non-skiing children from two years of age.

Most of the accommodation at Superbagnères is in apartments and the remainder in the two hotels, the Isard and the Aneto. Club Med has a base in the resort. There are two restaurants, two cafeterias and a supermarket. Activities outside skiing are a disco, swimming, indoor tennis, parapente and a thermal spa centre. Luchon's accommodation comprises more than 30 hotels including a three-star, the Corneille. The dozen restaurants range from pizzerias to those serving local cuisine.

TOURIST OFFICE
Tel 33 5 61 79 21 21
Fax 33 5 61 79 11 23

Chamonix

ALTITUDE 1035m (3,396ft)

Intermediates ✱✱ Advanced ✱✱✱ Snowboarders ✱✱✱

Chamonix is the climbing and skiing capital of Europe. It is not so much a single resort as a chain of unconnected ski areas set along both sides of the valley dominated by Mont Blanc. On stormy days, of which there are many, it is a brooding place, menaced by razor-sharp peaks and tumbling walls of ice. On sunny days, it is glitteringly beautiful and deceptively tranquil. The resort's focus is the town of Chamonix, a core of hotels and villas built at the turn of the century and subsequently hemmed in by the neo-brutalist architecture of post-war tourism. In recent years complacency has been the biggest foe of what is a year-round holiday destination. Lack of investment in the lift system, internecine squabbles between Chamonix and neighbouring **Les Houches** and a complete lack of visionary perspective over future development of the valley made even the most dedicated of its fans question their loyalty. New lifts, along with facilities for snowboarders on Les Grands Montets, have gone a long way to restoring Chamonix's reputation, but the valley is still steeped in territorial dispute. The result is an impossibly complicated series of conflicting lift passes. Study the options carefully before purchasing.

✔ Unsurpassed scenery
✔ Large vertical drop
✔ Extensive off-piste skiing
✔ Outstanding mountain guides
✔ Short airport transfer
✔ Wide choice of non-skiing activities
✔ Cosmopolitan atmosphere
✔ Vibrant nightlife
✘ Poorly linked ski areas
✘ Unsuitable for families
✘ Unpredictable weather patterns
✘ Decrepit lift system
✘ Heavy traffic

Chamonix lies in the lee of the highest mountain in Western Europe. It is home to the Compagnie des Guides de Chamonix, the oldest and best mountain guiding service in the world. As in many other parts of the Alps, the pioneering climbers were British. The celebrated British explorer Richard Pococke and his 24-year-old companion, William Windham, arrived in the Chamonix Valley from Geneva in 1741. Their party of 13 had expected to meet 'savages' along the way and was consequently armed to the teeth. To further confuse the peaceful peasants they encountered along what is now the Autoroute Blanche, Pococke was dressed as an Arab (for reasons best known to himself).

Forty-five years later, local-born doctor Michel-Gabriel Paccard and his reclusive partner Jacques Balmat conquered Mont Blanc; this was the

most famous of many first ascents that have made Chamonix pre-eminent in climbing lore.

Over the past 30 years Chamonix has acquired a comparable status among skiers and snowboarders due to the first descents made by radical extremists like Jean-Marc Boivin and Patrick Vallençant, who now lie buried in the local churchyard. Today, the *ski extrème* torch is carried by Pierre Tardivel, the one-time Chamonix bank clerk whose descents include Everest.

163

Ski and board
top 3842m (12,605ft) bottom 1035m (3,396ft)

The Chamonix Valley caters for all levels of skier but not in the same place, making it difficult for mixed-ability groups to ski on the same mountain. With Les Houches (not included in the Cham'Ski lift pass), there are five main base-stations, most of which are a bus ride from the town centre. The closest is the celebrated Aiguille du Midi cable-car, which takes skiers and snowboarders up on to the shoulder of Mont Blanc for the descent down the Vallée Blanche. Le Brévent and La Flégère provide the bulk of the intermediate skiing. The toughest and easiest skiing lie further up the valley at **Argentière** and **Le Tour** respectively. A chair-lift off the back of Le Tour at Tête de Balme gives access to some delightful skiing down towards Vallorcine.

Les Houches has broken away from the Chamonix umbrella and is now seeking to align itself with its other big-name neighbour **St-Gervais/Megève.** A much-discussed gondola would make it part of a separate 350-km linked ski circus centred on Megève.

A cable-car now links Le Brévent and La Flégère, making one good ski area out of two smaller ones. At the Grands Montets a gondola has replaced the ancient Bochard chair-lift and takes 3,000 snow-users per hour to the summit of Bochard. The adjacent Herse chair remains a sad, slow and consequently cold reminder of what lifts used to be like. New pistes (notably the Chamois) and increased grooming have made Argentière more user-friendly for less accomplished skiers and for groups of mixed ability.

The lift pass situation is 'messy and confusing'. The main choice lies between no less than 10 permutations of the Cham'Ski pass and the Ski Pass Mont Blanc. You can also buy a whole range of half-day and one-day passes valid for certain areas only. The Ski Pass Mont Blanc is slightly more expensive but covers **Courmayeur**, Les Houches and a number of other outlying resorts.

Beginners

Learn to ski in Chamonix if you must but do not necessarily expect to like it. The town has small training areas for absolute beginners at Les Planards and Le Savoy, but once you have mastered the basics the best practice slopes are at Le Tour, the most far-flung of the valley's outposts. As Le Tour is tree-free, the light is often hostile, but on a clear day the comfortable gondola access to Charamillon and the wide, empty slopes that fan out across the Col de Balme above it are very user-friendly. The best-protected area from bad weather is the small network of blue (easy) runs at the top of Prarion in Les Houches, but this is not included in any of the Chamonix lift passes.

Intermediates

Such is the diversity of pistes that skiers and snowboarders with the skills to tackle a red (intermediate) run with confidence can spend a week in the valley without going to the same place twice. The most convenient starting point is Le Brévent, where the six-seater gondola to Planpraz gives access to a choice of inviting blue runs down to the Col Cornu chair. This in turn opens up several moderately challenging reds, the longest of which goes to the bottom of La Charlanon drag-lift. Planpraz is also the launch point for the dramatic cable-car ride up to Le Brévent itself, a 2525-m crag with unsurpassed views of Mont Blanc. From this point, the return to the mid-station is via a sweeping red piste or a bumpy black (difficult) trail. Only genuinely confident intermediates should attempt the return to Chamonix down the black run from the bottom of La Parsa chair.

La Flégère is reached from the suburb of **Les Praz,** a ten-minute bus ride from the town centre. The terrain is similar to that of Le Brévent, with long red and blue runs from the top of L'Index to the mid-station and a black descent back to base. The cable-car link with Le Brévent greatly enhances the area.

No visit to Chamonix is complete without a ride up the two-stage Aiguille du Midi cable-car, the highest in Europe. This is the departure point for the 20-km glacier run down the Vallée Blanche, a gentle cruise through some of the most grandiose mountain scenery in the world. As it can be tackled readily by low intermediates, it provides thousands of snow-users with their first unforgettable taste of high-mountain off-piste adventure. The trickiest part comes early in the shape of the infamous steps cut into the spine of the ridge from the cable-car station and the skiing start-point.

Experienced mountaineers ignore both the safety rope and the vertical drop-offs on either side, trotting down effortlessly as if in Chamonix's main street; but first-timers, burdened with skis on their backs, can freeze with the horror of it all. Some guides rope their clients together; this precaution can increase the feeling of danger if several people slip at once – the reality is that everyone gets down safely in the end.

This is not true of the Vallée Blanche itself, a minefield of deathtrap crevasses that should never be skied without a guide. It can also be accessed from the Courmayeur side via Punta Helbronner, a route that eliminates the ridge hazard altogether.

Advanced

When enthusiasts talk of Chamonix, they really mean Les Grands Montets at Argentière. This is a truly magnificent mountain for expert skiers and snowboarders – steep, complex and dramatic with seemingly unlimited possibilities. It is accessed either by the 80-person cable-car to Lognan or by the high-speed quad-chair to Plan Joran, both of which terminate at the Argentière base-station. When the cognoscenti arrive at Lognan, they join the rush – and almost inevitably the queue – for the Grands Montets cable-car.

The huge popularity of this lift is undiminished by both the 28FF supplement payable on top of the Mont Blanc lift pass and the 200 slippery metal steps leading from the top-station to the start of the skiing. This reveals itself to be a bumpy defile divided into two black runs, Les

Pylones (under the cable-car) and the awkwardly cambered Point de Vue, which, as its name suggests, provides stunning views of the glacier as it tracks down its edge. The Bochard gondola opens up another huge section of the mountain, including the 4.5-km Chamois descent to the Le Lavancher chair.

Most riders here are out to shred some of the steepest and most demanding powder in the world. However, Les Grands Montets also houses an important funpark that is managed by the Chamonix Snowboard Club. There is also a funpark at Charamillon, the mid-station at Le Tour and a half-pipe near the Kandahar chair in Les Houches.

Off-piste
On powder mornings the rush for Les Grands Montets is fierce, but the area is so enormous that skiing it out quickly is beyond even the powers of Europe's most dedicated first-track pack. Although open snowfields, bowls and gullies abound between the marked pistes, this is wild and dangerous terrain. The glacier is a web of crevasses and seracs that changes position from season to season. Although the more macho of the temporary residents claim to know the mountain well enough to ski it alone, the truth is that to ski here without a qualified guide is to court death. From a skiing point of view, the most challenging descent is the Pas de Chèvre, a run from the top of Bochard via one of several extreme couloirs down the Mer de Glace to the bottom of the Vallée Blanche.

Another classic is the Envers route down the Vallée Blanche, reached from the top of the Aiguille du Midi cable-car, but far removed from the regular run in terms of degree of difficulty.

Tuition and guiding
The Chamonix branch of the French Ski School (ESF) and the Compagnie des Guides share an office in the downtown area. The less traditional Ski Sensation takes a wilder approach to the learning curve, which is said to be popular with British clients. The ESF also has an office in Argentière, while Les Houches is served both by the ESF and the International Ski School (ESI).

Mountain restaurants
The Chamonix Valley is not recommended for those who like to lunch on the mountain seriously. Le Brévent and La Flégère have crowded self-service cafeterias, while Le Tour's Hotel Olympique is acclaimed for its sunseeker's terrace, although its food is dismissed as 'so-so' and service as 'the worst in the valley'. Those who ski the Vallée Blanche have little choice but to eat at the spectacularly sited Requin refuge.

Ironically, the best restaurants are on Les Grands Montets, the place where snow-users are least likely to linger over lunch. It is necessary to book in advance for La Chavanne, a tin hut under the Bochard lift station that is decidedly more promising inside than out. The spacious Plan Joran has an extensive self-service area, with decent, reasonably priced hot and cold food, and a small wait-service restaurant offering more sophisticated fare. However, it is usually extremely crowded.

The refurbished Chalet Refuge de Lognan serves 'an enormous *croûte savoyarde* for 50FF'. La Crèmerie du Glacier in the woods at the bottom of Les Grands Montets is warmly praised ('fair prices and a really friendly welcome').

The resort

Chamonix took shape before cars took over, and its current concerns are primarily with traffic management. Most visitors to the valley rightly consider a car to be essential, the alternative being a local bus service that links the base-stations with moderate efficiency but little comfort, especially at peak hours.

The original village square is fully pedestrianised and the main street is closed to traffic during daylight hours. This allows for the free flow of shoppers at the cost of considerable congestion on the outskirts, especially in the ever-expanding new township of Chamonix Sud. The problem has not been improved as much as was hoped by the addition of a 300-space car park at St Michel. The shopping facilities are so comprehensive here that one reporter comments: 'Almost a range of shops that one would expect to find in any British town'.

Accommodation

Chamonix offers the full spectrum, from dormitory-style youth hostels to four-star hotels, plus a wide choice of chalets and apartments. The seven privately owned Les Autannes apartments in a former old stone-built hotel near Le Tour are some of the best appointed accommodation here.

The most luxurious hotels are the Albert 1er and Auberge du Bois Prin, owned by brothers Denis and Pierre Carrier. Le Hameau de l'Albert 1er is a new complex of 12 suites with a swimming-pool and a rustic restaurant. In the three-star category, the Sapinière recalls the heyday of the British Empire, both in its furnishings and its clientèle. The pleasant Hotel Richemond also trades on the faded glories of yesteryear, but from a more central location. The Alpina is a central, quality three-star hotel.

Eating in and out

No one denies that the Michelin-rated Albert 1er hotel has the best food in Chamonix, but prices have risen to such a level that even the seriously wealthy hesitate to go there except on special occasions. The Auberge du Bois Prin follows it closely in both quality and price, and the food at the Hotel Eden in Les Praz is also recommended. La Bergerie serves Savoyard specialities, while the Bistro de la Gare is known for its cheap daily special. Le Sarpe in Les Bois is praised for quality combined with good value. L'Impossible, the ancient barn in Chamonix Sud converted by Sylvain Saudain, is a winner for atmosphere. Other recommendations include La Cantina for Mexican cuisine and Le Cafeteria, which is said

Skiing facts: Chamonix

TOURIST OFFICE

85 Place du Triangle de L'Amitié,
F-74400 Chamonix Mont Blanc,
Haute Savoie
Tel 33 4 50 53 00 24
Fax 33 4 50 53 58 90
Email info@chamonix.com
Web site www.chamonix.com

THE RESORT

By road Calais 900km
By rail station in resort
Airport transfer Geneva 1½hrs
Visitor beds 54,994
Transport free ski bus included in lift
pass

THE SKIING

Linked or nearby resorts Argentière (n),
Courmayeur (n), Les Houches (n),
Megève (n), St-Gervais (n), Le Tour (n)
Longest run Les Grands Montets, 8km
(black/red)
Number of lifts 52
Total of trails/pistes 140km
(52% easy, 36% intermediate,
12% difficult)
Nursery slopes 17 beginner runs
Summer skiing none
Snowmaking 80 snow-cannon

LIFT PASSES

Area pass Cham'Ski (covers all valley
ski areas except Les Houches),
930FF for 6 days. Ski Pass Mont Blanc
(covers region), 1,080FF for 6 days
Day pass Cham'Ski 230FF, 120–185FF
for separate ski areas
Beginners no free lifts
Pensioners 20% reduction for 60yrs
and over
Credit cards yes

TUITION

Adults ESF, 770FF for 6 days
Private lessons ESF, 190FF per hr
Snowboarding ESF, 660FF for 3 after-
noons, private lessons 520FF for 2hrs
Cross-country ESF, prices as regular ski
lessons. Loipe 42km between Les
Bossons and Le Tour
Other courses heli-skiing
Guiding Compagnie des Guides de
Chamonix, Association Internationale
des Guides, Stages Vallençant,
Mont Blanc Ski Tours, Sensation Ski
International

CHILDREN

Lift pass Cham' Kid, 4–11yrs, 651FF for
6 days, 161FF per day, Cham' Jnr,
12–15yrs, 791FF for 6 days, 196FF per
day. Ski Pass Mont Blanc, 12yrs and
under, 756FF for 6 days
Ski kindergarten ESF, 4–12yrs, 1,300FF
for 6 days including lunch, Panda-Ski,
3–12 yrs, 1,425FF for 6 days including
lunch
Ski school ESF, 4–6yrs, 670FF for 6
days. 6–12yrs, 630FF for 6 days
Non-ski kindergarten Halte-Garderie,
18mths–6yrs, (Mon–Fri) 8am–6.15pm,
220FF per day, extra 19FF per day for
lunch. Panda Club, 6mths–3yrs, 1,450FF
for 6 days including lunch

OTHER SPORTS

Indoor tennis and squash, ice-driving,
snowshoeing, hang-gliding, parapente,
curling, skating, swimming, helicopter rides

FOOD AND DRINK

Coffee 15FF, glass of wine 15–20FF,
small beer 15–20FF, dish of the day
60–75FF

to provide 'very reasonably priced, wholesome food'. Self-caterers are well served by specialist food shops and supermarkets.

Après-ski

The ski-mad early evening trade may concentrate on the fashionable video bars of Le Choucas and Driver but there is no shortage of alternative entertainment. Floodlit skiing takes place at Les Bossons, and Chamonix Sud has a bowling alley and billiard school. After dinner the action focuses on Arbat, which has the best live music in town. Wild Wallabies, inspired by St Anton's Krazy Kangaruh, is another top choice, while real late-nighters end up at the Blue Night, which stays open until 5am.

The Bumble Bee and the Mill Street Bar in Chamonix are both recommended, as is The Office Bar in Argentière. Jekyll and Hyde and The Ice Rock Café in Chamonix Sud are both popular; the latter is a large basement bar incorporating half a truck and various motorbikes and is packed until the early hours.

Childcare

The ESF schools in Chamonix and Argentière have classes for children aged between 4 and 12 years of age. The Panda Club in Argentière provides care for children aged six months to three years, every day of the week. For three- and four-year-olds, Panda-Ski offers daily sessions in the Jardin des Neiges near the Lognan lift station. In addition, a municipal crèche provides entertainment for children aged between 18 months and 6 years of age.

Linked or nearby resorts

Argentière
top 3842m (12,605ft) bottom 1240m (4,067ft)

In winter, Argentière's main street becomes 'Ski Bum Alley', with a large proportion of its rooms let out cheaply for the season. After dark, the bars hum with macho talk of the day's achievements. The Office Bar, now relocated in larger premises, is the favoured British watering hole. The Rusticana is more cosmopolitan, while the Savoie dares to remain resolutely French. The Dahu Hotel, a prominent landmark on the congested road from Chamonix to Martigny, is recommended both for comfort and food.

TOURIST OFFICE
as Chamonix

Les Deux Alpes

ALTITUDE 1650m (5,412ft)

Beginners ✱ Intermediates ✱✱✱ Advanced ✱✱ Snowboarders ✱✱✱

This efficient and only partly purpose-built resort lies between Grenoble and Briançon within easy reach of **Alpe d'Huez** in one direction and **Serre Chevalier** in the other. Its primary asset is the height of the skiing (3600m), which means that snow is assured at any stage of the season, and the glacier is also open during the French summer holidays.

Les Deux Alpes began as a ski resort shortly before the outbreak of the Second World War. Pride of place was a Heath-Robinson-style rope-tow which fell down 15 minutes after the opening ceremony. It was not until the late 1950s that a new gondola and one of France's first ski passes – costing 2.50FF per day – paved the way for Les Deux Alpes to develop into a proper ski area.

- ✔ Snow-sure slopes
- ✔ Modern lift system
- ✔ Excellent child facilities
- ✔ Beautiful scenery
- ✔ Lively après-ski
- ✔ Summer skiing
- ✘ Large and spread-out village
- ✘ Heavy traffic
- ✘ Lack of tree-level skiing
- ✘ Crowded pistes

Today, Les Deux Alpes has 63 lifts, which distribute a potential 61,000 skiers an hour to every conceivable point on the mountain, resembling a large ski factory, but with fresh air and impressive scenery. Both village and ski area are long and narrow, and there is less skiing terrain than one would imagine for such a long vertical drop. However, the skiing links with **La Grave**, which is one of the most dramatic off-piste ski areas in Europe.

A quieter, alternative base is **Venosc**, a small, attractive village in the Vénéon Valley below Les Deux Alpes. Its ancient cobbled streets are lined with craft shops and studios. More than half-a-dozen craft shops sell a range of high-quality goods with local mountain gems their speciality. It has three extremely pleasant and inexpensive restaurants: 'The crêperie has wonderful food at realistic prices in an idyllic rustic setting'. The village is linked by an efficient, modern gondola that you have to take down again at the end of the day as you cannot ski back.

Snowboarding takes pride of place here each October as an apéritif to the winter ski season. Les Deux Alpes is the venue for the World Snowboard Meeting and the Grand Prix des Deux Alpes, which claims to be 'the highest and biggest exhibition of snowboarding on the planet'. Fixtures held on the Glacier du Mont de Lans at 3200m include slalom, giant slalom and half-pipe competitions which attract some 15,000 visitors.

Ski and board

top 3600m (11,808ft) bottom 1600m (5,249ft)

The chamois hunters and shepherds who once roamed what are now the ski slopes would scarcely recognise their traditional haunts today. Indeed, it is easy for skiers to be confused by such a multitude of lifts and 200km of piste within a relatively confined area. Apart from a smaller, uncrowded sector to the west of the village, between Pied Moutet at 2100m and the Alpe du Mont de Lans, the bulk of the skiing is between the village and La Toura (2600m) to the east. Reporters criticise the 'sameness' of the pistes: 'A huge array of blue (easy) and green (beginner) runs, all of which are rather dull,' and 'it seems to be something of a damning indictment that a resort that claims 200km of piste has so few runs of any real interest,' were two disgruntled reporters' verdicts.

The principal lift is the Jandri Express jumbo gondola, which deposits skiers on the glacier in 20 minutes. It is prone to rush-hour queues, and reporters unanimously suggest using the alternative network of fast chairs to reach the mid-station. Above La Toura the terrain narrows down to a bottleneck. At this point, it can sometimes be difficult to thread your way through skiers and pylons until the Col de Jandri at 3200m. Here the terrain widens again to include some good intermediate cruising down towards Roche Mantel before reaching the broader glacier plateau. This sector offers easy slopes and even a sub-glacial funicular for novice skiers who find wind-blown drag-lifts daunting. There is also some skiing below the village if conditions are favourable. The new La Fée chair-lift opens up a wide area to the skier's right from the 2600m mid-station.

WHAT'S NEW
La Fée chair-lift

Beginners

Those who learn to ski at Les Deux Alpes will be surprised at how much more convenient skiing can be when they move on to another resort. The most extensive nursery slopes are at the top of the ski area on the Glacier du Mont de Lans, and the only way down for novices is by taking a series of gondolas. The slopes immediately above the village are steep, and learners also have to download to the resort by lift at the end of the day. A compensation is the excitement of being able to experience your first slither on skis high up the mountain with magnificent views of the Oisans mountain range.

Intermediates

Intermediates can enjoy themselves on most of the upper slopes at Les Deux Alpes, although less experienced skiers may find themselves somewhat overwhelmed by the steep homeward-bound runs, which can become crowded at the end of the day. One way to escape from the mainstream skiing is to try one of the rare runs through the trees. There is an enjoyable piste down to the village of Bons at 1300m, while Mont de Lans can be reached from both ski areas. Les Gours, the run down to

La Voute quad-chair, is a conversion of a celebrated off-piste itinerary into an easy red (intermediate) run.

Advanced

Experienced skiers inevitably gravitate towards the Tête Moute area, which provides some of the steepest terrain on the mountain. They will be tempted to go straight from the Venosc end of the village by gondola to Le Diable at 2400m, which can also be reached by a more roundabout route via the Thuit chair-lift. From here, the Grand Diable chair reaches the Tête Moute itself, where steep, north-facing runs lead to Lac du Plan and onwards towards the Thuit chair. Le Diable run offers a challenging and often mogulled 1200-m descent to the village. There are seven other black (difficult) runs.

The snowpark is on La Toura piste in winter and moves to the glacier where camps are held in the summer. The park includes boarder-cross, a half-pipe, plus a barbecue and sound system.

Off-piste

Les Deux Alpes has enclosed bowl-skiing, which is ideal for those wanting to try off-piste for the first time. For seasoned deep-snow skiers there are a number of easily accessible (but not so easily skiable) couloirs. La Grave, one of the most exciting and scenic off-piste ski areas in the Alps, is on the doorstep – there is an 'over-the-top' link from Les Deux Alpes via the Glacier du Mont de Lans, which involves a 20-minute walk. A wonderful descent takes you 'off the back' towards the unspoilt little climbing village of **St-Christophe.**

Tuition and guiding

The main ski schools are the French Ski School (ESF) at Les Deux Alpes and the rival International Ski School (ESI) at St-Christophe. Both offer group and private lessons: special courses include snowboarding and telemark. The British-run European Ski School offers tuition (in English) to classes of up to four pupils ('I cannot speak highly enough of the teachers, who explained everything fully and taught with a high degree of understanding and patience', said one reporter). Courses are for two hours each day and include video analysis and computerised ski simulators; all classes have priority in the lift queues. Primitive Snowboard School is the specialist for wannabee riders.

Mountain restaurants

Les Deux Alpes receives few bouquets for its six mountain restaurants, and if it were not so inconvenient more skiers might consider lunching in town. 'Uninviting' and 'overpriced' are among the comments expressed by reporters. The Panoramic is 'friendly but a bit crowded at peak hours'. The highest restaurant, Les Glaciers, is as its name suggests on the glacier. Chalet de La Toura over the back of the mountain is 'a useful find in an area otherwise bereft of gastronomic comforts'. La Patache at Les Crêtes is recommended 'but not when ski school has just finished'. La Meije offers a 'friendly, efficient service of local specialities at very reasonable prices'. La Petite Marmite is also recommended.

The resort

This narrow, rather higgledy-piggledy and bustling small town developed on a somewhat haphazard basis from the two separate farming communities of Mont de Lans and Alpe de Venosc. Although the town itself is not attractive, it is by no means the worst example of modern French architecture. The resort links with the quaint old hamlet of Venosc. Les Deux Alpes will score highly for après-ski among those who like lively, noisy bars and discos and do not mind bumping into lots of other British people (more than 25 per cent of non-French visitors are British).

Accommodation

Most of the accommodation is in apartments, with the remainder in the resort's 40 hotels and pensions. The top end of the market boasts three four-star establishments, of which the Bérangère is particularly praised. There are nine three-star hotels and 21 two-stars. The Edelweiss is acclaimed for its 'wonderful gourmet dinners, with local produce properly cooked and well presented; the staff were patient and helpful and the bedrooms large, if a little spartan'. Hotel Les Marmottes is 'superb, with a five-course dinner, and large bedrooms'. Ten rental agencies deal with self-catering apartments.

Eating in and out

L'Abri and La Spaghetteria are warmly recommended for pizza and pasta. Blue Salmon Farm specialises in fish dishes. Il Caminetto is a much-praised Italian restaurant. Le P'tit Polyte is 'smart, expensive, and worth every centime'. Le Four à Bois is renowned for its regional specialities. Le Saxo serves Tex-Mex cuisine. Les Deux Alpes appears to have a higher turnover of restaurants than any other major resort. As one reporter said: 'We marvelled at the value of more than one restaurant – only to find it had closed down by next season'. There is a good range of supermarkets, plus a spread of boulangerie, boucherie and pâtisserie shops to make life easier for the many self-caterers.

Après-ski

Les Deux Alpes teems with après-ski opportunities. Pub Windsor is a lastingly popular haunt. Rodéo Saloon, at the Venosc end of town, has a bizarre mechanical bull which inevitably attracts the wilder element of après-skiers. The Asterix Bar, in the hotel of the same name, is 'not very pretty, but has friendly service'. Le Pressoir and Le Tonic are described as 'useful watering-holes'. A watering-hole of a different kind, Le Tanking Center, provides a therapeutic sensory deprivation experience whereby you float in warm water in total darkness. Sensory deprivation is far from absent at the four discos of La Casa, Le Club 92, L'Avalanche and L'Opéra Music Temple. The ice grotto is well worth a visit.

Skiing facts: Les Deux Alpes

TOURIST OFFICE
BP 7, F-38860 Les Deux Alpes, Dauphiné
Tel 33 4 76 79 22 00
Fax 33 4 76 79 01 38
Email Les2alpes@icor.fr
Web site www.les2alpes.com

THE RESORT
By road Calais 953km
By rail Grenoble 70km
Airport transfer Grenoble 1½ hrs,
Lyon 2hrs
Visitor beds 35,000
Transport free ski bus

THE SKIING
Linked or nearby resorts La Grave (l),
Alpe d'Huez (n), Serre Chevalier/Briançon
(n), St-Christophe-en-Oisans (l),
Venosc (l)
Longest run Les Gours, 5km (blue)
Number of lifts 63
Total of trails/pistes 200km (62% easy,
28% intermediate, 10% difficult)
Nursery slopes 2 free lifts and 2 runs
Summer skiing mid-June–Sept, 16 lifts
Snowmaking 30 hectares covered

LIFT PASSES
Area pass 928FF for 6 days (includes 1
free day in Alpe d'Huez, Serre Chevalier,
Puy-St-Vincent or the Milky Way)
Day pass 186FF
Beginners 3 free lifts
Pensioners reduction for 60yrs and over
Credit cards yes

TUITION
Adults ESF, 750FF for 6 mornings
(9.15am–12.15pm), 615FF for 6 afternoons (2.30–5pm). ESI, 9.30am–midday
and 2.30–5pm, 680FF for 6 half-days

(am or pm), European Ski School,
700FF for 5 days (2hrs per day)
Private lessons ESF 190FF per hr,
ESI 195FF per hr, European 170FF per hr
Snowboarding ESF 605FF, ESI 660FF,
both for 6 x 3hrs. Primitive Snowboard
School, 990FF for 6 x 2hrs
Cross-country ESF and ESI prices on
request, loipe 20km
Other courses ski-touring, monoski,
telemark, slalom
Guiding Aventures Verticales, ESF
Bureau des Guides, Nano Pourtier,
European Ski School

CHILDREN
Lift pass 4–13yrs, 681FF for 6 days,
free for under 4yrs
Ski kindergarten ESF, 4–6yrs, 595FF
for 6 mornings, ESI, 505FF for 6 days
(am or pm)
Ski school ESF, 6–12yrs, 985FF for 6
days (5½hrs per day). ESI, 6–12yrs,
970FF for 6 days (5hrs per day),
European, 5–8yrs, 650FF for
5 days (2hrs per day)
Non-ski kindergarten La Crèche
du Clos des Fonds, 6mths–2yrs, 180FF
per day including lunch. Le Bonhomme
de Neige, 2–6yrs, 950FF for 6 days
including lunch

OTHER SPORTS
Parapente, bungee-jumping, swimming,
skating, curling, helicopter rides,
ice-climbing, indoor tennis and squash,
climbing wall

FOOD AND DRINK PRICES
Coffee 6–12FF, glass of wine 10–15FF,
small beer 15–18FF, dish of the day
50–70FF

Childcare

Among the bridges, tunnels and animal characters at the Espace Loisirs playground there is a trampoline, a small slalom course, toboggan run, ski-biking, inner-tubing and an inflatable bob run, with organised races most days. Qualified staff welcome children from six months to two years old at the slope-side Crèche du Clos des Fonds, and Le Bonhomme de Neige caters for two- to six-year-olds.

The ESF operates a kindergarten slope in the centre of town close to the Jandri Express, and the ESI has its own kindergarten. Both ski schools offer half- or full-day courses for children over four years of age who wish to ski, snowboard or monoski. Yellow Cab Surfing has created a snow garden, Papoose Valley, and runs snowboarding courses for children over four years old. We have mixed reports of the ESF children's ski school: 'The French instructors spoke adequate English and even in the worst of the weather they took the wee souls out for at least part of the three-hour lesson. When they got cold, wet and fed up they returned to the ESF chalet to dry out and watch videos'. However, another reporter says: 'Frankly, we were not impressed with the ESF ski kindergarten. On the first day we found our four-year-old son alone in the kindergarten hut, crying'.

Linked or nearby resorts

La Grave
top 3550m (11,647ft) bottom 1450m (4,757ft)

This ancient, rugged village straggling the road up to the Col du Lauteret has in the past earned its reputation as a climbing centre rather than as a ski resort. It crouches in the shadow of the 3983-m La Meije, which was one of the last great European peaks to be conquered in 1876. Its reputation is founded on the fact that it has just one short piste and two lifts. This may sound insignificant until you realise that one of those lifts takes you up over 2000m vertical. It does not normally open until late January, although the ski area can be reached from Les Deux Alpes. The steep, unpisted routes down provide some of the most challenging advanced skiing in Europe. As the glacial area is heavily crevassed and the couloirs are steep, skiers are strongly advised to use the services of a local guide at all times. La Grave has only a couple of simple hotels and little to offer anyone who does not climb or ski off-piste to an advanced standard.

TOURIST OFFICE
Tel 33 4 76 79 90 05
Fax 33 4 76 79 91 65

Flaine

ALTITUDE 1600m (5,248ft)

Beginners ✱✱✱   Intermediates ✱✱✱   Advanced ✱✱   Snowboarders ✱✱✱

Flaine lies at the core of France's fourth largest ski area. Architectural visionaries may view it as an interesting example of the Bauhaus school of design, but most visitors view it as a disaster area created in the 1960s at the same time as **Les Menuires, Chamrousse** and other French resorts of its generation. The liberal use of grey, unfinished concrete is depressing enough even when the resort is cloaked under a blanket of fresh snow, but in the spring, when the white disappears and the rains come, it defies description. However, one reporter commented that 'compared with the area of east London where I work, Flaine is quite pretty'.

Its surprisingly international following, a fair proportion of which is British, hinges upon a number of factors: the resort is within easy reach of Geneva; its skiing is extensive and varied; and its proximity to Mont Blanc provides it with an unnaturally favourable snowfall for its altitude. The original aim in Flaine was to provide doorstep-skiing at affordable prices, but this resort is no longer cheaper than most of its rivals in the French Alps. Expansion over the years means that ski-in ski-out convenience is not to be found at all the resort's accommodation. Visitors come here for the skiing, not for the ambience which, as one reporter put it, 'simply doesn't exist'.

Flaine connects with the three lower and more traditional resorts of **Samoëns**, **Morillon** and **Les Carroz**, and a piste also takes you down the Combe de Gers to the charming village of **Sixt**.

✔ Large ski area
✔ Excellent family facilities
✔ Skiing convenience
✔ Short airport transfer
✔ Car-free resort
✔ Reliable resort-level snow
✔ Lack of queues
✔ Variety of off-piste skiing
✘ Lack of alpine charm
✘ Limited après-ski

Ski and board
top 2480m (8,134ft) bottom 700m (2,296ft)

Flaine is the core of the large ski area of Le Grand Massif, which comprises around 265km of linked skiing served by 80 lifts. It divides naturally into separate segments. Flaine's own skiing is ranged around the north-facing part of its home bowl, with lifts soaring to nearly 2500m around the rim. Most of the skiing is open and unsheltered.

The main mountain access from the village centre is a huge gondola up to Grandes Platières, a high, wide plateau with panoramic views. A large number of runs go from here down to the resort; most are graded red (intermediate) or blue (easy). In general, the skiing in the enclosed Flaine bowl is somewhat limited, and its real attraction lies in its link with the remainder of Le Grand Massif area; this is via the Grand Vans chair-lift, which, because of its exposed top-station, is usually the first to close in bad weather.

The Tête du Pré des Saix is the central point of the entire Grand Massif system. From here, north-facing runs drop down steep mogul slopes towards Samoëns. Halfway down, the descent is broken by the lifts which go up to **Samoëns 1600**. On the other side of the valley the parallel easier pistes towards Morillon comprise long and gentle trails in the tree-line, passing a couple of restaurants. An efficient gondola goes from Morillon village to Morillon Grand Massif.

The runs to Les Carroz are short but offer a wide variety of trails, including more difficult sections at the top of the red runs and some good off-piste. The blue run to the village is often crowded and bare of snow. We have received complaints that L'Airon chair-lift, which provides the best link to Flaine, is often closed; without it a long traverse or a 180-m uphill walk are necessary. Access to the slopes is via the Kédeuse gondola, which is reported to have long queues in the mornings.

Sixt, along the road from Samoëns, has its own small ski area linking with Samoëns and Morillon. The resort is directly linked into the Grand Massif via a piste down the Combe de Gers. This begins with the Styx black (difficult) run, served by its own drag-lift, and continues with a 6-km blue run. One reporter complained that narrow, plunging pitches alternate with uphill sections 'where we encountered cross-country skiers coming towards us'. A bus connects skiers and snowboarders with Samoëns.

Beginners

Flaine has good novice slopes in the middle of the village. Improvers can try wide, snaking blues on the bowl's west-facing slopes. Crystal and Serpentine are long, sweeping runs around the shoulder of the mountain that beginners will be able to tackle by the end of their first week.

Intermediates

The whole area is essentially designed for intermediates. Day-long forays into the far corners of Le Grand Massif are well within the capabilities of most snow-users with a few weeks' experience. However, it is important to allow plenty of time for the return journey. The Tourmaline blue from Les Grands Vans down to Le Forêt is usually well-groomed and is one of the classic runs of the resort.

Advanced

The more difficult skiing sections of the Flaine bowl are in the middle, graded black under the gondola and red to each side. The black Diamant Noir is an enjoyable mogul slope. Unlike some other large linked areas, there are plenty of steep runs and a good variety of terrain, making Flaine a suitable destination for advanced skiers and snowboarders.

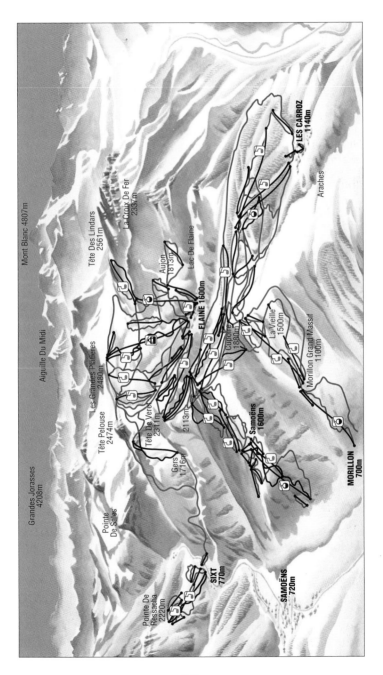

Grandes Jorasses 4208m

Mont Blanc 4807m

Aiguille Du Midi

Pointe De Sales

Pointe De Ressacha 2220m

SIXT 770m

Tête Pelouse 2474m

Les Grandes Platières 2480m

Tête Des Lindars 2561m

La Croix De Fer 2337m

Tête De Vere 2311m

Gers 1716m

2113m

Aujon 1813m

Lac De Flaine

FLAINE 1600m

Cupoire 1880m

La Vieille 1500m

Morillon Grand Massif 1100m

Samoëns 1600m

SAMOËNS 720m

MORILLON 700m

LES CARROZ 1140m

Araches

SAMOËNS 720m

Flaine is home to one of the best snowparks in Europe. The 3km-long park offers enough jumps and obstacles of all varieties to keep even the most hardcore freestyler happy. At the bottom of the park is a well-prepared half-pipe. A reduced-price snowboard pass gives access to the park's drag-lift as well as to some of the other nearby runs. Flaine is also popular with alpine riders because of the large number of wide and fairly flat pistes.

Off-piste

Flaine and Le Grand Massif area offer outstanding off-piste possibilities. The rocky terrain means that powder hunts can all too easily end on a cliff and the services of a local guide who really knows the region are essential.

Tuition and guiding

Flaine now has four ski schools. We have mixed reports of the French Ski School (ESF): 'Large classes, but our instructor was extremely helpful,' and 'we found our instructor typically volatile and he twice committed the cardinal sin of skiing on without waiting for all the class to catch up'. We continue to receive disastrous criticism of the International Ski School (ESI): 'Little or no teaching – little more than two pieces of advice in 12 hours of tuition might be described as frugal'. Another reporter comments: 'Never, in 30 years of skiing, have I seen such disorganisation. Our children hardly ever had the same teacher from morning to afternoon, let alone from day to day'.

Flaine Super Ski offers half-day improvement courses. Ski Action-Ski Passion was set up by two former members of the French ski team and has a growing reputation. Fantasurf is a dedicated funpark for children aged 6 to 10 years. Instructors provide equipment and two hours of lessons per day.

Mountain restaurants

Those in the immediate Flaine vicinity are limited, especially in the Aujon area, but there is a wide choice further afield. Close to the resort the Blanchot is recommended, and Chalet Bissac is 'busy, but has quick hot food'. Bar L'Eloge, by the Flaine gondola, has a simple choice of food and friendly service. La Combe, in the Morillon area, has 'terrific ambience'. The Oréade, at the top of the Kédeuse gondola is recommended for its food and large, sunny terrace. The restaurant on the Chariande piste at Samoëns has reasonable prices and an excellent view from the terrace. Le Pativerdans at Vercland is reported to be good value, and has English hosts who have become part of the local community.

The resort

The first view down into Flaine is a surprising one; it sits ostentatiously in an isolated bowl where you would not expect to find any habitation at all. The grey concrete matches the grey rock formation. Reporters' opinions of Flaine vary from 'no soul' and 'a ski ghetto, which does not give one the feeling of being in France,' to 'a pleasant atmosphere'. In counterpoint to this grey image, Flaine has developed a reputation as a centre for fine art. Sculptures by Picasso, Dubuffet and Vasarely are dotted around the village, and other works are housed in the resort's arts centre. Two enclosed people-mover lifts operate day and night between the higher and lower villages. Le Hameau de Flaine area is served by a free bus, which runs from the chalets to the nursery slopes every 15 minutes during the day but is apparently not reliable at night.

Accommodation

The heart of the resort is Flaine Forum, where the main shops and restaurants and the ski school meeting-place are based. The Totem, with Picasso's statue of the same name standing outside, is the main piste-side hotel. Reporters' views range alarmingly from 'expensive with clinical, modern décor,' and 'still living on its old reputation,' to 'a truly grand establishment'. The food is praised by most. Les Lindars, Flaine's most famous, family-oriented hotel, is now a Club Aquarius. One reporter commented: 'The hotel's previous reputation as being ideal for families and small children is no longer justified'. The two-star Aujon is the popular alternative: 'The bedrooms are so tiny they hardly fit two beds, but the breakfast is excellent'.

Flaine Forêt, on a shelf above Flaine Forum, has mainly self-catering accommodation and its own shops and bars. Most of the rental apartments in the resort have been refurbished. The apartments are small, even by French standards ('thank goodness we had booked an apartment for eight for the six of us'). Le Hameau de Flaine, on the mountain at 1800m, is a later development of attractive Scandinavian-style chalets inconveniently situated for the ski area. It has its own sports shop, a bar, restaurant and supermarket.

Eating in and out

Chez La Jeanne is 'small and friendly with excellent pizzas and good house wine'. La Perdrix Noire in Flaine Fôret is voted best restaurant by a number of reporters. La Pizzeria in the Forum is 'excellent and reasonably priced,' and La Trattoria has a 'pleasant, almost Italian atmosphere and good wine'. There are well-stocked supermarkets on both Forum and Forêt levels.

Après-ski

People do not come to Flaine for the nightlife and many tend to opt for quiet evenings in, especially those with small children. The Cîmes Rock Café in Flaine Forum has live music. The White Grouse Pub, that little piece of Scotland that is forever France, has raised its standards and is reported to have fought its way back to being one of the principal meeting places of the resort. The Bodega is the main disco.

Childcare

The Green Mouse Club (Souris Verte) at the ESI takes children all day, as does the ESF Rabbit Club, which is the more French-oriented of the

Skiing facts: Flaine

TOURIST OFFICE
Galerie des Marchards, 74300 Flaine
Tel 33 4 50 90 80 01
Fax 33 4 50 90 86 26
Email flaine@laposte.fr
Web site www.flaine.com
UK Agent: Erna Low (see *Which tour operator?*)

THE RESORT
By road Calais 890km
By rail Cluses 25km, frequent bus service to resort
Airport transfer Geneva 1½ hrs
Visitor beds 6,500
Transport free ski bus between Flaine and Le Hameau

THE SKIING
Linked or nearby resorts Les Carroz (l), Morillon (l), Samoëns (l), Sixt (n)
Longest run Cascade, 14km (blue)
Number of lifts 28 in Flaine, 80 in Le Grand Massif
Total of trails/pistes 150km in Flaine (13% easy, 31% intermediate, 43% difficult, 13% very difficult), 265km in Le Grand Massif
Nursery slopes 6
Summer skiing none
Snowmaking 17 hectares covered (Flaine)

LIFT PASSES
Area pass Grand Massif (covers Flaine, Les Carroz, Morillon, Samoëns and Sixt) 860FF for 6 days
Day pass Flaine 155FF, Grand Massif 177FF
Beginners 4 free lifts in area, beginner pass 80FF per day
Pensioners 640FF for 6 days
Credit cards yes

TUITION
Adults ESF and ESI, 700FF for 6 x 4hrs
Private lessons 370FF for 2hrs, 960FF for 6hrs
Snowboarding as ski schools, 695FF for 6 x 3hrs
Cross-country as private ski lessons. Loipe 10km at Flaine, 72km at Samoëns
Other courses race camps
Guiding through ski schools

CHILDREN
Lift pass Flaine, 11yrs and under, 580FF for 6 days, free for 4yrs and under. Grand Massif, 640FF. Both for 6 days. Beginner pass, 65FF per day
Ski kindergarten ESF Rabbit Club, ESI Green Mouse Club, both 3–12yrs, 1,200FF for 6 days including lunch
Ski school 390–430FF for 6 x 2hrs not including lunch
Non-ski kindergarten Les Petits Loups, 6mths–4yrs, 9am–5pm, 160FF per day not including lunch

OTHER SPORTS
Parapente, snowshoeing, hang-gliding, snowmobiling, ice-driving, climbing wall, swimming, skating

FOOD AND DRINK PRICES
Coffee 8–10FF, glass of wine 7.50–14FF, small beer 13–18FF, dish of the day 50–75FF

two. Both collect children from their accommodation each morning and return them at the end of the day. Non-skiing children can still be cared for at Les Petits Loups kindergarten, but priority is given to the families of resort workers and you need to book at least two months in advance. Club Aquarius has its own kindergarten.

Linked or nearby resorts

Les Carroz
top 2480m (8,134ft) bottom 1140m (3,739ft)

Les Carroz is large and, in the view of most correspondents, more pleasing to the eye than Flaine. Its drawback is its low altitude. The resort spreads across a broad, sunny slope on the road to Flaine and attracts many families, and weekend visitors, who use it as an access point for this substantial ski area.

The gondola and chair-lift are a steep walk from the centre of the village, but within easy reach of some attractive, simple old hotels including Les Airelles and the Croix de Savoie. The well-located Hotel des Belles Pistes, run by an English couple, is said to be decorated 'Cotswolds style with little local character, but the chef is French and very good'. The Front de Neige is reported to cope well with the needs of small children.

Most of the self-catering accommodation is much less conveniently placed. The bus is not included in the lift pass and only three services per day run to Flaine; late-night taxis between the two resorts are hard to find.

TOURIST OFFICE
Tel 33 4 50 90 00 04
Fax 33 4 50 90 07 00

Samoëns
top 2480m (8,134ft) bottom 720m (2,362ft)

The beautiful old town of Samoëns in the Giffre Valley has been a ski resort since 1912 and is the only one in France to be listed as a historical monument. It was once a thriving stone-cutting centre, and twice a week the tourist office organises guided tours around the town's architectural sites. Traditional-style bars and restaurants abound in what is a resort largely undiscovered by other nationalities. The Neige et Roc and Les Sept Monts hotels are recommended, together with Les Drugères. One reporter spoke highly of Le Pierrot Gourmet restaurant. Samoëns has its own ski school, a crèche for children from six months old and a ski kindergarten for children aged three to six years old. It also has 72km of loipe and a cross-country ski school.

TOURIST OFFICE
Tel 33 4 50 34 40 28
Fax 33 4 50 34 95 82

Megève

ALTITUDE 1100m (3,608ft)

Beginners ✱✱✱ Intermediates ✱✱✱ Snowboarders ✱

Megève, one of France's oldest and once most chic resorts, has made a comeback after a decade in the doldrums. A combination of extensive gentle skiing, excellent child facilities, lavish hotels and enticing restaurants all set in a village rich in ambience acts as the lure for a new generation of family skiers. The upmarket image is still here, with the resort's exclusivity due largely to the high prices in hotels, restaurants and nightclubs, which keep the mass-market out.

✔ Long runs
✔ Range of non-skiing activities
✔ Large choice of restaurants
✔ Ideal for family skiing
✔ Lively après-ski
✔ Short airport transfer
✔ Tree-line skiing
✔ Medieval town centre
✗ Unreliable resort-level snow
✗ Heavy traffic outside pedestrian area

The village is built around a fine medieval church and carefully restored old buildings. The streets are colourful, with designer boutiques and 32 brightly painted sleighs, which are owned and driven by local farmers. There are no noticeable architectural eyesores, and recent additions have been built in a sympathetic chalet-style.

In 1916, while holidaying in Switzerland, Baroness Maurice de Rothschild decided to find a resort in her home country to rival St Moritz. She took advice from her Norwegian ski instructor and visited the tiny village of Megève. So impressed was she that five years later she returned to build the Palace Hotel Mont d'Arbois, which helped transform Megève into an international resort.

Later on in its history, Megève boasted that at the height of the season it was home to more crowned heads of state than any other ski resort in Europe. The Aga Khan and celebrities including Rita Hayworth, Roger Vadim and Brigitte Bardot, have in the past installed themselves for the winter. During the boom years of the 1960s a week-long visit to Megève, staying in the Mont Blanc Hotel with its Jean Cocteau murals, was mandatory for anyone with international social aspirations. Then its reputation faded. The stars migrated to brighter galaxies, more certain snow and better skiing. Courchevel 1850 took on its mantle.

Ski and board
top 2350m (7,708ft) bottom 850m (2,788ft)
The skiing takes place on smooth and well-groomed pistes. Two of the three areas, Mont d'Arbois and Rochebrune, are connected at their bases

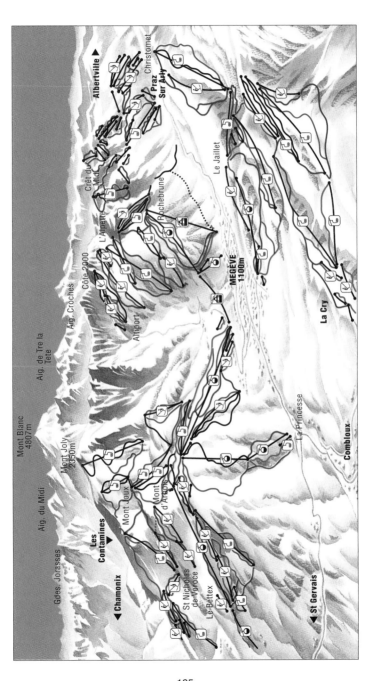

by cable-car. Mont d'Arbois is the most extensive and in turn is accessed by separate gondolas from La Princesse outside **Combloux**, **Le Bettex** above **St-Gervais**, and **St-Nicolas-de-Véroce**. The skiing around Mont d'Arbois is mainly gentle, although some more challenging runs are higher up on Mont Joux.

The only access to the Rochebrune area used to be by Megève's original cable-car, which was built in 1933 and still runs from the outskirts. The less creaky alternative is a swift 12-person gondola which starts from the town centre. Rochebrune offers arguably the most attractive runs in the area in delightful tree-lined settings, and reporters claim that it is less crowded than Mont d'Arbois.

Megève's third skiing area is Le Jaillet, which is completely self-contained and reached by gondola only after a lengthy walk or ski-bus ride from the middle of town. Its runs are mainly gentle and do not hold their snow well.

Piste-grading in the area, according to reporters, is not always consistent: some black (difficult) runs are said to be easier than the red (intermediate) trails due to careful grooming, while some blue (easy) runs have difficult sections.

Beginners

The nursery slopes at Mont d'Arbois are easily accessible by cable-car or ski bus. The resort also abounds in green (beginner) slopes and gentle blues for the next stage of learning. From Mont Joux, long easy runs descend to Les Communailles near Le Bettex, with drag-lifts back up to the ridge. The runs into Megève itself are mostly wide and easy and include a long green piste. There is a drag-lift in the trees at the top-station of Le Jaillet for novices, and the runs in this area are both mild and pleasant, being suited mainly to beginners and early intermediates.

Intermediates

The scope of skiing at Mont d'Arbois has been greatly increased by the chair-lift rising over an open slope to the highest point of the area at 2350m. A choice of long and fairly gentle red runs takes you down into the attractive little village of St-Nicolas-de-Véroce. The large ski area is well suited to intermediates, although lack of snow makes the season a short one.

Advanced

Megève is not recommended for advanced snow-users, although, provided you have a car, this is the most pleasant resort in the Mont Blanc area in which to base yourself to enjoy the 13 resorts (including **Chamonix** and **Argentière)** covered by the Ski Pass Mont Blanc. Mont Joux, the next peak along from Mont d'Arbois, on the ridge that climbs towards Mont Joly, has some of the steeper slopes around the bowl. The pistes on the north-facing La Princesse side of the mountain are wooded and more challenging than most in the area, but the black grading is not altogether justified.

From the top of the gondola at Rochebrune, further lifts take you on up to Alpette, the start of Megève's downhill course. The highest point, Côte 2000, provides some of the toughest skiing in the area.

Off-piste
The area through the trees towards La Princesse provides excellent powder skiing after a fresh snowfall, as does Côte 2000. The off-piste is far less skied than in most of the other Mont Blanc resorts and is therefore likely to remain untracked for far longer. You can also ski from the top of Mont Joly, after a 20-minute uphill walk, over to the resort of **Les Contamines-Montjoie.**

Tuition and guiding
Megève's ski schools have fine reputations, particularly for beginners, who progress speedily from the nursery areas to the long and flattering easy and intermediate slopes. 'I can't praise the ESI enough,' said one reporter, 'My father, who is in his 70s and not very fit, felt very confident after three lessons'. The resort has its own guiding company, Bureau des Guides de Megève, which is warmly recommended. Its 16 mountain guides take skiers off-piste and organise ski-tours in the area.

Both the French (ESF) and International (ESI) ski schools offer group courses for all standards of snowboarder. The ESF also runs special snowboarding classes for children.

Cross-country
Langlaufers have a choice of four circuits totalling 75km, including a long, tricky but wonderfully scenic track from the Mont d'Arbois cable-car to Le Bettex and St-Nicolas-de-Véroce; another links with the resort of **Praz-sur-Arly.** Unusual activities for cross-country enthusiasts include one-day guided outings off-piste between Val d'Arly and Beaufortain, plus night cross-country racing through the village streets.

Mountain restaurants
Megève certainly has no shortage of lunch venues, adding to its gourmet attraction. The ski area is home to about 30, most of which are marked on a special walker/cross-country skier lift map. However, reporters note that eating on the mountain is expensive. Particularly recommended is a trip to the Alpette restaurant. Its position on the piste high above the Rochebrune cable-car and gondola station would normally restrict its customers to skiers, but the restaurant runs a 45FF snowcat service from the lift station. L'Auberge du Grenand, also in the Rochebrune area towards Praz-sur-Arly, offers typically French cuisine and local specialities. Radaz Ferme Auberge has 'a great atmosphere but slow service, so go early'.

In the Mont d'Arbois sector, Côte 2000 restaurant is recommended for 'fresh, well-cooked food'. Le Rosay is a 'reasonable self-service with an excellent balcony'. Chalet Idéal Sport, a popular place for the fur-coated, at the top of La Princesse gondola has superb food and 'not

prohibitive' prices. Les Mandarines has 'first-class food in perfect surroundings'. L'Igloo ('pricey but excellent, particularly if you are a cheese
addict') has a terrace with magnificent views of Mont Blanc.

The resort

Megève has grown to become one of France's largest ski towns, with a
mass of suburbs stretching out in all directions. The attractive medieval
heart is made up of a traffic-free main square with four streets branching
off it, all teeming with an 'abundance of fur coats and matching dogs'.
Reporters praise the town as 'a window-shopper's paradise'. This includes
jewellers, perfumeries, delicatessen, antique shops, chocolate-makers,
children's clothing shops, designer boutiques ('cashmere dressing gowns
at 68,000 francs') and popular fashion outlets such as Poivre Blanc,
Cacharel and Benetton, as well as the famous Aallard department store.

Traffic is a problem, particularly during the main window-shopping
hours of between 4 and 7pm; a main road runs through the town,
although the actual centre is bypassed. Ski buses link the mid-town with
the lifts, and coaches run to other nearby resorts covered on the Mont
Blanc lift pass. Megève is one of the easiest of the Mont Blanc ski resorts
to reach. Not only is it close to Geneva (70km) but it also has two
Motorail termini close by at Sallanches and at St-Gervais.

Accommodation

Megève has more than 50 hotels, as well as both sumptuous and more
utilitarian private chalets. The standard of its six four-stars and some of
its 15 three-stars is outstanding. Chalet du Mont d'Arbois is located
some distance from the town near the Mont d'Arbois cable-car. The
Hotel Mont Blanc, owned and interior-designed by Jocelyne and Jean-
Louis Sibuet, is now one of the finest hotels in Europe. The style is very
New England, and each of the 43 rooms is individually decorated. At the
bottom of La Princesse ski area is the four-star Hotel Princesse de
Megève, which has only 14 rooms.

Les Fermes de Marie, another Sibuet-owned hotel, is a ten-minute
walk from the centre of town. The
heart of the hotel is a sixteenth-century
cow shed with vaulted ceiling; a collection of farm buildings in the grounds
have been converted into luxury suites.
The hotel has a fitness and beauty centre with a swimming-pool. The
four-star Lodge Parc de Megève has recently been bought and restored
by the Sibuets; it boasts 53 bedrooms and the atmosphere of a private
club. Le Fer à Cheval is a centrally placed chalet-style hotel. We also have
good reports of Hotel Au Coin du Feu and La Chauminé. Hotel Le
Sévigné is 'cheap and has a great atmosphere'.

Megève is not for those who count their centimes, but budget-con-
scious visitors would be wise to stay in one of the self-catering résidences
such as Gollet or Richmond.

> **WHAT'S NEW**
>
> Lodge Parc de Megève hotel refurbished

Eating in and out

A reporter comments on the 'extensive quantity and variety of eating places to suit all budgets'. This is certainly true; Megève has more than 70 restaurants and is, along with Courchevel 1850, one of the gourmet dining centres of the French Alps. However, it also offers a reasonable choice of less exotic places. Le Bar du Chamois is a lively bistro with local white wines and fondues. Good-value restaurants include Les Griottes, which has à la carte specialities, and La Maisonnette. La Sapinière and Tire Bouchon are both warmly praised.

At the top of the range, the Hotel Mont Blanc's Les Enfants Terribles has 'delicious but expensive food'. The Chalet du Mont d'Arbois used to be the Rothschild family home and is now a high-quality restaurant with interesting wines. Les Fermes de Marie offers good Savoyard cooking, and Le Fer à Cheval serves a fine dinner but is also recommended for its English breakfast. Le Phnom Penh offers unusual Cambodian food. Crêperie Grand Marnier and Marroniers Chez Maria are both recommended for crêpes.

Après-ski

This is taken almost more seriously here than the skiing, and the choice of venues is enormous, ranging from the simplest of bars to the most exotic of nightspots. The Milady, which has 'delectable apple tart', and Le Prieuré are recommended for tea and cakes at 5pm. Le Chamois is a traditional place with a warm atmosphere. The Village Rock Café is popular with teenagers.

Later on the nightlife is not cheap and revolves largely around Megève's piano bars and nine nightclubs. Club de Jazz Les Cinq Rues is one of the most popular evening venues, set in cosy surroundings complete with open fire; during the season it attracts some of the big international names in jazz. Bar St Paul is 'cheap and frequented by locals'. The casino, originally a 1930s bus station, has been given a new look and also houses a restaurant.

The most popular nightclubs include L'Esquinade, which is also a casino with Sacha Distel and Charles Aznavour among its regulars. Le Rols Club is the place for those who like their evening entertainment on the decadent side. The Glamour is half piano bar and half disco. Les Caves de Megève has a young atmosphere. The Pallas and Harri's bar are open until dawn.

The Palais de Sports contains an Olympic-size skating-rink and a vast swimming-pool; you can also learn to curl, rock climb and trampoline. Electric-powered ice-bumping cars are a new sport available on the skating-rink.

Childcare

In keeping with its family values, Megève has some of the most comprehensive childcare facilities of any resort in France, with a separate ski kindergarten conveniently situated at the foot of each ski area. The non-ski kindergarten, Meg'Loisirs, is housed in a well-equipped two-storey

Skiing facts: Megève

TOURIST OFFICE
BP 24, F-74120 Megève, Haute Savoie
Tel 33 4 50 21 27 28
Fax 33 4 50 93 03 09
Email megeve@laposte.fr

THE RESORT
By road Calais 890km
By rail Sallanches and St-Gervais,
regular bus service to resort
Airport transfer Geneva 1½hrs
Visitor beds 13,330
Transport free ski bus with lift pass

THE SKIING
Linked or nearby resorts Chamonix (n),
Combloux (l), Flumet (n), Le Bettex (l),
Les Contamines-Montjoie (n), Les
Saisies (n), Notre-Dame-de-Bellecombe
(n), Praz-sur-Arly (n), St-Gervais (l),
St-Nicolas-de-Véroce (l)
Longest run Milloz, 3.6km (red)
Number of lifts 82 in Megève, 190 in
Mont Blanc ski area
Total of trails/pistes 300km in Megève
(30% easy, 45% intermediate, 25%
difficult), 700km in Mont Blanc ski area
Nursery slopes 4 runs and 4 lifts
Summer skiing none
Snowmaking 60 hectares covered

LIFT PASSES
Area pass Ski Pass Mont Blanc (covers
region),1,080FF for 6 days
Day pass Megève only 159FF, Ski Pass
Mont Blanc 230FF
Beginners single lift tickets available
Pensioners 60 yrs and over as children
Credit cards yes

TUITION
Adults ESF (5 centres), 9.30–11.30am,
490FF for 6 half-days. ESI, 10am–

midday, 580FF for 6 half-days
Private lessons ESF 185FF, ESI 200FF,
both per hr
Snowboarding ESF 875FF, ESI
680–780FF, both for 6 half-days
Cross-country ESF (Mont d'Arbois), as
regular ski school. Loipe 75km
Other courses telemark, monoski, race
training, freestyle, off-piste, heli-skiing
Guiding Bureau des Guides de Megève,
and through ESI

CHILDREN
Lift pass Ski Pass Mont Blanc, 12yrs and
under, 756FF for 6 days. Free for 4yrs
and under (pass required on cable-cars)
Ski kindergarten Alpage, 3–6yrs,
9.15am–5.15pm, 390FF per day.
Princesse, 3–6yrs, 9am–5pm, 280FF per
day. Caboche, 3–10yrs, 9am–5.30pm,
350FF per day. (All prices include lunch).
ESI, as regular ski school
Ski school ESF, 5–12yrs, 9.30–11.30am
and 3–5pm, 750FF for 6 days. ESI, 4–12
yrs, 10am–midday and 3–5pm, 875FF
for 6 days. ESI Club 7 (max 7 children),
1–3pm, 780FF for 5 days
Non-ski kindergarten Meg'Loisirs,
1–6yrs, 8am–6pm, 210FF per day
including lunch

OTHER SPORTS
Parapente, hang-gliding, skating, curling,
indoor tennis, climbing wall,
snowmobiling, snowshoeing, winter walks,
dog-sledding, snow polo, ice hockey,
sleigh rides, swimming, night-skiing,
snow-biking, light-aircraft flights

FOOD AND DRINK PRICES
Coffee 12FF, glass of wine 10–14FF,
small beer 18–23FF, dish of the day
75FF

building next to the Palais de Sports. Creative children who want to take a break from skiing can attend Megève Matériaux, run by Marie-Christine Ours on the outskirts of town. Here, 6- to 13-year-olds can try their hand at stencilling, painting on wood and fabric, plaster moulding and lots more for 85FF per morning.

Linked or nearby resorts

Les Contamines-Montjoie
top 2500m (8,202ft) bottom 1164m (3,818ft)

This unspoilt Savoyard village is near the head of the narrow Montjoie Valley just over the hill from Megève. It has a keen following despite the fact that the whole set-up is badly planned; the long village is on one side of the river and the ski area on the other, and Le Lay base-station is a kilometre-long uphill walk from the centre. However, a shuttle bus runs between the village and the gondolas. Prices here are, on the whole, below average for this area of France, and the accommodation is modest.

The east-facing bowl, which makes up the ski area, tends to hold its snow well and offers a good alternative when neighbouring resorts like Megève have none. We have experienced some excellent and virtually untouched powder all over the area after a fresh snowfall.

Two efficient gondolas, Auberge du Télé and Le Pontet (reporters recommend the latter as it is further down the valley and therefore less busy) take skiers up to a plateau at 1470m, where the gondola to Le Signal and the start of the main skiing can become a bottleneck. The parallel chair does not take you as high. The small nursery lift at Le Signal at 1900m can often be busy when snow is poor on the L'Etape nursery slopes at 1500m.

Of the 44 runs, half are intermediate; the higher runs towards Mont Joly are steeper and more testing. A large number are spread around a vast, mainly northeast-facing bowl behind Le Signal. The Col du Joly at 2000m separates the main bowl from a smaller but open area. The six mountain restaurants include the rather basic one at Le Signal, which has views of Mont Blanc. However, one reporter found it 'crowded, even on a quiet day, with no charm,' and another calls it 'the pits'. Ferme La Ruelle is a 'rather rustic establishment, which is worth a visit'. Another of the mountain eateries, Auberge de Colombaz, is on an off-piste itinerary towards the village.

The village runs along a single street with an old church, old-fashioned hotels and a few shops and cafés. The best location is on the east side of the river near the gondola. The Chemenaz is the only three-star hotel; the rest have one or two stars, and there is a wide variety of self-catering apartments. The 18 restaurants include half-a-dozen crêperies. Two well-stocked supermarkets cater for those staying in apartments. Nightlife is severely limited ('virtually dead after 7pm') with a skating rink, two discos and concerts in the village church being the only entertainment.

La Galipette garderie, housed in an attractive wooden chalet, accepts children from one to seven years old and can combine its service with half-day ski lessons.

TOURIST OFFICE
Tel 33 4 50 47 01 58
Fax 33 4 50 47 09 54
Email les.contamines@wanadoo.fr
Web site www.lescontamines.com

St-Gervais
top 2350m (7,708ft) bottom 850m (2,788ft))

As a spa, St-Gervais has attracted tourists since 1806. The town is an informal if busy one. It is popular with families wanting a cheaper alternative to Megève. A reporter recommends it as an ideal base for visiting other resorts in France, Italy and Switzerland. Nearby Le Bettex at 1400m is a quieter village with a few comfortable hotels and some cross-country skiing.

The main ski area of St-Gervais is on the slopes of Mont d'Arbois and is linked with that of Megève. It now has a funpark with half-pipe, and the area is accessed by a fast, 20-person gondola from the edge of the resort to Le Bettex. The second stage goes up to what is known on this side of the mountain as St-Gervais 1850. This is a popular and often crowded entrance to Megève's ski area. Skiing on the Mont Blanc side of St-Gervais is served by the Tramway, a funicular that climbs slowly to the Col de Voza at 1653m, where it links to the skiing above **Les Houches.** The only run back to St-Gervais is off-piste and sometimes unskiable. Hotel-Restaurant Igloo and the Terminus in Le Fayet area both have good reputations for their cuisine.

St-Gervais has three nursery-slope lifts and its own kindergarten, which takes children between six months and six years old. The ESF St-Gervais and ESI at Le Bettex both teach snowboarding, monoski, telemark, slalom and off-piste, as well as the usual group classes. There is also a local mountain guiding company.

Hotels here include the Carlina which has a swimming-pool, the Val d'Este and the Edelweiss. A reporter recommends the Regina, with its simple rooms, reasonable prices and friendly staff. At Le Bettex, the quiet Arbois-Bettex has a heated outdoor swimming-pool, and the Flèche d'Or is also recommended. St-Gervais has a moderate range of restaurants, with two of particularly good value: 4 Epices and L'Eterle. Le Four and Le Robinson are popular eating places serving a variety of local specialities. La Tanière and La Chalette are traditional. Après-ski is said to be 'extremely limited'. The only disco is La Nuit des Temps, although the Chardon Bleu restaurant in Le Fayet has a dance floor.

TOURIST OFFICE
Tel 33 4 50 93 48 07
Fax 33 4 50 93 54 34
Web site www.saintgervais.com

La Plagne

ALTITUDE 1250–2100m (4,100–6,889ft)

Beginners ✷✷✷ Intermediates ✷✷✷ Advanced ✷ Snowboarders ✷✷✷

La Plagne, which for 30 years has maintained its position as France's most popular mass-market resort, is now struggling to project a fresh image in the face of increasing competition from its neighbours. However, it remains one of the greatest of all the intermediate playgrounds in the Alps, with statistics that speak for themselves: 113 lifts, which are being upgraded steadily as finance allows, serving 211km of groomed piste, of which 66 per cent is classified as easy. Combine this with guaranteed snow at the top altitude of 3250m and a vertical drop of 2000m, and the result should be a near-perfect destination for intermediate skiers and snowboarders.

Indeed, skiing convenience is so superior that the resort regularly heads the popularity charts in the French domestic market: 70 per cent of La Plagne's snow-users are French, and the British make up 37 per cent of all foreign visitors.

> ✔ Large integrated ski area
> ✔ Skiing convenience
> ✔ Beautiful scenery
> ✔ Extensive off-piste
> ✔ Geared to family skiing
> ✔ Summer skiing on the glacier
> ✘ Limited hotel accommodation
> ✘ Shortage of non-skiing activities
> ✘ Limited nightlife
> ✘ Some satellites lacking in atmosphere

In spite of all of this, La Plagne is stuck with the image of having cheap apartments in buildings reminiscent of 1960s urban shopping centres. In Val d'Isère and Tignes the municipal health authority insists on a minimum living space, but in the older parts of La Plagne it is still possible to find the 18-m square unit in which four people are expected to spend a week.

A total of 27 tour operators offer holidays here in villages and accommodation of vastly varying character and quality, so it is vital to choose both with care.

La Plagne's six high-altitude villages lie in the central area at altitudes ranging from 1800m to 2100m. In the order in which they were built, they are **Plagne Centre** (built in 1961–2), **Aime La Plagne** (1970), **Plagne Villages/Plagne Soleil** (1972), **Plagne Bellecôte** (1974), **Belle Plagne** (1980) and **Plagne 1800** (1981). Most people agree that Belle Plagne is the most attractive of the resort's purpose-built villages. The four lower villages, **Montchavin**, **Montalbert**, **Les Coches** and **Champagny-en-Vanoise,** lie on different access roads in far-flung parts of the mountain but all are connected with the central complex by lift.

Although the farming village of Montchavin was adapted to become a satellite ski resort in the early 1970s, a rural smell still lingers in the air. It has a gondola link to neighbouring Les Coches, which is a modern ski complex with its own wooded slopes.

Champagny-en-Vanoise, at the base of the south-facing back side of the mountain, is a series of hamlets in a quiet valley linked to the ski area by an efficient gondola. Montalbert and its satellite holiday centre have inferior snow conditions on west-facing slopes in the immediate vicinity and less convenient connections into the main bowl.

Ski and board
top 3250m (10,660ft) bottom 1250m (4,100ft)

La Plagne represents the ultimate in ski-in ski-out convenience. To point your skis in any direction from the nexus in Plagne Centre is to lock into the network of lifts on the shallow gradients of La Grande Rochette, Les Verdons and Le Biolley. The Bellecôte gondola provides the most efficient connection with Roche de Mio, a steeper mountain with more challenging terrain; from here you can take the lift up to the Bellecôte Glacier, which is the highest point in the resort. The Montchavin/Les Coches area is connected to the central arena through Arpette, a direct quad-chair ride from Bellecôte. The predominantly wooded Plagne Montalbert-Longefoy pistes lie on the other side of the resort below Aime La Plagne. Access to Champagny-en-Vanoise is via Les Verdons, the mid-way point on the rim of the main bowl, or Roche de Mio.

With 113 lifts, which include five swift six-seater chairs, La Plagne has few queues in good weather, but the links to the outlying areas close down rapidly as soon as storms move in, causing congestion in the centre. Reporters have mixed views on the lift map, ranging from 'easy to follow, the signposting is good and the pistes are well groomed' to 'the ski map was one of the worst I have come across. It does not indicate that there is a substantial ridge between the main valley and the Bellecôte, Roche de Mio and beyond'. La Plagne has 100km of marked cross-country trails in the lower villages but only 11km spread between the high-altitude satellites.

Beginners

With the exception of Champagny-en-Vanoise, all parts of the mountain have extensive beginner slopes. Those in the other three low-altitude villages gain in visibility by being below the tree-line, but this is balanced by less reliable snow conditions, especially in spring when the slopes are icy in the morning. Aesthetics aside, there can be no more encouraging place to learn to ski than La Plagne's central area in fine weather. The pistes on either side of the Arpette ridge above Bellecôte offer gradients so gentle that even the most fearful novice should gain in confidence, while the web of blue (easy) runs between Belle Plagne and Plagne Centre make for a natural second-week progression.

Dôme de Bellecôte 3416m

Glacier de Bellecôte 3250m

Le Grande Motte 3650m

Le Grande Casse 3852m

La Grande Rochette 2505m

Le Verdons 2500m

Le Becoin 2594m

Le Biolley 2350m

Aime La Plagne 2100m

Le Fornelet 1970m

Plagne Montalbert 1350m

PLAGNE CENTRE 1970m

Plagne 1800m

Champagny ▶

Roche de Mio 2700m

Plagne Soleil 2050m

BELLE PLAGNE 2050m

Plagne Bellecôte 1930m

L'Arpette 2400m

Dos Rond 2300m

Les Coches 1450m

Les Bauches 1800m

Montchavin 1250m

Intermediates

As befits a state-of-the-art ski area, La Plagne offers most to those snow-users dedicated to racking up the kilometres. This can be done most readily on the red (intermediate) runs on the eastern side of the bowl above Aime La Plagne. However, Roche de Mio has more varied terrain, with the run back to Belle Plagne via a long tunnel particularly recommended. An adventurous alternative is the Crozats piste down to Les Bauches 1800, which has a link back to the main circus via two chair-lifts. The summer ski drag-lifts at the top of the glacier are not usually open in winter, but La Combe and Le Chiaupe runs to the Bellecôte gondola base-station hold no terrors for committed motorway cruisers. Enterprising intermediates will enjoy the exhilarating Mont de la Guerre run from Les Verdons to Champagny-en-Vanoise, but check conditions first as the descent is extremely rocky when snow is sparse. The same applies to the more wooded route from the Roche de Mio, via Les Borseliers.

Advanced

The resort has a general lack of black (difficult) runs, with most pistes described as 'fairly intermediate'. One reporter commented: 'this is definitely a family resort – tough runs are scarce. However, the wide pistes and the lift system are ideal for snowboarders'. Although glaciers are not generally known for steep skiing, La Plagne's is one of the exceptions. The disadvantage is the 45-minute trek to the top from the centre of the resort, but once in place advanced skiers and snowboarders will find plenty to test them, especially the black Bellecôte and Le Rochu runs to the bottom of the Chalet de Bellecôte chair. The other steep area is off Le Biolley ridge above Aime La Plagne. When conditions are good (which often they are not), the Morbleu piste is a compellingly direct drop to Le Fornelet cross-country area; return is via the Coqs chair. On the east-facing side of the ridge, the Emile Allais descent to the bottom of the outlying Charmettes chair at the side of the Olympic bob run is the longest black run in the resort. Riders congregate at the Col de Forcle snowpark between Plagne Bellecôte and Plagne Village.

Off-piste

If La Plagne is not a favourite among dedicated powder skiers and snowboarders, it is because of its lack of ambience rather than lack of opportunity. As with the advanced pistes, the best areas are on the fringes of the resort, with the long, sweeping descent from the top of the glacier down to Les Bauches high on most experienced snow-users' lists. From here, the choice lies between an easy blue piste to Montchavin, a return to Arpette via the Bauches chair or, more dramatically, an itinerary down to **Peisey-Nancroix** in the adjacent valley. The other prime off-piste area lies on the western slopes of Le Biolley; it is especially enjoyable towards the end of the season, when spring snow is at its best. The back of the Bellecôte Glacier offers the demanding Col du Nant run into the remote valley of **Champagny-le-Haut**, followed by a return to Champagny-en-Vanoise by shuttle bus. The woods above Montchavin and Les Coches provide exciting powder skiing in the trees, but access is often restricted, at least as far as downtown La Plagne is concerned, by the closure of the link through Arpette.

Tuition and guiding

The French Ski School (ESF) has offices spread throughout the resort. The numbers wanting to learn are so great that one reporter said the process of dividing up beginners into separate classes was 'reminiscent of a cattle market with up to 16 steers in each'. On the plus side the volume of business means that the ESF has been able to introduce teenage ski classes for greater peer-group pleasure. It also has guided off-piste courses in La Plagne and the surrounding outposts of the Tarentaise Valley. One reporter criticised the ESF half-day children's courses for their timing, which was 'altered due to the Parisian holidays to an extremely inconvenient 12.30 to 3pm. My son was in an all-French class with an instructor who spoke little English'. Other ski schools are Elpro at Belle Plagne and Evolution 2 at Montchavin; we also have good reports of Oxygène at Plagne Centre, where instructors are said to be 'friendly and professional'. Oxygène offers a free, 45-minute introduction to snowboarding at the end of the day at Plagne Centre.

Mountain restaurants

In an area that is not known for its mountain restaurants, there are two outstanding choices. The Au Bon Vieux Temps, just below Aime La Plagne, is recommended for its sunny terrace, traditional Savoyard dishes and efficient service. The Petit Chaperon Rouge, on the edge of the nursery slope just above Plagne 1800 ('quiet, pleasant, with nice food for a reasonable price') is the wiser choice on a snowy day because of its open fires. Good value is represented by the Dou du Praz above Plagne Villages and La Rossa at the top of the Champagny gondola. Reporters favour Chez Pat du Sauget, an old summer farm on the pastures above Montchavin, which has recently been elevated to auberge status, with the addition of simple bedrooms. Polly's, next to the skating rink at Plagne Bellecôte, is said to have 'wonderful food – the Salad Blue is fantastic and it is reasonably priced in general'. The Bec Fin in Plagne Centre is recommended by reporters for its omelettes and is described as value-for-money. The Plan Bois, above Les Coches, has 'rustic charm and is a great spot for lunch'.

> **WHAT'S NEW**
>
> Drag-lifts between Champagny, Plagne Centre, and Plagne Bellecôte ski areas replaced by a six-seater chair
> Snowpark at Col de Forcle
> A second Balcons de Belle Plagne résidence and new apartments at Plagne Soleil

The resort

La Plagne's success lies in its diversity: whatever visitors want, they will be sure to find it somewhere. As far as modern architecture is concerned, the later the better: Belle Plagne's attractive village centre, with its integrated arcs of apartment buildings, is a fine example of imaginative design, while the low-rise wood-clad complexes at Plagne 1800 and Plagne Villages are inspired by Savoyard tradition. These are a far cry from the monolithic 'battleship' at Aime La Plagne or the square slabs at Plagne Centre. Aime's apartments are currently being redecorated, although no one is prepared to knock two into one to extend the size of the cramped studios, as this would mean losing lucrative business.

Skiing facts: La Plagne

TOURIST OFFICE
Le Chalet, BP 62, 73211, Aime Cedex
Tel 33 4 79 09 79 79
Fax 33 4 79 09 70 10
Email ot.laplagne@wanadoo.fr
Web site www.skifrance.fr/~laplagne
UK Agent Erna Low (see *Which tour operator?*)

THE RESORT
By road Calais 930km
By rail Aime 18km
Airport transfer Lyon 2hrs, Geneva 3hrs
Visitor beds 45,000
Transport inter-resort link by télébus, télémetro and télécabine (15FF return). Free ski bus between Plagne 1800, Plagne Centre and Bellecôte

THE SKIING
Linked or nearby resorts Les Arcs (n), Peisey (n), Vallandry (n), Trois Vallées (n), Val d'Isère (n), Tignes (n)
Longest run Roche de Mio–Montchavin, 10km (red)
Number of lifts 113
Total of trails/pistes 211km (66% easy, 28% intermediate, 6% difficult)
Nursery slopes 1 lift in each centre
Summer skiing 4 lifts and 2 runs on Bellecôte Glacier open July and August
Snowmaking mobile snow-cannon at Montalbert, Les Coches and Montchavin

LIFT PASSES
Area pass 1,005FF for 6 days (covers Les Arcs and 1 day in L'Espace Killy or Trois Vallées)
Day pass 216FF
Beginners free lift in each centre
Pensioners 754FF for 60–72yrs, free thereafter
Credit cards yes

TUITION
Adults ESF in all centres, Evolution 2 (Montchavin), Oxygène (Plagne Centre), Elpro (Belle Plagne) all 170FF per half-day, 850FF for 6 days
Private lessons 185FF per hr, 690FF for 3hrs, 1,300FF per day
Snowboarding ESF, 850FF for 5 x 3hrs, 210FF per half day. Oxygène (Plagne Centre) 780FF for 3 days,1,380FF for 6 days, Elpro (Belle Plagne) prices and times on application
Cross-country as regular ski school. Loipe 111km in area
Other courses off-piste, speed skiing, ski-touring, teenager lessons, freestyle, heli-skiing, monoski, telemark, disabled
Guiding through ESF

CHILDREN
Lift pass 7–15yrs, 755FF for 6 days, free for 7yrs and under
Ski kindergarten ESF in all 10 villages, 1,260FF for 6 days including lunch, crèche at Plagne Centre from 3mths
Ski school ESF in all villages for under 14yrs, times as adults,1,260FF for 6 days including lunch
Non-ski kindergarten in all villages, times, prices and ages vary, example: ESF Belle Plagne, 18mths–3yrs, 1,110FF for 6 days including lunch

OTHER SPORTS
Snowmobiling, snowshoeing, freestyle stadium, night-skiing, parapente, swimming, skating, bob-rafting, taxi-bob, bobsleigh, squash, hang-gliding, paragliding, climbing wall, winter walks

FOOD AND DRINK
Coffee 15FF, glass of wine 20FF, small beer 18–20FF, dish of the day 65FF

Bellecôte's semi-circle of high-rise reddish blocks is an acquired taste. Belle Plagne is the firm favourite. Inevitably, the complexities of the area are confusing at first, which may explain why regulars prefer to book the same apartment in the same block from one year to the next, rather than take a chance on unknown territory. All ten villages are self-sufficient, with their own selection of shops, bars and restaurants. The six high villages are connected by bus or covered lifts from 8am to 1am. As its name suggests, Plagne Centre has the lion's share of essential services – banks, a post office, police and doctors – in the environs of its bleak, subterranean commercial precinct. Aesthetic it is not, but it scores high for convenience, as does Bellecôte, which also has banks and a post office.

Accommodation

Two-thirds of La Plagne's 45,000 beds are in the high-altitude villages, and one-third are in the satellites down the valley. Only eight per cent of all accommodation is in hotels, so the vast majority of visitors opt for self-catering apartments. Many are owned by Maeva or Pierre et Vacances – studio-style rabbit hutches with bunks in the passage and sofas that convert into beds in the only living area. The Centaur apartments at Belle Plagne have 'awkward-shaped studios with a fixed bed under the window which is too cold to sleep in. They are poorly equipped, with no cooking utensils and a microwave without suitable dishes to use in it'. However, property owners have been offered grants and free lift passes to upgrade their old-fashioned apartments, but as a spokesperson for the tourist board said: 'We can make the apartments more attractive but we cannot do anything about their size'. As with the architecture, newer tends to be better (and more spacious), which gives the edge to Plagne Soleil and Plagne 1800. The Hotel Eldorador is the only high-altitude hotel in the resort, with ski-in ski-out convenience being its main advantage, but otherwise suitable for a no-frills family holiday with, according to one reporter, 'very good food and wine included in the net price'.

Club Alpina, in Champagny-en-Vanoise, is a chalet-style building containing apartments. It is recommended for its sports centre with swimming-pool and for its restaurant. Les Balcons de Belle Plagne is a résidence/hotel, which provides much-needed high-quality accommodation. The luxurious Chalet/Hotel Les Montagnettes in Belle Plagne represents a welcome wind of change with its chalets and apartments of varying sizes; they can be rented for self-catering or with full hotel services. Self-caterers in search of a taste of rural France can rent one of 200 gîtes on the lower slopes of La Plagne. They are rated as normal, comfortable or luxurious and cost about half the price of the higher, purpose-built accommodation.

Eating in and out

La Soupe aux Schuss in Aime La Plagne is an expensive restaurant serving specialities from the Périgord region. Le Matafan in Belle Plagne stays closer to home, with a range of medium-priced Savoyard dishes including raclette and fondue. Le Loup Garou, a short sleigh ride (or walk) down the path from Plagne Centre to Plagne 1800, serves similar dishes in a festive atmosphere. However, as one reporter put it: 'La Plagne is definitely not a gastronome's resort'. All the villages have supermarkets for the self-catering brigade, but there is a shortage of specialist food shops.

Après-ski

By comparison with its Tarentaise neighbours, Val d'Isère and Courchevel, La Plagne's nightlife is decidedly low profile. ('Our pack of cards was quite well used.') Clubs are confined to Plagne Centre and Bellecôte. The current favourites in Plagne Centre are Le King Café, which has live music most nights, and Le Must disco. Le Mat's Pub is a faithful recreation of a British pub, making it a winner among Brits staying in Belle Plagne ('popular with holidaymakers and workers alike. I have seen people in there at 1am still in ski gear and ski boots'). The watering-hole of choice in Bellecôte is Le Show Time Café/Le Jet Discotheque, while the Lincoln is the winner in Plagne Soleil. The most exhilarating non-skiing activity in La Plagne is the Olympic bob-run, which is open to the public whenever conditions permit. The Taxi-Bob is the genuine experience, with two rookies sandwiched between a professional driver and a brake man for a breathtaking 50-second descent at speeds of up to 105km per hour ('£50 for less than a minute of sheer terror seems a lot to pay'). The softer option is the Bob-Raft, a four-man, foam-rubber cocoon that hurtles down in gravity-propelled mode in 90 seconds.

Childcare

The ESF has learn-to-ski programmes for children aged two to seven in specially designed snow gardens in all of the villages. 'We found the Belle Plagne kindergarten to be both friendly and flexible. However, in practice the one at Bellecôte involves less walking for toddlers'. The Montchavin/Les Coches nursery has a mixed programme of skiing and other learning activities for children aged three and upwards.

La Plagne has ten nurseries for toddlers and upwards; those in Montchavin/Les Coches, Belle Plagne and Plagne Centre accept children as young as nine months old. The Eldorador Hotel has its Mini-Eldo children's club (4- to12-year-olds) from 9am to 5pm, plus a supervised children's table in the hotel restaurant and babysitting by arrangement in the evening.

Portes du Soleil

ALTITUDE Avoriaz 1800m (5,904ft), Châtel 1200m (3,936ft),
Morzine 1000m (3,280ft)

Beginners ✱✱✱ Intermediates ✱✱✱ Advanced ✱✱ Snowboarders ✱✱✱

The Portes du Soleil might be considered as one of Europe's greatest overall ski areas were it not for one major fault: it is too low. With a top height of only 2350m and the villages mostly below 1200m, snow cover is by no means guaranteed at any stage of the season, and the links are liable to rupture at any time. Nevertheless, it is one of Europe's three largest circuits. It straddles the French–Swiss border close to Geneva and is an uneasy marketing consortium of a baker's dozen of ski villages; these range from large, internationally recognised resorts to the tiniest of unspoilt hamlets. The published statistics talk about 650km of piste served by 219 lifts, a well-linked circus covering vast tracts of land bordered by Lac Léman; in reality Les Portes du Soleil consists of a series of naturally separate ski areas. Most are joined by awkward and often confusing mountain links, while a few like **St-Jean d'Aulps/La Grande Terche** and **Abondance** are entirely independent.

- ✔ Large ski area
- ✔ Extensive cross-country trails
- ✔ Good childcare facilities
- ✔ Car-free resort of Avoriaz
- ✔ Short airport transfer
- ✘ Low altitude (except Avoriaz)
- ✘ Few activities for non-skiers
- ✘ Lack of skiing convenience (Morzine)

While it is possible to complete a tour of the main resorts in one day, this actually involves limited enjoyable skiing and a considerable amount of time spent on lifts. To explore the region fully, you need four weeks, at least two bases, a car and exceptional snow conditions.

Out of the 13 resorts, only Avoriaz can be recommended as a snow-sure base and, when cover is poor or non-existent elsewhere, the over-crowding here becomes a complete misery. However, keen skiers and snowboarders should base themselves at this end of the circuit, where the slopes are the most challenging.

Signposting has been vastly improved, as has the overall Portes du Soleil piste map, which indicates the links from area to area, as well as rather over-optimistic figures for the suggested times they take. Snow-users who want to explore more than the main circuit still, infuriatingly, have to obtain separate piste maps on arrival in each resort. After a pilot experiment the previous year, last season saw the introduction of maps depicting a series of five daily 'discovery' circuits – each illustrated by a different bird or animal – for different standards of skiers. For example, a family with small children takes the blue bear cub route, while strong skiers and snowboarders follow the black ibex signposts. The idea is to reduce piste confusion and disperse snow-users who would otherwise follow their inescapable sheep instincts. The initial verdict from one reporter was 'pretty signposts but not really very helpful at all'.

When the snow is good there are few better playgrounds in Europe for intermediate skiers and snowboarders who enjoy fast cruising and want to feel that they are actually going somewhere each day. Snow-users are advised to carry passports as well as two sets of currency; both countries accept both types of franc but not always at an advantageous rate.

Ski and board
top 2350m (7,708ft) bottom 1100m (3,608ft)

Avoriaz was the first resort in Europe to appreciate the importance of snowboarding when the sport was in the early stages of its development, and was also the first to build a half-pipe. It is now recognised as the world's snowboard capital. The resort has special areas around Arare which are set aside for a half-pipe and a slalom run. A special reduced-price restricted-area pass gives access to these facilities.

The skiing around Avoriaz is ideal for all standards of snow-users. Above the village is an extension of the main nursery slopes (Le Plateau), with a variety of drag-lifts serving a series of confidence-building green (beginner) runs, which link with the lifts coming up from Morzine. In the opposite direction are pistes down to Les Marmottes, from where lifts branch off towards Châtel; these runs are by no means always easy and are often crowded. From Les Marmottes a satisfyingly easy red (intermediate) run goes on down a beautiful gorge to Ardent, where you can take a jumbo gondola back up. This also provides a useful access point to the best skiing for those staying in Châtel, **Torgon** and the other lower resorts at this end of the system.

At the bottom of Avoriaz you are faced with three choices. Directly to the south is the main Arare sector, which from Avoriaz looks steeper than it really is; the skiing here is mainly above the tree-line. Such is the volume of traffic that the separate marked runs amalgamate to form a complete pisted face to the mountain. The runs are mainly easy, with a few more difficult pitches towards the bottom. This sector is much frequented by ski schools, and parts are often closed for slalom practice, so it can become seriously congested. A long chair-lift from the same area at the bottom of the village takes you up to Hauts Forts, which offers the most challenging skiing in Avoriaz.

Several routes take you down all or part of the way to **Les Prodains**, 650m below Avoriaz and a full 1300m vertical from Hauts Forts. The often heavily mogulled pistes here narrow considerably as you descend into the trees, and are prone to ice. The black (difficult) runs are genuinely black, and the main red from the Arare sector has an extremely testing pitch, which causes major problems for otherwise confident intermediates. The lower runs are usually busy in the late afternoon and particularly popular when visibility is poor elsewhere.

The third direction is by chair- and drag-lift to the northwest-facing

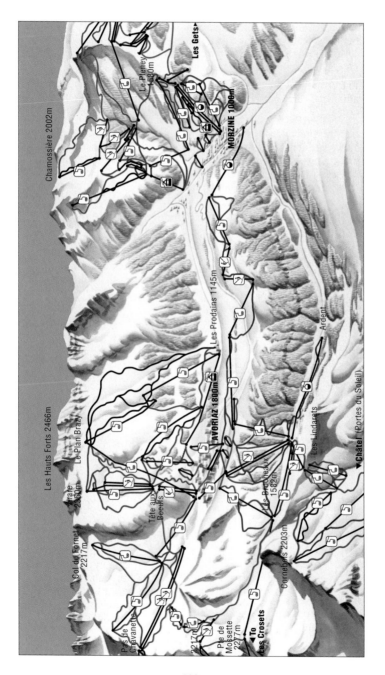

bowl between Pas de Chavanette and the Col du Fornet. This is another area of wide, open intermediate skiing above the tree-line. More adventurous snow-users can return from Chavanette through the next valley; after an initial mogul field a pleasant run leads down to Les Marmottes.

The border point, where Avoriaz meets the open pastures of the three Swiss resorts in the area, starts with the Chavanette (also known as the Wall); it is the most notorious black run in Europe, but the hype is greater than the degree of difficulty. The faint-hearted or the sensible can take the chair down in icy conditions. Below the Wall, acres of open snowfields are served by the lifts on either side of the Chavanette chair, connecting with the slopes of Planachaux above **Champéry** and with the adjacent bowl of **Les Crosets.** Planachaux is reached from Champéry by cable-car or by chair-lift from Grand-Paradis. The run down at the valley end is a delightful one, winding its way gently through sleepy hamlets and across the river against the dramatic backdrop of the Dents du Midi; snow disappears early in the season here. Irregular and crowded buses connect Grand-Paradis with Champéry.

WHAT'S NEW

Quad chair-lift from Pré-la-Joux to Plaine-Dranse

Toboggan run at Pré-la-Joux

Les Crosets sits above the tree-line surrounded by abundant wide pistes, some of them north-facing but most of them sunny. There are lifts up to the French border. The connection with **Champoussin** and **Morgins** is via the Pointe de l'Au, and a series of linked drags serve easy to intermediate pistes. The mountainside above Champoussin is wide but has little variety of terrain; the addition of a quad-chair from above Champoussin to the ridge has greatly improved the skiing. The pistes here are ideal for intermediates who need to build up their confidence.

Morgins has little skiing on the approach side from Champoussin, but it includes an excellent north-facing intermediate run cut through the woods above the village. Those who wish to continue skiing the circuit must walk across the village or take a short bus ride to the nursery slopes and the lifts for **Super-Châtel** and France. In strong contrast to the sometimes bleak ski-fields of Avoriaz and Planachaux, the pistes here wind through the trees and are connected by a series of short drag-lifts.

The Morclan chair from Super-Châtel up to 1970m serves the most challenging slope – a moderately difficult mogul field. The black piste down to the village presents no real problems provided snow cover is reasonable. The top of this chair is the departure point for Torgon, one of the further extremities of the Portes du Soleil, back across the border in Switzerland. The remainder of the skiing around Super-Châtel is mostly blue (easy) and red, on wide areas both above and below the lift station. The valley runs catch the afternoon sun and can be tricky in poor snow conditions.

The Portes du Soleil circuit breaks down at **Châtel** and whichever way you are travelling, the link cannot be made on skis. If going in a clockwise direction, a green traverse from the Linga lift delivers you to Châtel's nursery slopes, leaving you with a walk across the village to the

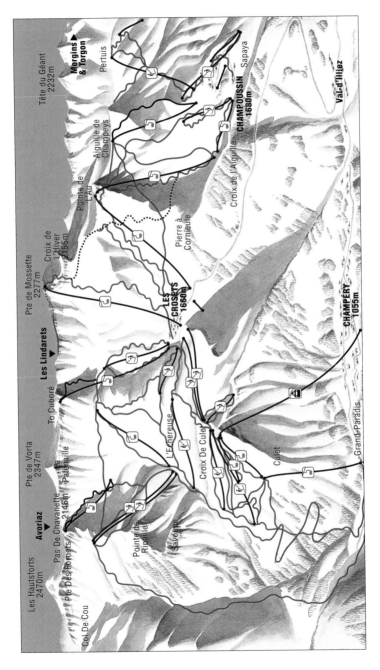

jumbo gondola for Super-Châtel. If travelling anticlockwise, a bus ride takes you from Châtel to the ten-person gondola up to Linga; this is the first of a long chain of lifts and pistes towards Avoriaz and to the new quad-chair from Pré-la-Joux. The skiing in this sector offers more variety than other major legs of the circuit and includes a long, challenging black beside the Linga gondola for clockwise snow-users or those with time to play en route.

The fairly steep slope above the gondola, served by chair-lift, has a blue traverse cut into it, as well as the red and black routes shown on the local piste map. The run down by the Combes chair-lift towards Avoriaz is a satisfying red; the Cornebois chair, which goes up from the same point, has good intermediate pistes of its own and it also connects with the top of the Chaux des Rosées chair-lift from Plaine-Dranse; the runs below this chair are seriously challenging. One more lift and one easy run bring you down to Les Marmottes for the return to Avoriaz.

A cable-car from the satellite of Les Prodains connects Morzine with Avoriaz, and on the other side of Morzine, a gondola and a cable-car climb steeply to Le Pleney (1500m), which is more of a sunny ridge than a peak. From the lifts you look down on the less enticing sections of the direct black run down from Le Pleney, which is fairly steep and often scraped to an icy glaze by too many snow-users. Easy skiing can be found on the northwest side of the mountain, including a long blue down to the resort. An attractive area on the eastern side provides a series of mainly red runs complicated only by a number of piste crossroads.

From Les Fys at the eastern end of this area, a quad-chair gives access to Plateau de Nyon. The Fys chair climbs back to the top of the ridge (Belvédère), where easy link-runs go down both wooded flanks of the ridge; southwestward runs take you to **Les Gets**, southeastward pistes to the junction of Le Grand Pré, where a chair and a drag-lift link with Nyon, and the long Charniaz chair climbs gently up to the Tête des Crêts. This lift is the usual access route to Les Gets ski area and the runs beneath it; a red, which is mostly a schuss, followed by a green along the road, are the only ways back to Morzine. Morzine shares in the glory as the home of snowboarding, and the percentage of riders found at this end of the circuit is 18 per cent – higher than in any other ski area in Europe.

The Plateau de Nyon can be reached by cable-car from just outside **Morzine**. Its appeal is mainly for good snow-users: the Pointe and Chamossière chairs reach the high points of the system and serve its most challenging summits – shadowy north-facing ridges beneath the sharp peaks, which tower over Morzine's ski area and keep the early sun off much of it. The wide bowl below the Chamossière lift provides plenty of off-piste opportunities. Behind Chamossière is a pleasant red run, which offers interesting off-piste alternatives before following a road through the woods to Le Grand Pré. From the Plateau de Nyon you can either ski down to the bottom of the cable-car or the whole 11.5km directly back to Morzine via a flimsy-looking but well-protected bridge over a gaping river gorge.

The Tête des Crêts is near the top of the north-facing half of Les

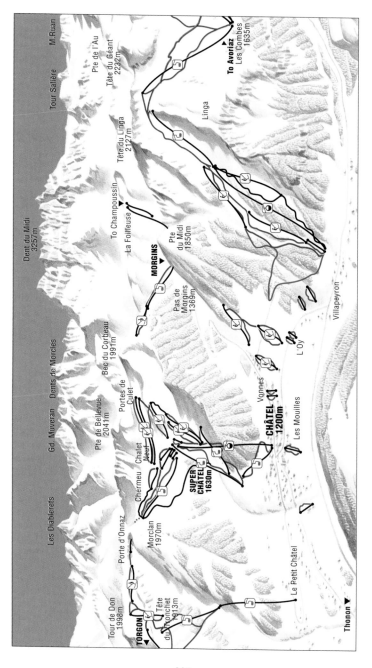

M.Ruan
Les Combes 1635m
To Avoriaz
Pte de l'Au
Tête du Géant 2232m
Tour Salière
Linga
Tête du Linga 2127m
Dent du Midi 3257m
To Champoussin
La Foilleuse
Pte du Midi 1850m
MORGINS
Villapeyron
Pas de Morgins 1369m
Bec du Corbeau 1991m
Dents de Morcles
Gd. Muveran
L'Oy
Vonnes
Portes de Culet
Pte de Bellevue 2041m
Chalet Neuf
Chermeu
CHÂTEL 1200m
Les Mouilles
Les Diablerets
SUPER CHÂTEL 1630m
Porte d'Onnaz
Morclan 1970m
Le Petit Châtel
Tour de Don 1998m
Tête du Tronchet 1413m
TORGON
Thonon

Gets ski area. This is gentle, with long runs over lightly wooded slopes to the resort. These pistes pass through **Les Chavannes**, a cluster of restaurants and hotel buildings with a nursery-slope area, walking trails and cross-country loipes that link up with Le Pleney. It is accessible by road as well as by lift from Les Gets. Only one of the drags at Les Chavannes climbs to Tête des Crêts, for access not only to Morzine but also to a broad, upper bowl. The direct blue run to Les Gets from here is not obvious; the piste down La Turche drag to the edge of the village is an equally gentle alternative.

The south-facing skiing of Les Gets is on Mont Chéry and is reached by a six-seater gondola; its base-station is a short walk across the road from Les Chavannes lifts and runs. Good snow on the lower red and black runs is a rarity for much of the winter. The top half of the mountain has easier, open skiing, with magnificent views to the south of the Mont Blanc massif. The fairly steep, open slope behind Mont Chéry has satisfying black and red runs to the Col de l'Encrenaz.

Most queuing problems in Les Portes du Soleil are in the Avoriaz sector; this is more because of the great volume of snow-users here than any major deficiencies of the lift system in this quarter.

Beginners
Given acceptable snow conditions, it does not really matter which end of the circus you choose. Châtel and Morgins both have easy nursery slopes and plenty of tree-level skiing to which novices can graduate after a few days. Morzine, and in particular the runs around **Super-Morzine**, are ideally suited to learners.

Intermediates
The whole Portes du Soleil is ideal cruising territory. Less confident snow-users will prefer the long, sweeping runs at the Châtel end of the circuit. Stronger skiers and snowboarders will look towards the greater challenges of Champéry and Avoriaz. Les Gets is also an ideal base from which to explore some of the best intermediate skiing. Little resorts like St-Jean d'Aulps/La Grande Terche, Abondance and **La Chapelle d'Abondance** can also provide excellent skiing when the rest of the region is crowded.

Advanced
Ideally, advanced snow-users should base themselves at the Avoriaz end of the circuit, although Champéry is a delightful alternative with easy access to the Avoriaz area. The Wall is the most notorious run in the area; a sign at the top warns that it is only to be attempted by experts, and certainly the initial angle of descent is such that you cannot see what lies ahead. But the Wall itself is wide and after the first 50m it flattens out considerably, although it still maintains an average gradient of 34 degrees. Like all black runs, the degree of difficulty depends on snow conditions; it is normally heavily mogulled within hours of a major dump of snow. Great care should be taken, not least because of the volume of less competent snow-users

who attempt it. This run certainly has to be skied, but there are plenty of other equally challenging pistes in the region, including the World Cup run from Le Plan Brazy above Avoriaz all the way down to Les Prodains.

The whole Arare area offers great freeriding terrain, and the detachable chair provides fast access. La Bleue du Lac piste is particularly recommended for freestylers. The funpark, which features a permanent half-pipe, is situated on the Bleue du Lac run. For alpine riders, the Arare piste is hard to beat for high-speed carving.

Off-piste

Again, the best powder runs are to be found above Avoriaz on both sides of the Swiss border. After a fresh snowfall various itineraries parallel to The Wall can be far more exhilarating than the actual run itself. The area is prone to considerable avalanche danger, and the services of a qualified guide are essential. Off-piste opportunities for riders include the Crêtes, Le Fornet and La Suisse.

Tuition and guiding

Avoriaz now has the International Ski School, as well as the ESF. Both also teach snowboarding in healthy competition with Emery Snowboard School, Free Ride, and the much-praised British Snowboard School. Reporters in Morzine recommended the ESF for its 'friendly instructors'. The ESF at Châtel also has a solid reputation and a new rival in Ecole de Ski Francis Sports. Virages Snoways specialises in off-piste. We have positive reports of the Swiss Ski School (ESS) in Champéry and in Morgins. However, the establishment that has received rave reviews is the British Alpine Ski School in Morzine and Avoriaz. This enterprise, set up by a couple of BASI instructors (who have passed the tough *équivalence* exam that allows them to teach legally in France), is described by one reporter as 'everything the ESF is not – small classes and good technical advice in one's mother tongue. Highly recommended and deserves a gold medal'. You need to book their services well in advance, especially during school holidays.

Mountain restaurants

The Portes du Soleil has a mixed bag of restaurants ranging from over-crowded self-services to wonderful old huts off the beaten track. Prices are generally high on both sides of the border, and all our reporters agree: there are simply not enough restaurants. Coquoz at Planachaux has a circular open fire and offers wonderful local Swiss specialities. Les Lindarets, the hamlet just north of Avoriaz, has the best concentration of eating-places with competitive prices. La Crémaillère is considered to be outstanding ('delicious chanterelle omelettes and wild myrtilles tart'), and Les Marmottes and the Pomme de Pin are also recommended.

Les Prodains, at the bottom of the Vuarnet run from Avoriaz, is much praised, not least for its reasonable prices. The restaurants at Plaine-Dranse are singled out as 'inexpensive and good'. Two restaurants at the top of Le Pleney are said to be always busy, 'but the wait is worth it'. The one at the top of the Super-Morzine gondola receives compliments for its 'appetising food and prices and spectacular view'. Les Raverettes at Les Gets is a handy stop before skiing back to Morzine. The Perdrix Blanche at Pré-la-Joux is recommended for its warm atmosphere and good-value food. Chez Gaby in Champoussin is highly praised ('we were ecstatic about the tomato fondue, but get here early or you won't find a free table'). Le Corbeau above Morgins is said to be 'a rustic, family-run affair with thoroughly reasonable prices'.

The resorts

Avoriaz is mainly a collection of apartment blocks perched on the edge of a cliff far above Morzine and built in what for the 1960s was a truly futuristic style. Unfortunately, many of the older blocks are showing their age, and no amount of face-lifts can improve the lack of space in their interiors. The resort is reached from the valley either by a narrow, winding road or by cable-car from Les Prodains. You are strongly advised to leave your car 'downstairs', or indeed to leave it at home. One reporter comments: 'There are too many cars already in Morzine, so don't spoil the environment even further by bringing one'. Certainly it has no useful application in car-free Avoriaz, and the charges in either car park are iniquitous.

Transport to your apartment block or hotel is via horse-drawn sleigh, piste machine or on foot. Between snowfalls, the amount of horse manure combined with dog-dirt deposited on the resort's 'roads' does little to improve the ambience. When not on skis, moving around is made easier by public lifts within the apartment blocks to different levels of this steep resort. The busiest part is the middle section around the foot of the nursery slopes; there are lots of bars and restaurants linking the slopes, and shops for ski gear, fashion and food. The best supermarket is, by consensus, the Codec near the tourist office.

Châtel is still a farming village, but caring for livestock and tilling the fields takes a poor second place to the more lucrative business of tourism. Unfortunately, precious little planning has gone into the development of the village, which is a huge, ungainly straggle of buildings up towards the Morgins Pass and Switzerland, as well as down the hillside and along the valley towards the Linga lift and the connection with Avoriaz. One reporter describes it as 'an excellent resort for a couple not too worried about après-ski, but who want to ski gently in breathtaking scenery'.

The valley lift departures are linked by free ski buses. These buses are crowded in the afternoon and have to fight their way through a village centre that is often choked with traffic. The disparate nature of the resort makes a car an advantage for reaching the out-of-town lift stations and for travel to the other unlinked resorts on the circuit.

Morzine is a market town and long-established resort with a Gallic atmosphere at the foot of the road to Avoriaz. It has all the appeal of an old-style chalet resort set in charming, wooded surroundings. Its biggest fault is its lack of altitude (1000m), which means that resort-level snow is scarce. The town covers a large area on both sides of a river gorge and is on several levels. It has a serious traffic problem, but a high footbridge over the river makes getting around less tortuous for pedestrians than for motorists. The main congested shopping street climbs from the old village centre beside the river to more open ground at the foot of Le Pleney, where the resort has developed, with hotels and shops around the tourist office.

Such is the diffuse nature of the resort that the free buses and a miniature road train are an essential form of transport. Horse-drawn taxis are an alternative means of getting around. Being a real town, the range of shops is far above the standard of most ski resorts.

Accommodation

The accommodation in Avoriaz is nearly all in apartment blocks, which vary in quality according to their age. The Alpage 1 apartments are said to be 'clean, but fairly cramped,' La Falaise units are similarly well-scrubbed but 'seriously short of storage space and maybe a bit cramped,' and La Thuya apartments are 'rather dilapidated'. In general, it seems prudent to halve the number of advertised bed spaces. The two hotels are Les Dromonts and La Falaise. Location within the resort is of no importance for skiing purposes, although some of the village streets, which are also pistes, may prove difficult for novices.

Châtel has a wide choice of hotels, most of them chalet-style and simple. Location is important and it is well worth checking out the distance from a main lift before booking. The Améthyste is said to be 'excellent and cheap,' the Résidence Yeti is recommended, and Hotel Fleur de Neige is praised for the quality of its food: 'more like a restaurant with rooms than a hotel'. The Flèche d'Or apartments are 'clean and comfortable, provided you halve the recommended occupancy figure'. Hotel Les Rhododendrons is 'perfectly located and typically French'.

Morzine has a plentiful supply of hotels in each price bracket; most are chalet-style and none is luxurious. In the central area, Les Airelles is one of the more comfortable, while Hotel Concorde is family-run and has a relaxed atmosphere. Hotel Le Tremplin is on the edge of the piste with a grandstand view of the night-skiing arena ('delightful family-run establishment with comfortable rooms and good food'). We continue to receive rave reports of the Hotel Dahu ('excellent and friendly, with lovely rooms – the children loved the pool'). In the Hotel Sporting 'staff could not do enough for us, even buying our 15-month-old son a new high-chair'.

Eating in and out

Avoriaz has a choice of around 30 restaurants, most of which are rather overpriced. Les Intrets is a favourite with reporters for its raclette, fondue and pierrade. Le Petit Vatel serves rustic fare including fresh trout, frogs' legs and snails. The Bistro opposite the Children's Village is 'good, but expensive'. Les Fontaines Blanches is 'reasonably priced, with a wide range of excellent food, a French atmosphere and occasional live music'. Le Savoyard has plenty of local flavour. In Châtel, La Bonne Menagère is popular, as is the Vieux Four ('slow service but food is good, basic French'). The Fleur de Neige has some of the best cuisine.

In Morzine, Le Dahu is again recommended for its 'mouth-watering dinners, night after night'. The Neige Roc at Les Prodains and Le Tremplin are also highly rated by reporters. L'Etale serves regional specialities in a 'wonderful, authentic mountain atmosphere'. In Les Gets, the Tyrol is recommended for '*châteaubriand* cooked on an open fire'.

Après-ski

The Place in Avoriaz has live, non-French music and an 'excellent atmosphere'. Le Choucas is recommended by reporters; it has live music and is usually not too crowded. Pub Le Tavaillon is described by one reporter who spent five weeks here as 'the nerve centre of Avoriaz'. The nightclubs are said to be generally overpriced and empty, except on striptease nights, when audience participation is invited. Le Festival and Midnight Express discos both have entrance fees. Midnight Express has a free 'bucking bronco'.

Châtel has a bowling alley and an ice-rink, but otherwise the after-slopes entertainment is mainly limited to a handful of bars, including the popular L'Isba, which has a lively atmosphere and shows ski videos. One reporter claimed: 'There was nothing to do and nowhere to go after 2.30am'. Morzine abounds with civilised tea-rooms and bars. Inside the Wallington complex are a bowling alley, pool hall, bar and disco. Le Pacha is another popular disco, which becomes extremely lively later on.

Childcare

Le Village des Enfants in Avoriaz has a justified reputation as one of the better childcare establishments in France. Children from three years of age are taught in the centre of the village, using methods developed by celebrated French ski champion Annie Famose. Younger non-skiing children are looked after in Les P'tits Loups day nursery of which we have good reports. Le Village Snowboard is for children from 6 to16 years of age – a dedicated secure area for learning and practising all disciplines.

Châtel has Le Village des Marmottons for children as young as 14 months, with a mixture of games and skiing for the older ones. The ESF operates classes for five-year-olds and upwards.

The Morzine crèche takes infants of two months to four years old, with one-hour ski lessons for children of three years and over. One reporter was dissatisfied with the service: 'The instructor did not speak English, the location was awkward, and the attitude was unsympathetic to slow starters'.

Linked or nearby resorts

Abondance
top 1800m (5,906ft) bottom 930m (3,050ft)
This tiny, historic village lies 7km from La Chapelle d'Abondance and is not linked into the main Portes du Soleil system. A bus service runs from

Châtel and La Chapelle d'Abondance. It has its own small ski area on the slopes beneath the Col de l'Ecuelle, served by a gondola and a series of drags.

TOURIST OFFICE
Tel 33 4 50 73 02 90
Fax 33 4 50 73 04 76

Champéry
top 2350m (7,708ft) bottom 1053m (3,455ft)

This traditional Swiss village is set in dramatic surroundings at the foot of the Dents du Midi. The one-way main street is lined with attractive wooden chalets, most of the hotels, shops and restaurants. The 125-person cable-car up to Planachaux is based on the hill down to the valley road that skirts the village. The lift is served by a free minibus that circles the village. Champéry's accommodation includes two centrally placed and long-established hotels: Hotel Suisse, which has a formal dining-room and old-fashioned bedrooms, and Hotel de Champéry, which is 'pleasant, comfortable and welcoming'. Auberge du Grand-Paradis and Hotel du Nord are also recommended. Pension Souvenir is a no-frills, cheaper option.

One of the best restaurants in the area, the Grand-Paradis, is 2km outside the village at the foot of the slopes. It has an atmospheric, wood-panelled interior with an open fire. Le Vieux Chalet is 'reasonably priced by Swiss standards'. Grill Le Mazot in the Hotel Champéry has the best and most expensive steaks in town. The village is not known for its nightlife. Le Pub bar and restaurant and the Farinet Bar are recommended.

Champéry has a gentle nursery slope with a simple rope-tow right in the middle of the village; snow permitting, this provides an ideal beginners' area for small children. The ESS Mini Club takes children up the mountain for the whole day.

TOURIST OFFICE
Tel 41 24 479 20 20
Fax 41 24 479 20 21
Email champery-ch@portesdusoleil.com
Web site www.champery.ch

Champoussin
top 2350m (7,708ft) bottom 1580m (5,182ft)

Champoussin represents more of an attempt to create a mini-resort than Les Crosets does. Its new, rustic-style buildings are almost all apartments, but most of our reporters stayed in the main hotel, the Résidence Royal Alpage Club, which receives mixed reports. It has a sauna, swimming-pool and disco. Its adjoining apartments are highly recommended. The hotel runs its own kindergarten and mini-club, and parapente school. Après-ski, which is limited to the hotel, Chez Gaby, and Le Poussin bar/restaurant, is 'almost non-existent'. Champoussin now has floodlit skiing on Wednesday evenings. The thermal baths 10km away at Val d'Iliez are worthy of a visit.

The resort is dominated by Dutch visitors. The small ski school does not receive impressive ratings, and reporters have mixed views on the resort: 'Great for family holidays, but singles and extreme skiers and snowboarders should look elsewhere,' and: 'Champoussin is so small and remote that just looking at it could give you cabin fever'.

TOURIST OFFICE
as Les Crosets

La Chapelle d'Abondance
top 1700m (5,577ft) bottom 1010m (3,313ft)

This small resort lies 6km down the valley from Châtel. It is an old farming community, straddling both sides of the road, without any defined centre. On one side, two long chairs take you up to Crêt Béni at 1650m, from where a series of drags serve a choice of mainly easy runs through the pine forest. On the other side of the road a recently built gondola and a chair-lift link into Torgon, Châtel and the main Portes du Soleil system. Hotels Les Cornettes du Bis and the Alti Mille both have swimming-pools and fitness centres. The Cornettes restaurant provides one of the best gastronomic experiences in the Abondance Valley.

TOURIST OFFICE
Tel 33 4 50 73 51 41
Fax 33 4 50 73 56 04

Les Crosets
top 2350m (7,708ft) bottom 1660m (5,445ft)

Les Crosets is a tiny ski station in the heart of the open slopes on the Swiss side of Les Portes du Soleil. It is popular with riders and has its own snowboard school as well as a funpark.The hamlet is fairly functional and, apart from a visit to the Sundance Saloon disco, has no obvious appeal to anyone but serious snow-users who want an early night. The main uphill transport from here is a detachable quad-chair. The Hotel Télécabine is simple, British-run and serves excellent food.

TOURIST OFFICE
Tel 41 24 477 20 77
Fax 41 24 477 37 73

Les Gets
top 2350m (7,708ft) bottom 1175m (3,854ft)

Les Gets is situated on a low mountain pass 6km from Morzine, with lifts and pistes on both sides and good nursery slopes on the edge of the village and higher up at Les Chavannes (1490m), which is reached by road or gondola. This attractive village, an old farming community that has expanded almost out of recognition, has a large and under-used floodlit piste. Parts of the ski area and many of the restaurants within it are accessible on foot. There is a bus service to Morzine for access to Avoriaz but it starts late in the morning and is infrequent.

Les Gets has three ski schools, and we have generally favourable reports of them all. Ski Plus specialises in 'excellent private tuition in English'. The Ile des Enfants kindergarten ('quite Gallic but lots of fun, they don't take the skiing too seriously') receives better comments than the ESF. The non-ski Bébé Club takes children from three months to two years of age.

Much of the accommodation is in tour-operator chalets. Hotel L'Ours Blanc is 'comfortable, with good service, and we would go back there again'. Hotel Régina is well placed in the quieter part of the village, and the Labrador and the Boomerang are both recommended. Le Meridien, La Cachette and the Clé des Champs chalets are recommended. The limited choice of restaurants includes Le Tyrol for pizzas.

Most of the nightlife centres around hotel bars, but there are also two discos. The English-run Pring's and the piano bar in the Hotel Régina are popular. An open-air skating-rink in the centre, a motor-tricycle circuit, a mechanical museum and two cinemas are other alternatives.

TOURIST OFFICE
Tel 33 4 50 75 80 80
Fax 33 4 50 79 76 90

Montriond
top 2350m (7,708ft) bottom 950m (3,116ft)

Montriond is little more than a suburb of Morzine, with no discernible centre and a number of simple, reasonably priced hotels. A bus links it to the resort's gondola, which provides direct access into the main lift system.

TOURIST OFFICE
Tel 33 4 50 79 12 81
Fax 33 4 50 79 04 06

Morgins
top 2350m (7,708ft) bottom 1350m (4,428ft)

Morgins is a few kilometres from Châtel and is the border post with Switzerland. It is a spacious, residential resort spread across its broad valley, but it is not the ideal base for keen snow-users because the best skiing is elsewhere. A car is useful for visiting other resorts in the region, but traffic is a problem at the beginning and end of the day due to day-trippers from other parts of Les Portes du Soleil.

Most of the accommodation is in chalets and apartments. We have received poor reports of the once-popular Hostellerie Bellevue, which is described as 'rather tatty with dinners uninspiring at best'. The resort is relaxed but short of any real character. It has a crèche, of which we have extremely positive reports. The large nursery slope in the centre of the

Skiing facts: Avoriaz

TOURIST OFFICE
Place Central, F-74110 Avoriaz, Haute-Savoie
Tel 33 4 50 74 02 11
Fax 33 4 50 74 18 25
Email Avoriaz@wanadoo.Fr
Web site www.ot-avoriaz.Fr

THE RESORT
By road Calais 889km
By rail Thonon les Bains 43km, Cluses 40km
Airport transfer Geneva 2hrs
Visitor beds 16,000
Transport traffic-free resort, ski bus service 30–60FF

THE SKIING
Linked or nearby resorts Abondance (n), Champoussin (l), Champéry (l), La Chapelle d'Abondance (l), Châtel (l), Les Crosets (l), Les Gets (l), Montriond (l), Morgins (l), Morzine (l), St-Jean d'Aulps/La Grande Terche (n), Torgon (l)
Longest run Abricotine 7km
Number of lifts 42 in Avoriaz, 219 in Portes du Soleil
Total of trails/pistes Avoriaz 150km (8% beginner, 55% easy, 27% intermediate, 10% difficult), 650km in Portes du Soleil
Nursery slopes 4
Summer skiing none
Snowmaking 180 hectares covered

LIFT PASSES
Area pass Portes du Soleil (covers 13 resorts), 946FF for 6 days
Day pass Portes du Soleil 203FF
Beginners 399FF for 4 days

Pensioners 60yrs and over, 134FF per day
Credit cards yes

TUITION
Adults ESF and ESI 800FF for 6 days (5hrs per day), 610–660FF for 6 half days (3½ hrs per day)
Private lessons ESF 175FF per hr or 1,250FF per day (7hrs)
Snowboarding Ecole de Glisse, Emery, Free Ride, Village Snowboard, all 800FF for 6 x5hrs. British Snowboard School, details on request
Cross-country 88FF (am) or 130FF (pm) Loipe 47km at Super-Morzine
Other courses telemark
Guiding through ski schools

CHILDREN
Lift pass 5–16yrs, Portes du Soleil 624FF for 6 days, free for 4yrs and under
Ski kindergarten Village des Enfants, 3–16yrs, 9.30am–5.30pm, 1,132FF for 6 days including lunch
Ski school ESF, 5–18yrs, 660FF for 6 days not including lunch. Le Village Snowboard, 6–16yrs, details on request
Non-ski kindergarten Les P'tits Loups, 3mths–5yrs, 9am–6pm, 1,280FF for 6 days including lunch

OTHER SPORTS
Parapente, hang-gliding, sleigh rides, snowmobiling, skating, swimming, squash

FOOD AND DRINK PRICES
Coffee 12FF, glass of wine 20FF, small beer 15–18FF, dish of the day 70FF

Skiing facts: Châtel

TOURIST OFFICE
F-74390 Châtel, Haute-Savoie
Tel 33 4 50 73 22 44
Fax 33 4 50 73 22 87
Email chatel@icor.fr.
Web site www.skifrance.fr/~chatel

THE RESORT
By road Calais 900km
By rail Thonon les Bains 45 mins, regular bus service to resort
Airport transfer Geneva 2hrs
Visitor beds 18,000
Transport free bus between village and Pré-la-Joux lift, and around resort

THE SKIING
Linked or nearby resorts as Avoriaz
Longest run Linga, 1km (red/black)
Number of lifts 38 in Châtel, 219 in Portes du Soleil
Total of trails/pistes 82km in Châtel (15% beginner, 30% easy, 43% intermediate, 12% difficult), 650km in Portes du Soleil
Nursery slopes 6 runs
Summer skiing none
Snowmaking 30 hectares covered

LIFT PASSES
Area pass Portes du Soleil (covers 13 resorts), 946FF for 6 days. Châtel only 696FF for 6 days
Day pass Châtel 158FF, Portes du Soleil 203FF
Beginners no free lifts
Pensioners 60yrs and over, Châtel 522FF for 6 days, Portes du Soleil 612FF for 6 days. Free for 75yrs and over

Credit cards yes

TUITION
Adults ESF, 460FF for 6 days (2hrs per day). Other schools, prices on request
Private lessons ESF 175FF per hr, ESI 175FF per hr
Snowboarding ESF, 2.30–5pm, 380FF for 3 lessons. ESI, 2–5pm, 690FF for 5 afternoons
Cross-country ESF, 9.30am–midday, 480FF for 6 days.
Loipe 24km
Other courses telemark, monoski, slalom, moguls, Skwal
Guiding through ski schools

CHILDREN
Lift pass Châtel, 5–16yrs, 522FF for 6 days, Portes du Soleil 612FF for 6 days, free for 4yrs and under
Ski kindergarten Le Village des Marmottons, 14mths–8yrs, 9.30am–4pm, 1,100FF for 6 days including lunch
Ski school ESF, 5–14yrs, 480FF for 6 x 2½ hrs. ESI, 8yrs and over, 660FF for 6 afternoons
Non-ski kindergarten Le Village des Marmottons, 14mths–3yrs, 8.30am–5.30pm, 685FF for 6 days including lunch

OTHER SPORTS
Parapente, snowshoeing, skating

FOOD AND DRINK PRICES
Coffee 7FF, glass of wine 12FF, small beer 12–18FF, dish of the day 50–65FF

Skiing facts: Morzine

TOURIST OFFICE
Place de la Crusaz BP 23, F-74110
Morzine, Haute-Savoie
Tel 33 4 50 74 72 72
Fax 33 4 50 79 03 48
Email touristoffice@morzine.com
Web site www.morzine.com

THE RESORT
By road Calais 880km
By rail Cluses or Thonon les Bains 30km
Airport transfer Geneva 1½ hrs
Visitor beds 16,000
Transport free bus service runs
throughout Morzine and to Les Prodains

THE SKIING
Linked or nearby resorts as Avoriaz
Longest run Piste Chamossière,
11km (red)
Number of lifts 82 in Morzine,
219 in Portes du Soleil
Total of trails/pistes 133km in Morzine
(13% beginner, 33% easy, 42%
intermediate, 12% difficult),
650km in Portes du Soleil
Nursery slopes 2 lifts
Summer skiing none
Snowmaking 130 hectares covered

LIFT PASSES
Area pass Portes du Soleil (covers 13
resorts), 946FF for 6 days. Morzine/Les
Gets, 726FF for 6 days
Day pass Morzine/Les Gets 145FF,
Portes du Soleil 203FF
Beginners special prices for some lifts
Pensioners as children
Credit cards yes

TUITION
Adults ESF, 800FF for 6 days,
British Alpine Ski School, details
on request
Private lessons ESF, 170FF per hr
Snowboarding ESF, as regular
ski school. Private lessons,
170FF per hr
Cross-country ESF private lessons,
170FF per hr. Loipe 97km
Other courses competition,
Skwal, telemark
Guiding through ESF

CHILDREN
Lift pass 5–15yrs, Morzine/Les Gets
532FF for 6 days, Portes du Soleil
598FF for 6 days, 109–115FF per day,
free for 5yrs and under
Ski school ESF, 4–12yrs,
445FF for 6 half-days
Ski kindergarten Halte Garderie,
3yrs and over, 8.30am–6pm,
1,295FF for 6 days including lunch
Non-ski kindergarten Halte Garderie,
2mths–4yrs, 8.30am–6pm, 885FF
for 6 days including lunch

OTHER SPORTS
Night-skiing, hang-gliding,
parapente, dog-sledding,
snowshoeing, ski-jumping, ice-hockey,
skating, curling, climbing wall,
swimming, ice-snorkling, cascade
climbing, heli-skiing

FOOD AND DRINK PRICES
Coffee 7FF, glass of wine 15FF,
small beer 14FF, dish of the day 65FF

village is prone to overcrowding.

Après-ski is limited to a natural skating-rink, indoor tennis courts and a few bars. The Hotel Bellevue's disco provides some measure of lively late-night entertainment in season, and its swimming-pool is open to the public. Several reporters have enjoyed the thermal baths at **Val d'Illiez.** The three cross-country loipe total 15km, and there is a long, marked but unprepared route to Champoussin. The village has three supermarkets as well as a butcher's shop and a bakery.

TOURIST OFFICE
Tel 41 25 77 23 61
Fax 41 25 77 37 08

St-Jean d'Aulps/La Grande Terche
top 1800m (5,906ft) bottom 900m (2,952ft)

St-Jean is the village, and La Grande Terche is the name given to a tiny development of apartments at the foot of the lifts, which are a 15-minute drive from Morzine. The skiing is not as yet fully linked into the system but it is surprisingly good and well worth a visit if you are staying elsewhere in the area. It has a combined ski area with **Bellevaux.**

TOURIST OFFICE
Tel 33 4 50 79 65 09
Fax 33 4 50 79 67 95

Torgon
top 2350m (7,708ft) bottom 1100m (3,608ft)

Torgon is perched above the Rhône close to Lac Léman on the outer edge of Les Portes du Soleil. Although it is in Switzerland, it is linked in one direction with La Chapelle and in the other with Châtel, both of which are in France. The distinctive and none-too-pleasing A-frame architecture contains comfortable apartments. There is little else to do here but ski.

TOURIST OFFICE
Tel 41 25 81 31 31
Fax 41 24 81 46 20

Risoul 1850

ALTITUDE 1850m (6,068ft)

Beginners ******* Intermediates ****** Snowboarders *******

Although it is increasing in popularity, Risoul is still an underrated purpose-built resort with extensive and convenient family skiing and a reputation for reliable late-season snow. The main reason for its low-profile image is its remoteness from any international airport. It is situated on the edge of the Ecrins National Park, at least three-and-a-half hour's drive from Turin, Lyon, Grenoble, or Marseilles. It was first planned as a ski resort back in the 1930s but the area never actually came into being until 1977. Its ski area of 54 lifts and 170km of pistes is shared with neighbouring **Vars 1850** and is known as the Domaine de la Forêt Blanche.

Its difficult location means that it is free of weekend overcrowding. The resort's clientèle is both family- and budget-oriented. Risoul is on the way to becoming a major snowboarding centre – the best in France according to some riders.

- ✔ Sunny and scenic tree-level skiing
- ✔ Value-for-money
- ✔ Skiing convenience
- ✔ Suitable for families
- ✔ Lack of queues
- ✔ Good snow record
- ✔ Late-season skiing
- ✘ Long airport transfer
- ✘ Limited chalet and hotel accommodation
- ✘ Lack of restaurants
- ✘ No activities for non-skiers

Ski and board
top 2750m (9,020ft) bottom 1650m (5,412ft)

Risoul is primarily a beginner and intermediate resort, although there are also off-piste opportunities. Lifts fan out from the village base, but the lift system still has a predominance of drag-lifts and is in need of upgrading. As one reporter put it: 'If you can't handle a long poma, do not come to Risoul. They are the longest, steepest, multi-directional pomas I have ever seen'. The new Mélèzert quad-chair does not go high enough to link directly with Vars 1850 so you have to take a further drag-lift. The skiing looks easy and most of it is, although experts can find some challenging terrain. Risoul offers three slalom race-training areas, a mogul-training course and a speed-skiing piste.

Beginners
It is possible to ski from Risoul to Vars 1850 and back on blue (easy) runs. The green (beginner) runs, with a children's park and snowmaking at the bottom of Risoul, are some of the most attractive in Europe.

Tête de Paneyron 2785m

Crête de l'Eyssina 2837m

Grand Parpaillon

Col de Vars

Châtelret 2431m

Col de Crevoux

Crête de Chabrières 2750m

Pic de Boussolenc 2809m

Pic St. André 2938m

Grand Morgon

Lac de Serre-Ponçon

Embrun

L'Homme de Pierre 2361m

Pic du Clocher 2473m

Gap

Briançon

Col Cherine

Payrefolle 2457m

RISOUL 1850m

Col de Valbelle

Pte de Razis 2571m

La Mayt 2678m

Le Forest

Lac

Peyniet 2273m

Les Plans

VARS 1850m

Vars Ste Marie

Vars St Marcellin

Vars Ste Catherine

221

The French Ski School (ESF) beginner area has its own lift. Two chair-lifts from Risoul give access to easy terrain for wobbly second-weekers.

Intermediates

A number of readers have complained that the resort has arbitrarily changed some of its blue runs to reds (intermediate). The official explanation is that these runs can be exactingly narrow for beginners. However, more cynical observers suggest that Risoul wants to upgrade its 'too easy' image. Most interesting are the ridge-line run from Risoul's high point, Crête de Chabrières, and the return to the village from the liaisons on Razis (numbers 21 and 22), which requires a hike back up from below the car park. Virtually unskied are the long, wide, mogul-free reds into **Vars-Sainte-Marie**.

Advanced

There are only eight black (difficult) runs, which readers say are graded thus more for their lack of grooming than their gradient. This is not a place for advanced piste-bashers. The Surfland snowboard park on L'Homme de Pierre is regularly used for boardercross competitions. It has a Renault 16 to jump over, a quarter-pipe, and numerous obstacles to 'bonk' (snowboard jargon for bump into and slide off).

Off-piste

Risoul has neither glaciers nor couloirs but it does have a lot of gladed powder skiing in fresh snow conditions. In the back bowl by Valbelle is a natural half-pipe shared by skiers and boarders. It is possible, given enough snow and the taxi fare home, to ski below the resort to the old village of Risoul. The ungroomed area to the skier's left of the Chardon chair also offers reasonable challenges.

Tuition and guiding

The ESF claims an average of ten skiers per class, but reporters have spotted groups of 15 and complain that not enough instructors are available during peak holiday periods. The rival International Ski School (ESI) guarantees no more than eight pupils per class, 'even during school holidays'.

Mountain restaurants

If skiing with a sandwich is ever to make a comeback it may be in Risoul, where the eating-places are cheap enough but lacking in both cuisine and character. Barjo at the bottom of the Mayt chair on the Vars 1850 side offers overnight accommodation and food. Vallon and Valbelle are small, spaghetti and steak-frites joints. Vars L'Horizon at the top of the Sainte-Marie chair-lift is 'typically French, no English here'.

The resort

Attractive as the skiing and wood-and-stone apartment complexes are, the small downtown section is blighted by illegally parked cars, a lack of proper pavements and a ghastly profusion of billboards. All except 200 of Risoul's guests stay in self-catered apartments. There is no shuttle bus, nor is there shopping of any note. Risoul has a small cinema and a skating-rink but no swimming-pool. The resort features live bands and fireworks during holiday periods, plus night-time snowboard-jumping contests.

Accommodation

The two-star Le Morgan is the only hotel in Risoul 1850 and is right in the centre. Some chalet accommodation is available, but most visitors opt for self-catering apartments. Les Mélèzes is functional but seriously lacking in space: 'If we had gone with another couple, rather than our children, we would have known each other intimately by the end of the week'. Another reporter complained that: 'The corridors and stairs were filthy. The apartments have nice balconies but they overlook a communal area blowing with litter and contaminated by half-eaten pizzas'. Le Belvédère is bigger and better.

Eating in and out

Most of the eateries are unambitious in price as well as menu. Cheap and plentiful are the burgers and frites at Snack Attack, and Au Point Chaud is the place to go for pizzas. Phil Good and Le Cesier Snowboard Café have low prices. L'Assiette Gourmand is the closest thing to gourmet cuisine.

Après-ski

The Grotte du Yeti is the young person's haunt for happy hour after the lifts close. Phil Good has live bands and is open until 2am. Readers commented that late-night noise in the resort is a serious problem: 'If you got to sleep before 2am you were woken up by revellers trying to find their way home. This contradicts the resort's family image'.

Childcare

Les Pitchouns crèche is conveniently located above the tourist office and takes children from six months to six years of age. A packed lunch must be provided if children are to be left all day. Both the ESF and ESI have children's learning areas.

Linked or nearby resorts

Vars 1850
top 2750m (9,020ft) bottom 1850m (6,068ft)

Vars 1850 is less attractive than Risoul and also less welcoming to the British. No tour operators currently come here. The old village is linked

Skiing facts: Risoul 1850

TOURIST OFFICE
Risoul 1850, F-05600 Guillestre,
Hautes-Alpes
Tel 33 4 92 46 02 60
Fax 33 4 92 46 01 23

THE RESORT
By road Calais 1024km
By rail Montdauphin 30 mins,
bus connection with Risoul
Airport transfer Grenoble 3½ hrs,
Marseilles 3½ hrs
Visitor beds 16,600
Transport free bus service

THE SKIING
Linked or nearby resorts Vars 1850 (l),
Vars-Sainte-Marie (l)
Longest run Les Marmottes, 2.1km
(blue)
Number of lifts 54
Total of trails/pistes 170km (24% easy,
69% intermediate, 7% difficult)
Nursery slopes 6 lifts
Summer skiing none
Snowmaking 30 hectares covered
in area

LIFT PASSES
Area pass (covers Risoul and Vars)
800FF for 6 days
Day pass 150FF
Beginners 80FF per day, 1 free lift
Pensioners 60yrs and over, 700FF for 6
days. Free for 70yrs and over
Credit cards yes

TUITION
Adults ESF 410FF, ESI 410FF,
both for 6 x 2hrs
Private lessons ESF 140FF per hr,
ESI 160FF per hr, for 2 people
Snowboarding ESF 460FF, ESI 460FF,
both for 6 x 2hrs
Cross-country ESF 85FF for 2hrs. ESI,
prices on request. Loipe 30km
Other courses monoski, Skwal,
telemark, slalom
Guiding through schools

CHILDREN
Lift pass 5–11yrs, 700FF for 6 days,
free for 5yrs and under
Ski kindergarten ESF Mini-Club,
2–12yrs, 1,380FF for 6 x 6hrs. ESI
3–12yrs, 280FF for 6hrs.
Both including lunch
Ski school ESF, 3yrs and over, 1,380FF
for 6 x 6hrs including lunch. ESI, 2–3yrs,
115FF for 3hrs
Non-ski kindergarten Les Pitchouns,
6mths–6yrs, 9am–5pm, 600FF for 6
days not including lunch

OTHER SPORTS
Snowshoeing, parapente, snowmobiling,
ruissiling (hiking with crampons and ice
axes on frozen rivers), skating

FOOD AND DRINK PRICES
Coffee 7FF, glass of wine 10FF,
small beer 12–18FF, dish of the
day 60–90FF

by drag-lift to the modern station, but you have to hike across town to
access the Vars gondola and high-speed chair back to Risoul.

TOURIST OFFICE
Tel 33 4 92 46 51 31
Fax 33 4 92 46 56 54

Serre Chevalier/Briançon

ALTITUDE 1200–1500m (3,936–4,920ft)

Beginners ✳✳ Intermediates ✳✳✳ Advanced ✳✳ Snowboarders ✳✳✳

Serre Chevalier is not a resort in its own right, but the collective description of over a dozen villages and hamlets that line the main valley road between the Col du Lautaret and the ancient garrison town of **Briançon**. Turin and Grenoble are the two nearest cities of international repute. Briançon is also directly linked by gondola into this substantial ski area. Of the three main villages, **Villeneuve/Le Bez** (marketed as Serre Chevalier 1400) is the most central and lively, while **Monêtier-Les-Bains** (Serre Chevalier 1500) is both the sleepiest and prettiest. **Chantemerle** (Serre Chevalier 1350) and Villeneuve share most of the visitor accommodation and have the best after-skiing facilities. Briançon is a pleasant town in a beautiful setting, with the added attraction of hilltop fortifications built by France's great seventeenth-century military engineer, the Marquis de Vauban.

A car is a definite asset for taking advantage of the off-slope facilities in the various conurbations as well as the Grande Serre Chevalier lift pass, which covers five nearby resorts, including **Montgenèvre** in the Milky Way area, 15 minutes down the road. The skiing is for all standards but is particularly well-suited to the adept intermediate, who will enjoy the 250km of cruising and the well-linked, albeit now rather old-fashioned, lift system.

Reporters are unanimous in their praise of the resort and its skiing: 'Serre Chevalier is one of France's best-kept skiing secrets. I loved being here and would unhesitatingly come again and bring all my friends'. Friendly locals are another plus.

✔ Large ski area
✔ Good artificial snow cover
✔ Varied off-piste
✔ Tree-level skiing
✔ Extensive cross-country trails
✔ Recommended for families
✔ Value for money
✘ Heavy traffic along main highway
✘ Strung-out resort
✘ Unreliable resort-level snow
✘ Long airport transfer (except Turin)

Ski and board
top 2800m (9,184ft) bottom 1200m (3,936ft)
The three main mountain access-points are by gondola and cable-car from Villeneuve/Le Bez, Chantemerle and Briançon, with most of the lifts and pistes concentrated in the area above Villeneuve and Chantemerle. The Monêtier section also has its own lifts starting from

the base and is the most appealing in the whole area, although the least accessible. Reporters complain there are too many ancient drag-lifts. Serre Chevalier's upper slopes are open and rather exposed to the weather, but the lower slopes are well protected by trees. Briançon has a floodlit piste for night-skiing. Snowmaking is extensive on the lower runs, and a reliable bus system links all the villages. According to reporters 'the piste-marking leaves a lot to be desired'. However, the area is praised for its lack of queues.

Beginners

Novice snow-users are well catered for with a choice of ten nursery slopes, and ski schools offering beginner tuition in all the main villages.

> **WHAT'S NEW**
>
> Snowpark at 2400m
> Peyra Juana mountain restaurant

The Grand Alpe area above Chantemerle has a decent but sometimes busy beginner area, and Briançon has a beginner area of its own at the 1625m gondola mid-station. Both Monêtier and Villeneuve have commendable nursery slopes and beginner lifts at their bases. A long green (beginner) run from Col Méa at the top of the ski area, all the way down to Villeneuve/Le Bez, is the next step.

Intermediates

The area is best suited to intermediate skiers. One reporter notes: 'For an average skier there are few better places'. Monêtier has some enjoyable red (intermediate) pistes through the woods. The Vallon de la Cucumelle above Fréjus is a recommended red but it can become icy in spring – 'varied from being wide and treeless at the top to narrow and mogulled in a few places. From Bachas at 2180m down to the valley at Monêtier there is a wide choice of intermediate runs through the woods. Le Bois is a short but fun red piste through the trees.

Advanced

Overall, Monêtier is the best area of the mountain for advanced skiers, although the high and exposed link with Villeneuve can sometimes be closed, both in harsh weather conditions and at the end of the season, when the slopes quickly lose their snow. Isolée is an exciting black (difficult) run, which starts on the ridge from L'Eychauda at 2659m and plunges down towards Echaillon. Tabuc is a long black through the woods with a couple of steep and narrow pitches. The Casse du Boeuf, a sweeping ridge through the trees back to Villeneuve, is 'outstanding' and 'the best black run we have ever skied'. Its natural snow is supplemented by snow-cannon when necessary. There is a half-pipe at the bottom of the Yret chair-lift.

Off-piste

The Fréjus–Echaillon section above Villeneuve provides some of the best runs for experienced skiers, with short and unprepared trails beneath the

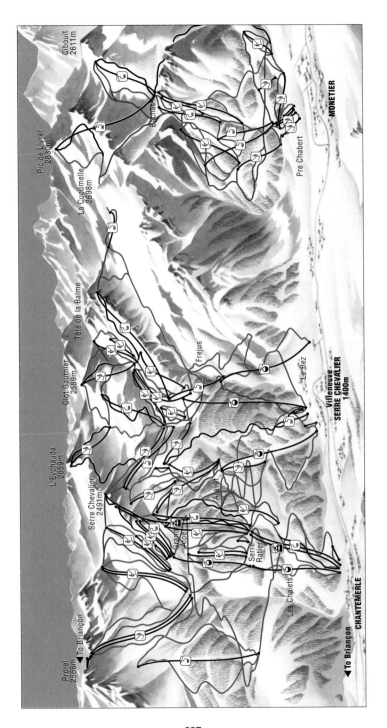

Skiing facts: Serre Chevalier

TOURIST OFFICE
BP 20, F-05240 Serre Chevalier,
Hautes-Alpes
Tel 33 4 92 24 98 98
Fax 33 4 92 24 98 84
Web site www.serre-chevalier.com

THE RESORT
By road Calais 1159km
By rail Briançon 6km, regular bus
service to resort
Airport transfer Lyon 3hrs, Turin 2hrs,
Grenoble 2½ hrs
Visitor beds 30,000
Transport free ski bus with lift pass
and regular bus service between
all centres

THE SKIING
Linked or nearby resorts Alpe d'Huez
(n), Briançon (l), Montgenèvre (n),
La Grave (n), Les Deux Alpes (n),
Puy-St-Vincent (n)
Longest run L'Olympique, 2.8km (black)
Number of lifts 72 in Grand Serre
Chevalier area
Total of trails/pistes 250km in linked
area (19% beginner, 69% intermediate,
12% difficult)
Nursery slopes 10 runs
Summer skiing none
Snowmaking 13km covered

LIFT PASSES
Area pass Grand Serre Chevalier
(covers all centres) 900FF for 6 days
including 1 day in each of Les Deux
Alpes, La Grave, Montgenèvre,
Puy-St-Vincent and Alpe d'Huez
Day pass 180FF
Beginners 1 day lift pass 60FF
Pensioners 60 yrs and over as children
Credit cards yes

TUITION
Adults ESF (1350, 1400, 1500) and ESI
(1350, 1400), 670–820FF for 6 days,
Buisonnière, details on request
Private lessons ESF and ESI,
175–1,235FF per hr, Buisonnière, details
on request
Snowboarding ESF and ESI, prices as
regular ski school. First Tracks,
2,700–3,400FF for 6 days, with tuition,
lifts and accommodation. Generation
Snow (1350), details on request
Cross-country ESF and ESI, 160FF for
3hrs, licence 30FF per day. Loipe 45km
Other courses telemark, monoski,
Skwal, competition
Guiding seven guiding companies

CHILDREN
Lift pass 7–12yrs, 600FF for 6 days, free
for 6yrs and under
Ski kindergarten Kids Club (1500),
180–210FF per day, 1,450FF for 5 days
Ski school ESF 540–730FF for 6 days,
ESI 780FF for 6 days
Non-ski kindergarten Les Poussins,
6mths and over, 9am–5pm, 205FF per
day including lunch. Les Schtroumpfs,
6mths and over, 9am–5pm, 180FF per
day not including lunch. Halte de Pré
Chabert, 18mths and over, 180FF per day
not including lunch, 1,000FF for 6 full days

OTHER SPORTS
Ice-driving, snowshoeing, aeroclub,
parapente, hang-gliding, swimming,
skating, husky rides, winter walks, sleigh
rides, ice-climbing, snowmobiling, horse
riding, ice-skating

FOOD AND DRINK
Coffee 14FF, glass of wine 12FF, small
beer 15–20FF, dish of the day 40–75FF

mountain crest. The Yret chair gives easy access to some off-piste runs including the testing face under the lift, which has a gradient of 35 degrees at its steepest point and often becomes mogulled. The Serre Chevalier lift map includes a separate map of off-piste itineraries.

Tuition and guiding

We have generally favourable reports of the ESF in both Serre Chevalier and Briançon, although a sound knowledge of spoken English is not always high on the list of the instructors' talents. There are five ski schools in Serre Chevalier and seven mountain guiding companies for off-piste skiing. We have continuing favourable reports of the Buisonnière Ski School – 'excellent, with small groups; the instructor had a sense of humour and the tuition was clear'. Another reader commented: 'Despite the instructor's limited English the lessons were really worthwhile and we skied much better afterwards'. Both the ESF and Buisonnière's private lessons are recommended. All the ski schools offer snowboarding lessons for all ages. First Tracks, which is run by the ESF, is a specialist snowboarding school in Villeneuve, and Generation Snow is in 1350.

Mountain restaurants

The choice of eating-places is small for an area of this size, and the quality is mixed. Café Soleil above Chantemerle attracts the crowds both at lunch-time and at the end of the day ('very well-prepared food and a great atmosphere, the best *vin chaud* and clean toilets, too'). L'Echaillon is 'pretty and off the beaten track, with friendly staff,' but is also said to be the 'poorest value for money'. Le Grand Alpe serves 'big portions'. Père et Noëlle at the bottom of the same gondola has 'large, beautiful salads'.

The resort

Monêtier is the furthest resort from Briançon and is the quietest and least-affected by modern architecture. It is a charming, rural spa village, which attracts fewer tourists than its neighbours. Next along the valley is Villeneuve, with its oldest section, Le Bez, at the top of the village and closest to the slopes. At the bottom of the village, beside the river, is an attractive narrow street with bars and restaurants. In the centre and above the main road is Villeneuve itself, which is a collection of modern apartment buildings including a small shopping centre. Chantemerle is the closest village to Briançon and acts as a base-station for commuters staying elsewhere in the valley. It has a good shopping centre.

The old town of Briançon became a ski resort when the Prorel gondola was built nine years ago. It is the main commercial centre of the region and the last major town before the Italian border. It does not have the atmosphere of a typical ski resort. However, the advantages of staying in a real town like this are many, including the large choice of shops and restaurants, and favourably priced hotels.

Accommodation

Most of Serre Chevalier's accommodation is in apartments, some 40 hotels throughout the three main villages and more than 20 in Briançon. The Altea, Vauban and Parc hotels are Briançon's three-stars. The Pension des Ramparts is a small and simple hotel with a loyal following. Le Clos de Chantemerle is a popular two-star with good food. Club Hotel Yeti is said to be 'very basic with paper-thin walls, but the food is good'. L'Alliey in Monêtier is a charming and central hotel with a fine menu. L'Auberge du Choucas, also in Monêtier, is known for its gastronomic cuisine. Le Lièvre Blanc, also in Villeneuve, is a British-owned two-star, which is recommended as 'one of the nicest hotels we have stayed in on any skiing holiday'. Another reporter commented: 'No praise is high enough. The staff were friendly, the food was exceptionally good, and the wine list extensive'.

Eating in and out

A car is useful for visiting the many restaurants along the valley. Le Petit Duc is a friendly crêperie beside the river in the lower part of Villeneuve/Le Bez. Le Petit Lard is 'rustic, French and fantastic value – but you have to book'. Pastelli in Le Bez has been criticised for its 'unimaginative food'. Le Bidule in Le Bez ('excellent, with a huge choice') has a friendly ambience and specialises in fresh fish and seafood. L'Auberge du Choucas in Monêtier serves fine regional cuisine. L'Aigle Fin in Chantemerle's commercial centre is recommended. Le Passé Simple in Briançon has a historic Vauban menu with dishes from the seventeenth century. Le Napoleon is praised for its pizzas. The Rallye hypermarket in Briançon is the best place for food shopping.

Après-ski

All three villages are quiet after dusk, with nightlife confined mainly to the bars. These include Le Sous Sol in Villeneuve. Le Yeti and the Underground are the best late-night drinking places in Chantemerle; both have live bands and stay open until 2am. Le Frog, L'Iceberg and La Baita discos in Villeneuve come alive only at weekends. Le Lièvre Blance has weekly live music. Both Briançon and Chantemerle have extensive health and fitness facilities. There is an ice rink in Chantemerle, and snowmobiles can be hired in Villeneuve.

Childcare

Each village has its own crèche and children's ski school. Kids de l'Aventure in Monêtier is a fully catered course for children aged between 10 and 15 years old; this includes ski tuition and a variety of other activities. Le Petit Train, a toy train on road wheels that ferries skiers and non-skiers around Villeneuve, is extremely popular with small children.

The Trois Vallées

ALTITUDE Courchevel 1300–1850m (4,264–6,068ft), Méribel 1450–1700m
(4,756–5,576ft), Val Thorens 2300m (7,544ft), Les Menuires 1850m (6,068ft)

What puts the Trois Vallées ski-lengths ahead of its rivals in the super-circus league is the range and sophistication of the resorts it contains, coupled with the variety of skiing on offer. Ideal topography means that even the links between each valley are serious runs in their own right. Its critics claim that 90 per cent of the skiing is geared towards intermediates, but then 90 per cent of skiers are intermediate. However, the Trois Vallées still provides more than adequate scope for those of greater or lesser ability. This substantial chunk of the French Alps is covered by what is considered to be the most efficient overall lift system in the world.

Collectively, it is the most popular ski destination for the British in France, and the French, who rarely venture beyond their own mountains, claim with dubious justification that it is also the largest in the world. While the true winner in this category is almost certainly the Sella Ronda in the Dolomites, the Trois Vallées team is top on the international podium for best all-rounder.

At one end, above the Bozel Valley, sits chic **Courchevel 1850**, with its not-so-smart satellites of 1650, 1550 and **Le Praz** beneath it. At the other end the pastoral Belleville Valley is dominated by functional **Val Thorens** and the *bête noire*, **Les Menuires**. In the middle is cosmopolitan **Méribel**, with its British bulldog overtones. The skiing is reached by two winding mountain roads from Moûtiers, or by an under-used gondola from **Brides-Les-Bains.** A fourth valley, the Maurienne, has no road access, but the skiing is linked by lift over the Cime de Caron above Val Thorens. The small town of **St-Michel-de-Maurienne,** previously known only for the quality of its carved choir stalls, has become a new tourist gateway into the Trois Vallées. The area can be reached by car in two hours from Turin via the Fréjus Tunnel.

The combination of cable-cars, gondolas, detachable chairs and tows is of gargantuan proportions and improves each year. Mammoth, the

---

COURCHEVEL

Beginners ✷✷✷
Intermediates ✷✷✷
Advanced ✷✷✷
Snowboarders ✷✷

✔ Big vertical drop
✔ Long cruising runs
✔ Tree-level skiing
✔ Resort-level snow (1850m)
✔ Gourmet restaurants
✔ Choice of luxury
   accommodation
✔ Skiing convenience
✔ Large ski area
✗ Fragmented resort
✗ High prices in Courchevel
   1850
✗ Crowded pistes at peak times

largest US resort, has 30 lifts; the Trois Vallées has 200, all of them linked by a mighty 600km of prepared slopes and uncounted hectares of off-piste terrain. Méribel alone has an extraordinary 17 gondolas.

Given a single week's holiday, a competent skier will barely scratch the surface. It takes a whole 20-week season based in at least two different resorts to get to grips with it.

However, the area is not without faults. The mountains are managed by an uneasy alliance of five separate lift companies, each of which looks after itself extremely well and pays lip service to its agreement with the others. As a result ski passes are checked at almost every lift.

The French regard the Trois Vallées as their premier destination. At peak holiday times all 115,000 beds will be taken, but even at New Year it passes the acid test of good ski resorts: when the whole area is operational you will struggle to find serious queues anywhere on the mountain, although the main motorway pistes will inevitably be overcrowded. As one reporter comments: 'The trouble is that the lift capacity is simply too high for the runs served'.

Each resort has its own character as well as its individual ski area, aside from the hundreds of kilometres they share. Méribel has such a strong British chalet-holiday tradition that in some bars French is either the second language or not spoken at all. Courchevel is ultra-chic and international, at least at 1850, where designer ski-suits outnumber their chain-store counterparts. 'The prices made us wince,' said one reporter. Les Menuires could not be a bigger contrast: it is a budget resort where the main evening entertainment for the bourgeois French, who make up its winter inhabitants, is watching the rented television set in their apartment, or walking the dog. Val Thorens, architecturally slightly more pleasing, is for skiers who want to be as sure of finding snow in early December as in late April. **La Tania** and the lower villages of Courchevel provide the middle ground for the more price-conscious. Brides-Les-Bains, in the valley below Méribel, is connected by a 25-minute gondola ride and provides a budget base and useful back door into the system.

MÉRIBEL
Beginners **✷✷**
Intermediates **✷✷✷**
Advanced **✷✷**
Snowboarders **✷✷**
✔ Superb mountain access
✔ Large ski area
✔ Choice of luxury chalets
✔ Resort-level snow (at Mottaret)
✘ Fragmented resort
✘ Skiing inconveniently located
✘ Heavy traffic and limited parking
✘ Poor reputation of ski school
✘ Crowded pistes at peak times

Ski and board
top 3300m (10,825ft) bottom 1300m (4,264ft)
Each resort has its own large ski area, which is covered by a single-valley local pass. Less-than-confident intermediates are strongly advised to take stock of what is on offer in their immediate location before buying

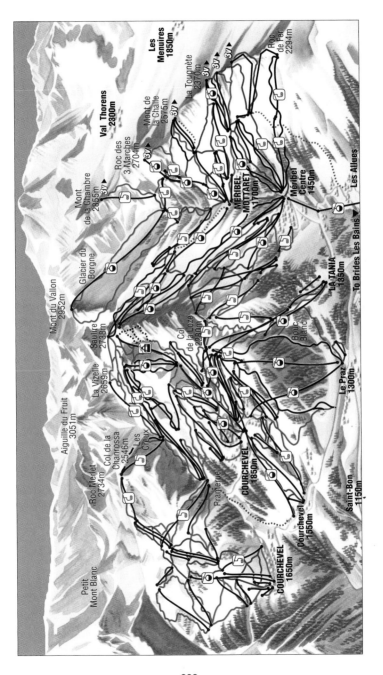

the more expensive Trois Vallées pass. The links between the three valleys are liable to be suspended when snow-cover is insufficient or in storm conditions. You should also note that the Trois Vallées lift map is printed back to front; **Courchevel 1650**, which appears to be the most westerly resort in the complex, is in fact the most easterly. What appear to be south-facing slopes are therefore north-facing and consequently hold the snow well.

Les Allues Valley, dominated by Méribel and its higher satellite of **Mottaret**, lies in the middle and provides the ideal jumping-off point for exploring the whole area. However, it does not necessarily give the easiest access to the most rewarding skiing.

Both sides of the open valley are networked with modern lifts for all standards of snow-users. The western side culminates in a long skiable ridge, which separates it from the beautiful Belleville Valley and the resorts of Val Thorens, Les Menuires and **St-Martin-de-Belleville.**

The eastern side rises to the rocky 2738-m summit of Saulire and the Col de la Loze at 2274m. Beyond lies the Bozel Valley and Courchevel – not one but four separate resorts at different altitudes – as well as the purpose-built addition of **La Tania**. At the head of Les Allues Valley lies the 2952-m Mont du Vallon – the most easterly of the horseshoe of 3300-m peaks accessed from Méribel and Val Thorens – which provides some of the most scenic and demanding off-piste in the region.

The ski area has been extended over the back, beyond Val Thorens and the Cime de Caron, into the Maurienne. The red (intermediate) run of 660m vertical takes you down to the Chalet Refuge de Plan Bouchet at 2350m, from where a fast chair takes you back up to the Col de Rosaël. A gondola carries skiers from Orelle (880m) in the Maurienne up to Plan Bouchet.

VAL THORENS
Beginners *
Intermediates **
Advanced **
Snowboarders **
✔ Resort-level snow
✔ Long season
✔ Large ski area
✔ Glacier skiing
✔ Ski-in ski-out convenience
✘ Lack of tree-level skiing
✘ Exposed and cold in mid-winter
✘ Limited for non-skiers
✘ Lack of après-ski
✘ Late-season lift queues

Beginners

Facilities for beginners are good in all the major resorts, although the sheer volume of visitors here necessitates impersonal instruction, which is not conducive to the early-learning process. The runs surrounding the altiports at both Courchevel and Méribel are excellent beginner areas with enough length to help build confidence. The green (beginner) Truite run connecting Mottaret with Méribel is popular with novice ski classes, but more proficient skiers taking the whole run 'in the tuck' on their way to lunch can be unnerving.

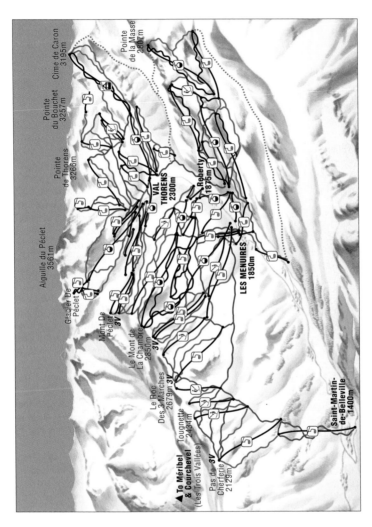

Once the basics have been conquered, the area lends itself to easy exploration. Les Teppes Noires, followed by Le Gros Tougne and L'Allée take you from Méribel via the Tougnette gondola down to Les Menuires. It is an ideal chance for second-week skiers to feel they are really going somewhere.

Intermediates

The Trois Vallées constitutes what many skiers rightly regard as the greatest intermediate playground in the world: a seemingly endless network of moderately graded runs that provide a challenge to all levels of skier. The Combe de Vallon is a magnificent cruise of 1100m vertical from the top of Mont Vallon all the way down to Méribel Mottaret. The Cime de Caron above Val Thorens is more famous for its Combe du Caron black (difficult) descent, but there is also a red intermediate variation around the shoulder, as well as the long and scenic Itinéraire du Lou. The blue (easy) Arondiaz trail from the top of Courchevel 1650 back down to the resort is a great last run of the day, and its north-facing aspect usually ensures excellent conditions.

Advanced

With a maximum gradient of about 38 degrees, the couloirs of Courchevel are among the most radical black runs marked on any piste-map in the world. Take the 150-person cable-car up from the Courchevel side of Saulire and exercise special care on the entry route, which can be dangerously icy. In most conditions, the runs are not as difficult as they look from below, but as one reader puts it :'Actually getting to them is a life-threatening experience'.

The Courchevel side of Saulire is the starting point for a magnificent descent of 1400m vertical to Le Praz. It is more tiring than technically difficult, apart from the black Jockeys piste on the final section, which is shaded for most of the winter and consequently icy. La Masse above Les Menuires boasts Les Enverses and the usually icy La Dame Blanche.There is a funpark above Rond Point des Pistes in Méribel and a designated snow-board area below the second Plattières station above Mottaret. At Courchevel impossibly high moguls are interspersed with steep canyons on the Verdons piste for the use of skiers as well as snowboarders. Plantrey has a funpark with an obstacle course as well as a dedicated trick space and a giant half-pipe. This season both have more snow-cannon, and a third funpark has been created at Biolley.

LES MENUIRES

Beginners ✷✷
Intermediates ✷✷✷
Advanced ✷✷
Snowboarders ✷✷

✔ Large ski area
✔ Long cruising runs
✔ Sunny slopes
✔ Off-piste skiing
✔ Well-run children's village
✔ Budget prices
✔ Extensive snowmaking
✘ Ugly architecture in centre
✘ Heavy traffic
✘ Limited après-ski
✘ Lack of tree-level runs
✘ Limited for non-skiers

Off-piste

The guided off-piste opportunities are outstanding, and one of the great charms of the Trois Vallées is that after a major snowfall the best powder runs are some of the most accessible. The long runs down to Les Menuires from the Méribel ridge are exhilarating.

The summit of La Masse on the far side of the Belleville Valley is also the starting point for long itineraries towards St-Martin as well as into the Vallon du Lou. Roc Merlet above Courchevel 1650 is the jump-off point for a glorious descent around the shoulder into the Avals Valley, which brings you back, after a short walk, to 1650. Mont Vallon and the Col du Fruit offer further thrills.

Tuition and guiding

Courchevel has the Supreme Ski and Snowboard School, formerly known as both Masterclass and the British Ski School. It is run by Alan Hole with Kenny and Sue Dickson and has 11 BASI instructors, all of whom have passed the rigorous *équivalence* test, which allows them to work legally in France. Ski Cocktail, which originated in Méribel now has a branch here and we also have positive reports of Ski Académie.

The ESF in Méribel is in danger of eclipsing the reputation of the Swiss Ski School in Zermatt as the most consistently criticised in the Alps. Classes of more than 12 skiers are not uncommon, and reporters complain that two levels are sometimes merged into one class. One experienced tour operator rep said that 85 per cent of his clients complained about the ESF in one way or another. 'A two-hour private lesson in Mottaret was a complete waste of time. The instructor gave little or no instruction. He just expected us to ski around after him.'

However, Ian and Susan Saunders, BASI instructors who work for the ESF, are strong exceptions. They have their own company, Ski Principles, which provides 'great instruction by sympathetic teachers'. Méribel's Ski Cocktail, formerly praised as a viable alternative to the ESF, has 'lost its edge' according to reporters, who criticised 'classes of up to 12 and only four levels of instruction'. Another reader complained about the poor time-keeping of teachers. Magic in Motion is currently the best school in Méribel and also the most expensive, 'but you get what you pay for'. All instructors are said to be 'full of enthusiasm and keen to teach'. Classes are restricted to seven skiers. It is important to note that all ski lessons in the Trois Vallées must be pre-booked during high season.

Val Thorens also has alternatives to the ESF. Ski Cool limits class sizes and claims 'a different approach to lessons'. Jardin Prosneige and Ski Surf Nature L'Ecole structure specialist courses on demand. Les Menuires offers the regular ESF and ESI classes.

Mountain restaurants

The majority of mountain restaurants in the Trois Vallées serve bland fast-food at truly shocking prices. As one reporter commented: 'even with a strong pound they are eye-wateringly expensive, and this is particularly galling when the food is merely average'. Regular visitors tend to head down into the resorts at lunch-time where prices are not necessarily lower but the standard is generally higher. Reporters staying in Courchevel 1650 criticise the lack of lunchtime eateries: 'The lack of good-value mountain restaurants is our only criticism of an otherwise perfect little resort'.

Reporters recommend Bel-Air at the top of the Courchevel 1650 gondola, which has the best views; booking is essential ('waiter-service and freshly-cooked food at high, but not extortionate prices'). La Soucoupe above Courchevel 1850 is also praised. Chalet de Pierres above Courchevel 1850, with liveried waiters hovering on the edge of the piste, is a gastronomic delight, but expensive. Cap Horn, just above the Courchevel altiport has 'outstanding food at an extortionate price'. Le Bouc Blanc at the top of La Tania gondola is always welcoming ('good pasta, tasty salads, but at all costs avoid the house *vin rouge*'). Pub Le Ski Lodge down in La Tania offers 'the cheapest lunches in the Trois Vallées'. Le Petit Savoyard in Courchevel 1650 is also singled out: 'three-course meal for only 105FF'.

WHAT'S NEW IN COURCHEVEL

Avalanche protection system on La Loze and La Saulire
Reshaping of summit of La Loze to improve lift linkage to pistes
Improvements to Plantrey and Verdons funparks including more snow-cannons
Creation of a third funpark at Biolley

Quatres Vents at Les Bruyères has reasonable prices. La Sitelle above the first stages of the Plattières lift above Mottaret is also praised. Les Crêtes above St Martin has a 'great atmosphere but is not suitable for vegetarians'.

Les Castors, at the foot of the Truite run in Méribel, has spaghetti cooked in individual copper pans. Roc des Trois Marches offers consistently good value. Plein Soleil at Mottaret is 'perfect for a sunny day lunch'. Les Rhododendrons offers 'smashing burgers and chips'. Les Crêtes, at the top of the Tougnètes gondola, is recommended for its atmosphere but not for its 'unspeakable' vegetable sausages ('thick pig inner tubes filled with all sorts of animal bits with strands of something green, which must have been the vegetable element').

L'Ours Blanc is the smartest hotel in Les Menuires and serves 'excellent-value lunches'. Chez Alfred is an old hut just off the piste above Les Menuires. Alfred doesn't always cook but, when the mood takes him, his are the finest and cheapest *steak frites* on the mountain. The Panoramique at Saulire is said to be 'good, but 40 per cent more expensive than anywhere else'.

The resorts

Courchevel is not one but four quite separate resorts at different altitudes, linked on piste but with nothing else in common. Before booking a holiday here it is crucial to ascertain exactly where you will be staying. Courchevel 1850 is the international resort with the jet-set image, and most tour operators are happy for you to think their accommodation is here, even when it is not. Courchevel 1850 is the most fashionable of all French ski destinations. Like its rival, Megève, a high proportion of its designer-clad visitors come here to see and to be seen. The only exercise they take is to ferry gastronomic delights from plate to mouth at the resort's clutch of fine restaurants.

Unlike Megève, **Courchevel 1850** offers seriously challenging skiing that is some of the best and most accessible in the whole of the Trois

Vallées; its high altitude ensures early and late snow cover.

A covered mall houses expensive boutiques, and a couple of super-markets cater for the more mundane needs of self-caterers. Two chic boutiques are entirely devoted to the kind of exotic lingerie that, in terms of money for weight, is matched only by rare postage stamps. The secluded Jardin Alpin sector is a Millionaire's Row of sumptuous chalets and shockingly expensive hotels tucked discreetly away in the trees; it provides at least an illusion of privacy.

Courchevel 1650 is 200 vertical metres lower down both the mountain and the price scale. Many would argue that this is *le vrai* Courchevel, with its year-round population and atmosphere of the farming community it once was. One reporter commented: 'We are passionate about 1650 and would not go anywhere else. It is a completely separate resort and we have never felt we were missing out on the glitzier village above us'. The intermediate skiing here is both extensive and isolated from the main Trois Vallées thoroughfares; consequently, it remains wonderfully uncrowded even at peak times.

Courchevel 1550 is off the beaten track and away from the heart of the skiing. It is little more than a cluster of apartment buildings and a few hotels and is popular with self-catering French families. **Le Praz** (some-times known as **Courchevel 1300**) is a farming village at the foot of the lift system and is becoming an increasingly popular and cheap base for Courchevel's skiing ('if the road was rerouted and the snow a little more reliable, this would be a heavenly place'). Indeed, snow cover is by no means guaranteed in the hamlet, but two gondolas ('always free of queues') swiftly take you up towards the Col de la Loze or to 1850.

So many British people holiday or work in **Méribel** during the winter months that any attempt to order a drink or a meal in French can be met with a look of blank incomprehension. It is an expensive resort, which offers more luxury-class chalets and apartments with en-suite bathrooms than any other ski destination.

Méribel was founded by an Englishman; dedicated pre-war skier Colonel Peter Lindsay built the first lift here in 1938. Amazingly, the resort has stayed faithful to his original concept of a traditional chalet village: every building has been constructed in local stone and wood in harmony with the mountain setting. Today, it has stretched with little or no long-term

WHAT'S NEW IN MÉRIBEL
Detachable six-seater chair-lift to replace two-seater Adret chair-lift
Beginners' drag-lift in Mottaret below the Plattières gondolas
Quad-chair to connect Méribel Village to the altiport
Blue run down to Méribel Village
Increased snowmaking
Pas du Lac gondola from Mottaret to Saulire upgraded to eight-person capacity

planning into a hotch-potch of confusingly named hamlets at different altitudes. Their convenience for skiing, shopping and nightlife varies considerably. 'The Heart of The Trois Vallées' is Méribel's marketing slogan, but because of its diffuse layout it is devoid of a single heart and its atmosphere is muted accordingly. Méribel Centre (1450m) is now known generally as Méribel and is the commercial core – a one-street village with the tourist office 'square' as its focal point. It has a number of boutiques and souvenir shops beyond the usual sports shops and one main supermarket. The bi-weekly street market provides colour and the occasional clothing bargain.

Méribel Mottaret (1700–1800m), now 24 years old, is a separate satellite further up the valley, and is also now divided into separate hamlets. The higher altitude of Mottaret ensures good snow cover and is the starting grid for the best 'motorway' skiing. This may explain why Alain Prost built his winter home here, but Mottaret has few other obvious temptations. The different sectors of Méribel are all connected by a regular, free bus service which runs efficiently every 20 minutes until midnight. Traffic, parking and pollution from petrol fumes remain serious problems, which are not adequately addressed.

At 2300m, **Val Thorens** is the highest ski resort in Europe. Consequently, it is one of only a handful where you are virtually guaranteed snow at resort level over both Christmas and Easter. On a sunny day its functional, purpose-built architecture is positively attractive compared with its nearest neighbour, Les Menuires. You can ski into the centre of the car-free village, and the horseshoe of surrounding peaks are dramatic. In bad weather, this far above the tree-line, you may be forgiven for thinking you have been stranded amid the mountains of the moon; few places in the Alps are colder, and a white-out is just that.

WHAT'S NEW IN VAL THORENS

Plein Sud chair-lift upgraded to detachable six-seater

Les Menuires, down the valley from Val Thorens at 1850m, has a reputation as the ugliest resort in the Alps. Certainly, the original centre of La Croisette is a prime example of the alpine architectural vandalism of the 1960s. Minuscule apartments are housed in anonymous, box-like buildings clad in unpainted concrete. The more modern satellites of **Reberty** and **Les Bruyères** are far more appealing, and you can holiday in comfort, hardly ever venturing into La Croisette. Both are on the piste and have their own hotels and restaurants as well as all the shops you might need, apart from a chemist (there is one in La Croisette). The main skiing here is exceptionally sunny. A bank of snow-cannon keeps the home run in good condition until late in the season.

Accommodation

Courchevel 1850 has a host of four-star de luxe hotels (there are no five-stars in France), which pamper their exotically wealthy guests. The Byblos de Neige is the star. Les Airelles is more discreet. Hotel des Neiges is an established favourite, and the Trois Vallées is 'intimate and charming'. The family-run three-star La Sivolière provides four-star comfort and has a health centre. The reasonably priced Courcheneige is situated on the edge of the piste near the altiport; during the school holidays the hotel is over-run by British families mainly from the Home Counties and the more fashionable parts of south-west London. Le

Mélèzin, Les Ducs de Savoie, Le Dahu, Les Grandes-Alpes, and L'Aiglon are singled out for praise. The quality of some of the luxury catered chalets here ranks alongside the smartest hotels. The Forum apartment complex is praised by reporters ('modern, with a perfect location'), although both the apartments themselves and the staircases are showing signs of wear-and-tear. **Courchevel 1650** consists mainly of chalets. Hotel du Golf has 'modern rooms with balconies, superb food, and it is situated right on the edge of the piste'. **Le Praz** has the comfortable Hotel Les Peupliers ('a delightful base from which to ski Courchevel without paying through the nose').

Méribel began as a chalet resort and so it remains. In the short summer months the village rings to the sounds of saw and hammer as new luxury establishments sprout in response to demand. Of the hotels, the four-star Grand Coeur was one of the resort's first and remains its finest: 'the food and service are excellent; its understated luxury appeals equally to the Brits and the French'. Other four-star hotels include L'Antarès and Le Chalet. The Marie Blanche is 'small and friendly'. Le Yeti and the Merilys are also recommended. In **Mottaret**, La Tarentaise is warmly praised. Most guests stay in apartments that vary in size and standard.

Accommodation in **Val Thorens** is divided between the standard French apartments and mainly unremarkable hotels. The four-star Fitz-Roy is the exception. Readers report that the apartments in the Naska block of the Temples du Soleil complex are 'surprisingly spacious, with enormous bathrooms'. Résidence Altineige is said to be 'extremely noisy thanks to the Ski Rock Café next to the reception area'. Le Bel Horizon and Le Sherpa ('the best hotel in town, very friendly') are reporters' favourites, along with Le Val Chavière where 'staff are actually pleased to see you'.

Les Menuires is also apartment territory: the older ones in La Croisette are cramped and largely to be avoided. Their more modern counterparts in **Les Bruyères** are beginning to show signs of exhaustion. Hotel Les Latitudes in Les Bruyères offers some of the best-value accommodation and five-course dinners in the region ('quite exceptional food, pleasant rooms and ideally situated on the edge of the piste. Don't tell anyone else'). Reporters praise the Necou apartments at **Reberty 2000** ('a high-quality, well-designed ski-in ski-out complex').

Eating in and out

Courchevel 1850 abounds in good restaurants at truly outrageous prices. The Chabichou Hotel has two coveted Michelin stars, as does Le Bâteau Ivre. The seafood restaurant at Byblos de Neige is a wonder to behold; however, few reporters found themselves in this envious price bracket. La Saulire (Jacques' Bar) in the square at 1850 offers fine cuisine at far more friendly prices and is without doubt the most welcoming and best-value restaurant in town: 'a resort institution with a passionate following'. Le Plancher des Vaches and La Chapelle are warmly praised.

Restaurants at **Courchevel 1650** are less Parisian in price. La Poule au Pot is recommended for classic French fare, and Le Yeti for its fresh seafood. In **Courchevel 1550** the Oeil de Boeuf is 'good, but rather smart'. La Cortona and Le Caveau are warmly recommended: 'great atmosphere and food in both'. **Le Praz** is famed for the outrageously expensive but nevertheless compelling Bistrot du Praz and Charley, its *bon viveur* host. A *dégustation* of four different types of foie gras is the house speciality. Hotel Les Peupliers, the original village inn, is also worth a visit for lunch or dinner and is more modestly priced. One reporter described Le Ya Ca in Le Praz as 'a true French bistro that is proud of its food. A *gigot d'agneau* was roasting slowly in the fireplace when we arrived. By the time we left it had completely disappeared'.

Méribel has a surprisingly limited choice of recommended restaurants for a resort of its size, mainly because such a large proportion of its clientèle eat in their self-catered chalets. La Cava is good for fondue, and Le Jardin d'Hiver has fresh seafood. La Taverne offers pizzas and Savoyard dishes and has established itself as one of the resorts' main rendezvous. Chez Kiki specialises in charcoal grills, and the surroundings are appealing. Santa Marina is praised for its 'excellent pizza and pasta'. In **Mottaret**, Ty Sable is strongly recommended. El Poncho is a friendly Tex-Mex at Méribel 1600 offering some of the best-value food in the resort. Le Rib is 'smoky, noisy, packed with resort workers,' and has a weekly live band. In Mottaret, Hotel Tarentaise, on the edge of the piste, is British-managed and popular with the French for its food. The central Côte Brune restaurant is still a culinary mainstay. Pizzeria du Mottaret is the restaurant with the best ambiance and reasonable prices.

Val Thorens has a limited choice of restaurants. Le Galoubet is recommended at lunch-time for its dish of the day. La Joyeuse Fondue, Le Vieux Chalet and Bloopers are all recommended. El Gringo's Café in the Péclet shopping centre is among the most popular.

Les Menuires is no gastronomic delight, but the half-board food in Hotel Les Latitudes was described as 'much more exciting than we could have hoped for'. Better restaurants include La Bouitte in nearby **St-Marcel**, and La Mascotte and Chalet Necou in Les Menuires.

Self-caterers heading for the Trois Vallées are strongly advised to stock up at the large hypermarket on the outskirts of **Moûtiers** before beginning the climb up to the resorts: prices are markedly cheaper at lower altitude.

Après-ski
At Prends Ta Luge Et Tire-toi (grab your toboggan and go) in the Forum complex at **Courchevel 1850** you can surf the Web, buy a snowboard or get a tattoo. The 5 à 7 beneath the Hotel Albatross is popular. L'Accord and Le Grenier are two usually crowded piano bars. The Koyote is a Tex-Mex restaurant with live music and 'a buzzy bar'. La Grange and Les Caves are the main late-late but prohibitively expensive venues ('where the French glitterati buy vodka by the bottle while dancers gyrate to Euro anthems on podiums overlooking the dance floor'). Le Kalico is a much cheaper 2am alternative ('no entry fee and reminiscent of a student disco with Brits dancing ankle-deep in beer').

At **Courchevel 1650**, Le Signal is the bar-restaurant where the locals meet. Le Phlouc (it means clown in France or pimple in Scotland) is a small, smoky and busy bar. By night Le Green Club has a modest entry fee, a British DJ and 'the best music at any altitude in Courchevel'. Rocky's Bar is also always busy. At **Courchevel 1550** après-ski revolves around La Taverne ('very French, very friendly') and the Glacier Bar ('full of British resort staff'). Chanrossa provides the late-night action.

Le Praz is not the place for raucous nightlife. The crêperie has 'the best *vin chaud* in the business'. The Bar Brasserie (it bears no other name) is 'the only place with any life'.

In **Méribel** Jack's Bar close to the piste has a popular après-ski happy hour, 'lively, happy atmosphere, value for money'. Le Rond Point is equally busy as the lifts close. L'Artichaud, located above the ice-rink, has live music, a fun atmosphere and stays open late. Dick's T-Bar, a branch of the Val d'Isère original, is extremely popular.

Childcare

All the main resorts are well-served with both ski and non-ski kindergarten. However, it is important to note that the facilities offered may not be conducive to the enjoyment of your holiday as parents. The Gallic approach to childcare may seem harsh by northern European standards, with a serious emphasis on learning to ski without any accompanying element of enjoyment. The number of children who dig in their heels and tearfully refuse to return to these French establishments on day two of their holiday has led most major tour operators to set up their own, more sympathetic crèches and even ski classes.

The ESF runs children's villages in all the resorts. The best reports came from **Les Menuires**, where staff at Village des Schtroumpfs are praised for their friendliness and dedication in looking after children from three months to two-and-a-half years old in the nursery and up to seven years in the kindergarten section. The village has a rope-lift for beginners and a longer drag. ESF teachers also take classes out on the mountain, and there are play facilities and a video room for non-skiing children.

The equivalent in **Courchevel 1850** is criticised as being 'too serious' in its approach ('needs to be more organised'). Many parents staying here feel that **Le Praz** has a better ski school, and the instructors will come up to 1850 to collect children. However, at Le Praz kindergarten 'at least a third of the children were British, but the staff didn't make a big effort to speak English. Our three-year-old was not overly impressed, but enjoyed it enough to go back'. We have favourable reports of the ESF children's ski school in **Courchevel 1650**.

Reporters praise the **Méribel** ski school: 'Although the classes were large, the teachers made the lessons fun. This was the first time my son really enjoyed ski school and wanted to go back each day'.

In **Val Thorens**, the ESF runs a children's village with a non-ski kindergarten for children from three months old and upwards. Stage Etoile is for skiers from 5 to 16 years old.

Skiing facts: Courchevel

TOURIST OFFICE
BP37, La Croisette, F-73122 Courchevel
Tel 33 4 79 08 00 29
Fax 33 4 79 08 15 63
Email pro@courchevel.com
Web site www.courchevel.com

THE RESORT
By road Calais 925km
By rail TGV Moûtiers 25km, frequent buses
Airport transfer Chambéry 2hrs, Geneva 3hrs, Lyon 2½hrs
Visitor beds 32,000
Transport free ski bus with lift pass

THE SKIING
Linked or nearby resorts La Tania (I), Méribel (I), Val Thorens (I), Les Menuires (I), St-Martin-de-Belleville (I)
Longest run Les Creux, 4.2km (red)
Number of lifts 67 in Courchevel, 200 in Trois Vallées
Total of trails/pistes 151km in Courchevel (26% beginner, 27% easy, 36% intermediate, 11% difficult), 600km in Trois Vallées
Nursery slopes 26 slopes
Summer skiing at Val Thorens
Snowmaking 479 snow-cannon

LIFT PASSES
Area pass Courchevel 880FF, Trois Vallées 1,080FF, both for 6 days
Day pass Courchevel 184FF, Trois Vallées 220FF
Beginners 12 free lifts
Pensioners reductions for 60 yrs and over, free for 75 yrs and over
Credit cards yes

TUITION
Adults ESF (1850) 1,125FF and (1650) 900FF for 6 days, (1550) 550FF for 6 half-days. Ski Académie, 510FF for 5 days. Supreme S&S-S 750FF for 5 days, Ski Cocktail 696–795FF for 5 days
Private lessons (1850), (1650) and (1550) 1,450FF per day Ski Académie 590–720FF for 3hrs, Ski Cocktail 1,750FF per day
Snowboarding ESF (1850) 9.30am–midday 630FF, 2.30–5pm 700FF for 6 days
Cross-country all ski schools. Loipe 66km
Other courses slalom, ski-touring, skwal, telemark, monoski, competition
Guiding through ski schools

CHILDREN
Lift pass Courchevel, 5–16yrs 660FF, Trois Vallées, 5–15yrs 702–810FF, both for 6 days, free for under 5yrs
Ski kindergarten ESF (1850) Village des Enfants, 3–12 yrs, 1,020FF for 6 days. ESF (1650) Vacances des Petits, 3–5 yrs, details on request. ESF (1550) Jardin des Neiges, 3–6 yrs, 920FF for 6 days
Ski school (1850) ESF Village des Enfants, 4–12 yrs, 255FF per day including lunch. ESF (1650) Vacances des Petits, 3–5 yrs, 720FF for 6 days not including lunch. ESF (1550) 4–7yrs 960FF
Non-ski kindergarten (1850) Village des Enfants, 18mths and over, 9am–5pm, 265FF per day. (1650) Les Pitchounets, 2–7yrs, 1,290FF for 6 days

OTHER SPORTS
Parapente, flying club, skating, lugeing, ice-climbing, squash, swimming, snow-shoeing, snowmobiling, climbing wall, ski-jumping, ice hockey, ice-driving

FOOD AND DRINK PRICES
Coffee 12FF, glass of wine 20FF, small beer 20–28FF, dish of the day 65–75FF

Skiing facts: Méribel

TOURIST OFFICE
BP1, F-73551 Méribel, Savoie
Tel 33 4 79 08 60 01
Fax 33 4 79 00 59 61
Email meribel@laposte.fr
Web site www.meribel.net

THE RESORT
By road Calais 920km
By rail TGV Moûtiers 18km, regular bus service to resort
Airport transfer Chambéry 2hrs, Geneva 3hrs, Lyon 2½hrs
Visitor beds 30,000
Transport free ski bus included with lift pass

THE SKIING
Linked or nearby resorts La Tania (l), Courchevel (l), Val Thorens (l), Les Menuires (l), St-Martin-de-Belleville (l)
Longest run Campagnol (Mont Vallon), 3.6km (red)
Number of lifts 75 in Méribel, 200 in Trois Vallées
Total of trails/pistes 150km (15% easy, 71% intermediate, 14% difficult), 600km in Trois Vallées
Nursery slopes 4
Summer skiing at Val Thorens
Snowmaking 83 hectares covered

LIFT PASSES
Area pass Méribel Valley 897FF, Trois Vallées 1,080FF, both for 6 days
Day pass Méribel Valley 188FF, Trois Vallées 220FF
Beginners 1 free lift at Le Rond Point and 1 in Méribel Mottaret (beginner's pass also available)
Pensioners reductions for 60 yrs and over, free for 75 yrs and over
Credit cards yes

TUITION
Adults ESF, 220FF per day (5hrs). Ski Cocktail, 795FF for 6 mornings. Magic in Motion, 840FF for 12hrs. Ski Principles, details on request
Private lessons ESF 190FF per hr, 1,500–1,550FF per day. Ski Cocktail details on request. Magic in Motion 550FF 2hrs, 1,750FF per day
Snowboarding ESF, 645FF for 5 half-days
Cross-country ESF, prices as regular ski school. Loipe 33km
Other courses slalom, telemark, moguls, off-piste, heli-skiing
Guiding through ski schools

CHILDREN
Lift pass Méribel Valley, 5–16yrs, 583–673FF, Trois Vallées, 5–15yrs, 702–810FF, all for 6 days, free for under 5yrs
Ski kindergarten Les P'tits Loups (at Méribel and Méribel Mottaret), 3–5yrs, 9am–5pm, 200FF per day, 1,037FF for 6 days. Supervised lunch 640FF for 6 days
Ski school ESF, 5–13yrs, 1,087–1,349FF for 5 days including 6-day Méribel Valley ski pass (not including lunch)
Non-ski kindergarten Les Saturnins, 18mths–3yrs, 9am–5pm, 1,037FF for 6 days. Supervised lunch 500FF for 6 days

OTHER SPORTS
Skating, snowshoeing, parapente, hang-gliding, swimming

FOOD AND DRINK PRICES
Coffee 12FF, glass of wine 20FF, small beer 20–28FF, dish of the day 65–75FF

Skiing facts: Val Thorens

TOURIST OFFICE
F-73440 Val Thorens, Savoie
Tel 33 4 79 00 08 08
Fax 33 4 79 00 00 04
Email valtho@valthorens.com
Web site www.valthorens.com

THE RESORT
By road Calais 928km
By rail TGV Moûtiers 37km, frequent buses to resort
Airport transfer Chambéry 2hrs, Geneva 3hrs, Lyon 2½hrs
Visitor beds 22,000
Transport free ski bus

THE SKIING
Linked or nearby resorts La Tania (l), Méribel (l), Les Menuires (l), Courchevel (l), St-Martin-de-Belleville (l)
Longest run Col de Laudzin,12km
Number of lifts 30 in Val Thorens, 200 in Trois Vallées
Total of trails/pistes 140km in Val Thorens (40% easy, 50% intermediate, 10% difficult), 600km in Trois Vallées
Nursery slopes 3 lifts
Summer skiing 3 lifts and 3 runs on Péclet Glacier
Snowmaking 92 snow-cannons

LIFT PASSES
Area pass Val Thorens 810FF, Trois Vallées 1,080FF, both for 6 days
Day pass Val Thorens 180FF, Trois Vallées 220FF
Beginners 3 free lifts
Pensioners 20–50% reduction depending on age. Free for 75yrs and over
Credit cards yes

TUITION
Adults ESF 690FF for 6 mornings. ESI Ski Cool, 600FF for 5 half-days
Private lessons ESF 180FF per hr, ESI Ski Cool 190FF per hr
Snowboarding ESF 590FF for 5 days (3hrs per day), Ski Surf Nature L'Ecole 600FF for 5 days, Ski Cool 700FF for 6 days
Cross-country ESF 140FF per half-day, 605FF for 6 half-days. Loipe 5km
Other courses telemark, moguls, competition, skwal
Guiding through ESF

CHILDREN
Lift pass Val Thorens 5–15 yrs 527–583FF, Trois Vallées 5–15yrs 702–810FF, both for 6 days, free for under 4yrs
Ski kindergarten ESF Miniclub, 5yrs and over, 9am–5.30pm, 1,350FF for 6 days including lunch. Bambi ski courses, 2–4yrs, 1,350FF for 6 days
Ski school ESF, 5–12yrs, 810FF for 6 days (5½hrs per day). ESI Ski Cool, 4–12yrs, 1,290FF for 6 days including lunch. ESF Stage Etoile, 5–12yrs, 9am–5pm, 1,350FF for 6 days including lunch. Jardin Prosneige, from 4yrs, inclusive package with lessons, ski pass and equipment from 1,120FF for 6 days
Non-ski kindergarten ESF, 3mths–3yrs, 1,350FF for 6 days including lunch

OTHER SPORTS
Parapente, snowmobiling, swimming, snowshoeing, skating, indoor tennis and squash, golf simulator, volleyball, climbing wall

FOOD AND DRINK PRICES
Coffee 12FF, glass of wine 20FF, small beer 20–28FF, dish of the day 65–75FF

Linked or nearby resorts

St-Martin-de-Belleville
top 3300m (10,825ft) bottom 1400m (4,593ft)

Two contrastingly different villages provide alternative bases for skiing the Trois Vallées while avoiding the hustle of the mainstream resorts and their high prices. The first is St-Martin, the 'capital' of the Belleville Valley, a farming community at pastoral counterpoint to the high-tech world of the ski network above it. Reporters praise it as 'quiet and lived-in, unlike the larger towns in the area'. The old cheese-making village has considerable charm and a couple of fine restaurants: L'Etoile de Neige is a lunchtime favourite with ski guides, while Les Airelles, on the main road out of the village, is said to offer 'delicious food'. La Bouitte in neighbouring St-Marcel is a serious exercise in gastronomy.

St-Martin is connected into the system by a slow triple-chair. However, the second stage has now been upgraded to a high-speed quad chair that takes you directly to the top of Tougnette. Nevertheless, if you are staying in Méribel do not linger too long over lunch – allow a full 40 minutes to reach the ridge of the valley on your way home.

TOURIST OFFICE
Tel 33 4 79 08 93 09
Fax 33 4 79 08 91 71

La Tania
top 33C0m (10,825ft) bottom 1350m (4,429ft)

The second, and more modern, alternative ski base for the Trois Vallées is the purpose-built but pleasing village of La Tania, a couple of kilometres by road from Le Praz. It is linked by piste to Courchevel 1850 as well as to Méribel via the Col de la Loze. It was constructed as a dormitory satellite for the Albertville Olympics.

It is a pleasant and reasonably priced base served by a jumbo gondola and, despite its youth, has developed its own village atmosphere. During a heavy snowfall, the tree-lined slopes above it provide some of the most enjoyable powder skiing in the whole of the Trois Vallées area, yet are always under-used. La Tania has its own branch of the ESF: 'The level of the instructors' English was not good – describing the subtle art of knee bending is quite difficult with a vocabulary of only 30 words'. Hotel Montana is 'excellent, modern and clean with large rooms. It now has a small swimming-pool'. Both Pub Le Ski Lodge and La Taiga are described as 'welcoming and serve tasty, (relatively) inexpensive food'. The supermarket has a limited stock. One reporter was also unmoved by the nightlife ('the place is a cemetery after dark').

TOURIST OFFICE
Tel 33 4 79 08 40 40
Fax 33 4 79 08 45 71
Web site www.latania.com

Val d'Isère/Tignes

Val d'Isère 1850m (6,068ft), Tignes 2100m (6,888ft)

Intermediates ✱✱✱ Advanced ✱✱✱ Snowboarders ✱✱✱

Whenever two or three skiers are gathered together anywhere in the world, the conversation will inevitably turn towards Val d'Isère. Early each December – if snow permits – the self-crowned capital of modern European skiing traditionally hosts the first World Cup men's downhill. Between then and the May Bank Holiday, more British skiers visit this remote and rather unprepossessing resort at the head of the Tarentaise Valley than anywhere else.

- ✔ Large well-linked ski area
- ✔ Extensive off-piste
- ✔ Summer skiing
- ✔ Reliable snow record
- ✔ Excellent lift system
- ✔ Lively après-ski (Val d'Isère)
- ✔ Skiing convenience (Tignes)
- ✘ Few activities for non-skiers
- ✘ Lack of tree-level runs

It is a destination for serious enthusiasts, which somehow manages to blend a cocktail of high ski-tech and mass-market tourism with a smooth topping of sophistication. It is a social melting pot, and although it may not attract as many millionaires as Courchevel 1850, those that it does can usually ski like a dream because they visit a resort of this calibre so often. The ski area is directly linked to neighbouring Tignes and is jointly marketed as L'Espace Killy, after its most revered son who swept the board of gold medals at the 1968 Winter Olympics. The fact that Jean-Claude Killy comes from lowland Alsace bothers no one at all.

The quality of the skiing in the area is so varied and demanding that it has raised a whole genre of international experts who never ski anywhere else. A vertical drop of 1890m, coupled with 100 lifts, including two high-speed underground railways, six gondolas and four cable-cars, form the hardcore infrastructure. For the expert, however, the real joy lies in the unlimited off-piste opportunities to be found in this wild region on the edge of the Vanoise National Park. Prices are high, but as one reader commented: 'It may not be cheap, but it probably has the best all-round lift-served skiing on the planet'.

Ski and board
top 3439m (11,279ft) bottom 1550m (5,084ft)

Val d'Isère alone has eight major points of mountain access including a high-speed underground train. The ski school rush hour (adults and children) must be avoided, and the French February holidays are inevitably crowded, but otherwise queuing is not a problem. The long

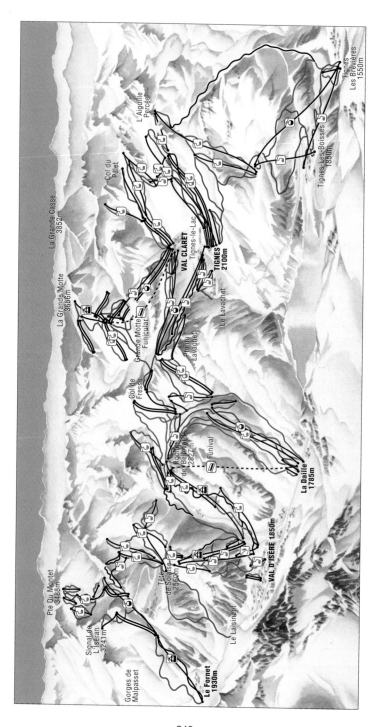

Pte Du Montet
3488m

Signal de
L'Iseran
3241m

Gorges de
Malpasset

La Grande Casse
3852m

Col du
Palet

La Grande Motte
3656m

L'Aiguille
Percée

Tignes
Les Brévières
1550m

Tignes-les-Boisses
1850m

Grande Motte
Funiculaire

VAL CLARET

Tignes-le-Lac

TIGNES
2100m

Le Lavachet

Col de Fresse

Pte du Lavachet

Rocher
de Bellevarde
2827m

Funival

La Daille
1785m

VAL D'ISÈRE 1850m

Le Laisinant

Tête
de Solaise
2550m

Le Fornet
1930m

valley floor is covered by an efficient ski-bus service known as Le Train Rouge, and with a little experience you can avoid even the smallest of rush-hour lift lines.

L'Espace Killy divides naturally into six separate ski sectors. On the Val d'Isère side there are Col de l'Iseran/Pissaillas, Solaise and Bellevarde, which are strung in a row along the curving road between the satellites of **Le Fornet** and **La Daille.** The first two sectors are linked by lift at altitude, but Solaise and Bellevarde link only at valley level just beside the main resort. Bellevarde links with Tignes via the Tovière ridge/Col de Fresse.

The skiing at Tignes is divided into three areas – Tovière, Grande Motte and the glacier, and Palet/Aiguille Percée. Tignes also has a state-of-the-art underground railway. Passengers are whisked at high speed up through the rock and permafrost from **Val Claret** at 2100m to the Panoramic restaurant at 3030m in just six minutes.

An alternative network of lifts takes you from **Tignes-Le-Lac** up towards the dramatic rock formation of L'Aiguille Percée in one direction or towards the greater demands of Val d'Isère's ski area in the other. For most of the season there is more skiing in Tignes down to the lower lying hamlets of **Les Boisses** at 1850m and **Les Brévières** at 1550m. A new lift from Tignes-Le-Lac to this area opens this winter. Once up the mountain it is the dispersal of snow-users that is so clever. The lie of the terrain encourages you to ski further into the mountain range, rather than immediately returning towards the valley.

Piste-grooming is of a high standard. However, the severity of the terrain makes it hugely prone to avalanches. Those in the know take a day out on the protected pistes of **Sainte-Foy**. In windy conditions both Val d'Isère and Tignes benefit enormously from their underground railways. The Funival at La Daille gives guaranteed access to the Rocher de Bellevarde and some of the best runs in the resort. Snowmaking is extensive.

Beginners

Val d'Isère is unfairly denigrated as a resort for beginners. In fact, it has acceptable nursery slopes right in the centre of the village and a wide choice of ski schools. The problem stems from the fact that it is suitable for absolute novices only, and not for wobbly second-weekers. The nursery slopes are free, but the big problem is where to go next. Do not trust the piste-map; some of the runs marked green (beginner) could frighten the daylights out of you. One solution is to ski on Solaise and take the chair-lift or cable-car back down. The Col de l'Iseran sector has some gentle runs, but here, as in other parts of the resort, it is too difficult to ski back to the valley. Tignes has a good choice of blue (easy) runs on the glacier but it is a cold place in which to be falling about.

Intermediates

Piste-grading is not Val's strongest point, and colour-coding is on the dark side – some blues would be red (intermediate) runs elsewhere, and you may find the odd red that is positively black (difficult) by Tyrolean standards. The Bellevarde sector provides plenty of variety. The Solaise Bumps down the front face of the 2560-m Tête de Solaise are classic, and the moguls can be awkward. The L (check to see if it is open) off the back of Solaise takes you down to the hamlet of **Le Laisinant** and is a superb cruise. The OK run around the shoulder of the Rocher de Bellevarde is the World Cup downhill course; when it is not prepared for racing this trail provides another excellent cruise.

> ## WHAT'S NEW IN VAL D'ISÈRE
> Trifollet piste at La Daille
> Privilege card points offering shopping discounts

Advanced

The Face de Bellevarde, reached by the Funival funicular railway, became the men's downhill course for the Albertville Olympics in 1992. The legacy is a superb black run, which leads you back to Val in rather more than the two minutes it took winner Patrick Ortlieb and his fellow competitors. Sache, a superb long black, starts from the blue Corniche run below L'Aiguille Percée and takes you almost down to **Tignes-Les-Brévières** where it merges with the red Pavot. The run down through the trees from the top of Le Fornet can, at times, be the best in the resort. The steepest piste is the Epaule du Charvet ('when groomed, you can play at being a downhiller; otherwise, the bumps are legendary'). Val snowpark is above La Daille on the upper slopes of Bellevarde.

Off-piste

The starting points for some of the most challenging itineraries are marked on the piste-map. Once you begin, you are on your own and it is easy to get lost – or worse. It is imperative to have a local guide who can read the snow conditions and knows which routes are safe. In fresh powder the Charvet area is a particular favourite. One resident reporter commented; 'there is no greater thrill than cutting first tracks on the Face du Charvet or the Couloir Mont Blanc before skiing the Bec d'Aigle'. The Signal de l'Iseran/Glacier de Pissaillas sector provides some of the most dramatic runs, but the beauty of Val and Tignes is the accessibility of good off-piste throughout the region.

Tuition and guiding

To get the best out of the ski area you need some expert help: the two resorts now boast over 20 ski and snowboarding schools. Back in 1976 the French Ski School (ESF) had the monopoly throughout the country on instruction. Patrick and Jean Zimmer, two young ex-racers from Alsace, took on the ESF in true David and Goliath fashion – all the way to the French high court – and won the right to open their own ski school in Val d'Isère. Since their precedent, alternative schools have sprung up in almost every resort, but the Zimmer brothers' Top Ski has a cult following. The secret of its success is that it has remained small. Jean and Patrick take groups of six skiers off-piste in the mornings and guarantee to find you the best snow in the resort. They also give instruction on piste technique in the afternoons and arrange ski-tours, heli-skiing in Italy, summer skiing, and tuition for children aged eight and over.

The ESF operates in both resorts, but Anglo-Saxons tend to favour the alternatives, which are more linguistically and emotionally geared towards the needs of the calibre of skier who wants to get the best out of this extraordinary area. We have continuing good reports of Snow Fun: 'The instructors were personable, spoke fluent English and made the effort to learn the names of their pupils', and 'we were highly impressed by their organisation and emphasis on group grading'. We have encouraging reports of Mountain Masters, which has been criticised in the past. One reporter described a guide from Alpine Experience as: 'The best I have ever come across anywhere'. Evolution 2, in both Val and Tignes, also receives complimentary reports.

Hors Limites Surf School in Val runs free introductory snowboard lessons, with equipment included, on the nursery slopes on Sunday afternoons. It takes riders from as young as five years old in groups of six to eight. Most of the ski schools offer lessons. Surf Rider Snowboard Club specialises in off-piste snowboarding and heli-surfing in Italy. In Tignes, Surf Feeling and Kébra Surfing are the specialist schools.

Mountain restaurants

Good mountain restaurants are both sparse and expensive. It costs about as much to build a new WC up a mountain as it does to install a lift, and L'Espace Killy concentrates on the latter. The better establishments are on the Val side and include Trifollet ('good pizzas'), which is halfway down to La Daille, and La Folie Douce, at the top of La Daille gondola. La Fruitière, next to the Folie Douce, is decorated as a Savoyard dairy, has some of the best food on the mountain as well as the best WCs, and should be booked in advance during high season. La Datcha at the foot of the Cugnai chair was criticised: 'The food is expensive, the staff surly and the service poor'.

At lunch-time many snow-users return to the valley, where restaurants are as busy as they are by night. The family-run Crech'Ouna, near the Funival station, and Bananas are the favourites among reporters. Clochetons is also praised for its 'reasonably priced *table d'hôte*'. The Arbina in Lac de Tignes has 'delicious local Savoie salads'. The Bouida, by the gondola at Les Brévières, is said to be good value for money, although one reader waited an hour for a drink. The newly rebuilt restaurant at the Col du Palet was described as 'very welcoming'.

The resort

Apart from the eleventh-century church, precious little remains of the old village of Val d'Isère, which used to be called L'Aval de Tignes and was home to the hunting lodges of the Dukes of Savoie before becoming a winter sports resort in 1932. Today, it has grown into a hotchpotch of a ski town, which sprawls from the apartment blocks of La Daille at one end to Le Fornet at the other. Until the mid-1980s the centre was an ill-defined area where the petrol stations, concrete résidences and the occasional pleasing chalet gave way to a row of shops and bars on either side of the wide and busy main road.

However, a cluster of 'old-style' stone buildings (created for the 1992 Olympics) house the smarter boutiques and restaurants and provide the village with a pleasing focal point, which it previously lacked. Attempts to limit the traffic, which tends to clog this long, drawn-out resort, have been partially successful. Anyone who does not use the underground car park or the parking lots on the edge of town risks a hefty fine. The old village of Tignes disappeared beneath the waters of the Lac du Chevril when the valley was dammed in 1952. Its replacement, a series of high-rise housing estates at varying altitudes around 2000m, represents some of the most ghastly excesses of French alpine architecture of the 1960s.

> ## WHAT'S NEW IN TIGNES
> £70-million investment plan over five years
> Chaudannes quad chair-lift
> Remodelled *front de neige*

The hamlets of Val Claret, Tignes-Le-Lac, **Le Lavachet** and even the much lower community of **Tignes-Les-Boisses** would all benefit from a compulsory demolition order. Only the valley farming community of Tignes-Les-Brévières should be reprieved. The village fathers have announced plans to invest some £35 million in lift improvements by 2004 and have ambitiously earmarked a similar sum to give the resort an entire new look by 2001. During the summer of 1998 major construction work was started in the resort centre to create a new *front de neige*. A new 320-space covered car park was built at Le Lavachet. A new people-mover lift now links the car park at Val Claret with the funicular station, and the new Chaudannes quad chair-lift from Lac de Tignes provides extra easy access to the L'Aiguille Percée sector.

Skiing is a year-round commitment in Tignes. Permanent winter conditions on the Grande Motte Glacier allow racers and dedicated recreational snow-users to practise on its wide and open slopes even in July and August. In winter, at least, the ugliness of the resort is counterbalanced by the glory of the skiing.

Buses between Val d'Isère and Tignes are neither frequent nor cheap, and taxis can be extortionate. If you have your own car and want a change of scenery, day-trips to **Les Arcs**, **La Plagne**, **La Rosière** and Sainte-Foy are all possible.

Accommodation

In Val d'Isère a cluster of four-stars heads a choice of 39 hotels. The Blizzard and the Christiania are the most comfortable, while the Savoyarde and the Tsanteleina have a strong British following. Most snow-users stay in chalets or in self-catering apartments. YSE is the largest specialist chalet operator here and runs Mountain Lodges, a seventeenth-century farmhouse divided into two units.

In Tignes, most accommodation is in self-catering apartments, which vary dramatically in quality in direct relation to their age. The more

Skiing facts: Val d'Isère

TOURIST OFFICE
BP 228, F-73155 Val d'Isère, Savoie
Tel 33 4 79 06 06 60
Fax 33 4 79 06 04 56
Email info@val-disere.com
Web site www.val-disere.com

THE RESORT
By road Calais 960km
By rail Bourg-St-Maurice 30km
Airport transfer Geneva or Chambéry
2½hrs, Lyon 3hrs
Visitor beds 26,500
Transport free ski bus between La Daille
and Le Fornet

THE SKIING
Linked or nearby resorts Tignes (l),
Sainte-Foy (n)
Longest run OK, 4.8km (red)
Number of lifts 100 in L'Espace Killy
Total of trails/pistes 300km in L'Espace
Killy (15% easy, 47% intermediate, 38%
difficult)
Nursery slopes 7 free lifts
Summer skiing 7 pistes and 14 lifts on
Grande Motte Glacier, and limited on
Glacier de Pissaillas
Snowmaking 125 snow-cannon in
Val d'Isère

LIFT PASSES
Area pass L'Espace Killy, 1,005FF
for 6 days
Day pass L'Espace Killy 217FF
Beginners free for under 5yrs
Pensioners 60yrs and over 810FF for 6
days, 70–74yrs half-price, free for 75yrs
and over
Credit cards yes

TUITION
Adults ESF 1,050FF and Snow Fun

1,020–1,030FF, both for 6 days. Other
schools, details on request
Private lessons ESF, 9.30am–5pm,
1,500FF per day
Snowboarding ESF, 695FF for 6 half-
days. Other schools, details on request
Cross-country ESF private lessons,
530FF for 2½hrs. Loipe 44km in
L'Espace Killy
Other courses telemark, slalom,
competition, carving, Big Foot,
snowblading, monoski
Guiding Top Ski, Snow Fun, Altimanya,
Bureau des Guides, Evolution 2, Alpine
Experience, Mountain Masters

CHILDREN
Lift pass 5–12yrs, 705FF for 6 days,Val
d'Isère and Tignes, free for 4yrs and under
Ski kindergarten Snow Fun Teddy Bear
Club, 3–6yrs, 168FF for 3hrs. Snow Fun
Club Marmottons, 4–7yrs, 9.30am–midday and 2.15–4.45pm, 990FF for 6 days
Ski School Snow Fun, 6–13yrs,
9.30am–12.30pm and 2.30–5pm, 890FF
for 6 days. Snow Fun Stage courses,
8–13yrs, 9.30am–5pm, 1,700FF for 6
days including lunch and equipment. ESF
159FF per day, details on request
Non-ski kindergarten Garderie Isabelle,
2–8yrs, 220FF per day. Petits Poucets,
3–8yrs, 9am–5pm, 220FF per day

OTHER SPORTS
Parapente, snowshoeing, quad- and
ice-driving, dog-sledding, snowmobiling,
skating and curling, ice-climbing,
swimming, helicopter rides

FOOD AND DRINK
Coffee 10–15FF, glass of wine 12–16FF,
small beer 15–20FF, dish of the day
75–80FF

modern developments are much more spacious, and it is important to check carefully before booking. Hotels range from the comfortable four-star Le Ski d'Or to a clutch of two-stars which includes Hotel de la Vanoise ('convenient, with an excellent breakfast and five-course dinner, and a fine room with bathroom and large balcony').

Eating in and out

In Val d'Isère the Grand Ourse is 'in a lovely setting but the service is not always dependable'. Perdrix Blanche is unpretentious and renowned for its fresh seafood. Chalet du Crêt is a 'wonderfully gastronomic' smart restaurant in a 300-year-old chalet. The restaurants in the three-star Savoyarde and Blizzard hotels are both excellent for dinner. Bananas is an old favourite among reporters. Pacific Pizzeria 'has good food, including fish at sensible prices'. Crêpe Val, close to the post office, is recommended for regional specialities as well as crêpes. L'Arolay in Le Fornet has 'fine food'. Val d'Isère has two supermarkets and several specialist food shops.

In Tignes, L'Osteria in Le Lavachet is recommended for raclette and pierrade. L'Arbina (upstairs restaurant) is 'outstanding, a *crêpe des escargots* to die for'. The Wobbly Rabbit in Val Claret serves Mexican food and fondues. The Codec supermarket in Val Claret is expensive but has a wide range of goods for self-caterers.

Après-ski

Val d'Isère buzzes with a fun-seeking après-ski crowd unparalleled elsewhere in France. 'Have An Affair in Val d'Isère' proclaimed the T-shirt of the 1980s as it gyrated sensually in the strobe-lighting of Dick's T-Bar. The T-Bar is still here and it continues to be one of the most celebrated discos in the Alps. Café Face and Bananas are riding high. G Jay's has cheap beer, sausages and beans, chalet girls and a crush of homesick ex-pat ski bums. The Morris Pub has a lively, young following.

'What après-ski?' said one reporter of Tignes. Certainly it is limited in comparison with that of its smoother and more sophisticated neighbour. Harri's Bar and the predominantly British-frequented Cavern Bar in Le Lavachet have a strong following. The Caves du Lac in Tignes-Le-Lac has a small dance floor. Other discos are the Xyphos in Le Lac, and Les Chandelles and Graffiti in Val Claret. One reporter summarised it: 'When the lifts close skiers and snowboarders just melt back to their apartments without stopping off for one or two drinks before dinner'.

Childcare

Facilities for small children in Val d'Isère have improved enormously over the last few seasons, although if you want to take non-skiing children on holiday, there are still more convenient resorts to go to. Garderie Isabelle takes children from two years. Les Petits Poucets kindergarten collects and delivers children from your chalet or hotel. The Bibou Nanny Agency provides day and evening babysitting.

Families with children at ski school should choose accommodation

Skiing facts: Tignes

TOURIST OFFICE
BP 51, F-73321 Tignes, Savoie
Tel 33 4 79 40 04 40
Fax 33 4 79 40 03 15
Email tignes@laposte.fr
Web site www.tignes.net

THE RESORT
By road Calais 960km
By rail Bourg-St-Maurice 26km
Airport transfer Geneva or Chambéry
2½hrs, Lyon 2½hrs
Visitor beds 28,000
Transport free ski bus between Les
Boisses and Val Claret

THE SKIING
Linked or nearby resorts Val d'Isère (l),
Sainte-Foy (n)
Longest run Double M, 5.5km (red)
Number of lifts 100 in L'Espace Killy
Total of trails/pistes 300km in L'Espace
Killy (62% easy, 29% intermediate, 9%
difficult)
Nursery slopes 3 lifts
Summer skiing 7 pistes and 14 lifts on
Grande Motte Glacier
Snowmaking 125 snow-cannons in
Tignes

LIFT PASSES
Area pass L'Espace Killy, 1,005FF for 6
days
Day pass L'Espace Killy 217FF
Beginners 5 free lifts
Pensioners 60–69yrs 850FF for 6 days,
70–74yrs half-price, free for 75yrs and over
Credit cards yes

TUITION
Adults ESF 1,104FF for 6 days. Evolution
2 and Ski Action, details on request
Private lessons ESF 230FF per hr,
1,400FF per day
Snowboarding ESF 720FF for 6 half-
days. Beginners 395FF for 3 half-days.
Other schools, details on request
Cross-country ESF, 600FF for 5
mornings. Loipe 44km in L'Espace Killy
Other courses slalom, competition,
moguls, heli-skiing
Guiding Bureau des Guides, Association
9 Valleys, Stage 2000

CHILDREN
Lift pass 5–12yrs, 705FF for 6 days,
free for 4yrs and under
Ski kindergarten Les Marmottons,
8.30am–5pm, 2–7yrs, 1,450FF for 6
days including lunch
Ski school ESF, 4–10yrs, 1,044FF for
6 days. ESI, details on request
Non-ski kindergarten Les Petits Lutins
3mths and over, Les Marmottons
3yrs and over at Le Lac and
Val Claret, both 1,500FF for 6 days
including lunch

OTHER SPORTS
Ice-diving, bowling, skating, squash,
tennis, parapente, hang-gliding,
climbing-walls, husky sleigh-rides

FOOD AND DRINK PRICES
Coffee 8–15FF, glass of wine 12–16FF,
small beer 15–20FF, dish of the day
60–80FF

close to the Front de Neige to minimise the inconvience of travelling backwards and forwards on the bus. ESF, Snow Fun and Evolution 2 all cater for young beginners from three to four years. Surfer Kids run by Hors Limites takes riders from six years, and BillaBong Snowboard School from six years.

Snow Fun is highly recommended by reporters – 'We wouldn't consider sending our children to any of the other ski schools in the resort'. Its Teddy Bear Club is for small beginners and Club Marmottons is for those who can manage to ski a green run. Children from eight years of age who have completed the highest ski school class can join Snow Fun's Stage course during the school holidays only, which includes slalom skiing, snowboarding, Big Foot and SnowBlading.

In Tignes, the Petits Lutins takes babies from three months old, and Les Marmottons from three years. The ESF offers ski lessons from four years of age, and the International Ski School (ESI) from five.

Linked or nearby resorts

Sainte-Foy
top 2620m (8,596ft) bottom 1550m (5,084ft)

Sainte-Foy is an unremarkable old hamlet that you drive through on the road up from **Bourg-St-Maurice** to Tignes and Val d'Isère. But just above it, reached by a side road, lies the ski resort of the same name. To call it a resort is an exaggeration; the lift ticket office, ski shop and bar provide the main base facilities of this raw and exciting ski area. The locals come to Sainte-Foy to enjoy untracked powder after a fresh fall. When high winds or unstable conditions shut down the main components of L'Espace Killy, this is the place to spend the day. The mid-station mountain restaurant, an old cow barn, is renowned for its omelettes.

Three chair-lifts take you up to the Col de l'Aiguille and the starting point for 600 vertical metres of challenging piste and some dramatic powder descents. There are two simple but atmospheric mountain eating-places. At the moment Sainte-Foy remains remarkably unspoilt; plans to extend the lift system and to build accommodation may change all this. The simple but pleasant Hotel Le Monal in the old village is recommended. The Ski Company has a delightful lodge here which is said to be 'the most luxurious chalet in the Alps'. One reporter praised the British-owned Auberge sur la Montagne in the neighbouring hamlet of La Thuile: 'Excellent cuisine, warm welcome.

TOURIST OFFICE
Tel 33 4 79 06 95 19
Fax 33 4 79 06 95 09

Valmorel

ALTITUDE 1400m (4,592ft)

Beginners ✳✳✳ Intermediates ✳✳✳ Advanced ✳

Valmorel is an attractive family resort in the Tarentaise, which is reached by road from Moûtiers. It shares a network of 53 lifts and 151km of pistes with the popular French destination of **St François-Longchamp** in the Maurienne Valley and the beginner resort of **Doucy Combelouvière**. Together they market themselves as Le Grand Domaine and offer a wide range of skiing, mainly below advanced level. Unlike its purpose-built forerunners, the village is architecturally pleasing and fits so snugly into its mountain environment that it is hard to believe that it was only constructed in 1976. Central Valmorel is often referred to as Bourg-Morel to distinguish it from the satellite residential areas called *hameaux* lying some distance outside the centre. There are a further 20km of cross-country pistes below Valmorel where wild boar have been sighted, even in winter.

- ✔ Protected learning areas
- ✔ Sympathetic architecture
- ✔ Family atmosphere
- ✔ Central pedestrian area
- ✔ Value for money
- ✘ Few non-skiing activities
- ✘ No shuttle bus around residential satellites

Readers have pointed out that the colour-coding of the local lift map flies in the face of all accepted procedure in Europe for reasons that are not at all clear. Green is listed as easy, blue as intermediate, red as difficult, and black as very difficult. The tourist director is unable to shed any light on this.

Ski and board
top 2550m (8,364ft) bottom 1250m (4,100ft)

Valmorel is a planned family resort with exceptional nursery slopes (for adults and children), which are closed off to passing skiers and snowboarders. It also has testing enough terrain to keep competent skiers and snowboarders interested for a week. Mountain access is from various satellite hamlets at different altitudes. The Télébourg gondola runs from Bourg-Morel in two stages up to the hamlets of Crève-Coeur and Mottet, but is designed more as a people-carrier than a ski lift.

The old Beaudin chair-lift, which was heavily prone to queues, has been replaced by the new Altispace covered quad-chair, which acts as the link to St François-Longchamp. The skiing is mostly as easy as it appears. Le Grand Domaine network is divided into the bowl above Valmorel and a straight up-and-down system of lifts between Longchamp and St

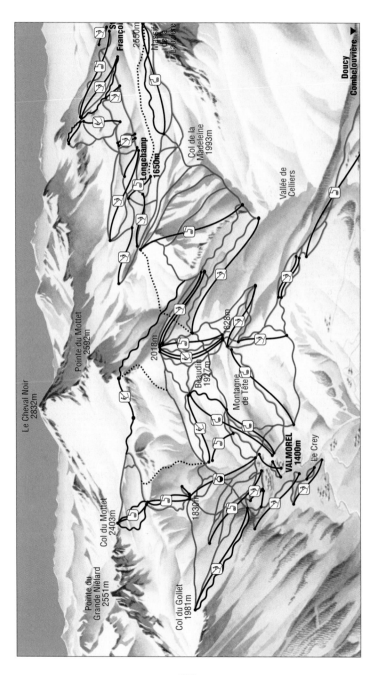

St
Françoi

2650m

Massi
Lauz

Doucy
Combelouvière

Col de la
Madeleine
1993m

Longchamp
1650m

Vallée de
Celliers

Pointe du Mottet
2592m

2018m

1828m

Le Cheval Noir
2832m

Beaudin
1927m

Montagne
de Tête

VALMOREL
1400m

Le Crey

Pointe du
Grande Niélard
2551m

Col du Mottet
2403m

1830m

Col du Gollet
1981m

François across the Col de la Madeleine. All three sectors are accessible by blue (intermediate) pistes. It is important to allow enough time to make the journey back to Valmorel at the end of the day, as a taxi ride of two hours is the only alternative. The installation of a drag-lift and a chair at St François have greatly eased late-afternoon congestion.

Beginners

Valmorel is one of the best resorts in the Alps for beginners – both adults and children. The latter have a protected nursery area with a rope-tow at the Saperlipopette kindergarten down by the Télébourg tower, as well as a totally enclosed area with toys and a lift up the mountain in the Pierrafort area. Unusual, if not unique in the Alps is a similarly enclosed adult training area by the Bois de la Croix drag-lift. It has hillocks and slalom snowplough runs specially designed to give confidence. The linked resort of Doucy Combelouvière has a network of the easiest of green (easy) runs.

> **WHAT'S NEW**
>
> Covered quad-chair provides link to St François-Longchamp

Second-week skiers and snowboarders should be able to make the traverse to St François and Longchamp, which have the best easy slopes in the network. The Biollène piste is ideal for novice riders.

Intermediates

This is a resort where you always feel you are going somewhere, rather than skiing the same runs or similar pistes in the same bowl over and over again. The long runs down into the Celliers Valley and the exciting descents off the Col de Gollet provide classic skiing. Bump bashers will want to hit the two red (difficult) runs under the Madeleine chair where the snow keeps cool and crisp. Both runs (numbers 86 and 87) off the Lauzière chair are steeper options.

Advanced

There are not many black (very difficult) runs, nor are they especially ferocious, though the monster bumps (number 31) under the Gollet chair have been used in championship competitions. The Mottet chair also leads to some testing bumps (number 44) and is the setting-off point for the longest and most interesting black (number 74) which, after a short drag-lift, takes you all the way to the valley floor.

Off-piste

The beauty of Valmorel's off-piste is that even during the high-season weeks you can usually find whole stretches of untracked powder long after a snowfall. With its family image, the resort does not normally attract advanced skiers and snowboarders. However, it is also part of the Nine Valleys ski safari, for which a guide is required. Most terrain is rolling rather than steep and narrow. Excellent powder skiing after a snowfall can be found down the ridge between Mottet and Gollet.

Tuition and guiding

Classes meet at the French Ski School (ESF) headquarters at the top of the Télébourg people-mover. Lessons given in English are held in the afternoons from Sunday to Friday; and in French in the mornings, from Monday to Saturday. The 70 permanent instructors seem dedicated and professional. ESF instructors/guides take private clients off-piste. There is an independent mountain guides bureau, which has no office but can be contacted by phone.

Mountain restaurants

These are mostly self-service and offer value for money rather than haute cuisine. The Alpage at the top of the Altispace chair-lift is recommended: 'A basic cafeteria with ample space and inspiring views'. Le Prariond under the Pierrafort is under new ownership. Altipiano on Pierrafort is smarter, while the Banquoise 2000 refuge on Col de la Madeleine is self-service but characterful, with rustic tables and a log fire. Les 2 Mazots has the best *croûte au fromage*, and Le Grenier, next to the ski school, is still extremely popular. Le Slalom opposite the St François nursery slopes 'serves excellent food and beers from around the world'.

The resort

The wood-and-stone cladding of its six residential developments makes Valmorel the least offensive of French planned communities. There is no shuttle bus around the hamlets, and the Télébourg people-mover delivers residents either too high or too low for convenience. Shopping is limited to a single car-free street, which is not without charm, and shopkeepers are friendly and helpful. An inordinate number of stray dogs and wailing children create hazards underfoot and discord to the ears. Valmorel is within easy driving distance of **Courchevel**, **Méribel**, **La Plagne** and **Les Arcs**.

Accommodation

The resort has only three hotels, none of which is in the luxury class. Self-catered apartments, all less than 15 years old, are generally larger and better designed than their counterparts in other French purpose-built resorts. Most apartments have balconies and provide easy access to the pistes. The two-star Hotel du Bourg, used by most British tour operators, is situated in the main village centre. Its rooms are unadorned boxes, and the beds are as narrow as coffins. The Hotel la Fontaine has bigger, better rooms. Hotel Planchamp, above the main village, is convenient for skiing down from but not handy for evenings out.

Eating in and out

If proof were needed that the French now live off pizza and fast food, then Valmorel is it. This is not a resort renowned for fine dining, although reporters note recent improvements. La Grange has the ubiquitous range of Savoie specialities. Planchamp is 'cosy with a great

Skiing facts: Valmorel

TOURIST OFFICE
La Maison de Valmorel, Bourg-Morel,
F-73260 Valmorel, Savoie
Tel 33 4 79 09 85 55
Fax 33 4 79 09 85 29
Web site www.skifrance.fr/valmorel

THE RESORT
By road Calais 910km
By rail Moûtiers 15km, regular bus
service to resort
Airport transfer Geneva 3hrs,
Lyon 2½hrs
Visitor beds 8,500
Transport traffic-free village centre,
Télébourg gondola between village
sectors

THE SKIING
Linked or nearby resorts St François-
Longchamp (l), Doucy Combelouvière (l)
Longest run La Madeleine, 3.5km (blue)
Number of lifts 53 in Le Grand Domaine
Total of trails/pistes 151km in Le Grand
Domaine (34% easy, 38% intermediate,
28% difficult)
Nursery slopes 4
Summer skiing none
Snowmaking 40 hectares covered

LIFT PASSES
Area pass Valmorel 682–857FF,
Le Grand Domaine (covers Valmorel
Doucy Combelouvière and St François-
Longchamp) 750–954FF, both for 6 days
Day pass Valmorel 128–161FF,
Le Grand Domaine 141–178FF
Beginners no free lifts

Pensioners 60yrs and over, as children
Credit cards yes

TUITION
Adults ESF, 585FF for 6 half-days.
Beginners' course 1,169FF for 6
half-days including lift pass
Private lessons ESF, 174FF per hr
Snowboarding 585FF for 6 half-days
Cross-country 585FF for 6 half-days.
Loipe 20km
Other courses monoski,
competition, telemark
Guiding independent mountain
guides bureau

CHILDREN
Lift pass Valmorel, 4–12yrs, 630–816FF
for 6 days, Le Grand Domaine,
603–768FF for 6 days
Ski kindergarten Saperlipopette,
3–7yrs, 8.30am–5pm, 91–108FF
per day not including lunch
Ski school ESF, 4–12yrs, 545FF.
Beginners' courses, 1,169FF including lift
pass. Both for 6 x 2½hrs
Non-ski kindergarten Saperlipopette,
6mths–3yrs, 8.45am–12pm or
1.30–5pm, 153–174FFper day

OTHER SPORTS
Parapente, snowshoeing, dog-sledding,
winter walks, micro-light, sleigh rides

FOOD AND DRINK PRICES
Coffee 7–10FF, glass of wine 13FF,
small beer 14–18FF, dish of the day
60–75FF

atmosphere'. L'Aigle Blanche, just outside the village, is worth the visit. Ski-Roc is best for rabbit filet with garlic. Le Perce Neige can also be recommended. Jumbo Lolo serves Tex-Mex, and La Marmite advertises couscous and paella, but you should stick with the steak-frites. Chez Albert is best for pizza. Self-caterers have a wide choice of tempting *traiteurs*, and the Superette du Bourg and Etoile des Alpes, right across the main street from each other, have a full range of groceries.

Après-ski

It is not that there isn't any, but it is all rather uninteresting. Jean's Club under the Télébourg tower is the only disco. Loud Top-20 type music is played in the Perce Neige, Café de la Gare and at La Cordée. The Shaker Bar in the Hotel la Fontaine has comfortable sofas and karaoke evenings.

Childcare

The only childminding service is the Saperlipopette nursery. The school has bedrooms and playrooms for infants from six months of age. Children from 18 months to three years of age have their own enclosed outdoor area. Older children have their own fenced-off ski slope with a rope-tow. Reservations should be made well in advance of leaving Britain, as the school keeps to a strict ratio of five children per nanny. 'Good English, good care, and exceptionally well-organised,' was one of a number of positive comments.

Round-up

La Clusaz
top 2600m (8,528ft) bottom 1100m (3,608ft)

La Clusaz is a large, spread-out resort off the Autoroute Blanche on the way to Chamonix, less than two hours' drive from Geneva Airport. Consequently, it is extremely attractive to skiers from Britain and Holland, some of whom have bought apartments here and visit for weekends. However, the real drawback is its lack of altitude. The village itself is only 1100m, which is extremely low by Haute-Savoie standards, and the ski area, with its 56 lifts, only goes up to 2600m. The 40 lifts of nearby **Le Grand-Bornand** are included in the regional lift pass, as is the connecting ski bus.

La Clusaz has five ski areas spread around the sides of a number of neighbouring valleys. Mountain access to Beauregard and L'Aiguille is by lifts from the resort centre. The other three areas (Balme, L'Etale and Croix-Fry/Merdassier) are reached from various points along the valleys via a satisfactory ski-bus network. Despite roads and rivers all five are linked by lift or piste.

The best novice slopes are at Crêt du Merle in L'Aiguille sector and on the top of Beauregard. The skiing is best suited to intermediates, and the pistes are of limited appeal to advanced skiers.

The resort has two ski schools: the French Ski School (ESF) and Ski Académie. We have reports of oversubscribed classes run by the ESF ('our instructor just could not remember 15 names'). The ESF and Ski-Académie both teach snowboarding, and there is a funpark.

The heart of the village is mainly traditional, built around a large church, with a stylish modern shopping precinct beside it and a fast-flowing stream below. Non-skiing activities include swimming and snowshoe excursions. Accommodation is divided between tour-operator chalets and a number of hotels of varying quality. We have glowing reports of the three-star Hotel Beauregard ('extremely well-fitted, modern pine interior, the food is excellent and it really deserves a four-star rating'). The skiing convenience here is one of the lowest we have found among French resorts, and location of accommodation is crucial. The Alpenroc, Hotel Nouvel, Hotel Christiania and Hotel Floralp all receive favourable reports.

La Clusaz has a much wider choice of restaurants than you would expect in a resort of this size. Le Foly is an attractive and expensive log-cabin in the Confins Valley. Le Symphonie in the Hotel Beauregard offers 'excellent cuisine with a cheerful service in a warm atmosphere'. Le Coin du Feu is recommended for its 'delicious *crêpe sucré*'. The Crémaillère specialises in fondue and raclette. One reporter raved about the chili and burgers at the Tex-Mex Café.

Après-ski centres around a few bars. Le Pressoir is the 'in' place for snowboarders. Resort workers meet in the Lion d'Or. L'Ecluse is said to be the best of the discos, with a glass dance-floor over the river, while Le Club 18 has live bands and attracts the locals and an older clientèle. Nightlife is quiet during the week, some would say too quiet, but can become extremely lively during weekends.

La Clusaz has a '3 Kids' rating as one of the best-equipped French resorts for children.

TOURIST OFFICE
Tel 33 4 50 32 65 00
Fax 33 4 50 32 65 01

Isola 2000
top 2610m (8,561ft) bottom 1800m (5,904ft)

Isola is a purpose-built resort and the most southerly ski area in France. In reasonable weather conditions it is 90 minutes' drive north of Nice along the dramatic road beside the Tinée Ravines. The resort was built by a British property company in the 1960s. Created with families in mind, it has a convenient complex of shops, bars, economically designed apartments and hotels, and a large, sunny nursery area. Isola is not accessible from the north, which in part accounts for why so few tour operators offer it in their brochures. However, British skiers make up a big slice of the winter business, and many of them own apartments in the resort.

The resort's original building, the ugly and soulless Front de Neige Centre, is right on the slopes. In an attempt to dress it up, the more attractive, wood-clad additions of Le Bristol, Le Hameau and Les Ardets were built behind it. These are less convenient but contain bigger and better apartments and a luxurious hillside hotel. This has greatly helped the overall look of Isola 2000, dissipating some of its claustrophobic atmosphere.

The ski area is limited, but varied enough for beginners, families with small children and intermediates. There are 46 pistes covered by 24 lifts with 35 hectares of snowmaking. The resorts of **Auron** and **Valberg** are both within easy reach for a day's skiing.

TOURIST OFFICE
Tel 33 4 93 23 15 15
Fax 33 4 93 23 14 25

Pra-Loup
top 2500m (8,202ft) bottom 1600m (5,249ft)

This small resort in the Alpes de Haute-Provence was named after the wolves that once frequented these pine forests. It has a surprisingly extensive range of beginner and intermediate trails but few advanced. The 167km of piste is shared with neighbouring **La Foux d'Allos**. The skiing takes place on two main mountains, accessible by cable-car from the top of the village at 1600m. Intermediates will find open-bowl skiing and good tree-line runs with spectacular scenery. There is extensive off-piste, for which you will need a guide, but only five black (difficult) runs. Weekend queues are said to be 'fearsome'.

The resort is split into the two villages of 1500 and 1600, which are linked by a chair-lift and consist of a collection of hotels and apartments built in the 1960s, along with some older chalets. Prices at the restaurants and bars are lower than in better-known French resorts. Hotel Berger is recommended. Lou Foque and Mamas are the popular après-ski spots. There are a couple of discos, indoor tennis courts, and night-skiing takes place from 6 to 8pm.

TOURIST OFFICE
Tel 33 4 92 84 10 04
Fax 33 4 92 84 02 93
Email praloup@baratel.fr

Puy-St-Vincent
top 2750m (9,022ft) bottom 1350m (4,429ft)

Puy-St-Vincent is an established resort, which was extremely popular with British families in the 1970s and is now staging a major comeback. It is situated 20km from **Briançon**, three hours from Grenoble or Turin, and on the edge of the Ecrins National Park. It has a microclimate that usually ensures solid late-season snow cover along with 300 days of sunshine per year.

Puy-St-Vincent 1400 is an unspoilt mountain village with three two-star hotels. It is connected by a double chair-lift and a drag-lift to the higher *station de ski* of **Puy-St-Vincent 1600**, which is dominated by a central apartment block that has seen better days. Newer résidences have been built on the edge of the piste. The ski area is small but challenging, with enough variety to suit all standards of skier. Queues are a rarity. Two chair-lifts and a gondola give easy access to the main skiing, which goes up to 2750m. The ESF and ESI both offer group lessons and a range of courses. The ESI runs classes for British children during the peak holiday weeks.

Accommodation is mainly in apartments, and après-ski is strictly limited: 'Puy 1600 goes to bed at 9pm,' said one reporter, and 'Puy 1400 is cut off after the lifts close'. The St-Vincent and Cadran Solaire restaurants are both warmly recommended. As one reporter put it: 'Puy is a resort which visitors either love or hate. To some it is too small, with not enough to occupy avid skiers by day or après-skiers by night. To others it has great charm, character and intimacy. I have already booked again for next year'.

TOURIST OFFICE
Tel 33 4 92 23 35 80
Fax 33 4 92 23 45 23

Valloire
top 2600m (8,528ft) bottom 1430m (4,690ft)

Valloire is an attractive, reasonably large village set in an isolated bowl above the Maurienne Valley. It is still very much a traditional French farming community, and the odd whiff of manure mingling with the aroma of freshly baked bread is all part of the atmosphere.

This is a friendly, medium-priced resort, uncrowded except in high season. However, its proximity to the Italian border means that it can be busy and very noisy. The 150km of skiing comprises 86 pistes divided between two areas – La Sétaz and Le Crey du Quart – on adjacent mountains reached by lifts that start a few minutes' walk away from the village centre and rise to 2600m. The terrain is varied, and some of the runs are as long as 1000 vertical metres. The skiing is not difficult – even the black runs would be red (intermediate) by many other resorts' standards.

Mountain access to La Sétaz is by a six-person gondola from the village up to Thimel, followed by a chair- and drag-lift to the summit. Served by artificial snow-cannon and groomed to a high standard, the area provides a good choice of runs from the wide reds to the gently meandering blues. Access to Le Crey du Quart is either by the Montissot and Colerieux chair-lifts via Les Myosotis, or directly from Valloire on two long chairs. A gondola is planned for this area in the near future. The skiing at Le Crey du Quart is mainly of the red motorway variety, with gentler slopes going down towards Valloire.

Accommodation includes the Grand Hotel, and there are 20 restaurants and 13 bars to choose from. The other après-ski activities are skating, squash and snowmobiling.

TOURIST OFFICE
Tel 33 4 79 59 03 96
Fax 33 4 79 59 09 66
Email valloire@laposte.fr

Italy

Extremely favourable exchange rates have quadrupled Italy's share of the snow market in recent years, and with the lira riding higher than ever, its future as a major player is – at least for the present – assured. However, in the longer term price alone may not be enough for it to maintain its advantage. Italy now has to stand, so to speak, on its own two skis and will be judged by skiers and riders alike on the quality of its snow, lift systems and tourist infrastructure.

Price remains the leading, but by no means the only, criterion for choosing Italy, but France and, in particular, Austria are fighting back in the war of the wallets. Italy now has to prove that it really has what it takes to compete in real-time with the big boys.

Certainly, the Dolomites offer some of the most scenically charming and extensive skiing to be found anywhere. The Milky Way has attained new popularity and Cortina d'Ampezzo thrives as the most fashionable ski town in Italy. Madonna di Campiglio has excellent intermediate skiing. The Monte Rosa has established its own niche both as a family destination (Gressoney) and as holy ground for powderhounds (Alagna). A whole host of less heralded resorts are also vying for their stall in the international market place. But the fragile fabric of Italian skiing remains largely unchanged. Lift systems have been slowly improved, but enormous investment is needed in areas such as the Sella Ronda and the Milky Way to bring them into line with the likes of the Trois Vallées and even Ski-Welt.

First-time visitors will be delighted by the Italian zest for enjoyment both on and off the slopes, and as a nation Italy has raised the pastime of eating on the mountain to an art form. From long before midday, delicious scents wafting from every wayside hut in resorts such as Courmayeur are enough to tempt you in for a lunch that can last way into the afternoon. The Italian penchant for partying extends to the après-ski, which starts early and carries on well into the early hours.

Although the Italians are well-known for their love of children, the major resorts are mysteriously lacking in childcare facilities. This is possibly due to the fact that Italian families often travel as a whole – complete with granny to look after the *bambini*.

Whether Italy's simplistic but not necessarily durable formula of price-and-snow is enough to sustain it in an increasingly sophisticated and competitive market remains to be seen.

Bormio

ALTITUDE 1225m (4,018ft)

Beginners ✳✳✳   Intermediates ✳✳✳

Bormio is one of Italy's most important ski towns, although the amount of skiing is limited in comparison with the larger and better-known circuits. A high top-lift altitude and a neighbouring glacier allow the season to last well into April. The resort shares a lift pass, but not a lift link, with the neighbouring village of **Santa Caterina** and with the small Valdidentro ski area above the village of **Oga** on the opposite side of the valley. The lift pass is also valid for **Livigno**, which is an hour's drive away over a pass to the west. **St Moritz**, across the Swiss border in the Engadine, is another option for a day's excursion.

Bormio's history dates from Roman times, when its location at a crossroads in the Valtellina in the mountains of Lombardy made it a natural staging-post for trans-Alpine traffic. Attracted by hot springs and spectacular views over what is now the Stelvio National Park, the Romans built a town and thermal bath complex at the foot of the pass. The town prospered during the Middle Ages, and its ancient cobbled streets date from that time. In subsequent centuries it was sidelined by history, but the post-Second World War tourist boom has restored some of its former vitality. Today its ugly suburbs spread over the broad valley floor but do not impinge on the charm of the pedestrianised centre.

✔ Lack of crowds on the slopes
✔ Late-season skiing
✔ Attractive medieval town centre
✔ High standard of restaurants
✔ Range of activities for non-skiers
✗ Long airport transfer
✗ Unattractive suburbs
✗ Lack of childcare facilities

Ski and board
top 3012m (9,879ft) bottom 1225m (4,018ft)

Bormio's first lifts opened in the 1960s, but the resort came of age in 1985 when it hosted the World Alpine Skiing Championships. The slopes rise steeply on a single broad mountain served by two base-stations, both within a few minutes' walk of the town centre. The main one is the starting point for the two-stage cable-car to the Cima Bianca via **Bormio 2000**, a substantial mid-station with a large family hotel and a small shopping mall. This can also be reached by car in most conditions. The alternative is the six-seater gondola to **Ciuk**, a lower mid-station, which also has accommodation and restaurants. The top third of the mountain is above the tree-line, with a network of chair-lifts providing a variety of choices. Lower down, the skiing is in glades cut from the forest, ensuring good visibility when the weather closes in.

Beginners
The only nursery slopes are at Bormio 2000; this is a mixed blessing as everyone has to buy a lift pass from day one. On a more positive note, it means that everyone learns halfway up the mountain, which gives more of a feeling of what skiing is all about. After a few days of mastering the basic manoeuvres, beginners will find plenty of easy pistes in the wooded area down to Ciuk. By the end of the week, many will be skiing the blue (easy) runs from the top of the cable-car.

Intermediates
For the two-week-plus brigade, Bormio's slopes are to die for; there are no particularly steep sections and lots of high-speed cruising. The 14-km descent from the Cima Bianca to the town is just one of many exhilarating options. The bottom section of the Bosco Basso piste has been widened to provide an alternative route back to the gondola station.

Advanced
Strong piste-skiers may be frustrated by the lack of challenge on Bormio's slopes, as the two short runs that are graded black (difficult) might well be red in a steeper resort. The Stelvio FIS course, which runs from just above La Rocca past Ciuk to the bottom of the gondola, is an occasional choice for the World Cup circuit.

Off-piste
The powder opportunities off the Cima Bianca more than compensate for the shortage of black bump runs. To the west of the main piste a steep, open bowl leads down to some shallow-gradient, tree-level skiing. Those who plan to go below the right-hand turn-off to Bormio 2000 should check first that the Ornella drag-lift is running. To the east of the pistes, a wider choice of terrain gives access to a more heavily wooded area. A long trail leads back to the Praimont chair. An alternative is to ski down the flattering run to Santa Caterina. Those who are prepared to hire a guide and climb on skins will find magnificent terrain in both winter and summer on the Stelvio Glacier.

Tuition and guiding
Of the six competing ski schools in Bormio the Alta Valtellina, based near the nursery slopes at Bormio 2000, is highly recommended for its young, friendly, English-speaking instructors. The more traditional alternatives include the Nazionale and Bormio 2000. The Anzi School is for hotel guests only. The Sertorelli and the Capitani organisations specialise in summer ski-touring, retaining only a skeleton winter staff for valued clients.

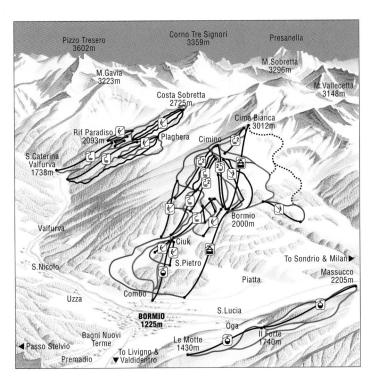

Mountain restaurants

The favoured stopping-off point for lunch or refreshments is La Rocca, an old-fashioned hut on the main trail from the top of the mountain to Bormio 2000. It has two rooms, each with a wood-burning stove and friendly service. It also hosts dinner followed by a torchlight descent whenever there is sufficient demand. The Rhondendri near the top of the Rocca chair is also recommended ('quiet, small and pleasant, with a splendid viewing position at the top of a black mogul run'). The Girasole Hotel and the self-service cafeteria at Bormio 2000 are equally convenient, though less traditional, alternatives.

The resort

Bormio is the most Italian of resorts, with a strong sense of style in its immaculate shops and restaurants. In the early evening, chattering crowds stroll down the narrow cobbled streets and fill the bars and cafés on the historic Via Roma, the centre of activity in the old town. The new town, with its modern hotels and high-rise apartment blocks, makes a stark contrast. As one reader summed it up: 'Bormio is much nicer than the brochures suggest. It is upmarket, yet cheaper than the UK. It is

Skiing facts: Bormio

TOURIST OFFICE
Via Roma 131B, I-23032 Bormio, Sondria
Tel 39 342 903300
Fax 39 342 904696
Email aptvaltellina provincia.so.it

THE RESORT
By road Calais 1146km
By rail Tirano 39km
Airport transfer Milan or Bergamo 4hrs
Visitor beds 6,035
Transport free ski bus with lift pass

THE SKIING
Linked or nearby resorts Livigno (n),
Santa Caterina (n), San Colombano (n)
Longest run Pista Stelvio, 14km (red)
Number of lifts 17
Total of trails/pistes 50km in Bormio
only (23% easy, 68% intermediate, 9%
difficult)
Nursery slopes 4 on the mountain at
Ciuk and Bormio 2000
Summer skiing 20km on Stelvio Pass
(May–November)
Snowmaking 11km covered

LIFT PASSES
Area pass Alta Valtellina (covers Bormio,
Livigno, S. Caterina, S. Colombano)
L225,000–250,000 for 6 days
Day pass Bormio only, L46,000–49,000
Beginners points tickets
Pensioners 65yrs and over as children
Credit cards yes

TUITION
Adults Alta Valtellina, 9–11am or
11am–1pm, L120,000–150,000 for
6 x 2hr lessons. Nazionale,
10am–12.30pm or 2–4.30pm, L150,000
for 6 half-days. Other schools, details on
request
Private lessons L50,000–60,000 per hr
Snowboarding all ski schools, details on
request
Cross-country Scuola Sci Fondo Alta
Valtellina, L88,000–92,000 for 6 days.
Loipe 12.5km
Other courses telemark
Guiding Scuola di Alpinismo Guide Alpine
Ortler Cevedale, Associazione Guide
Alpine Alta Valtellina

CHILDREN
Lift pass Alta Valtellina, 5–12yrs,
L100,000 for 6 days
Ski kindergarten none
Ski school all ski schools, 4yrs and over,
prices and times as adults
Non-ski kindergarten through Girasole
Hotel

OTHER SPORTS
Climbing-wall, swimming, snowmobiling,
indoor tennis and squash, skating,
thermal baths

FOOD AND DRINK PRICES
Coffee L1,500, glass of wine L1,500,
small beer L4,000, dish of the day
L10,000–15,000

authentically Italian and ideal for families and couples but not suitable
for those looking for a rowdy nightlife'.

Bormio's nearest airports are Bergamo and Milan, both officially four
hours away, although reporters have experienced transfer times of up to
six-and-a-half hours from Bergamo. The drive from Milan includes a dramatically beautiful section along the shore of Lake Como.

Accommodation

The modernised four-star Hotel Posta, on a pedestrianised street in the
old town, offers luxurious accommodation, a swimming-pool and fitness
centre. The alternative four-star recommendations are the Rezia and the
Palace. Those who prefer to be near the lifts should consider one of the
modern three-star options: the Derby, the Nevada or the Funivia. In the
two-star category, the family-run Dante and the atmospheric Gufo offer
exceptional value in central locations. Hotel Aurora is praised by
reporters: 'The hotel was very clean and warm, the staff friendly and
helpful, and the food excellent. However, few rooms with baths were
available.'

As the town of Bormio is only ski-in ski-out when snow conditions
are good in January and February, there is an excellent case to be made
for staying in the three-star Girasole at Bormio 2000. This is especially
true for holidays over the Easter period when the main resort begins to
wind down. The hotel is run with a strong emphasis on family entertainment by the hospitable Alfredo Cantoni and his English wife, Elizabeth.

Eating in and out

Although *pizzocheri,* a rather gritty indigenous pasta, is something of an
acquired taste, the Valtellina also offers an interesting range of specialities including charcuterie, mushrooms and locally produced wines. The
best places to try them are the Rasiga (a beautifully converted saw mill),
the Vecchia Combo, the Taulà and Osteria dei Magri. All four restaurants will prepare multi-course gourmet feasts at modest all-inclusive
rates, provided they are booked in advance. Bormio also has five pizzerias and a spaghetteria. Self-catering is not the norm in a resort with a
wide choice of cheap eating-places, but the specialist grocery shops on
the Via Roma certainly stock all the necessary ingredients for home
cooking on a magnificent scale.

Après-ski

The Bagni Vecchi, a few miles out of town, is a natural sauna and curative hot baths in a cave in the hillside. It includes a very atmospheric turn-
of-the-century spa complex offering a range of treatments for weary
skiers. In town, the natural hot water has been put to good use in the
large public swimming-pool. The Gorky on the Via Roma and the
Vagabond in the church square are the current pubs of choice, both after
skiing and after dinner. Late nightlife focuses on the King's Club disco,
which is open until 3am, with the piano bar at the Aurora Hotel a less
frenetic option.

Childcare

The ski schools will take children from four years of age, provided there are other children with whom to make up a class. Older children have to fit in with the adult classes. There is no formal crèche service, but the Girasole Hotel can arrange local babysitters during the day and in the evening.

Linked or nearby resorts

Santa Caterina
top 3296m (10,814ft) bottom 1737m (5,697ft)

Santa Caterina, or San Cat as it is known, is a quiet, attractive village 30 minutes away by bus up a mountain road that is a dead-end in winter when the Gavia Pass is closed. It usually has better snow than its larger neighbour, Bormio, with which it shares a lift pass. Local skiing is on the north-east-facing slopes of the Sobretta. The higher slopes are fairly steep and graded black; there are also some winding, intermediate trails down between the trees.

The Santa Caterina Ski School receives mixed but generally favourable reviews. The two cross-country trails are Pista Valtellina which is 10km and challenging, and the 8-km Pista La Fonte, which is classified as easy. Skating takes place on a natural rink.

The San Matteo Hotel is recommended for comfort and food. Self-caterers have a choice of two well-stocked supermarkets. Nightlife is limited, with one fairly large disco and a number of cosy bars that remain open until after midnight.

TOURIST OFFICE
Tel 39 342 93 55 98
Fax 39 92 55 49

Cervinia

ALTITUDE 2050m (6,724ft)

Beginners ✶✶✶ Intermediates ✶✶✶

Cervinia is Italy's most snow-sure resort, set at 2050m in the Aosta Valley within easy reach of Turin and Geneva. It is dominated by Il Cervino, which is considerably better known under its Swiss name of the Matterhorn. The substantial ski area is linked with **Zermatt**, and finally, after ten years of international hag-gling between the two lift companies, the adjacent resorts now operate a joint lift pass. Cervinia has a reputation as a resort best suited to beginners and intermediates, and the real advantage of this arrangement is that accom-plished snow-users can enjoy the greater challenges offered on the Zermatt side of the mountain.

✔ Excellent snow record
✔ Value for money
✔ Alpine scenery
✔ Sunny slopes
✔ Extensive skiing season
✔ Long runs
✘ Heavy traffic
✘ Inconvenient lift access
✘ Lift queues
✘ Unattractive village

Mussolini, who was instrumental in the resort's construction in the 1930s, decreed the name should change from Breuil to the more Italian-sounding Cervinia. A nucleus of original build-ings reflect the austere imperial style of the time. Post-war concrete edi-fices, thrown up without regard for the extraordinarily beautiful mountain environment, resemble 1960s council flats. More recent addi-tions have façades of wood and natural stone.

Even under its customarily secure winter blanket of snow, the resort is not aesthetically pleasing. Nevertheless, Cervinia's large bed-base has earned it the unassailable title of the most popular resort in Italy with the British; from December to April, about 1,000 British skiers a week holiday here and not all of them can be wrong. The ambience remains overwhelmingly Italian, making weekends and school holiday periods chaotic and prone to queues, though these are cheerful and unaggressive.

Cervinia's skiing is linked to the nearby village of **Valtournenche** (1524m), and a new 12-person gondola has greatly enhanced this end of the ski area.

Cervinia is more expensive than the Italian resorts that are further from Switzerland and is not as chic as Cortina or even Courmayeur. However, it has a vibrant atmosphere and, although by no means any-one's image of a fairytale resort, Jack (of bean stalk fame) would appre-ciate the mysterious sign in English outside the Plan Maison gondola, which reads: 'Do not go on if you have not the ticket for going up plants'.

Ski and board
top 3490m (11,447ft) bottom 1524m (4,999ft)

For years Italy's highest resort has been unfairly dismissed by competent snow-users as a playground for beginners and lower intermediates – no match for its swanky Swiss neighbour. Certainly it is true that despite warnings of *solo per esperti* (only for experts), most of the handful of black (difficult) runs would be graded red on the Swiss side of the mountain.

The amalgamation with the Zermatt ski area is not as complete as the tourist board suggests. The joint lift pass covers all 25 Italian lifts, but only 16 Swiss ones – in the Klein Matterhorn/Trockener Steg sector of Zermatt (it would be impractical for Cervinia snow-users to stray further afield). The joint pass is considerably cheaper if purchased in Italy rather than in Switzerland. However, the majority of snow-users will be perfectly content with the wide, open motorway cruising that Cervinia has to offer. The length and quantity of Cervinia's flattering red (intermediate) and blue (easy) runs provide hours of effortless cruising and an opportunity to hone technique.

Mountain access is most direct from the queue-prone gondola and cable-car, which are an irritating hike uphill from the village. Access is also possible from drag-lifts to the left of the village in the nursery area, or from the satellite areas of **Cieloalto** and Valtournenche. Plan Maison is the mid-mountain station from which the main lifts fan out, with cable-cars rising to Plateau Rosa and the Swiss border.

When the resort opened in 1936 the lift system was considered state-of-the-art but it has since been updated only in parts, and considerable investment is now needed. On paper, some 34,000 snow-users per hour can be transported uphill, although not without annoying queues at weekends and during peak periods for some of the most essential links.

Beginners

If you learn to ski in this resort you will wonder what all the fuss is about. Beginners tend to spend no more than two days on the conveniently accessed nursery slopes at the village edge. Cervinia's excellent snow record means that novices have good conditions on the nursery slopes beside the village, before moving up to the network of green (beginner) and blue (easy) pistes at Plan Maison. There are few resorts where beginners can graduate so quickly and are able to ski runs as high as the top-to-bottom, wide and well-groomed blue piste from Plateau Rosa down to the village, which is a drop of nearly 1500 vertical metres. Plan Maison provides ideal terrain for novice riders, but the predominance of drag-lifts and lack of jumps, natural or otherwise, do not make this a serious snowboarding destination.

Intermediates

The 8-km Ventina (no 7 on the piste map) from Plateau Rosa down to the resort is a classic alpine run. The series of runs from the Klein

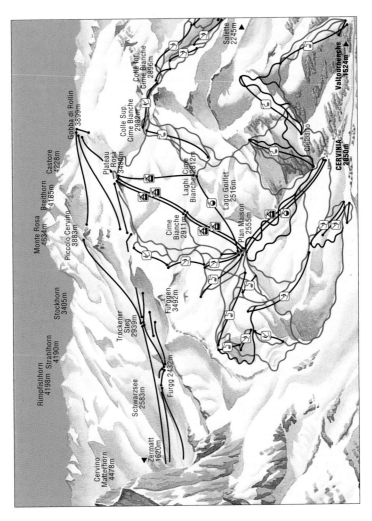

Matterhorn to the farming village of Valtournenche measures a total of 22km and is enough to transform even the toughest skier's knees to noodles. Many red runs in Cervinia would be graded blue in Switzerland. In fact, snow-users used to the intimidating steeps in Chamonix or Val d'Isère will find the gradual pitch of Cervinia's pistes both ego-boosting and useful for advancing technical skills.

Advanced

The one true pisted challenge was the run down from Furggen, on the shoulder of the Matterhorn, from where you could see both resorts simultaneously. This was reached by an ancient cable-car and began from a cliff face after a walk down an internal staircase of nearly 300 steps. However, the piste became inaccessible when the cable-car was closed three years ago after failing a safety test. It now looks as if the closure is permanent. The marked black runs on Cieloalto and down from Plan Maison will not increase anyone's insurance premium. Zermatt's skiing is considerably more challenging.

Off-piste
On powder days, especially when the wind closes upper lifts, the skiing among the trees on the shoulder above Cieloalto is a good off-piste option. More ambitious routes require guides and mountaineering gear. Heli-skiing is available on the Zermatt side of the mountain and, in addition to ski-touring, provides access to a wealth of glacier runs.

Tuition and guiding
The main Cervino school continues to receive some criticism but still appears to be more organised than the smaller school in Cieloalto. Reporters said of the Cervino: 'unsatisfactory instruction without much enthusiasm,' and 'having children and adults in the same class did not work'. Another reader noted that teachers at the Cervino seemed to do whatever they felt like, rather than following a strict and regimented method – 'the way they do in Austria'.

> **WHAT'S NEW**
> Chair-lift from Plan Maison to Fornet

Valtournenche has its own ski school. Mountain guides from the local bureau in Cervinia charge considerably less than their Swiss counterparts but have equal expertise on the border peaks.

Mountain restaurants
The piste map now shows where to stop for lunch. Cervinia's mountain meals are not cheap by Italian standards but are still much better value than over the other side of the Matterhorn. Bar Ventina on the eponymous run down from Plateau Rosa, Bar Bontadini on the slope of the same name and Chalet Etoile near the Rocce Nere chair-lift are among the best for polenta and fondue. Baità Cretaz da Mario on the nursery slopes receives outstanding reviews for its cuisine, relaxed and attentive service and 'lovely linen tablecloths'. The Igloo – run by Pauline, an English exile – at the top of the Bardoney chair, is praised for its tasty food and large portions. La Motta da Felice at the top of the Motta drag-lift is not to be missed.

The resort
Cervinia is functional rather than fashionable. Despite some tarting up, the buildings have no authentic mountain charm, nor do the shops have much class. The Italian side of the Matterhorn, unlike Zermatt, is not car-free. Attempts to create a pedestrian zone are obviated by

Skiing facts: Cervinia

TOURIST OFFICE
Via J.A. Carrels 29, 11021
Breuil-Cervinia, Aosta
Tel 39 166 949086
Fax 39 166 949731

THE RESORT
By road Calais 1000km
By rail Châtillon 27km, regular buses
to resort
Airport transfer Turin or Geneva 2hrs
Visitor beds 5,700
Transport free bus from Camper's
Square to the church

THE SKIING
Linked or nearby resorts Zermatt (I),
Valtournenche (I)
Longest run Ventina, 8km (red)
Number of lifts 25 in Cervinia, 41 with
Klein Matterhorn (Zermatt)
Total of trails/pistes 80km in Cervinia
(34% easy, 53% intermediate,
13% difficult), 180km with Zermatt
Nursery slopes 2 lifts
Summer skiing on Plateau Rosa, 8 lifts
and 1 cable-car
Snowmaking 7 hectares covered

LIFT PASSES
Area pass (covers Cervinia,
Valtournenche and Klein Matterhorn)
L320,000 for 6 days
Day pass L50,000
Beginners points tickets, L20,000
Pensioners 60yrs and over,

20% reduction on 6-day pass
Credit cards yes

TUITION
Adults Cervino and Cieloalto ski
schools, both 10am–1pm, L200,000
for 6 days
Private lessons both ski schools,
L50,000 per hr
Snowboarding Cervino Ski School,
10am–1pm, L200,000 for 6 days,
private lessons L50,000 per hr
Cross-country Cervino Ski School,
details on request. Loipe 6km on edge
of village
Other courses telemark, heli-skiing
(Zermatt)
Guiding Guide del Cervino

CHILDREN
Lift pass 6–9yrs, 20% reduction on
adult pass. Free for 5yrs and under
Ski kindergarten none
Ski school both ski schools, 5yrs
and over, 10am–1pm, L200,000
for 6 days
Non-ski kindergarten none

OTHER SPORTS
Parapente, skating, snowmobiling,
swimming

FOOD AND DRINK PRICES
Coffee L1,300, glass of wine L1,500,
small beer L2,000, dish of the day
L25,000

anyone who feels like shunting aside the movable barrier. Parking at weekends is chaotic, since the influx from Milan and Turin insists on parking in the street instead of in the five free and one fee-paying parking areas.

There is no free ski bus, but a municipal bus makes circuits every 20 minutes as far as Cieloalto until 8pm.

Accommodation

Cervinia has virtually no chalet or self-catering accommodation. Most of its hotels date from the 1930s and are seldom convenient for the lifts. The Hermitage is in the super league of five-star alpine hotels, with the highest standards of service, cuisine and price. The four-star Punta Maquignaz is an attractive wood-clad hotel close to the ski school and drag-lifts. You can ski back to the Petit Palais, which is close to the cable-car and five minutes from the village centre. The Cristallo is the oldest hotel, an ugly arc of white concrete, though agreeably decorated inside and with a swimming-pool. The Jumeau is 'pleasant, quiet and well-run'. The Compagnoni on the main street is 'simple, convenient and welcoming'.

Eating in and out

The resort has a reasonable range of restaurants, which are priced rather highly compared with tourist expectations of Italy, but are mostly good value. The Hermitage has 'truly outstanding cuisine'. Il Capriccio in the resort centre is a close contender. Le Nicchia is similarly rich for pocket and paunch. La Tana is recommended for wild boar, venison and everything with porcini mushrooms. La Maison de Sausure is the place to try the typical Valdostana specialities. It is hard to beat the pizzas at Al Solito Posto, which is the locals' favourite.

Après-ski

Lino's Bar beside the ice rink is busy when the lifts close and just as popular later in the evening. Skating is a passionate pastime here, but reporters complain that the nightlife lacks lustre. 'Like the skiing,' said one reporter, 'it is all intermediate'. The Garage is the hippest disco. Yel Matrob cocktail bar is the liveliest, thanks to its animated patron, Renzo. The Copa Pan Irish bar is popular and serves Murphy's beer. The Dragon Bar, which had the cheapest beer in town, is sadly no more.

Childcare

Italians appear to bring their grandmothers or nannies with them, as Cervinia still does not have a daycare centre for those too young for regular ski lessons. The tourist office has a list of officially sanctioned babysitters but admits that few speak English.

Cortina d'Ampezzo

ALTITUDE 1224m (4,015ft)

Beginners ✹✹✹ Intermediates ✹✹✹ Advanced ✹✹✹

If we had to single out one ski resort in the world for the sheer beauty of its setting, combined with an attractive town and a truly all-round winter-sports resort, it would be Cortina d'Ampezzo in the craggy Dolomite mountains. However, Cortina's upmarket reputation can deter those skiers who see Italy as the destination for cheap and cheerful holidays, although by international standards it is not an exclusive or overtly expensive resort. There are plenty of pleasant, family-run hotels with reasonable prices as well as simple, characterful bars. As one reporter put it: 'Our holiday here cost no more than previous ones in Val d'Isère and Verbier. We were constantly surprised by the value for money that we experienced both on and off the slopes'.

Cortina sits in isolated splendour in the Ampezzo Valley, a two-hour journey by road from Venice. Unlike its neighbours in the German-speaking Sud Tirol, Cortina is Italian to its voluptuous core and largely devoid of German and Austrian tourists. Some 90 per cent of its visitors are Italian. The resort was extensively developed for the 1956 Winter Olympics,

✔ Extensive nursery slopes
✔ Variety of restaurants
✔ Long runs
✔ Activities for non-skiers
✔ Beautiful scenery
✔ Extensive cross-country
✔ Tree-level skiing
✔ Resort ambiance
✔ Lively après-ski
✘ Spread-out ski areas
✘ Limited for late-season holidays
✘ Heavy traffic outside pedestrian area
✘ Limited facilities for children
✘ Oversubscribed ski bus system

although the ice stadium is now looking down-at-heel, and no one can decide whether to pull it down or restore it to its former splendour. Cortina has some of the best nursery slopes anywhere, as well as long, challenging runs for intermediate to accomplished skiers.

Ski and board
top 3243m (10,640ft) bottom 1224m (4,015ft)

The skiing is divided between the main Tofana-Socrepes area to the west of town, which is reached via the Freccia nel Cielo (arrow in the sky) cable-car, and Staunies-Faloria on the other side of town, which consists of two sectors separated by a minor road. A scattering of smaller ski areas along the Passo Falzarego road still belong to individual farmers.

One of these areas, Cinque Torri, reached by an isolated two-stage chair-lift, is small and uncrowded with reliable snow (it is north-facing), long runs and breathtaking scenery. Passo Falzarego, further down the road and a 20-minute bus ride from the town centre, links with the **Sella Ronda** ski area.

If Cortina has one major flaw, it is its inefficient transport system. The buses linking the town with the various fragmented ski areas are both infrequent and hopelessly over-subscribed at peak hours. To enjoy the skiing to its full, you need your own car and a driver mentally equipped to cope with the stress of securing rare and much sought-after parking spaces against fearless Roman opposition in supercharged Alfa Romeos.

WHAT'S NEW

Col Drusciè–Ra Valles cable-car replaced
Rio Gere–Plan de Ra Bigontina new 3-seater chair
Drag-lift at Guargnè

Both Tofana and Faloria can be reached on foot from most of the accommodation if you are prepared for a hearty hike in ski boots. Morning queues for the Tofana cable-car are not a problem, owing to the late rising-time of the average Cortina visitor – the morning rush-hour never starts before 10.30am. The top section of Tofana is designated for sunbathers and sightseers only.

Beginners

A long serpentine blue (easy) piste takes you down from Tofana's mid-station to link with Socrepes, one of the best nursery slopes in Europe. Socrepes looks like a kind of sloping Kensington Gardens interspersed with easily negotiable lifts and covered by snow-cannon. The more isolated Pierosà-Miétres is an equally gentle sector.

Intermediates

The majority of Cortina's skiing is of intermediate standard, with long runs in both the main ski areas. Between the resort and Col Drusciè the Tofana cable-car travels over gentle, tree-lined terrain and open fields with wide and easy trails, which cross rough roads without much warning to either skiers or drivers. Poor snow conditions often make these runs testing, which gives them their red (intermediate) and black (difficult) gradings. The second stage of the cable-car climbs the sheer, rocky mountainside to Ra Valles, in the middle of a pleasant bowl.

A day-trip into the Sella Ronda ski area should not be missed for anyone of intermediate standard and upwards. The good-value Superski Dolomiti lift pass covers both Cortina and the Sella Ronda.

Advanced

Higher up at Tofana, the Ra Valles sector at 3000m offers the best snow in the resort. Near the bottom of the Tofana bowl, a gap in the rock gives access to an exhilarating black (difficult) trail, which has a fairly steep south-facing stretch in the middle. The run ends up at the Pomedes chair-lifts, an area which itself offers some excellent runs including a

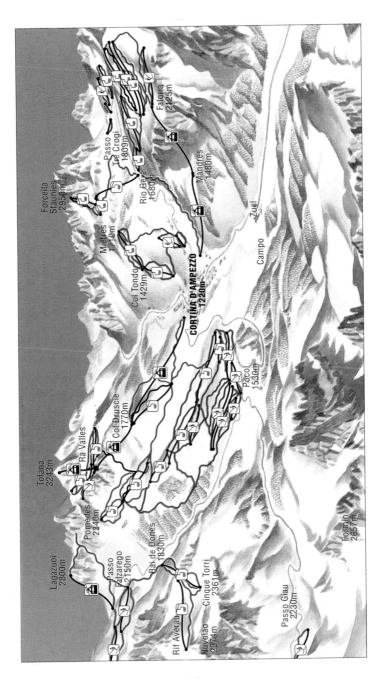

couple of good blacks and the spectacular Canelone downhill race-course.

The most dramatic skiing is found between Cristallo and Cresta Bianche, two soaring cathedrals of granite that dominate the landscape. From the foot of Monte Cristallo a four-stage chair climbs to Forcella Staunies, which starts with a steep black mogul field so sandwiched between the rock walls that it creates an illusion of narrowness. Half-way down, the bumps flatten out into a wide red race track ('Each of us managed 150 linked turns on the deserted slope all the way down to the Padeon chair-lift').

Off-piste

After a fresh snowfall Forcella Staunies becomes an appealing off-piste area, as do the higher reaches of Tofana. Gruppo Guide Alpine, the resort's ski guiding organisation, arranges day ski-tours.

Tuition and guiding

The main Scuola Sci Cortina has meeting places at Socrepes, Pocol, Rio Gere and Pierosà-Miétres. The standards appear to be mixed, depending mainly on the standard of English spoken by the instructor. Scuola Sci Azzurra and Scuola Sci Cristallo-Cortina are smaller alternatives. There are no special facilities for snowboarding on the mountain, but lessons are available through the Scuola Sci Cortina and Scuola Sci Cristallo-Cortina.

Mountain restaurants

Eating is a memorable experience in Cortina, and the choice of restaurants is extensive in the main ski areas. Rifugio Duca d'Aosta is recommended for its wood-panelled walls and heart-warming local dishes. Simple mountain fare can be eaten at Rifugio Son Forca, which is reached by a modern chair-lift from Rio Gere on the road separating the Cristallo and Faloria ski areas. Rifugio Berghaus Pomedes has hand-carved furniture and a varied menu. Reporters praise El Farel at the foot of Socrepes, and Col Taron in the same area, which serves delicious pasta.

Next stage down the mountain from the Duca d'Aosta is Baità Pie Tofana, a relaxed eating place with a sun terrace and attractive interior. Rifugio Averau at Cinque Torri has stunning views and was voted best restaurant in the ski area by one reporter. Rifugio Lagazuoi is situated a steep but worthwhile walk from the top of the Falzarego cable-car.

Other recommended eating places are the Tondi restaurant, and Rifugio Scotoni on the long run down to Armentarola in the Sella Ronda.

The resort

Cortina is a large, attractive town centred around the main shopping street of Corso Italia and the Piazza Venezia with its green-and-white bell tower. The large, frescoed buildings have an air of faded grandeur, and the views of the pink rock-faces of Monte Cristallo are sensational. More recent architectural additions display a sympathetic Italian alpine style in keeping with the town's dramatic surroundings. The centre is mercifully traffic-free, with cars confined to a busy one-way perimeter road. Parking is a problem in the centre, and reporters have warned: 'If your hotel provides a private parking space at extra cost, pay up and don't complain'. Drivers should aim to avoid the huge Friday night/Saturday morning exodus, with queues that tail back all the way to the motorway exit.

Accommodation

Hotels range from the large international variety to simple, family-run establishments. A large number of private apartments and chalets are also available. The resort's smartest hotel, the Miramonti Majestic, is 2km out of town. The four-stars include the attractive Hotel de la Poste in the heart of Cortina, which is especially noted for its food. The Parc Hotel Faloria is another recommended four-star. Also well-located is the charming Hotel Ancora on the Corso Italia, run by the indomitable Flavia Sartor, who uses the hotel to house her enormous collection of antiques and paintings. The Parc Victoria is advantageously placed and comfortably furnished by the Angeli family, who own the hotel. The three-star, family-run Aquila is highly recommended. The Italia is a popular two-star with wholesome food and a loyal following. Although inconveniently positioned, the Menardi is praised for its food and reasonable prices. The Olimpia is one of the cheapest and most central bed-and-breakfasts and is said to be comfortable with large rooms.

Eating in and out

Dining is taken seriously in Cortina. More than 80 restaurants cater for all tastes, from simple pizzas to gourmet dining. Michelin-starred Tivoli on the edge of town has a warm ambience with delicious and often unusual cooking. El Toula is a converted barn with a rustic atmosphere. The Croda Caffé, Il Ponte and the Cinque Torri are all good for pizzas. Lunch at the Hotel de la Poste is delicious and expensive. Leone e Anna specialises in Sardinian cuisine, while El Zoco has grilled meats. For self-caterers or those trying to save money, the Cooperativa department store has 'an outstanding wine selection at very reasonable prices'.

Après-ski

'In one week you can only scratch the surface of Cortina's après-ski', commented one reporter. At about 5pm the early evening *passeggiata* along the pedestrianised Corso Italia heralds the start of the off-slope festivities. The street becomes alive with promenading, fur-clad Italians: 'Like a fashion show with mobile phones'. Cortina's shopping is absorbing and varied and includes antique and jewellery shops, sportswear and designer boutiques, interesting delicatessen and the six-storey Cooperativa department store, an Aladdin's Cave that seems to sell everything, with reasonable prices to match. As one reporter commented: 'It's the only town we know where the Co-op has marble floors and sells designer clothes'.

Skiing facts: Cortina d'Ampezzo

TOURIST OFFICE
Piazzetta San Francesco 8, I–32043
Cortina d'Ampezzo, Belluno
Tel 39 436 3231
Fax 39 436 3235
Email apt1@sunrise.it
Web site www.sunrise.it

THE RESORT
By road Calais 1200km
By rail Calalzo–Pieve di Cadore 35km
Airport Transfer Venice 2hrs
Visitor beds 22,800
Transport free bus connects the town
centre with the main lifts

THE SKIING
Linked or nearby resorts Armentarola
(I), San Cassiano (I), San Vito di Cadore
(n), Kronplatz (n)
Longest run Lagazuoi 11km (red)
Number of lifts 52 in area
Total of trails/pistes 140km in area
(44% easy, 49% intermediate,
7% difficult)
Nursery slopes 5 runs, 3 lifts
Summer skiing none
Snowmaking 70km covered

LIFT PASSES
Area pass Superski Dolomiti (covers 450
lifts), L260,000 for 6 days Cortina only,
L286,000 for 6 days
Day pass Superski Dolomiti L58,000,
Cortina L52,000
Beginners coupons available
Pensioners 20% reduction for over 60yrs
Credit cards yes

TUITION
Adults Scuola Sci Cortina, 9.30am–midday, L280,000 for 6 days. Scuola Sci

Azzurra, 9.15am–1pm, L620,000 for 6
days. Scuola Sci Cristallo-Cortina
9–11am L240,000 per day
Private lessons Cortina or Azzurra
L62,000 per hr
Snowboarding as ski lessons
Cross-country Scuola Italiana Sci
Fondo, private lessons L73,000 per hr.
Loipe 58km in the valley north and
east of Cortina
Other courses race training, off-piste,
carving, telemark, ski-touring
Guiding Gruppo Guide Alpine
Cortina

CHILDREN
Lift pass Superski Dolomiti L200,00,
Cortina L182,000, both for 6 days for
14 yrs and under
Ski kindergarten none
Ski school Scuola Sci Cortina,
9.30am–midday, L280,000.
Scuola Sci Azzurra, 15 yrs and under,
9.15am–1pm, L620,000.
Scuola Sci Cristallo-Cortina,
9–11am, L240,000.
All are for 6 half days
Non-ski kindergarten none

OTHER SPORTS
Bobsleigh, taxi-bob, skating,
snowmobiling, ski-joring, swimming,
ice hockey, curling, parapente,
hang-gliding, indoor tennis,
ice-polo, dog-sledding, ski jumping,
snowshoeing

FOOD AND DRINK PRICES
Coffee L1,600, glass of wine
L1,500–2,500, small beer
L2,800–3,000, dish of the
day L12,000

After dinner the action starts at the Enoteca wine bar, a serious drinking spot with a magnificent cellar. Jerry's Wine Bar is another popular meeting place. Later on, the Hyppo, Area and VIP discos are extremely lively. The entrance fee for the nightclubs does not subsidise the drink prices, as in some comparably smart resorts; partying is consequently an expensive occupation here.

Childcare

Cortina has some of the most extensive nursery slopes we have ever encountered and used to be a resort we could recommend for families. However, the children's ski school only runs group lessons in the mornings and the ski- and non-ski kindergarten have now been disbanded completely.

Linked or nearby resorts

The Sella Ronda

Cortina links, in one direction only, into the Sella Ronda circuit at Lagazuoi and shares the Superski Dolomiti lift pass. You need to start early in the day in order to achieve any distance on skis. The trip starts at Passo Falzarego, where a dramatic cable-car soars 640 vertical metres up a cliff-face to Lagazuoi, linking into the Sella Ronda area via a beautiful 11-km red run past a shimmering turquoise ice-fall and several welcoming huts to **Armentarola** and **San Cassiano** beyond.

Reporters recommend taking an early bus from Cortina to Passo Falzarego, skiing down from Lagazuoi to the restaurant at Sare, and from there catching a taxi-bus to Armentarola and skiing over to Corvara. However, the whole day is a rush and can be stressful. To return to Cortina you either take a bus from Armentarola to Falzarego or one of the waiting taxis at Armentarola to Lagazuoi.

Kronplatz
top 2275m (7,464ft) bottom 900m (2,953ft)

This interesting resort on the Italian–Austrian border is covered by the Superski Dolomiti lift pass. It is little-known outside Italy and Germany, yet is an easy day-trip just 60km from Cortina. Eighty-five kilometres of piste are serviced by 31 lifts, of which an astonishing 12 are cable-cars. The resort has four ski schools and three kindergarten. Reporters comment on its excellent lifts, wide variety of runs and 'excellent snowmaking. It claims to have the most modern lift system in Europe and it may well be so'.

TOURIST OFFICE
Tel 39 474 555 447
Fax 39 474 530 018

Courmayeur

ALTITUDE 1230m (4,034ft)

Beginners ✳ Intermediates ✳✳✳ Advanced ✳✳ Snowboarders ✳

Courmayeur is a delightful old village, which established its reputation first as a climbing base for the forbidding, granite peaks of Mont Blanc, Western Europe's highest massif, and second as a popular nine-teenth-century spa for its curative, pungent-smelling waters. Its role as an internationally acclaimed ski resort did not begin to take shape until 11.31am on 14 August 1962. That was the moment when a delighted Italian miner thrust his fist through a hole in the rock-face five kilometres beneath Mont Blanc and swapped a bottle of Asti Spumante for a bottle of Veuve Clicquot with his French counterpart. The Mont Blanc Tunnel, then the longest underground road route in the world at 11.6km, ended Courmayeur's international isolation and linked it with **Chamonix**. Suddenly, Geneva Airport was only a 90-minute drive away. Today Courmayeur remains an attractive medieval village, with the narrow cobbled streets and alleyways of its pedestrianised centre lined with smart boutiques and welcoming bars. While serious Chamonix shivers throughout much of the winter in the northern shadow of the great mountain, bubbly Courmayeur basks in the sunshine.

- ✔ Beautiful scenery
- ✔ Village atmosphere
- ✔ Easy resort access
- ✔ Excellent restaurants
- ✔ Lively après-ski
- ✔ Varied off-piste skiing
- ✔ Long vertical drop
- ✔ Tree-level skiing
- ✔ Extensive snowmaking
- ✔ Cross-country skiing
- ✘ Lack of skiing convenience
- ✘ Peak-period queues

Courmayeur is the favourite resort of the Milanese, a clientèle for whom lunch is frequently a greater priority than skiing, and as a result it proudly boasts some of the finest mountain restaurants in the Alps.

Ski and board
top 3470m (11,381ft) bottom 1370m (4,494ft)

The main mountain access is via a cable-car across the river gorge, and the arterial Mont Blanc Tunnel road. This takes you up to Plan Chécrouit, a sunny plateau from where, annoyingly, you have to plod a further 75m to the foot of the lifts. At the end of the day there is no alter-native but to take the cable-car back down. It is possible to leave boots and skis in lockers at Plan Chécrouit, but the procedure is nevertheless inconvenient. Plans to build a piste to the bottom have never been

Mont Blanc 4810m
Mont Maudit 4468m
Mont-Blanc Du Tacul
Aiguille Du Midi
Chamonix
Vallée Blanche
Punta Helbronner 3470m
Summer Skiing
Rifugio Torino 3325m
Ghiacciaio Del Toula
Pavillon 2130m
Aiguille Noire 3773m
Mont Blanc Tunnel
Aiguille Des Glaciers
Ghiacciaio del Miage
Val Veny
Zerotta 1520m
Peindeint
Pre de Pascal 1912m
Arp Vieille
Mt Chetif 2345m
Plan Checrouit 1706m
Dolonne
M. Favre
Cresta D'Arp 2755m
Cresta Youla 2624m
Lago Chercrouit 2256m
COURMAYEUR 1230m

289

realised and are now unlikely to be so. The mountain can also be reached by cable-car from **Val Veny**. Queues at the bottom of the Plan Chécrouit cable-car can be a problem at peak times, but all this fails to detract from the overall appeal of Courmayeur as a ski resort.

Reporters consistently remark on the friendliness of the locals, in startling contrast to the dour Gallic attitude of those on the other side of the tunnel. Extensive investment in snow-cannon has done much to improve skiing on the lower slopes down to Plan Chécrouit and, over the mountain, down to Val Veny. However, the skiing is not satisfactory for everyone; the pisted runs are mainly short and lack challenge. Advanced skiers will be more interested in the separate off-piste ski area shared with Chamonix, reached by the three-stage Mont Blanc cable-car at **La Palud**, near the village of **Entrèves** on the tunnel side of Courmayeur.

Beginners

The nursery slopes are somewhat hazardous, with those at Plan Chécrouit cramped by buildings and crowds of skiers descending from the main pistes. The baby slopes at the top of Val Veny and Dolonne are quieter, and beginner snowboarders need to go to Val Veny.

Intermediates

The east-facing Chécrouit bowl has many quite short intermediate runs served by a variety of lifts including a six-seater gondola. The pistes are often crowded, especially at the bottom where they merge. There are some surprisingly steep and narrow passages, even on some of the blue (easy) runs. The wooded, north-facing Val Veny side of the mountain is linked in a couple of places with the Chécrouit Bowl; it has longer and more varied pistes with two red (intermediate) runs and a black (difficult) trail following the fall-line through the trees. Queuing for the Plan Chécrouit and Mont Blanc areas is much worse at weekends when the crowds arrive from Turin and Milan. Quad-chairs at La Gabba and Zerotta have eased some of the other bottlenecks on the mountain, but the Youla cable-car can still be a problem. Plan Chécrouit has plenty of intermediate runs for snowboarders around the main ski area.

Advanced

The pistes served by the Gabba chair at the top of the ski area and to the west of Lago Chécrouit keep their snow well. The off-piste run underneath them is testing. The Youla cable-car above Lago Chécrouit opens up a deep and sheltered bowl, which serves a single, uncomplicated red run with plenty of space for short off-piste excursions. It is also possible to ski (with a guide) the long itinerary run off the back of Youla down into Val Veny.

Off-piste

The top of the two-stage cable-car at Cresta d'Arp is the starting point at 2755m for a couple of long and demanding powder runs. One takes you down through 1500m vertical to the satellite village of Dolonne or to the river bank near **Pré-St-Didier;** the other brings you through the beautiful Vallon de Youla to La Balme, a few kilometres from **La Thuile**. The second stage of the cable-car only runs until 11.30am because of the high risk of avalanche later in the day, and you are strongly advised to use a local guide.

From the nearby hamlet of La Palud, the Mont Blanc cable-car rises over 2000m to Punta Helbronner, giving easy access to the Vallée Blanche by avoiding the dreaded ice steps. There is an afternoon bus back from Chamonix. Alternatively, you can cruise the 10km back down the Toula Glacier to La Palud; it is steep at the top and involves a clamber along a fixed rope and the hair-raising negotiation of an exposed and awkward staircase; again, you are strongly advised to take a guide. The bottom stage of the cable-car from Pavillon has a long, uncomplicated red trail that is rarely skied. The off-piste at Cresta d'Arp makes for some excellent snowboarding.

Tuition and guiding
We continue to receive mixed reports of the Scuola di Sci Monte Bianco. The standard of spoken English has greatly improved in recent years, and the general verdict is that private instructors and guides are excellent value, but that group instructors are often jaded: 'Our instructor gave the impression that he wasn't interested in our skiing at all. He was never enthusiastic or encouraging.' However, the strong presence of Interski, a British tour operator that has been allowed to establish its own private British Association of Ski Instructors (BASI) ski school for a mixed clientèle of adults and schoolchildren, has served to raise standards dramatically.

Cross-country
Opportunities for cross-country are enormous here, with a major nordic centre at **Val Ferret,** a five-minute drive away at the foot of the Grandes Jorasses. The centre offers four loipes totalling 35km, which wind through spectacular scenery. Cross-country tours can be arranged in the spring through the ski school.

Mountain restaurants
In our experience there is nowhere you can eat better for less money in a greater variety of mountain restaurants than in Courmayeur. In fact, food in Courmayeur is taken just as seriously as skiing. By midday on the mountain the scent of cooking wafting from 24 restaurants scattered across the area weakens the resolve of even the most dedicated skier. The prices in these restaurants are lower than in the resort itself. One reporter comments: 'It is really hard to ski when you could be eating. The atmosphere in the huts scattered around the mountain is an integral part of our annual visit here.'

The Christiania at Plan Chécrouit is singled out for special praise ('the freshest seafood I have ever tasted; the owner comes from Elba and obviously pines for home'). The Château Branlant serves full meals with

Skiing facts: Courmayeur

TOURIST OFFICE
Piazzale Monte Bianco, I -11013
Courmayeur, Aosta
Tel 39 165 842060
Fax 39 165 842072
Web site www.courmayeur.com

THE RESORT
By road Calais 921km
By rail Pré-St-Didier 5km, regular buses
from station
Airport transfer Geneva 2hrs, Turin 3hrs
Visitor beds 5,800
Transport ski bus not included in lift
pass

THE SKIING
Linked or nearby resorts Cervinia (n),
Champoluc (n), Chamonix (l), Gressoney-
La-Trinité (n), Pila (n), La Thuile (n)
Longest run Internazionale,7km (red)
Number of lifts 25
Total of trails/pistes 100km (44% easy,
52% intermediate, 4% difficult)
Nursery slopes 3
Summer skiing none
Snowmaking 52 hectares covered

LIFT PASSES
Area pass (Courmayeur Mont Blanc)
L221,000–255,000 for 6 days
Day pass L50,000 (Courmayeur only)
Beginners 3 free lifts
Pensioners no reduction
Credit cards no

TUITION
Adults Scuola di Sci Monte Bianco,
10am–1pm, L190,000 for 5 days,

L210,000 for 6 days.
Private lessons L220,000 for 4hrs.
L350,000 for 7hrs
Snowboarding through ski school,
details on request
Cross-country through ski school,
L5,000. Nordic centre and 24km loipe
at Val Ferret and Dolonne
Other courses monoski, slalom,
ski-touring, heli-skiing, race camps
Guiding Società delle Guide di
Courmayeur

CHILDREN
Lift pass L255,000 for 6 days, free for
accompanied children under 1.1m
Ski kindergarten Kinderheim at Plan
Chécrouit, L400,000 for 5 days or
L450,000 for 6 days including lunch and
3hrs daily tuition
Ski school Scuola di Sci Monte Bianco,
3hrs per day, L190,000 for 5 days,
L210,000 for 6 days
Non-ski kindergarten Kinderheim at
Plan Checrouit, 6mths–12yrs,
9am–4pm, L360,000 for 6 days including
lunch. Kinderheim at sports centre,
9mths–6yrs, details on application

OTHER SPORTS
Parapente, skating, ski-jumping,
hang-gliding, indoor tennis and squash,
dog-sledding, climbing wall

FOOD AND DRINK PRICES
Coffee L1,500–1,800, glass of wine
L2,000–4,000, small beer
L4,000–6,000, dish of the day
L25,000–30,000

wait-service and 'heavenly desserts'. La Grolla at Peindeint on the Val Veny side is outstanding ('expensive, but worth it and difficult to find – thank goodness'). Other recommendations are the Petit Mont Blanc at Zerotta, Chiecco and Le Vieux Grenier for pasta. On the Mont Blanc side there are bars at each lift stage. The Rifugio Pavillon at the top of the first stage of the cable-car is reportedly excellent and has a sun terrace. Rifugio Torino, at the next stage, is also said to be good. Rifugio Maison Vieille at Col Chécrouit, which has a large wood-burning stove, and Rifugio Monte Bianco, between the Zerotta and Peindeint chairs, both serve pasta, polenta and sausages, and have a long wine list.

The resort

The heart of the old village is a charming maze of cobbled alleys, which are largely traffic-free and lined with fashion boutiques, delicatessen, antique shops, and even a good-value toy shop. There are more bars, cafés and restaurants than could ever seem necessary, with a lively clientèle. The atmosphere is, as one reader puts it, 'completely compelling – this is real Italy, garnished with real skiing'. These days the suburbs stretch endlessly outwards, and for anyone interested in observing and therefore contributing to the prolonged après-ski *passeggiata* along Via Roma, it is important to find accommodation within easy walking distance of the pedestrian precinct.

Accommodation

The four-star Gallia Gran Baità is described as 'wonderfully worthy of its rating, but too far out of town unless you have a car'. Few of the great variety of hotels, apartments and chalets are well-situated for the main cable-car. Several reporters stress the undesirability of hotels located on the main road as it is used by countless lorries on their way to the Mont Blanc Tunnel (not to be confused with the main street through the village).

The comfortable and expensive Hotel Pavillon is well-situated 150m from the cable-car and has a swimming-pool and sauna. Hotel Courmayeur is 'friendly, with a roaring log fire in the sitting area'. The Edelweiss and the three-star Berthod are good value for money. The Bouton d'Or is located just off the main square and the Roma is 'simple and cheap'. The resort has three new hotels: Auberge de la Maison, the Tavernier and the Walser.

Eating in and out

Restaurants are varied, plentiful and lively. Pierre Alexis rates as one of the best restaurants in town ('owner Ino Cosson has an extraordinary wine list to complement great food'). Chalet Proment da Floriano on the cross-country track at Val Ferret combines fine cuisine with an intimate atmosphere. The Coquelicot is recommended for its grills. Le Bistroquet offers 'wonderfully prepared regional dishes'. La Palud is known for its fresh fish.

Courmayeur also has plenty of pizzerias, including Mont Frety with its regional dishes, and La Terrazza. La Maison de Filippo at Entrèves is an exercise in unparalleled gluttony; it offers a fixed-price menu of at least 30 courses. Self-caterers are advised to shop at the supermarket on the Via Regionale, directly above the cable-car station, as there are no supermarkets in town.

Après-ski

After-skiing entertainment begins with early-evening cocktails in Steve's Privé or the American Bar, and evolves into a hanging-out situation, with certain times for certain bars, and often more than one in a night or a return visit after dinner. The Bar Roma, with its comfortable sofas and armchairs, fills up early and is especially recommended if you are tired after skiing. Ziggi's is beer-oriented, and Cadran Solaire is where the sophisticated Milanese go.

The swimming-pool is 5km away at Pré-St-Didier, and the floodlit skating-rink is open every evening until midnight, complete with disco music.

Childcare

The Kinderheim up at Plan Chécrouit has excellent facilities and looks after children from six months old. Staff pick up children from the bottom of the cable-car in the village and return them if parents want a day off from the mountain. A new Kinderheim at the sports centre now cares for children aged nine months to six years and is particularly useful for parents wanting to ski on the Mont Blanc side.The Scuola di Sci Monte Bianco has private and group lessons for children, with lunch included.

Livigno

ALTITUDE 1820m (5,970ft)

Beginners **✱✱✱** Intermediates **✱✱** Snowboarders **✱**

Livigno – the cheapest of all Alpine resorts – is a duty-free village in one of the highest and remotest corners of Italy. It is user-friendly for skiers and revellers alike, but you have to suffer a three- to five-hour transfer from Bergamo, Milan or Zurich airports. What you get during your stay is a large, exposed ski area with a fine snow record, which is best suited to beginners and intermediate snow-users. The resort's main problem has always been access. The community developed near but not on the Roman road from Milan to Innsbruck, a route that crossed the neighbouring Passo di San Giacomo. As frontiers moved back and forth, the Spol Valley became a distant border outpost of Switzerland, Italy and the Austro–Hungarian Empire in turn. Today it has slow road links with **Bormio** to the east, **St Moritz** to the west and **Davos**, via the one-way Munt La Schera tunnel, to the north.

✔ Ski-in ski-out convenience
✔ Reliable snow cover
✔ Low prices
✔ Choice of restaurants
✔ Recommended for telemark
✘ Long airport transfer
✘ Poor road links
✘ Bleak location
✘ No real resort centre
✘ Heavy traffic

Livigno's fiscal privileges date from 1600 and were confirmed in 1805 when Napoleon, then the ruler of the Kingdom of Italy, granted 'customs benefits' that were validated by the Austro–Hungarian Empire in 1818, and by the European Community in 1960. With vodka selling in duty-free shops at less than £3 a litre, it can compete on price with Andorra – and the skiing is superior.

Ski and board
top 2798m (9,180ft) bottom 1820m (5,970ft)

International visitors began skiing in Livigno in 1964 when the Munt La Schera tunnel opened the resort up to northern Europe. In those days there was one lift; today there are 30, serving 110km of predominantly gentle slopes on both sides of the valley. The core of the skiing is the ski-in ski-out south-east-facing Carosello, which catches the morning sun. The two-stage Carosello 3000 gondola provides rapid access from the town to the highest point. The Carosello links with two supplementary areas, one served by the Federia drag-lift on the back side of the mountain, where the snow is better protected from the sun, and the other on Costaccia, where the high-speed Vetta quad along the ridge gives various options.

The skiing is generally steeper on the west-facing side of the valley, where the setting sun attracts skiers late into the afternoon. The gondola station for Mottolino is at the suburb of **Teola**, a long walk or a short bus-ride from the town centre. There are notoriously chilly chair-lift connections with Monte della Neve, the departure point for the best skiing in the resort, and Trepalle, a windswept outpost on the road to Bormio.

In recent years, Livigno has become the self-appointed telemark capital of the Alps, thanks to the Skieda International Festival, which takes place in the spring.

Beginners
Livigno is justly proud of a lift system that provides blanket coverage of sun-soaked, resort-level nursery slopes within a stone's throw of the main street. The runs straggle along the flank of the mountain on the Carosello side, leaving beginners with no excuses for not practising when classes are over. The best graduation slopes for progressive novices are from Monte della Neve and Mottolino to **Trepalle**.

Intermediates
The heart of the skiing is Carosello and the linked area of Blesaccia, which together offer the widest choice of long descents. The toughest intermediate options in a generally flattering environment are on the slopes above Val Federia. On the other side of the valley, the rolling red (intermediate) runs from Mottolino, Monte Sponda and Monte della Neve back to Teola are rewarding, but those to Trepalle are rather short.

Advanced
The creators of the piste map have taken pains to include some statutory black (difficult) runs, but the grading is strictly complimentary. This is not a resort for advanced snow-users. Livigno's two main mogul fields are at the extremes of the resort, below Costaccia and on the descent from Carosello. A longer and much better black run winds down from Monte della Neve to the bottom of the Monte Sponda chair.

Off-piste
Very few visitors to Livigno have any intention of skiing off-piste, but extensive possibilities exist for those prepared to hire a guide and go exploring. The most accessible options are from Carosello 3000 and the ridge above Costaccia to Val Federia, or from Monte della Neve down the Vallaccia to Trepalle – but be prepared for long walk-outs.

Tuition and guiding
Livigno has four ski schools. As far as British clients are concerned, Sci Livigno Italy is the major player. However, minority interests are better served by the Azzurra and Inverno-Estate schools, which offer telemark, touring and mountaineering in addition to regular tuition. All schools teach snowboarding, and there is also a specialist nordic ski school.

Borchetta
Di Federia

Caroselio
2737m

Vetta Blesaccia
2796m

P.Ta Campacci
3007m

P. Campone
2904m

Lago Salin
2694m

Val Federia

M. Delle Rezze
2958m

Costaccia
2328m

Pizzo Orsera
3032m

Tresenda

S. Rocco

P. Paradisin
3302m

LIVIGNO
1820m

Teola

Lago Di Livigno
1805m

Colle Di Val Nera
3000m

Pemonte

M. Della Neve
2725m

P. Filone
3133m

M. Sponda
2576m

Il Mottolino
2349m

P. D'elra
2210m

La Pare
2393m

M. Foscagno
2927m

Trepalle
2096m

M. Crapene
2430m

297

Mountain restaurants

The main self-service restaurants at the top of the Mottolino and Carosello gondolas offer consistency at competitive prices, while the restaurant La Costaccia is known for its outdoor barbecue. More atmospheric mountain lunches can be found in the Teas, the mountain huts once used by herdsmen working the summer pastures. The Tea Borch, below Carosello, and the Tea del Plan, below Costaccia, specialise in *pizzoccheri*, the brown local pasta that is traditionally prepared with cabbage and cheese. Tea Bourk is warmly recommended ('oodles of rustic mountain charm and noodles to match'). Mottolino's Passo d'Eira has a range of typical dishes while the Fior di Bosco concentrates on local cheese and salami.

The resort

Although many of the individual buildings are very attractive, Livigno's lack of town planning makes it unsympathetic overall. Its high, bleak location has earned it the nickname 'Piccolo Tibet' (Little Tibet), a description that is particularly apt in bad weather. An efficient free bus-service links the four hamlets of **Santa Maria**, **San Antonio**, **San Rocco** and Trepalle, which, stretched over 12km, make up the resort. Evening taxis are numerous but expensive. A pedestrianised zone has been achieved by blocking off the centre section of the main road through San Antonio. It provides a rather tacky focus, crammed full of hotels, restaurants and noisy bars. Santa Maria, a neighbourhood in which the original stone and wooden houses cluster round the church, is more distinguished architecturally, but its charm is diluted by heavy traffic in its narrow streets.

Livigno's *raison d'être* is shopping, with stores dedicated to cheap alcohol, clothing and consumer durables. Anyone who is not perceived as Italian is addressed in German by over-eager assistants.

Accommodation

The two four-star hotels, the Golf Parc and the Intermonti, are in Teola on the hillside overlooking the town – a suitable place to stay for the Mottolino lifts but not for the nightlife. In the pedestrian zone, the three-star Albergo Bivio has a swimming-pool and a terrace. Also convenient for both nursery slopes and après-ski are the Alpina, the Helvetia, the Victoria, the Sonne and the Alpenrose. In Santa Maria, Damiano Bormolini, an ex-Italian freestyle champion and fourth-generation hotelier, offers two quiet and expertly run family hotels, the Livigno and the St Michael ('nothing was too much trouble'). The Pedrana Rocco apartments are 'basic, but fairly big'.

Eating in and out

Livigno is not short of choice, but the emphasis is on quality local fare rather than haute cuisine. The Pesce d'Oro daringly advertises 'fresh fish every week' but still enjoys a sound reputation. So, too, do La Mirage, La Stua, La Pioda and Il Passatore. The Camana Veglia has a notably good chef, while the Bellavista wins many friends for its pizzas.

Skiing facts: Livigno

TOURIST OFFICE
Via da la Gesa 65, I-23030 Livigno, Sondrio
Tel 39 342 996 379
Fax 39 342 996 881
Email aptminfo@livnet.it
Web site www.livigno.com

THE RESORT
By road Calais 1107km
By rail Tirano 2½ hrs
Airport transfer Milan 3½–5hrs, Zurich 3–5hrs, Bergamo 4hrs
Visitor beds 8,455
Transport free ski bus

THE SKIING
Linked or nearby resorts Bormio (n), St Moritz (n) Valdisotto (n), Valdidentro (n), Santa Caterina (n)
Longest run Femminite, 4.8km (red)
Number of lifts 30 in Livigno, 36 in linked area
Total of trails/pistes 110km in Livigno (44% easy, 45% intermediate, 11% difficult)
Nursery slopes 12 lifts, 5km of runs
Summer skiing Stelvio Pass and Diavolezza/St Moritz
Snowmaking 15km covered in Livigno

LIFT PASSES
Area pass (covers Bormio, Santa Caterina, Valdidentro, Valdisotto and 1 day in St Moritz) L245,000 for 6 days
Day pass L45,000–49,000 (Livigno only)
Beginners no free lifts

Pensioners 65yrs and over, as children
Credit cards yes

TUITION
Adults Sci Livigno Inverno-Estate, Sci Livigno Azzurra, Sci Livigno Italy, Sci Livigno Soc Coop, all L120,000 for 6 days (2hrs per day), 9–11am or 11am–1pm
Private lessons L45,000 per hr
Snowboarding all ski schools, L190,000 for 6 days (2hrs per day)
Cross-country Scuola Italiana Sci Fondo Livigno, L115,000 for 6 days. Loipe 40km
Other courses monoski, telemark
Guiding Lodovico Cusini

CHILDREN
Lift pass 14yrs and under, L170,000 for 6 days
Ski kindergarten Inverno-Estate from 3yrs, L250,000 for 6 days not including lunch
Ski school all ski schools, 3yrs and over, L115,000 for 6 days (2hrs per day)
Non-ski kindergarten Inverno–Estate, from 3yrs, L200,000 for 6 days

OTHER SPORTS
Ice-driving, horse riding, snowmobiling, skating, snowshoeing, parapente, sleigh rides, swimming

FOOD AND DRINK PRICES
Coffee L1,300–1,500, glass of wine L1,500–2,000, small beer L3,000–3,500, dish of the day L10,000–12,000

Après-ski
Tea del Vidal is a cheerful pit-stop on the Mottolino side. In town, the most popular watering holes are Foxi's Pub, with a slide for an entrance, which is said to be the 'home of a ritual where you put on a Viking helmet, drink tequila, and then get hit on the head with a baseball bat'.

Marco's Bar offers ski videos. Noisy alternatives favoured by the British include the Underground and Galli's Fun Pub in San Antonio ('lots of Brits singing silly songs'). Il Cielo, which sometimes has live music, is rated as the smartest disco by the Italians, but the Kokodi is generally preferred by British visitors; both are quiet until after midnight but gather momentum towards closing time at 4am. Other attractions include a modern cinema showing up-to-date (but usually dubbed) American and British films, and an ice-driving school.

Childcare

Skiing tuition is available at Livigno's four ski schools. Ski School Inverno-Estate takes non-skiing children in its kindergarten from three years of age, but there is no other formal childcare for toddlers.

Madonna di Campiglio

ALTITUDE 1520m (4,987ft)

Beginners ✱✱✱   Intermediates ✱✱✱   Advanced ✱   Snowboarding ✱✱✱

Madonna di Campiglio is one of Italy's two smartest resorts, pocket-sized in comparison with equally expensive but more sophisticated **Cortina d'Ampezzo**. However, it is a definite rival in terms of social prestige. Madonna is situated in a narrow valley in the Brenta Dolomites on an arterial thoroughfare, which is a 60-km climb through galleried tunnels past spectacular drops from the autostrada and the valley town of Trento. The nearest airport is two hours' drive away at Verona. The ski area, which last season celebrated its fiftieth birthday, is officially rated as Italy's premier for piste-grooming and regularly hosts international winter sports events, including World Cup ski races and snowboarding champion-

> ✔ Beautiful scenery
> ✔ Extensive snowmaking
> ✔ Intensive piste-grooming
> ✔ Excellent nursery slopes
> ✔ Attractive cross-country
> ✔ Nightlife
> ✘ High prices (for Italy)
> ✘ Peak-season traffic

onships. Long stays are the rule, with the better hotels booked out for the whole season. Ninety-five per cent of the resort's clientèle is Italian. Very few British visit, and those who do, share Italian tastes, especially for relaxed and unintimidating skiing.

Although there are now some ultra-modern covered chair-lifts and swift gondolas, with more upgraded each year, much of the lift system dates from the 1950s. Today it counts a modest 26 lifts covering 90km of pistes in the Madonna core area, although an additional 25 lifts and 60km of pistes can be accessed with the Skirama lift pass, including the separate but linked resorts of **Folgarida** and **Marilleva**.

Ski and board
top 2505m (8,219ft) bottom 1520m (4,987ft)

Madonna is a resort with flattering skiing and excellent nursery slopes, as well as a good range of far-flung intermediate terrain. However, it has little to offer expert or off-piste snow-users. What initially appear to be three entirely separate zones are cunningly interlinked at valley level by a snow-cannon-maintained piste that winds beneath a series of road bridges. An ancient cable-car climbs slowly up to the first area, 5-Laghi, from the centre of town. The second is reached by a fast jumbo gondola north of the town centre, whisking you up to Pradalago at 2100m, which is linked to Marilleva and Folgarida. The third area of Monte Spinale/Grosté is dramatically positioned beneath the towering granite cliff faces of Petra Grande and is reached by high-speed gondola from the east side of town.

The resort has accommodation for 27,000 visitors, who in theory can be carried uphill in less than an hour. January and March are the best months in which to visit – you largely have the slopes to yourself. Overcrowding is the norm at Christmas and New Year, as well as during the February school holidays, particularly at the budget resorts of Marilleva and Folgarida.

When viewed from the village, the mountains appear steep; above, they open into a civilised network of wide trails. Only the Grosté sector is entirely above the tree-line and is not covered by the exhaustive system of about 500 snow-cannon covering a total 72km of piste. Proficient skiers need to invest in the slightly more expensive regional Skirama lift pass that covers Folgarida and Marilleva. Snow-users are somewhat redundantly issued with a separate ticket as soon as they cross into the neighbouring zones of these two resorts.

Madonna is rated as one of the best snowboarding resorts in Italy, although the two pistes on Grosté set aside as a snowpark are neither roped-off to skiers nor equipped with a dedicated lift.

Beginners

Novices taking tuition should not buy a lift pass, as they will be taken by bus to the private Campo Carlo Magno nursery area five minutes' drive away. Beginners who are not enrolled at the ski or snowboard school pay a small fee for both the shuttle bus and the use of the nursery lifts. This is a superb learning area, serviced by its own drag-lifts and snowmaking. Another private nursery area called Bambi is run by Des Alpes Ski School on the east side of Madonna.

All of Madonna's terrain is accessible to inexperienced snow-users; blue (easy) runs make up 21 of the 45 named slopes in the main Madonna area. The Zeledria blue continues for more than 3km all the way down to town from Pradalago, as does the Pozza Vecia on the other side of the mountain; this run can be combined with the Boch blue providing a non-stop beginner cruise of 5km. Snowboard Paradise is a blue piste from the top of Passo Grosté.

Intermediates

Madonna's ski area is ideal for intermediate skiers and boarders, with lots of long cruises on attractive tree-lined trails. Folgarida and Marilleva also provide a supply of flattering cruising pistes including the long red (intermediate) Genziana. The two highest runs in the resort, reached by the Grosté chairs, are suitable for anyone who can ski parallel. The scenery in the form of dramatic granite cliffs rising to the skier's right are truly spectacular. However, this is the most popular area of the resort with Italian visitors and should be avoided at peak holiday times. At the top of the Boch chair you can ski or board Nube d'Oro, the resort's most challenging red piste that continues into the trees to meet Fortini.

Advanced

There is little challenge for mogul skiers in a resort where each night every bump is systematically flattened by a fleet of piste machines. None of the five runs listed as (black) difficult on the inadequate piste map is truly worthy of the colour grading. However, the Canalone Miramonti is a short, steep shock, and the FIS 3-Tre racecourse in the 5-Laghi area provides some challenge. Up on Grosté a dual slalom racecourse is open to the public. Spinale Direttissima is a long black from Spinale down to the resort. Snowboarders can use the half-pipe and boarder-cross park on Grosté, although the former is not maintained and the latter is unimpressive.

Off-piste

The ski schools seldom break away from the prepared pistes, although snowboarders do. Tempting lines run through the trees but do not always bring you back to the piste. Above Spinale and towards the Cima Brenta is a wide couloir, which requires a mountain guide and ski-touring equipment.

Tuition and guiding

Confusingly, Madonna has six ski and snowboard schools, all affiliated to the national Scuola Italiana Sci, each of which changes its uniform colour every season. English is indifferently spoken. Children's lessons are for three hours each morning in large classes of ten or more. Adult group lessons may have between 8 and 12 pupils and run for two hours in two shifts during the mornings. Nuova Campiglio and Nazionale receive good reports. The Scuola Alpinismo is recommended for ski-touring in the Dolomites.

Mountain restaurants

'All furs and no food' is how one reporter, expecting a truffles-and-caviar experience, responded to the self-service inns that are all you get in Madonna. For a resort of this stature, cosy mountain restaurants are sadly absent. Most of the converted *malga* (old wooden barns that once served as summer shelters for farmers and cows) have been transformed into high-volume self-service establishments. One exception is Cascina Zeledria, tucked away in the woods, which offers *delizie alle piastra* – steaks that you cook yourself on a hot stone. A free snowcat tows you back up to the piste after lunch. Malga Boch has a pine interior and sometimes a DJ from Zangola. La Grotte, in Albergo Fortini at the base of the Grosté gondola, is recommended by reporters. Agostini, on Pradalago, serves *picchiorosso*, a secret-recipe grappa.

The resort

Madonna is the site of a mountain hospice dating back 800 years, and was developed as a summer holiday and skiing centre in the 1950s. Today, it is compact and congenial with a mix of mostly modern architectural styles and a high standard of accommodation. The village runs north–south with the slopes coming right down to the town on either side. Traffic is a serious problem in high season when the one-way system goes into operation and parking becomes near impossible. A bypass tunnel scheduled for completion in time for the 1999–2000 season should restore Madonna's tranquillity. The ski bus is not free although it covers the region well.

The many elegant boutiques in the resort include Martini for Trentino-Tyrolean clothing and carved wooden artifacts, and Chalet Ferrari for designer clothing. One reporter commented: 'The Italians in Madonna wear furs to the floor, orange fluorescent moonboots and sunglasses at midnight, and parade their tiny rat-dogs outside the Bar Suisse. You will see them sunbathing with silver reflectors by the skating lake, hear them shouting on the slopes as they collide, and you wonder who still makes hand-painted ski suits that run in the rain'.

Professional Snowboarding is a hole-in-the-wall rental shop with English-speaking teachers. Other sports available in the resort include parapente, skating, snowshoeing and dog-sledding.

Accommodation

Most guests stay in the resort's 14 four-star and 24 three-star hotels, which are booked for most of the season. Relais Club des Alpes (four-star) carries the most cachet and is the most central. The Savoia Palace is smart and well-positioned. The Lorenzetti is also four-star, though more rustic in setting and décor, and has its own free shuttle bus. The Diana is friendly, close to the lifts and furnished to a high standard. Arnica is a conveniently central, modern bed-and-breakfast. Equally central is the old-style Villa Principe, which has some of the cheapest rooms in town. There are chalet-apartments and self-catering establishments such as the Ambiez apartments, which have a swimming-pool and a fitness centre.

Eating in and out

A must in Madonna is piling into heated snowcats and jolting up to the mountain restaurants of Malga Montagnoli, Cascina Zeledria or Malga Boch, where the service and food are better by night. In town, Antico Focolare is the in place to eat, serving typical Trentino food in atmospheric surroundings with open fires. Artini has good cuisine but lacks atmosphere. Papagallo has a generous set menu on Wednesdays. Cliffhanger serves fish platters. The Golden River has the only non-Italian menu, Tex-Mex with influences, but even here Gorgonzola makes an appearance. La Sfizio is vegetarian. Le Roi has the best pizzas until 2am, and like the Belvedere it does take-aways. There are numerous supermarkets and speciality delicatessen.

Après-ski

Right after skiing, those wearing furs gather at Bar Suisse or the Franz-Josef Stube to flutter eyelashes under dark glasses and make dates for later. Café Campiglio in the piazza is popular for coffee and cakes. However, although Madonna is often said to be lively it doesn't really get into the groove until the early hours. The population then goes wild until 4 or even 8am in what has been for 25 years one of the most famous discos in the Alps: the old cow barn, Zangola, 3km out of town but serviced by late-night buses. The disco features male strippers and dancing girls. Des Alpes has techno music as well as an upstairs piano bar. The Stork Club's clientèle is seriously under-age and closes when the school holidays end. Not to be confused with the bar of the same name, Cantina del Suisse has a live band and is a warm-up nightspot for Zangola. Cliffhanger disco is open until the early hours and shows heli-skiing videos. La Stalla has karaoke and live music.The two garish video-game centres and billiard bar are extremely popular with Italian boys.

Childcare

Most Italians leave the little ones at home or bring nanny or granny. Relais Club des Alpes has informal childminding for guests and an outdoor playground by the skating rink. Hotel Spinale has a children's club. A new childcare service is organized by the Campiglio Holiday Agency in the resort. The ski schools accept children from five years for morning lessons only.

TOURIST OFFICE
Tel 39 465 442000
Fax 39 465 440404
Email aptcampiglio@well.it
Web site www.aptcampiglio.tn.it

The Milky Way

ALTITUDE Montgenèvre 1850m (6,068ft),
Sauze d'Oulx 1500m (4,920ft), Sestriere 2035m (6,675ft)

Beginners ✳✳ Intermediates ✳✳✳ Advanced ✳✳

The Via Lattea, or Milky Way, straddles the Franco–Italian border, and is reached more easily from Turin than from Grenoble. Its southerly location is compensated for by the height of the main resorts, and snow cover is therefore sound. Spring arrives earlier here than in the Haute-Savoie, and this factor should be taken into account in choosing when to visit.

✔ Large ski area
✔ Skiing convenience
✔ Extensive tree-line skiing
✔ Varied off-piste
✔ Value for money
✔ Lively après-ski (Sauze d'Oulx)
✔ Reliable snow cover (Sestriere)
✘ Lack of activities for non-skiers
✘ Limited mountain restaurants

The Milky Way is one of the great and still surprisingly undiscovered ski circuits of Europe. **Sestriere** hosted the 1997 Alpine Skiing World Championships and the events televised worldwide did much to raise awareness of this important dual-nation ski area which has 400km of groomed pistes served by 91 lifts. However, British skiers are inevitably familiar with its naughty sister **Sauze d'Oulx** in the neighbouring valley, which despite local efforts at rehabilitation is still better known for its lager-oriented après-ski than for the quality of its slopes.

The other major resort is **Montgenèvre** (the only French component). All three have markedly different characters. Montgenèvre is an old stone village perched on the col separating France from Italy. It has been developed for tourism in a pleasant-enough manner and retains considerable charm. Sauze d'Oulx (pronounced Sow-zee Doo) has tried to clean up its act by heading upmarket, a feat at which it cannot succeed until more luxurious hotels are built to cater for a better class of clientèle – the new three-star Park Hotel Bosco is a positive step. The main part of the village, adjacent to the slopes, is a largely uninspiring collection of modern edifices constructed with budget rather than beauty in mind. In contrast, Sestriere, which used to be one of the most fashionable wintering holes in Europe, is intent on rebuilding its reputation, and this has been backed by huge financial investment over the past three years.

The Milky Way is bounded by Montgenèvre at one end and by Sauze d'Oulx at the other. In between lie the villages of Sestriere, **Clavière**, **Cesana Torinese** and **Sansicario**, as well as a handful of small hamlets that are little more than ski-lift access points. The area is very spread out;

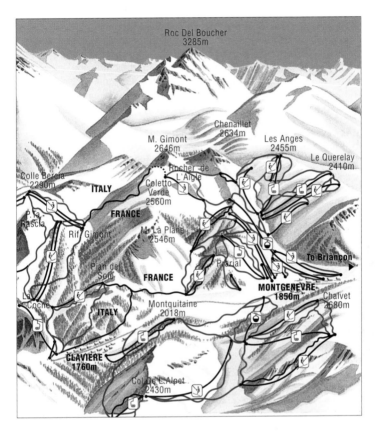

it takes a long time to work one's way from one sector of the circuit to another, so a car is useful.

Ski and board
top 2820m (9,250ft) bottom 1350m (4,428ft)

Montgenèvre's slopes are on both sides of the Col de Montgenèvre. The south-facing side, Chalvet, is slightly higher with runs up to 2600m, and is usually less crowded than the north-facing pistes, which create the main link with the Italian Milky Way resorts. Mountain access on the other side of the pass is by gondola from the **Briançon** end of the village, as well as by drag-lifts and a chair from the centre. These serve easy runs through woods, opening into wide nursery slopes above the road. From the top of the gondola there is a choice of three small ski areas. The wide, sheltered bowl of Le Querelay/Les Anges has ruined fortress buildings around the crest with some red (intermediate) and black (difficult) runs beneath them, but no challenging skiing overall.

The Milky Way link from Montgenèvre starts with a poorly sign-posted traverse around the mountain, which is easy to miss in bad light. Otherwise, it is not difficult and leads to a long run, which starts as red and becomes blue (easy) past the Gimont drag-lifts and down to Clavière. The north-facing slopes of Monti della Luna above Clavière and Cesana Torinese offer plenty of challenge, including some vast trails through the woods and satisfying off-piste.

Reporters are unanimous in their opinion that the best skiing in the Milky Way is above **Sestriere**. This end of the lift system was upgraded for the 1997 Alpine World Championships. The bulk of it is on mainly north- and west-facing slopes on two mountains, Sises and Banchetta, which are separated by a deep valley.

The **Sauze d'Oulx** slopes face west and north, and the majority of them are below the tree-line. The lifts are positively old-fashioned in comparison with those of Sauze's smart neighbour, Sestriere, even though they are run by the same company. A quad-chair takes you up to the centre of the skiing at **Sportinia**, a sunny woodland clearing with a few hotels, a small busy nursery area and a variety of restaurants. Above it is some wide, open intermediate skiing served by several chairs and drags. Below Sportinia wide runs back through the woods are graded red and black; these are quite steep in places, although never really demanding. There are also blue and black runs down to the hamlet of **Jouvenceaux**.

Queues in Montgenèvre are bad only at weekends and when snow in the nearby resorts is poor. The main queue problems at the Italian end of the Milky Way are on the Sauze side of the mountain, which a reporter who was there during an Italian bank holiday described as 'horrendous'. The local lift map has been improved, but it is still difficult at times to work out exactly where you are. Irritatingly, it names only the lifts and not the pistes. A number of reporters describe trail-marking as virtually non-existent to the point of being dangerous, which adds to the problems of orientation.

Beginners

A dozen nursery slopes are scattered around the different resorts of the Milky Way on both sides of the border, and the area is ideal learner territory. The main nursery slope for Sauze is at Sportinia; it is open and sunny but often very crowded. Nursery slopes are also available at Belvedere on the Genevris side, as well as in the village when there is snow. Sauze d'Oulx and Montgenèvre in particular are geared towards international clients. The Montgenèvre end of the circuit has the best choice of blue runs for those who have graduated from the novice slopes.

Intermediates

The long red runs down to Sansicario from Monte Fraiteve are satisfyingly varied and some of the best on the circuit. Red run 29, back through the trees to Sauze, is the favourite of several reporters. Old hands say that high-season crowds are a problem throughout the Milky

Way, but particularly around Sestriere. The secret is to ski the remote Genevris/Moncrons/Bourget sector on Saturdays and Sundays ('a pleasure to ski and no queues at all').

Advanced

An assortment of difficult runs scattered throughout the Milky Way makes this an underrated playground for advanced skiers, who will find plenty of challenge. The Sauze sector quite wrongly has a novice label attached to it because of the predominance of beginner and early-intermediate skiers that it attracts. In fact, some of the reds here could easily be graded black in other resorts, and a few of the blacks (notably 33 and 21) are seriously challenging in difficult snow conditions. The best of the skiing is found above Sansicario and Sestriere, although this may not be apparent from the local map.

The steep Motta drag-lift and chair serve the highest and toughest of Sestriere's skiing and reach the top point of the Milky Way. Here the slopes beside the drag can have gradients of up to 30 degrees and are often mogulled.

Off-piste

Monte Fraiteve is an exposed crest with impressive views of the French mountains, where the ski areas of Sauze d'Oulx, Sestriere and Sansicario meet. It is also the start of the famous Rio Nero off-piste run, which is a long descent that follows a river gully down to the Oulx–Cesana road, 1600m below. An infrequent bus service takes you back to the lifts at Cesana. The long dog-leg drag, La Crête, travels through magnificent rocky scenery to Rocher de l'Aigle and the start of an outstanding off-piste bowl and an alternative steep couloir. Anyone attempting the latter draws admiring glances from those on the piste below. Heli-skiing drops on the top of Valle d'Argentera and Val Thuras can now be arranged from Montgenèvre.

Tuition and guiding

We have sound reports of the Ecole de Ski Français (ESF) at Montgenèvre ('first class – patient instructors all with good spoken English') for all grades of skier and for private lessons. The Sauze d'Oulx Ski School has two rivals, Sauze Project and Sauze Sportinia. We have much improved reports of the Sauze d'Oulx ('after Zermatt, the attitude of the instructors was like a breath of fresh air. Lessons were made to be fun'). Sportinia has a high standard of teaching, but one reader complained that his instructor had only a few English phrases. We have encouraging reports of the Sestriere school, which has in the past been the subject of criticism. As one reader commented: 'Clearly the publicity surrounding the Alpine Skiing World Championships has jolted improvements. Our instructor spoke excellent English and tuition was friendly and competent'.

Mountain restaurants

'You can eat out in the mountain restaurants on the Italian side for the cost of a drink in Courchevel,' enthused one reporter. Montgenèvre is seriously short of mountain restaurants, with just the Altitude 2000 and Gondrands. The excellent and inexpensive bars and restaurants above Clavière (particularly La Coche) help make up for this shortfall. Ciao Pais in the Clotes sector is warmly praised.

The five busy restaurants at Sportinia maintain a high standard ('but eating in Piccadilly Circus is not my idea of a fun holiday'). Chalet Genevris at Genevris is renowned for its barbecue, with all you can eat or drink for around £10 per person ('very friendly with an excellent atmosphere of camaraderie at lunch-times, which often stretched well into the afternoons').

Sestriere's Bar Chisonetto, half-way down Red 8 on Banchetta, is recommended for its hamburgers. Bar Conchinetto is a traditional wood-and-stone restaurant noted for its polenta, and La Gargote has plenty of atmosphere but is more expensive. Alpette is praised for its glühwein and pasta.

The resorts

The first impression of **Montgenèvre** is of a rather untidy and higgledy-piggledy collection of bars, restaurants, shops and hotels lining an extremely busy main road where skiers joust with pantechnicons. The real village is tucked away on the northern side and has plenty of atmosphere, despite the heavy traffic. Shopping facilities are limited, but the weekly open-air market adds considerable colour and the occasional bargain. Prices are markedly lower than in most other French resorts. Italy begins at the border post on the outskirts of town, and both currencies are in circulation here.

In its heyday, the main street of **Sauze d'Oulx** was at its noisiest at 3am. Raucous revellers, still in their ski boots and awash with cheap lager and tequila slammers, staggered homewards from the infamous Andy Capp Bar to a dozen shabby two-star hotels for a few hours of further recreation before hitting the slopes once more. To the 2,000 young British skiers (50 per cent of the resort's customers) who flocked to this corner of Piedmont each winter in search of snow, sex and mind-shattering amounts of alcohol, it was known as 'Suzy does it'. Suzy, it seems, has matured beyond the gratifying excesses of her youth and is trying to cultivate a more married and maternal

> ## WHAT'S NEW
> TGV direct from Paris to Oulx, 20km away
> Heli-skiing

image. If she still does it, she has at least drawn the curtains and turned down the lights. At the height of the recession the number of weekly British visitors slumped into the hundreds, but the resort has climbed back gradually without the extreme yobbo element, which has moved on to fresh grazing elsewhere.

Sestriere was purpose-built in 1930 by Giovanni Agnelli, the founder of Fiat, who was frustrated by the fact that members of his family spent so much of their winter skiing abroad. Its position on a high, cold and barren pass is not enchanting but high-quality snow cover is the norm rather than the exception. The sky line is dominated by the twin towers of the Albergo Duchi d'Aosta, once one of the smartest hotels in Europe but now a Club Med. The village is compact, but despite being essentially Italian, lacks soul. As one reporter put it: 'There is no continuity, resulting in a confusion of styles, which seem to compete rather than harmonise.' Buses run to and from **Borgata**, **Grangesises** and the end of the Rio Nero run (on the Oulx–Cesana road). Stena Line is the only tour operator offering holidays to Grangesises.

The more shrewd Italians have now swapped Sestriere for nearby

Sansicario, which is a smaller, more sophisticated and modern development with its own ski area. It is linked to Sestriere and Sauze on the one side and Cesana Torinese on the other.

Accommodation

Montgenèvre's accommodation is mostly in apartments scattered along the road, in the old village and on the lower south-facing slopes; there are also a few catered chalets. Access to the skiing is easy from most places, but the Italian end of the village is more convenient. The pick of Montgenèvre's half-a-dozen less than luxurious hotels are the Napoléon, which is convenient but basic, and the more attractive Valérie, near the church.

Accommodation in Sauze is mostly in cheap hotels, which reporters generally find adequate. The best location is around the bottom of Clotes, with the hotels in this area the Hermitage ('very basic food'), Stella Alpina, and the Sauze ('clean and spacious'). The Gran Baità is recommended as 'excellent – very clean, the staff are pleasant and the hotel is five minutes' walk from everything'. San Giorgio is far from luxurious and badly placed, but friendly and inexpensive. The Chaberton is a basic bed-and-breakfast, and the Savoia is close to the lifts. The Palace is the biggest and the most expensive hotel, although not particularly stylish. Il Capricorno at Clotes is expensive and attractive. You can be first on the nursery slopes by staying at the Monte Triplex or the Capanna at Sportinia. The Ciao Pais above Clotes offers cheap and cheerful accommodation. The three-star Park Hotel Bosco is new.

Sestriere's accommodation is in hotels, modern apartments and at Club Med. The restored Principi de Piemonte Hotel is a couple of kilometres out of town but has its own access lift to the Sises ski area. A third distinctive tower block in the style of 1930s architect Vittorio Bottino was built to house competitors for the championships and opens this season as a hotel. Albergo Il Fraitevino is 'very simple for a four-star, but convenient'. The Hermitage and Banchetta are also recommended. The Biancaneve is just outside the town and provides its own mini-bus service to the slopes. Hotel du Col is 'warm, comfortable and clean'.

Eating in and out

Montgenèvre boasts more than a dozen eating-places, including the Ca Del Sol for pizzas, Les Chalmettes, L'Estable ('quality home-cooked cuisine'), Pizzeria Le Transalpin, and smart Le Jamy. Chez Pierrot is recommended for its home-made pizzas at about 75FF a head, including wine and 'a homely atmosphere with an open log fire'.

In Sauze, La Griglia is strongly recommended. Del Falco is praised for its relaxed and friendly service ('food great and not expensive'). Albertino's is more of a café than a restaurant, with prices to match. Del Borgo has 'a pleasant buzz' and is famed for its tiramisù.

Eating places in Sestriere range from pizzerias to smart, international restaurants. Ristorante du Grandpère in the nearby hamlet of **Champlas**

Janvier is praised for its wild boar stew and polenta. Antica Spelonca has 'a wonderful atmosphere and fine food'. Antica Osteria is an ancient chalet with considerable charm. L'Teit Pizzeria has 'the best pizzas we have ever eaten'. Jolly Market is said to be the most reasonably priced of the five supermarkets.

Après-ski
After-skiing activity in Montgenèvre is extremely limited and there is little for non-skiers apart from snowmobiling. However, a good choice of inexpensive bar-restaurants is on offer; three have nightclubs attached. The Ca del Sol and Le Graal are both popular bars. The Blue Night is the disco. The village has a good skating-rink.

In Sauze, the infamous Andy Capp and the New Scotch Bar near the bottom of the home run catch the early evening crowd and are awash with pints of Tartan long before dark. Later on, the action moves to the Cotton Club, Hotel Derby Bar and Moncrons. Max's Bar shows British sport on satellite TV. Osteria da Gigi and The Village Gossip both have live music six nights a week. The Chicchirichi, Schuss, New Life, and Rimini Nord discos 'keep you dancing as long as you want'. One reporter noted that entry to all clubs is free, which is a pleasant contrast to France.

Sestriere's après-ski is fairly lively and stylish when the Italians are in residence at weekends and in holiday periods, although at other times it is quieter. The Black Sun and Tabata discos are popular at weekends. Brahms Pub is Irish and serves Guinness. Anno Zero, Pinky Bar and People Pub are all popular. Maialetto has live music.

Childcare
Montgenèvre has a non-ski kindergarten, which takes children from 12 months to four years of age. The ESF takes three to five-year-olds in its ski kindergarten. Italy is not renowned for its childcare facilities, but the Milky Way is an important exception. Sauze now has Dumbo, which takes non-skiing children all day – parents must provide their children's lunch, which staff will heat up. The ski schools take children from four years of age. Sestriere has no public crèche, but Club Med looks after its smallest members from four years of age, as does the ski school, and there is a mini club at nearby Grangesises.

Linked or nearby resorts

Bardonecchia
top 2750m (9,022ft) bottom 1312m (4,303ft)
This is a large and traditional market town set in a sunny valley and surrounded by beautiful scenery. Although it is not part of the Milky Way circuit, it lies close to both Montgenèvre and Sestriere. It is a popular place with Italians, who swarm in from Turin at weekends and on public holidays. The skiing is spread over three areas, linked by a free ski bus,

with a total of 140km of piste served by 24 lifts, and offers a surprising amount of challenge. The nightlife is limited to a couple of rather dull bars ('a walk up the main drag at 9pm was a silent, empty experience'). Hotels include La Bettula, close to the shopping centre ('basic rooms, good food,') the Tabor ('nothing to commend it') near the ski bus stop, and Des Geneys ('very fine food') set well back from the road. Facilities for small children are non-existent.

TOURIST OFFICE
Tel 39 122 99032
Fax 39 122 980612

Borgata
top 2820m (9,250ft) bottom 1840m (6,035ft)
This is a small resort five minutes by road from Sestriere, with an infrequent bus service between the two. Hotel Hermitage is recommended ('nice rooms, but the food was not up to much'). Reporters who stayed in the Nube d'Argenta self-catering apartments praised them as 'clean, modern and convenient for the lifts'. There are complaints about the ski school ('very poor, with limited spoken English; little progress was offered in the lessons, but the teachers were pleasant enough'). Shopping is almost non-existent ('a poor selection of postcards and no stamps'). The après-ski is quiet ('a couple of sleepy bars with miserable staff and no, or few, customers'). As another reporter put it: 'When the sun goes down, it is time to eat and go to bed'.

TOURIST OFFICE
Tel/fax *as Sestriere*

Cesana Torinese
top 2820m (9,250ft) bottom 1350m (4,428ft)
This attractively shabby old village dates from the twelfth century and is set on a busy road junction at the foot of the Italian approach to the Montgenèvre Pass. It is rather confined and shaded, and accommodation is mainly in apartments and a few hotels. The chair-lifts up to the skiing above Clavière and Sansicario are a long walk from the centre, and the place can be safely recommended only to those with a car. The Chaberton is a three-star hotel and there are half-a-dozen small one-stars. Restaurant La Selvaggia specialises in regional dishes, La Noblerot is for French cuisine, and the smart Fraiteve serves truffles; Brusachoeur is a popular pizzeria. Après-ski spots include the Pussy-Cat pub and the Cremeria Rinaldo e Luciana bar. Two British tour operators offer accommodation in the resort.

TOURIST OFFICE
Tel 39 122 89202
Fax 39 122 811315

Skiing facts: Montgenèvre

TOURIST OFFICE
F-05100 Montgenèvre, Hautes-Alpes
Tel 33 4 92 21 52 52
Fax 33 4 92 21 92 45

THE RESORT
By road Calais 978km
By rail TGV direct to Oulx (Italy) 20km, Briançon 10km
Airport transfer Turin 1hr 20mins, Grenoble 3hrs
Visitor beds 8,000
Transport bus service throughout the resort

THE SKIING
Linked or nearby resorts Bardonecchia (n), Borgata (I), Clavière (I), Cesana Torinese (I), Grangesises (I), Jouvenceaux (I), Sansicario (I), Sauze d'Oulx (I), Sestriere (I), Sportinia (I)
Longest run Le Chalvet, 2.5km (red)
Number of lifts 35 in Montgenèvre-Monti della Luna, 91 in Milky Way
Total of trails/pistes 100km in Montgenèvre/Monti della Luna (37% easy, 43% intermediate, 20% difficult), 400km in Milky Way
Nursery slopes 1 free lift
Summer skiing none
Snowmaking 26 hectares covered

LIFT PASSES
Area pass Montgenèvre-Monti della Luna 750FF for 6 days, extension pass for Milky Way 100FF
Day pass Montgenèvre-Monti della Luna 140FF, Milky Way 240FF
Beginners 1 free lift. Beginners pass (covers 7 lifts), 90FF a day for adults, 70FF for children
Pensioners 60–69yrs 560FF, free for 70yrs and over
Credit cards yes

TUITION
Adults ESF, 510–527FF for 6 x 2½hrs
Private lessons ESF, 169FF per hr
Snowboarding ESF, as regular ski school
Cross-country ESF, 499–515FF for 6 half-days. Loipe 50km
Other courses moguls, slalom, competition
Guiding through ski school

CHILDREN
Lift pass Montgenevre-Monti della Luna, 6–12yrs, 560FF for 6 days. Milky Way, 190FF per day
Ski kindergarten ESF Jardin d'Enfants, 3–5yrs, 164FF per day
Ski school ESF, 475–496FF for 6 x 2½hrs
Non-ski kindergarten Haute Garderie, 12mths–4yrs, 9am–5.30pm, 120FF per day, not including lunch

OTHER SPORTS
Horse-riding, parapente, skating, snowmobiling

FOOD AND DRINK PRICES
Coffee 8FF, glass of wine 7FF, small beer 15FF, dish of the day 60FF

Skiing facts: Sauze d'Oulx

TOURIST OFFICE
Piazza Assietta 18, I-10050 Sauze
d'Oulx, Piedmont
Tel 39 122 858009
Fax 39 122 850497

THE RESORT
By road Calais 998km
By rail Oulx 5km, frequent buses to
resort
Airport transfer Turin 1hr
Visitor beds 4,350
Transport ski bus, L9,000 for 6 days

THE SKIING
Linked or nearby resorts Bardonecchia
(n), Borgata (l), Clavière (l), Cesana
Torinese (l), Grangesises (l), Jouvenceaux
(l), Montgenèvre (l), Sansicario (l),
Sestriere (l), Sportinia (l)
Longest run no. 12, 7.2km (red)
Number of lifts 21 in Sauze d'Oulx, 91 in
Milky Way
Total of trails/pistes 120km in Sauze
d'Oulx (27% easy, 61% intermediate,
12% difficult), 400km in Milky Way
Nursery slopes 3 lifts
Summer skiing none
Snowmaking 12km covered

LIFT PASSES
Area pass Milky Way (covers Sauze
d'Oulx, Sestriere, Sansicario, Cesana

Torinese and Clavière),
L210,000–260,000 for 6 days
Day pass L48,000 (Milky Way)
Beginners points tickets
Pensioners 60yrs and over,
L193,000–239,000 for 6 days
Credit cards yes

TUITION
Adults Sauze d'Oulx, Sauze Project and
Sauze Sportinia, 10am–1pm,
L160,000–220,000 for 6 x 3hrs
Private lessons all ski schools,
L48,000–50,000 per hr
Snowboarding as regular ski schools
Cross-country loipe 3km
Other courses heli-skiing, carving,
disabled skiing.
Guiding through ski schools

CHILDREN
Lift pass 8–12yrs, L193,000–239,000
for 6 days. Free for 7yrs and under
Ski kindergarten none
Non-ski kindergarten Dumbo, L280,000
for 6 days
Ski school all schools, prices as
adults

FOOD AND DRINK PRICES
Coffee L1,400, glass of wine L2,000,
small beer L3,000–3,500, dish of the day
L25,000

Clavière
top 2820m (9,250ft) bottom 1760m (5,773ft)
Clavière is a small village on the Franco–Italian border. During the eighteenth century it was part of Montgenèvre. The village consists of a few
hotels and a row of shops (including several good supermarkets) on the
Italian side, specialising in food and cheap local alcohol, with prices in
both francs and lire. Reporters say Clavière has a pleasant, relaxed
atmosphere; it is tightly enclosed by wooded slopes, and the nursery area

Skiing facts: Sestriere

TOURIST OFFICE
Piazza Agnelli, I-10058 Sestriere,
Piedmont
Tel 39 122 755444
Fax 39 122 755171
Web site www.agora.stm.it/sestriere

THE RESORT
By road Calais 1020km
By rail Oulx 22km, buses to resort
Airport transfer Turin 1½hrs
Visitor beds 4,200
Transport ski bus L3,000 per day

THE SKIING
Linked or nearby resorts Bardonecchia
(n), Borgata (l), Clavière (l), Cesana
Torinese (l), Grangesises (l), Jouvenceaux
(l), Montgenèvre (l), Sansicario (l), Sauze
d'Oulx (l), Sportinia (l)
Longest run Sestriere-Pariol, 7.3km
Number of lifts 19 in Sestriere, 91 in
Milky Way
Total of trails/pistes 120km in Sestriere
(39% easy, 42% intermediate, 19%
difficult), 400km in Milky Way
Nursery slopes 12 in area
Summer skiing none
Snowmaking 75km covered

LIFT PASSES
Area pass Milky Way (covers Sauze
d'Oulx, Sestriere, Sansicario, Cesana
Torinese and Clavière),
L210,000–260,000 for 6 days

Day pass L48,000 (Milky Way)
Beginners points tickets
Pensioners 60yrs and over,
L193,000–239,000 for 6 days
Credit cards yes

TUITION
Adults Sestriere Ski School,
10am–1pm, L45,000 per day,
L180,000 for 6 days
Private lessons L47,000 per hr
Snowboarding as regular ski school
Cross-country private lessons through
ski school, details on request. Loipe 15km
Other courses heli-skiing
Guiding through ski school

CHILDREN
Lift pass 8–12yrs L193,000–239,000
for 6 days, free for 7yrs and under
Ski kindergarten Sestriere Ski School,
4yrs and over, 10am–1pm, L45,000 per
hr, L180,000 for 6 days
Ski school as ski kindergarten
Non-ski kindergarten Mini Club of
Grangesises, 3–12yrs, 9am–1pm and
3–7pm, L15,000 per day

OTHER SPORTS
Dog-sledding, snowmobiling,

FOOD AND DRINK PRICES
Coffee L1,500, glass of wine L2,000,
small beer L3,500, dish of the day
L25,000

is small and steep. Lifts give access to the skiing above Montgenèvre and
Cesana, with easy runs back from both. Queuing is not usually a problem, although it does tend to become busier at weekends. Mountain eating-places close to the village are the Località Gimont and La Coche.
There is a cross-country trail up to Montgenèvre and back. The ski
school has some English-speaking instructors and, outside high season,
mainly English-speaking pupils. At weekends the village suffers from

heavy through-traffic.

There are eight hotels along the road; the two-star Hotel Roma, close to the main chair-lift, is recommended ('good value, plenty of food and comfortable rooms'). Others include the Passero Pellegrino, Pian del Sole and the Savoia. The recommended restaurants are the Ski-Lodge, the Sandy and the Gran Bouc crêperie. Clavière is 'not a place for those interested in a hectic après-ski'. It has half-a-dozen bars, including the Bar Caffé Torino and the Pub Kilt, plus La Scacchiera disco. Clavière has become increasingly popular with tour operators, and five offer accommodation here.

TOURIST OFFICE
Tel 39 122 878856
Fax 39 122 878888

Sansicario
top 2820m (9,250ft) bottom 1710m (5,609ft)

The village is in a sunny position halfway up the west-facing mountain-side, and is well placed for exploring the Milky Way. It is purpose-built, consisting mainly of apartment buildings linked to a neat commercial precinct by shuttle-lift. Facilities for beginners, and especially children, are generally good. A ski- and non-ski kindergarten (the Junior Club), provides daycare, including lunch, for 3- to 11-year-olds. Sansicario has its own ski school. There is little variety among the après-ski facilities – only a disco and a handful of restaurants and bars. Accommodation is of a generally high standard, mostly in apartments, but with a few comfort-able and expensive hotels. The most attractive of these is the Rio Envers, a short walk from the centre. Others include the four-star Monti della Luna and the simpler San Sicario.

TOURIST OFFICE
Tel 39 122 831596
Fax 39 122 831880

Monte Rosa

ALTITUDE Champoluc 1568m (5,144ft), Gressoney-la-Trinité 1624m (5,327ft), Alagna 1200m (3,936ft)

Beginners ✱✱ Intermediates ✱✱✱ Advanced ✱ Snowboarders ✱

The Monte Rosa ski area comprises the villages of **Champoluc**, **Gressoney-la-Trinité** and **Alagna** on the southern side of the border with Switzerland and within easy reach of France via the Mont Blanc tunnel. The Matterhorn is more pimple than peak from this perspective, but the Monte Rosa range, with its crags and glaciers, provides spectacular views. The valleys were settled by the Walser people in the Middle Ages and their geographical isolation has resulted in a distinctive culture and a strong Germanic/French dialect that persist today. Although the three villages are close as the crow flies and well connected by the lift system (at least in the case of Champoluc and Gressoney), it takes two to three hours to drive between any two of them.

✔ Excellent off-piste
✔ Strong regional identity
✔ Rustic charm
✔ High-quality local cuisine
✔ No crowds or queues
✘ Shortage of non-skiing activities
✘ Limited nightlife

Gressoney, in particular, has developed a strong following among British families in recent seasons, and the off-piste skiing of Alagna is no longer the best-kept secret of the Alps. A mountain guide of our acquaintance, a member of the esteemed Compagnie des Guides de Chamonix, confided to us: 'Alagna is more challenging, more exciting and certainly as scenically beautiful as the Grands Montets. As a Chamonard it hurts me to say it, but it is true'. The hopeless piste map resembles 'the footwork of a drunken spider'. However, on-piste signposts are plentiful and accurate.

Ski and board
top 3370m (11,056ft) bottom 1200m (3,936ft)

In the Monte Rosa ski area all pistes eventually lead to **Stafal**, a modern hamlet above Gressoney-la-Trinité, which is the central link in the chain of 53 lifts. Head up in the cable-car and chair-lift to the west and you reach the Colle Bettaforca, the departure point for the descents to Champoluc. Take the two-stage gondola to the east and you come to the Passo del Selati, the start of the Alagna connection. With slopes on both sides of the valley, Gressoney has the lion's share of the skiing in an area which totals 200km of piste, and the fastest lifts.

There are two points of departure from Champoluc, one on the outskirts of the village and the other up the hill in **Frachey**, which provides much quicker access to the main area. Three small satellite areas – **Antagnod**, **Brusson** and **Gressoney-St-Jean**, are not connected to the central system. Alagna's facilities consist of a venerable three-stage cable-car, which is almost empty except on Sundays and is supplemented by four minor lifts. Although its impressive vertical drop and its extensive powder fields attract rugged skiers, its links with Gressoney are unpisted in both directions, which makes it unsuitable for anyone else.

Beginners

The best place to learn is the sunny nursery slope at Crest, at the top of the first stage of the Champoluc gondola. In Gressoney, beginners congregate around the Punta Jolanda lift, then progress via the 70-person cable-car to the wide plateau above Stafal on the Champoluc side.

Intermediates

Both Gressoney and Champoluc have plenty of interlinked intermediate cruising, rather more in fact than the piste map suggests; it is so badly printed that most of the blue (easy) runs appear to be black (difficult).

Advanced

The best black piste in the area is the 7-km descent from the top of the Punta Indren in Alagna, but even that would not be so severely rated in other resorts. The same could be said of the only mogul field, which is at Sarezza in Champoluc. The blue-ish red from Gabiet back to Stafal has been regraded into an undeserved black.

Off-piste

In the right conditions, all three resorts present challenges that are made all the more testing by bumpy terrain and narrow defiles between rock walls. The Mos and the Bertolina in Gressoney are excellent examples of this and they should not be attempted without a guide. The same is true of most of the skiing in Alagna, where the cable-car provides rapid access to huge snow fields that – inevitably in a predominantly south- and west-facing resort – are prone to avalanche.

The north-facing slopes in the Alta Valsesia National Park give a sense of extreme adventure, especially when accessed by the couloir at the top of the Malfatta. Alternatively, there is extensive heli-skiing, with glacier drops at over 4000m in the Monte Rosa range. Some of the routes take skiers down to **Cervinia** for the 25-km return to Champoluc. A qualified alpine guide can be hired for off-piste, heli-skiing and heli-boarding expeditions.

Tuition and guiding

English-speaking ski instruction can be hard to come by. In Gressoney, only 5 out of 30 instructors speak the language, so you should request one of them when booking lessons in advance. Qualified alpine guides are available through the respective tourist offices, but again the language can be a problem.

In Alagna, the young mountain guide Roberto Valzer arranges exciting off-piste adventures, as well as accommodation and evening meals in restaurants that are more like private homes.

Mountain restaurants

'The food was invariably good and we never had a bad lunch,' commented one reporter who also warned that the local *zuppa d'Aostano* is a cabbage soup so thick that it has to be eaten with a knife and fork. Rifugio Guglielmina, reached by a short off-piste route from Passo del Salati, is praised for both its food and the view. The Lys Rifugio at Gabiet is recommended for its local meats and cheeses as well as its ambience. The Edelweiss at Crest serves a reasonably priced set lunch in the restaurant and snacks in the bar. In Alagna, La Baità Refuge has superb mushroom pasta and exceptionally friendly service.

The resorts

Champoluc, at the top of the Ayas Valley, is set around a church and a fast-running mountain river. The old quarter was built in the fifteenth century, but the village has expanded in recent years to accommodate the requirements of a small ski resort. Gressoney-la-Trinité is on a similar scale, with a network of cobbled streets and wooden chalets surrounded by contemporary buildings. Gressoney-St-Jean, 5km down the valley, is larger and more attractive, while the outpost of Stafal tries to make up in convenience what it lacks in soul. Given its remote location, Alagna is built on a puzzlingly large scale, with decaying buildings surrounding a church where bell-ringing rules. This is a genuine oddball of a place, which has unique wooden houses with built-in hay frames, and a charm all of its own.

Accommodation

In Champoluc the best choice is the central, two-star Farvre, which according to its extremely enthusiastic British clients, is small, well-managed and friendly. The three-star Petit Prince in Champoluc-Antagnod also finds favour, but the welcome is less warm at the awkwardly located though authentically rustic Villa Anna Maria in Champoluc. The four-star Monboso at Stafal was criticised by one reporter ('rooms spacious, clean and comfortable but the food and service gave cause for complaint'). The Scoiàttolo, in Gressoney-la-Trinité, is equally comfortable but with a better ambience. In the same resort, Hotel Residence is popular with reporters ('the rooms were comfortable, the food good, the staff helpful and the wine was reasonably priced'). In Alagna the Bar Mirella, a bed-and-breakfast with rooms over a cake shop, is a must if you can get in. If not, try the Genzinella. The Cristallo is the most comfortable hotel in Alagna and is 200m from the lifts.

Eating in and out

Le Sapin in Champoluc looks unpromising, not least for its multi-lingual tourist menus, but the food is something of a revelation. Otherwise, the

Favre is consistently good, with a bias towards gargantuan feasts of local game. Cuisine at the Villa Anna Maria was described as 'variable, but the restaurant has an honest wine list'. In Alagna the Servan is surprisingly sophisticated and should not be missed.

Après-ski

This is the kind of area where the nightlife is described by tour operators as 'informal and relaxed' – often a euphemism for dead in the winter. What there is takes place in the bars of family hotels, where locals and tourists drink and play cards. The Champoluc disco scene centres on the Gram Parsons in Frachey, while Gressoney-St-Jean offers Il Futuro. Gamblers with their own transport can visit the casino in St-Vincent (25km from Champoluc, 70km from Gressoney). The relaxed nightlife in Gressoney-la-Trinité consists of cafés such as the Hirsch Stube and the Petit Bar. Other activities include squash, swimming, skating, and winter walks.

Childcare

Childcare in the area is extremely limited, with no crèche or kindergarten facilities in Champoluc. The ski school at Champoluc takes children from five years of age. Hotel Monboso, above Gressoney, has a mini-club for its residents' children aged four to eight years old. Those over six years must join the adult classes at the ski school.

TOURIST OFFICE
(Monte Rosa Ski)
Tel 39 125 303111
Fax 39 125 303145

Passo Tonale

ALTITUDE 1884m (6,181ft)

Beginners ✳✳✳ Intermediates ✳✳✳ Snowboarders ✳

Passo Tonale is one of a group of Italian resorts which, with the lure of good snow and low prices, are dramatically increasing in popularity. It is situated a three-hour drive from Bergamo Airport and shares its skiing with the charming village of **Ponte di Legno**, 600m along the pass to the west. Together they offer 30 lifts with the capacity to carry 30,000 snow-users per hour to 80km of pistes.

> ✔ Excellent snow record
> ✔ Value for money
> ✔ Varied off-piste itineraries
> ✔ Lack of weekday queues
> ✘ Through-village traffic
> ✘ Lack of alpine charm

The resort is a thin line of settlement running for 1700m east to west along both sides of a high mountain pass, with a steep glacier to the south and open, rolling snowfields to the north, which mark the border between Lombardy and Trentino. The clientèle is a combination of families, ski clubs and school groups. The resort has become popular with British skiers and Eastern Europeans.

Ski and board
top 3069m (10,069ft) bottom 1270m (4,167ft)

Passo Tonale is a resort with exceptional snow quality, ideal beginner and easy intermediate terrain, as well as extensive ski-touring and off-piste. Mountain access is on either side of the main road, with most of the chair- and drag-lifts starting from the south-facing snowfields. The only cable-car is a 1-km walk west from the village; at the top is a chairlift which leads to four drags on the Presena Glacier. The cable-car is the only lift prone to queues, but these are only on Sundays and then are rarely longer than 15 minutes.

The skiing looks temptingly easy and open; it is, apart from the off-piste adventure routes. Even the glacier run would not daunt a mildly experienced intermediate. Until recently there have been no dedicated facilities for snowboarders, however the Contrabbandieri covered chair serves a 3-km run and accesses an ungroomed area which is being promoted for riders.

Ponte di Legno is a separate sector, normally accessible on skis or by bus, with a handful of lifts starting at the edge of the forest.

Beginners
Few resorts offer such a wide scope of blue (easy) runs. As one reporter commented: 'Of all the resorts we have visited this is probably one of the

best for beginners, although high-altitude and exposed pistes can make it very cold'. Six lifts rise up the south-facing side of the valley to access easy blue pistes; Valbiolo, the longest, is nearly 3km. The blue run off the Tre Larici drag-lift is fenced in on both sides of its carpet-like expanse and frightens no one. Beginners who insist on going to the top should think twice before tackling the blue glacier runs as they involve skiing some red (intermediate) sections to get back to the cable-car.

Intermediates

The 3-km Bleis run (now served by a covered chair) takes you all the way back to town and is easy cruising terrain. The two glacier reds, accessed by drag-lifts, connect with the single red piste down to the cable-car station for the best snow in the resort. Adventurous intermediates might try the Alpino, a 4.5-km excursion around the back of Monte Serodine and out of sight of the pistes. However, this sunny run can lose snow earlier than others and it is not groomed.

Advanced

The Sinistro black (difficult) run on the glacier is really a reclassified red. Its 300-m vertical drop in the space of 1km makes it steep enough to be a regular training slope for the Italian ski team. The only run under the cable-car is also marked as black, but skiers from Chamonix or Verbier would scarcely give it a red rating.

Off-piste

Italians adore ski-touring, and the best itineraries usually require some uphill walking. The 16-km Pisgana Glacier route runs from the drag-lift down the back of the Presena Glacier, with an optional climb up Monte Adamello at 3554m. It follows on over open snowfields into the ravine of Valnarcanello and at least 1km of flat skating into Ponte di Legno. This run is safe only from mid-March and demands a guide, available from any of the ski schools.

Tuition and guiding

Passo Tonale has a choice of three ski schools. Instructors at both Tonale-Presena and Ponte di Legno-Tonale are described by one reporter as 'unspoilt, simple and sympathetic; they try just as hard with beginners, love a joke, and even if they are not technically the best teachers, they put their hearts into it'. We have also received a favourable report for the third school, Il Castellaccio. G & G is a snowboard school that also hires out equipment. However, the terrain around Passo Tonale is too tame for freestylers looking for natural jumps and dips.

Mountain restaurants

Negritella serves 'very good local dishes in a warm, friendly, efficient environment'. The Mirandola Hospice is 'an interesting building but has little atmosphere'. Malga Viabola is 'lacking in atmosphere and serves poorer-quality food than elsewhere'.

The resort

For centuries the Mirandola Hospice sheltered pilgrims crossing Passo Tonale, but tourism dates only from the 1960s. Prosperity has brought some new paint, three 12-storey tower blocks and rows of condominiums that resemble army barracks. Hotels hug the single roadway, but fortunately there is little through-traffic by night. You can walk across the village in ten minutes. The only bus runs seven times daily to Ponte di Legno. British tour operators collaborate on a weekly coach trip to the ski slopes of **Folgarida** and **Marilleva,** touching on the **Madonna di Campiglio** area. There are few shops and the latest technical ski equipment is not available for hire. The old indoor swimming-pool is now defunct.

> **WHAT'S NEW**
>
> Three-star Hotel Pian di Neve and Paradiso disco
> Serodine covered chair-lift

Accommodation

Passo Tonale's 3,000 beds include only one chalet and limited self-catering apartments. Hotel Redivalle is the oldest hotel and a landmark by which directions are given. Orchidea is the most recent and one of the most attractive hotels, along with the historic Mirandola Hospice, where resident guests can rely on snowmobile transport until 2am. Pian di Neve is a new 300-bed hotel for the 1999 season.

Eating in and out

For fine dining, the snowmobile ride up to the Mirandola Hospice is mandatory. Intimate décor and delicious gorgonzola *Spätzle* are found at Il Focolare ('impressive but not cheap'). La Torretta is praised for 'the best thin, crispy-base pizza'. The newly opened Antares is recommended for pasta. Supermarket Sossi is the best of the two supermarkets.

Après-ski

Bar Cady, Nico's and the UFO are popular bars. Monti and Cantuccio offer sports events on television. El Bait is quiet and cosy. The Embassy disco gives free entrance to British visitors. Antares features live music several nights a week. Paradiso is a new disco. Other sports available include snowmobiling, dog-sledding in Ponte di Legno, and ice-skating

Childcare

The kindergarten in the Hotel Miramonti takes children from four years.

TOURIST OFFICE
Tel 39 364 903838
Fax 39 364 903895
Email turismvaldisole@well.it
Web site www.turismvaldisole.well.it

Sella Ronda

ALTITUDE 1440–1563m (4,724–5,128ft)

Beginners ✳✳✳ Intermediates ✳✳✳ Advanced ✳✳ Snowboarders ✳✳

The Dolomites are home to the largest and scenically the most beautiful ski area in the world. Others try to compete but nowhere else actually manages 1180km of pistes served by 464 lifts in one region. Similarly, the backdrop of craggy peaks and dramatic granite cliff faces, which take on a distinctive and glorious shade of rose pink in the light of the setting sun, is without parallel.

- ✔ Outstanding scenery
- ✔ Range of mountain restaurants
- ✔ Extensive ski-touring
- ✔ Good children's facilities
- ✔ Excellent-value lift pass
- ✘ Unreliable snow record
- ✘ Skiing convenience
- ✘ Lift queues
- ✘ Heavy traffic

By no means are all of these runs and resorts linked by lift, but all are included in the Superski Dolomiti lift pass, which represents the best value in the northern hemisphere. At the core of it all lies the Sella Ronda, a celebrated circuit of four valleys involving 90 minutes of lifts, 120 minutes of downhill skiing, and an always undetermined Joker factor of queuing time. It can be skied in both directions, but clockwise involves less poling and skating. Miss the crucial lift home because of deteriorating weather or volume of people and you are in for an expensive taxi ride.

Much has been done in recent years to improve the antiquated lifts which blighted the Sella Ronda, but despite continuing innovations queues can still become chronic at weekends and during the Italian holidays ('It was the first time we have ever seen staff specifically employed to pack skiers into gondolas – we thought only the Tokyo underground needed these'). One reporter said the problem was exacerbated 'by the persistent Italian refusal to either queue sensibly or to share chair-lifts with strangers'. Skiers and riders are strongly advised to stray from the actual circuit, which anyway is short of enchanting, and explore and enjoy individual valleys for their own merits.

The best-known, but by no means the most important of these valleys is Val Gardena. **Selva Gardena**, or Wolkenstein as it is also known in this bilingual border area of Italy, is the actual name of the resort, which is barely more than a small village strung along the valley road. The second most popular resort is **Canazei**, in the Italian-speaking Val di Fassa. This large and bustling village acts as one of the major holiday bases for skiing the region, and is the best for those in search of non-skiing activities and a good nightlife.

On the periphery of the Sella Ronda circuit lies a whole range of

resorts, from established international ski towns like chic **Cortina d'Ampezzo** to the sleepy and essentially Italian villages of **San Martino di Castrozza** and **Vigo di Fassa**. You cannot hope to ski it all in a week, or even a season. Vastly improved services to the upgraded airports at Venice and Verona, coupled with two-and-a-half-hour motorway transfers to most Dolomite resorts, have reopened this unspoilt corner of the European ski map.

The layout of the Sella Ronda and the whole Superski Dolomiti region is not as confusing as it sounds, and you will soon get your bearings, provided you invest in the Ordnance Survey-style map of the region, called Sellaronda e Valli Ladine Carta Sciistica, which costs the equivalent of £3 from any newsagent in the resorts. It shows all the lifts and gives fairly accurate colour gradings. The Val di Fassa now produces a similar and moderately accurate map, although the piste gradings are suspect. Other local piste maps – of which there are many variants – raise more questions than they answer.

Ski and board
top 2950m (9,676ft) bottom 1225m (4,018ft)

With its mainly blue (easy) and unproblematic red (intermediate) runs, the Sella Ronda is better for seeing some wonderful scenery than for really challenging skiing. Although the peaks of these mountains are high, virtually all the skiing takes place lower down; this is the main cause of the Dolomites' variable snow records, a handicap that has been offset by heavy investment in modern snowmaking techniques. Nevertheless, south-facing slopes in particular can become very worn and unpleasant. One reporter recounted having to remove her skis and walk certain sections of the circuit during a mild spell, and indeed short walks between lifts are not uncommon, even when conditions are good.

The Sella Ronda can be skied in either direction with all kinds of variations. Clockwise mountain access from Selva Gardena is via the Dantercëpies gondola to the start of a long and mainly red cruise through 730m vertical all the way to **Colfosco**. From here a chair-lift takes you to **Corvara**, and a 12-person gondola brings you to Boè and the Crep de Munt for a short red run down to **Campolungo**. You can take a drag-lift up to the Rifugio Bec de Roces, which is the start of a pleasant red and blue run with dramatic backdrops down into **Arabba**. Queues here can be unacceptable during busy weeks ('a 40-minute wait mid-morning for a four-minute uplift'). A chair-lift is the most direct, but not necessarily the quickest onward route. The cable-car to Belvedere involves more skiing and a much more challenging piste that allows you to rejoin the blue route before Pont de Vauz. A desperately slow chair-lift, which is scheduled for replacement, is followed by a fast detachable quad-chair that brings you up to Sas Becè and the red run down to Lupo Bianco. Take a short red off the circuit into Canazei, or continue via a gondola up to Col Salei. From here, a short red and a long blue cruise through 700m vertical return to Selva.

Beginners
The best of the novice skiing is found in the Alta Badia sector, bordered by **Armentarola** in the east, Corvara in the west and **La Villa** in the north. The wooded meadows here are reminiscent of the Austrian Tyrol. At the other end of the circuit, try the long blue that starts above the Passo Sella at 2400m and takes you all the way down to Selva at 1550m.

Intermediates
The whole of the Sella Ronda is ideally suited to cruisers who really want to put some mileage beneath their skis each day in this outstanding setting. Where to base yourself is a matter of personal choice. The Selva Gardena–Canazei end of the circuit has some of the better long runs, though fans of Corvara and Colfosco would strongly disagree. The favourite run among reporters is the Armentarola piste from Lagazuoi.

Advanced
Arabba is the Argentière of Italy and the place to base yourself for the toughest skiing in the area. Anyone who imagines that the Dolomites consist solely of scenic blue cruising runs is in for a wicked shock here. From the edge of the village a two-stage jumbo gondola and a cable-car take you up nearly 900m over the granite cliffs off the Soura Sass to the start of what is, by any standard, some serious advanced skiing. The black (difficult) runs down the front face are testing in the extreme.

Alternatively, from the halfway stage of the gondola you can ski off the Sella Ronda on a wonderful 20-km journey down usually deserted pistes to the town of **Malga Ciapela**. From here you pay a L30,000 supplement to your lift pass for the two long cable-cars to the top of the 3269-m Marmolada, revered by mountaineers in the same breath as the Matterhorn, the Eiger and Mont Blanc; the lift opens only in February. After admiring the views from the top, a long red run takes you to within a couple of slow lifts of the home run back down to Arabba. Powderhounds can also enjoy moderately priced heli-skiing on the Marmolada. Colfosco, Plan de Gralba-Piz Sella, Belvedere and Seceda areas all have half-pipes.

Off-piste
Passo Pordoi, between Arabba and Canazei, is the base-station of the Sas Pordoi cable-car, which takes you up to the Rifugio Maria at 2958m. Piste-grooming machines have never made it up here, and all the skiing is as nature intended. The long run down the Val de Mesdi is one of the most taxing in the Dolomites and should not be attempted without a guide. The front face of Sas Pordoi is a shorter, difficult challenge, with a steep and usually icy entrance guaranteed to get anyone's adrenalin pumping; falling is not advised.

Tuition and guiding
The Selva Gardena Ski School continues to generate excellent reports, and tuition appears to be of a high standard ('good teaching and no silly

end-of-week races'). Reporters note that the standard of English spoken by instructors throughout the Sella Ronda appears to have improved dramatically in recent years. The other two ski schools in Val Gardena are at **Santa Cristina** and **Ortisei**.

Cross-country
The Superski Dolomiti area claims a mighty 1033km of prepared loipe scattered throughout the region; some of the most scenic (98km) are situated in Selva Gardena.

Mountain restaurants
The Dolomites abound with mountain eateries, but the standard between the Italian- and German-speaking regions varies markedly, with the better food found in the former. Rifugio Lagazuoi is singled out as 'spectacular value with amazing views'. Rifugio Bec des Roces is said to be 'over-priced'. Rifugio Pralongia is singled out for 'well-prepared meals at nice prices'. Rifugio Padon is popular with the ski patrol. Rifugio Portoa Vescovo has 'a wide range of food at reasonable prices'. Pizzeria El Table in Arabba is strongly recommended. Plan Boè above the village is popular for traditional Austro–Italian fare. Trapper's Bar, on the Passo Campolungo between Corvara and Arabba, has a sun terrace and live music. Forcelles above Colfosco is warmly praised. Rifugio Crep de Munt, above Corvara, also has a terrace and a warm welcome. Try Mesules – its position on the edge of the road and the piste between Selva and Colfosco means it can be reached by skiers and non-skiers alike.

Rifugio Scotoni is a welcome wayside warming hut on the run down from Lagazuoi if you are unable to make it to the even cosier Alpina, 2km further on. Either way, you may need some refreshment before the next lift, which is one of the quaintest in the region – a horsedrawn tow (L2,000 supplement).

A more gastronomic lunch can be found at the Hotel Grand Angel on the edge of the Armentarola cross-country track. Baità del Gigio, on the nursery slopes above Malga Ciapela, is worth the long run down and is exceptionally good value. Chez Anna, on the run from Seceda to Ortisei, is said to be worth a visit for spectacular ham-and-eggs. Baità Fredarola, near Belvedere, is recommended for its pizzas. Way off the beaten track is the Ospizio di Santa Croce, reached by a ski bus from La Villa to **Pedraces** and two lifts up to the Abbey of the Holy Cross. Ristorante Lé, at the top of the chair, is renowned for the best gulaschsuppe in the Sud Tirol.

The resort
Selva Gardena is an unassuming village, which sprawls in suburban style up the Val Gardena. Traffic is heavy and weary skiers are more at risk crossing the road than they ever are on piste. For all that, the village maintains a quiet, unsophisticated charm, which makes it popular with

families. Examples of the local woodcarving industry colourfully adorn houses and even lamp-posts.

Accommodation

In Selva Gardena, Hotel Gran Baità is the pick of the four-stars, together with the Aaritz and the Alpenroyal. Hotel Laurin is a favourite amongst visitors and is renowned for its food. Accommodation is mainly in small hotels, most of which are very comfortable. We have good reports of the Hotel Solaia and, in particular, its buffet breakfast. The centrally situated Hotel Antares is praised, as is the simple Stella. Inexpensive bed-and-breakfasts include the Eden and the Somont. The more comfortable Savoy also has a restaurant. Hotel Continental is well located for skiers beneath the Dantercëpies gondola, but 'non-skiers should note that the ten-minute walk into town can be steep and icy'.

> **WHAT'S NEW**
>
> Covered quad chair-lift from Lezuo to Rifugio Sass Becce
> Piz Seteur and Piza Pranseies chair-lifts both upgraded

Eating in and out

In Selva Gardena, reporters say one of the best restaurants is Pizzeria Rino. A wider selection of dishes can be found at Café Mozart and the restaurant of the Hotel Laurin. Other eateries include Armin, Lo Scoiàttolo, Freina, the restaurant in the Hotel Gran Baità, and in Santa Cristina, Plaza and Dosses. Pizzeria Miravalle is praised for 'its high standard of cuisine with an excellent, varied menu'.

Après-ski

At first sight, Selva Gardena does not appear to have much of a nightlife. Half-a-dozen cafés serve home-made cakes and pastries, but the resort is quiet in the evening, with few lights, seemingly little activity and none of the buzz of a serious party resort. In fact, behind the shutters is a thriving après-ski scene and a wide choice of nightspots, but light sleepers are unlikely to have their slumber disturbed. The Luisl is the most popular haunt after skiing ('the only place with any real life between skiing and dinner'). Bar La Stua has twice-weekly folk-music evenings. Also recommended are the Hotel Laurin Bar, Villa Frainela, the Monica and Mozart bars. The Dali and Stella Club discos throb through the night. In nearby Santa Cristina, Yeti's Ombrella Bar is popular, and other bars include Calés and I Tublà.

Childcare

Selva Gardena is an excellent area for children of all ages to learn to ski. The nursery slopes are based below the Dantercëpies gondola at the northern edge of the village. At the kindergarten at the bottom of the Biancaneve drag-lift toddlers and small children are taught the rudiments of skiing among cartoon characters. Instructors are plentiful and patient and there seems to be none of the 'here is an entire generation to be put off skiing' attitude that you encounter in some French resorts. The surrounding area is ideal for older children to learn or improve their skiing.

Linked or nearby resorts

Arabba
top 2950m (9,676ft) bottom 1600m (3,808ft)
This small, unspoilt village is tucked away in a fold of the landscape and is surrounded by the most challenging skiing in the area. The village itself is hopeless for non-skiers, and facilities for babies and toddlers are non-existent. The language here is Italian, although Arabba is only a couple of kilometres south of the Sud-Tirol border. The Sport is the smartest hotel, but the three-star Portavescovo ('lovely hotel – highly recommended') is more lively and houses the Stübe Bar, which along with Peter's Bar just about sums up the nightlife. The Rue de Mans is an excellent restaurant just outside the village.

TOURIST OFFICE
as Canazei

Campitello
top 2950m (9,676ft) bottom 1440m (4,723ft)
A small collection of old buildings make up this quiet village set beside a stream, well back from the main road. The Col Rodella cable-car (45-minute queues reported) goes up to the ski area and there is no piste back down again. The village is ideal for complete beginners as some of the area's best nursery slopes are right on its doorstep. Hotels include the Fedora, next to the lift station, and the Medil, which is a modern hotel built in traditional alpine style with its own fitness centre and bar with music. Hotel Sella Ronda is an alpine-style hotel owned by a priest. Hotel Rubino has a swimming-pool and piano bar among its many facilities.

TOURIST OFFICE
Tel 39 462 750 525
Fax 39 462 750 242

Canazei
top 2950m (9,676ft) bottom 1440m (4,724ft)
Canazei is a large, attractive and lively village on a busy main road in the Italian-speaking Val di Fassa. It is the best place to stay for those in search of non-skiing activities and a lively nightlife. The village itself is a tangle of narrow streets with a mixture of old farm buildings, new hotels and some delightful shops. Such is the scramble for beds in the Val di Fassa that tour operators offer hotels in outlying villages as far away as **Pera**, **Pozza**, **Vigo di Fassa**, and even distant **Moena**.

The Croce Bianca is the best hotel in town, with hand-painted pine furniture in abundance. The Campagnola is 'friendly, comfortable and three minutes from the gondola station'. The Dolomiti is built in grand hotel style, while the newly upgraded four-star Astoria has the friendliest atmosphere. Hotel Bellevue is well placed for the skiing, which is inconvenient from many of the village hotels. Hotels Freina and Serena have both been renovated for this season.

Canazei boasts many modestly priced restaurants. Rosticceria Meleser was singled out for praise ('you must book at weekends'). Rosengarten has 'simple décor, but good food'. The Italia is popular with the locals and has live music. Try Al Vecchio Mulino for local Italian dishes. Dolomiti is said to be 'pretentious and overpriced'. The Montanara Bar is the place to meet after skiing, as is the Frogs Pub, a few kilometres up the valley road in **Alba**. Peter's Bar by the Belvedere gondola is popular immediately after skiing. The Gatto Nero and Veruschka discos in Canazei and Alba are for the late-night crowd. Other sports available here are parapente, swimming, tobogganing and winter walks.

Organisation is said to be poor at the Canazei Marmolada Ski School: 'Hardly any English spoken. Two different queues of different ability led to a long, slow and totally confusing grading system with 16 in a class'.

TOURIST OFFICE
as Campitello

Colfosco
top 2950m (9,676ft) bottom 1650m (5,412ft)
Colfosco has easy access to both Selva and Corvara's skiing, although the village also has a small ski area of its own with good nursery slopes. Recommended hotels are the Kolfuschgerhof and the Centrale. Speckstube Peter, Mesoles, Stria, and the Matthiaskeller are the most popular eating-places; the Capella is the smartest.

TOURIST OFFICE
as Selva

Corvara
top 2950m (9,676ft) bottom 1550m (5,085ft)
This pleasant Sella Ronda resort fails to attract any British tour operators, but it is strategically placed for some of the best skiing in the region. Hotel Posta-Zirm, the old post house at the bottom of the Col Alto chairlift, is the place to stay. The building dates from 1808 and has been carefully renovated; the hotel also keeps alive the tradition of the tea dance ('it's good fun – when did you last see a man in a purple and silver one-piece suit with the zip pulled halfway down to reveal a giant gold medallion as he grooved away to hits from the 1970s?'). The Pensione Ladina nearby is a less expensive alternative and renowned for its home-made

Skiing facts: Selva Gardena

TOURIST OFFICE
Str. Mëisules 213, I-39048 Selva
Gardena
Tel 39 471 795122
Fax 39 471 794245
Email selva@val-gardena.com
Web site www.val-gardena.com

THE RESORT
By road Calais 1226km
By rail bus service from Bressanone
35km, Bolzano 40km,
Chuisa 27km
Airport transfer Munich and Milan
3–4hrs, Verona 2–3hrs, Innsbruck
1½hrs
Visitor beds 16,500 in Val Gardena
Transport free ski bus between Ortisei
and Selva Gardena

THE SKIING
Linked or nearby resorts Arabba (I),
Armentarola (I), Campitello (I), Canazei
(I), Colfosco (I), Cortina d'Ampezzo (I),
Corvara (I), La Villa (I), Ortisei (I),
Pedraces (I), San Cassiano (I), Santa
Cristina (I)
Longest run Seceda–Ortisei, 9km (red)
Number of lifts 464 in region
Total of trails/pistes 175km in Val
Gardena/Alpe di Suisi, 1180km in region
(30% easy, 60% intermediate, 10%
difficult)
Nursery slopes 10 runs
Summer skiing none
Snowmaking 90km covered in Val
Gardena/Alpe di Suisi

LIFT PASSES
Area pass Superski Dolomiti (covers
464 lifts), L249,000–286,000 for 6 days

Day pass Superski Dolomiti
L50,000–58,000
Beginners points tickets
Pensioners 20% discount for 60yrs
and over
Credit cards yes

TUITION
Adults Selva Gardena, L230,000 for 6 x
4hrs
Private lessons Selva Gardena, L54,000
per hr
Snowboarding Selva Gardena, private
lessons L54,000 per hr
Cross-country Selva Gardena, L54,000
per hr. Loipe 98km
Other courses freestyle, competition,
slalom, telemark
Guiding Mountain School Catores Val
Gardena, L190,000 for 3 days

CHILDREN
Lift pass 6–14yrs, Superski Dolomiti
L174,000–200,000, free for 5yrs and
under
Ski kindergarten as ski school
Ski school Selva Gardena, 4–12yrs,
L365,000 for 6 days
Non-ski kindergarten Selva Gardena,
from 12mths, L50,000 per day including
lunch

OTHER SPORTS
Skating, indoor shooting range, sleigh
rides, parapente, indoor tennis and
squash, swimming

FOOD AND DRINK PRICES
Coffee L1,800, glass of wine L3,000,
small beer L3,000, dish of the day
L15,000–25,000

blueberry grappa. Cross-country skiing is available, and the village boasts a skating-rink. The ski school has a kindergarten for children from three years of age, but English is not widely spoken.

TOURIST OFFICE
as Selva

San Cassiano
top 2950m (9,676ft) bottom 1537m (5,041ft)

A small, roadside village with mainly new Dolomite-style buildings, San Cassiano has some excellent skiing for beginners and early intermediates who want to avoid challenges. Long, easy runs go down to the village from Pralongia and Piz Sorega. Reporters mention the lack of spoken English in the resort, which attracts mainly wealthy Italians. The downside of this is being the sole English speaker in a ski class where lessons become 'laborious, with everything spoken in German and Italian'.

The Rosa Alpina is a large and comfortable hotel in the village centre and, with a live band, is also the focal point for après-ski. The Ski Bar is recommended for tasty, cheap pizzas and the Capanna Alpina, Saré and Tirol are all busy restaurants. La Siriola, Rosa Alpina, Fanes and the restaurant in Hotel Diamant are more expensive. There is bowling at the Daimant, but otherwise the village tends to be on the quiet side. Armentarola, with its own hotels and restaurants, is a kilometre away.

TOURIST OFFICE
as Selva

La Thuile/La Rosière

ALTITUDE La Thuile 1450m (4,757ft), La Rosière 1850m (6,070ft)

The overriding importance of this extensive but gentle ski area, which stretches in an uneasy *entente cordiale* across the Italian–French border, is the lack of crowds on its pistes – even at New Year. On the French side skiers tend to drive on up the Tarentaise past the turn-off at Bourg-St-Maurice to the more sophisticated charms of L'Espace Killy, while remote road access in the Aosta Valley keeps the Italians in Courmayeur.

LA THUILE
Beginners ✱✱✱
Intermediates ✱✱✱
Advanced ✱
Snowboarders ✱

✔ Lack of crowds
✔ Off-piste opportunities
✔ Choice of restaurants
✘ Lack of resort atmosphere
✘ Limited nightlife
✘ Few mountain restaurants
✘ Lack of childcare facilities

La Thuile is an old mining town clawing its way back to tourist-led prosperity, while La Rosière is a third-generation purpose-built resort content to rely on the rustic charm of its 1970s chalet-style architecture and the popularity of its low prices. Development at La Rosière on the French side in recent years has been restricted to a single high-speed quad and one large block of apartments; this is a source of much irritation to its go-ahead Italian neighbour.

In summer the resorts are joined by road over the Col du Petit-St-Bernard – in winter the car journey via the Mont Blanc Tunnel takes four hours. It is widely held that Hannibal led 30,000 men, 8,000 horses and his 30 elephants over the pass in the course of his epic journey from Spain to Rome in 218 BC. Under continuous attack from a murderous army of local Celts, who rained down rocks upon his column from every vantage point, it took him 15 days to cross from Bourg-St-Maurice.

The lift pass includes a day-out in Les Arcs, easily reached by funicular from Bourg-St-Maurice, and in Sainte-Foy, the best-kept secret of the Tarentaise. However, none of this is made easy. You first have to go to La Rosière's tourist office to obtain a (free) special ticket for the day, which then has to be exchanged for yet another ticket at the main lift station of the resort you are visiting.

Ski and board
top 2642m (8,668ft) bottom 1150m (3,773ft)
Both La Thuile and La Rosière have wide open slopes well suited to beginners and intermediates. In La Thuile these are supplemented by much tougher runs through the steeply wooded area just above the

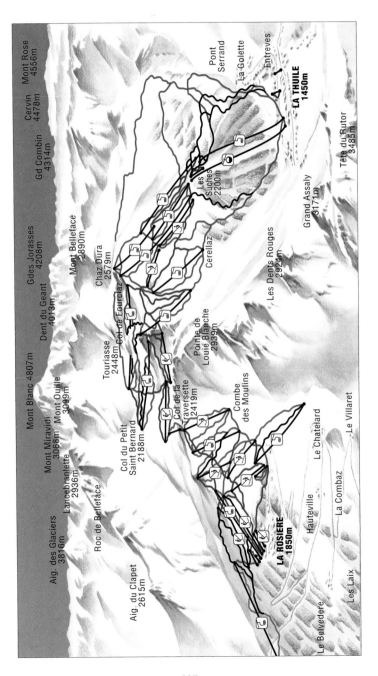

resort. In La Rosière, due to the greater height of the base, the slopes are predominantly above the tree-line. The highest point in the linked area is Belvédère, where lifts are often closed due to high winds. There are plans to extend the ski area to the top of Mont Valaisan (2891m), opening up the Bella Valetta Valley in the process. Plans are also being made to install lifts on Mont Miravidi (3068m) in the early years of the new century, further increasing the ski area by 50 per cent. However, for the moment they just remain plans.

La Thuile's main slopes face east, with a steeper north-facing area going down to the Col du Petit-St-Bernard. By taking the long, loopy alternative routes, it is possible for novices to cover the whole area. Most of the skiing in La Rosière faces south; these slopes are generally easier, with gentle blue (easy) pistes above the resort giving way to red (intermediate) ones on the higher part of the Col de la Traversette. As a result of being on different sides of an Alpine divide, each resort has its own microclimate; this often means that one is shrouded in cloud while the other is bathed in sunshine. By checking at the respective base-stations before deciding where to go, it may be possible to turn an unpromising day into a brilliant one. However, the infamous Vent du St Bernard, which cuts through even the most technical ski clothing – especially on the long slow lifts on the Italian side – must be borne throughout most of the winter. La Thuile has a half-pipe and a snowpark.

> **LA ROSIÈRE**
> Beginners ✱✱
> Intermediates ✱✱
> ✔ Ski-in ski-out convenience
> ✔ Facilities for children
> ✘ Unsuitable for non-skiers
> ✘ Limited nightlife
> ✘ Disappointing mountain restaurants

Beginners

Although there is a small nursery slope at resort level, the steepness of the lower mountain at La Thuile means that beginners soon take Les Suches gondola to the green (beginner) pistes served by La Combe lift. In La Rosière, there are several short nursery slopes near the resort, with more at the altiport nearby. Adventurous learners will soon move up the mountain to Les Echerts, La Poletta and Roches Noires lifts, which serve a network of blue runs.

La Combe, an encouragingly wide, flat area above Les Suches, is ideal learner riding territory. The transition to blue runs is best made in the catchment area of the Chalet Express, a chair-lift that is particularly easy to get on and off; board cred requires regular visits to the noisy La Clotze Bar at the bottom of it.

Intermediates

The area's 135km of mainly red pistes provide challenges for the average motorway cruiser. La Thuile offers a long run around the edges of the ski area from Chaz Dura and Belvédère, augmented by more aggressive terrain towards the Col du Petit-St-Bernard road (a piste in winter), which usually holds the best snow. The main link with La Rosière has a tricky start, but the runs below the Col de la Traversette are mainly short reds with plenty of blue alternatives on the way down to lunch.

Advanced

The most testing black (difficult) runs are in the Touriasse sector, from Belvédère or Chaz Dura to the Col du Petit-St-Bernard, between the San Bernardo and Fourclaz chair-lifts. In bad light, the Europa World Cup track through the woods from Les Suches to Golette is more user-friendly. The Ecureuil and Eterlou runs down to Les Ecudets below La Rosière do not deserve their black gradings, although their severity is frequently increased by indifferent snow conditions.

Off-piste

First-time visitors to the resort will be surprised by the variety and quality of La Thuile's off-piste possibilities. Wannabe powderhounds will find the regular pitch they need to gain confidence on the ungroomed sections under the chairs, while experts will enjoy the challenge of wooded, north-facing slopes between the pistes on the Touriasse. Better still is the heli-skiing, which begins on the Italian side as it is forbidden in France.

The 20-km run from the Ruitor Glacier to La Rosière is suitable for intermediates and upwards, but the descent to La Thuile is a real adventure, complete with a short rope section across an ice gully and a long walk at the bottom. There are further extensive heli-skiing options in neighbouring **Valgrisenche**.

Tuition and guiding

The simple choice is between the Italian Ski School in La Thuile and the French Ski School (ESF) in La Rosière. Accounts are divided as to the standard of spoken English, especially on the Italian side. We have conflicting reports of the Italian Ski School: 'The instructor's English was excellent and the standard of tuition high,' and 'our instructor's English was so limited she had problems understanding our questions'.

Mountain restaurants

La Thuile is the exception to the rule that skiers invariably eat well on Italian mountain tops. This is not so much a question of quality as of availability. Les Suches self-service is undeniably soulless ('a motorway-style cafeteria, but the food was not bad'), while Le Foyer, higher up on the same hill, offers substantial but unsophisticated fare; both restaurants are criticised by reporters for their 'hole-in-the-ground style loos; it is not easy to balance in ski boots'. At the top of the pass on the Italian side is an old fort that has been converted into an atmospheric restaurant specialising in grilled meats. The WCs are in the dungeons.

There are two fashionable Blues bars: the Roxi at the bottom of the Fourclaz chair and nautical Off Shore by the Belvédère chair. Both serve sandwiches and drinks to an aggressive backing track. The Bar du Lac at the bottom of the San Bernardo chair – the meeting-point for the weekly torchlight procession – serves a simple selection of Italian dishes at lunch-time. The on-mountain options in La Rosière are Plan Repos, an adequate but crowded self-service restaurant with a large and sunny terrace, and L'Ancolie, a pleasant inn with home-made food above the cross-country track at **Les Eucherts**.

The resort

The heart of La Thuile is the Planibel, an integrated tourist unit with a hotel, apartments, a sports complex and a selection of shops and bars. There are two swimming-pools (one is for children) and good facilities for squash and fitness training. The shops major on ski clothing and equipment, with no thought for the chic boutique factor that dominates in neighbouring Courmayeur. The efficient, but discouragingly clinical, complex contrasts sharply with the rest of the resort, which sprawls haphazardly through the surrounding woods.

> **WHAT'S NEW**
>
> Free mini club in La Thuile

La Rosière is situated at 1850m on the French side of the col named after St Bernard of Clairvaux, patron saint of the Alps. The original hamlet was the home of Jean Arpin, one of France's first ski instructors, who earned his bronze badge in 1939 at the age of 18 shortly before he and the other inhabitants of the hamlet were forced to evacuate their houses at an hour's notice as Mussolini invaded over the pass.

After the Second World War, Arpin set about developing La Rosière as a ski resort, but the first drag-lifts were not built until 1961. The ski area was linked to that of La Thuile on the far side of the col in 1984. The village has slowly developed along the bends of the mountain road from Seez to the Col du Petit-St-Bernard. The result is an attractive, neo-Savoyard tiered village with low-rise accommodation built out of wood and local, roughly-hewn stone. In winter, the road ends in a bank of snow outside the Relais du Petit-St-Bernard hotel. Just beyond lies the kennels of the St Bernard dogs, which on and off have maintained a presence here as rescuers of snowbound travellers since the seventeenth century. No matter what the weather, the brandy-bearers are ready and willing to pose for snaps in exchange for scraps.

Accommodation

The four-star Planibel Hotel in La Thuile is the most convenient and luxurious place to stay, but reports suggest that the warmth of the reception can leave much to be desired. This is certainly not true of the Chalet Alpina, a 500-m walk away across a stream. Eddy Nico (South African-born but of Italian descent) and his British wife, Debbie, extend a warm welcome and provide a very extensive service on and off the slopes to clients who return year after year. The Entreves has a cheerful family atmosphere. The Planibel Apartments have the advantages of the hotel with none of the disadvantages. Early booking is recommended for the bargain spacious two-, four- and six-person units.

In La Rosière, the emphasis is on self-catering apartments, which can be reserved through one of four local agencies. Hotel accommodation is limited, but the Relais du Petit-St-Bernard, the Roc Noir, the Vanoise and the Plein Soleil offer simple facilities in central locations. The family-run Solaret in the outlying hamlet of Les Eucherts (linked to La Rosière by a free bus-service while the lifts are open) is also recommended.

Eating in and out

Valdostana cuisine, with its emphasis on game, polenta and mushrooms, is well represented in La Thuile. Le Rascard specialises in guinea-fowl stuffed with green peppers and spinach, while the long-running La Bricole, a converted barn, is known for its chamois, polenta and extensive wine list. Fish lovers can enjoy lake perch at La Fordze, as well as 'excellent beef with juniper berries'. Lo Creton Pizzeria and the Fast Food Spaghetti House are sound budget choices. For ice-cream lovers the Cremeria in the Planibel complex is 'unmissable'. In the old village, La Grotta specialises in pizza.

Much of La Rosière's off-slope life focuses around two restaurants: the Relais du Petit-St-Bernard, which serves local specialities, pizza and crêpes, and Bar Le Relais, the most popular bar in town. Favoured alternatives include La Pitchounette, L'Ancolie and Le Plein Soleil. However, gourmets should make the 7-km trek to La Chaumière, a converted Savoyard farmhouse in the village of **Montvalezan**.

Après-ski

Given their attraction to families, it is hardly surprising that neither La Thuile nor La Rosière is known for its riotous nightlife. In La Thuile, Planibel's Rendezvous bar is 'decidedly laddish, especially late at night when the karaoke gets going'. Bar La Bouvette near the gondola station attracts the later afternoon crowds. La Bricole video-disco has a genuine pub atmosphere that appeals to British visitors, as well as live music at weekends. Dedicated night owls go to the Fantasia disco. The piano bar in the Hotel Planibel attracts a more sedate crowd. La Rosière's entertainment starts at Bar Le Relais when the lifts close and continues at the Yeti and the Arpin, which has karaoke. The resort has one disco.

Childcare

La Thuile now has a free non-skiing kindergarten for children from three years of age, but there is no crèche for younger children. In La Rosière, Le Village des Enfants takes care of children from 12 months from 8.30am to 5.30pm. The programme includes skiing, organised games and lunch. Specialist family operator Ski Esprit has a strong presence here and runs its own crèche in an apartment block beside the piste.

Skiing facts: La Thuile

TOURIST OFFICE
I-11016 La Thuile, Aosta
Tel 39 165 884179
Fax 39 165 885196

THE RESORT
By road Calais 938km
By rail Pré-Saint-Didier 10km
Airport transfer Geneva 2½hrs, Turin 3hrs
Visitor beds 3,123
Transport free bus service in the village

THE SKIING
Linked or nearby resorts La Rosière (l), Courmayeur (n)
Longest run San Bernardo, 11km (red)
Number of lifts 15 in La Thuile, 33 in linked area (with La Rosière)
Total of trails/pistes 130km (44% easy, 36% intermediate, 20% difficult) in linked area
Nursery slopes 4 lifts
Summer skiing none
Snowmaking 44 hectares covered

LIFT PASSES
Area pass Aosta Valley L267,000 for 6 days. La Thuile/La Rosière L211,000–237,000 for 6 days
Day pass L49,000
Beginners 1 free baby lift
Pensioners no reductions

Credit cards yes

TUITION
Adults Scuola di Sci La Thuile, 10am–12.30pm, L180,000 for 6 days
Private lessons Scuola di Sci La Thuile, L53,000 per hr, L360,000 per day (7hrs)
Snowboarding through ski school, prices and times as regular ski lessons
Cross-country through ski school. Loipe 12km
Other courses moguls, disabled skiing, slalom, competition, heli-skiing, telemark
Guiding through ski school

CHILDREN
Lift pass 20% reduction for 6–12yrs, free for 5yrs and under
Ski kindergarten none
Ski school La Thuile, 5yrs and over, 10am–12.30pm, L180,000 for 6 days
Non-ski kindergarten Mini Club 3–8yrs (10am–12.30pm and 2.30pm–4.00pm) free. Lunch extra and by arrangement

OTHER SPORTS
Swimming, snowshoeing, squash, indoor football

FOOD AND DRINK PRICES
Coffee L1,800, glass of wine L1,800, small beer L3,500, dish of the day L10,000–L25,000

TOURIST OFFICE
La Rosière
F-73700 La Rosière de Montvalezan, Savoie
Tel 33 4 79 06 80 51
Fax 33 4 79 06 83 20
Email la.rosiere@wanadoo.fr
Web site www.skifrance.fr/~rosiere

Round-up

RESORTS COVERED Macugnaga, Madesimo, San Martino di Castrozza, Val di Fassa

Macugnaga
top 2984m (9,790ft) bottom 1327m (4,353ft)

The resort of Macugnaga is made up of the two adjoining and attractive villages of **Staffa** and **Pecetto**. Staffa forms the centre while Pecetto is at the quieter end of town. They lie on the opposite side of the Monte Rosa to **Gressoney**, close to the Swiss border and two hours' drive from Turin. Macugnaga's proximity to the border has resulted in a style of architecture far more in keeping with Switzerland than with Italy.

Staffa and Pecetto have their own small ski areas, which are linked by ski bus. One reporter summed up the area as 'a marvellous introduction to skiing'. Reporters praised the 'short queues, if any at all; often you can finish your run and ski right back on to an empty chair-lift'. Staffa has better skiing for beginners ('only ten people on the nursery slopes at the very busiest'), a cable-car rising to the summit, and a number of longer runs. We have encouraging reports of Scuola Sci Macugnaga: 'excellent value for money'. Off-piste enthusiasts can hire a local mountain guide to ski over the back of Monte Moro to **Saas-Fee** in Switzerland.

Hotel du Four in Staffa's main square is 'clean and friendly, with plentiful and delicious food'. Hotel Zumstein is close to the resort centre and the cable-car. Recommended restaurants include the Miramonti at the Mt Belvedere base ('good lunchtime pizzas and great fondue nights'), and the Glacier ('you must book at weekends'). There are various other bars and restaurants in town, as well as a few small shops, but on the whole après-ski is rather limited. The Big Ben disco 'appears to be in a 1960s time warp'. Skating, night-skiing and cross-country are the other activities on offer.

TOURIST OFFICE
Tel/Fax 39 324 65119

Madesimo
top 2884m (9,459ft) bottom 1530m (5,018ft)

This small, attractive resort, centred around an old church, is a two-hour drive north of Bergamo. It is right on the Swiss border and close enough for a shopping spree in **St Moritz**. The old village has narrow streets with a few shops and some old converted farm houses, as well as some less pleasing concrete buildings. Madesimo's appeal is that it is cheaper than other, better-known resorts and offers excellent value for money.

The skiing is mostly intermediate and is concentrated on the usually uncrowded slopes of the 2984-m Piz Groppera, with long runs leading down into the neighbouring Valle de Lei. The high altitude normally ensures reasonable snow conditions. Seventeen lifts serve 45km of mostly red (intermediate) pistes and some challenging black (difficult) trails, including the famous Canelone run. The nursery slopes are pleasant and served by a new quad chair-lift. The lower slopes have snow-cannon, and the ski school has a reputation for small classes ('excellent, with plenty of English-speaking instructors').

Hotels include the central Emet and the family-run Andossi, which has a fitness room and a lively bar. The Alrecchino has 'small rooms, but a brilliant location and delicious hot chocolate in the hotel bar'. Hotel Cascata e Cristallo has excellent facilities including a swimming-pool, piano bar and a mini-club for 4- to 12-year-olds. You can ski back to most of the accommodation.

TOURIST OFFICE
Tel 39 342 53015
Fax 39 342 53782

San Martino di Castrozza
top 2385m (7,825ft) bottom 1450m (4,7572ft)

San Martino is on the eastern edge of the Trentino Dolomites, surrounded by wild forest with pink mountain peaks above. In 1700, the violin-maker Stradivari used to go into the same woods to select the spruce for his violins. Due to this historic connection, the area soon became known as the Forest of Violins. Skiing started at San Martino di Castrozza in the early 1930s. It has developed into three separate areas (two of which are linked) of 60km and 25 lifts. **Passo Rolle** is a small nearby village, which is reached by ski-bus and has five chairs and one drag-lift.

San Martino has two ski schools, Nuova Scuola Italiana di Sci and Scuola Saas Maor. The mountain guiding company Gruppo Guide Alpine supplies guides for the long and exciting off-piste descents of the steep slopes of the Pale Highlands, from Val Canali towards Primiero or from Val delle Comelle towards the Agordino area. The Rosetta cable-car is open in February and March for ski-touring and snowshoeing expeditions. The local cross-country skiing takes place on several circuits including one around the lake. Accommodation in the resort includes Hotel Des Alpes, Hotel Savoia, and Hotel Colfosco.

TOURIST OFFICE
Tel 39 439 768867
Fax 39 439 768814
Email info@sanmartino.com
Web site www.sanmartino.com

Val di Fassa
top 2949m (9,676ft) bottom 1320m (4,330ft)

The main resorts in the valley for tourism are **Canazei** and **Campitello** (see 'Sella Ronda'), which act as gateways to the giant Sella Ronda ski area. These, together with the villages of **Vigo di Fassa**, **Moena**, **Pozza di Fassa**, **Soraga** and **Mazzin**, are all connected by a free – albeit slow, crowded and irregular – ski bus. Each of these little Italian communities has its own tiny ski area, suitable mainly for beginners. The Skipass Fassa covers all the separate ski areas in the region, but if you want to ski Canazei and the Sella Ronda from here you need a car.

Moena is the principal town of the valley and has 56 hotels including the Hotel Alle Alpi, Belvedere, and Rosengarten, and two renowned restaurants: the Malga Panna and the Navalge. Other accommodation is available in the neighbouring hamlets of **Alba**, **Forno**, **Medil** and **Passo San Pellegrino**. Vigo di Fassa was the administrative centre of the valley during the fourteenth century as well as a transit station for merchants travelling across the Costalunga Pass to the Tirol. Today it is home to 40 tourist hotels including the comfortable Park Hotel Corona, where Olympic champion Alberto Tomba is often a guest. Pozza di Fassa has a further 55 hotels including the Hotel Arnika and Garni Roseal.

Moena is the starting point for the annual Marcialonga Di Fiemme e Fassa cross-country marathon. Floodlit cross-country skiing is available at Pozza di Fassa.

TOURIST OFFICE
Tel 39 462 60 24 66
Fax 39 462 60 22 78
Web site www.dolomititour.com/fassa

Switzerland

Switzerland is the cradle of alpine skiing that has been rocked to the limits of endurance by high domestic prices. These were enforced by unfavourable exchange rates which, in the darkest days of recession, left all but its most ardent and well-heeled devotees with little option but to desert the most beautiful skiing grounds of the world and turn to fresh and more affordable pastures. For many of those winters visitors experienced the joys of skiing elsewhere, not least in North America. Happily, with British skiers on the receiving end of SF2.5 to the pound last season, the number of snow-users now returning to Switzerland is rapidly increasing, although how lasting the damage to the Swiss tourist industry is remains to be seen.

First-time visitors will be pleasantly surprised to discover that while table wine is expensive, prices in general are now much on a par with France and Austria, and, in cases such as mountain restaurants, the value for money is greater.

Modern skiing began in Switzerland at the turn of the century, and, while it may well be an exaggeration to suggest that British holidaymakers introduced the sport, they certainly helped to promote it in the Parsenn, the Bernese Oberland and the Engadine. Ecological pressure to preserve the natural mountain environment has largely prevented the overdevelopment of Swiss ski villages.

The 1960–70s concept of the giant, linked ski area was never fully realised here; even the Portes du Soleil only marginally brushes into Switzerland. As a result, most resorts remain traditional villages, still largely unspoilt by the demands of mass tourism. The downside of this has been lack of investment in uphill transport in comparison with Switzerland's more free-spending neighbours. Despite – or because of – this the skiing remains unhomogenised, with natural rather than man-made runs against outstanding Alpine backdrops.

Mountain restaurants, for those who enjoy the relaxed ski lunch, are among the best in Europe, and the standard of hotels and apartments is consistently high.

Almost all Swiss resorts can be reached by train from Geneva and Zurich airports. Crossair Saturday flights to Sion are an added bonus.

Switzerland has two types of rail pass, which can be purchased from the Swiss Tourist Board before leaving home. These vouchers allow either airport transfers to and from your resort, or 'rover' facilities for the duration of your stay.

As expected in Switzerland, trains run to the strictest of timetables. You are strongly advised to send your luggage in advance wherever possible; the Swiss themselves rarely travel with more than hand luggage; trolleys are consequently scarce, and there is little provision for suitcases on trains.

Crans Montana

ALTITUDE 1500m (4,920ft)

Beginners ✱✱ Intermediates ✱✱✱ Advanced ✱ Snowboarders ✱✱✱

Crans Montana was the venue in 1911 for the world's first downhill race, the inaugural Roberts of Kandahar Challenge Cup, which was won by Cecil Hopkinson of Great Britain. For the occasion he donned his trusted tweed plus-fours which had already seen active service on a Scottish grouse moor the previous summer, and reached the finishing gate in 61 minutes. His fellow competitors were somewhat slower as they stopped to talk to spectators on the way.

The resort sits on what is claimed to be the sunniest plateau in the Alps, dotted with larches and lakes. The view across the Rhône Valley of 150km of the Alps from the Breithorn to Mont Blanc is the most spectacular of all Alpine panoramas.

Crans Montana is the official umbrella name for the agglomerations of **Crans**, **Montana** and **Aminona**. It is

✔ Short airport transfer
✔ Exceptional sunshine record
✔ High standard of hotels
✔ Ample non-skiing activities
✔ Superb mountain views
✔ Glacier skiing
✔ Facilities for children
✘ Urban landscape
✘ Heavy traffic
✘ Spread-out resort

a traditional spa resort that cultivates an élite, older clientèle in search of much more than a daily bash down what are irretrievably intermediate slopes. It has evolved from its early days as a centre for tuberculosis clinics into an interlinked skiing complex on the mountainside above. Its chic shopping is advertised as the finest in the Alps. Some 50 per cent of winter visitors are Swiss; French, Germans and Italians account for most of the rest, but the the British can now be found here in significant numbers.

Last season Crossair introduced a weekly direct service on winter Saturdays between Heathrow and Sion, which is only 30 minutes' drive from the resort. This, coupled with the strong pound and attractively priced accommodation, has encouraged major British tour operators to return after a long price-enforced absence. Consequently, the number of UK skiers has increased this season by 30 per cent.

What they will find is a fashionable 40,000-bed town of little architectural merit, dotted with smart hotels that vie with each other for the number of stars and the quality of their cuisine. The whole urban conglomeration sprawls untidily for over a mile along a busy main road. At peak times the traffic problem becomes so serious it often results in gridlock. It is sometimes hard to remember that the two towns, which started life separately and grew together over 20 years ago, owe their existence to the once pure mountain air so beneficial to convalescents from tuberculosis.

Last season a new funicular opened: it takes only 12 minutes to carry skiers up to Montana from the valley town of Sierre, encouraging visitors to either arrive in the valley by train or at least to leave their cars down below.

Ski and board
top 3000m (9,840ft) bottom 1500m (4,920ft)

Crans Montana is an intermediate's resort with good beginner terrain. All the pistes are easier than their rating suggests. Mountain access is via five points spread from west to east across the base of the mountains between Crans and Aminona. The free underground parking at the lift stations is some of the best in the Alps.

A smart 30-person Funitel gondola gives direct access to the top of the ski area at Plaine-Morte. A new gondola this season replaces the old 'egg' from Crans to Cry d'Err.

Queuing is not a serious problem here. The red (intermediate) run from Cry d'Err towards Pas du Loup is, according to reporters, 'the only area that could occasionally be described as congested'. Most visitors are content with making a few casual runs in the sunshine each day on the 160km of groomed piste served by 41 lifts. Of these, two are modern high-speed quads, but more than half are antiquated drag-lifts.

A single gondola from Montana and the new eight-person Cry d'Err gondola at Crans lead up through the woods to Cry d'Err, where a cable-car and chair-lift continue to the 2600-m summit of that sector. Between Montana and Aminona, the glacier skiing at 3000m on Plaine-Morte is reached by the Funitel gondola continuing upwards from the Violettes gondolas, which start from the outskirts of Montana at Barzettes. The resort's longest run is the 1500-vertical-metre drop from the glacier to town-level here.

From Crans Montana a bus takes skiers to Aminona, where a gondola rises to Petit Bonvin at 2400m. All sectors except the glacier are mutually accessible, but not without traversing multiple lifts.

Beginners

Starting at the top, beginners have three short but easy runs on the Plaine-Morte Glacier, where good snow is guaranteed. The nursery slopes down by the golf course in Crans are even easier but susceptible to sun. Cry d'Err has the most beginner runs; a handful accessible by no fewer than eight lifts providing skiing all the way down into Crans or Montana. However, it is impossible to ski back to Aminona entirely on blue (easy) runs.

Intermediates

Despite the generally superior standard of piste-grooming everywhere, passages between rock walls, such as on the long red (intermediate) run from Plaine-Morte, add a genuine thrill. The largest conflux of intermediate pistes is in the Violettes sector, with winding trails through the woods. The Toula chair- and drag-lifts lead to steeper reds. Most excit-ing are the Nationale World Cup piste and Chetseron, which are well-groomed but have the occasional banked drop-off designed to make the stomach flip at high speed. One reporter described the Nationale as 'an excellent run with some testing sections – a proper red run'. Two short sections in the middle of a couple of red pistes are more difficult; one is the women's downhill racecourse on Chetseron, the other is an innocu-ous link between the Violettes mid-station and the long red coming down from the glacier.

Advanced

The only officially graded black (difficult) run in the entire resort is a bumpy fall-line pitch on the ridge under the Toula chair-lift ('no more than a red really'), which is often impeccably groomed on the lower sec-tion. The Plaine-Morte run is said to be the most avalanche-prone in Switzerland. Although perfectly safe when officially open, its gunbarrel pas-

> **WHAT'S NEW**
>
> Eight-person gondola between Crans and Cry d'Err

sages and changes in direction require a high level of commitment from even the most adept skier.

Crans Montana is an active snowboarding centre, with parks in Aminona and **Merignou**, and a half-pipe at Cry d'Err. Aminona is equipped for snowboarding jumps.

Off-piste

Crans Montana has no death-defying couloirs, but three of its unmarked itineraries require guides. From the Plaine-Morte Glacier it is possible to ski across open slopes and through three bands of rock down to the lake at **Zeuzier**. Walking through tunnels (torches required) and skiing a summer roadway leads to the ski lifts in the neighbouring resort of **Anzère**. Another route from the glacier guarantees fresh tracks in pow-der straight down into the Vallon d'Ertenze. The only way out at the bot-tom is by helicopter.

Tuition and guiding

There are two branches of the Swiss Ski School (SSS) in Crans and in Montana. Teaching in Montana is said to be 'imaginative, with a lot of emphasis on technique – most instructors speak good English'. Surf Evasion, affiliated with the Montana Ski School, offers group snow-board lessons during holiday periods, private lessons at other times and heli-boarding.

The Swiss Snowboard School in Crans, part of the SSS, is another learning centre.

Cross-country

Crans Montana has 50km of tracks including a 12-km loipe unusually set at an altitude of 3000m on the Plaine-Morte Glacier and therefore with guaranteed snow. A 15-km touring trail starts at Plans Mayens and winds across the pistes and through the woods all the way to Aminona.

Mountain restaurants

The Crans Montana clientèle prefers to eat in town. Lift station eateries at Cry d'Err, Petit Bonvin ('we were revolted to find horse meat on the menu') and Plaine-Morte are adequate but not inspiring. The Cabane des Violettes is an authentic alpine club touring hut with simple meals. The Café de la Cure alongside the blue run down to Aminona has character, but the best inns are Merbé for its tortellini, and Plumachit for its wild strawberry tart; both are old chalets with sunny terraces.

The resort

The resort sprawls along its three communities with few pretensions to charm. The tower-block Résidence Vermala, sticking out like a sore thumb on a hill above Montana, is arguably the greatest eyesore in the Alps. Life in Montana revolves around the central open-air skating-rink where the action is lazily invigilated by the clientèle lounging in the Café Rendez-vous beside it.

Crans has no such focal point. The main lift complexes are a five-minute walk uphill from their respective town centres. Gucci, Hermès, Valentino and Vuitton are some of the designer boutiques in Crans Montana. In addition to half-a-dozen cellulite centres and four major medical complexes, the resort features a resident astrologer, four reflexologists and three funeral homes.

Accommodation

In the past, Crans was traditionally the smartest of the three towns, followed by mass-market Montana and sleepy Aminona. Today the social divisions have gone down as the concrete has gone up, and Crans and Montana have equally impressive four- and five-star establishments as well as a host of more reasonably priced hotels. The Crans-Ambassador and the Grand Hotel du Parc in Montana, together with the Royal in Crans head the luxury cast.

The three-star Mont Blanc, on a hill above the resort, has 'the biggest terrace and best views'. Hotel de la Forêt caters for vegetarians. Hotel St George in Montana is 'conveniently placed and has good food and service. However, the rooms are shamefully pokey for a four-star'.

Eating in and out

The modestly priced Diligence in Montana is run by a Lebanese family and specialises in Middle Eastern cuisine ('the locals eat here along with regular weekenders, so booking is essential'). Otherwise, the most celebrated non-hotel gourmet dining is at the Cervin, the chic Rôtisserie de la Reine, and La Poste. The Mont Blanc, in the woods above Crans, has a marmot zoo for children and serves delicious sea bass. Dun Huang is Cantonese, and the Christina has Portuguese specialities. Valais-style raclette and fondue are on offer at the Bergerie du Cervin and Le Chalet. Pizza and pasta are taken seriously at Il Padrino and La Casa della Pizza.

Après-ski

The Absolut Disco in Crans heads the surprisingly long list of late-night entertainment spots. Immediately after skiing the younger crowd gathers at Amadeus; Le Pub 7 in Crans is popular. Teenagers flock to the Number One Club, then on to the Number Two Bar for late drinking. The Pascha Club in Crans has mostly techno music. The Memphis in Crans is a comfortable piano bar for the older set, who are also found in the Miedzor, Aida Castel and Crans-Ambassador hotels. Other sports on offer in the resort include curling, indoor tennis and squash, winter horse-riding, hot-air ballooning, parapente, swimming, hang-gliding, a climbing-wall, and luge-ing.

Childcare

Infants from two months old can attend the Fleurs des Champs kindergarten, next to Hotel Eldorado in Montana. Les Libellules, also in Montana, takes toddlers from two years of age. The Montana Ski School has its own Jardin des Neiges up on the Grand Signal mid-station. The Crans Ski School also accepts children at its kindergarten, which is by the golf course.

TOURIST OFFICE
Tel 41 27 485 04 04
Fax 41 27 485 04 60
Email crans_montana@scopus.ch
Web site www.crans-montana.ch

Davos/Klosters

ALTITUDE Davos 1560m (5,117ft), Klosters 1130m (3,706ft)

Beginners ✷ Intermediates ✷✷✷ Advanced ✷✷✷ Snowboarders ✷✷✷

An entrepreneurial Swiss saddle-maker with an eye for a winner is credited with bringing skis to the Parsenn and publicising their use via the creator of fiction's greatest detective. Tobias Branger first saw 'Norwegian snowshoes' in 1889 in the shadow of the Eiffel Tower at the Paris World Fair and ordered a few pairs of these 240-cm long elm planks for his Davos shop. He and his brother, Johannes, devised leather straps to attach them to their boots and tried them out under cover of darkness to avoid the ridicule of their fellow citizens. In 1894 they crossed the Maienfeld Furka Pass to **Arosa** on skis with Dr Arthur Conan Doyle, the creator of Sherlock Holmes. The novelist wrote about his experiences in *Strand Magazine* and captured the imagination of the then 400 British residents in Davos.

- ✔ Long runs
- ✔ Large linked ski area
- ✔ Good restaurants at all levels
- ✔ Off-piste for all standards
- ✔ Ski-touring opportunities
- ✔ Tree-level skiing
- ✔ Good-value lift pass
- ✔ Village atmosphere (Klosters)
- ✘ Straggling town (Davos)
- ✘ Lack of skiing convenience
- ✘ Dull nightlife (Klosters)

The transformation of Davos from a remote farming community into an international resort had begun in 1860 when Dr Alexander Spengler opened the first tuberculosis clinic. As the town grew, the Dutch entrepreneur Jan Holsboer founded the Rhätische Bahn railway to provide easier access to the high Alpine valley. He also secured financial backing for further spas and boarding houses, making Davos the leading health resort in Switzerland, with 700,000 annual overnight bookings by the turn of the century.

The slopes of the Parsenn, which Davos shares with **Klosters** its much more attractive neighbour, developed gradually with the introduction of the annual Parsenn Derby race in 1924, the opening of the funicular railway in 1931, and the installation of one of the earliest T-bars in Switzerland in 1934. With the decline of tuberculosis after the Second World War, many of the old clinics were converted into hotels to serve the tourists who now come in winter and summer. The opening of the Davos Congress Centre, since 1971 the venue for the annual meeting of the prestigious World Economic Forum, has allowed Davos to develop a lucrative parallel role as a conference town.

Klosters, which welcomed its first winter sports enthusiasts in 1904, has prospered from its connection with the British royal family, in particular Prince Charles. His passion for skiing and the resort has not been affected by the avalanche that killed his equerry, Major Hugh Lindsay, and threatened his own life in 1988.

Ski and board
top 2844m (9,328ft) bottom 813m (2,667ft)

The core of the Davos/Klosters ski area is the Parsenn, accessed most directly by funicular from Davos Dorf, but also connected to Davos Platz via the Schatzalp/Strela lift system, and to Klosters by the two-stage Gotschna cable-car. It is dominated by the Weissfluh, the highest point on the piste map, and it also includes the lowest – the marked run down to **Küblis**. The piste linking the two is a 12-km red (intermediate) descent. This is the terrain that made Davos famous – the wide, sweeping runs that flatter more often than they deceive.

This skiing heartland is supplemented by four further lift systems, three of them on the other side of the Davos Valley, and the fourth beyond Klosters. In the Davos catchment area, the three peaks are Pischa, Jakobshorn and Rinerhorn. They are accessed respectively by bus from Dorf, directly from Platz, and by bus or train from **Glaris** (the next stop on the line down to Chur). In Klosters, the alternative is the Madrisa, where the slopes stretch up to the Swiss–Austrian border.

When people talk queues in Davos/Klosters – and they frequently do – they are talking Parsenn. Whether you start from Dorf or Platz, you are faced with a slow journey in a funicular before you reach more modern forms of transport; even these may not be as modern as you would like, given that the T-bar, largely phased out in many parts of the Alps, still rules on the Parsenn. Improvements are not happening as quickly as effective crowd-management requires. By contrast, the quartet of outlying areas, with their lower profiles and more progressive lift systems, are enticingly empty.

Throwing tradition out of the window, the Parsenn has embraced snowboarding with enthusiasm and admirable commercial acumen. There is even a piste map symbol to suggest where it may best be done, but as it appears on all the mountains its value is debatable.

Beginners
Like many large, non-purpose-built resorts, Davos is not the place to learn to ski from scratch. If you must, the wide Bolgen nursery slope at the bottom of the Jakobshorn, a short walk from Platz, is the best starting point. In Dorf the equivalent is Bunda, which is a longer but steeper pitch. In Klosters, the sunny user-friendly nursery slopes are up the mountain on the Madrisa, which means buying a full lift pass and downloading by gondola at the end of the day. Once the basics are mastered, there is no shortage of blue (easy) runs to progress to.

Intermediates
Those who profit most from the Davos/Klosters area are intermediates with the energy to ski all the hours the lift company allows. Nearly all the

marked runs are red or blue, most are invitingly wide and several are over 10km long. The ones from the top of the Weissfluh to the valley villages of Kübils, **Saas** and **Serneus** start high above the tree-line, then track down through the woods to the railway line, providing a sense of adventure that is definitely not available in more tightly knit places. Another unmissable cruiser starts at the top of the Madrisa lift system and descends to Klosters Dorf via the Schlappin Valley. All five ski areas offer lots of easy terrain, so there is no excuse for not ranging far and wide. The result, in terms of variety at least, is a lift pass of remarkable value.

Advanced

As the mountains in the area become steeper near the bottom, the black (difficult) runs are mostly confined to the lower sections, which means that they can be icy in all but the most favourable snow conditions. The upside is that they are generally among trees, and therefore the visibility is always good. The best conditions are usually on the north-facing Klosters side; the Gotschnawang, which is no longer marked as a piste and is in any case rarely open, and the Drostobel provide serious challenges. Turn right from the Gotschnagrat and you come instead to a prime mogul-basher under the Schwarzeealp chair. Further gruelling bump runs on the Standard Ersatz and the Unterer Standard immedi-

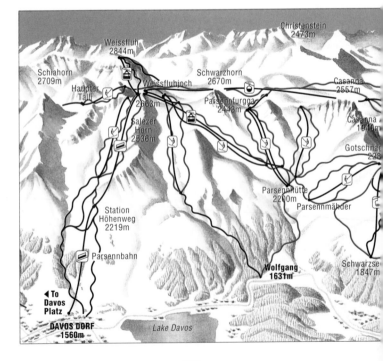

ately above Davos Dorf offer considerable challenge. The most highly recommended black run starts on the Meierhofer Tälli at the top of the Parsenn and goes on down to **Wolfgang**, a hamlet that makes a peaceful lunch stop. A funpark on the Parsenn includes two half-pipes.

Off-piste

Those who are prepared to put on skins and climb a bit can explore the huge potential for deep-snow adventure in one of Switzerland's most extensive ski areas. The longest, but by no means the most exciting, of the runs are the 18-km descents to Fideris and Jenaz, each with short climbing sections along the way. The Madrisa provides excellent possibilities for learning powder technique and is also the starting point for the trans-border loop to the hamlet of **Gargellen** at the head of the Montafon Valley. The best part of the tour is the section down to the attractive village of **St Antönien**.

Skiing to Arosa in the tracks of Conan Doyle is a more serious business, with a three- to four-hour climb to the Maienfeld Furka Pass above **Frauenkirch**, followed by a benevolent descent through woods to the bottom of the valley and a bitter sting in the tail: a 40-minute plod up through the town to the railway station for the three-hour return to Davos.

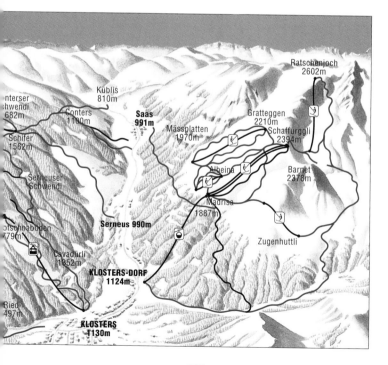

Tuition and guiding

The Swiss Ski School (SSS) in both resorts has classes for adults and teenagers, either in groups or with private guides. Half-day safety classes for off-piste debutantes (for a maximum of six per group) are available on the use of ABS-rucksacks and avalanche transceivers. Daily or weekly guided ski-tours can be arranged from January until Easter. Bruno Sprecher also runs the Saas Ski and Snowboard School (Saas S&S-S) in Klosters, which receives complimentary reports, and from February each year an exclusive off-piste guiding service. The three snowboard schools are Top Secret Snowboarding School in Platz, Snowboard School Davos (part of the SSS) and the PaarSenn in Dorf.

Cross-country

Davos offers 75km of prepared langlauf trails on the valley floor and in the Sertigtal and Dischmatal areas. Evening expeditions can be made on the 2.5-km floodlit section, and dogs are allowed on some of the trails. The SSS has a cross-country division, which teaches both the classic and the skating methods in group classes or privately. The highlight of the cross-country year is the 20-km Volks Langlauf, held in early March. Klosters has 50km of prepared trails.

Mountain restaurants

Go low is the main recommendation in an area where skiing to lunch should be an integral part of a long adventure run. Intelligent use of the piste map makes it possible to locate the many small establishments in the woods on the way down to the outlying villages. The restaurant at the Teufi on the off-piste descent from the Jakobshorn is recommended, as is the Hotel Kulm (known as Jakob's) in Wolfgang. Another winner is the pizzeria at the end of the Schlappin run in Klosters Dorf, but enterprise should yield gastronomic dividends. The Conterser Schwendi is recommended for its rösti and other local specialities, as is the Serneuser Schwendi ('popular, but a bit noisy and smoky'). The Strelapass Hut is praised, as is the Bahnhof Buffet in Küblis.

The resorts

Davos is a straggling no-nonsense town built along a major road, with all the traffic problems that suggests. In recent years these problems have been partially solved by a one-way system that at least keeps things moving. There is also a highly efficient bus service, which is included in the lift pass. It runs primarily between the two main centres: Davos Dorf, quiet and stately with handsome old hotels, and Davos Platz, the bustling commercial heart. Dorf has the most direct access to the Parsenn, but Platz has excellent facilities and the lion's share of the nightlife; the choice of where to stay therefore depends on where your priorities lie. Davos attracts a wealthy cosmopolitan crowd whose tastes are catered for by designer boutiques, and exclusive shops specialising in furnishings, art and jewellery. Enthusiasts will enjoy the Wintersport Museum, which traces the development of equipment and clothing through the years.

Klosters is also divided into Platz, an extensive traditional village clustered around the railway station and the Gotschna cable-car, and Dorf, a sleepy outpost at the bottom of the Madrisa lift system. Again, the two are connected by a regular bus service, but only those of a reclusive disposition should consider staying in Dorf. Platz is conveniently compact, with a range of hotels in each category and the kind of shops required by lovers of designer clothes and fine wines.

Accommodation

Davos has two five-star hotels: the Steigenberger Belvédère, up on the hillside above Platz, and the Flüela, opposite the railway station in Dorf. Both offer old-fashioned comfort in the stolid Swiss manner, a style copied by many of their competitors in the four- and three-star brackets. In Platz, the Waldhotel Bellevue is rich in tradition, though rather far removed from the mainstream. The same can be said of the Berghotel Schatzalp, a converted sanatorium offering turn-of-the-century grandeur. The Jakobshorn is popular with riders because of its dedicated snowboard hotel, the Bolgenschanze, which is conveniently close to the lift station. Kleines Palace für Snowboarder offers low-budget accommodation especially for riders.

In Klosters, the smart choice is the Hotel Vereina, which has impressive public rooms and comprehensive facilities, including a swimming-pool and crèche. The Steinbock is less conveniently situated but it offers a warm welcome and good food. The Wynegg is run by the incorrigible Ruth Guler, who rules with a broad smile and an iron handshake. The overspill can find a quieter refuge in the Bundnerhof next door.

Eating in and out

As in all resorts with a huge choice of restaurants in every category, the main criterion must be price. In Davos, as elsewhere in contemporary Switzerland, those who stray outside half-board deals must be prepared to pay highly for the privilege unless they are prepared to eat in chains like Burger King or Charly's Bakery. Money should be well spent in the Davoserhof, Hubli's Landhaus, the Magic Mountain Restaurant in the Bellevue, and the Stübli in the Flüela hotel. The Montana Sporthotel, opposite the Flüela, served 'the best pizza I have ever eaten at a very reasonable price,' according to one reporter. Try the Zauberberg restaurant in the Hotel Europe for Chinese, the Steinhof for Thai, and the Cascada in the Hotel Seehof for Mexican cuisine. Localised dining at correspondingly lower prices can be found in the outlying villages of Frauenkirch, Wolfgang and **Laret**.

In Klosters, the Chesa Grischuna has to be booked three days in advance, and tables at rival establishments require at least one day's notice. This is certainly true of the Wynegg, which profits from its royal connections to sell meals that are more rustic than gastronomic. The Walserhof is expensive but good, and the Vereina's pizzeria is popular.

Skiing facts: Davos

TOURIST OFFICE
Promenade 67, CH-7270 Davos Platz
Tel 41 81 415 21 21
Fax 41 81 415 21 00
Email davos@davos.ch
Web site www.davos.ch

THE RESORT
By road Calais 1000km
By rail Davos Dorf and Davos Platz
stations in resort
Airport transfer Zurich 2½hrs
Visitor beds 24,111
Transport free ski bus with lift pass,
free ski train with Rega Pass

THE SKIING
Linked or nearby resorts Arosa (n),
Klosters (l), Wolfgang (l), St Moritz (n),
Gargellen (n), Glaris (l), Küblis (l), Saas
(l), Serneus (l)
Longest run Weissfluh–Küblis, 12km
(black/red)
Number of lifts 22 in Davos, 55 in area
Total of trails/pistes 344km in area
(30% easy, 40% intermediate, 30%
difficult)
Nursery slopes 1 lift on Bunda
Summer skiing none
Snowmaking 24km covered

LIFT PASSES
Area pass Rega Pass (covers all Davos
and Klosters lifts, buses and railway),
SF259 for 6 days
Day pass Jakobshorn SF46, Parsenn
SF52, Pischa SF38, Rinerhorn SF40,
Schatzalp SF25

Beginners no free lifts
Pensioners women 62yrs and over,
men 65yrs and over, 20% reduction
Credit cards yes

TUITION
Adults SSS, 10am–midday and 2–4pm,
SF185 for 5 days
Private lessons SF165 per half-day,
SF270 per day
Snowboarding SSS, Top Secret
Snowboarding School, PaarSenn, all
SF185 for 5 days. Private lessons SF145
per half-day
Cross-country SSS, SF220 for 5 days,
times as regular ski school. Loipe 75km
Other courses telemark
Guiding Stefan Welz, SSS

CHILDREN
Lift pass 6–16yrs,
Gotschna/Strela/Parsenn SF134, Rega
Pass SF155, both for 6 days, free for
5yrs and under
Ski school SSS, 4–16yrs,
8.30–11.30am and 2–4.30pm, SF185
for 5 days not including lunch
Ski kindergarten Snow Playground
(3–7yrs) SF49 not including
lunch
Non-ski kindergarten Pinocchio
Kindergarten, 3–5yrs, 8.30am–4.30pm
SF49 not including lunch

FOOD AND DRINK PRICES
Coffee SF3.80, glass of wine SF8–10,
small beer SF4–5, dish of the day
SF15–25

Skiing facts: Klosters

TOURIST OFFICE
CH-7250 Klosters, Graubunden
Tel 41 81 410 2020
Fax 41 81 410 2010
Email info@klosters.ch
Web site www.klosters.ch

THE RESORT
By road Calais 1000km
By rail Klosters Dorf and Klosters Platz stations in resort
Airport transfer Zurich 2½hrs
Visitor beds 8,800
Transport free ski bus with lift pass, free ski train with Rega Pass

THE SKIING
Linked or nearby resorts Davos (l), Arosa (n), Gargellen (n), Küblis (l), Saas (l)
Longest run Weissfluhgipfel–Küblis, 12km (black/red)
Number of lifts 30 in Klosters, 55 in area
Total of trails/pistes 344km in area (30% easy, 40% intermediate, 30% difficult)
Nursery slopes 4 lifts
Summer skiing none
Snowmaking 4.3km covered, plus 1 mobile snow-cannon on Madrisa

LIFT PASSES
Area pass Rega Pass (covers all Davos and Klosters lifts, buses and railway), SF259 for 6 days
Day pass Parsenn SF52, Madrisa SF42
Beginners no free lifts
Pensioners women 62yrs and over, men 65yrs and over, 20% reduction
Credit cards yes

TUITION
Adults SSS, 9.45am–midday and 1.45pm–4pm, SF200 for 5 days. Saas S&S-S, 9am–midday and 1.15–3.30pm, SF295 for 6 days
Private lessons both ski schools, SF60 per hr, SF270 per day
Snowboarding SSS, SF170 for 3 days. Saas S&S-S, as regular ski school, Swiss Duty Snowboard School Madrisa, SF200 for 3 days
Cross-country SSS, SF148 for 6 half-days. Loipe 50km
Other courses telemark, carving, competition
Guiding Bruno Sprecher, or through ski schools

CHILDREN
Lift pass 6–16yrs, Gotschna/Parsenn/Madrisa SF134, Madrisa SF113, Rega Pass SF155, all for 6 days, free for 5yrs and under
Ski school SSS, 4–12yrs, times as adults, SF166 for 6 half-days, extra SF16 per day for lunch. Saas S&S-S, 4yrs and over, SF175 for 6 half-days. Swiss Duty Snowboard School Madrisa, 6–10yrs SF170 for 3 days, 11–16yrs SF185 for 3 days
Ski kindergarten all schools, 4–16yrs, SF113–155 for 6 days
Non-ski kindergarten Hotel Vereina, 3yrs and over, prices on request. Madrisa Kindergarten, 3yrs and over, SF25 per day not including lunch

OTHER SPORTS
Davos/Klosters: curling, parapente, hang-gliding, indoor tennis and squash, badminton, swimming, sleigh rides, skating, snowshoeing, climbing-wall

FOOD AND DRINK PRICES
Coffee SF3.80, glass of wine SF8–10, small beer SF4–5, dish of the day SF15–25

Après-ski

In the late afternoons, the high-lifers at Davos congregate in the Café Schneider in Platz and the Café Weber in Dorf, both specialists in temptation cakes. The most favoured bar is the rustic Chämi, which is full to bursting with revellers of all ages until closing time. In the pre-dinner hours, there are major league ice-hockey matches in the handsome Sports Centre, plus facilities for skating (on the largest natural ice rink in Europe), curling, indoor tennis and squash, and swimming. The Montana has a pool bar, with four good tables.

The area's pulsing nightlife can be found in Davos Platz, and especially in the Ex-Bar, which has developed the novel idea of shutting at 11pm in order to re-open from 2am to 7am. The laser show at the Cabanna Club disco attracts the very young, while the Pöstli in the Posthotel Morosani caters for an older crowd. The Cava Grischa has live folk music, and there is a popular Piano Bar in the Hotel Europe. Graubunden's largest casino, also in the Hotel Europe, is now up and running despite gambling options that are limited to 150 slot machines and a boule table. The Scala restaurant in the same building stays open until 3am.

After-skiing activities in Klosters start with tea and cakes at A Porta's. However, when it comes to nightlife, this resort, with its many chalets and few bars, is not a major player. The Hotel Vereina has two popular bars, the Brasserie and the Scotch, while the Steinbock Bar attracts locals as well as tourists. Alternative watering holes include the Verruckte Baustellen in the Hotel Kaiser, the piano bar in the Aldiana Club, and the cellar bar in the Chesa Grischuna. For late nights try the Casa Antica, once Princess Diana's favourite disco, the Kir Royal in the Aldiana Club, or Rufinis in Klosters Dorf.

Childcare

The Pinocchio Kindergarten in Davos takes care of children over three years of age throughout the day from Monday to Friday. Its programme includes playing in the snow and an introduction to skiing. More advanced group instruction is available to the over-fours during the week, with a race every Friday. There is also a special course at Bolgen on Sundays.

In Klosters, the Hotel Vereina offers a crèche and evening baby-listening service. Alternatively, there is a kindergarten on the Madrisa for the over-threes; this is an inconvenient arrangement as parents have to take their children there for a 10am start, while they themselves would probably choose to ski in another area a bus-ride away.

Jungfrau

ALTITUDE Wengen 1274m (4,180ft), Grindelwald 1034m (3,391ft),
Mürren 1650m (5,412ft)

Beginners (except Mürren) ✱✱✱ Intermediates ✱✱✱ Advanced ✱✱
Snowboarders ✱✱

The Jungfrau region is the most popular in Switzerland with British
visitors and one which is once again flourishing, thanks to favourable
exchange rates and excellent snow cover for much of last season. It is
recognised as the Edwardian nursery of modern skiing and has always
had an edge on quality, which it has
somehow managed to maintain over
the years. Trains are a crucial part of
any holiday to the region's principal
resorts of **Wengen**, **Grindelwald**, and
Mürren; the mountain railway, which
dates from the 1880s, is still the backbone of the lift system today, making
both Wengen and Grindelwald ideal
bases for non-skiers. Wengen and
Mürren remain traffic-free and
remarkably unspoilt by the passage of
a century. The three resorts share a lift
pass that covers 45 lifts in the Jungfrau

✔ Beautiful scenery
✔ Variety of slopes
✔ Car-free villages (Wengen/Mürren)
✔ Convenient for family skiing
✔ Facilities for non-skiers
✘ Poorly linked ski areas
✘ Lower slopes can become icy or worn

Top Ski region, offering 195km of wonderfully scenic skiing against the
awesome backdrop of the Eiger, Mönch and Jungfrau mountains.

This was one of the birthplaces of modern alpine skiing. Henry Lunn,
a Methodist minister, a non-skier, and one-time lawn tennis equipment
salesman, is credited with introducing the first-ever ski package holidays
here in the winter of 1910–11. To encourage the class-conscious British
to come on his tours he founded the Public Schools Alpine Sports Club
and somehow managed to persuade the Swiss to continue to operate
their mountain railways during the winter. His more distinguished son,
Sir Arnold, went on to found the Kandahar Ski Club in Mürren, where
slalom racing was first introduced in 1922.

Ski tourism started in Wengen with the Downhill Only Club, a pioneer band of British skiers formed in February 1925 to race against the
Kandahar Club rivals in Mürren. The club name developed from its
members' customary train ride up the mountain in order to ski down, a
process considered distinctly unsporting by the standards of the day,
when people thought there should be no gain without pain. Both British
ski clubs are alive and functioning in the resorts today.

Wengen, Grindelwald and Mürren are all reached by rail from
Interlaken. The track divides at Zweilutschinen, with the left-hand fork

veering to Grindelwald. The right-hand fork goes to **Lauterbrunnen**, which is more of a railway halt than a resort, although it does have a number of hotels and some reporters consider it a convenient and much cheaper base from which to ski the area. Trains from Lauterbrunnen run steeply up to Mürren on one side of the valley and up to Wengen on the other. The railway climbs as high as the main ski area at Kleine Scheidegg, above Wengen, before descending into Grindelwald. Trains stop at wayside halts throughout the area to pick up and set down skiers. They run as accurately as a Swiss watch to a timetable printed on the back of the piste map. However, this form of transport is painfully slow, and the trains can be as crowded as the London Underground at rush hour, although the network has been augmented by conventional cableways and chairs.

Ski and board
Wengen: top 2320m (7,610ft) bottom 1274m (4,180ft)
Grindelwald: top 2486m (8,154ft) bottom 943m (3,093ft)
Mürren: top 2970m (9,724ft) bottom 796m (2,611ft)

To a great extent the runs are dictated by the contours of the mountains and the prevailing weather. The pistes are not arbitrarily cut out from forest nor bulldozed down scarps but simply follow the best, easiest or most exciting ways down. Slight variations in both bearing and difficulty are influenced each season by the amount of snow and the direction in which the wind was blowing when it fell.

WHAT'S NEW
Gummi lift up graded to quad chair-lift

A circuit of lifts around the Lauberhorn and Tschuggen peaks links the ski areas of **Wengen** and **Grindelwald** through the Männlichen and Kleine Scheidegg. From the centre of Wengen a cable-car rises to the Männlichen, while the train climbs up to Kleine Scheidegg and Eigergletscher. Between Eigergletscher and Kleine Scheidegg are high alps served by chairs and tows. On the long run down from Kleine Scheidegg to Wengen is an interesting diversion off to **Innerwengen**. From Grindelwald a gondola rises to the Männlichen, while the train also carries on up to Kleine Scheidegg. On the other side of Grindelwald, the First area is easily accessible, even for Wengen-based skiers. The areas complement each other well, and one of the pleasures of visiting any of them is to spend days exploring the others.

Mürren, separated from the other two resorts by the Lauterbrunnen Valley, sits on an east-facing shelf. Its skiing is spread across three parallel ridges – the Schiltgrat, the Allmendhubel and the Maulerhubel – that run roughly north and south above the village. These slopes provide decent skiing conditions whatever the weather: powder on the north slopes, spring snow on the south, high bowls for fine weather, trees for shelter and visibility in blizzards.

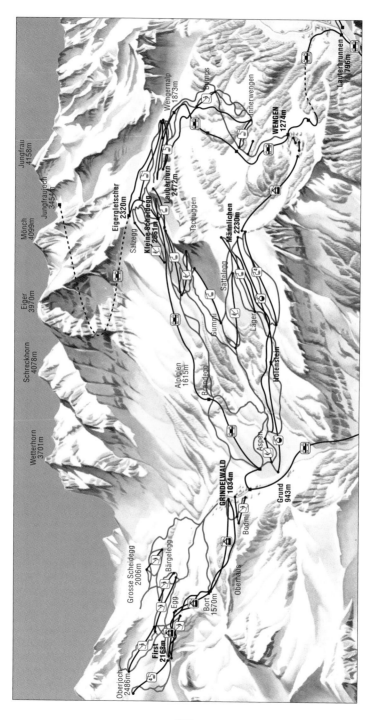

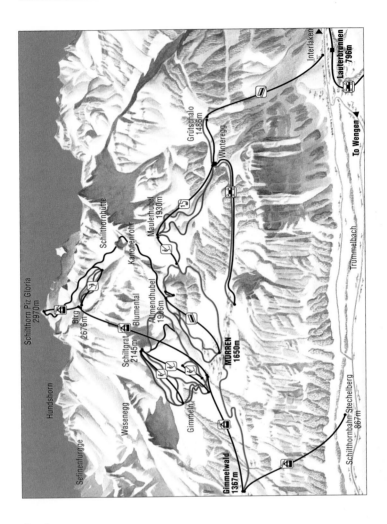

Beginners

Wengen has an excellent nursery area in the middle of the village with two babylifts and an unusual three-person drag-lift, which is surprisingly easy for snowboarders to use. There are also satisfyingly long blue (easy) runs on which even those with little technique can stretch their legs. From Kleine Scheidegg, a broad tree-lined road down Schattwald leads to Brandegg. If, instead of the train, you take the Männlichen cable-car from Wengen, you arrive at the top of a big sunny scarp, which is served by several lifts. The easiest route is down under the Männlichen chair.

Grindelwald also has nursery slopes right by the village and others up on the Hohwald and Bargelegg lifts, although beginners will want to return to base via the First gondola. Mürren is not an ideal resort for beginners. The small nursery slope is on the upper road behind the Jungfrau Hotel; this is historic ground where the world's first modern slalom was set. Another small beginners' area lies at the top of the Allmendhubel lift and is served by a small tow. The next stage is to move to the Allmendhubel area, which is not particularly easy.

Intermediates

Wengen and Grindelwald owe much of their popularity with families to their long, medium to difficult runs. You can take the Männlichen cable-car and explore the route under the gondola right down to **Grund**. From there the train goes up to Kleine Scheidegg, which has a similarly well-networked area recently improved by the installation of a detachable quad on the Lauberhorn. The famous World Cup racecourse, at two-and-a-half kilometres the longest in the world, forms a fairly testing descent. The nearby Standard run offers an easier way down.

From Grindelwald, the First gondola leads to the Stepfi, a satisfying red (intermediate) run from Oberlager down to the Hotel Wetterhorn. As you pass the hotel you can see the old cable-car cabin, which was built in 1908 to take summer climbers up to the Gleckstein Hut on the Wetterhorn. The lift was closed in 1914 after being damaged by avalanche, and the cabin was left as a relic. This is a satisfying stop-off before returning by bus to Grindelwald.

At Mürren, some very pretty intermediate skiing can be reached by taking the Allmendhubel railway and then a small T-bar to the Hogs Back area; turn right towards the Maulerhübel T-bar, at the top of which is a wide area of open slopes leading either back to the bottom of Maulerhübel or off to the mid-station on the main railway. You can return to the village from the bottom of the Maulerhübel on the wide Palace Run.

The Muttleren and Kandahar chair-lifts halfway up the Schilthorn give access to plenty of intermediate skiing in a snow-sure bowl. However, the only way out for those unwilling to face the often icy Kanonenrohr piste is by a steep and uncomfortable T-bar. This is one of the very few places where queues form.

Advanced

From Wengen, the train up to Eigergletscher leads to the black (difficult) runs of Blackrock and Oh God. In sunny weather these are best left until late morning, as they can be hard and icy before the sun reaches them. The Aspen run is the steepest way down from the Männlichen towards Grund. Grindelwald's First area has a challenging black piste under the gondola.

At Mürren, the extremely steep run from the top of the Schilthorn can be followed by another steep pitch alongside the new Muttleren chair-lift, and then the Kanonenrohr, to give an almost continuous black run with plenty of challenge. Kleine Scheidegg has an excellent funpark with equally easy access from both Wengen and Grindelwald.

Off-piste

All three resorts have a great deal of easily accessible off-piste skiing between the trails. In Mürren, the Blumental is famous for its powder, Tschingelchrachen off the Schilthornbahn should be treated with care as it is very steep and often closed, and Hidden Valley from the summit of the Maulerhubel to Grutsch is a delight. The White Hare, which starts from the foot of the Eigerwand, is a dramatic and exciting powder run; it can be accessed from both Wengen and Grindelwald.

Local mountain guides are essential here, and Grindelwald's Bergsteigerzentrum is one of the most famous guiding establishments in the world; both ski-touring and heli-skiing can be organised through the centre. Day tours over to the Lötschental and other separate areas can be arranged, weather permitting.

Tuition and guiding

The Swiss Ski and Snowboard School (SSS) operates in each village, and the standard of service varies alarmingly. Lessons are given daily, excluding Sunday. Most, but by no means all, instructors speak more than adequate English. One reader encountered a class of 14 in Grindelwald: 'Our instructor was just interested in skiing madly down-hill; it took a sit-in at the ski school office to get the teacher we wanted'. Another reader who went to Wengen complained: 'I did not receive one word of advice about my skiing'.

We have more positive reports of the Privat Ski and Snowboard School run in Wengen by Tino Fuchs. A reporter in Mürren complained that his mountain guide 'didn't speak English, kept losing people and wouldn't say where he was going'. Grindelwald has two dedicated snow-board schools: Backside and Lupo.

Mountain restaurants

The area is littered with enjoyable eating places. The Hotel Jungfrau at Wengernalp is among our top ten mountain restaurants in the Alps; it has beautiful views and a friendly atmosphere, not to mention the high standard of cooking. At Wengen the Brandegg restaurant is famed for its 'quite extraordinarily delicious' apple fritters. The Kleine Scheidegg station buffet is much more interesting than it looks, and besides its variety of Swiss fare offers its own *Röstizza*, a cross between rösti and pizza. The Eigergletscher restaurant has 'the best rösti and the best views'. The Jagerstübli is a farmhouse below Männlichen, with a 'cosy ambience and delicious home cooking on a bitterly cold day'. The Aspen above Grund has a loyal clientèle. Mary's Café just above Wengen is recommended for its raclette. Café Oberland is an agreeable alternative and is right on the piste. The Hotel Victoria-Lauberhorn, near the skating-rink, has a pizze-ria/crêperie with quick service. The rösti in the stübli of the Eiger Hotel is also recommended.

The restaurant at Bort above Grindelwald is 'pleasant and reasonably priced, but the food is not exceptional'. The big self-service at First boasts 'a glorious hamburger'. The Hotel Wetterhorn on the way down

Skiing facts: Wengen

TOURIST OFFICE
CH-3823 Wengen, Bernese Oberland
Tel 41 33 855 1414
Fax 41 33 855 3060
Email information@wengen.com
Web site www.wengen.com

THE RESORT
By road Calais 835km
By rail station in resort
Airport transfer Zurich 3hrs, Geneva
4hrs
Visitor beds 5,000
Transport traffic-free resort

THE SKIING
Linked or nearby resorts Grindelwald
(l), Grund (l), Lauterbrunnen (n),
Mürren (n)
Longest run Mettlen–Grund, 8.5km
(blue)
Number of lifts 45 in Jungfrau Top Ski
Region
Total of trails/pistes 195km in
Jungfrau Top Ski region (28% easy,
57% intermediate, 15% difficult)
Nursery slopes 3 lifts
Summer skiing 1 lift at Jungfraujoch
Snowmaking mobile snow-cannon on
nursery slopes

LIFT PASSES
Area pass Jungfrau (covers Wengen,
Grindelwald and Mürren), SF232
for 6 days
Day pass Kleine Scheidegg/Männlichen

SF52
Beginners points tickets
Pensioners 62yrs and over, SF206
for 6 days
Credit cards yes

TUITION
Adults SSS, SF204 for 6 days
(3hrs per day)
Private lessons SSS, SF125 for 2hrs
Snowboarding Swiss Snowboard
School, SF204 (3hrs per day)
Cross-country 12km
Other courses telemark, skiing for
partially sighted
Guiding through SSS

CHILDREN
Lift pass 6–16yrs SF116, 17–20yrs,
SF186, both for 6 days, free for 5yrs and
under
Ski kindergarten SSS, as below
Ski school SSS, 4–12yrs, SF204
for 3hrs
Non-ski kindergarten at Sport Pavilion,
3–7yrs, 8.45am–4.30pm, SF150 for 6
days including lunch

OTHER SPORTS
Skating, ice-hockey, parapente,
hang-gliding, curling, swimming, indoor
climbing wall, indoor tennis and squash

FOOD AND DRINK PRICES
Coffee SF3, glass of wine SF3, small beer
SF3, dish of the day SF17

to Grindelwald has a convivial atmosphere and delicious food.

Above Mürren the Birg restaurant is 'nothing to write home about,'
but the Gimmeln has 'tasty raclette and *Apfelküchen*'. We have a whole
series of complimentary reports of the revolving Piz Gloria on the summit of the Schilthorn ('not expensive and good value'). One reporter had
'an imaginative salad – it took a full revolution to demolish it'. Another

claimed it to be 'the best and the cheapest menu to be found in Switzerland – what a surprise!'. The Schilthornhütte, on the descent from here, is a mountain refuge serving simple dishes, with a 'fun atmosphere and wonderful views'. Sonnenberg chalet in the valley between the Hogs Back and the top of the Schiltgrat maintains a high standard. Winteregg, at the halfway station on the railway, is acclaimed for its *rösti mit speck*.

The resorts

A car is of little or no use in the area. **Wengen** is almost car-free, although a handful of four-wheel drive vehicles are allowed to operate as taxis. Otherwise, luggage is carried by electric buggy. Many of the visitors are still British – the same families who return year after year to create their own entertainment. The presence of Club Med at the northern end of town seems incongruous in this otherwise neo-Edwardian setting. The handful of old hotels have been refurbished and others built, but the village remains much as it was – a single pedestrian street of unremarkable shops and a cluster of chalets around one of the best nursery slopes in the Alps. There is also a magnificent skating-rink. At the heart of it all on a sunny balcony above the Lauterbrunnen Valley is the railway station.

    Grindelwald is the oldest of the three villages, a large and busy year-round resort spread along the valley floor between the soaring peaks of the Wetterhorn and the Eiger on the one side, and the gentler wooded slopes of its First ski area on the other. There are

WHAT'S NEW

Schiltgrat T-bar upgraded to chair-lift

few more cosmopolitan resorts to be found in the world, with every nationality imaginable listed among its guests, not least the Japanese, who come here in numbers to visit the Eiger and the Jungfraujoch, which at 3454m is the highest station in Europe. The scenery around Grindelwald is spectacular, and many reporters consider it the best place to stay in the Jungfrau: 'Having seen it all and skied for 22 years, no member of my family would now consider skiing anywhere else'. However, its low altitude means that snow cover in the village and on the lower mountain is extremely uncertain.

    Mürren has few rivals as the prettiest and most unspoilt ski village in Switzerland. Old chalets and hotels line the paths between the railway station at one end and the cable-car at the other. The car-free village is on a sunny shelf perched on top of a 500-m rock face above **Lauterbrunnen**. Again, the same British families, nearly all of them members of the Kandahar Club, have been returning here for generations and have forged firm links with the villagers.

Accommodation

In **Wengen** the accommodation is split between hotels, apartments and chalets. The attractive resort is quite spread out and distinctly steep.

Skiing facts: Grindelwald

TOURIST OFFICE
CH-3818 Grindelwald, Bernese Oberland
Tel 41 33 854 1212
Fax 41 33 854 1210
Email touristoffice@grinderwald.ch
Web site www.grindelwald.ch

THE RESORT
By road Calais 835km
By rail station in resort
Airport transfer Zurich 3hrs, Geneva 4hrs
Visitor beds 11,700
Transport ski bus free with lift pass

THE SKIING
Linked or nearby resorts Wengen (l),
Mürren (n), Lauterbrunnen (n), Grund (n)
Longest run Lauberhorn–Grindelwald,
13km (red)
Number of lifts 45 in Jungfrau Top
Ski region
Total of trails/pistes 195km in Jungfrau
Top Ski region (28% easy, 57%
intermediate, 15% difficult)
Nursery slopes 2 lifts
Summer skiing none
Snowmaking 20km covered

LIFT PASSES
Area pass Jungfrau (covers Wengen,
Grindelwald and Mürren), SF232 for
6 days
Day pass Kleine Scheidegg/Männlichen
SF52, First and Mürren SF50
Beginners points tickets

Pensioners 62yrs and over,
SF206 for 6 days
Credit cards yes

TUITION
Adults SSS, SF192 for 5 days
Private lessons SSS, SF288 per day,
SF170 per half-day
Snowboarding SSS, Lupo and Backside
snowboard schools, SF140 for 5 x 2hrs,
private lessons SF170 per half-day
Cross-country SSS, SF122 for 5
half-days. Loipe 35km
Other courses telemark, heli-skiing,
skiing for partially sighted, competition
Guiding Bergsteigerzentrum
Grindelwald

CHILDREN
Lift pass 6–16yrs SF116, 16–20yrs
SF186, both for 6 days. Free for 5yrs
and under
Ski kindergarten as ski school
Ski school SSS, 3–14yrs, times and
prices as adults
Non-ski kindergarten Children's Club
Bodmi, 3yrs and over, SF44 per day

OTHER SPORTS
Skating, parapente, curling, glacier
ski-tours

FOOD AND DRINK PRICES
Coffee SF3, glass of wine SF4.50, small
beer SF4.50, dish of the day SF15–20

While location is of little importance for the skiing (if staying high up you can ski down to the train which will take you back to your hotel), a long uphill slog after midnight tends to deter many a holidaymaker from exploring what limited nightlife there is. The Hotel Eiger (Wengen) is central and has long been a favourite among the British. The Falken is variously described as 'delightfully old-fashioned,' 'ramshackle,' and 'very comfortable'. The Hotel Regina is 'spacious, clean and comfort-

Skiing facts: Mürren

TOURIST OFFICE
CH-3825 Mürren, Bernese Oberland
Tel 41 33 856 86 86
Fax 41 33 856 86 96
Email info@muerren.ch
Web site www.muerren.ch

THE RESORT
By road Calais 835km
By rail station in resort
Airport Transfer Zurich 3hrs,
Geneva 4hrs
Visitor beds 2,000
Transport traffic-free resort

THE SKIING
Linked or nearby resorts Grindelwald
(n), Grund (n), Lauterbrunnen (n),
Wengen (n)
Longest run Schilthorn–Lauterbrunnen,
15.8km (black/red)
Number of lifts 45 in Jungfrau Top Ski
region
Total of trails/pistes 195km in
Jungfrau Top Ski region (28% easy, 57%
intermediate, 15% difficult)
Nursery slopes 2 runs and 1 lift
Summer skiing none
Snowmaking limited

LIFT PASSES
Area pass Jungfrau (covers Wengen,
Grindelwald and Mürren), SF232
for 6 days
Day pass Mürren SF50
Beginners points tickets
Pensioners 62yrs and over, SF206
for 6 days

Credit cards yes

TUITION
Adults SSS, 10am–midday, SF130
for 6 half-days
Private lessons SSS, SF110 per half-day
Snowboarding Swiss Snowboard
School, SF49 per half-day, private
lessons SF130 for 2hrs
Cross-country lessons not available.
Loipe 3km
Other courses heli-skiing, carving
Guiding Bergführervermitlung
Lauterbrunnen/Wengen/Mürren

CHILDREN
Lift pass 6–16yrs SF116, 17–20yrs
SF186, both for 6 days, free for 5yrs
and under
Ski kindergarten none
Ski school SSS, 4yrs and over, prices
and times as adults
Non-ski kindergarten guest
kindergarten at the sports centre, 3yrs
and over, SF192 for 6 days including
lunch, 2–3yrs old (half-days only),
SF192 for 6 half-days, not including
lunch

OTHER SPORTS
Skating, ice-hockey, parapente,
hang-gliding, curling, swimming, indoor
climbing wall, indoor tennis and squash,
snowmobiling

FOOD AND DRINK PRICES
Coffee SF3, glass of wine SF3, small beer
SF3, dish of the day SF12–20

able,' and is renowned for its English breakfast. Hotel Brunner, situated on the piste a ten-minute walk above the village centre, is described as 'one of those alpine secrets that visitors – many of them with children – like to keep to themselves'. Hotel Wengener Hof, five minutes' walk from the station, was strongly criticised by one reporter ('food only just better than my work canteen').

Hotel Silberhorn is 'excellent, with multi-national and very friendly staff, superb and substantial food'. Hotel Alpenrose is said to be of an exceptionally high standard ('we particularly liked the large lounge area with its log fire'). Hotel Bellevue is also recommended. The three-star Hotel Belvédère is a seven-minute uphill walk from the station and has 'grand art-deco public rooms'. The four-star Hotel Sunstar has family 'maisonettes', a swimming-pool and is one of the most conveniently placed hotels. Club Med here has a fine reputation, although the presence of large, noisy French-led classes on crowded pistes can lead to Agincourt-style confrontations with the more conservative British element.

Grindelwald has the five-star Grand Hotel Regina, which is partly decorated with eighteenth-century antiques and is famous for the ice sculptures in its grounds. A host of four-star hotels include the 'excellent' Hotel Spinne. Hotel Jungfrau is praised for 'good and plentiful food; we would have paid twice the price for the view from our window'. The Hotel Alpenhof, a few minutes' walk from the village, has a sound reputation. Hotel Derby and Hotel Hirschen are both recommended. Hotel Bodmi on the nursery slopes is convenient for families, and Parkhotel Schönegg is warmly acclaimed. Hotel Bernerhof is centrally located close to the station and has 'friendly and attentive service'.

In **Mürren** the Hotel Eiger, across the road from the railway station, has some luxurious suites as well as standard hotel rooms and apartments. The Palace Hotel is central but keeps changing hands. One reader stated that the Jungfrau is 'the best hotel in Switzerland'. The Alpenruh at the Schilthornbahn end of the village has an excellent restaurant. The popular Edelweiss is 'convenient, clean and friendly', and the Bellevue-Crystal and Blumental are both recommended, together with the simpler Belmont. The supermarket is said to be adequate and there is also a butcher's shop.

The village of **Lauterbrunnen** in the valley below is well placed for those who want less expensive accommodation and the chance to try a different area each day, but it does suffer from being hemmed in by sheer mountains on all sides.

Eating in and out

Most restaurants in Wengen are in hotels, but Sina's Italian is warmly recommended for pizzas, pasta and steak ('good value for money in a warm and friendly ambience'). Mary's Café offers cheese fondue accompanied by alpenhorn-blowing contests. Restaurant Wengen in the Hotel Hirschen specialises in fondue *chinoise*. The Felsenkeller in the Hotel Silberhorn is also praised. The Berghaus is known for its fresh fish and the Bernerhof for fondue and raclette. The restaurant in the Schönegg

Hotel in Wengen is popular. On sunny days, the Hotel Eiger has outdoor tables next to the railway station.

The à la carte Bahnhof Restaurant is one of the best places to dine in Grindelwald. Reporters also speak warmly of the Schweizerhof. The restaurant in the Hotel Alte Post is popular with the locals. The Alpina is good for fondue. The Cava restaurant in the Hotel Derby has 'the best fondue and pasta in town'.

In Mürren the Hotel Eiger's stübli has an excellent, if somewhat expensive, menu. At the other end of the village, the Alpenruh comes well recommended and the Belmont offers 'excellent value'.

Après-ski

Wengen's nightlife remains muted in comparison with other Alpine resorts. The last ski trains of the day are full of families with toboggans going up to Wengernalp for the four-kilometre descent back to the village. The TeePee Après Ski Bar at Kleine Scheidegg is busier during the skiing day. Crowds gather in Café Oberland and in Mary's Café, and the ice-bar outside the Hotel Brunner is lively. In the village itself the twin skating-rinks at times offer ice-hockey matches on one and curling on the other. In the afternoons it seems that there are almost as many people skating as there are skiing.

Reporters complain that Wengen has no real tea-and-cakes places, apart from Café Grübi, which is full of atmosphere but rather cramped. The Hotel Eiger's stübli is packed out, as is the independent Eiger Bar in the main street. The Tanne, Sina's Pub and Hot Chilli are the most popular bars, while Tiffany's in the Silberhorn is the disco. Terry's Bar in the Caprice offers 'big beers and friendly service'.

In Grindelwald the Expresso bar draws a young crowd after skiing, while the Gepsi attracts a slightly older clientèle. Later on the Chälli bar in the Hotel Kreuz and Post, the Cava in the Derby, and Herby's in the Regina are the most popular. The Plaza Club and the Spyder disco rock on into the small hours. Snow go-karting and daily llama treks around the First ski area are new attractions.

For such a small village, Mürren is surprisingly lively after skiing. The Ballon bar in the Palace Hotel, together with the Grübi in the Jungfrau and the Pub in the Belmont, are all popular. The Tächi bar in the Hotel Eiger is one of the main meeting places. The Bliemlichäller disco in the Blumental and the Inferno disco in the Palace Hotel are packed at week-ends and in season. The village boasts an excellent sports centre.

Childcare

We have pleasing reports of high standards of tuition in all three resorts. However, the decision by Wengen SSS to run group lessons only in the mornings seriously detracts from its erstwhile reputation as an ideal resort for families with young children ('some unhappy parents found their skiing day curtailed at lunch-time'). Mürren has little easy skiing and is not suitable for small children. The non-ski kindergarten in Wengen has a sound reputation.

St Moritz

ALTITUDE 1800m (5,904ft)

Beginners ✱   Intermediates ✱✱✱   Advanced ✱✱   Snowboarders ✱

St Moritz is an urban resort on two levels, above and along the shores of a fir-lined lake in the Engadine, which is Switzerland's most scenic valley. It is four hours by road from Zurich, and winter holidays were invented here – by the British. Twice host to the Winter Olympics, the resort sets the world standard for luxury and indulgence. Skating, curling, golf, cricket, polo and a number of exotic horse-racing events take place throughout the winter on the frozen lake. The Cresta Run, still closed to women, has been the ultimate test of male machismo for more than a hundred years, and the bobsleigh made its debut here. The truly international clientèle is dominated by Germans.

- ✔ Exceptional climate
- ✔ Choice of winter sports
- ✔ Wealth of luxury hotels
- ✔ Cross-country facilities
- ✔ Good snow record
- ✔ Extensive snowmaking
- ✘ Lift queues at peak times
- ✘ Widely dispersed skiing sectors
- ✘ High prices
- ✘ Lack of architectural charm

St Moritz is not simply a ski area, but a winter-sports resort. Warmed by the Engadine sun and vitalised by the local 'champagne climate', the first visitors took to tobogganing in 1864. The Upper Engadine regional ski pass covers 55 lifts and 350km of pistes from one end of the valley to the other. **Celerina, Pontresina, Silvaplana** and **Sils Maria** are outlying villages with ski lifts. **Dorf** is the name used for St Moritz proper, and **Bad** is down on the lake below.

Ski and board
top 3303m (10,834ft) bottom 1720m (5,642ft)

Few skiers in St Moritz are fanatics. However, there is a wide range of skiing, with sunny blue (easy) slopes, abundant red (intermediate) runs and adequate advanced and off-piste routes scattered around the dozen lifts rising from the valley floor. The region divides into the sectors of Corviglia, Corvatsch and Diavolezza-Lagalp. From St Moritz itself, the home mountain is Corviglia, accessed by a funicular from the centre of town or from Suvretta, with skiing up to 3057m at Piz Nair. Celerina and Bad also give access to the mostly red runs of Corviglia. Corvatsch, on the other side of the valley, has more advanced terrain and is accessed from Sils Maria and **Surlej**. Diavolezza and Lagalb, both at nearly 3000m, lie in a side valley and are reached by train or bus. Skiing here is less crowded and more challenging.

The renovated funicular at Corvatsch should do much to reduce the once notorious queues. Elsewhere, steady investment in modern chair-lifts in recent years has done much to diminish waiting time, although a bottleneck remains at Piz Nair. Snowmaking ensures skiing on six Corviglia pistes, to the bottom of Corvatsch at Surlej, and from top to bottom of Diavolezza.

Beginners

There are nursery slopes at Corviglia, and guests at the Suvretta Hotel even have their own beginner lift. However, because of the spread-out nature of St Moritz and high prices, this is not the ideal resort in which to learn.

Crucial for ski-to-lunch addicts is the long, gentle blue run down from the Marmite restaurant on Corviglia, through the woods back into St Moritz, or all the way across to the cable-car at Bad. Every sector has some blue runs suitable for second-week snow-users. The Furtschellas drag-lifts go up to blue runs at 2800m above Sils Maria, but beginners will have to ride the cable-car down.

Intermediates

Corvatsch has the highest skiing and links with even more red runs on Furtschellas via the Curtinella drag-lift. South-facing Corviglia has a number of flattering reds. The run under the Piz Grisch chair always has excellent snow. However, the best intermediate skiing, with the least crowds, is out of St Moritz in the Lagalb sector at nearly 3000m. The Giandas red under the cable-car has the longest and most direct fall-line skiing in the Engadine.

Advanced

The black (difficult) Hahnensee run from the top of Corvatsch winds over open snow fields and into the woods at the edge of Bad, providing 8km of non-stop skiing for 1600 vertical metres. At Diavolezza, the Schwarzer Hang black piste drops through bands of rock for some excellent steep skiing down on to the Bernina black run all the way to the bottom. At Corviglia (accessed by the Munt da San Murezzan chair-lift) there is a snowpark with a half-pipe and obstacle course.

Off-piste

The steep face of Piz Nair provides incredible thrills when there is enough powder snow to cover the sheer rock. The long glacier itinerary from the top of Diavolezza, around and over crevasses to Morteratsch is one of the classic off-piste routes in the Alps.

Tuition and guiding

The St Moritz and Suvretta ski schools are both branches of the Swiss Ski School (SSS) that together employ about 300 instructors. The Palace Hotel has its own school.

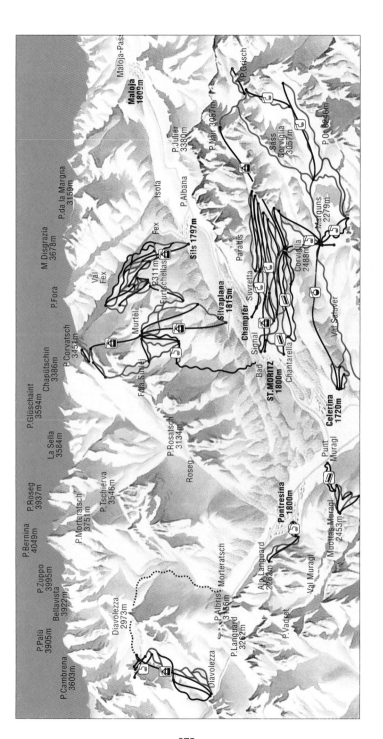

Off-piste guiding is not widely in demand. Snowboard School St Moritz and The Wave Snowboard School both offer lessons.

Cross-country

The frozen lakes of the Engadine and the forest trails make St Moritz one of the most interesting and beautiful cross-country areas in the Alps, with loipes of every standard. Ideally, serious langlaufers should stay in Bad, as this is where the tracks are based. The 42-km Engadine Marathon is held here each season and attracts thousands of entrants.

Mountain restaurants

Renowned among snow-users and gourmets alike, the Marmite on Corviglia has been radically rebuilt. Reservations are necessary for both the

> **WHAT'S NEW**
>
> Renovated funicular at Corvatsch

midday and 2pm sittings. Owner Reto Mathis, whose father Hartly was the first man to bring haute cuisine to the high mountains, counts caviar and truffles by the kilo. But his daily specials in the Brasserie or self-service sections of the restaurant are always budget-priced. Also on the Corviglia mountain, the Skihütte Alpina is great for pasta and rustic charm. Cheese specialities are best at the Piz Nair.

The resort

Since tourism began here in 1864, St Moritz has been a hotel town. No other resort has so many luxury hotels – 63 per cent are four- or five-star rated. The urban architecture is bland at best. St Moritz's beauty lies not in the views of the resort itself but in the views from it. It is small enough to walk around, although most hotels have shuttle vans, and buses and trains provide adequate public transport to all regions. Designer boutiques are as prevalent as furs, but the old-fashioned shops remain.

Accommodation

The Palace Hotel, with its grotesque tower, is the most famous of the five-stars and has its own ski school. The pastel blocks of the Kulm are preferred by the Cresta crowd. The Suvretta House is less central and attracts older, European money. The Carlton has a country-house atmosphere. The four-star Schweizerhof and Steffani hotels, both with active après-ski, are downtown and affordable. There is also a reasonable choice of less exalted accommodation.

Eating in and out

Hanselmann's in the town centre has been around for more than 100 years and serves coffee, pastries and ice-cream to die for. Lunch at the Chesa Veglia, an architectural museum-piece owned by the Palace Hotel, is not expensive compared with dinner. All the top hotel restaurants require jacket and tie. Out in Celerina, Peter Graber's lamb marinated in herbs and served on hay at the Stuvetta Veglia is a local legend.

Skiing facts: St Moritz

TOURIST OFFICE
Via Maistra 12 CH-7500 St Moritz,
Graubunden
Tel 41 81 837 33 33
Fax 41 81 837 33 66
Email kvv@stmoritz.ch
Web site www.stmoritz.ch

THE RESORT
By road Calais 1047km
By rail station in resort
Airport transfer Zurich 4hrs
Visitor beds 12,500
Transport bus free with ski pass

THE SKIING
Linked or nearby resorts Celerina (l),
Champfèr (n), Pontresina (n), Samadan
(n), Sils Maria (l), Silvaplana (l), Surlej
(l), Zuos (n)
Longest run Morteratsch, 9km (black)
Number of lifts 23 in St Moritz, 55 in
linked area
Total of trails/pistes 80km in St Moritz
(10% easy, 70% intermediate, 20%
difficult), 350km in linked area
Nursery slopes 3 lifts in St Moritz
Summer skiing on Diavolezza Glacier
Snowmaking 11km covered

LIFT PASSES
Area pass Upper Engadine (covers St
Moritz, Celerina, Silvaplana, Pontresina,
Sils), SF258 for 6 days including a day's
skiing in Livigno
Day pass St Moritz/Celerina SF50, linked
area SF54
Beginners no free lifts
Pensioners no reductions
Credit cards yes

TUITION
Adults St Moritz, 10am–midday or

1.30–3.30pm, SF230 for 5 days. Suvretta,
10am–midday and 2–4pm, SF220 for 5
days. Palace Hotel, details on request
Private lessons St Moritz and Suvretta,
both SF140 for 2hrs, SF250 per day
Snowboarding Snowboard School St
Moritz and The Wave, SF220 for 5 days
Cross-country St Moritz, SF90 for 3
half-days. Loipe 150km in area
Other courses competition, freestyle,
slalom, hang-gliding, telemark
Guiding The St Moritz Experience, All
Activities Agency (AAA)

CHILDREN
Lift pass 50% reduction for 6–16yrs,
free for 5yrs and under
Ski kindergarten St Moritz, 4yrs and
over, 10am–3.30pm, SF40 per day, SF25
per day for lunch
Ski school St Moritz, 6–12yrs, SF380
for 6 days including lunch. Suvretta,
12yrs and under, 10am–midday or
2–4pm, SF170 for 6 half-days. AAA,
details on request.
Non-ski kindergarten Parkhotel
Kurhaus SF29, Hotel Carlton, SF22,
Hotel Schweizerhof SF34, all per day,
3yrs and over, 9am–4.30pm
including lunch

OTHER SPORTS
Skating, curling, horse-racing, polo,
cricket and golf on the frozen lake,
swimming, parapente, Cresta Run,
Olympic bob-run, hot-air ballooning,
hang-gliding, winter walks, climbing wall,
indoor tennis and squash

FOOD AND DRINK PRICES
Coffee, SF3.50–4.50, glass of wine
SF5–7, small beer SF3.60–5.50, dish of
the day SF20–25

Après-ski

At the Palace Hotel's Kings Club an orchestra plays until 4am (jacket and tie required). The stübli at the Schweizerhof has late-night dancing on tables, but after 10pm it is so crowded that you could not possibly fall off. The Cresta Bar across the street is less popular than the Vivai disco. Muli Bar has country-and-western music. Bobby's Bar is for the under-20s. The Cascade Bar and the Cava Bar in the Hotel Steffani are both praised.

Childcare

The kindergarten in the Schweizerhof, Carlton and Parkhotel Kurhaus all accept children over three years old on a daily basis, with lunch included. The Parkhotel Kurhaus is next to the cross-country track in Bad. The Suvretta and St Moritz ski schools accept children over four years old.

Linked or nearby resorts

Celerina
top 3057m (10,030ft) bottom 1720m (5,643ft)
A village atmosphere, old stone houses painted with the local graffito designs, and ski access to Corviglia make Celerina a quiet alternative. Chesa Rosatsch is a 350-year-old inn now run by a British couple.

TOURIST OFFICE
Tel 41 81 830 00 11
Fax 41 81 830 00 19

Pontresina
top 2262m (7,421ft) bottom 1800m (5,904ft)
With no big lifts of its own, Pontresina is about midway between the out-lying Diavolezza sector and Corviglia. It has good indoor-sports facilities and a loyal clientèle of Italian and German families. Kochendorfer's Albris is an inexpensive hotel with its own bakery and chocolate shop. The Steinbock and Engadinerhof are comfortable, traditional hotels.

TOURIST OFFICE
Tel 41 81 842 6488
Fax 41 81 842 7996

Verbier

ALTITUDE 1500m (4,920ft)

Intermediates ✷✷   Advanced ✷✷✷   Snowboarders ✷✷

Verbier is home to Europe's best lift-served off-piste skiing and what in the past have been the worst queues. Glaciers, couloirs, bowls and day-long itineraries, none requiring mountaineering gear, are nowhere in the world more abundant or varied. Val d'Isère, Chamonix and Zermatt are routinely beaten by Verbier skiers in annual resort-versus-resort extreme competitions held in Argentière.

It is the antithesis of purpose-built; none of its limited hotel accommodation (only 1,500 beds out of 15,000) is ski-in ski-out, and its haphazard lift network has developed over the years without the benefit of a long-term masterplan. The attractions include 90-minute motorway access from Geneva and more than 300 days of sunshine per year. The British clientèle tends towards the loud and boorish,

- ✔ Easy rail and road access
- ✔ Wealth of off-piste
- ✔ Excellent sunshine record
- ✔ Summer glacier skiing
- ✘ Queues and overcrowding
- ✘ High prices for après-ski
- ✘ Minimal hotel accommodation
- ✘ Inadequate mountain restaurants
- ✘ Traffic and difficult parking

but has declined from a peak of 26 per cent to less than 10 per cent of all visitors, leaving Verbier to the Swiss (52 per cent), most of whom own chalets or apartments in the four- to six-storey blocks which sprawl across the plateau.

The lift company, Téléverbier, has made gargantuan efforts to improve the skiing experience – efforts unmatched by local restaurateurs – and this season the infamous Tortin bubble is replaced by a long-awaited eight-person gondola. With an uphill capacity of 2,000 skiers and snowboarders per hour, it should dramatically reduce queues here which at peak times could be as long as an unacceptable two hours.

Verbier is the chief component of the Four Valleys circuit, a linked network of 96 lifts serving 410km of piste. At the beginning of last season this was savagely cut to 68 lifts and 290km of piste when **Thyon** opted out in a dispute over revenue sharing. We are assured by Verbier that the argument has now been resolved.

In addition to the Four Valleys circuit, which also extends to **Nendaz** and **Veysonnaz**, Verbier's skiing includes the separate family resorts of **Bruson**, **Fouly** and **Vichères**. The delightful little ski area of **Champex-Lac** is under new ownership and has removed itself from the Four Valleys.

Ski and board

top 3330m (10,925m) bottom 1500m (4,920m)

Verbier's best skiing is not visible from the resort and almost impossible to decipher from the cramped piste map which comes in for universal criticism from readers: 'Runs on the map are missing from the mountain'. Lifts passes here are extremely complicated, and therefore we have listed only the Four Valleys and Family Pass in our skiing facts table. You are advised to assess the area you want to cover before parting with any money. The Family Pass, which includes children up to 20 years old, provides substantial savings.

The quickest route from Verbier's Medran base area is via the six-person gondola. From the Ruinettes mid-station, a modern (1994) 30-person Funitel gondola zips up to Attelas at 2740m. From here skiers can ride a cable-car up to Mont Gelé (3023m), ski down into the intermediate Lac des Vaux sector for chair-lift access to Tortin and further cable-cars to Mont-Fort (3330m), or ski over to the south-facing intermediate runs of La Chaux, where the 150-person Jumbo cable-car rises to the glacier slopes of Gentianes and Mont-Fort.

Savolèyres is a separate intermediate mountain, accessed by an old (1970) gondola, with sunny south-facing slopes towards Verbier and longer, better runs down its back side to **Tzoumaz**. This season, the return drag-lift has been upgraded to a double chair-lift. Every lift in Verbier is subject to queues. These can be as brief as 15 to 30 minutes, and readers have commented on a definite improvement over the last few years, especially mid-week and in low season.

Verbier has funparks with half-pipes and obstacles at both Mont-Fort and Les Ruinettes.

Beginners

A beginner in Verbier, as one reporter noted, is better described as 'an aspiring expert'. There is one short nursery slope mid-town on the Moulins golf course, and another extremely crowded area on Esserts. Those certain of their snowploughing technique can ski blue (easy) runs higher up the mountain on the usually excellent snow at Lac des Vaux.

Intermediates

Savolèyres and its north side down to Tzoumaz, along with La Chaux and Lac des Vaux, are about the limit for intermediate skiing. It is impossible to ski all the way down to Savolèyres base-station on piste, which is a cause of much complaint, as skiers are diverted sideways across the mountain to a dead-end bus stop. Verbier's main arterial highway, the pistes from Attelas to Ruinettes and the inescapable roadway to Medran, are unreasonably overcrowded. The bottom road is made even more dangerous by a profusion of pedestrians, children on sledges, and dogs.

Advanced

Aside from the one run down Mont-Fort, all of Verbier's interesting black (difficult) pistes have been reclassified as 'ski itineraries' to avoid

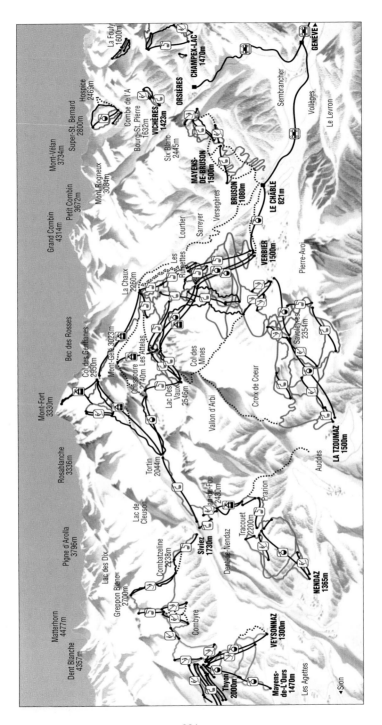

legal responsibility in case of accident. Skied by thousands on a daily basis, such itineraries are essentially pistes, though not groomed. Most notorious is Tortin, a steep, wide slope usually pounded into bumps and often dangerous to access because of exposed rocks at the top. Gentianes, the run under the eponymous cable-car, offers a huge scope of bumps and ravines. Col des Mines, an open, south-facing slope returning to Verbier, and Vallon d'Arbi, a tremendously scenic, steep-sided valley leading eventually to Tzoumaz, are both accessed by a traverse beginning in Lac des Vaux. It is important to respect signs warning that this traverse is closed as it is an area where several deaths have occurred. Marked itineraries down to **Le Châble** from Verbier are very seldom skiable, due to poor snow cover, and always dangerous, due to unmarked obstacles.

WHAT'S NEW

Eight-person gondola at Tortin
Etablons lift upgraded to double-chair

Off-piste

You could devote an entire book to describe the best of Verbier's off-piste. Only a decade ago Creblet, the front face of Mont Gelé and the back of Mont-Fort down to Cleuson were considered radical descents. Now, like Stairway to Heaven and Hidden Valley, they are skied out within an hour of fresh snowfall. Bec des Rosses (3220m) is now the venue for snowboarding extreme contests, and skiing off the back down into Fionnay wins jealous admiration. The 'North Face' of Mont-Fort, with its B52 and Poubelle variants is routinely skied, despite its if-you-fall-you-die entry. The Grand Banana and Paradise are examples of off-piste sectors, which are not so much difficult to ski as dangerous to access. Off-piste skiers without guides should note that Cleuson, Col de Mouche, Marlenaz, Rock Garden and Vallon d'Arbi have all witnessed death by avalanche in recent years. Off-piste freeriding possibilities are exceptional, and annual extreme snowboarding contests prove the test of Verbier's tough terrain.

Tuition and guiding

We have more positive reports of the Swiss Ski School (SSS), which has expanded its programmes and moved meeting places. All children and beginner adults now gather in the Medran parking lot; other adults meet at Ruinettes: 'Generally sensible tuition from a sympathetic teacher'. 'La 6' is a four-hour off-piste course with mountain guides for experienced skiers. The rival Ecole du Ski Fantastique, with 20 qualified mountain guides, is better for off-piste, ski safaris and heli-skiing. No Bounds is the dedicated snowboard school. Off-piste skiers should beware of local ski bums in Pub Mont-Fort offering illegal and uninsured guiding.

Mountain restaurants

Nowhere in the Four Valleys is there a gourmet restaurant to compare with those in Zermatt or St Moritz, except in price. Chez Dany at Clambin, perennially overcrowded and serving nothing more ambitious than cheese dishes, is the best of an indifferent lot. Worst are the fast-food terraces at Attelas and La Chaux with their blaring loudspeakers. The Ruinettes cafeteria has tempting pastries and an acceptable sit-down restaurant upstairs. On Savolèyres, the primitive Buvette de la Marlenaz is far off-piste but authentically olde worlde, as is Cabane Mont-Fort, a real Haute Route touring hut with simple fare under the Jumbo cable-car. The station café at Le Châble is warmly recommended by one reporter: 'Don't tell anybody, as the seating is limited'. The wooden shacks at Tortin and Gentianes are gold-mines for their owners and hunting grounds for ski bums scavenging leftovers at the outdoor tables but offer meagre sustenance.

The resort

Verbier was nothing but Alpine pasture before the 1950s. Today its sprawling chalets are jammed cheek-by-jowl with virtually no interven-ing spaces, and many larger apartment blocks are seriously dilapidated. Recession has led to hundreds of properties being put on the market. There is no village parking garage, and skiers hiking up to Medran are forced into the middle of a narrow, heavily trafficked roadway. Shopping is limited but there is a Timberland shop and some excellent supermar-kets. British-owned Mountain Air, off-piste and telemark headquarters, is considered to be one of the best ski shops in the Alps. Ski Adventure features Armani and Polo Ralph Lauren. The free bus around the village receives praise for its service: 'Always polite and very frequent'.

Accommodation

The vast majority of visitors stay in tour-operator chalets – almost always apartments in large blocks – or in the wealth of self-catering apartments, which comprise 90 per cent of Verbier's 15,000 beds. Most of Verbier's 26 hotels will not accept bookings for less than seven days. Verbier is the only Swiss resort of note with no five-star hotels. And even the four-star Rosalp, Verbier's flagship, suffers from cramped rooms and lacks a swimming-pool. The modest Hotel Verbier in the village square is friendly, as are Serge Tacchini's Mazot around the corner and the hid-den-away, modern and elegant Rois Mages, near the church. The Montpelier, near the sports centre, is Verbier's best all-round hotel, and Les Touristes at the village entrance is the best value. Hotel Bristol was recommended by one reporter because: 'There is not a more convenient location in Verbier'. However, 'the hotel houses a disco on the first floor, which can provide some noise late into the night'. It has the advantage of a small, free parking area, which is a rarity in the resort.

Eating in and out

The excuse for the lack of excellent cuisine in Verbier is that most visitors eat at home in their chalets. The exception is the Rosalp, which remains a true gourmet treat. Of the cheeseries, the best are the unpretentious and homey Les Touristes and the Vieux Valais. The Channe Valaisanne (in

Hotel Bristol), Chamois and Robinson are all equally undistinguished. Borsalino ('the best'), Chez Martin and Al Capone serve pizzas. Harold's in the square is famous for burgers. Grotte à Max has an interesting range of rösti dishes, with kangaroo and ostrich. The Hacienda Café features Tex-Mex, with indifferent success. The Bouchon Gourmand wins good reviews for its south-western French dishes. The Relais des Neiges is recommended for simple home cooking at modest prices.

Après-ski

The Swedish-owned Farinet, in the central square, has an enclosed terrace, live bands and is popular immediately after skiing. Fer à Cheval, sometimes serving free pizza, is packed out as soon as the lifts close. The coolest hangout remains the Offshore, famed for its pink VW Beetle. At night all the world – especially chalet girls and ski bums – flocks to the Pub Mont-Fort. Haunt of Fergie, the Farm Club these days is too expensive and too boring for most. One reporter commented: 'The Farm is OK if you are stinking rich and want to pose'. Ravers prefer the Scotch ('very basic') or Marshall's ('techno'). Crok No Name is Verbier's most sophisticated bar, although the over-50s will find Jacky's piano bar more to their taste. Sub-teens will enjoy the video games and pool tables at the Big Ben. The Nelson is, according to one reporter: 'Crowded and with the décor and atmosphere of a Birmingham pub'.

Childcare

Chez les Schtroumpfs has an excellent reputation for day-long indoor childminding (ages five months to seven years). More expensive is the Kids Club skiing programme for children over three years, which is run by its SSS at their Moulins nursery site with its own lift and restaurant.

Linked or nearby resorts

Bruson
top 2445m (8,022ft) bottom 1100m (3,543ft)

Verbier's lift company has plans for a direct gondola from the valley train station in Le Châble to the top of Bruson. But for the moment Bruson remains uncrowded, with some of the very best steep powder skiing, especially in its off-piste larch forests, on the Verbier skipass. Two chairlifts and two T-bars make up the lift system, serving only 30km of groomed pistes. But with some hiking, long excursions down to **Sembrancher** and **Orsières** over snow-filled pastures, and a free train-ride back to Le Châble, are possible. Access is by free bus from Le Châble, itself connected to Verbier by gondola or another free bus. Bruson has some self-catering flats midway up the mountain and a simple restaurant.

TOURIST OFFICE
Tel 41 27 776 1682
Fax 41 27 776 1541

Skiing facts: Verbier

TOURIST OFFICE
CH-1936 Verbier, Valais
Tel 41 27 775 38 88
Fax 41 27 775 38 89
Email verbiertourism@verbier.ch
Web site www.verbier.ch

THE RESORT
By road Calais 998km
By rail Le Châble 15mins
Airport transfer Geneva 2hrs
Visitor beds 15,000
Transport free ski bus

THE SKIING
Linked or nearby resorts Bruson (n),
Champex-Lac (n), La Fouly (n),
Nendaz (l), Super-St-Bernard (n), La
Tzoumaz (l), Thyon (l), Veysonnaz (l),
Vichères (n)
Longest run Mont-Fort to Verbier, 13km
(red/blue/black)
Number of lifts 96 in area
Total of trails/pistes 410km in area
(39% easy, 43% intermediate, 18%
difficult)
Nursery slopes 4
Summer skiing 2 lifts, June–July
Snowmaking 12km in Verbier, 30km
in area

LIFT PASSES
Area pass Four Valleys SF282. Family
Pass (covers whole area) SF282 for 1st
adult, SF169 for 2nd adult, SF85 for
6–16yrs, all for 6 days
Day pass SF56 whole area
Beginners no free lifts

Pensioners SF169 for 65yrs and over
Credit cards yes

TUITION
Adults SSS, 9.15–11.45am, SF123 for
6 half-days
Private lessons SSS SF115, Fantastique
SF110, both for 2hrs
Snowboarding SSS, Fantastique, No
Bounds, all SF35 per half-day, SF138 for
6 half-days
Cross-country SSS and Fantastique,
details on request. Loipe 9km in Verbier,
43km in Four Valleys
Other courses telemark, skiing for the
blind, heli-skiing
Guiding SSS and Fantastique

CHILDREN
Lift pass free for 5yrs and under.
6–16yrs, SF169 for 6 days
Ski kindergarten SSS Kids Club,
3–10yrs, 8.30am–5.30pm, SF66 per day
including lunch
Ski school SSS Kids Club (see above)
Non-ski kindergarten Chez les
Schtroumpfs, 7yrs and under, SF288 for
6 days (54hrs), including lunch

OTHER SPORTS
Swimming, squash, climbing-wall,
indoor golf, hang-gliding, ice-climbing,
parapente, skating, winter walks,
snowshoeing

FOOD AND DRINK PRICES
Coffee SF3, glass of wine SF2.80, small
beer SF3.50–4, dish of the day SF15–20

Champex-Lac
top 2188m (7,178ft) bottom 1470m (4,823ft)

The narrow, hairpin road up to Champex guarantees that this delightfully forested, family resort with its scenic frozen lake, never sees a queue. Unfortunately for Verbier-based skiers, the resort has now opted out of the Four Valleys lift pass, and you must buy a separate ticket. Skiing is limited: two chair-lifts access no more than 10km of pistes, which are very steep if taken off-piste directly under the main chair. Powder on the north face remains good for weeks, and Champex's family clientèle rarely ventures into the untracked snow among the trees.

The Belvédère is an outstandingly characterful hotel, its few bedrooms panelled in broad Arolla pine and decorated with antiques. The food is of a higher standard than anywhere except the Rosalp in Verbier, but modestly priced. Champex has a small branch of the Swiss Ski School (SSS). The kindergarten has closed.

TOURIST OFFICE
Tel 41 27 783 1227
Fax 41 27 783 3527

Nendaz
top 3330m (10,925ft) bottom 1365m (4,478ft)

Nendaz offers cheaper accommodation than Verbier but complicated and inefficient access to the best of the Four Valleys skiing, although a free bus does run from Nendaz to Siviez.

TOURIST OFFICE
Tel 41 27 289 5589
Fax 41 27 289 5583
Email otnendaz@scopus.ch
Web site www.nendaz.ch

Siviez
top 3330m (10,925ft) bottom 1730m (5,676ft)

Skiers desperate to save money and determined to be first up Mont-Fort, might consider Siviez. It is sunny and is the hub of the Four Valleys, with a high-speed chair link to the Gentianes–Mont-Fort cable-cars. Accommodation is limited to one hotel, a concrete apartment block, and a youth hostel.

TOURIST OFFICE
Tel 41 27 289 5589
Fax 41 27 289 5583

Zermatt

ALTITUDE 1620m (5,314ft)

Intermediates ✱✱✱　Advanced ✱✱✱　Snowboarders ✱

If you take your skiing with sugar and cream, then Zermatt is the resort in which to stay, provided, of course, you have both the wherewithal and the luck to find a vacant room in a tourist centre that has no low season at all. Arriving off the train from the end-of-the-road hamlet of Täsch is an astonishing experience, regardless of financial status. At the station backpackers mingle with fur-clad socialites surrounded by mounds of Louis Vuitton, but everyone is equally awe-struck by the mountain setting that greets them. Zermatt – dominated by the Matterhorn – is Switzerland's southernmost skiing terrain, with 30 summits of over 4000m. It is one of the most scenically beautiful ski resorts in the world.

Zermatt was an isolated hamlet until it was adopted as a mountain base-camp by British climbers and, later, skiers. The canny burghers began milking the cash cow in earnest during the nineteenth century, committing communal funds to building the Gornergrat cog railway and passing local legislation forcing every inhabitant of the village to labour on construction of the Zermatterhof Hotel. The lift system dates from the construction of the Gornergrat cog railway in 1898. The new express trains run twice as fast as the older carriages, which are still in use. However, due to a single track, the express trip is only ten minutes shorter than the standard 40-minute trip, which stops at every station. The free ski-bus system has dramatically improved resort transport. A combined lift pass with **Cervinia**, which is linked off the back of the Klein Matterhorn, is available.

- ✔ Superlative scenery
- ✔ Excellent mountain restaurants
- ✔ High standard of accommodation
- ✔ Alpine charm
- ✔ Lively après-ski
- ✔ Activities for non-skiers
- ✔ Long runs
- ✔ Extensive ski area
- ✔ Car-free resort
- ✔ Extensive snowmaking
- ✔ Glacier skiing
- ✘ Inadequate ski school
- ✘ High prices
- ✘ Long airport transfer

Ski and board
top 3899m (12,788ft) bottom 1620m (5,314ft)

Zermatt is a resort for the adept skier with deep pockets and a taste for good living. No competent skier will find him- or herself outclassed by any groomed slope in Zermatt, but 20-minute queues for the Klein Matterhorn cable-car and longer for the Gornergrat cog railway – not to mention packed crowds coming down to the village at the end of the day on narrow, icy trails – will keep even experts on the edge. One reporter notes that Zermatt suits 'bump lovers and people who like skiing on paths'.

An underground funicular begins by the mainline train station and runs up to the Sunnegga sector, with sunny slopes continuing up to Blauherd and Rothorn, which are connected by an efficient 150-person cable-car. The Gornergrat mountain railway station, just across from the main railway terminus, is the start of a trip up past Riffelalp and Riffelberg to Gornergrat, from where cable-cars go onwards to Hohtälli, Rote Nase and Stockhorn. At the Matterhorn edge of Zermatt, a cable-car and various gondolas head out to Furi. From there, lifts branch left for the Trockener Steg and Klein Matterhorn sectors and right for the Schwarzsee area, with Furgg straight up the middle. Zermatt retains 18 antiquated drag-lifts among its impressive cable-cars.

Zermatt used to be known for the awkward connections between its three ski areas. The resort, from a skier's point of view, began to get better with the introduction of a free bus system to provide cross-town linkage. It will further improve with the introduction of a new cable-car, which should be running at the start of this season. It is being built between Gant and Hohtälli to link properly the Sunnegga and Gornergrat areas for the first time. It should therefore become possible to ski all three Zermatt sectors in one day, and to ski from one to another in both directions.

Reporters complain of inconsistent piste-grading: 'Some blue (easy) runs seemed more like red (intermediate) ones and yet the reds were very straightforward, especially on Trockener Steg'. Zermatt is now one of Switzerland's leading resorts for artificial snowmaking which covers more than 55km of the area.

Beginners

Zermatt cannot be recommended for novices, but beginners do have the rare chance to ski at exceptionally high altitude on the glacier, particularly when snow is sparse elsewhere. Guaranteed skiing on the glacier above 3000m is flat and easy on the blues alongside the Gandegg and Theodulpass drag-lifts, going over to Cervinia from Trockener Steg, as well as on the Plateau Rosa and Testa blues well above 3500m. Normally, the ski school takes beginners to Blauherd, where the blue run, marked 2A on the piste map, returns over flattering terrain to the Sunnegga lift station. But be careful not to turn right on to the National black (difficult) run.

At Sunnegga, beginners have a short blue called Easy Run. Tuftern, although marked as a blue from Blauherd all the way down to Patrullarve, is actually quite tricky in parts. Gornergrat appears to offer more beginner terrain, but it is important to get off the train at Rotenboden, one stop earlier, to avoid a 'nasty bit' at the top.

There is a half-pipe in the Klein Matterhorn sector, but Zermatt is not overly adoring of the snowboard ethos.

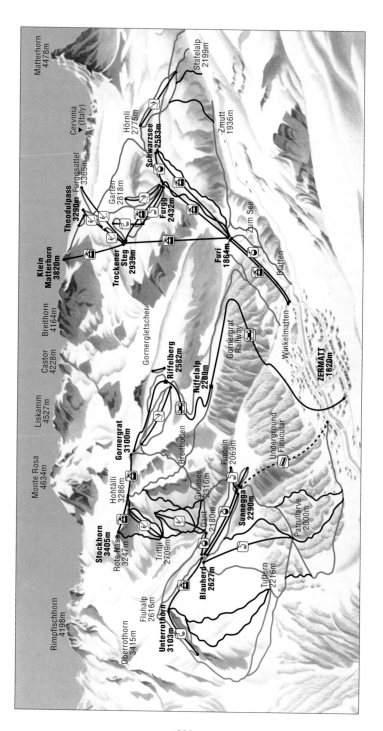

Matterhorn 4478m

Cervinia ▶ (Italy)

Statelalp 2199m

Hörnli 2775m

Schwarzsee 2583m

Zmutt 1936m

Furggsattel 3365m

Theodulpass 3290m

Gartern 2818m

Furgg 2432m

Zum See

Klein Matterhorn 3820m

Trockener Steg 2939m

Furi 1864m

Blatten

Breithorn 4164m

Gornergletscher

Gornergrat Railway

Winkelmatten

Castor 4228m

ZERMATT 1620m

Liskamm 4527m

Riffelberg 2582m

Riffelalp 2209m

Monte Rosa 4634m

Gornergrat 3100m

Breithoden

Underground Funicular

Findeln 2069m

Hohtälli 3286m

Grünsee 2316m

Sunnegga 2290m

Stockhorn 3405m

Rote Nase 3247m

Gant 2180m

Patrullarve 2000m

Triftji 2709m

Rimpfischhorn 4198m

Oberrothorn 3415m

Fluhalp 2616m

Blauherd 2627m

Tuftern 2216m

Unterrothorn 3103m

389

Intermediates

Zermatt's red runs often become more than ordinarily testing due to icy conditions and extreme overcrowding on narrow sections down to the village. The highest and easiest intermediate skiing is up in the Klein Matterhorn and Trockener Steg sectors. From the Klein Matterhorn, the long KL red flows alongside blue-ice crevasses down past the Plateau Rosa T-bars to the Führer piste and over to the Testa T-bar.

Aggressive intermediates will be thrilled by the Kelle run from Gornergrat, passing over a 'scary' ridge to link up at Breitboden with the classic White Hare red, which begins with a narrow, challenging passage up at Hohtälli. Both reds proceed on terrain bordered by woods all the way to Furi – a good 30 minutes on skis without stopping.

Intermediate skiing on the Sunnegga–Blauherd sector is sunnier and smoother, making ideal 'ski to lunch' terrain. The Fluhalp red leads down to the Gant drag-lift, which gives access to the black runs back down from Rote Nase, but also links with the start of the red White Hare and the Furi sector.

Advanced

Triftji is one of the most famous black runs in the Alps. Unfortunately, this and the other black trails down under the Hohtälli–Rote Nase sector require so much snow to make them skiable that they are often closed until mid-January. Together, the Stockhorn and Grieschumme blacks make an almost perfect fall-line descent from Rote Nase down to Gant, a bone-jarring bump bonanza that only the most rubber-legged will achieve without stopping. Further afield, and invisible to spectators, is Zermatt's least crowded, best black-run skiing.

Sloping sharply down from the Stafel–Hörnli drag-lift into the tree-line, Tiefbach and Momatt are steep runs which dive towards Zmutt and the borders of the resort. Notorious as an accident black-spot as well as an expert run, the Furgg–Furi stretch is described as being 'like the M25' in late afternoon, when it is the main homeward-bound route. But early in the morning, when Furgg–Furi has yet to be scraped clean of snow, it makes an excellent downhill course for more advanced skiers.

Off-piste

The Schwarzsee sector is cold and uncrowded. The Aroleid trail under the cable-car is normally a bump run all the way to Furi. Less skied are the Garten gullies. From the top of the Furgg–Garten drag, and to the left of the Garten red run, the two Garten couloirs offer a choice of narrow chutes, which are very steep for the first 40m but not life-threatening should you fall. At the bottom there is a favourite 'sky ramp' jump of about 20m, which has the attractions of a perfect landing and good views for spectators from the Garten lift. Down from Rothorn on the sunny side of the mountain, three itineraries (Chamois, Marmotte and Arbzug) become wide-open powder routes after a good storm.

A day's heli-skiing excursion to **Monte Rosa** or the Alphubeljoch above Zermatt is a popular way to escape the pistes.

Tuition and guiding

Few ski schools have been so heavily criticised as the Swiss Ski School (SSS) here. Zermatt's 50-plus mountain guides also have a reputation, even among the Swiss, for aloof indifference. One explanation is that many guides and instructors work as a hobby, making their real living from local shops or hotels. A reporter comments: 'Neither of the two instructors we experienced bothered to ask the names of the class members. Nor did many of the instructors show any respect for each other; on several occasions one ski class would cut straight through another'. Another reporter says: 'The instructor seemed more concerned with getting a sun tan than anything else'.

> **WHAT'S NEW**
>
> Kids' park and kindergarten at Riffelberg
> Cable-car from Gant to Hohtälli

Ski classes are often overpopulated and somewhat chaotic, despite a pool of about 175 teachers. 'The instructor failed to make sufficient allowances for the weaker skiers, frequently skiing on far ahead and often going on again before the last members of the class had caught up' commented an unhappy reporter. Another reporter notes: 'A large proportion of teachers seemed to be over 60 years old, and very little technical instruction was offered'.

The SSS has around 20 snowboard instructors. Julen Sports houses a snowboard school called Stoked, which is described by one reader as 'very dynamic'.

Mountain restaurants

Lunching on a wooden terrace comes a close second to gazing at the Matterhorn as the main occupation in Zermatt. This is no place to pack a picnic – not when old wooden barns like Chez Vrony provide crystal glass, starched napkins, sofas on the terrace and intimate nooks and crannies for serious dining. The Findeln plateau also offers Chez Adler, which some reporters prefer to Vrony, perhaps because Max, the host, is so genial. Both Enzian and the Findlerhof (formerly Enzo's) are both warmly recommended.

The centuries-old hamlet of Zum See houses an inn of the same name, which is run by Max and Greti and has a rising reputation as Zermatt's best – it is worth trying the curried noodles and king prawns here. Higher up in the Furi sector, Simi is the rösti headquarters but also serves delicious salads at reasonable prices. Tony's Grotta has delectable pasta.

Fluhalp, at the top of Rothorn, has pancakes and the best panorama of the Matterhorn. The Gandegg Hütte is very popular: 'The restaurant was so full we ate outside in a blizzard, but they did provide rugs, and the atmosphere was still amazing'. Paradies, below Sunnegga, has 'memorable rösti and wonderful salads'. At Furi in the Schwarzsee area, the Farmerhouse is popular, and Aroleid is a good stop-off point on the way home.

The resort

Zermatt was a settlement from the early Middle Ages and inaugurated its first three tourist beds in 1838. Development has since been constrained by steep valley walls, leaving nothing between the Matterhorn and the village edge but open pasture dotted with wooden barns.

In Zermatt's narrow lanes, sheep are still shorn outside centuries-old wooden mazots (ramshackle barns on stilts fitted with stone discs to keep rats at bay), but the conflux of electric taxis and horse-drawn carriages on the main thoroughfare is so frantic that radar traps have been installed.

There are a number of expensive jewellery shops and some good ski clothing shops, but few of the chic boutiques one finds in Crans Montana or St Moritz. 'Expensive for food and wine, otherwise not too bad for ski gear, T-shirts and gifts,' comments one reporter. Computers can be rented at Laser-Druck, and software is obtainable at Easy-Hot, giving a measure of the type of clientèle.

Accommodation

Hotel-keepers rule in Zermatt (there are 113 of them), and chalet accommodation is popular. It is important to choose a hotel close to where you want to ski and spend your evenings. For indulgent romantics nothing compares to the five-star experience of the venerable Zermatterhof Hotel, right in the village centre near the bronze sculpted marmots. Its interior was recently completely overhauled and redecorated in palatial style. The central, five-star Mont Cervin has fewer balconies but has opened sumptuous apartments in a recently built annex. All have private saunas, whirlpools, fireplaces, and most have kitchens. The four-star Alex Schlosshotel Tenne is an Alpine-Byzantine architectural mélange. The Monte Rosa, a favourite of Sir Winston Churchill and the base from which Edward Whymper, the Victorian mountaineer, set off to conquer the Matterhorn, exudes understated opulence. The chalet-style Malteserhaus has generously sized apartments. The Albana Real is 'modern and comfortable'.

Many reporters express satisfaction with the medium-priced (for Zermatt) Bristol, which is renowned for its cuisine. Hotel Parnass, located close to the Sunnegga Express and with a bus stop outside the door, is said to have 'a quiet and relaxed atmosphere – not wildly luxurious, but good value for money'. Hotel Bijou, two minutes' walk from the Klein Matterhorn lift, is praised as 'small and friendly with rooms even better than four-star; the food was a culinary delight each evening'. The Excelsior is 'central, next to a bus stop, and caters for vegetarians'. We also have glowing reports of Le Petit Hotel and the Darioli.

Eating in and out

Zermatt's restaurants (there are more than 100) have a deserved reputation for high quality and price. As elsewhere in the Alps, world-class cuisine is hard to find. Excepting menus at the Chinese restaurant next to the London Bar and the Fuji Japanese restaurant in the Hotel Albana, meat, cheese and potatoes prevail. Le Mazot and Le Gitan are at the top

Skiing facts: Zermatt

TOURIST OFFICE
Bahnhofplatz, CH-3920 Zermatt
Tel 41 27 967 0181
Fax 41 27 967 0185
Email zermatt@wallis.ch
Web site www.zermatt.ch

THE RESORT
By road Calais 1076km
By rail station in resort, or Visp 36km
Airport transfer Geneva 4hrs, Zurich
5hrs, Milan 3hrs
Visitor beds 13,000 (6,500 in hotels,
6,500 in chalets/apartments)
Transport ski bus included in the
ski pass, also electric taxis and horse-
drawn sleighs

THE SKIING
Linked or nearby resorts Cervinia (I),
Grächen (n), Saas-Fee (n), Riederalp (n),
Crans Montana (n)
Longest run Klein Matterhorn–Zermatt,
15km (red/black)
Number of lifts 73 with Cervinia
Total of trails/pistes Zermatt only
150km, 245km including Cervinia (33%
easy, 42% intermediate, 25% difficult)
Nursery slopes 3 nursery slopes
Summer skiing 25km of trails and
10 lifts on Klein Matterhorn Glacier
Snowmaking 55km covered

LIFT PASSES
Area pass SF218–296 for 6 days
Day pass SF54–60 including Cervinia.
Half price from 1pm
Beginners no free lifts.
Pensioners 25% reduction for men
65yrs and over, women 62yrs and over
Credit cards yes

TUITION
Adults SSS, SF215 for 6 days
(4hrs per day)
Private lessons SSS, SF145 for 3hrs,
SF270 for 6hrs)
Snowboarding SSS group lessons,
SF125 for 3 half-days (2hrs per day),
private lessons, SF270 per day. Stoked
Snowboard School, details on request
Cross-country SSS SF110 per morning.
Loipe 7km Zermatt, 15km Täsch
Other courses off-piste, heli-skiing,
telemark, carving, Big Foot
Guiding Zermatt Mountain Guide
Association, Alpin Center

CHILDREN
Lift pass 9–15yrs SF27–30 per day,
SF109–148 (6 days), free for 8 yrs and
under
Ski kindergarten SSS, 4–6yrs,
1–3.15pm, SF60 per day– (4½hrs)
Ski school SSS, 6–12yrs, SF255 for 6
days (4½hrs per day) including lunch
Non-ski kindergarten Kindergarten
Hotel Nicoletta, 2–8yrs, 9am–7pm, SF55
including lunch. Kinderclub Pumuckel at
Hotel La Ginabelle, 2½–6 yrs, 9am–5pm,
SF90 per day including lunch

OTHER SPORTS
Skating, curling, sleigh rides, winter
walks, ice-climbing, ice-diving,
helicopter rides, parapente, heli-skiing,
snowshoeing, tennis, squash,
rock-climbing, dog-sledding

FOOD AND DRINK
Coffee SF3.30, glass of wine SF3–3.50,
small beer SF4.30, dish of the day
SF20–28

of most lists for haute cuisine, although the Buffet Royal in the Zermatterhof Hotel is more luxurious. American-style steaks are grilled at the Viktoria-Centre and Cheminée Steak house. Fish, even in fondue, is good at the Coquille Fischstube. Lamb from the Julen's own flock (watch out for the sheepdog in the foyer) is excellent at the Schäferstübli. The Whymperstube in the Hotel Monte Rosa serves traditional fondues in Edwardian setting. Chez Gaby is a warm and friendly place and recommended for its fondue Bourguignon. Enzo Vrony is a new Italian, but looks Californian. Since its opening in the 1998 season it has fast become the most chic place in town.

Zermatt has about 15 grocery shops. The best is said to be La Source, but one reader recommends Martin Welschen, opposite the skating-rink, for the lowest prices.

Après-ski

Elsie's Place, by the church, is expensive, crowded, but irresistible for champagne and oysters after skiing or late at night. The Post Hotel complex caters for everybody: its Brown Cow snack bar boasts the best sandwiches in Europe; the Pink Elephant has a high standard of live jazz; Le Village is for a young age group, and Le Broken disco incites dancing – to '70s, '80s and '90s music – on huge beer barrels until 3am. However, the Post's Boathouse bar, not to be confused with the Zermatt Yacht, Golf and Country Club, is a tiny haven of cocktail civilisation decorated like the inside of a sloop. For a whale of a time, Moby Dick's Dancing Pub is open until late and has pool tables. The Alex Hotel's nightclub is sedate, but it is the only place where 30-somethings and upwards can dance to music that allows conversation. Grampi's Pub is a glass-fronted haunt with the cheapest beer in Zermatt. The T-Bar in Hotel Pollux was new for the 1998 season, and the Vernissage Cinema/Bar is the coolest après-ski spot in town.

Childcare

The SSS takes children from four to six years old, but only in the afternoons as the school considers mornings to be too cold for teaching on Sunnegga. Often there are no more than two children per instructor, although up to six are accepted. At the Nicoletta Hotel, Seiler's Children's Paradise takes kids from two years old. Childminding, with optional ski lessons on a baby slope by the river, is available at Hotel La Ginabelle's Kinderclub Pumuckel for children from two-and-a-half years old.

Zermatt used to have a reputation as a resort that was unsuitable for small children. However, the introduction last season of a kindergarten at Riffelberg goes some way towards redressing the situation. A special train from Gornergrat takes small, non-skiing children up to Riffelberg from the village and down again at the end of the day. Unfortunately, this does not link up with small skiers who are at ski school in the Sunnegga area for half a day.

Round-up

RESORTS COVERED Andermatt, Arosa, Flims, Gstaad, Kandersteg,
Lenzerheide/Valbella, Saas-Fee, Villars/Les Diablerets

Andermatt
top 2965m (9,725ft) bottom 1445m (4,740ft)

Andermatt is a retreat for a dedicated skiing minority. Its enormous off-piste opportunities and reputation for generous dumps of snow make it one of Switzerland's lesser-known little gems. It is situated at a major Alpine crossroads on the route to the St Gotthard Pass into Italy and was once one of the busiest of Swiss resorts. Now the high Urseren Valley, of which Andermatt is the main village, is underpassed by the Gotthard road and rail tunnels, making it a virtual dead-end in winter.

There are four ski areas along the sides of the Urseren Valley, between the Furka and Oberalp passes. The two main ones lie at either end of Andermatt; the two smaller and less popular areas lie to the south-west, above the villages of **Hospental** and **Realp**. Descents down the shaded face of Gemsstock, which has 800m of severe vertical and treacherous off-piste skiing in the bowl, should not be tackled without a guide; nor should some of the long off-piste alternatives in other directions from the top-station.

Andermatt itself has cobbled streets and a traditional character; however, it is one of Switzerland's major centres for the training of alpine troops, and severe barrack buildings are a feature of the architecture. The heart of the old village receives little sun as it is hemmed by mountains. There is not much traffic and no public transport. Accommodation is in a mixture of hotels and appealing old chalets.

TOURIST OFFICE
Tel 41 41 887 1454
Fax 41 41 887 0185
Email verkehrsverein-andermatt@bluewin.ch
Web site www.centralswitzerland.ch/andermatt

Arosa
top 2653m (8,702ft) bottom 1800m (5,904ft)

In 1883, ski-tourer Dr Otto Herwig-Hold stumbled across the tiny village of **Inner Arosa** high in the Swiss Graubunden. He climbed to the top of the 2512-m Hörnli, looked down at the village and realised that it was the perfect site for his new tuberculosis sanatorium. The hospital was built and, with its wide range of international patients, soon put Arosa on the Alpine map. Today it remains one of the truly all-round ski resorts of the Alps.

Arosa's skiers are not here to bash the pistes from dawn until dusk. Instead, they are in search of the complete winter-sports experience. The ski area consists of wide, sunny slopes mostly above the tree-line and covering the three peaks of Hörnli, Weisshorn and Bruggerhorn. It is well linked and although small with only 16 lifts, boasts a total of 70km of piste. Much of this is made up of blue (easy) and red (intermediate) runs over hilly rather than mountainous terrain. One of the only hazards of Arosa's skiing is the number of pedestrians and tobogganers on the piste; non-skiers can buy hiking passes that allow them to use gondolas and some chair-lifts.

The lift system is modern and efficient by Swiss standards. Main mountain access from **Obersee** is by chair-lift, drag-lift or two-stage cable-car. Access from Inner Arosa is by gondola. The top of the Hörnli is the starting point for a variety of ski-tours, involving skins and public transport, to neighbouring resorts. The more difficult piste-skiing is reached from the top of the 2653-m Weisshorn, a treacherous black (difficult) run that brings you down to the Carmnennahütte, which is the best of half-a-dozen mountain restaurants. Arosa has a dramatic half-pipe and is keen to promote snowboarding.

Waldhotel National is 'convenient for the slopes, comfortable, but lacking in style'. The choice of restaurants and nightlife is limited. Access to the village is not easy, with 244 bends in the dramatic 32-km road from the busy medieval valley town of Chur. Taking the train through stunning scenery is the better option. Once in the village, a toboggan is the essential form of transport.

TOURIST OFFICE
Tel 41 41 887 1454
Fax 41 41 887 0185

Flims
top 2980m (9,774ft) bottom 1080m (3,542ft)

This year-round destination lies in the heart of the Graubunden on the road from Chur to Andermatt. Together with its neighbours, **Laax** and **Falera**, it serves the wide south-facing ski area known as the White Arena. Dorf is a livelier and more convenient part of town in which to stay. The hotels in **Waldhaus** are not within easy walking distance of the lifts, but the larger ones have a courtesy minibus service to the Dorf base-station. The pleasant old village of Laax is 5km to the west, with a modern satellite base-station at **Murschteg** and low-cost, on-mountain accommodation at Crap Sogn Gion. The farming hamlet of Falera provides a rustic alternative.

Waldhaus has a nursery area, and some gentle practice slopes are near the base-stations and higher up the mountain. Motorway-style pistes give the intermediate snow-user the run of the whole mountain. The longest black run is the FIS downhill from Crap Sogn Gion to Murschteg. The off-piste potential is unexpectedly high with tree-level runs above Laax.

In Flims, the choice of tuition is between the Swiss Ski School (SSS) and the Swissraft Ski School. The Swiss Snowboard School and

Swissraft give boarding lessons, and a half-pipe is available at Crap Sogn Gion. Flims has extensive langlauf trails along the valley floor, including one loipe that is floodlit at night. The Flims SSS has classes for children from four years old, and we have excellent reports of the ski kindergarten. Both the Park Hotel Waldhaus and the Hotel Adula have crèches.

The best mountain eateries are at the lower levels and therefore not on the skiing trails, although the Runca hut below Startgels and the Tegia at Larnags are both worth the detour. Among the higher alternatives, the Segnes-Hütte is welcoming, the Foppa is an old wooden chalet with a sun terrace, and Nagens has a varied menu. The Elephant restaurant at Crap Masegn has excellent food.

The choice of accommodation is wide, ranging from the five-star Park Hotel Waldhaus, which comprises five buildings with opulent rooms, to the well-run two-star Encarna in Falera. Hotel Adula is praised for its child facilities. Sunstar Surselva is said to be 'excellent and central'. The top choice in Laax is the Posta Veglia. Recommended restaurants include Pizzeria Pomodoro, the Barga in Hotel Adula, La Cena in the Waldhaus, and the fish restaurant in Hotel National. The all-glass Iglu Bar opposite the Dorf base-station is the height of Flims chic for après-ski drinks. Later on the action focuses on the MacGeorge Pub in the Albana, and the quieter Segnes Bar.

TOURIST OFFICE
Tel 41 81 920 9200
Fax 41 81 920 9201

Gstaad
top 2979m (9,744ft) bottom 1000m (3,280ft)

To serious skiers, the lure of Gstaad is a mystery of its own. However, skiing is only a decorative accessory to the charm of this small but smart resort. The village stands at 1050m, with none of the local skiing above 2200m, which means that snow cover is unreliable even during a good winter. The redeeming factor is the nearby presence of the Glacier where the lifts go up to 2979m. Regulars argue that the sheer extent of the skiing included in the Ski Gstaad lift pass – 69 lifts covering 250km of piste (nearly half of it rated as easy) and 10 villages – makes up for the lack of challenge.

The local skiing is inconveniently divided into three separate areas. Regular ski buses to the surrounding villages of **Rougemont**, **Saanenmöser** and **Schönried** give access to slopes offering considerably more scope. The other villages covered on the lift pass are **St Stephan**, **Zweisimmen**, **Lauenen**, **Gsteig**, **Saanen** and **Château d'Oex**.

The Snowboard Schule Gstaad has a good reputation. Gstaad has snowboard funparks at Hornberg above Saanenmöser, at Rinderberg above Zweisimmen, and on the Diablerets Glacier. Heli-skiing and ski-touring are available through the ski schools, and there are 140km of cross-country loipe. The ski schools in Gstaad, Saanen, Schönried and Saanenmöser take children from four years of age. Recommended mountain restaurants include Chemihütte above St Stephan, and Cabane de la Sarouche at Château d'Oex. Ruble-Rougemont at the bottom of the Gouilles chair-lift is 'half the price of anywhere else'.

Gstaad is filled with top-quality hotels and a cluster of well-preserved wooden buildings in the newly traffic-free village centre. The best known hotel is the Palace, which has fairytale turrets and sits on the hill like a feudal castle dominating the village and its daily life. The opulent Gstaad Hotel Park is downhill but not necessarily downmarket. The four-star Bernerhof is conveniently close to the station, and the Christiania has individually designed bedrooms. The three-star Olden is family-run and cosy, as is the Posthotel Rössli, while Sporthotel Rutti is the most basic but has a high standard of food and is said to be good value. Most of the cheaper hotels are in the surrounding villages of Schönried and Saanenmöser. Some hotels can arrange babysitting and the Palace Hotel has a nursery.

Recommended restaurants include La Cave in the Hotel Olden and the sixteenth-century Chlösterli. The Bären at Gsteig offers traditional Swiss fare. Café du Cerf in Rougemont is a typical Swiss restaurant with live music at weekends. The Palace's Greengo nightclub is the main late-night venue for those who can afford it. The locals meet at Richi's. Other haunts include the Hotel Boo in Saanen, Club 95 at the Sporthotel Victoria and the Grotte in the Hotel Alpin Nova in Schönried.

TOURIST OFFICE
Tel: 41 33 748 8181
Fax: 41 33 748 8183
Email tvsl@gstaad.ch
Web site www.gstaad.ch

Kandersteg
top 1920m (6,299ft) bottom 1200m (3,937ft)

Kandersteg is a delightful village in the Bernese Oberland much favoured by langlaufers of all standards for its 75km of loipe. It also has attractive alpine skiing for beginners ('the perfect resort for our first-ever skiing holiday') and a ski school with a sound reputation. Mountain access is via a chair-lift to Oeschinen, where a couple of drag-lifts take you on up to a small assortment of blue (easy) and red (intermediate) runs. A cable-car outside the village also gives access to a drag-lift that serves two blue runs, as well as a long and more challenging descent to the valley. Hotels include the four-star Victoria ('wonderful food and lovely indoor swimming-pool'). Recommended restaurants include the Berestübli, the Alfa-Soleil, Au Vieux Chalet and the Bahnhof Buffet. Evening entertainment centres around the High Moon Pub and the hotel bars; Hotel Alpenblick provides folkloric dance displays.

TOURIST OFFICE
Tel 41 33 675 80 80
Fax 41 33 675 80 81

Lenzerheide-Valbella
top 2865m (9,397ft) bottom 1500m (4,920ft)

These two resorts used to attract a fair number of British families but in recent years they have decreased in popularity. The area has considerable charm, as well as magnificent cross-country skiing. The skiing is in two separate sectors, Rothorn and Danis/Stätzerhorn, on either side of the inconveniently wide pass. The skiing terrain in both is half wooded and half open. None of these pistes is particularly difficult, although the Rothorn cable-car opens up some off-piste skiing. A total of 37 lifts serve 150km of piste.

The villages of Lenzerheide and Valbella lie at either end of a lake in a wide, wooded pass with high mountains on either side. Transport is based on an efficient system of buses travelling clockwise and anti-clockwise. The main street of Lenzerheide has some attractive old buildings. Valbella has less identity; it is no more than a large community of hotels and concrete holiday homes crammed on to a hillside, but it is less of a roadside strip than Lenzerheide and gives direct access to the eastern and western ski areas.

TOURIST OFFICE
Tel 41 81 385 11 20
Fax 41 81 385 11 21

Saas-Fee
top 3600m (11,811ft) bottom 1800m (5,904ft)

Saas-Fee is a delightfully unspoilt and picturesque resort set against one of the most dramatic glacial backdrops in the Alps. Its narrow streets are lined with some 56 hotels interspersed with ancient barns and chalets of blackened wood. Designer ski shops stand beside working farmhouses where you can buy fresh milk by the pail, even in the centre of the village.

At this high altitude, snow cover is virtually guaranteed, and the long vertical drop of 1800m (5,904ft) provides a total of 100km of varied runs. However, these are few in number because the possible groomed area is severely limited by the 'active' glaciers. The risk of falling down crevasses is extreme for anyone foolish enough to stray beneath the ropes without a local guide.

Saas-Fee has been a pioneer in the development of hi-tech ski lifts, and the main mountain access is by the sophisticated Alpin Express cableway and the world's highest underground funicular system, the Metro Alpin. The area boasts 39 lifts including the smaller, separate areas at the nearby villages of **Saas-Almagell**, **Saas-Balen** and **Saas-Grund**.

Five drag-lifts at the bottom of the mountain are part of an excellent nursery slope complex flanked by a horseshoe of eight of the highest glaciers in Europe. The Swiss Ski and Snowboard School (SSS) in Saas-Fee is run both as a co-operative and a monopoly and suffers from poor organisation and overcrowding, especially during peak holiday periods. Weekend and afternoon group lessons are not available.

Snowboarding is big business here, and the SSS suffers fierce and healthy competition from the refreshingly radical Paradise Snowboard School. Possibilities for ski-touring are exceptional, and the separate mountain guide association, Bergsteigerschule Saastal, has an impressive programme of ski-tours.

Saas-Fee is traffic-free. On arrival you must leave your vehicle at the edge of the village in the car park, which costs SF13 for the first day and SF9 for each subsequent day. There are no buses, and electric taxis are not readily available. Where you stay is consequently of some importance if you want to avoid a long trek to the ski area. Recommended hotels include the Walliserhof and the Schweizerhof. The Burgener is a small, single-storey family hotel close to the lifts, and the four-star Saaserhof is also conveniently situated.

The Fletschorn Waldhotel is rated as one of Switzerland's better restaurants. The Hofsaal in the Schweizerhof is recommended for fish, and the Cheminée for flambées. The Crazy Night is the hippest techno après-ski venue. John's Pub, in the Metropol Hotel, tries for an English ambience. Rowdy drinking is frequent at Nesti's Ski Bar, the Go-Inn and the Why-Not pub. Recommended mountain restaurants include the rustic Berghaus Plattjen and the Gletschergrotte. The world's highest revolving restaurant at Mittelallalin was said to have 'the worst food at the highest prices'.

The SSS Pulvo ski kindergarten takes children from four years old for one-and-a-half hours on weekday afternoons only, and the regular ski school takes children from five years old for weekday mornings only. The Bären-Klub in the Hotel Garni Berghof offers all-day care for children from two-and-a-half to six years old.

TOURIST OFFICE
CH-3906 Saas-Fee, Valais
Tel 41 27 958 1858
Fax 41 27 958 1860
Email to@saas-fee.ch
Web site www.saas-fee.ch

Villars/Les Diablerets
top 2979m (9,744ft) bottom 1128m (3,700ft)

Villars, situated on a sunny balcony above the Ollon Valley, is reached either by a winding road or a quaint Edwardian mountain railway. It has a strong international following as a family resort. The impressive intermediate skiing is linked directly by a quad-chair with the neighbouring resort of Les Diablerets. Together, the two areas provide 120km of pistes, with two snowparks, served by 45 lifts. The Diablerets Glacier provides high-altitude, snowsure skiing but can get crowded when conditions are poor in nearby Villars and **Gstaad**.

The quickest access to the hub of the skiing in Villars is by gondola from the edge of town. A second gondola from the nearby village of **Barboleusaz** also feeds into the system. The nursery slope at Bretaye is gentle, and first-timers quickly graduate to a wide choice of blue runs. A new drag-lift connects Bretaye with Roc d'Orsay. A separate ski area, Isenau, offers easy but limited skiing.

The Swiss Ski School (SSS) in Villars is commended for its friendly instructors. The Modern Ski School uses the *ski évolutif* method of teaching beginners and also offers snowboarding and parapente. The Villars SSS children's classes are praised by reporters, and the Pré Fleurie ski kindergarten is said to be 'quite excellent'. Hotel Le Chamois in Diablerets runs a kindergarten for children aged from three to six years old.

The Lac des Chavonnes, above Villars, is one of the great Alpine restaurants tucked away in a delightful lakeside setting, and the Buffet Col de Soud is an attractive chalet with superb views of Les Diablerets Glacier. Hotel Bristol, in the town centre, has a comfortable and modern interior. Hotel du Cerf has 'home-style cooking'. Three-star Hotel Elite, next to the gondola, reopened in December 1997. The large Eurotel is an eyesore but contains 'spacious and clean apartments'. The three-star Hotel du Golf opposite the station is praised by reporters. La Crémaillère in Barboleusaz is a good-value option. Vieux Villars and Café Carnotzet specialise in fondue and raclette. Le Mazarin in the Grand Hotel du Parc is the smartest restaurant in town.

Les Diablerets is a sprawling village with mainly chalet accommodation. The few hotels seem out of place, but the overall atmosphere is relaxed. The Eurotel, Le Chamois and the Mon Abri hotels are recommended. Dining in Villars varies between a few good restaurants and informal stüblis, with the Auberge de la Poste and the Buvette du Pillon singled out for praise. Hotel Les Sources is said to be 'incredibly inconveniently located, but clean and friendly'. The nightlife in both Les Diablerets and Villars is quiet and centres around a few bars.

TOURIST OFFICES
Tel Villars: 41 24 495 32 32 Les Diablerets: 41 24 492 33 58
Fax Villars: 41 24 495 27 94 Les Diablerets: 41 24 492 23 48
Email Villars@pingnet.ch Les Diablerets: diablerets@bluewin.ch
Web site www.villars.ch Les Diablerets: www.alpes.ch/diablerets

North America

Canadian and US resorts now attract for over 20 per cent of the British ski market, and the number of skiers and snowboarders prepared to make the long journey across the Atlantic each winter continues to rise beyond all expectations. In recent years, flying to destinations in the American Rockies has been a protracted and frustrating business involving up to three changes of aircraft. However, this season a daily scheduled British Airways service to Denver has been introduced, along with the existing tour operators' weekly charter service. This should enormously improve access to the main Colorado resorts and even further increase their desirability. But for the present, the majority of British visitors continue to congregate in Banff/Lake Louise, which is served by bi-weekly charter flights to Calgary.

The favourable exchange rate of the pound against the Canadian dollar means that tour operators can offer holidays here at prices comparable to those of European destinations. However, we are frequently told by readers that their reasons for returning each winter are by no means based on price alone. They point out that even the most famous Alpine resorts fail to measure up to the expectations they now have after skiing in North America. As one reporter put it: 'If you take into account the warmth of the welcome, the standard of service and accommodation, the lower prices, the fact that English is the language spoken, and the overall cultural experience, then the enjoyment factor is greater'.

The first point to strike the European visitor is the smaller size of the average North American ski area. The second is that each North American resort is owned and operated by a single company. The result is a coordinated policy of keeping customers happy.

In general, the skiing is blander in North America (some might say homogenised) and nearly always consists of man-made trails cut through wooded slopes, their exotic names belying the similarity of those graded the same colour. It is important to note that Americans operate a different colour-coding system from that in Europe: green is easy, blue is intermediate, black is difficult, black-diamond is very difficult or advanced, and double-black-diamond is expert. The standard of piste-grooming and trail-marking, fuelled by the threat of skier litigation, is outstanding.

Off-piste, in the European sense, does not really exist. While a few major resorts permit vast tracts of mountainside to be left untouched by machines (calling it 'back-country' skiing), leaving the designated ski area is absolutely forbidden, and you face confiscation of your lift pass – or even arrest – if you do so. With the exception of chalet holidays, most packages to North America are offered on a room-only basis, and the extra cost of food and a more expensive lift pass, must be taken into consideration.

Aspen

ALTITUDE 7,945ft (2422m)

Beginners ✲✲ Intermediates ✲✲✲ Advanced ✲✲✲ Snowboarders ✲✲

Aspen still suffers from its dated image as Hollywood-on-ice, being more of a winter playground for the rich, the famous and the wannabees than a ski resort for serious skiers. Certainly it continues to attract a handful of big names in showbusiness and sport, some of whom, such as Jack Nicholson, Kevin Kostner, Martina Navratilova and Chris Evert, have made their homes here. What these celebrities have in common is that they are all fanatical skiers. Aspen has some of the best skiing in North America for all standards, from complete beginner to advanced.

- ✔ Excellent children's facilities
- ✔ Attractive Victorian town
- ✔ Wide choice of restaurants
- ✔ Ideal for non-skiers
- ✔ Lively nightlife
- ✘ Ski areas not linked
- ✘ High prices

The town's first claim to fame was as a silver-mining centre. The brave and sometimes desperate miners defied vicious weather and marauding Ute indians to set up their first rickety camp in Colorado's Roaring Fork Valley in the late 1870s. During the boom years Aspen's population reached 12,000, and the town was served by two railroads, six newspapers, three schools, ten churches and a notorious red-light district. But by 1893 it was all over; the silver market collapsed, and the town virtually died.

However, during the 1936 Winter Olympics at Garmisch-Partenkirchen, Theodore Ryan, a wealthy American, compared notes with the bob-sleigh champion William Fiske III about the need for good ski resorts in America. The following summer they were approached by an Aspen mine-owner, who was convinced that the snowfields of his home town would make an ideal setting for their plans. He was right. Fiske and Ryan encouraged other investors to help them develop the resort. War intervened, and when America joined the fighting, the US Army's 10th Mountain Division trained in Aspen. One of those troops was an Austrian, Friedl Pfeifer, and after the war he and Walter Paepcke, a Chicago industrialist, formed the Aspen Ski Company.

Ski and board
Aspen top 11,212ft (3418m) bottom 7,945ft (2422m)
Snowmass top 12,510ft (3813m) bottom 8,104ft (2470m)
Aspen Highlands top 11,675ft (3559m) bottom 8,040ft (2451m)
Buttermilk top 9,900ft (3018m) bottom 7,870ft (2399m)
Aspen has four completely separate mountains: **Aspen Mountain**, which

is also known as Ajax (a name taken from an old mining claim); **Aspen Highlands**; **Buttermilk**; and **Snowmass**, 12 miles (19km) out of town which now boasts the longest vertical drop in the USA. Aspen Mountain is strictly the reserve of good skiers and has no beginner slopes. Anyone less than a strong intermediate will struggle to cope with the home-run gradient here, although there are less demanding trails. Buttermilk is ideal beginners' and children's terrain, with no hidden surprises but plenty of variety for novices. Snowmass, which has skiing for all levels, is the furthest of the separate ski areas from Aspen and is a resort in its own right under the same ownership. Aspen Highlands has the toughest, most radical terrain and greatly adds to Aspen's appeal for advanced skiers.

> **WHAT'S NEW**
>
> New lifts on Aspen Mountain and at Snowmass

The four mountains are linked by ski bus. A useful extra is the equipment transfer – at the end of the day you can have your skis or snowboard and boots taken from any of the ski areas to another for $2, and they will be waiting for you the next morning. Snowboarding is not permitted on Aspen Mountain, but the other three mountains encourage it.

Beginners

Buttermilk is one of North America's best mountains for beginners, and Snowmass also has excellent novice slopes. The area below Buttermilk's West Summit is packed with green (easy) runs like Westward Ho and Homestead Road, and more advanced beginners will thrive on a large network of long blue (intermediate) runs with an impressive vertical drop of more than 1,800ft (549m). The nursery slopes at Snowmass hug the lower slopes and most are accessed by the Fanny Hill high-speed quad. At Aspen Highlands the main nursery slopes, such as Apple Strudel, Riverside Drive and Nugget, are concentrated mid-mountain and are reached most quickly by the Exhibition quad-chair. The Skiwee lift at the base also serves a small beginner area.

Intermediates

Of Aspen's four mountains, Snowmass has the largest intermediate appeal. Almost every run mid-mountain and below provides good cruising, and the region below Elk Camp at the far perimeter of the ski area (with runs like Bull Run, Grey Wolf and Bear Bottom) is another popular intermediate haunt. Snowmass is famous for its Big Burn area, where a clutch of blue trails separated by a few trees provide almost unlimited scope for cruising. Although the runs have individual names (Whispering Jesse, Timberline, Wineskin, Mick's Gully, etc), the Big Burn is effectively one huge intermediate trail as much as a mile wide in places.

Plenty of strong intermediate skiing with top-to-bottom cruising is to be found on Aspen Mountain. Straying on to more difficult terrain by mistake is less likely here than at many resorts; most of the black (difficult) runs tend to be hidden away from the main slopes. The best area for middling skiers at Highlands is near the top of the mountain,

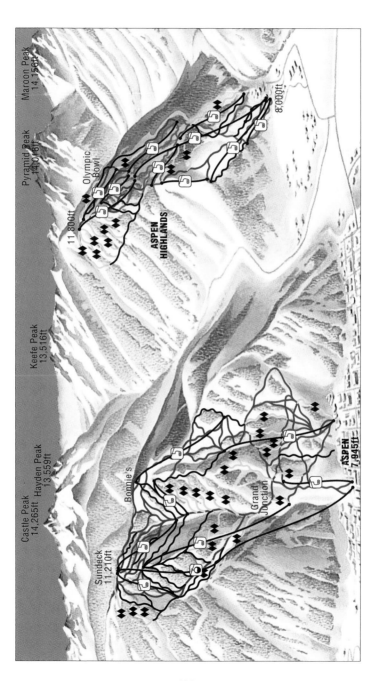

Maroon Peak
14,156ft

Pyramid Peak
14,018ft

Keefe Peak
13,516ft

Castle Peak
14,265ft

Hayden Peak
13,559ft

Olympic
Bowl

8,000ft

11,800ft

ASPEN
HIGHLANDS

Bonnie's

Sundeck
11,210ft

Grand
Junction

ASPEN
7,945ft

where the Cloud Nine lift accesses runs such as Scarlett's, Grand Prix and Gunbarrel. Golden Horn and Thunderbowl offer enjoyable cruising. All of Buttermilk is suitable for intermediates, but the lack of challenging runs means that stronger skiers will quickly become bored.

Advanced

Aspen Mountain is riddled with short, sharp and quite steep double-black-diamond (advanced) chutes, including the famous 'dump runs' like Bear Paw, Short Snort and Zaugg Dump, which were created by miners throwing out spoil as they were tunnelling their way into Aspen Mountain. Walsh's is considered to be the most challenging. Bell Mountain, a peak that juts out from Ajax, looking as if it has been stuck on, provides excellent opportunities for mogul skiers with its variety of individual faces, including Face of Bell, Shoulder of Bell and Back of Bell.

Much of the skiing at Aspen Highlands falls into the advanced category. The large and challenging gladed area to the left of the Exhibition quad-chair includes Bob's Glade, Upper Stein and Golden Horn Woods, which are all double-black-diamond trails. At Snowmass, real challenges are to be found in the largely gladed chutes in the Hanging Valley Wall and Hanging Valley Glades, and The Cirque has even steeper terrain mainly above the tree-line; access to these runs is on the new Cirque lift. Buttermilk has a funpark off Spruce Trail. Highlands has enough double-black-diamond trails to suit experienced riders, while Snowmass caters for all levels.

Off-piste

Aspen Highlands has some of the most exhilarating off-piste terrain in the valley, much of it accessed by the Loge Peak quad-chair at the top of the ski area. The chair follows a ridge with steep terrain on both sides. As you ride up, a dramatic area known as Steeplechase opens up on your left; this comprises about half-a-dozen steep chutes. On your right is even steeper terrain in Olympic Bowl, although the gradient is not always fully appreciable until you have progressed some way down the slopes. Deception is aptly named; it starts off at a fairly moderate pitch, but the further down you ski, the steeper it becomes.

Snowboarders are not allowed in the ski area but excellent riding and skiing can be accessed by snowcat off the back through Aspen Mountain Powder Tours.

Tuition and guiding

As well as traditional lessons, the Aspen Ski School offers Discover Aspen and Snowmass, and Master the Mountains courses, which all include accommodation, lift tickets and lessons. Ski Ambassadors are based on all four mountains to give free mountain tours at 10am and at 1.30pm.

Aspen Highlands offers the graduated-length method (GLM), which is similar to the French ski évolutif instruction, as well as race and telemark clinics and extreme terrain lessons. Snowmass Ski School

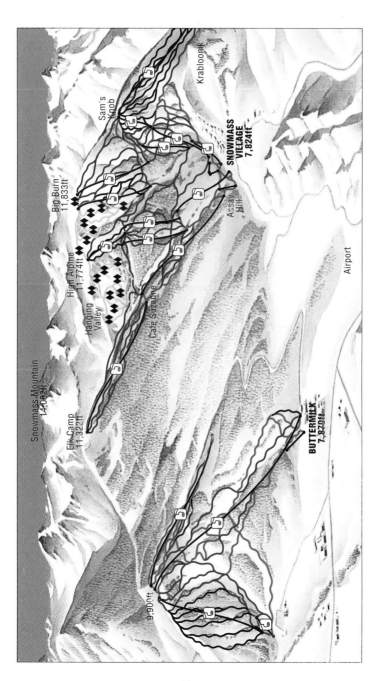

Krabloonik

SNOWMASS VILLAGE
7,824ft

Sam's Knob

Big Burn
11,833ft

Assay Hill

Airport

High Alpine
11,774ft

Hanging Valley

Café Suzanne

Snowmass Mountain
14,092ft

Elk Camp
11,322ft

9,900ft

BUTTERMILK
7,870ft

offers special bumps, powder, telemark and racing programmes. At Buttermilk it is claimed: 'We guarantee you will be able to ski from the top to the bottom by the third day!'

Three-day First Time on Snowboard lessons are available at Aspen Highlands, and Snowmass has special snowboard clinics.

Mountain restaurants

Only in Aspen could you find no less than three mountain restaurants – The Sundeck on Aspen Mountain, Bumps at Buttermilk, Gwyn's High Alpine at Snowmass – where you can have a massage along with your lunch – at $1 a minute. All of them are good for eating as well as relaxing. The fourth altitude restaurant at Aspen Mountain is Bonnie's ('an intimate place with superb strudel and hot apple dumplings'). La Baità, at the bottom of Ruthie's and Roch Run, has wait-service and specialises in Italian food. At the base of the Silver Queen gondola the Ajax Tavern serves Mediterranean food.

Snowmass has six restaurants including Up 4 Pizza at the top of the Big Burn lift, which is warmly praised. Ullrhof, at the bottom of the same lift serves 'a hearty skier's breakfast, and has a wood-burning stove and sun-deck'. Sam's Knob restaurant and cafeteria also feature home cooking, including soups, pizzas, pasta and fish. The Café Suzanne, at the bottom of the Elk Camp lift, features a southern French menu, and Krabloonik, near the Campground parking lot, specialises in smoked meats and wild game.

At Aspen Highlands, the Merry Go Round Restaurant at mid-mountain offers home-made soups, chilli and burgers. The Highlands Café is another breakfast and lunch spot at the base. Buttermilk boasts three mountain restaurants: the Café West near the bottom of Lift 3, which is designed in the style of a French café; Bump's, at the base, includes a rotisserie and grill; the Cliffhouse, at the top of the Summit Express, has food indoors and outdoors along with some of the best scenery on the mountain.

The resorts

The town is situated at the foot of Aspen Mountain and has about 200 appealing shops and a large variety of restaurants. Planners have managed to conserve the low-rise appeal of the original Victorian mining town; the older buildings have been authentically refurbished, and recent additions are in sympathetic style. Although considerably larger than most US ski resorts, the centre is relatively compact, and outlying hotels and the ski areas are served by a highly efficient bus service. Celebrity status attracts higher prices, and day-to-day living in Aspen is more expensive than in any of its Colorado counterparts. However, with a little care in your choice of restaurants and nightlife it is still possible to have a moderately priced holiday.

Snowmass is an alternative and cheaper accommodation base, but having come so far it seems a pity not to fully partake of Aspen's greater facilities. Aspen has its own airport, served by flights from Denver, which must at all times be booked. Eagle County Airport has direct flights from a number of hub cities.

Accommodation

In Aspen, skiers who can afford to live like celebrities should try the Little Nell and the Luxury Collection, although many people's favourite is the historic Hotel Jerome. Those on limited budgets can try one of the numerous modestly priced lodges such as the Limelite, the Alpine and the Christiania. The Christmas Inn, the Snow Queen and the Innsbruck Inn are all recommended. The Aspen Bed and Breakfast is a little more expensive but is also praised.

Top-of-the-range accommodation at Snowmass includes the Silvertree, the Snowmass Lodge and Club, the Chamonix and Crestwood. More reasonably priced are the Snowmass Mountain Chalet, the Stonebridge Inn and Shadowbrooks.

For those counting their cents, the Pokolodi Lodge and the Snowmass Inn are both close to the slopes, as are the Aspenwood and Laurelwood condominiums. The so-called Inn at Aspen (really at Buttermilk) has mid-range prices.

Eating in and out

Aspen has a huge variety of restaurants, with almost every type of cuisine imaginable. Bentley's is a Victorian-style pub and restaurant at the Wheeler Opera House, featuring American food and a selection of 35 beers from around the world. The Jerome provides excellent fare at its Century Room. The Chart House on East Durant is well known for steaks and seafood. L'Hostaria is an authentic Italian restaurant. Wabi Sabi serves Thai, Vietnamese and Pacific Rim cuisine. Farfalla's, on East Main Street, is another fashionable restaurant, which specialises in Italian cooking.

Pacifica has a fine selection of seafood and a caviar menu. Poppies Bistro Café has 'Victorian charm', while the Red Onion on East Cooper serves food at more modest prices. Aspen has three Japanese restaurants – Kenichi, Takah Sushi and Matsuhisa, plus a Japanese take-away (Sushi Ya Go-Go). Baang Café has a mixture of Asian cuisine. The Hard Rock Café and Planet Hollywood chains both have restaurants here.

Après-ski

Aspen has wall-to-wall après-ski in dozens of nightspots. The Jerome Bar (better known as the J-Bar), where miners once congregated to celebrate when they struck silver, is always lively. The sun-deck at the Ajax Tavern attracts the crowds at the bottom of Ajax when the lifts close. Shooters is a Country-and-Western saloon with live bands. The Howling Wolf is a late-night coffee bar. Aspen Billards is casually elegant and smoke-free. The Cigar Bar has fine liqueurs and cigars. The Caribou Club is a smart members-only establishment.

Skiing facts: Aspen

TOURIST OFFICE
425 Rio Grande Place, 81611 Aspen,
C081611
Tel 1 970 925 1940
Fax 1 970 920 1173
Email acra@aspeninfo.com
Web site www.aspen.com
(and) skiaspen.com

THE RESORT
Airport transfer Eagle County 1¼hrs,
Aspen 10mins
Visitor beds 16,000 in area
Transport shuttle bus between all 4
mountains (daytime free)

THE SKIING
Linked or nearby resorts Snowmass (n)
Longest run Big Burn to Fanny Hill at
Snowmass, 4.1 miles (7km) – blue
Number of lifts 41 in area
Total of trails/pistes 4,416 acres
(1787 hectares) – 16% easy,
40% intermediate, 24% difficult,
20% expert (4 mountains)
Nursery slopes 3 slopes and
5 beginner lifts (Snowmass 4,
Buttermilk 1)
Summer skiing none
Snowmaking 558 acres (226 hectares)
over 4 mountains

LIFT PASSES
Area pass (covers all 4 mountains)
$304 for 6 days
Day pass $59
Beginners no reduction
Pensioners 65–69yrs, $192 for 6 days,
free for 70yrs and over
Credit cards yes

TUITION
Adults All four mountains,
10/10.15am–3.15/3.30pm,
from $149 for 3 x 5hrs
Private lessons $285 for 3hrs
Snowboarding as regular ski school
Cross-country Snowmass Club Touring
Center, $30 per day, private lessons
$45 per hr. Loipe 80km
Other courses Nastar racing,
moguls, telemark, dynamic stunts,
women's ski seminars
Guiding Aspen Mountain Powder Tours

CHILDREN
Lift pass 7–12yrs, $35 per day, free for
6yrs and under
Ski kindergarten Snow Puppies at
Highlands, 3½–6yrs, 9.30am–3.30pm,
$75 per day. Powder Pandas at
Buttermilk, 3–6yrs, Bears and Grizzlies
at Snowmass, 3½–6yrs, both
8.30am–4pm, $370 for 5 days
Ski school Buttermilk, Snowmass and
Highlands, 7–12yrs $289 for 5 days,
13–19yrs $174 for 3 days, both
9.30am–3.15pm
Non-ski kindergarten Kid's Club at
Aspen, 12mths–3yrs, $315 for 40hrs,
Snow Cubs at Snowmass, 6wks–3½yrs,
8.30am–4pm, $370 for 5 days

OTHER SPORTS
Climbing-wall, hang-gliding, helicopter
rides, indoor tennis, parapente, skating,
snowmobiling, snowshoeing, swimming

FOOD AND DRINK PRICES
Coffee $2, glass of wine $5, small beer
$3.50, dish of the day $10–15

Childcare

Aspen has an in-town nursery service and a nursery ski-school programme in each resort. At Snowmass, Snow Cubs caters for children aged between six weeks and three years. Older children can join the Big Burn Bears. Snowmass also runs a series of Kid's Ski Weeks. The Powder Pandas Ski School is at Buttermilk. Parents register their children at Aspen Mountain, and the Max the Moose Express brings them to Buttermilk, where they can take part in The Brave Good Eagle Great Feather Chase and the Max the Moose Challenge race.

Banff/Lake Louise

Beginners ✱✱ Intermediates ✱✱✱ Advanced ✱✱ Snowboarders ✱✱

Banff is the most popular destination in North America for British skiers. Last winter an estimated 25,000 made the journey to this remote and beautiful corner of Alberta, and no doubt it came as a surprise to many of them to discover that Banff is not a ski resort at all. Instead it is an attractive little town in the Banff National Park, which each summer plays host to four million tourists, and each winter acts as the main accommodation base for three small (by European standards) ski areas up to 35 miles (56km) apart as well as a sprinkling of smaller ski areas. Anyone expecting to find hundreds of kilometres of linked skiing on the scale of the Trois Vallées or L'Espace Killy is in for a disappointment. However, the region does have sufficient skiing to keep most skiers happy for a ten-day holiday, and even the most jaded of powderhounds could not fail to be impressed by the scenery and the lack of blatant commercialisation.

- ✔ Spectacular scenery
- ✔ Reliable snow record
- ✔ Long skiing season
- ✔ Extensive children's facilities
- ✔ Few queues
- ✗ Strung-out resorts
- ✗ Extremely low temperatures
- ✗ Lack of slopeside lodging

Just eight years ago the shopkeepers and restaurant owners of Banff were lucky if 400 British skiers passed through their portals in an entire season. Now, charter flights from London and Manchester bring up to 1,000 skiers a week for bargain-priced skiing amid spectacular scenery. However, one reporter warned: 'There seems to be a high proportion of the 'ere-we-go type of British skier. I certainly didn't fly half-way around the world to ride a chair-lift with two louts swearing about Tottenham and Arsenal'. Fellow skiers apart, the nine-hour flight, two-hour transfer and seven-hour time difference have to be taken into consideration, and it really requires a visit of at least ten days to adjust and relax fully in such unfamiliar surroundings.

The area has reliable snow conditions, but temperatures on the mountain can be extreme, falling to as low as −40°C for three or four weeks between December and mid-February. The daytime average in the valley at Banff is −7°C in January.

Lake Louise, 39 miles (63km) from Banff, is by far the most important of the three ski areas. **Mount Norquay**, the closest, is the smallest, while **Sunshine Village**, 10 miles (16km) away, has good skiing for all standards. A free and rather slow bus service links Banff with the three resorts, but a car is a real asset. The distances are such that it is not really worth trying to ski more than one area in a day. Rivalry between the three

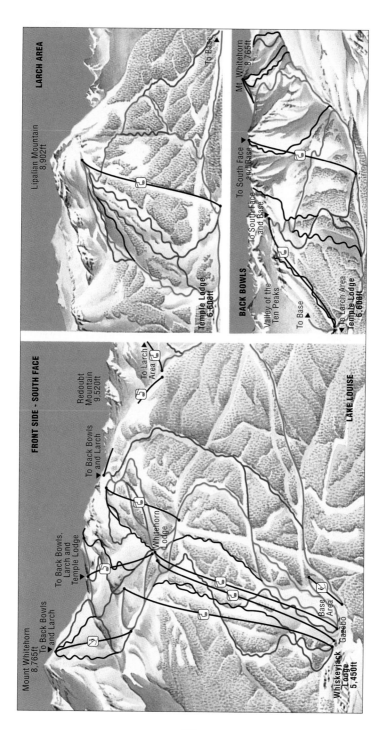

LARCH AREA

Lipalian Mountain
8,902ft

To Base

Temple Lodge
6,608ft

BACK BOWLS

Mt Whitehorn
8,765ft

To South Face and Base

To South Face and Base

Valley of the Ten Peaks

To Base

To Larch Area
Temple Lodge
6,608ft

FRONT SIDE - SOUTH FACE

Mount Whitehorn
8,765ft
To Back Bowls and Larch

To Back Bowls, Larch and Temple Lodge

To Back Bowls and Larch

Redoubt Mountain
9,520ft

To Larch Area

Whitehorn Lodge

LAKE LOUISE

Base Area

Gazebo

Whiskeyjack Lodge
5,450ft

has resulted in considerable discounts and incentives being offered to catch your custom. Reporters recommend taking time out to visit **Nakiska**, a small ski area situated a one-hour drive from Banff. It was the site of the men's downhill at the Calgary Olympics in 1988: 'beautiful runs planned by computer, immaculately groomed and virtually deserted'. **Fortress Mountain**, a further 30 minutes by bus from Banff, is dramatically positioned at the foot of sheer, granite cliffs. Skiing here is a more primitive experience and it is particularly popular with riders. In the right conditions, some excellent off-piste can be accessed by snowcat.

Ski and board
top 8,954ft (2730m) bottom 5,350ft (1631m)

Lake Louise itself is the furthest from Banff but has easily the largest and most varied ski area. The skiing begins three miles (5km) from the tiny village of Lake Louise; its 11 lifts attract the majority of daily skiers, who make the bus journey from Banff. Importantly, Lake Louise boasts that every difficult run is matched by an easy one, allowing families and groups of mixed ability to ski together. From the Mount Whitehorn base at Whiskyjack Lodge, the choice of three chair-lifts includes the Friendly Giant Express quad, which takes skiers to mid-mountain at Whitehorn Lodge. From here the Top of The World Express is another high-speed quad, providing the fastest way up and over to the Back Bowls or down to Mount Lipalian's Larch area. The four faces of Whitehorn and Lipalian share some 4,000 acres (1619 hectares) of terrain.

WHAT'S NEW
Additional quad-chair at Sunshine

Sunshine Village is the highest of the three resorts and has predominantly medium-length, moderately steep, intermediate terrain above the tree-line. Despite its name, sunshine is not guaranteed and it can be a bleak and cold place on a grey day. The addition of Goat's Eye Mountain has virtually doubled the size of the ski area and provides more advanced terrain. Mount Norquay is four miles (6km) from Banff and is mainly a beginner area. However, the development of Mystic Ridge has given it more intermediate appeal.

Beginners

Because of Lake Louise's policy of ensuring an easy way down from each major lift, novices can share the pleasure of roaming the mountain almost at will. Although riding high-speed quads could seem daunting in other resorts, here you can board them confidently and meander down the green (easy) Saddleback and Pika trails to the Larch chair. This leads to runs like Marmot and Look-out before returning to the main base via Eagle Meadows. Alternatively, you can warm up on the Sunny T-bar and try skiing the long but gentle Wiwaxy trail, although one reporter warned this can be intimidating when very crowded. Cameron Way is a new parallel run, which should ease this congestion.

At Sunshine, the best choice of novice runs is served by the Wheeler double chair-lift from the Gondola mid-station. The Strawberry triple-chair and the Standish double-chair also give access to gentle terrain. A long, green trail starts from the top of Lookout Mountain, but in all cases beginners need to take care not to stray accidentally on to neighbouring black (difficult) runs. Beginners at Norquay are recommended to ski the runs off the Cascade chair, or the Sundance tow.

Intermediates

At Lake Louise, intermediates can clock up huge mileage over all the terrain, with the possible exception of some of the steeper bowls. Skyline is a steepish blue (intermediate) from the high point of the ski area. Larch is a wide, fast-cruising blue. Stronger skiers will want to sample the black-diamond (difficult) Ridge Run and Whitehorn One on the Back Bowls side. Most of the runs at Sunshine are within the grasp of intermediates. Nearly all of the Mystic Ridge trails were specifically created for skiers of medium experience.

Advanced

At Lake Louise, the Front Face has challenging men's and women's downhill runs. Other tough black-diamond pistes – Outer Limits, Sunset and the Flight Chutes – start higher up. Ptarmigan and Raven are testing glade runs on the Back Bowls side, and Exhibition has the additional challenge of exposing skiers to the gaze of people riding the Ptarmigan chair. Whitehorn 1 is steep and usually holds the snow. Lynx is the one advanced trail (the others are off-piste) in the Larch area. Fall Line Glades, a 100-acre (40-hectare) area between Exhibition and Ptarmigan provides some of the best tree-skiing in this part of Canada. The funpark is accessed from the top of the Olympic chair. Lone Pine, which is fiercely steep and mogulled, is the big challenge at Norquay. At Sunshine, runs like Little Angel, Ecstasy and Big Angel offer steep chute skiing from the top of Lookout Mountain. Goat's Eye Mountain has a number of long and tricky runs including Hell's Kitchen and Freefall, as well as the Wild Side and the Far Side at the top of the ski area.

Off-piste

Large areas of the Back Bowls at Lake Louise are permanently closed because of avalanche danger. These are well marked, but sometimes bowls that are normally skiable can be closed too. Paradise Bowl and East Bowl provide challenging off-piste skiing. Serious powder skiers who do not mind a hike claim Purple Bowl provides the best fresh tracks on the mountain. Some of the most rewarding tree-skiing can be found between the upper parts of the Larch chair and the Bobcat run below. Goat's Eye Mountain has some excellent untracked terrain.

Tuition and guiding

Lake Louise offers a special package for beginners, which includes equipment rental, a beginner area lift ticket and a half-price pass valid for

Skiing facts: Banff/Lake Louise

TOURIST OFFICE
Ski Banff/Lake Louise
PO Box 1085, Banff, Alberta
Tel 1 403 762 4561
Fax 1 403 762 8185
Email info@skibanfflakelouise.com
Web site www.skibanfflakelouise.com

THE RESORT
Airport transfer Calgary Airport 1½hrs
Visitor beds Banff 9,920,
Lake Louise 2,400
Transport ski buses from hotels to
all 3 ski areas

THE SKIING
Linked or nearby resorts Sunshine
Village (n), Mount Norquay (n)
Longest run Lake Louise, 5 miles
(8km) – blue
Number of lifts 11 at Lake Louise, 12 at
Sunshine Village, 5 at Mount Norquay
Total of trails/pistes 62 miles (100km)
at Lake Louise, 52 miles (83km) at
Sunshine Village, 10 miles (16km) at
Mount Norquay (area: 19% easy, 47%
intermediate, 34% difficult)
Nursery slopes 1 tow-rope at
Lake Louise
Summer skiing none
Snowmaking 1,600 acres (648
hectares) at Lake Louise

LIFT PASSES
Area pass CDN$303 for 6 days
Day pass Lake Louise CDN$45, Sunshine
Village CDN$45, Mount Norquay CDN$33
Beginners tow-passes available
Pensioners Lake Louise and Sunshine
Village, 65yrs and over, CDN$37 per day.
Mount Norquay, 55yrs and over,
CDN$28 per day
Credit cards yes

TUITION
Adults CDN$144 for 3 days, times vary
between areas
Private lessons CDN$65 per hr
Snowboarding group lessons only
available with Club Ski Program,
CDN$38 for 3hrs, private lessons,
CDN$39 per hr, CDN$134 for
3 days (9hrs)
Cross-country private lessons only,
CDN$20 for 1¼ hrs or $55 for
half-day. Loipe 56km
Other courses heli-skiing, telemark,
moguls, race training
Guiding Yamnuska Mountain Ski School

CHILDREN
Lift pass 6–12yrs, CDN$111 for 6 days,
reductions for 13–17yrs, free for
5yrs and under
Ski kindergarten Lake Louise Kinderski,
3–6yrs, 9am–4pm, CDN$31 per day
Ski school Lake Louise, 7–12yrs,
CDN$39 per day including lunch,
Club Ski program (all areas), 6–12yrs,
details on request, teen ski, 13–19yrs,
CDN$39 per day
Non-ski kindergarten Lake Louise,
3wks–18mths, 8am–4.30pm, CDN$21
per day, Sunshine, 19mths–6yrs,
8am–4.30pm, CDN$3.75 per hr.
Norquay 19mths–6yrs, 9am–4pm
$22–32 per day

OTHER SPORTS
Broomball, dog-sledding, ice-fishing,
skating, sleigh rides, snowmobiling,
snow volleyball, swimming

FOOD AND DRINK PRICES
Coffee CDN$1.25, glass of wine
CDN$4.00, small beer CDN$3.50,
dish of the day CDN$9.00

all areas for the following day, as well as a ski lesson. Instruction at Sunshine is said to be 'friendly and positive'. The Club Ski and Snowboard programme enables skiers to stay with one instructor for three hours a day, visiting all three areas. All the resorts offer a free piste-guiding service, and Yamnuska Mountain Ski School organises guided off-piste skiing.

Mountain restaurants

Whiskyjack at the main Lake Louise base has been entirely rebuilt. The self-service is described as 'still dire, but the food is OK'. The wait-service section upstairs is unanimously praised. Nearby Beavertails is 'pleasantly unpretentious'. Another reporter recommended taking the free bus down to Chateau Lake Louise ('a longer lunch break but the deli is great value'). At Sunshine Village, Mad Trapper's Saloon has 'Tex-Mex, good beer, good atmosphere and unlimited free peanuts'. Norquay's new lodge, rebuilt after a fire, contains the Lone Pine Pub, a cafeteria and a delicatessen.

The resorts

'Banff is an ordinary little tourist resort in mountainous country, with hills and a stream and snow-peaks beyond,' wrote the First World War poet Rupert Brooke a year before his death, 'but Lake Louise – Lake Louise is of another world'. Little has changed. Banff is a small, attractive community with a frontier-town atmosphere, just 10 miles (16km) inside Banff National Park. Apart from the breathtaking scenery, the town is famous for its railway history and wildlife. It is quite common to see elk grazing on vegetation protruding through the snow, or even rummaging through dustbins. 'In 39 miles (62km) on the back road from Lake Louise to Banff we saw just two other cars and were halted by a traffic jam caused by a family of elk crossing'. Banff has a wide variety of shopping and dining opportunities.

After Canadian Pacific Railways started bringing tourists here to marvel at the scenery, the company built the neo-Gothic Banff Springs Hotel in 1888 and promptly looked for a second site. It found it in a dramatic glacial setting at Lake Louise. The magnificent Chateau Lake Louise, Canada's most celebrated hotel, opened its doors in 1890. Lake Louise remains no more than a railway halt; the shopping mall barely constitutes a village. Sunshine Village is simply a ski area with nominal accommodation up the mountain and nothing but a snack bar at the bottom.

Accommodation

Unfortunately, not everyone has the budget to stay at the two Canadian Pacific hotels. Winter rates are considerably lower than those in summer, but these have inevitably risen because of the increase in the resort's global popularity in recent years. However, there is plenty of choice elsewhere. In Lake Louise, the Post Hotel and Deer Lodge are both recommended. In Banff, the Mount Royal is conveniently located on Banff

Avenue. The King Edward, the town's original hotel, has been completely modernised and is 'surprisingly quiet, with extremely helpful staff'. Caribou Lodge is also recommended, along with the Inns of Banff. Siding 29 Lodge is described as 'a no-frills hotel with large comfortable rooms and a heated underground car park'. Rundle Manor apartments are 'spacious, comfortable, and cheap'. Norquay has no lodging of its own, and the only on-mountain accommodation at Sunshine is the Sunshine Inn.

Eating in and out

Banff has a surprisingly wide range of restaurants serving cuisine from at least a dozen countries. 'If you haven't been to Bumper's, you haven't been to Banff', is the motto of Bumper's Beef House. Joe Btfsplk's Diner looks like a misprint but serves 'meals like Mom used to make', including apple pie. Silver Dragon is Chinese, while Sukiyaki House is one of six Japanese restaurants. El Toro is a Greek restaurant despite its Spanish-sounding name; similarly, the Magpie and Stump is not an English pub but a Mexican cantina. Guido's Spaghetti Factory is long established and has 'good-value Italian food at reasonable prices, so don't be put off by the tatty entrance'. The Barbary Coast has 'plenty of atmosphere and a wide range of dishes including vegetarian options'. Melissa's serves fish steaks and 'potent home-brewed ale'. Caboose Steak and Lobster at the railway depot is 'superb in every way'. The Post Hotel is 'Canadian fine dining at its finest'. In Lake Louise, The Station, which was used as a location for *Dr Zhivago*, is warmly recommended.

Après-ski

One reader described Banff's nightlife as 'refreshingly unsophisticated, plenty of cowboy bars and line dancing'. Another said it reminded him of Söll in his youth: 'After dinner the streets get busy with Brits and Germans noisily moving from bar to bar'. There is rock 'n' roll at Eddy's Back Alley, country-rock at Wild Bill's, blues at The Barbary Coast, live entertainment at Bumper's, and live bands at the Silver City Beverage Co. The Caboose has karaoke. The Rose and Crown is one of Banff's most popular bars. Constables and the Mount Royal have 'pitchers of beer and lots of atmosphere'. Après-ski at Lake Louise is largely confined to drinking in the Glacier Saloon at the Chateau. Charlie Two's Pub and the Outpost in the Post Hotel are the alternatives.

Childcare

This is a great place for kids if your children can stand the low temperatures ('I saw an eight-year-old crying with cold at Sunshine Village'). At Lake Louise, the nursery takes babies from newborn. The Kinderski programme is geared for three to six year olds. There is also a Club Ski programme where children are guided around the mountain with instruction along the way. At Sunshine Village, the kindergarten takes toddlers from 19 months. Young Devils provides tuition and care for children aged 6 to 12 years old. Mount Norquay also has a crèche.

Breckenridge

ALTITUDE 9,600ft (2927m)

Beginners ✱✱✱ Intermediates ✱✱✱ Advanced ✱ Snowboarders ✱✱✱

Breckenridge was the beachhead for the British skiers' invasion of America in the 1980s. In the heart of the Rockies and boasting the infrastructure of a small city as well as the restored charm of an old mining 'boom town', Breckenridge remains a leader in the evolution of American skiing and snowboarding; it was the first resort in Colorado to permit boarders and has won America's top prize for its snowpark. These days it is under the same ownership as Vail/Beaver Creek, which has also acquired Keystone – consequently it has benefited from the huge sums ($74 million last season) that Vail Resorts is prepared to invest in its portfolio of resorts.

✔ Good base for skiing other resorts
✔ Attractive town centre
✔ Choice of dining and après-ski
✔ Range of ski school courses
✔ Reliable snow record
✘ Persistent overcrowding
✘ Poor mountain connections
✘ High altitude can cause sickness
✘ Skiing exposed to weather

The four resorts share a lift pass (if purchased for three or more days and with various restrictions) and are served by a heavily subsidised shuttle bus. Nearby **Copper Mountain** and **Arapahoe Basin** were not included in the buy-out but provide alternative skiing if you can find the time.

Breckenridge was the first resort in the world to install a high-speed detachable quad chair-lift (it now has six) and has responded to demands from American skiers for more 'European-style off-piste terrain' by opening huge, above-tree-line bowl areas to skiers – who must prove their stamina and determination to ski such steeps by first walking uphill, which is not easy at this height. Long criticised for its unchallenging intermediate terrain, the resort now successfully exploits its high altitude and ample natural snow to attract hard-core snowboarders and telemark skiers, as well as the spoilt-for-choice Denver market, who arrive by the thousands with each substantial snowfall. Getting from one peak to another involves tiresome and complicated traverses.

Skiing began here in 1961, on Peak 8, and expanded a decade later to Peak 9; Peak 10 opened in 1985, and Peak 7 in 1993. A total of 14 chair-lifts and five drag-lifts carry 28,600 skiers per hour to 138 well-manicured pistes and half-a-dozen wilderness bowls spread across 2,031 acres (822 hectares). Complaints about both the early closing of the pistes (3.45pm) and overcrowding in town and on the mountain are common. Easily accessed bowls and chutes make Breckenridge hugely popular with boarders, who voted the resort's snowpark and half-pipes the best in North America. Away from groomed runs, boarders vastly outnumber skiers, especially on powder days.

Ski and board
top 12,998ft (3962m) bottom 9,600ft (2927m)

Breckenridge's skiing – exceptionally high-altitude by Alpine standards – fans out above the town from left to right across four awkwardly inter-connected mountains, numbered from 7 to 10, in the Ten Mile Range of the Rockies. Most skiing faces roughly north, exposed to weather that gives the resort its nickname 'Breckenwind'. Skiing is mostly below tree level, and Peaks 7 and 8 require 30- to 60-minute climbs to reach their summits. Peaks 8 (intermediate to expert) and 9 (beginner to intermedi-ate) account for most of the resort's groomed skiing, sharing about the same lift capacity and number of runs, though Peak 8 has double the amount of skiing terrain. Peak 10 has only one lift, and Peak 7 has no lifts whatsoever. Actual skiing and snowboarding experiences range from the tedious, though scenically forested, flats at the resort base to steeps and deeps in the ample chutes above tree level – as good as any-thing in the Alps – on Peaks 7 and 8.

Beginners

Advanced snow-user's dismay is beginner's luck: vast tracts of the lower slopes are as flat as a pancake. At least half of Peak 9 is beginner terrain, with strictly enforced slow-skiing zones. On Peak 8, chairs 5 and 7 access half-a-dozen beginner runs effectively barred to faster skiers. All this beginner terrain is beautifully dot-ted with widely spaced trees.

WHAT'S NEW

2 additional quad chair-lifts
50% increase of snowmaking on Peak 8
Drag-lift on Peak 8
2 'magic carpet' lifts for children
Funpark improvements
New restaurant between Peaks 9 and 10

Intermediates

Peak 9 is medium-standard cruising, marked as blue (intermediate) and green (easy) from top to bottom. There is an intermediate way down from everywhere except for the Peak 8 T-bar. Union connects Peak 10 to Peak 9, and subsequently Peak 8, from the top. Four O'Clock and Lehman are long, easy ways home from Peaks 8 and 9 respectively.

Advanced

The best advanced skiing in Breckenridge is accessed from Chair 6 and the Peak 8 T-bar, both of which offer skiing above 3500m. From the T-bar to the skier's right are six black (difficult) runs in the North Bowl area. To the skier's left, just past the warming hut, are Horseshoe, Contest and Cucumber bowls, all marked double-black-diamond (very difficult) but all wide open and less than threatening. A dozen marked

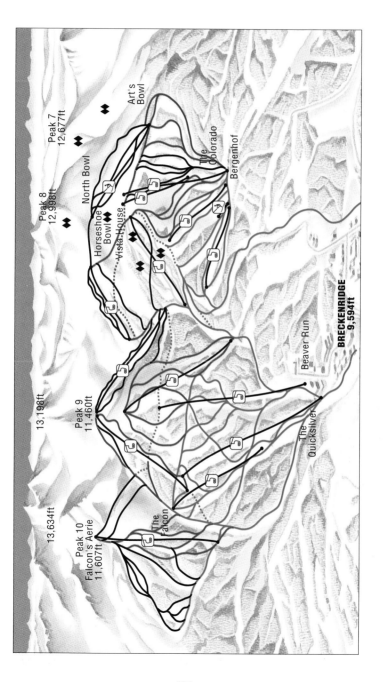

Art's Bowl

Peak 7
12,677ft

Peak 8
12,998ft

North Bowl

Horseshoe Bowl

Vista House

The Colorado

Bergenhof

13,198ft

13,634ft

Peak 9
11,460ft

Peak 10
Falcon's Aerie
11,607ft

The Falcon

The Quicksilver

Beaver Run

BRECKENRIDGE
9,594ft

chutes in the Way Out sector below the Lake Chutes feed into the black Psychopath under Chair 6 for a ride up Chair E to the longest-lasting powder on the mountain in the 41 acres (17 hectares) of the North Chutes.

Off-piste

Piqued by its reputation for less than adrenaline-inducing skiing, Breckenridge has in the past few years gone to extremes and has opened (when safety conditions permit) the Lake Chutes sector, which offers 20 acres (8 hectares) of 656-vertical-ft (200-m) pitches of up to 50 degrees. The Lake Chutes can be accessed by climbing some 820 vertical feet (250 vertical metres) to the top of Imperial Bowl on Peak 8 from the top of the Horseshoe Bowl T-bar. Less taxing is the climb of 492 vertical feet (150 vertical metres) from the same spot to the summit of Peak 7 for the open, untracked Whale's Tail, Peak 7 and Art's bowls. It is also possible to cheat on the climb by traversing into the lower sectors of these bowls from the T-bar.

Tuition and guiding

Breckenridge Ski School is big – 450 instructors – but diversified, with specialised clinics such as the 50-plus seminars (taught by oldies for oldies), women's workshops, and teen-only programmes. The Adventure Guides course is for advanced skiers who want to find the best 'tree shots and sweet shots'. Instructors try their hardest, as work is assigned according to reports of client satisfaction. Snowboarding is big here, and the school teaches everything 'from carving and riding to busting out of the half-pipe'.

Mountain restaurants

Piz Otto's at the Vista House on Peak 8 is by far the best in Breckenridge for spacious, sit-down comfort and cuisine, and serves both à la carte and buffet spreads of Northern Italian meat and pasta, with a good choice of Barolo wines. By contrast, Falcon's Aerie on Peak 10 is little more than a warming hut that serves cold fare for skiers on the move. Peak 9's eponymous eatery exhausts the shortlist of high-altitude dining spots, as well as the patience of skiers queuing for cafeteria fodder. Down below, American blueberry muffins, hot dogs and other fast but filling fare are indifferently on offer at the expanded and remodelled Bergenhof at the base of Peak 8.

The resort

Breckenridge is a bustling town that prides itself on accommodating 26,000 skiers in its 254 restored structures downtown, which date from 1859, and in its self-contained resort/shopping complexes closer to the slopes. Breckenridge is the oldest continually occupied community in Colorado and has embraced conservation with a fervour that European visitors might regard as verging on the kitsch or over-cute. However, international visitors, who exceed 10 per cent of all skiers, are courted ardently with events including World Cup races, a hot-air balloon festival, the Ullr Fest winter carnival and an international snow sculpture competition. The extremely low humidity and altitudes in excess of 12,000ft (3937m) can cause dehydration and headaches – made worse by exercise – which can be avoided by resting and abstaining from alcohol.

The resort is chock-a-block with boutiques, art galleries and ski shops. Scores of designer discount shops can also be found in nearby Silverthorne. The town has a free bus service and, as parking private cars is almost impossible, driving the icy roads is best left to the professionals.

Accommodation

Nearly all the accommodation in Breckenridge is non-smoking. Most convenient for the lifts are the huge shopping and hotel complexes of the Beaver Run Resort, Breckenridge Hilton and the Village at Breckenridge, in descending order of altitude. All of these attract large conference groups, as does the Lodge & Spa outside the Breckenridge town limits. Restored 'Victorian' houses featuring bed-and-breakfast accommodation include the romantic Williams House, furnished with American antiques, and the Evans House, which are both downtown. Hunt Placer Inn is a European chalet-style bed-and-breakfast. Aspenglade Cabin is a rustic out-of-town retreat. The Safari Ranch and Muggins Gulch Inn, set in 160 acres (65 hectares) of land, are also out of town. Budget accommodation includes the family-oriented Breckenridge Wayside Inn and the old-fashioned Ridge Street Inn.

Eating in and out

Beware of local advice, as Americans often confuse cutesy décor – impossible to escape in Breckenridge – with decent cuisine. Reservations are essential – even though there are more than 50 eateries – and are unlikely to be honoured if you are so much as 15 minutes late. Casual dining favours Mexican cuisine at Mi-Casa. Spicy Louisiana Cajun fare can be found at Poirrier's. Fatty's and the Village Pasta Company offer exotic pizzas. The Bamboo Garden provides respectable Szechwan and Mandarin food. Café Alpine has won several local gourmet awards, but Pierre's River Walk Café is the sole 'real' French restaurant, eclipsed only by the Top of the World restaurant at the Lodge & Spa, where the red deer *carpaccio* and buffalo-stuffed pasta are exquisite. Curry enthusiasts should not miss out on Ghandi India's Cuisine. Downstairs at Eric's describes itself correctly as 'Breckenridge's most outrageous beer hall and pizza joint'.

Après-ski

Breckenridge is renowned as a 'party town'. 'Really friendly, even by American standards' is a frequent comment on the Breckenridge crowd, the rowdier section of which is to be found in the cheerfully seedy surroundings of Shamus O'Toole's Roadhouse Saloon. Jake T Pounders and the Gold Pan are typical 'cowboy' bars. Breckenridge Brewery

Skiing facts: Breckenridge

TOURIST OFFICE
PO Box 1058, Breckenridge, CO 80424
Tel 1 800 934 2485
Fax 1 970 453 3202
Email info@vailresorts.com
Web site www.snow.com

THE RESORT
Airport transfer Denver International
2hrs, Eagle County Airport 1¼hrs
Visitor beds 26,000
Transport free bus throughout resort.
Shuttle bus to Keystone and
Vail/Beaver Creek

THE SKIING
Linked or nearby resorts Arapahoe
Basin (n), Copper Mountain (n),
Keystone (n), Vail/Beaver Creek (n)
Longest run Four O'Clock, 3½ miles
(5.6km) – blue/green
Number of lifts 19
Total of trails/pistes 2,031 acres
(822 hectares), (14% easy,
26% intermediate, 60% difficult)
Nursery slopes children's areas at the
Village Center, Beaver Run and Peak 8
Children's Center
Summer skiing none
Snowmaking 504 acres (204 hectares)

LIFT PASSES
Area pass $234–240 for 6 days
(includes 3 days in Keystone or
Vail/Beaver Creek)
Day pass $47–49
Beginners no free lifts
Pensioners 65–69yrs, $180 for 6 days.
Free for 70yrs and over

Credit cards yes

TUITION
Adults Breckenridge Ski School (Peak 8,
Peak 9, Village), 9.45am–4pm,
$288 for 6 days
Private lessons $80 per hr
Snowboarding as regular ski school
Cross-country Breckenridge Nordic
Center, details on request. Loipe 38km
Other courses moguls, race-training,
women's seminars, 50-plus seminars,
family ski clinics, teen-only programmes
Guiding Adventure Guides course,
through ski school

CHILDREN
Lift pass 5–14yrs, $102 for 6 days
Ski kindergarten Peak 8 and Peak 9
Children's Centers, 3yrs and over,
8.30am–4.30pm, $390 for 6 days
including lunch
Ski school Breckenridge Ski School,
5–9yrs, 8.30am–4.30pm. 10–14yrs,
9.45am–3.45pm. Both $348–390 for
6 days including lunch
Non-ski kindergarten Peak 8 Children's
Center, 2mths and over. Peak 9, 3yrs
and over. Both $360 for 6 days
including lunch

OTHER SPORTS
Climbing-wall, ice-fishing, indoor tennis,
racket-ball, skating, sleigh rides,
snowmobiling, snowshoeing, swimming

FOOD AND DRINK PRICES
Coffee $1.30, glass of wine $5, small
beer $3, dish of the day $12–18

attracts a tumultuous throng. More sophisticated – and pretentious – is Cecilia's Cigar Parlor, which is the only smoking zone in town (Havanas prohibited). Computer nerds flock to the Reality Bytes cybercafé. The Back Stage Theatre is strictly amateur but entertaining. Tiffany's Nightclub has cheap drinks and techno. The Faust and Lewis bar features a new musical comedy routine each week. The Alligator Lounge presents live reggae, rock and blues acts of some note seven nights a week.

Childcare

Advance reservations are advised for either of the base-area kindergarten at Peaks 8 and 9. The former accepts infants as young as two months, the latter children from three years of age. Both have pagers for parents to hire, provide lunches and offer a non-skiing, outdoor snow-play programme. Two 'magic carpet' conveyor belts have now been added to the children's learning area. Children from five years can join the ski school programme; the school also runs a teens-only programme.

Jackson Hole

ALTITUDE 6,311ft (1924m)

Beginners ✶✶ Intermediates ✶✶ Advanced ✶✶✶ Snowboarders ✶✶✶

Jackson Hole is the Jerusalem of skiing and snowboarding, the pilgrimage point which all true adherents to the faith must finally visit to pay their obeisance to the god of snow. In the past they needed to be either a beginner or an expert to enjoy the experience. Anyone in-between risked having their confidence slaughtered by the daunting steepness of the rugged terrain of the Teton Mountains in this remote and beautiful corner of Wyoming. While other North American resorts make do with three colour codings for the degree of difficulty of their ski trails, Jackson needs five. Its hardcore of devoted fans around the world see it as one of the last wild frontiers of macho mountainside, a place where 'a man's gotta ski what a man's gotta ski', and a place where powderhounds compete for the number of vertical feet they can clock up in a day, in a season or indeed, in a lifetime. Its ancient lifts, including an antique tram (cable-car), were all part of the legend. However, times are changing. Jackson's new owners, who have renamed it Jackson Mountain Resort, need more visitors to make it commercially profitable. Consequently they are installing new lifts and are opening up tracts of intermediate terrain – much to the chagrin of the powderhound purists.

- ✔ Cowboy-town atmosphere
- ✔ Lively après-ski
- ✔ Ideal for non-skiers
- ✔ Beautiful scenery
- ✔ Attractive town
- ✔ Well-run kindergarten
- ✘ Distance from town to slopes
- ✘ Queues for tram (cable-car)
- ✘ Short ski season
- ✘ Remote location

Last season the Bridger gondola was opened; it takes 2,000 skiers per hour on a seven-and-a-half minute ride up to Headwall. The lift is part of $14 million's worth of initial mountain improvements. A further nine new lifts and three new mountain restaurants are on the drawing board, and snowmaking has been increased on the beginner and intermediate terrain of neighbouring Apres Vous Mountain. A new 17,000-square-foot base lodge, the Bridger Center, has been built.

Despite local opposition, the owners have been granted planning permission to triple the size of Teton Village, the ski base area, to cope with the 500,000 skiers expected annually. Until now, the resort's position on the edge of Grand Teton National Park and near an elk reserve 60 miles (97km) from Yellowstone National Park has meant that environmental considerations have taken precedence.

Jackson Hole Mountain Resort is situated beside Teton Village, 12 miles (19km) from the town of Jackson, which confusingly also has its

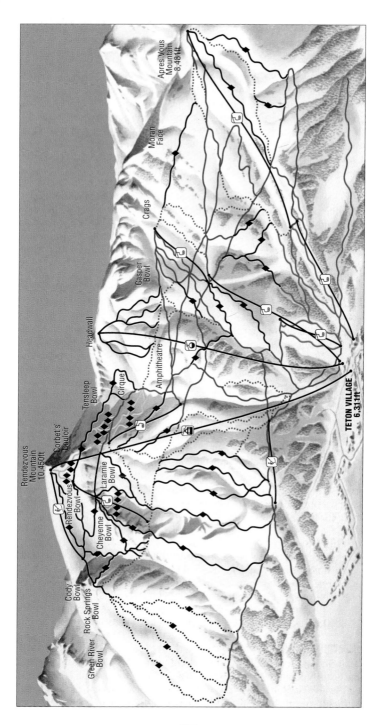

Rendezvous Mountain
10,450ft

Cody Bowl

Green River Bowl

Rock Springs Bowl

Corbet's Couloir

Rendezvous Bowl

Cheyenne Bowl

Laramie Bowl

Tensleep Bowl

Cirque

Amphitheatre

Headwall

Casper Bowl

Crags

Moran Face

Apres Vous Mountain
8,481ft

TETON VILLAGE
6,311ft

own resort of **Snow King**. Snow-users either choose the convenience of Teton Village or make the 20-minute commute from Jackson each day by ski bus or car. Jackson is a genuine Wild West town, complete with boardwalks, wooden Victorian shop fronts and tough bars, straight off the set of a Western movie. The locals derive their living not just from skiers and boarders but also from the summer tourists who stop here en route to Yellowstone National Park. Working ranches still surround the town, and the horse is the secondary means of transport behind the four-wheel-drive.

One criticism of Jackson Hole is that for a resort of such international fame the ski area is quite small, and there is little other skiing within driving distance. Snow King, overlooking the town of Jackson, is smaller still. **Grand Targhee**, 47 miles (76km) away, goes some way to offsetting this disadvantage. The early closure of Jackson's skiing in mid-April is dictated by the annual elk migration.

Ski and board
top 10,450ft (3186m) bottom 6,311ft (1924m)
Jackson Hole no longer offers the longest continual vertical drop in the USA (the title now goes by a whisker to Snowmass in Colorado). The main ski area is on the extremely challenging Rendezvous Mountain. It has mostly black (difficult) runs, steep chutes and unlimited off-piste, which is a rarity in America. Intermediate snow-users will find that even some of the blue (intermediate) runs are left

WHAT'S NEW
Headwall gondola
Bridger Summit restaurant
Outdoor skating rink

ungroomed. Easier runs are to be found below Headwall, reached by the new gondola, and on neighbouring Apres Vous Mountain.

A veteran 63-person cable-car tram is the other main means of uphill transport and the only way up to the peak of Rendezvous Mountain. You have the option of buying an all-inclusive lift pass or paying a $3 supplement for a single ride.

Beginners
All the beginner slopes are concentrated at the base of Teton Village, where both the adult and children's ski schools meet. The nursery slopes are serviced by two short chair-lifts, one of them a quad; this allows beginners to start on the easiest slopes and then graduate to steeper gradients. Second-week snow-users can find easier blue runs down Apres Vous Mountain and should tackle these before venturing up Headwall.

Intermediates
As in St Anton and Chamonix, the colour-grading is radical, and you must study carefully the unique colour coding system which is explained on the lift map; for most snow-users 'intermediate' means 'difficult', and 'difficult' means 'extreme'. While much of the terrain provides varied

skiing for good intermediates, gradients can change suddenly, and in certain conditions unpisted runs are unpredictable and difficult. The friendliest intermediate skiing can be found off the Headwall and the Casper Bowl triple chair. The runs are well-marked, but you must pay attention as several blues turn into black runs on the lower part of the mountain. Only the truly confident should stray up the tram. Plenty of mid-skill skiing can now be found here in most conditions.

Advanced

Most of the advanced skiing is in steep chutes and couloirs and on tree-lined runs. The skiing initially reached from the tram is all graded black. The simplest way down is to take Rendezvous Trail, which is the longest run. Here you can get into the Hobacks or into Laramie Bowl by taking the Upper Sublette Ridge quad-chair. You can also enter the steep Alta chutes from here. Upper Teewinot, under the chair on Apres Vous Mountain, is excellent in fresh powder. The new gondola opens up some magical terrain which could previously be reached only by hiking. A new groomed half-pipe opened on Apres Vous last season. Dick's Ditch also houses a natural half-pipe

Off-piste

Jackson Hole is one of the few US resorts with limitless off-piste skiing. The Hobacks, on the lower section of Rendezvous Mountain, are marked as black runs but are in fact one large, steep snowfield, which is best skied in the morning and is completely ungroomed. Many steep chutes, such as the Expert, Alta, and Tower Three Chutes, cut through the trees, and the steep bowls include Cody, Cheyenne, Rendezvous and Tensleep.

For those with plenty of nerve, Corbet's Couloir, off the top of Rendezvous Mountain, is a chute so steep it seems inconceivable that anyone could ski it and survive. It is entered by a 20-ft (6-m) jump off a cornice; if you manage to control your skis you will land on a ribbon of snow dropping away at 50 degrees, where you must either turn or fall.

Tuition and guiding

The ski and snowboard school, under the direction of Jim Kercher, emphasises having fun and being able to tackle simple slopes in a short time. Group, private and three-day courses are offered in alpine and nordic skiing and snowboarding. The ski school uses video evaluation for many of its classes. Special clinics include race camps, steep skiing, women's clinics, mountain experience classes, deep powder skiing and a guiding service.

Mountain restaurants

A new restaurant opens this season at the top of the gondola, but other-wise eating on the mountain is limited. Casper Restaurant serves both hot food and salads, and two small snack-bars are at the base of the Thunder chair-lift and at the top of the tram. A basic cafeteria at the bottom of the home run serves sandwiches and salads.

Skiing facts: Jackson Hole

TOURIST OFFICE
PO Box 290, Teton Village, WY 83025
Tel 1 307 733 2292
Fax 1 307 733 2660
Email info@jacksonhole.com
Web site www.jacksonhole.com/ski

THE RESORT
Airport transfer Jackson Airport 15mins
from Jackson and 20mins from
Teton Village
Visitor beds 12,000
Transport bus service between Jackson
and Teton Village ($2)

THE SKIING
Linked or nearby resorts Snow King (n),
Grand Targhee (n)
Longest run Rendezvous Trail,
7.2 miles (11.5km) – blue
Number of lifts 10 in Jackson Hole
Total of trails/pistes 2,500 acres
(1,011 hectares), (10% easy,
40% intermediate, 50% difficult)
Nursery slopes 10% of total slopes
Summer skiing none
Snowmaking 110 acres
(44 hectares) covered

LIFT PASSES
Area pass $234 for 6 days
($258 including tram)
Day pass $51 including tram
Beginners no free lifts
Pensioners 65yrs and over, $34 per day
Credit cards yes

TUITION
Adults Jackson Hole Ski School (S-S),
$150 for 3 x 5hrs

Private lessons $135 per morning
(2hrs), afternoon extension $90 (1¾hrs),
full day $320 (6hrs)
Snowboarding Jackson Hole S-S, prices
as ski lessons
Cross-country Jackson Hole Nordic
Center, $37 per day including lesson,
equipment hire and trail pass. Loipe
17km at base of resort
Other courses disabled skiing, moguls,
mountain experience, race camps,
women's ski clinics
Guiding Jackson Hole Alpine Guides

CHILDREN
Lift pass 14yrs and under, $129 for 6
days including tram. Free for 5yrs and
under on Eagle's Rest
Ski kindergarten Rough Riders at the
Kids Ranch, 3–5yrs, $68 per day
including daycare, lunch and lesson
Ski school Jackson Hole, 6–13yrs,
$245 for 5 x 4hrs including lunch
Non-ski kindergarten Tenderfoots
Infant Care (2–19mths), Wrangler
Childcare (18mths–5yrs), both
8.30am–4.30pm, $58 per day
including lunch

OTHER SPORTS
Climbing wall, dog-sledding, heli-skiing,
indoor tennis, parapente, skating,
snowcat skiing (Grand Targhee),
snowmobiling, snowshoeing,
swimming

FOOD AND DRINK PRICES
Coffee $1.75, glass of wine $2.75–3.50,
small beer $2.75, dish of the day
$6.50–8.50

Most skiers and riders head to the Rocky Mountain Oyster Bar downstairs at the Mangy Moose or to the Alpenhof, which is a Tyrolean-style restaurant.

The resort

Jackson is one of the few Western frontier towns which have been transformed into ski resorts and where the past does not clash with the present. Stetsons are as common on the slopes as in the bars. In the summer it is the gateway to Yellowstone National Park, and three million visitors pass through in their trailers on their way to see the wildlife and Old Faithful, the world's largest geyser. In winter the resort returns to its natural state, a small market-town with surprisingly individual shops and restaurants, as well as vast country bars.

The charismatic town of Jackson is made up largely of single- or double-story buildings, many of which are renovated saloon-type structures. The central square has gates fashioned from naturally discarded elk horns. At night their former owners are quite likely to amble across the road or forage in a dustbin. Teton Village, 20 minutes away by car, is – but not for much longer – a small cluster of hotels and condominiums centred around a picturesque clock tower, the tram and the new Bridger Center base lodge. A regular bus service links Teton and Jackson.

Accommodation

The Wort Hotel in Jackson is the original, rebuilt stagecoach inn. Other hotels include the Forty Niner, The Lodge at Jackson ('pleasant, but inconveniently located'), and the popular Parkway Inn. The Sundance is central and has a strong following. The Inn at Jackson Hole is in fact at Teton Village and is well positioned at the base of the slopes. Self-caterers need to go to Jackson for the supermarkets.

Eating in and out

Breakfast is a serious business in cowboy country. The real McCoy of 'eggs-over-easy', stacks of pancakes, hash browns and grits are on offer at the Mangy Moose in Teton Village. In the evening, the art-deco-style Cadillac Grille in Jackson has hamburgers, seafood and fresh pasta. J.J.'s Silverdollar Bar and Grill in the Wort Hotel has the ubiquitous ribs in various forms. Off Broadway is praised for 'freshly produced food with imagination'. Other options include Sweetwater and the Blue Lion as well as The Merry Piglets and Mama Inez for Mexican.

Après-ski

Unless you can prove you are 21 or over, you are not going to enjoy yourself outside skiing hours here. So strict are Wyoming's licensing laws that even young-looking 30-year-olds should carry identification at all times. The Million Dollar Cowboy Bar and J.J.'s Silverdollar Bar in Jackson are where the action is. The Cowboy Bar has the most atmosphere, with real leather saddles as bar stools and a full-sized, stuffed grizzly bear silently directing proceedings.

Teton Village has the Mangy Moose, one of the finest après-ski bars in the Rockies. It has live music in the evenings and a video room for those under age. The Wingback Lounge at the Inn is a quieter option, and the Stockman's Lounge at the Sojourner usually has ski videos and free appetizers. If you have hired a car you can drive to Wilson, on the road towards the Teton Pass, for an evening at the Stagecoach Inn with live music, cowgirls in flounced dresses, and good-value food. It is the kind of place where you eat with your hat on and go easy on the eye contact with strangers.

Teton Village has a new skating rink. Other après-ski activities include night-skiing at Snow King resort in Jackson, sleigh rides through the elk reserve, and snowmobile tours of Yellowstone National Park. Shops sell everything from cowboy boots to designer fashions, including the Polo Ralph Lauren Factory Store, which sells end-of-line designer clothes at a fraction of the normal prices.

Childcare

Kids Ranch (formerly the Kinderschule) in the Bridger Center is, in a country of excellent ski kindergarten, one of the best. Children are taught the 'Edgie Wedgie' technique where ski tips are clipped together with bright, bendy strips of plastic. This stops the skis from crossing and encourages children to make a wedge or snowplough. Children are taken to and from the nursery slopes in a snowmobile trailer. The non-ski kindergarten is for infants from two months to five years of age, with ski lessons from three years. Explorers is a ski course for children aged 6 to 14. Instruction is combined with scouting for moose, porcupines and eagles.

Linked or nearby resorts

Grand Targhee
top 10,230ft (3118m) bottom 8,000ft (2438m)

The small resort is 47 miles (76km) north-west of Jackson and just inside the Wyoming border. It is blessed with an excellent snow record, which is why the main attraction is snowcat skiing in the virgin powder. This is by previous arrangement only, as the cat takes a maximum of ten passengers, plus the guide and a patrolman. If you can't get a booking for snowcat skiing, the resort's own 3,000 skiable acres (1,214 hectares) are varied as well as exciting and served by a new detachable quad chairlift. They are often left ungroomed in fresh snow. The resort has a small shopping centre, but restaurants are limited. The Trap has 'friendly table service, ski videos, and a good variety of local beers'. Accommodation includes the Teewinot Lodge.

TOURIST OFFICE
Tel 1 307 353 2304
Fax 1 307 353 8148

Keystone

ALTITUDE 9,300ft (2835m)

Beginners ✱✱✱   Intermediates ✱✱✱   Advanced ✱✱ Snowboarders ✱✱✱

Set among forests of pine in the heart of the Rocky Mountains in Colorado, Keystone is a modern (28-year-old), purpose-built sprawl of multi-level complexes running west to east along Highway 6, 90 miles (145km) west of Denver's new airport. Designed to be all things to all families, Keystone has a superlative range of intermediate terrain, America's most comprehensive snowmaking and night-skiing operations, and has won numerous awards for its family facilities. Three of its restaurants rate among the best in American ski resorts, though overall standards are unexceptional. Children under 13 stay and children under 5 ski for free. Its three mountains, with 20 lifts and 91 trails are now owned by the same company as **Vail**, **Beaver Creek** and **Breckenridge** and are consequently undergoing major expansion. The four resorts are connected by shuttle bus, and you can now ski all of them on the same lift ticket (if purchased for three or more days and with various restrictions). Nearby **Arapahoe Basin** provides limited, but exciting, advanced skiing.

✔ Three of top US resort-restaurants
✔ Long ski season
✔ Extensive snowmaking
✔ Major night-skiing centre
✔ Recommended for families
✔ Excellent grooming and signposting
✔ Range of ski school courses
✘ Lack of ambience
✘ Limited nightlife
✘ High altitude can cause sickness
✘ Weekend and holiday crowds

Ski and board
top 11,980ft (3652m) bottom 9,300ft (2835m)

Keystone's skiing is laid out on three interlinked mountains, one behind the other, and each progressively more challenging. Facing the resort is Keystone Mountain with 16 lifts and 55 invitingly easy, meticulously groomed, rolling trails through forest. North Peak's three lifts access 19 shorter, more difficult runs, some of which are left ungroomed in sections. The huge Outback area, the size of both other mountains combined, is protected from the wind and is an excellent introduction to advanced skiing, especially in its two wilderness bowls. Queues can exceed 15 minutes at weekends, especially on the Skyway Gondola. Locals warn of the 'Keystone donut' effect: icy slopes whenever nearby Lake Dillon fails to freeze over.

Beginners

Progressing from the Energizer Bunny Slope even the most inept snow-user will be flattered by the wealth of ultra-simple green (easy) and blue (intermediate) runs, which comprise almost all of Keystone Mountain's front face. The longest and easiest run is Schoolmarm, running 3 miles (5km) from top to bottom via a traverse of the resort's western boundary.

Intermediates

Intermediates have the run of all three mountains. The Flying Dutchman blue trail takes the most direct line down Keystone Mountain's front face. North Peak has five gladed blue runs, with Star Fire taking the most direct and challenging line. In the Outback area, Elk Run is the widest, with Wolverine throwing up more trees to dodge, although it is still graded blue.

Advanced

Keystone's cautious grading puts black (difficult) runs within the scope of aggressive intermediates, who may first want to test their skills on the short black sections near Area 51 on Keystone Mountain's west border. North Peak has six fall-line blacks tumbling down to the Santiago chair. But it is the Black Forest in the Outback that is most testing, with four narrow, heavily bumped tree-line runs, particularly adored by snowboarders. Keystone has one of the biggest and best-designed funparks in America. Area 51 features numerous pipes in a 20-acre (8-hectare) terrain garden and is lit at night.

Off-piste

A short hike above the Outback lift at 11,980ft (3652m) opens up North and South bowls, which are within Keystone's boundaries. In powder conditions they provide a good mix of quite steep, untracked terrain leading down into the trees.

Tuition and guiding

Keystone Ski and Snowboard School is rated among America's top five and features a varied menu of special clinics for women, bump skiers and those convinced they will 'never-ever' be able to ski. Former racers Phil and Steve Mahre also run regular clinics, which have an avid following.

Mountain restaurants

The Alpenglow Stube is without question the best and highest – at 11,444ft (3488m) – haute cuisine in North America. Culinary delicacies served here include tenderloin of wild boar.

The resort

Keystone has been almost entirely rebuilt during the past few years, with the addition of $700-million condos in the River Run and Ski Tip Ranch quarters, together with new shops and restaurants. Nevertheless, fewer

Skiing facts: Keystone

TOURIST OFFICE
Box 38, Keystone, CO 80435
Tel 1 970 496 2316
Fax 1 970 496 4339
Email info@vailresorts.com
Web site www.snow.com

THE RESORT
Airport transfer Vail/Eagle County
Airport 1¼hrs, Denver 1¾hrs
Visitor beds 5,200
Transport free resort bus service,
also to Breckenridge
and Keystone

THE SKIING
Linked or nearby resorts Arapahoe
Basin (n), Breckenridge (l), Vail/Beaver
Creek (l)
Longest run Schoolmarm (3 miles)
Number of lifts 20
Total of trails/pistes 1,756 acres
(710 hectares), (13% easy,
36% intermediates, 51% difficult)
Nursery slopes 3
Summer skiing no
Snowmaking 100% capacity

LIFT PASSES
Area pass $234–240 for 6 days
(includes 3 days at Vail/Beaver Creek
and Breckenridge)
Day pass $47–49
Beginners no free lifts
Pensioners 65–69yrs, $180 for 6 days.
Free for 70yrs and over
Credit cards yes

TUITION
Adults Keystone Ski and Snowboard
School at Mountain House and River Run
10.30am–1pm or 1.30–4pm, $37 for
2½hr lesson
Private lessons $145 for 2hrs
Snowboarding at Mountain House and
River Run, 2½hrs $37, 4½hrs $48.
Private lessons as regular ski school
Cross-country $39 per day, moonlight
tour $30 (includes equipment).
Loipe 24km
Other courses women's clinics,
bumps, Mahre race-camps, teen
programs, backcountry nature tours,
carving, freestyle
Guiding through ski school

CHILDREN
Lift passes $102 for 6 days.
Free under 5yrs
Ski kindergarten 3yrs and over $72,
4–14yrs $74, both for full day
10am–3pm including lesson, lifts,
lunch and equipment
Ski school 4–14yrs, as ski kindergarten
Non-ski kindergarten Children's Centre,
2mths and over, 8am–5pm,
$56 per day including lunch

OTHER SPORTS
Indoor tennis, skating, sleigh rides,
snowmobiling, snowshoeing, swimming

FOOD AND DRINK
Coffee $1.30, glass of wine $5, small
beer $3, dish of the day $12–18

than 50 families are in residence year round, and consequently it lacks atmosphere. Bussing from one sector of this sprawling resort to another in search of some nightlife becomes tiresome. Headaches brought on by dehydration or altitude sickness are common and can persist for days.

Accommodation

The most characterful accommodation is the Ski Tip Lodge, which is intimate and appealing with the feel of the old stagecoach inn it once was. Keystone Lodge is a full-service hotel, with swimming-pool, fitness centre and hot tubs, but requires a bus-ride to the skiing and is, according to visitors: 'Rather spread out with a long walk to the rooms'. The Inn is closer to the lifts and has rooms with private hot tubs. Nearly a thousand condo flats and private homes of quite luxurious standards are also available.

Eating in and out

The Edgewater Café and the Bighorn Southwestern Grille at the Lodge are uninspiring. Soda Creek Homestead is a rustic cabin reached by horse-drawn sleigh. But truly memorable dining is reserved for two of the best resort-restaurants in America: the Ski Tip Lodge (Colorado's oldest such establishment) and the Keystone Ranch, which is rated by some US publications as the best resort-restaurant on the continent. Reporters praised The Lodge Garden for its à la carte menu.

Après-ski

Take a stagecoach to dinner, rip through the Arapahoe National Forest on a snowmobile or ski until 9pm. Aside from America's largest outdoor ice-skating lake and excellent indoor tennis courts, really exuberant nightlife is quashed by the preponderance of families with small children, though Bandito's tries its best to lower the tone. There is a factory outlet shopping mall about 15 minutes' drive from the resort.

Childcare

Babies from two months old are accepted into the nursery, which is open from 8am to 5pm. Telephone pagers are available for parents. The ski school takes children from the ages of 4 to 14. Fort Saw Whiskers is a children-only ski playground. Babysitting in resort accommodation must be reserved 24 hours in advance.

Killington

ALTITUDE 2,200ft (671m)

Beginners ✱✱✱ Intermediates ✱✱ Advanced ✱ Snowboarders ✱✱✱

Killington is the East Coast flagship of the giant American Skiing Company, which is currently devouring resorts across America. The large amount of skiing available, coupled with ease of access and an unusually vibrant nightlife make it one of the most popular US destinations for British skiers. A choice of direct flights to Boston, a journey that takes only seven hours from Britain and a three-hour transfer to the resort give Killington an edge over its Colorado rivals in this respect. Alternatively, visitors can fly to New York and take the Amtrack service to Rutland, a 15-minute drive away. The downside is the New England weather, which is often extremely cold or wet, with low cloud and icy conditions. To combat this all the Vermont resorts invest hugely in snowmaking equipment, and nowhere more so than Killington, where 24 hours a day (temperature permitting) state-of-the-art cannons mounted on 15-ft 'giraffe' pylons power out a white substitute for the snow that nature does not always manage to produce. So sophisticated is the system – they tested it to the full last winter when real cover was scarce – that the big business of skiing and snowboarding can continue here without weather worries.

- ✔ Excellent facilities for children
- ✔ Extensive snowmaking
- ✔ Modern lift system
- ✔ Lively après-ski
- ✔ Wide choice of restaurants
- ✘ Lack of charm
- ✘ Straggling layout
- ✘ Cold climate and icy slopes

Killington opened for skiing in 1958, when the first tickets were sold out of a ticket booth made from a converted chicken coop. The resort is currently at the midway stage of a US$50 million expansion. This includes a new gondola to the summit of Killington Peak, new chair-lifts, an on-mountain link with neighbouring **Pico**, and two new half-pipes. Killington hopes to have the largest lift system in the USA before the year 2000, with 35 lifts including seven high-speed quads.

The lifts are spread across seven mountains, but the resort still lacks a heart, with most of the hotels, condominiums, restaurants and bars lined up on either side of Killington Road, the five-mile link between the ski area and the junction to the main highway. Hopefully, the new $20 million Grand Hotel and Crown Club being constructed on the edge of the slopes will provide the village focal point that has previously been lacking. A large number of readers have complained that while Killington has plenty of intermediate skiing, it is lacking in character.

Ski and board
top 4,220ft (1287m) bottom 1,045ft (319m)

Killington's seven peaks provide plenty of skiing for all standards but with the emphasis on mileage rather than variety. At this low altitude, it is inevitable that the runs are in glades cut through the all-embracing forest. Although the pitch changes it is hard to tell one run from the next. On the plus side, different levels are catered for in separate areas, with beginners safely corralled on their own hill – an arrangement that benefits everyone. Killington has a special trail map for snowboarders, with essential advice on areas in which skating may be required to connect the trails. A new snowpark with a beginner, as well as a regular half-pipe has been constructed at the bottom of Highline, and a permanent boarder-cross course has been built on Middle Dream Maker. A new 1,200-ft (366-m) snowpark is also being built on Upper Bunny Buster, and Pico is to have its own park and half-pipe. The new gondola, capable of carrying 2,000 passengers per hour replaces the old Killington double-chair and takes snow-users to the top of Killington Peak in six minutes.

Beginners

The Rams Head area is the ultimate in luxury for first-timers. At the bottom of the hill the flattest slope is designated as a snowpark and is served by a 'magic carpet' conveyor belt and a hand-tow, but skiers soon graduate to a modern high-speed quad that gives effortless access to wide, sweeping descents. Once confident on the looping Caper, Great Bear and Vale trails, snow-users can tackle three easy intermediate trails: Timberline, Header and Swirl. The three-level base-lodge has a cafeteria, a ski rental shop and a selection of other shops. The original beginner slopes on Snowshed, a neighbouring base zone served by a quad and two double-chairs, also encourage a gentle learning curve.

Beginner snowboarders are advised to join a learn-to-ride programme in the enclosed novice area on Snowshed before heading for the beginner-pipe at Highline.

Intermediates

The most comfortable approach to Killington's slopes, especially in hostile weather, is via the two-stage Skyship up to Skye Peak. The eight-person gondola is described as the longest and fastest lift in the east, but more importantly it has the world's first heated cabins. Many of the runs from the top are green (easy), with Great Eastern providing a long, gentle return to the base-station. Those pistes starting from the complicated junction at the top are black (difficult), and it is necessary to take care when selecting a route. The blue (intermediate) trails to look out for are Needle's Eye, Home Stretch and Cruise Control. Halfway down Great Eastern, snow-users come to the Bear Mountain quad, which opens up another zone, again with more black and green runs than blue ones.

The focus of the whole ski area is the Killington Base, which has chair-lifts fanning out to Killington Peak, Skye Peak and Snowdon Mountain. Of the three, Snowdon, which is networked with green and blue trails, is recommended for lower intermediates, while more confident snow-users can graduate to the single black diamond (very difficult) runs on Skye.

Advanced

The most extensive area of double-black-diamond (advanced) trails is on Killington Peak, with Double Dipper, Cascade, Escapade and Downdraft among the names to look out for. Big Dipper is a gladed trail, but care should be exercised when conditions are icy. Killington's alternative macho challenge is the Outer Limits double-black-diamond mogul slope on Bear Mountain.

Off-piste

Although there are no powder fields, the resort has recently created two so-called Fusion Zones in the forest by thinning out the trees and clearing away the undergrowth. Squeeze Play, off Rams Head, is the logical starting point, with Julio, between Killington and Skye Peaks, providing a sterner test. The resort is also introducing Wild Things – trails that are left ungroomed and without artificial snow, but to date the only one in operation is a short section called Breakaway on Killington Peak.

Tuition and guiding

The Killington Skier Development Program offers courses in the perfect turn, whether it is executed on carving or regular skis. Ninety-minute clinics operate four times daily for a maximum of six pupils. Private lessons can be booked at the Snowshed and Killington Skier Development desks, and two daily two-hour advanced skier workshops for a maximum of five pupils are available, starting at 9.30am and 1.30pm. Specialist courses include a race-training week and a snowboard freeriding and carving camp in December, as well as mogul weekends, and clinics for women – both in skiing and snowboarding – throughout the season.

Mountain restaurants

Killington Peak Restaurant, which offers views of five US states as well as Canada, is a much-needed part of the improvement plan and should have been transformed in time for the 1998–99 season. All six day-lodges have extensive restaurant facilities. The Mahogany Ridge Eatery at the Killington base has a typically limited soup, sandwich and salad menu, but a comprehensive drinks list, with foreign beers, including Newcastle Brown. Their selection of hot alcoholic concoctions is welcome after a morning spent combating the wind-chill factor.

The resort

Killington would never win a beauty contest, either for its architecture or its design. Those without a car are tied to the shuttle bus service from their lodging to the mountain or, in many cases, between their lodging and any form of entertainment. Waiting for the bus is a bitterly cold experience. Lack of style aside, the resort has more to offer than any of its New England rivals. The après-ski starts early, with hot snacks available from 3pm onwards and heavy competition for complimentary chicken wings. Casey's Caboose, named after a turn-of-the-century train driver who died saving his crew, is judged the winner by popular acclaim. This sets the tone for the varied nightlife, with a choice of bars and clubs and cosmopolitan restaurants. Unlike the Rocky Mountain states, Vermont allows older teenagers into bars – but not clubs – provided they do not drink alcohol.

> **WHAT'S NEW**
>
> Gondola to Killington Peak
> Expanded snowmaking
> Two funparks
> Grand Hotel and Crown Club

Accommodation

The Killington Lodging and Travel Service is the central booking office for accommodation of all types, including condominiums, country inns, lodges and motor inns. The Villager Motel is within walking distance of the Snowshed chair-lifts, as are the Trail Creek, Whittletree, Edgemont and Fall Line condos. The most luxurious accommodation is the Cortina Inn, eight miles (13km) from the mountain. The Inn of the Six Mountains is close to the nightlife and runs its own courtesy bus to the lifts. The newest accommodation is the Killington Grand Hotel and Crown Club, which is a slopeside condominium-hotel with a health club.

Eating in and out

Hemingway's, the only four-star restaurant in Vermont, is designated as one of the top 25 restaurants in America by *Food and Wine Magazine*. Panache at the Woods Resort serves farm-raised African and American wild game, including giraffe, ostrich and lion. Claude's is known for its European cuisine, while Santa Fe and Casey's Caboose specialise in basic American surf and turf. PPeppers bar and grill is recommended for hamburgers, the Outback for oven pizzas, and Sushi Yoshi is Japanese. The Killington Market sells everything required for self-caterers, including fresh meat, groceries, local cheeses and wines.

Après-ski

The six-mile (9.6km) Killington Road is lined with pubs and clubs. Named by *Snow Country* Magazine as one of the top ten nightclubs in North America, the multi-level Pickle Barrel is the centre of the action, with a season-long schedule of big name bands playing every weekend. The Wobbly Barn is very popular, combining steakhouse dining with live rhythm and blues. The Outback and Mother Shapiros are local bars with pool tables. Teenagers can dance and listen to live music at Bumps, in the Killington Dance Club at the Rams Head base lodge, on Friday and Saturday evenings. Racquetball, skating and snowmobiling are the other sports available in the resort.

Childcare

The Friendly Penguin nursery at the recently-expanded Rams Head Family Center cares for children between six weeks and six years old. The First Tracks programme offers ski tuition for children from two years of age. Four-year-olds are encouraged to join the Mini Stars programme, which teaches the basics. Seven-year-olds graduate to the Superstars programme, with coaching for all levels in skiing and snowboarding.

TOURIST OFFICE
Tel 1 802 422 3333
Fax 1 802 422 4391
Email swright@killington.com
Web site www.killington.com

Lake Tahoe

Heavenly 6,500ft (1982m) Squaw Valley 6,200ft (1890m)

Beginners ✱✱ Intermediates ✱✱✱ Advanced ✱✱ Snowboarders ✱✱

California is a world unto itself, so it is not surprising that its ski resorts are also unique. The majority of them – 15 alpine and 8 cross-country – are clustered around the shores of Lake Tahoe, a glimmering stretch of cobalt blue water which lives up to its reputation as the second largest and most magnificent alpine lake in the world after Lake Titicaca in Peru.

✔ Spectacular scenery
✔ Diverse resorts share lift pass
✔ Facilities for children
✔ Extensive snowmaking (Heavenly)
✔ Recommended for cross-country
✔ Plenty of tree-level skiing
✔ Lively après-ski (South Lake Tahoe)
✘ No resort centre at Heavenly
✘ Lack of non-skiing activities

Heavenly (on the Nevada–California state-line) and **Squaw Valley** (on the far side of the lake) are the main players, but nearly all the others are worth a visit for a day's skiing. Transport is easy, and interchangeable lift tickets can be used at Heavenly, Squaw Valley, **Kirkwood**, **Northstar-at-Tahoe**, **Alpine Meadows** and **Sierra-at-Tahoe**. Kirkwood is a favourite among locals, and one reader described it as 'the star of the show'.

Heavenly is now part of the American Skiing Company's empire and is consequently undergoing major redevelopment. Last season the Tamarack Express six-person detachable chair-lift was built as the first stage of a ten-year masterplan of on-mountain improvements. This year two more lifts are being upgraded to detachable quads. It is a resort of extraordinary contrasts: from the top of the Sky Express chair-lift you can either turn left to ski in Nevada with views of the arid vastness of the Nevada Desert, or turn right to the Californian side overlooking the lush beauty of Lake Tahoe. Off the slopes, serenity switches to frenzy amid the clunk of one-arm bandits in the 24-hour casinos. Gambling is legal in **South Lake Tahoe** on the Nevada side of the state-line. Unfortunately, reporters agree that the view is the best part of Heavenly, which otherwise lacks charm and challenge: 'A classic linear development along one main road. Very tatty, very busy and the skiing was no compensation'.

Across the waters, Squaw Valley, which hosted the 1960 Winter Olympics, provides the steeper and altogether more demanding terrain in a corner of the Sierra Nevada that has a long skiing tradition. As far back as 1856 John 'Snowshoe' Thompson, a Norwegian immigrant, used to carry the mail on skis between the mining camps in these mountains. Until the railroad was built in 1872, he was the miners' only winter link with the outside world.

Ski and board

Heavenly: top 10,100ft (3079m) bottom 7,200ft (2195m)
Squaw Valley: top 9,050ft (2759m) bottom 6,200ft (1890m)

With 26 lifts, Heavenly is one of America's larger ski areas, and almost all of it is below the tree-line. It also has one of America's most extensive snowmaking programmes: 37 miles (59km) of terrain are covered by snow-cannon (a total of 66 per cent of the resort's pistes). The skiing is divided between the Nevada and the Californian sides of the mountain. The Nevada face consists mainly of blue (intermediate) runs; the advanced skiing is in the Mott Canyon area, a north-facing wall with a selection of chutes through the trees, and Killebrew Canyon, which has steep unpisted chutes. The green (easy) trails are mostly on the lower and middle slopes. The upper Californian side is mainly fast, blue, cruising terrain. The most difficult skiing on the Californian side is just above the Base Lodge and on the bowl runs. Higher up the mountain are some black-diamond (very difficult) runs off Skyline Trail.

The skiing at Squaw Valley takes place on six peaks: Granite Chief, Red Dog, KT-22, Squaw, Emigrant and Broken Arrow. The area is divided into three sectors, but the 30 lifts, rather than the runs, are colour-graded. All the main lifts on KT-22 and Granite Chief are black, while those on Squaw and Emigrant are blue. Intermediates will find a huge amount of skiing, with the highlight a 3-mile (5-km) trail from the High Camp area down to the mountain base. This season the main access gondola is replaced by the Gold Coast Funitel. It has a daily capacity of 8,200, and its dual cable allows it to continue to operate in winds of up to 70mph.

Heavenly has a snowpark on the Nevada side of the mountain. Central Park at Squaw is a dedicated snowpark served by the Riviera chair-lift and overlooking Lake Tahoe; it has rollers, quarter-pipes, half-pipes and a sound system, and is open until 9pm.

Beginners

Heavenly has three beginner areas: The Enchanted Forest at the California base, at Boulder Base Lodge, and midway up the mountain on the California side. Squaw's main beginner area is located at the High Camp Bath and Tennis Club, at the top of the mountain.

Intermediates

Medium-standard skiers will find they can ski virtually every run on the mountain at Heavenly. Most of the trails are long cruisers bordered by banks of pine trees, with the highlight the stunning view of the lake. You can take the Sky Express chair and try Liz's or Betty's, then head to Nevada for the Big Dipper, Sand Dunes, Perimeter and Galaxy runs. You need to make your way back to the state in which you started by 3.30pm.

Squaw Valley has three main intermediate areas: the runs off Squaw Creek and the Red Dog lifts, which are best tackled later in the day; the area off Squaw One Express; and the bowls on Emigrant Mountain and Shirley Lakes.

Advanced

Heavenly's Milky Way Bowl provides challenging skiing, but the most advanced skiing is in Mott Canyon and Killebrew Canyon. Steep chutes are cut through the trees, with runs such as Snake Pit. Heavenly has the odd black run – such as Ellie's from the Sky Express and the Face near the California base-lodge – as well as huge areas of tree-level skiing. Gunbarrel is a challenging mogul slope.

Squaw has some seriously steep terrain with couloirs and steep gullies as well as open bowl skiing. The most radical terrain is to be found off the KT-22, Headwall, Cornice II and Granite Chief chair-lifts.

Off-piste

At Heavenly many of the trees are packed tightly together, and some vast untracked areas are there to be discovered. The Milky Way, Mott Canyon and Killebrew Canyon are large expanses of off-piste; you need to arrive early on powder days as they are quickly skied-out. Black-diamond (difficult) runs cut through huge areas of forest, where you can always find untouched snow.

At Squaw Valley, the further away from the lifts you travel the more likely you are to find good powder snow. The locals ski by the cliffs behind the tram (cable-car), but tourists need to be accompanied by a local guide in this tricky area. Many skiers opt for Headwall and KT-22, but some excellent skiing is also found off Granite Chief and Silverado. Central Park West is a new funpark with a half-pipe and boardercross course and is situated between Mainline and Gold Coast chair-lifts. Central park East, located under the Riviera chair-lift, also has its own half-pipe and is open until 9pm.

Tuition and guiding

The ski and snowboard school at Heavenly offers private and group lessons. The school offers three-hour lessons for first-timers and improvers, Mountain Adventure (off-piste) and women's ski seminars. The Shred Ready Snowboard School at Heavenly gives lessons at both Boulder Lodge and California Lodge.

The Squaw Valley Ski and Snowboard School has programmes for all ages and abilities including Ski Your Pro, where you choose how long the lesson lasts. Advanced lessons and mogul clinics are also available, as well as X-Clinics (tuition in extreme skiing).

At Children's World, instructors teach snowboarding to children between 7 and 12 years old.

Mountain restaurants

The Monument Peak restaurant, cocktail lounge and cafeteria is at the top of the tram at Heavenly and boasts a sun-deck. This winter a new lodge housing three restaurants opens on the Californian side adjacent to Sky Deck ('cook your own barbecue' and 'very enjoyable and reasonably-priced'). Boulder Lodge offers a bar, cafeteria and sun-deck, while Stagecoach Lodge just has a cafeteria. East Peak Lodge is the place to go to soak up the sun. The Sushi Bar at the California Base Lodge is enthusiastically recommended along with the Slice of Heaven Pizza Pub at the Stagecoach Base Lodge.

At Squaw Valley the highly recommended Resort at Squaw Creek offers a daily barbecue. High Camp and Gold Coast, at the top of the Super Gondola, also have barbecues. Gold Coast has restaurants and bars on three levels. High Camp boasts five different restaurants and bars, and the main dining-room is open at night. At the base, several lunch places serve pizza and sandwiches.

The resorts

The blatant flashing lights, huge neon signs and monstrous casino complexes are such a contrast from the lake front and its simple, single-storey homes that it takes a while to digest South Lake Tahoe. 'Interesting sightseeing,' said one reporter about the casinos 'but if you don't know the rules, the gambling seems pretty daunting'. Après-ski includes taking in a show – some excellent cabaret acts and pop concerts are staged here and often feature top artists. Nero's disco may be stopped temporarily for 'The Best Buns' contest, or you can have a flutter at the tables.

Alternatively, you can ignore the tacky glitter and find a small restaurant for an intimate dinner. This is easier in **Tahoe City**, a 15-minute drive from Squaw Valley, where there are several fine restaurants on the lakeside. The drive to Squaw Valley along the lake is spectacular, passing a castle on the Emerald Lake inlet.

Accommodation

The ski area of Heavenly and the town of South Lake Tahoe are separate entities, although the Tahoe Seasons Resort hotel complex is close to the lifts at the California base. Harrah's and the Horizon Casino Resort in South Lake Tahoe are two of the bigger casino-hotels; others include Caesar's Tahoe and Harvey's Resort (all have good spas). On the quieter, Californian side, motels are stacked side by side, with the Station House Inn and the Timber Cover Lodge singled out by reporters. Much of the accommodation is in condominiums at the Nevada and California bases.

The Resort at Squaw Creek is a large ski-in ski-out complex near the base of Squaw Valley, which has its own restaurants, bars, fitness centre and skating rink. Squaw Valley Lodge is also close to the base lifts, and the Olympic Village Inn is nearby. The Squaw Valley Inn next to the tram is being extensively refurbished. There are also lodges in and around Tahoe City, which is the liveliest place to stay.

Eating in and out

In South Lake Tahoe the big casino resorts have numerous restaurants, some of which are excellent. Caesar's has Planet Hollywood, complete with movie paraphernalia. Harvey's Mexican restaurant is recommended, as is Chevy's. Zachery's and Dixie's specialise in Cajun cooking. The Swiss Chalet is recommended for fondue. Heidi's is 'great for breakfast'. The Station House Inn serves reasonably priced meals, and the Chart House is more expensive but affords great views. The Cal-Neva Lodge in Crystal Bay has two restaurants and an oyster bar, and the Dory's Oar serves good seafood.

At Squaw Valley, the Resort at Squaw Creek has excellent food, Glissandi is a high-priced Italian, and Graham's is cosy. The restaurants in Tahoe City and a couple in Truckee ('a characterful Wild West town'), half-an-hour away, are more fun. In Tahoe City, Za's is a basic Italian, while Christy Hill's is upmarket and overlooks the lake.

Après-ski

Heavenly has no après-ski apart from the California Bar at the base. All the after-skiing activities take place in South Lake Tahoe, with bars in all the hotels and Vegas-style celebrity shows. McP's is a lively Irish pub, Turtle's has dancing, and the Christiania Inn is close to the ski area and has a good atmosphere. The gaming tables attract money, and money attracts the top names in showbusiness.

At Squaw there is music every weekend at Gold Coast on the mountain and at Bar One in the base village. Other post-slope options include Salsa, the Squaw Valley Inn, and the Red Dog Saloon, which is where you will find the locals. The High Camp Bath and Tennis Club is open until 9pm with tubing and skating in winter, and swimming during the spring. Night skiing is included in the daily lift ticket.

Childcare

Heavenly has redesigned its Perfect Turn Children's Center and now takes care of children aged between six months and four years. There is also a mini-clinic and junior ski school for four- to 12-year-olds.

At Squaw, Children's World is a giant complex at the foot of Snow King and is convenient for families. Parents can deliver their offspring before buying their tickets and proceeding up the mountain on the Red Dog lift. Ten Little Indians is a kindergarten that takes two- to three-year-olds for snow play and arts and crafts. The Children's World Ski School is for children of four to 12 years of age.

TOURIST OFFICES
Tel Heavenly: 1 702 586 7000 Squaw: 1 916 583 5585
Fax Heavenly: 1 702 588 5517 Squaw: 1 916 581 7106
Email Heavenly: info@skiheavenly.com Squaw: squaw@sierra.net
Web site Heavenly: www.skiheavenly.com Squaw: www.squaw.com

Linked or nearby resorts

Public transport is efficient and frequent, but a car is useful to explore the enormous amount of skiing on offer. **Alpine Meadows**, next to Squaw, has similar steepish terrain. **Boreal** and **Tahoe Donner** are both beginner areas. **Diamond Peak** has upgraded its lifts and calls itself

'Tahoe's premier family ski resort'. **Donner Ski Ranch** has six chair-lifts and 45 runs geared mainly towards intermediates. **Granlibakken**, just outside Tahoe City, is the oldest resort on the lake and is open only at weekends. **Kirkwood** has some of the best snow and more advanced terrain. **Mount Rose** has 43 trails and is only 22 miles (35km) from Reno. **Northstar-at-Tahoe** has five lifts and a cross-country centre. **Sierra-at-Tahoe** is the third largest resort around the lake and has three high-speed quad-chairs. **Ski Homewood** on the West Shore has views of the lake on every run and is popular with snowboarders. **Soda Springs** is a small beginner area off highway I-80. **Sugar Bowl** has 58 trails and a 1,500-ft (457-m) vertical drop.

Mammoth Mountain

ALTITUDE 7,953ft (2425m)

Beginners ✱✱ Intermediates ✱✱✱ Advanced ✱✱✱ Snowboarding ✱✱✱

Mammoth, the final frontier of big-time independent skiing in the United States, has finally fallen for the lure of Mammon and sold out to corporate America. Intrawest, the Canadian resort development conglomerate, bought a 51 per cent holding and then swiftly increased it to 58 per cent. Founder Dave McCoy, who set up a portable rope-tow in 1941 and bought the resort in 1953 still runs the mountain with his family, but presumably without the financial worries. Most days he is out on the slopes skiing or checking lift tickets. Mammoth has expanded since those early days and now has 150 named runs and 31 lifts, most of them chairs which are systematically being upgraded – last season three new quad-chairs were introduced. Readers found the lack of lift safety bars 'disturbing and, at times, frightening'.

✔ Long ski season
✔ Large, varied ski area
✔ Extensive snowmaking
✘ Lack of ski resort atmosphere
✘ Long airport transfer
✘ Limited après-ski
✘ Few mountain restaurants

Ask how Mammoth got its name and there will be several answers. Some say it was named after the dinosaur bones found in the nearby meadows, others that the mountain owes its name to the Spanish, who dubbed this extinct volcano the 'big mountain'. It is not because the mountain is huge nor because it is shaped like a prehistoric elephant. The real reason stems from mining days when gold was discovered in 1878. The main mining company called itself the Mammoth Mining Company because it was so big, and gradually local geographical features including the mountain were named after it. **Mammoth Lakes**, the closest town, is 4 miles (7km) away. It is a sprawling place with not much nightlife and is supported by a year-round tourist business. Thirty minutes away by road is **June Mountain**, which offers more benign, tree-level skiing with magnificent views of the more jagged peaks in the Sierras; the McCoys opened this area in 1986, and today it has two detachable quads and five double-chairs. The Mammoth lift ticket covers both ski areas, but if you buy your pass at June Mountain (which costs less)you have to pay a nominal extra daily charge to ski at Mammoth. This 500-acre (202-hectare) ski area is a great place to ski at weekends while the Los Angelinos swarm to Mammoth.

The ski resorts lie 300 miles (480km) to the north of Los Angeles, necessitating a spectacular six-hour drive through the Mojave Desert, followed by a climb into the mountains. Reno is half the distance. Rent

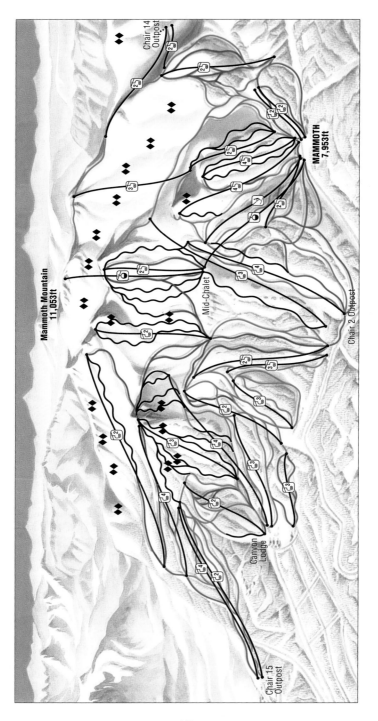

Mammoth Mountain
11,053ft

Chair 14
Outpost

MAMMOTH
7,953ft

Mid-Chalet

Chair 2 Outpost

Canyon
Lodge

Chair 15
Outpost

a 4x4 vehicle unless you enjoy fitting snowchains. While a car is useful, an efficient shuttle-bus service plies between Mammoth Lakes and the ski area during the main season. Shuttle taxis ($3 each way per person) are also available. But as one reader commented: 'Mammoth is crying out for a decent bus and taxi service'. The shuttle-bus only runs during ski hours and readers consistently complain that the lack of public transport during the evening detracts from enjoyment of their holiday.

Ski and board
top 11,053ft (3370m) bottom 7,953ft (2425m)

Mammoth has an impressive average annual snowfall of over 27ft (8m) and a tree-line going up to 9,000ft (2743m). Higher up, open bowl-skiing provides a variety of steep black (difficult) runs as well as wide blue (intermediate) trails. Grooming is efficient, but the piste map is inadequate, and piste marking is poor ('coming down from the top there are no signs to say which trail you are looking at. Skiers looking for the single-black-diamond Dave's Run can easily find themselves on the much steeper Huevos Grandes'). Above the trees are five small peaks accessed by chair-lifts. The rim of an old volcano runs right across the skyline. The top of the mountain is heavily prone to wind closure.

The six-seater Gondola 2 takes you up to the highest point, while a little further to the right as you look up the mountain the three-person Chair 23 takes you up to the next highest point. Between the two lifts are six double-black-diamond (very difficult) trails – Climax, Hangman's Hollow, three versions of Drop Out, and MJB's. For those of a more cautious nature, a single black trail takes you down a less forbidding gradient into Cornice Bowl.

Even though Mammoth is known for its sunny days and mild temperatures, the mountain does not receive its fantastic snowfalls without its share of white-outs and storms. Be prepared to spend days on end in limited visibility during the main winter months. Mammoth has four easy mountain-access points, each served by one or other of the shuttles. Mountain 'hosts' help you find your way around. A few lean years led Mammoth to expand its snowmaking facilities – which now cover 300 acres (121 hectares) and 22 runs – and can ensure skiing from early November.

Beginners
All the novice slopes are below the tree-line, with most runs concentrated on the Main Lodge, which is also where the ski school meets. The majority of the runs are green (easy) and can be reached by two chair-lifts. Another novice area is at the Canyon Lodge. A few beginner runs can be

found at Chair 15 but these are longer and less accessible. A choice of blue runs is available in both skiing areas.

Intermediates

Every area of the mountain has varied intermediate skiing, except the peak, which has some steep black runs. The Stump Alley Express quad, which has replaced chairs 2 and 18, gives swift access to some excellent middle-range terrain. The runs through the woods have been designed to offer some tight tree-skiing as well as some wide pistes. At 3 miles (4.8km), Road Runner is the longest run. It starts as a blue and then turns into a green before ending at the Main Lodge. A reader pointed out that signposting is limited and 'it is easy to end up on a difficult run by accident'.

Advanced

One look at the map scrawled with double-black-diamond runs will fire up any advanced skier. Mammoth offers steep chutes, challenging tree-level skiing, bowl-skiing and plentiful off-piste. On fresh powder days, of which there are many, exhaustion will hit you long before you have explored the whole mountain. When the snow cover is good, the black trails at the top of the mountain are steep but wide. Gondola 2 and chair 23 give access to some dramatic chutes and bowl skiing.

The Unbound, reached by the Thunder Bound Express quad, is the newly expanded funpark with two terrain parks, a half-pipe and a wide array of jumps and obstacles. It is floodlit in the evenings until 9pm at weekends. Riders should also try the Dragon's Back chute and Hemlock Ridge, which are steep and challenging runs. Upper Dry Creek has numerous walls and drop-offs, and you can follow the run into the trees to arrive at Lower Dry Creek, which is a natural half-pipe. June Mountain has a snowpark with a half-pipe.

Off-piste

The large bowls provide endless off-piste, and it is also easy to pick your own route through the trees. If there is fresh powder you should be able to ski it all day, although this is more of a challenge at the weekends. The pisteurs start work early in the morning from Main Lodge and Canyon Lodge; but to get to the good snow before they do you need to head high. Some of the best first runs of the day include Powder Bowl, Fascination, Stump Alley, Broadway, Mambo and St Anton. For off-piste boarding, hike up to Hole-in-the-Wall or Sherwin Ridge.

Tuition and guiding

Mammoth Mountain Ski and Snowboard School has packages that include group lessons, learn-to-ski specials and two-day weekend courses. Special courses incorporate bump lessons and steep skiing clinics. 'Good-quality instruction, thoroughly worthwhile,' said one reporter. Specialist three-day camps include a women's ski seminar and senior ski clinics.

Skiing facts: Mammoth Mountain

TOURIST OFFICE
PO Box 48, Mammoth Lakes, CA 93546
Tel 1 619 934 2571
Fax 1 619 934 8608
Email mmthvisit@qnet.com
Web site www.visitmammoth.com

THE RESORT
Airport transfer Mammoth/June Lake
15mins, Los Angeles 6hrs
Visitor beds 8,200
Transport Mammoth area free
shuttle bus

THE SKIING
Linked or nearby resorts June
Mountain (n)
Longest run Road Runner,
3 miles (4.8km) – blue/green
Number of lifts 31
Total of trails/pistes 3,500 acres
(1,400 hectares) – 30% easy, 40%
intermediate, 30% difficult
Nursery slopes 30% of ski area
Summer skiing none
Snowmaking 300 acres
(121 hectares) covered

LIFT PASSES
Area pass (covers Mammoth and June
Mountain) $205 for 5 of 6 days
Day pass $47
Beginners free for those taking
ski lessons
Pensioners 65yrs and over, $23 per day
or $102 for 5 of 6 days
Credit cards yes

TUITION
Adults Mammoth Ski and Snowboard

School, 10am–midday and
1.30–3.30pm, $230 for 5 days
Private lessons $60 per hr,
$390 per full day
Snowboarding Learn to Snowboard
package, $90 per day including board
and lifts. Group lessons $43 per day
Cross-country Tamarack
Cross-country Ski Center, details
on request. Loipe 50km
Other courses moguls,
race training, slalom, extreme skiing,
women's ski seminars, seniors
Guiding through ski school

CHILDREN
Lift pass 7–12yrs, $102 for 5 days,
13–18yrs, $153 for 5 days, free for
6yrs and under
Ski kindergarten Small World Day
Center, 4–12yrs, 8am–5pm,
$77 per day including lesson,
supervision and lunch
Ski school Woollywood Kid's Ski
and Snowboard School 4–12yrs,
10am–midday and 1.30–3.30pm,
$70 per day including lunch
Non-ski kindergarten Small World
Day Center, 0–12yrs, 8am–5pm,
$48–56 per day including lunch

OTHER SPORTS
Bobsleigh, dog-sledding,
hot-air ballooning, indoor tennis,
sleigh rides, snowmobiling,
snowshoeing

FOOD AND DRINK PRICES
Coffee $1.25, glass of wine $3, small
beer $3, dish of the day $6.95

Mountain restaurants

Mammoth has only one large restaurant on the mountain, at the Mid-Chalet. Chair 14 Outpost and Chair 15 Outpost are both for snacks, and June Mountain has one on-hill snack bar. The four base-areas all have cafeterias with generally reasonable prices ('Main Lodge has what comes closest to pleasant surroundings'). The best restaurant is in The Yodler, a Swiss chalet that was brought over from Europe and reconstructed plank by plank in the base area. The Mountainside Grill in the Mammoth Mountain Inn is recommended. The Austria Hof by Canyon Lodge lift station is also praised.

The resort

Keen skiers should stay in one of the hotels or condominiums at the ski base area. Readers comment that the problem is that the bus service to the town of Mammoth Lakes stops at 5.30pm, and unless you have a car you trade nightlife for daytime convenience. Mammoth Lakes has no real centre and, while there are a number of bars and restaurants, is without community feeling. The single main street has excellent shopping with numerous sports shops where you can buy equipment and clothing for considerably less than in the UK. The town also offers brand-name factory stores, including Polo/Ralph Lauren and Van Heusen, and designer ski-wear shops such as Patagonia.

Accommodation

Mammoth Mountain Inn is located at the base area and is 'large, comfortable, and ideal for keen skiers'. The complex contains a bar, restaurant and a whirlpool. The Austria Hof near the Canyon Lodge lift is 'good value with good rooms'. The 1849, Bridges, and Silver Bear are condominiums which also provide skiing convenience. Mammoth Ski & Racquet Club condos are said to be 'adequate, but not as good as we have found elsewhere in North America'.

In Mammoth Lakes, The Alpenhof ('well above average') is a cheerful place that looks as Tyrolean as its name suggests. Jägerhof Lodge is another recommended hotel, just out of town on the ski-shuttle route. The Austrian influence on the early days of American skiing is reflected in some other, more economical, establishments such as Holiday Haus. Sierra Lodge is a no-smoking hotel. One reporter favours the Shilo Inn.

Eating in and out

Mammoth Lakes has over 50 restaurants, delicatessen, ice-cream parlours and pizzerias. Alpenrose is 'a small, cosy Swiss restaurant'. Aspen Grill is recommended for its steaks, seafood and ambience. The Restaurant at Convict Lake, 15 minutes from town, has 'an interesting menu in smart surroundings'. The Lakefront has 'delicious elk and other venison. Save it for a special occasion'. Slocum's Italian and American Grill is ever popular. The Shogun is the resort's sushi bar. Grumpy's is a budget option. Self-caterers can shop at Von's supermarket, Pioneer Market or Gray Lake Grocery.

Après-ski

Directly after skiing, the Yodler offers great cocktails, and the Austria Hof has spiced wine and a variety of après-ski drinks. Late-night entertainment is limited. Check out Grumpy's, Slocum's or Gringo's, but midweek they can be quite subdued. The Clocktower is where the locals go. Whisky Creek has 'great food and dancing', while Ocean Harvest, Kegs and Cue's (for pool) are the other main nightspots. The pace hots up at weekends when the Los Angelinos hit town.

Childcare

Special learn-to-ski packages are available with prices that include lifts, lessons and equipment rental. The expanded Woollywood Ski and Snowboard School takes children from four to 12 years old, with a snowboard club for children aged seven years and over. Children six years and under ski free. The Mountain Inn's Small World Day Center takes newborn to 12-year-old children.

Mont Tremblant

ALTITUDE 870ft (265m)

Beginners ✱ Intermediates ✱✱ Advanced ✱✱ Snowboarders ✱✱✱

Located in the Laurentian Mountains, 75 miles (120km) north-west of Montreal, Mont Tremblant offers skiing in a cold climate, combined with a chance to appreciate Quebec culture and cuisine. A massive investment of CD$1 billion over a ten-year period by owner, Intrawest, has transformed – and is continuing to transform – the traditional ski village built in 1939 into a state-of-the-art resort. Intensive grooming and Canada's largest snowmaking system do much to combat the prevailing icy conditions.

✔ State-of-the-art lift system
✔ Recommended for families
✔ Extensive snowmaking
✔ Atmospheric village
✔ Choice of restaurants
✔ Car-free centre
✔ Short airport transfer
✘ Extremely low temperatures
✘ Peak season overcrowding

Ski and board
top 3,001ft (914m) bottom 870ft (265m)

Seventy years after the first chair-lift was built at Mont Tremblant, the resort now has 72km of varied pistes and 10 lifts, and these figures are still growing. A further five lifts are in the pipeline, including a much needed high-speed gondola. Currently, all the main lifts are chairs ('pretty uncomfortable in bad weather'), and only one is covered.

The lifts on both sides of Mont Tremblant – Versant Sud and Versant Nord – meet at Le Grand Manitou Lodge at the top. Part of the front (south) face of the mountain has been given over to Xzone, a large flood-lit snowpark with a half-pipe, jumps and obstacles.

Mont Tremblant claims to have Canada's most powerful snowmaking system, with 620 snow-cannon that guarantee season-long snow cover. However, reporters agree that the snowmaking is 'excessive', and 'on most days up to two-thirds of the runs were impassable and the noise of these infernal machines was deafening. Both views and sunshine were blocked out by the cloud of vapour rising into the sky'. Peak-week queues for the Tremblant Express quad-chair from the base of the mountain in the morning look horrendous but in fact they move quite quickly.

The piste map indicates a designated 'mogul zone' and a 'blade zone'. Mont Tremblant boasts 50 miles (80.5km) of cross-country trails. When Mont Tremblant is closed due to high winds – and unfortunately this is not a rare occurrence – the small neighbouring ski area of Gray Rocks at **St Jovite** usually remains open.

Beginners

As many as 20 per cent of the runs are for beginners, so second-weekers and early intermediates are able to go almost anywhere: 'Skiing as a family with two small children, we were able to go all over the mountain'. Enchanted Forest is a special beginners', and children's trail on the mountain, which is graded green (easy), and you can also travel from top to bottom of the south face on green trails. However, the downside of the resort is the extreme cold, which makes the first few days in a beginners' class – traditionally spent falling and standing around waiting for others who have fallen – not a lot of fun.

Intermediates

Those keen to bash the pistes will find plenty of scope on both sides of the mountain. Intermediate snow-users have 12 blue (intermediate) trails on the generally easier south face, while over the top the skiing is more challenging.

Advanced

The ski area on both sides of the mountain is surprisingly demanding, with over half designated as advanced or expert terrain. Dynamite is a double-black-diamond (very difficult) trail located on the north side of the mountain; it has a 42-degree pitch, making it one of the steepest trails in eastern Canada. Beside it, the legendary Expo piste is for lovers of tricky moguls, and Cossack has been the site of three world freestyle championships. The Edge is a corner of the mountain that has been set aside for advanced skiers and riders and is served by its own quad-chair. It has three demanding trails – Emotion, Action and Haute Tension – the difficulty of which is accentuated by the icy hardpack snow conditions which prevail in East Coast resorts. Despite all this, we received criticism on the limited amount of skiing: 'There is not quite enough of anything – Intrawest is promising to open up the mountain to the east but, until then serious skiers might be advised to head further west'.

Off-piste

Three intermediate runs among frozen spruces provide a dramatic introduction to tree-skiing. The Edge sector offers some difficult gladed skiing at the sides of its trails.

Tuition and guiding

The Tremblant Ski and Snowboard School offers lessons between 10am and midday and from 1.30 to 3pm. The school also offers a choice of courses ('a bewildering variety'). Ladies Love Wednesdays is a crèche- and lunch-inclusive midweek package for women skiers with children. Cybersnow Camp involves three hours of snowboarding in the morning and two hours of net-surfing in the afternoon. Other courses include Snowblade Camps, Parallel Perfection, moguls, powder skiing, telemark, cross-country, skiing for the physically challenged, and a 'discovery programme' for beginners.

Mountain restaurants

Mountain eating opportunities are disappointing; Le Grand Manitou at the summit is the only restaurant. It houses La Legende, which offers a 'fine dining experience' but not much ambience, as well as a self-service area. Many snow-users come down the mountain at lunch-time to warm up and to try one of the many restaurants in town. These include Le Shack in the square ('a good atmosphere at lunch-time and a view of the slopes').

The resort

The old part of Mont Tremblant has been meticulously restored, and the new section artfully designed to create steeply terraced main streets with painted wooden buildings that are modelled on the old quarter of Montrèal. The numerous boutiques in the Place du Village are enticing; the resort has a total of 70 shops and restaurants.

Accommodation

Six hotels have been built so far, including Château Mont Tremblant, which is undeniably the smartest and most comfortable place to stay on the slopeside. The Kandahar is one of the newest hotels. However, those who prefer self-catering can choose from a wide range of condominiums.

Eating in and out

Unlike the better-known Canadian resorts, such as Banff and Lake Louise, prices are not low in Mont Tremblant – indeed they are equivalent to those in any medium-sized French resort. However, the choice of eating places is wide, ranging from pizzerias to atmospheric establishments serving cuisine québéçoise. Le Gascon, a brasserie transported from the foothills of the Pyrenees, offers

> **WHAT'S NEW**
> High-speed gondola
> Le Lodge de la Montagne hotel
> Further major resort development

'outstanding cassoulet and robust bottles of vin rouge'. Pizzateria is lively and busy, and Mexicali Rosa's is recommended for its food and service. Coco Pazzo is an elegant Italian restaurant.

Après-ski

The nightlife is concentrated at Vieux Tremblant, which has a growing number of bars and clubs. Bizztrado is a no-go area for adults, where children up to 18 years of age can play pool and video games, listen to music and enjoy non-alcoholic drinks at the bar. The Aquaclub, which has a swimming-pool that has been modelled on a lake with an island in the middle and a 9-ft deep diving area with rocks to jump from, makes good early evening entertainment. Other activities include snowmobiling, dog-sledding, snowshoeing, skating, sleigh rides and deer observation outings.

Childcare

Low temperatures aside, this is an ideal resort for families. At the base of the slopes is the Kidz Club, which is served by a 'magic carpet' conveyor belt lift. The club organises ski and snowboarding lessons for 3- to 12-year-olds, and twice weekly après-ski for children, between 5.30 and 9.30pm, including a hot meal. Also in the evening is 'sliding fun for tots' at the base of the mountain.

TOURIST OFFICE
Tel 1 819 681 2000
Fax 1 819 681 5996
Web site www.tremblant.ca

Ski Utah

A group of distinctively different resorts make up Ski Utah, a market-ing consortium in the state that produces the finest, driest powder snow in the world. What they also offer is the most accessible skiing and snowboarding from any airport in both Europe and North America. You can either stay in Salt Lake City itself and drive 45 minutes to a different resort each day or you can base your-self in any one resort. The most central of these is **Park City**, which has its own ski resort of the same name and also acts as a bed base for the adjoining ski areas of **Deer Valley** and **The Canyons** (formerly Wolf Mountain). Even with-out the Canyons, which is currently being moulded at a cost of £125 mil-lion by the giant American Ski Company into one of the largest resorts in the USA, the other two make up the largest ski area in Utah. No doubt this was a contributory factor in the regions' successful bid to host the next Winter Olympics in 2002. **Snowbird**, the other major player, and **Alta**, its smaller, less sophisticated but exciting neighbour in Little Cottonwood Canyon, are only 6 miles (10km) away as the crow flies; however, the journey takes 45 to 60 minutes by road. Utah's two leading resorts could hardly be more dissimilar. While Snowbird is confined in its steep-sided canyon and trapped in purpose-built glitz, Park City sprawls along a much wider valley with little regard for convenience and none at all for land conservation.

> **PARK CITY**
> Beginners ✷✷
> Intermediates ✷✷
> Snowboarders ✷
> ✔ Wide choice of restaurants
> ✔ Ideal base for visiting other resorts
> ✔ Activities for non-skiers
> ✔ Tree-level skiing
> ✔ Excellent snow record
> ✘ Inconvenient resort layout
> ✘ Uninspiring scenery
> ✘ No daycare for small children

Since mining began here in the mid-nineteenth century, silver to the value of $400 million has been extracted from the hills surrounding Park City. George Hearst, father of William Randolph Hearst, made his for-tune here in the 1880s. Today, Park City has a reputation for being rather more than a ski resort. Its cultural aspirations have been enhanced by the emergence of the Sundance Film Festival. This event, which takes place over the last ten days in January under the patronage of Robert Redford's Sundance Institute, is now recognised as the premier show-case for independent American films.

Snowbird is generally considered to be the home of 'champagne powder', a dream substance of talcum-type flakes that have been freeze-dried in their journey over the desert from the distant ocean before being deposited in copious quantities on the steep slopes surrounding Little Cottonwood Canyon. The skiing terrain is prettier than in many Utah resorts, but the architecture is consideably less attractive. The resort is situated about 30 miles (48km) from Salt Lake City International Airport and is dominated by the Cliff Lodge, a huge 11-storey building of concrete and glass.

Other nearby resorts include **Snow Basin**, where former Swiss champion Bernhard Russi currently spends much of his time forging the course for the next Olympic Men's Downhill, which he promises will be the most demanding and dramatic of all time.

Ski and board
Park City: top 10,000ft (3049m) bottom 6,900ft (2104m)
Snowbird: top 11,000ft (3352m) bottom 7740ft (2359m)

As the year 2002 approaches we are seeing major on-mountain improvements in the region, both for the racers and for the tens of thousands of skiers who are expected to descend on Salt Lake City. The main Park City skiing lies on rolling, wooded terrain on the slopes of Jupiter Peak. Although the United States Ski and Snowboard teams use the resort as their headquarters, the skiing is much less challenging than at Snowbird. The general gradient of the slopes is comforting rather than challenging. The comparatively lower altitude makes for a greater percentage of glade-skiing on trails cut from the forest. Access to the top of the main ski area is by two high-speed six-passenger chairs, which take 12 minutes from the Resort Center (a moderately well-designed complex on three levels, with shops and cafés set around an open-air skating-rink) to the Summit House Restaurant. The highest point is Jupiter Bowl, which is reached by the two-seater Jupiter chair and is recommended for advanced snow-users only. Snow-users of all standards will find suitable runs from the summit to the bottom of the Silverlode six-person chair.

> **SNOWBIRD**
>
> Intermediates ✶✶
> Advanced ✶✶✶
> Snowboarders ✶✶
>
> ✔ Impressive scenery
> ✔ Excellent snow record
> ✔ Short airport transfer
> ✔ Variety of off-piste skiing
> ✔ Late-season skiing
> ✔ Doorstep skiing
> ✘ Unattractive resort
> ✘ Limited après-ski
> ✘ No real village centre
> ✘ Few mountain restaurants

Snowboarders are now allowed on the whole of the mountain, and snowboard workshops are available. However, riders are still not welcome at Deer Valley. Park City has night-skiing and snowboarding on the Pay Day and First Time trails.

Snowbird is no beauty. It is essentially a collection of concrete and glass buildings that were, according to the locals, primarily designed for

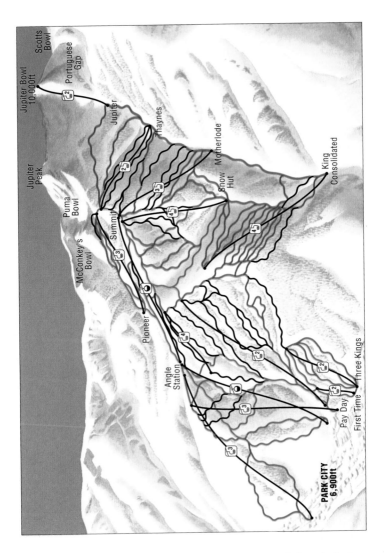

protection from avalanches. The resort boasts one of America's few cable-cars. The 'tram' carries 125 skiers almost 3,000ft (914m) to the top of Hidden Peak in eight minutes. There is only one relatively easy run down: Chips, a 3-mile (5.5-km) trail back to the base-area. Elsewhere, the higher skiing is dominated by bowls, chutes and gullies – an exciting arena for advanced skiers who enjoy powering through steep slopes on ungroomed snow. Although intermediates are well catered for, there is a shortage of real novice skiing.

461

Beginners

Park City has two beginner areas, one at the base of the resort with two lifts and another at the top of the gondola, where runs are concentrated around the Silverblade chair. Beginners can profit from a 3-mile (5.5-km) green (easy) descent from the Summit House to the Resort Center, via the top of Claimjumper, Bonanza and Sidewinder. This is broad, flat territory, which is perfect for discovering the pleasures of the beautifully groomed snow. The less experienced should avoid it late in the afternoon, when it becomes a race-track back to base as the lifts close. Claimjumper is a broad green boulevard curving round the mountain towards the Snow Hut restaurant.

Snowbird's Baby Thunder lift opens up a network of green runs and the slightly more demanding blue (intermediate) trail, Thunder Alley, which all end up below the village. Novice skiers should stay away from the top of Hidden Peak unless they really feel they can cope with Chips Run, which is a very long blue. If you only have the stamina for part of Chips, the Peruvian lift goes almost halfway. Complete beginners might want to ski off the Chickadee lift down by the Cliff Lodge. Otherwise, the Mid Gad lift (with a midway unloading station) and the Wilbere lift serve some of Snowbird's least intimidating terrain. This includes Big Emma, named after an old mining claim, which is one of the widest green slopes in the Rockies.

Intermediates

At Park City, 48 per cent of the trails are listed as intermediate and cover every area of the mountain except Jupiter Bowl. Confident snow-users will not find themselves unduly tested by Hidden Splendour, Mel's Alley, Powder Keg and Assessment. However, Prospector, Single Jack, Sunnyside and Parley's Park take rather more direct routes down the mountain. Reporters found the grading of blue (intermediate) runs unpredictable: 'The variation in the blues is quite alarming for lower intermediates'. Favourite runs include Blue Slip Bowl and 10th Mountain.

The ski area at Snowbird offers a number of well-groomed runs best suited to confident parallel skiers. Bassackwards, Election, Bananas and Lunch Run are all straightforward cruising trails. However, the ski area is littered with black (difficult) slopes and intimidating double-black-diamond (advanced) runs; considerable care should be taken to avoid embarking on a slope that may be too testing.

Advanced

Advanced snow-users at Park City have a choice of moderate black (difficult) runs, including The Hoist, Thaynes, Double Jack, Ford Country and Glory Hole, which all lead into Thaynes Canyon, a blue cruiser that marks the eastern boundary of the ski area. Halfway down, they can take the Motherlode chair-lift back to the Summit House or continue down to the King Consolidated chair-lift, which is the access point for ten short blue runs leading into Broadway and Hot Spot.

Snowbird's strong skiers are spoilt for choice, with everything from

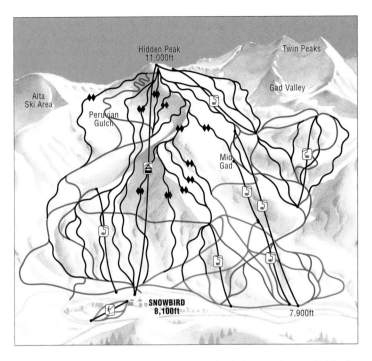

fairly easy, open-bowl skiing to very difficult bump chutes. With the exception of Chips, all the trails off Hidden Peak are classified as either black or double-black-diamond. Challenging black runs through spruce and lodgepole pine, such as Gadzooks and Tiger Tail, are reached from the Gad 2 lift. The Road To Provo traverse from Hidden Peak (also reached by the Little Cloud lift) leads to other demanding runs like Black Forest and Organ Grinder.

Off-piste

Those in search of adventure at Park City should take the Jupiter Access trail from the top of Pioneer chair-lift to the Jupiter chair-lift. This goes up to the top of the resort, a wind-blown ridge with a variety of ungroomed options. Shadow Ridge and Fortune Teller go straight down under the chair through sparsely wooded snowfields, but a ten-minute walk along the ridge to the east brings skiers to the top of Scott's Bowl. Further along, Portuguese Gap is a narrow, often heavily mogulled, field between the trees. A 20-minute walk along the ridge to the west leads to Jupiter Peak. Here there is a choice between the steep descent into Puma Bowl via the East Face, or back to the chair-lift via the West Face. All these runs are well worth the walk, but expert skiing in Park City is dependent on the Jupiter chair-lift being open.

When the wind gets up (as it frequently does) or the cloud closes in, the options are drastically reduced. The black alternatives to the west of the resort are six parallel descents through aspen trees, which are prone to closure because of poor snow conditions. A guided programme called Ski Utah Interconnect is a full-day off-piste adventure that covers five ski areas.

Snowbird's off-piste terrain is superb, and the key to it is the Cirque Traverse from Hidden Peak. From this narrow ridge skiers can drop off both sides into a large selection of chutes and gullies. Some are sandwiched between pines which have been twisted and stunted by blizzards; others are guarded by imposing outcrops of granite. Plunges into Silver Fox, Great Scott and Upper Cirque on one side and Wilbere Chute, Wilbere Bowl, Barry Barry Steep and Gad on the other can be exhilarating in fresh, deep snow and quite frightening in difficult conditions. There is also some awesome back-country (off-piste) skiing below Twin Peaks in Gad Valley.

Tuition and guiding

The Park City Ski and Snowboard School uses the American teaching system as prescribed by the Professional Ski Instructors of America (PSIA). Full-day and half-day adult group lessons are available for visitors aged 14 years and over. We have enthusiastic reports: 'The ski school is the best we have found anywhere'. The Mountain Experience programme takes good intermediate to advanced snow-users into the high bowls on Jupiter Peak. The other courses available are disabled skiing, women's clinics, race camps, and carving. Private lessons are also on offer.

The Utah Winter Sports Park is one of the few places in the world offering recreational ski-jumping on three days each week during the mid-winter months as well as bobsleigh and luge.

Beginners and low intermediate 'wedge turners' meet at the bottom of the mountain, and intermediate to advanced at the Summit Ski School area at the top of the Silverlode chair. Special courses include moguls, freestyle, slalom, off-piste, race clinics and women's ski performance workshops.

As well as normal lessons, Snowbird Ski School operates speciality workshops for style, bumps-and-diamonds and racing. A Mountain Experience clinic and free guided tours are also on offer.

Mountain restaurants

The Mid-Mountain restaurant at Park City is a low, clapboard building that was erected to serve the miners in 1898 and moved to its present site in 1987. It offers high-quality fast food ('simply heaven on a sunny day'). Its rivals, the Summit House at the Summit, and the Snow Hut at the bottom of the Silverlode lift, serve breakfast as well. Steeps, a cavernous ski-in ski-out bar at the bottom of the main run back to the Resort Center, has table service at lunch-time. It is also an essential après-ski stop, with live music, happy-hour prices and a party atmosphere.

The only real restaurant on the mountain at Snowbird is at Mid Gad. The Snowbird trail-map describes it as a 'fuel stop', which is exactly what it is. The Peak Express warming hut on Hidden Peak serves coffee and light snacks.

The resorts

A car is useful for exploring the area and the nearby resorts of **Alta**, **Solitude**, **Brighton**, **The Canyons**, **Sundance** and **Deer Valley**. All of them are less than 45 minutes' drive from Park City. Alternatively, Salt Lake City is the cheapest place to stay because you will not be paying inflated resort prices. It also offers the greatest variety of accommodation, restaurants and entertainment. However, nothing can match the atmosphere of a ski resort, and the daily drive could become a grind.

Park City, like many of its Colorado rivals, has artfully converted a mining past into a colourful touristic present. Its focus is Main Street, home to the Wasatch Brewery, the Egyptian Theater and a host of art galleries and boutiques. Between them are numerous bars, coffee shops and restaurants. A less cosmopolitan area is Prospector Square, where you can find Albertsons the supermarket, a video shop and one of Park City's two liquor stores (the other is on Main Street), which are the only places besides the bars where you can buy alcohol. Main Street is also the shopping area where specialities include pottery and native American artifacts. The Factory Stores at Kimball Junction, 4 miles (6km) away, is a large shopping centre selling end-of-the-line designer clothing, and is well worth the visit.

When Dick Bass, a fast-talking Texan oilman, built Snowbird almost 30 years ago he had apparently fallen under the spell of the latest concrete additions in the Alps. Officially, the heart of the resort is Snowbird Center, the departure point for the tram, but it is the mirrored walls of the Cliff Lodge with its 11-storey atrium that dominate the long, narrow sprawl of contemporary buildings and car-parking. The Center consists of the Plaza Deck, an open space surrounded by limited shops on three levels. Outlying buildings house condominiums, and the overall impression is of a single-function resort with few alternatives for non-skiers.

Accommodation

Much of the accommodation in Park City is in condominiums, many of which are on the ski slopes. One of the most convenient places to stay is the Silver King Aparthotel, a complex offering 85 units ranging from studios to penthouses. Most of the hotels are a few miles from Park City on the free bus route and include the Radisson Inn and Yarrow Hotel. The Chamonix Lodge is at the foot of the slopes, and the Prospector Square Hotel, which is about 15 minutes away by free shuttle-bus, resembles a collection of Nissen huts and is priced accordingly. The hotel also has a superb athletics club with an Olympic-sized indoor swimming-pool, four racquetball courts and an impressively mechanised gym. At the unusual Angel House each room is modelled on a different member of the Heavenly host ('delightful angelic antiques'). The Best Western Landmark Inn at Kimball Junction is good value and has its own sports complex.

At Snowbird most people stay either at the Cliff Lodge or at one of the three other condominium lodges nearby: The Lodge at Snowbird, The Inn and the Iron Blosam Lodge.

Eating in and out

Park City is a strong contender for the best dining in a US ski resort. An evening on Main Street could have a no more traditional start than dinner at The Claimjumper, an all-American establishment serving 'surf-and-turf'. The Irish Camel is more Mexican than its name: ('charismatic ambience, booking essential'). Chimayo is for Mexican and South-western cuisine. Ichiban Sushi has a wide selection of fresh fish. 'Excellent crab and enormous Pacific mussels' can be found at the Seafood and Oyster Company. Grappa is classic Tuscan. Zoom is owned by Robert Redford. Mercato Mediterraneo turns out stylish pizzas. The Riverhorse Café is American and trendy. Texas Red's is 'cheap and cheerful with great chili'.

Snowbird has a choice of 12 restaurants, including the Aerie at the top of Cliff Lodge, which is enclosed by glass and offers continental cuisine and a rather non-Japanese sushi bar. Keyhole Junction (also in the Cliff Lodge) specialises in South-western cooking. Pier 49 at Snowbird Center serves gourmet pizzas, and the Steakpit offers an all-American menu that includes king crab. The Wildflower Ristorante at the Iron Blosam Lodge specialises in Italian food.

Après-ski

As the Olympics draw near the stiff Mormon stance on the evils of alcohol is being visibly relaxed – at least in Park City where political correctness is noticeably less strict than in downtown Salt Lake City. In reality, licensing laws are no more severe than they were in England and Wales until a few years ago. Any establishment serving food is allowed to sell beer and usually wine. Restaurants need a spirits licence. Late-night bars must conform to the strictures of a private club licence, but temporary membership is easily obtained. This usually takes the form of a stranger asking the barman if he can find him a sponsor and he turns to the nearest drinker and asks him to oblige; he nods, you buy your sponsor a drink, and you and your party are members for the evening. Renting a hotel room entitles you to club membership on the premises.

In Park City, the Alamo Bar displays the local Park City Rugby Club memorabilia on its walls alongside stuffed moose and elk heads. By 1.30am, Main Street is as quiet as London's Bond Street on Christmas Day.

Snowbird's bars are few in number and formal enough to deter all but the most enthusiastic nightlifers. Immediately after the lifts close, skiers gravitate to the Forklift, just across the plaza from the tram (cable-car), and the Wildflower Lodge. Later on, the Aerie often has a pianist, but sitting here until closing time at 1am is not particularly exciting. If the roads are clear and no storms are imminent you could try a night-out in Salt Lake City, 25 miles (40km) away.

Other activities at Park City include an aeroclub, a climbing-wall, hang-gliding, helicopter rides, hot-air ballooning, ice-driving, indoor tennis and raquet-ball, parapente, skating and curling, sleigh rides, snowcat skiing, snowmobiling, snowshoeing, swimming, as well as bob-sledding, ice-rocketing (a one-person sled) and ski-jumping at the Olympic Sports Park. Snowbird's other sports are a climbing-wall, indoor tennis, racquetball and squash.

Childcare

The Park City Ski and Snowboard School divides its tuition into Youth (7 to 13 years) and Kinderschule (3 to 6 years) for six- and four-hour daily programmes respectively. The Kinderschule package also includes lunch and indoor supervision. The Kinderschule Mountain Adventure is for children aged three to six who can snow-plough. There are no crèche facilities for non-skiing children.

Daycare for children of two months and upwards at Snowbird is available at the Camp Snowbird Children's Center at the Cliff Lodge. The ski school offers programmes combining ski instruction with day-care. One reporter described Snowbird as 'the most child-friendly resort I have ever been to'.

TOURIST OFFICE Park City
Tel 1 435 649 6100
Fax 1 435 649 4132
Email pcinfo@pcski.com
Web site www.skiutah.com

TOURIST OFFICE Snowbird
Tel 1 801 742 2222
Fax 1 801 742 3344
Web site www.skiutah.com

Linked or nearby resorts

Alta
top 10,550ft (3216m) bottom 8,530ft (2600m)

This is an old-fashioned, unpretentious resort revered by powder skiers, ski bums and skiers in search of a cheap lift ticket and powder that can sometimes better Snowbird's. Alta, just a mile up the hill from Snowbird in Cottonwood Canyon, was here about 30 years before Snowbird and likes to remind you of that fact. It has rather more beginner/lower inter-mediate terrain but has phenomenal chutes and secret powder caches reached only by back-country (off-piste) hiking. Devotees refuse to accept that Snowbird is in the same class; realists count their blessings that two outstanding powder resorts are so close together. Many believe that eventually the two will be linked; they already form the most chal-lenging section of the back-country Interconnect circuit, which includes

Park City, Solitude and Brighton, in an attempt to reproduce the alpine concept of skiing from one resort to another.

On piste, Alta has eight chair-lifts and five drag-lifts. The resort limits its uphill capacity to 10,750 skiers per hour in order to make the skiing experience more pleasant. The Alf Engen Ski School was named after its founder, who taught skiing here in 1948; children's lessons are offered as well as adult tuition. The Alta Children's Center is a privately run daycare organisation. Alpenglow and Watson's Cafés are the two mountain restaurants, while Albion Grill, Alta Java and Goldminer's Daughter are located at the mountain base. Alta's oldest and most charming lodge is the Alta Pine Lodge, which has been attracting visitors since 1938 and was renovated in 1990. Other accommodation includes the Alta Peruvian Lodge and Goldminer's Daughter Lodge.

TOURIST OFFICE
Tel 1 801 359 1078
Fax 1 801 799 2340
Email info@altaskiarea.com
Web site www.altaskiarea.com

The Canyons
top 9,380ft (2859m) bottom 4,980ft (1518m)

The resort that started off as Park West, and was later sold and changed its name to Wolf Mountain, has now been bought by the giant ski real estate company the American Skiing Company, which plans to turn it into one of the largest resorts in the USA. The new Tombstone Peak area has 500 acres (202 hectares) of ski and snowboarding terrain served by a high-speed quad, making a total skiable area of 2,200 acres (890 hectares), nine lifts, including an eight-person gondola, and four half-pipes. By 2002 its owners hope to have developed 7,000 acres (2833 hectares) of varied terrain served by 22 lifts. Technically it is possible to link it easily to both Park City and Deer Valley. At present both the latter resorts insist that they will never sell, but 'never' in currently about six months in contempory US ski resort warfare. The resort is reached by a short, free shuttle-bus ride from Park City and offers a wide variety of terrain on three mountains. The Red Pine Lodge is a mid-mountain lodge and restaurant but for the present there is no slopeside accommodation.

TOURIST OFFICE
Tel 1 801 649 5400
Fax 1 801 649 7374
Email info@thecanyons.com
Web site www.thecanyons.com

Deer Valley
top 9,400ft (2865m) bottom 7,200ft (2195m)

Unashamedly luxurious, Deer Valley is one mile north-east of Park City up a winding mountain road lined with multi-million-dollar homes. It is a place where grooming counts, both on the meticulously pisted slopes ('like going skiing at Harrods') and with the clientèle, who are a walking advertisement for designer clothing. 'It is worth a visit for two or three days,' said one reporter, 'if only to observe the outfits'.

The skiing is on three mountains served by 14 lifts and is constantly being expanded. A further 640 acres (259 hectares) of Empire Canyon off the back of Flagstaff Mountain is served by a chair-lift. Snowmaking has also been improved on all three mountains. The Deer Valley Ski School offers group and private lessons, and special ski courses including black-diamond workshops, parallel breakthrough, style clinics, women's ski clinics, mountain extreme and teen equipe (for 13- to 18-year-olds). Children aged 2 months to 12 years are looked after by Deer Valley Child Care, and Deer Valley Children's Ski School takes children from 4 to 12 years of age. Snowboarding is not allowed at Deer Valley.

Deer Valley is a short, free bus ride from Park City. The resort does not have a town as such, but accommodation includes several large condominiums and a few small hotels, including the luxurious Stein Eriksen Lodge. Restaurants include the Mariposa, and the 'all you can eat' seafood buffet. The lounge at Snow Park Lodge is a popular après-ski bar.

TOURIST OFFICE
Tel 1 801 649 1000
Fax 1 801 649 1910
Email p_denny@deervalley.com
Web site www.deervalley.com

Solitude
top 10,035ft (3059m) bottom 7,988ft (2435m)

Just 28 miles (45km) and 45 minutes' drive from Salt Lake City, Solitude is in the heart of Big Cottonwood Canyon in Utah's Wasatch-Cache National Forest. Solitude is dedicated to creating and maintaining some of the best groomed slopes that you will find anywhere. State-of-the-art machinery ensures that 50 per cent of the mountain is groomed on a rotating basis – including the steeper terrain. Seven lifts serve 1,200 acres (486 hectares) of which 20 per cent is rated beginner standard, 50 per cent intermediate and 30 per cent advanced. Accommodation is available at the Inn or at Creekside. Six restaurants include a Mongolian-style hut, the Yurt, situated a third of a mile from the Inn at Solitude and reached either on snowshoes or cross-country skis through the trees.

TOURIST OFFICE
Tel 1 801 534 1400
Fax 1 435 649 5276
Email info@skisolitude.com
Web site www.skiutah.com

Smuggler's Notch/Stowe

ALTITUDE Smuggler's Notch 1,030ft (314m), Stowe 1,300ft (396m)

Beginners ***** Intermediates ***** Advanced ***** Snowboarders *****

The Smuggler's Notch pass in Vermont was given its name during the American War of Independence, when it was used for the illicit passage of supplies from Canada. Sensibly, given the nature of its mainly gentle pine-clad slopes, it has not tried to compete with its bigger sisters in Colorado and Utah but has carved a niche that no other resort has so far been able to match anywhere in the world. Smuggs, as the locals call it, has established itself at the cutting edge of the family market and regularly wins awards for its child-friendly facilities. You would not choose to come to Smuggs without children; the key is convenience, with the lifts and accommodation within a 300-yard (274-m) radius and apartments designed with the family in mind.

- ✔ Superb children's facilities (Smuggs)
- ✔ Lack of queues
- ✔ Outstanding ski school (Smuggs)
- ✔ Attractive village of Stowe
- ✘ Subzero temperatures

Over the mountain, the eighteenth-century village of Stowe is picturesque, with a white church and municipal buildings in the traditional New England style. Convenience is not a feature here because the village is separated from the skiing base by 5 miles (8km) of winding highway lined with the customary motels, rental shops and restaurants.

Ski and board

Smuggler's Notch: top 3,640ft (1109m) bottom 1,030ft (314m)
Stowe: top 4,393ft (1339m) bottom 1,300ft (396m)

The skiing at Smuggler's Notch is mainly benign, interspersed with some tricky mogul slopes, which are not widely publicised but keep the parents happy. Snow records are excellent, with an average of 250 inches (98cm) per season, but the 'frozen granular patches' for which the state is renowned are an all too common occurrence. The three mountains – Morse, Madonna and Sterling – are interconnected, and Sterling in turn links with Stowe's Spruce Peak via Snuffy's Trail. This requires a lot of poling in both directions. The old fixed double chair-lifts at Smuggler's Notch are in dire need of upgrading, but their low hourly uphill capacity means that the slopes manage to remain uncrowded.

Madonna at Smuggs has a large terrain park for intermediate and advanced skiers and boarders, with a 300-ft- (90-m)- long half-pipe and music that belts out above your head from speakers that are attached to the lift pylons.

The skiing at Stowe is on two mountains outside the village centre. The top of the skiing is Mount Mansfield, Vermont's highest peak, which is reached in comfort by an eight-seater gondola. Although the FourRunner quad to the Octagon Web Café (from where you can email friends and colleagues) is considerably more exposed, it opens up a much bigger part of the mountain, with a choice of runs for all standards. There are four funparks at Stowe.

Beginners
Morse is the beginners' mountain, conveniently situated in the village centre of Smuggler's Notch. From the top of Morse Mountain at 2,250ft (684m) you can ski along a green (easy) trail to the base of Madonna Mountain and back again. From the top of the Mountain Triple and Toll House Double lifts at Stowe are a network of blue (intermediate) trails to the Toll House base.

Intermediates
More adept snow-users quickly move on from Morse Mountain in Smuggs to the other two mountains, which are reached either by bus or on skis. Madonna Mountain has some pleasant trails such as the blue Upper and Lower Drifter and Upper and Lower Chilcoot. From the top of the FourRunner lift at Stowe there are some good blue cruisers, one of which – Rimrock – connects across to the second half of the mountain. Here the choice of trails back to base comprises three blues: Perry Merrill, Switchback and Gondolier.

Advanced
Smuggler's Notch has several sharp double-black-diamond (very difficult) trails, as well as The Black Hole, which is billed as 'the only triple-black-diamond in the east'. The trail directly below the Madonna 1 chair-lift is intimidating: 'Looking down from the chair at rocks covered in ice I could hardly believe they were actually skiable'. The skiing can also be near perpendicular in places at Stowe. It is said that if you can ski Stowe's celebrated Front Four, you can ski anywhere. Starr, Liftline, National and Goat are ready to test the most proficient of snow-users, especially when the familiar 'boilerplate' ice is in place. Chinchip is the sole black (difficult) trail back to base on Mount Mansfield.

Off-piste
There is some unpatrolled skiing through the trees, but snow-users in search of powder adventures would be better giving these resorts a miss and buying a plane ticket to Colorado or Utah.

Tuition and guiding
The Peter Ingevold Snow Sports University is the impressive ski and snowboard school at Smuggs. Special courses include 'Dad & Me' and 'Mom & Me', where you and your child are taught together, with the emphasis on picking up useful tips to teach your child yourself. Stowe's

Ski and Snowboard Training Center has adult workshops, race clinics, and even Quick Fix where you 'take a run with a personal ski trainer'.

Mountain restaurants

At Smuggs the only on-mountain eating place is a small, bleak hut rather exaltedly called Hearth & Candle at the Top of the Notch, with self-service drinks and snacks served during limited hours. Most snow-users return to the two bases where there is a choice of The Village Restaurant at Morse, which houses the Green Mountain Café & Bakery, and Snowsnake Pizzeria. At Madonna base there is the Green Peppers Pub for lunch, as well as a cafeteria with 'boring old hamburger, and uninspired pasta'.

The eight-seater gondola at Mount Mansfield runs in the evening so that visitors can dine in the gastronomic Cliff House Restaurant.

The resorts

Smuggler's Notch is a small, unadorned village consisting mainly of condominiums and is devoid of boutiques and bars. A single sports shop in the village provides the necessary balaclavas and neoprene face masks, and there is one grocery store. As a complete contrast, the 200-year-old town of Stowe has been a sophisticated tourist centre for more than a century and attracts wealthy Bostonians. It is a typical Vermont town of red-and-white weather-boarded houses set around a steepled white church on attractive Main Street, where most of the shops and accommodation is based.

Accommodation

The Village at Smuggler's Notch offers regular hotel rooms and self-catering apartments. The resort's condominiums are highly recommended for families: 'The best two-bedroomed apartment we have ever seen, with a separate 30-ft sitting room and a television in every room, including one angled above the family-sized whirlpool'. Stowe has more than 30 high-quality inns.

Staying in Stowe is civilised rather than riotous, especially at the Trapp Family Lodge four miles (2.5km) out of town, seemingly run by the survivors of *The Sound of Music*. Ye Olde England Inne plays heavily on its name and the expensive Inn at the Mountain is the only slope-side accommodation.

Eating in and out

All the restaurants in and around Smuggler's Notch are child-friendly – indeed you would feel left out if you came to the resort without a child. Breakfast is at The Mountain Grille, with children under 12 years old charged half their age in dollars for all they can eat. The Hearth & Candle restaurant is the only eatery that has a separate upstairs section – for adults without children. Café Bandito's is recommended: 'My children voted it their favourite après-ski spot. Three Mountain Lodge has an authentic Vermont atmosphere.

In Stowe, Winfield's in the Stoweflake Resort is recommended for fish. Copperfields at Ye Olde England Inne serves game and seafood.

Après-ski

Nightlife in Smuggs is geared to family entertainment, with tobogganing and karaoke evenings, torchlight parades, fireworks and dance parties. After skiing, hot chocolate awaits you as you gather around a camp fire at the foot of Morse Mountain, while a man in a Disney-style mouse suit and another dressed as a bear hand out sweets to children and pose for photos with them. Floodlit snowboarding and tobogganing on high-tech inner tubes down Sir Henry's Sliding Hill provide the later evening entertainment. There is also a family-friendly swimming-pool, tennis courts, snowmobile tours of the mountain by night and a skating rink.

At Stowe, Mr Pickwick's Polo Pub serves international ales. Next door, the Fox and Hounds provides further evidence that Stowe is an aspiring home from home for visiting Brits.

Childcare

Children is what Smuggs is all about, and everything centres around them. The only disadvantage is the numbingly low temperatures. Little ones from just six weeks of age spend their days at Alice's Wonderland Child Enrichment Center, which includes a children's zoo and an out-door pirate ship playground in the warmer weather. The ski school ('outstanding and put anything in Europe that we had experienced to shame') takes children to and from the slopes in a horse-drawn trailer, and in the cold weather classes frequently return to base for hot chocolate, videos and snacks. The amenities at Stowe's base include the Cubs Infant Care Center and the Children's Adventure Center.

TOURIST OFFICE
Smuggler's Notch
Tel (0800) 897159 (*freephone*)
Fax 1 802 644 2713
Email smuggs@smuggs.com
Web site www.smuggs.com

TOURIST OFFICE
Stowe
Tel 1 802 253 3000
Fax 1 802 253 3406
Email skistowe@sover.net
Web site www.stowe.com

Steamboat

ALTITUDE 6,900ft (2104m)

Beginners ✱✱✱ Intermediates ✱✱ Snowboarders ✱✱✱

Steamboat lies at the foot of Rabbit Ears Pass in north-west Colorado, a three-and-a-half-hour drive from downtown Denver. It is now part of the empire of the ever-expanding American Skiing Company, and we can expect to see major resort development over the coming seasons.

✔ Accessible nursery slopes
✔ Excellent snow record
✔ Easy tree-level skiing
✔ Choice of restaurants
✔ Range of non-skiing activities
✘ Limited ski area
✘ Distance from town to lifts

Legend has it that Steamboat Springs came into being in 1865 when three French trappers mistook a chugging noise on the River Yampa for a paddle-steamer, only to discover that it came from bubbling mineral springs. With Gallic logic they duly conjured up Steamboat Springs. The broad Yampa Valley was permanently settled 100 years ago by homesteaders raising cattle. In 1912 a Norwegian, Carl Howelsen, introduced ski-jumping lessons, followed two years later by the first Winter Carnival, with jumping competitions as the main attraction.

Skiing took off in the 1960s, triggered by the opening of the first double chair-lift on Storm Mountain in 1963, and the silver medal won by local boy Billy Kidd in the Innsbruck Winter Olympic Games the following year. When Kidd retired he was appointed Steamboat's Director of Skiing. He joined forces with World Champion cowboy Larry Mahan to found the Cowboy Downhill, a unique slalom with roping and saddling elements, which is held each January for more than 100 professional rodeo riders in full costume. Steamboat trades heavily on this cowboy motif in its marketing strategy, but the reality is that it has much less of a Wild West atmosphere than some of its Colorado rivals. As is often the case in the Rockies, what you actually get is a two-tier resort connected by a shuttle bus. Steamboat, at the base of the mountain, is all ski-in ski-out convenience, but the real action is in **Steamboat Springs**, 4 miles (6km) away in the valley.

Ski and board
top 10,568ft (3221m) bottom 6,900ft (2103m)
The skiing covers three interlinked mountains: Sunshine Peak, Storm Peak and Mount Werner (formerly Storm Mountain). Although the area is served by a modern lift system backed up by extensive snowmaking, the terrain is of even pitch. This limits the variety and challenge of the

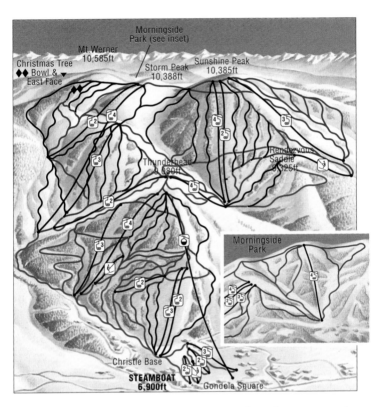

trails. The efficient Silver Bullet gondola takes skiers up to the Thunderhead mid-station, and two high-speed quads, Storm Peak and Sundown, allow them to fan out rapidly over the upper slopes. The development of Morningside Park, a 179-acre (72-hectare) bowl off the back of Storm Peak, provides more gentle terrain and offers better access to the rugged skiing off the face of Mount Werner, which is served by a triple-chair. The Thunderbird Express quad chair-lift has replaced both the old Thunderbird and Arrowhead chair-lifts.

This season development in the Pioneer Ridge sector continues, with the opening of the Pony Express detachable quad and 12 new trails mainly for advanced skiers. Riders are made extremely welcome in this resort with easily accessible nursery slopes and a specialist snowpark near the Elkhead lift. Snowboarders buy an estimated one in three of the lift tickets, and the Steamboat Snowboard School now has 45 instructors.

Beginners
The wide, flat area at the base of the gondola within two minutes' walk of Ski Time Square is an ideal place to learn to ski or snowboard. It is

served by six beginner lifts – several of them chairs – which are readily slowed down on request. Phase two is from the Christie Chairs, which rise out of the base area to give access to friendly green (easy) runs with names like Yoo Hoo and Giggle Gulch. By the third day, competent beginners should be able to ride the Silver Queen lift and return to base via Why Not and Right-O-Way.

Intermediates

As Steamboat has a relatively low altitude by Colorado standards, there are trees all the way up the mountain, which means that almost all the skiing is through glades cut out of the forest. Most of the trails are extremely wide and all are impeccably prepared, giving plenty of cruising on all three mountains.

Advanced

The best black (difficult) runs are the chutes on Mount Werner, on the extreme edge of the ski area. As you hike along the access ridge, you come to Chutes One, Two and Three, Christmas Tree Bowl and finally East Face, which are short descents that become progressively steeper. Otherwise, the toughest skiing is on Three O'clock, Two O'clock and Twilight, which quickly become mogulled.

Off-piste

Whenever new snow falls, Steamboat's great glory is the easy tree-skiing within the resort boundaries. At the top of Sunshine Peak, the forest is quite dense but it soon opens out to allow uninhibited action among the aspens between Closet and Shadows trails. Another good area is off the Storm Peak Express, between Cyclone, Typhoon, Tornado and Nelson's Run. The irrepressible Jupiter

> ### WHAT'S NEW
>
> Pony Express detachable quad-chair
> 12 new trails on Pioneer Ridge
> Additional snowmaking

Jones, owner of Steamboat Powder Cats, runs excellent day trips to Buffalo Pass in the Routt National Park, a few miles out of town.

Tuition and guiding

The Steamboat Ski School in Gondola Square offers a Beginner's Guarantee scheme for complete novices, plus group lessons for adults, children and teenagers. The Billy Kidd Center provides more advanced training in bumps, racing and other disciplines.

Mountain restaurants

In tune with the current trend in the Rockies, Steamboat provides gourmet lunches as a supplement to the customary cafeteria fare. The most sophisticated option is Hazie's at the Thunderhead mid-station, but the printed caveat against drinking alcohol in the course of a skiing day may not suit some European visitors.

The alternative sit-down choice, Ragnar's at Rendezvous Saddle, specialises in Scandinavian dishes. Both the Thunderhead and Rendezvous self-services have sun-deck barbecues.

The resort

Steamboat's commercial heart is Gondola Square, the focal point of the whole ski area, but the dominant element is the concrete and glass bulk of the Sheraton Hotel crouched on the hilltop above it. This is surrounded by malls and condominiums, which become progressively more attractive the further you fan out from the centre. The Steamboat Springs Old Town area consists almost entirely of Lincoln Avenue, a broad street that has not been prettified to the same degree as rivals like **Breckenridge**. Lincoln Avenue boasts a first-run multi-screen cinema, shops that go far beyond the normal range of ski-related goods, and the best restaurants.

Accommodation

The Sheraton is convenient, but once you are inside you could just as well be in Los Angeles or Houston. Those who need to be within a stone's throw of the lifts might prefer the Ptarmigan Inn, which has an outdoor pool and hot tub, plus a more cheerful après-ski bar. Steamboat Springs offers a choice between renovated old-style and simple new accommodation, represented most centrally by the Harbor Hotel and the Alpiner Lodge on opposite sides of Lincoln Avenue.

Eating in and out

For a resort of this size, the range and quality of the restaurants is impressive. Remingtons at the Sheraton represents hotel-chain grandeur and expense, but finer dining can be found at L'Apogee, Antares, Cipriani's and the Steamboat Yacht Club. Riggio's has a cheaper line in Italian fare, and the Chart House has the best salad bar in town. There is Chinese food at the Panda Garden and the Canton, excellent sushi at Yama Chan's, and Mexican at La Montana. Alternatively, you can ride the Silver Bullet by night and dine on the mountain at Hazie's, or plunder the eat-as-much-as-you-can buffet at the BK Corral. Another on-mountain option is the snowcat-ride to Ragnar's. Condo dwellers will appreciate the chain supermarkets, but they are inconveniently sited halfway between Steamboat and Steamboat Springs.

Après-ski

When the lifts close, beer lovers gather in the Heavenly Daze Brewery in Ski Time Square and the Steamboat Brewery and Tavern on Lincoln Avenue. Lively watering-holes include the Inferno, which often has alternative rock music, the Tugboat and Dos Amigos, which are all near the base of the mountain. In the downtown area, BW-3 (where you can hear live music) and the Old Town Pub, which first opened its saloon doors in 1904, have happy hours and pool tables. More active après-ski takes place on Howelsen Hill, a floodlit area overlooking Steamboat

Springs with facilities for night-skiing and skating. It also has a mile-long four-man bobsled track and two ski jumps. The natural springs at Strawberry Park Hot Springs, located a few miles out of town, provide a less stressful alternative. Murphy's Exchange Pub is lively until late, as is Harwigs. Those who are prepared to brave the locals should try ZZ, but be prepared for regulars to say 'this is my chair, so get out of it'. Other sports available at Steamboat are bungee jumping, dog-sledding, hot-air ballooning, ice-driving, sleigh rides, snowmobiling, swimming and winter fly-fishing.

Childcare

Children under six years ski free at Steamboat. For every parent who has bought a five-day ticket, one child under 13 can ski for free. Steamboat's Kids Vacation Center takes skiing children from two to six years of age from 8.15am to 4.30pm. Babies and non-skiing children are looked after at Kiddie Corrall Child Care.

TOURIST OFFICE
Tel 1 970 879 6111
Fax 1 970 879 7844
Email info@steamboat-ski.com
Web site www.steamboat-ski.com

Vail/Beaver Creek

ALTITUDE Vail 8,120ft (2475m) Beaver Creek 8,100ft (2470m)

Beginners ✳✳✳ Intermediates ✳✳✳ Advanced ✳ Snowboarders ✳✳✳

Vail is the velvet-lined showcase of American skiing. Other resorts, from Vermont to California, look in the window of this Colorado superstore and then race home to emulate what they have seen. Through enormous investment in recent years it has wooed and seduced both the jaded Wall Street banker and the international skier to its immaculately groomed slopes, and now delivers the largest area of ski terrain of any US resort, unbeatable service and guaranteed snow. The primping and pampering of an otherwise moderately bland stretch of mountainside has signalled the danger of reducing the skiing and snowboarding experience to the homogenised level of a Disney-style theme park. However, this cynical view is completely lost on its big-buck owners as well as on its flock of devotees, who sheepishly concur with its worldwide advertising slogan: 'Once Is Never Enough'. Indeed, so many skiers now make the two-and-a-half hour drive from Denver International Airport that a monorail train system over the mountains has now been proposed.

- ✔ Favourable snow record
- ✔ Large ski area
- ✔ Separate children's ski area
- ✔ Excellent ski school
- ✔ Easy introduction to off-piste
- ✔ Wide choice of resort restaurants
- ✘ Limited steep terrain
- ✘ Homogenised skiing
- ✘ Poor choice of mountain restaurants
- ✘ High prices

Anyone expecting a classic Rocky Mountain settlement at their journey's end is in for a disappointment. The pedestrianised village centre is built in neo-Tyrolean style with chalets clustered around a central clock tower. Its suburbs sprawl for 7 miles (11km) along the busy I-70 freeway. It shares a lift pass with sister resort **Beaver Creek**, 10 miles (16km) to the west, which is now linked European-style to the two smaller ski areas of **Bachelor Gulch** and **Arrowhead**. Beaver Creek was the first computer-designed ski area, and its expanding mass of luxury condominiums and five-star hotels consistently wins it awards as one of America's top resorts. Long, winding trails, lack of crowds and family-oriented facilities make Beaver Creek an altogether more peaceful place than Vail in which to base yourself. Vail's acquisition of nearby **Breckenridge** and **Keystone** means that multi-day lift passes at any of these resorts are interchangeable (if you buy your ticket in Vail/Beaver Creek) and there is a regular subsidised shuttle service between them.

Expansion and improvement is a continuous process here as Vail flouts its position at the head of the US resort league table. Next on the agenda is an 885-acre (358-hectare) extension of its fabled Back Bowls off-piste area. Vail has finally been granted planning permission, but the scheme is presently being thwarted by the lynx. Environmentalists say that the terrain is the ideal habitat of the cat, although the last sighting was over 20 years ago. Sceptics say that skiers dropping into the avalanche-prone chutes of East Valley are unlikely to endanger any species but their own.

Vail has enthusiastically embraced snowboarding and has a dedicated snowboard piste map, two half-pipes, funparks and several glades cut through the trees to give riders their own pistes.

While the number of lifts (30) is minuscule in comparison with Espace Killy or the Trois Vallées in France, their efficiency is such that you can clock up the vertical metres in a way that is not always possible in Europe. Queuing is not a problem except at the main access points during peak-season rush hour. As one reader put it: 'Vail does everything right. It overwhelms you with service and courtesy'. Indeed, if it does not, then they want to know about it at the best-named web site in the business: www.snow.com

Ski and board
top 11,450ft (3491m) bottom 8,150ft (2485m)

Vail's main skiing takes place on the north-facing side of the mountain above the resort and is reached from three main access points along the valley floor: the Vista Bahn in Vail Village, a gondola and high-speed quad in Lionshead, and the Riva Bahn Express at Golden Peak. There is also a slow two-person chair at Cascade Village. These lifts are served by an efficient ski bus system. The backside of the mountain is devoted to the largely unpisted Back Bowls area renowned for its powder. When the resort is busy you can take the new and much underused detachable quad-chair at Golden Peak, which connects with the Northwoods Express lift and provides direct access to the Back Bowls.

Typical Colorado conditions are on a par with exceptional days in Europe. Ice, crud, bare patches or uncovered rocks are a rarity. Ample fluffy snow and top-to-bottom skiing from mid-November until the end of April is usual. Vail and Beaver Creek have state-of-the-art snowmaking. A battalion of snowcats – increased by 30 per cent last season – manicure the slopes at the end of each day, all pistes are well-signposted, and any obstacles are marked. One criticism of Vail's skiing is its lack of variety. While many of the runs on the front face are indistinguishable apart from their names, some of the steeper trails are heavily mogulled and there is some exciting tree-skiing and plenty of long cruising runs.

The skiing at Beaver Creek covers four areas: Spruce Saddle, Grouse Mountain, Strawberry Park and Arrowhead. It is served by 14 lifts, and most of the 146 runs are enjoyably intermediate on rolling terrain, which offers plenty of variety. Grouse Mountain has a number of double-black-diamond (very difficult) runs.

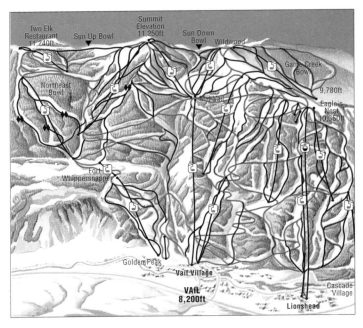

Beginners

The two beginner areas in Vail are at Golden Peak and Eagle's Nest. Golden Peak at the east end of the mountain has a number of easy runs and short lifts at the base area. Fort Whippersnapper, at the mid-station of the Riva Bahn lifts, is an extensive ski-in ski-out playground for children. At Eagle's Nest, reached directly by the gondola from Lionshead, are several easy runs and an activity centre including tubing, an ice-rink and snowpark. More advanced beginners can find suitable runs on all areas of the mountain by following the green (easy) runs on the piste map.

At Beaver Creek, the beginner areas are at the base of the Centennial Express lift and at Arrowhead. Another beginner area is at the top of the Stump Park lift.

Intermediates

Both Vail and Beaver Creek are essentially intermediate mountains. If you want to perfect your turns, the wide open pistes are a perfect training ground. Most skiers head to the top of the mountain via the Vista Bahn Express to mid-Vail, where two high-speed quads let you explore the central west side of the mountain. The Back Bowls can be reached from the Mountaintop Express or Wildwood Express lifts. Intermediates favour the long, cruising runs from the Northwoods chair, or the easier trails off the Game Creek Express lift. For fast and smooth cruising you can take the runs off Eagle's Nest Ridge, such as Lodgepole, Berries and Ledges, down to the Avanti chair or all the way to the base. Although the

Back Bowls are notorious, they are not at all steep, with the easier runs offering a gentle introduction to powder skiing. A few runs such as Poppyfields are groomed. The Slot black (difficult) piste can be icy in the early morning.

Beaver Creek has long, cruising runs off the Centennial lift and from Strawberry Park to Bitteroot, Stacker and Pitchfork. Bachelor's Gulch has some long runs such as Grubstake and Gunder's.

Advanced

Highline and Roger's Run are both double-black-diamond (expert) trails, which are steep and heavily mogulled. Little-skied Skipper, off the Windows Road catwalk, can provide considerable challenge. Some excellent tree-skiing is to be found at Ouzo Woods off Faro, Ouzo and Ouzo Glade. Look Ma and Challenge under the Wildwood Express chair are testing in good snow. Kangaroo Cornice, and North Rim under the Northwoods chair are also well worth skiing. Most advanced skiers congregate in the Back Bowls, which provide superb skiing and boarding in true powder conditions. However, they can be closed in bad weather or when cover is insufficient.

At Beaver Creek, Grouse Mountain has several double-black-diamonds, which are steep mogul runs such as Bald Eagle and Falcon Park. Screech Owl and Ptarmigan are also challenging.

Vail prides itself on the variety and challenge of its riding terrain, which includes dedicated pistes cut through the trees. These are marked on a separate snowboarding map. There are also two half-pipes at Eagle's Nest, which are floodlit for night-riding, and two funparks with obstacles. Beaver Creek has seven dedicated snowboard runs through chutes and gullies, a half-pipe on Moonshine, and Stickline Park between Harrier and Centennial, which has a combination of tabletops, banks and log slides. The separate snowboard map shows riders how to avoid the dreaded, flat catwalk.

Off-piste

The Back Bowls provide Vail's off-piste skiing and snowboarding, and it is rewarding to make fresh tracks here on a powder day. Chutes, drop-offs and fine tree-skiing are available in the Mongolia Bowls. Back-country (off-piste) skiing does require a guide. The Minturn Mile takes you down through some scenic and challenging terrain to the small town of the same name; margaritas or pitchers of beer at the Saloon in **Minturn** provide a pleasant end to the outing. In perfect weather conditions when the crowds hit the Back Bowls, the local powderhounds are to be found whooping it up on Beaver's Grouse Mountain.

Tuition and guiding

The Vail/Beaver Creek Ski and Snowboard School, with a total of 1,300 instructors, is one of the largest in the world. In Vail it has separate locations at the base of Golden Peak, Lionshead and in Vail Village, and at Two Elk, Mid-Vail and Eagle's Nest. The Beaver Creek Ski and

Snowboard School is at Village Hall and on the mountain at Spruce Saddle. Arrowhead has its own ski school. Readers continue to comment on the high quality of instruction and the friendly attitude of the teachers: 'What a change from Europe! Our instructor became a real pal, and we learned more from her in a week than in the previous three seasons in France'. The Vail/Beaver Creek Ski and Snowboard School has 150 snowboard teachers with dedicated classes in high season for teenagers.

Mountain restaurants

Size rather than intimacy seems to be the priority at most of the mountain restaurants in both Vail and Beaver Creek. Largest and most lavish is the Two Elk self-service (referred to as 'Too Elkspensive' by the locals). The smaller Wildwood Smokehouse is renowned for its tuna sandwiches. The Cookshack in Vail and Rafters in Beaver Creek both have wait-service. Buffalo's at Chair 4 is good for snacks. All the mountain restaurants are owned by the resort and are geared towards high turnover rather than the leisurely

> **WHAT'S NEW**
>
> Further major resort development

lunching enjoyed by most Europeans. To avoid the corporate pressure – and indeed the corporate fare which is priced according to altitude – you should eat at the (usually cheaper) independent restaurants at the base areas. Garfinkels, or Bart and Yeti's at Lionshead are recommended, as are Pepi's and Los Amigos in Vail Village.

The resorts

Vail Village itself is a small, mainly traffic-free precinct with smart hotels, restaurants and expensive boutiques in a pleasant riverside setting a decent distance from the I-70 freeway and bordered by pistes. While the nucleus of Vail is compact, there is more to explore in the Vail Valley by car. In Avon, check out Cassidy's Hole in the Wall, a bar decorated with mooseheads which often has live bands. Cordillera, 25 minutes from Vail, is a small luxury hotel with a wonderful spa. Here you can cross-country ski in the light of a full moon. Silverthorne, 40 minutes away towards Denver, has factory outlets such as Nike and Levis.

Accommodation

The Lodge at Vail and the Sonnenalp Hotel are the most luxurious. Vail Village Inn and Holiday Inn's Chateau Vail head the second rank. Marriott's Mountain Resort at Vail has spent $10 million upgrading its rooms and is warmly praised. Cheaper is the Roost in West Vail and West Vail Lodge.

The Hyatt Regency at Beaver Creek, which has an impressive lobby complete with vast log fire and enormous elk horn chandelier, is the last word in ski-in ski-out comfort. Also at Beaver Creek, Post Montane Lodge is 'small and comfortable'. The Charter is larger, and Beaver Creek Lodge has 'wonderfully comfortable suites'.

Eating in and out

The Vail Valley has an enormous choice of restaurants serving food of every nationality from Mexican to Thai and Japanese. Terra Bistro, in the Vail Athletic Club, and Sweet Basil are praised for their Californian cuisine. The Wildflower in the Lodge, La Tour, and the Left Bank are also strongly recommended for a special night out, as are The Tyrolean Inn and Lancelot. Vendetta's and Blu's are Italian. Montauk in Lionshead is excellent for seafood. The Jackalope in West Vail is warmly recommended, along with The Saloon at Minturn ('try their quail speciality'). Cassidy's in Avon is 'unique and truly wonderful'. For cheaper food in Vail try the Hubcap Brewery, Kitchen, and Pazzo's Pizzeria. Burgers are always good at the Bully Ranch in the Sonnenalp.

In Beaver Creek the Mirabelle and Tiamonti at The Charter are both smart Italian restaurants. Game Creek Club, up the mountain, is a members-only club for lunch but is now open to the public at night, as is Beano's Cabin.

Après-ski

Check out the sunset at the Blue Moon, a new bar at Eagle's Nest, or sip a margarita at Los Amigos at the bottom of the Vista Bahn lift. Mickey's Piano Bar at the Lodge is the place in which to spot celebrities. Other favourite post-ski hang-outs are the deck at Pepi's Bar, the Red Lion and the Hong Kong Café. In Lionshead go to Garfinkels, Trail's End or Bart and Yeti's. The Ore House in Vail has après-ski happy-hour prices. For coffee go to the Daily Grind, and for tea the Alpenrose. Later on,

Skiing facts: Vail/Beaver Creek

TOURIST OFFICE
PO Box 7, Vail, CO 81658
Tel 1 970 845 5720
Fax 1 970 845 5728
Email vailpr@vail.net
Web Site www.snow.com

THE RESORT
Airport transfer Eagle Country 45mins, Denver 2½hrs
Visitor beds 41,305
Transport Bus between Vail and Beaver Creek (nominal charge)

THE SKIING
Linked or nearby resorts Arrowhead (n), Beaver Creek (n), Breckenridge (n), Keystone (n)
Longest run Flapjack/Riva, 4½ miles (7km) – green/blue
Number of lifts 30 in Vail, 14 in Beaver Creek/Arrowhead
Total of trails/pistes 4,644 acres (1,879 hectares) in Vail (28% easy, 32% intermediate, 40% difficult), 1,625 acres (658 hectares) in Beaver Creek/Arrowhead (34% easy, 39% intermediate, 27% difficult)
Nursery slopes Golden Peak, top of Eagle's Nest, and Beaver Creek bases
Summer skiing none
Snowmaking 347 acres (140 hectares) covered in Vail, 550 acres (223 hectares) in Beaver Creek

LIFT PASSES
Area pass $300–312 for 6 days, (covers Vail, Beaver Creek, Breckenridge and Keystone)
Day pass $54–56
Beginners no free lifts
Pensioners 65–69yrs, $270 for 6 days. Free for 70yrs and over

Credit cards yes

TUITION
Adults Vail Ski and Snowboard School (at 6 bases) and Beaver Creek Ski and Snowboard School (2 bases), both $65–70 per day
Private lessons $100 per hr, $415–430 per day
Snowboarding as ski lessons
Cross-country $59 per day at Golden Peak and Beaver Creek. Loipe 32km
Other courses telemark, women's ski courses
Guiding Paragon Guides

CHILDREN
Lift pass 5–12yrs, $210 for 6 days. Free for 4yrs and under
Ski kindergarten Vail/Beaver Creek Ski School (Golden Peak, Lionshead and Beaver Creek), 3–6yrs, 8am–4.30pm, $76–79 per day including lunch, lessons and lifts
Ski school Vail/Beaver Creek Ski and Snowboard School, 3–13yrs, 9.45am–3.30pm, $76–79 per day including lessons and lift
Non-ski kindergarten Small World Nursery, 2mths–6yrs, 8.30am–4.30pm, $57–60 per day, $45 per half-day at Golden Peak, Lionshead and Beaver Creek

OTHER SPORTS
Bob-sledding, climbing-wall, dog-sledding, hot-air ballooning, ice-hockey, skating, snowcat tours, Snowmobiling, snowshoeing, squash, tennis, volleyball and basketball

FOOD AND DRINK PRICES
Coffee $2, glass of wine $4, small beer $2.75, dish of the day $10–15

Garton's has rock'n'roll and sometimes country and western, Club Chelsea has a disco, Sheika's is for rap-and-roll, while you could try Nick's or the Club for 1970s music. Booco's Station in Minturn has jazz and blues bands. In Beaver Creek the choice is more limited but includes the Coyote Café, Beaver Trap Tavern and Hyatt.

Childcare

The Small World Nursery at Golden Peak, Lionshead and Beaver Creek is a non-ski kindergarten. The Children's Ski and Snowboard School at all three centres is for kids from 3 to 13 years of age. Arrowhead has learn-to-ski or snowboard programmes. After-skiing children and family programmes include Kid's Night Out Goes Western for children aged 5 to13 with music, pizza and a Wild West show. Kids can ski with the Buckaroo Bonanza Bunch, a group of Western characters who tell stories about the Wild West. The children's ski school centres are at Lionshead, Golden Peak, Eagle's Nest and at the Village Hall in Beaver Creek. A playpark for children is open at Spruce Saddle.

Whistler/Blackcomb

ALTITUDE 2,214ft (675m)

Beginners ✹✹ Intermediates ✹✹✹ Advanced ✹✹✹ Snowboarders ✹✹✹

The now combined resort of Whistler and Blackcomb provides the most challenging skiing and the most cosmopolitan atmosphere of any ski resort in North America. Here you can ski or snowboard your heart out on two adjoining peaks that offer plunging powder bowls, sheer couloirs, and gladed skiing for all standards. Down below, the once separate villages of Whistler and Blackcomb have been skilfully melded into one charismatic resort by owners, Intrawest, with Blackcomb now renamed Upper Village.

Whistler Mountain stands at only 7,160ft (2182m) but affords over 4,920ft (1500m) of vertical – the longest continuous drop in North America. Its more rugged neighbour, Blackcomb Mountain, was originally developed in 1980 by a breakaway consortium. The contrastingly different, and often more demanding, terrain includes two glaciers and a set of truly awesome couloirs.

- ✔ Long vertical drop
- ✔ Large ski area
- ✔ Attractive village centre
- ✔ Modern lift system
- ✔ Long ski season
- ✔ Extensive off-piste
- ✘ Harsh maritime climate
- ✘ Short skiing days
- ✘ Weekend lift queues

The merger in 1997 between the two rivals resulted in CDN$31 million being spent immediately on mountain facilities, which included two replacement quad-chairs on Whistler Mountain. In the summer of 1998 a further CDN$24 million was spent on both mountains. Improvements include a new quad-chair to the peak of Whistler Mountain and a complete overhaul of the gondola. All this is in addition to the CDN$500 million already spent on developing the base area in recent years.

Whistler, which is the largest resort in Canada is indeed a world class resort – but with one major problem which no amount of investment can solve. Its maritime position means that much of the heavy winter precipitation falls as rain in the village and only as powder snow higher up. As one reporter put it: 'Bring your umbrella, wellies, and a full set of waterproofs along with your ski gear'. Sunshine days are statistically scarce in comparison with Whistler's Rocky Mountain cousins in the USA. Changes in temperature between village and summit can be frostbitingly dramatic, although not as extreme as in Banff/Lake Louise.

Such has been the scale of development that anyone who has not visited Whistler during the past four years would fail to recognise it. With the addition of new condominiums, hotels, shops and restaurants the resort has virtually doubled in size. The increased number of tourist beds has encouraged mass-market British tour operators to run two charter flights a week. The immediate effect has been to lower holiday costs dramatically. Purists argue that the character of the resort has already irrevocably changed.

High-season queues – particularly at weekends, when the number of snow-users on both mountains is augmented by day visitors from Vancouver – are a problem. The area is extremely popular with the Japanese, and during Tokyo holiday periods they can account for up to 50 per cent of the clientèle. The sight of so many smiling Orientals clad in Samurai-style ski clothing can come as a culture shock to other overseas visitors.

Ski and board
top 7,492ft (2284m) bottom 2,214ft (675m)

The two mountains of Whistler and Blackcomb stand side by side and share a lift pass, but they are divided by Fitzsimmons Creek and are at present linked only at the foot. Snow-users wanting to cross over from Blackcomb to Whistler have to travel all the way down to the bottom and take a green trail to catch the revamped Whistler Village Gondola up the other side. Similarly, Whistler snow-users have to return to the village to take the Excalibur Gondola up Blackcomb. Ambitious plans have already been drawn up by Intrawest to link the two at altitude by gondola.

Superficially, the two mountains are not dissimilar: each claims more than a hundred runs and each has long cruising trails. But whereas Whistler is known for its bowls, Blackcomb prides itself on its two glaciers and some dramatic couloirs. The new owners are concentrating mountain investment on the Whistler side, where some of the lifts were in serious need of improvement. Inevitably, some of the steeper terrain is being tamed to give it wider appeal. To the chagrin of true powderhounds, the peak of Whistler Mountain will no longer be an experts-only zone.

The terrain on both mountains is exceptionally well suited to snowboarders. Blackcomb has a snowpark where regular boardercross races are held.

WHAT'S NEW
Roundhouse restaurant rebuilt
Peak Chair upgraded to detachable-quad chair
Whistler Mountain gondola overhauled

The resort has two half-pipes, and some ski-patrol members use boards rather than skis to make riders feel they have equal status on the mountain. It is estimated that 50,000 snowboarders visit Whistler every year.

Beginners
Both areas have easy trails high on the mountain, so novices can enjoy the wide-open spaces and a vertical drop usually associated with intermediate ambitions. At Whistler, you can ride all the way up to the Roundhouse on the gondola, and also access ski trails such as Upper Whiskeyjack and Pony Trail (where packhorses once helped transport lift equipment). Papoose, Bear Cub and Expressway are other options lower down.

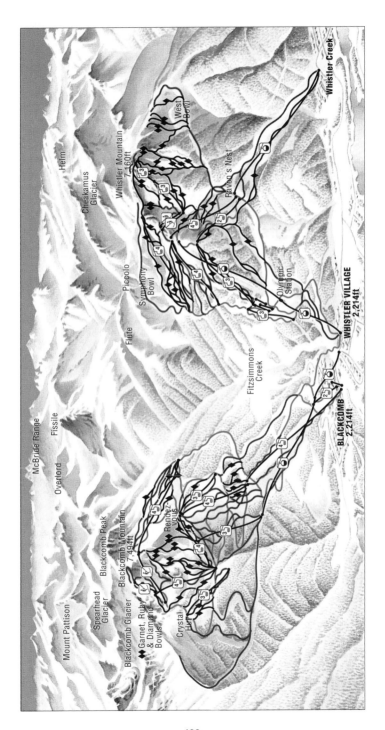

Mount Pattison

McBride Range

Spearhead Glacier

Overlord

Fissile

Helm

Blackcomb Peak

Cheakamus Glacier

Blackcomb Mountain 7,494ft

Whistler Mountain 7,160ft

West Bowl

Blackcomb Glacier

Garnet, Ruby & Diamond Bowls

Rendez-vous

Crystal Hut

Piccolo

Flute

Symphony Bowl

Raven's Nest

Fitzsimmons Creek

Olympic Station

BLACKCOMB 2,214ft

WHISTLER VILLAGE 2,214ft

Whistler Creek

At Blackcomb, take the Wizard Express quad-chair and switch to the Solar Coaster Express, which takes you to the easy Expressway link with the Seventh Heaven Express quad and Xhiggy's Meadow – a black-diamond (very difficult) run that is also the top of the easy Green Line trail. From here beginners can also ski from the top of Crystal Traverse that leads to the Jersey Cream and Glacier Express quads, both of which access some easy learner trails. Nursery slopes are also situated around Whistler gondola's Olympic Station and at the Blackcomb base area.

Intermediates

Whistler and Blackcomb both offer exhilarating top-to-bottom skiing, much of it below the tree-line. Half of the runs on the two mountains are graded intermediate. Both the Blackcomb and Horstman Glaciers have some impressive terrain for snow-users. Easier access routes to Whistler Bowl and West Bowl were built in the summer of 1998 to open up this huge area to intermediates. Franz's run offers cruising all the way from mid-mountain to Whistler Creek, where a gondola takes you back up to the mid-station in just seven minutes.

At Blackcomb, the Seventh Heaven Express quad-chair and Showcase T-bar to the Blackcomb Glacier serve mainly intermediate terrain at the top of the mountain. The mid-mountain area beneath the Solar Coaster Express quad-chair is dominated by a large number of medium-standard runs, including the long Springboard trail. Zig Zag and Cruiser are also popular pistes.

Advanced

At Whistler, much depends on whether the Peak chair or Harmony Express quad are open. If not, good advanced terrain can be found around Chunky's Choice and GS. Lower down, Seppo's and Raven off the Black chair-lift provide black-diamond skiing, and the Orange chair accesses the long Dave Murray Downhill and two expert cut-offs: Bear Paw and Tokum. Some of Blackcomb's most difficult runs are among the trees in a broad triangle between the lower sections of the Glacier Express and Crystal chair, which means you can inspect them before you ski. Trapline, Straight Shot, Rock'n Roll and Overbite are Crystal chair's featured runs, and The Bite, Staircase and Blowdown are on your right as you board the Glacier Express.

Off-piste

Blackcomb's couloirs and Whistler's bowls are the main areas of interest for off-piste snow-users. Couloir Extreme separates the advanced skier from the expert. It is the unlikely location for an annual extreme ski-race in which more than a hundred competitors, both professional and amateur, compete in a contest described as '2,500ft of thigh-burning hell'. Pakalolo is another couloir that attracts experienced snow-users. It has a fearsome reputation but is not in the same league as Couloir Extreme. The Blackcomb and Horstman glaciers usually provide excellent intermediate off-piste conditions. Whistler's five bowls – Symphony, Glacier,

Whistler, Harmony and West Bowls – offer a wide spectrum of off-piste challenges. First-time powder skiers and snowboarders can try the gentle run beside the T-bar at Blackcomb Glacier after a fresh snowfall. Two local companies run daily heli-skiing excursions. The best free-riding and off-piste snowboarding is accessed by the new Peak quad-chair. Heli-boarding is offered by Tyax Heli-skiing.

Tuition and guiding

Whistler/Blackcomb Mountain Ski and Snowboard School (SSS) is the new title of the amalgamated ski schools. Ski and Ride Esprit covers both mountains. We have encouraging reports of both 'Just the best instruction I have ever found anywhere' (Whistler/Blackcomb) and 'excellent value for money, good instruction and guiding' (Esprit). Whistler's free guiding programme is strongly recommended. The ski-patrol's Avalanche Awareness Course is described as 'a must for all advanced skiers, but you don't need to be an expert to do it'. There is also a summer training camp for boarders run by Craig Kelley, five-times World champion.

Mountain restaurants

At Whistler, the old Roundhouse was removed in the summer of 1998 to make way for an CDN\$8.5 million replacement with 1,750 seats, which promises 'everything from burgers and fries to fresh pasta and Asian cuisine'. Adjoining Pika's is currently the reporters' favourite. The Raven's Nest at the top of the Creekside gondola specialises in pasta and home-made soup. Dusty's is a popular lunch location.

At Blackcomb, Christine's Restaurant in the Rendezvous Lodge serves a leisurely 'linen and silverware' lunch, while the Rendezvous offers more casual but faster service. The River Rock Grill, upstairs at the Glacier Creek, is praised for 'a cosmopolitan choice of cuisine with wonderful glacier views'. Béla's in the Excalibur Base II Daylodge serves all-day breakfasts. Essentially Blackcomb at Excalibur Village Station has an outdoor barbecue. Crystal Hut at the top of the Crystal chair-lift is 'just like an atmospheric Swiss or Italian alpine hut with the same primitive toilets'.

The resort

Whistler – named after the cry of the marmot – is one of the world's most cosmopolitan resorts. Its position on the edge of the Pacific Rim attracts snow-users from Australia and Japan as well as Europe. As a consequence its shops and restaurants have an international ambience that is unusual in a North American ski resort.

Whistler Village is prime evidence that a purpose-built resort can be attractive. It is a mixture of chalet-style apartments, inns, lodges and condominiums, with weather boarding more in evidence than concrete. There are few large buildings, and the biggest hotel, the Chateau Whistler Resort, is built in a neo-Gothic style. The centre of Whistler is car-free and getting from the village square to Mountain Square at the base of the two gondolas involves a hearty walk. Whistler Village and the much smaller Upper Village (Blackcomb Base) and Village North are only a five-minute walk apart.

Accommodation

The 13-storey Chateau Whistler Resort sits on the edge of the piste at Blackcomb and dominates the skyline as you ski down to the resort. A new wing was added in 1998, and it remains one of the truly great ski hotels of the world – although prices have risen in proportion to demand. We also have good reports of the Delta Mountain Inn ('next to the mountain and very convenient'). Timberline Lodge is 'comfortable, well-situated and friendly'. The Crystal Lodge and the Listel Whistler Hotel are both popular. Condominiums at the Blackcomb Lodge and Mountainside Lodge are both recommended. Carney's Cottage is 'the best bed-and-breakfast in, or rather on the edge of, town'. Haus Stephanie is 'a friendly little bed-and-breakfast'.

Travel firms operate a growing number of catered chalets. It is worth checking the exact position before booking as many are situated an inconvenient distance from the lifts and village centre.

Eating in and out

As one reporter put it: 'Eating out in Whistler is nothing short of sensational. We ate Japanese, Chinese, Thai, Italian, Greek, French, American, and pub food. We did not have one bad or even mediocre meal'. Trattoria di Umberto and Il Caminetto di Umberto are both recommended along with La Rua. The Wildflower Restaurant in the Chateau Whistler Resort is warmly praised: 'Smart dining, not too expensive and very worthwhile'. Zeuski's Taverna at the gondola base is said to have 'soundly priced and tasty meals'. Sushi Village ('excellent but expensive') is one of eight Asian restaurants. Ristorante Araxi has Mediterranean cuisine and is 'absolutely delightful'. Monks Grill, Thai On One and the Garibaldi Lift Co. are all warmly praised. Brasserie des Artistes is cheap and cheerful, and there is a Hard Rock Café. Nester's is said to be the best-priced supermarket.

Après-ski

The Longhorn Saloon at the foot of the slopes catches skiers and snow-boarders as they come off the mountain but is much quieter in the evening. Tapley's Pub is 'friendly, cheap and used by the locals'. Garfinkel's, Tommy Africa's and the Savage Beagle are all extremely popular. Shopping is described as 'excellent and addictive', with ski clothing such as North Face at approximately half British prices, plus a Helly-Hansen outlet. Other shops worth visiting include a Guess Jeans shop, and Skitch Knicknacks & Paddywacks for original gifts.

Childcare

The Ski Scamps programme caters for children aged 18 months to 12 years on both mountains. Whistler/Blackcomb Mountain SSS also runs

Skiing facts: Whistler/Blackcomb

TOURIST OFFICE
4010 Whistler Way, Whistler, BC VON 1B4
Tel 1 604 932 3928
Fax 1 604 932 7231
Email reservations@whistler-resort.com
Web site www.whistler-resort.com

THE RESORT
Airport transfer Vancouver Airport 2hrs, frequent coach service to resort
Visitor beds 17,910
Transport free shuttle bus within the village loop

THE SKIING
Linked or nearby resorts Whistler Creek (l)
Longest run Whistler: Burnt Stew, Sidewinder, Olympic, 7 miles (11km) – blue/green. Blackcomb: The Green Line, 7 miles (11km) – green
Number of lifts 30
Total of trails/pistes 7,050 acres (2853 hectares), (20% easy, 55% intermediate, 25% difficult)
Nursery slopes 6 baby lifts
Summer skiing mid-June to mid-August on Horstman Glacier at Blackcomb Mountain
Snowmaking 1,500 vertical feet (457 vertical metres) of trails covered at Whistler, 4,000 vertical feet (1219 vertical metres) of trails covered at Blackcomb

LIFT PASSES
Area pass CDN$334–347 for 6 out of 7 days
Day pass CDN$61–63

Beginners no free lifts
Pensioners 65yrs and over, CDN$283–294 for 6 out of 7 days
Credit cards yes

TUITION
Adults Whistler/Blackcomb Mountain SSS, Ski and Ride Esprit, both CDN$219 for 4 days
Private lessons Whistler/Blackcomb Mountain SSS, CDN$270 for 3hrs
Snowboarding as skiing
Cross-country through ski schools. Loipe 28km
Other courses Dave Murray Ski Camps, women's clinics, slalom
Guiding Whistler Alpine Guides Bureau, Tyax Heli-skiing

CHILDREN
Lift pass 7–12yrs, CDN$164–170, 13–18yrs, CDN$283–294, both for 6 out of 7 days, free for 6yrs and under
Ski kindergarten Ski Scamps at Whistler and Blackcomb, 3–12yrs, 9am–3pm, CDN$69 per day including lunch
Ski school as ski kindergarten
Non-ski kindergarten 18mths–3yrs, CDN$69 per day including lunch

OTHER SPORTS
Indoor tennis, parapente, skating, sleigh rides, snowmobiling, snowshoeing, swimming

FOOD AND DRINK PRICES
Coffee $1, glass of wine CDN$6, small beer CDN$4.50, dish of the day CDN$7–15

special classes for teenagers. Parents with small children at the kindergarten are given optional pagers so they can be called anywhere on the mountain if their child needs them.

Round-up

ALBERTA

Jasper
top 8,533ft (2601m) bottom 5,640ft (1719m)

The most northerly and arguably the most beautiful of Canadian resorts is set among the glaciers, forests, frozen lakes and waterfalls of Jasper National Park. The ski area at Marmot Basin, a 15-minute drive from the town, is not large but the terrain is extremely varied, with open bowls, steep chutes and trails cut through the trees. The runs are split evenly between green (easy), blue (intermediate) and black (difficult) trails, and snowboarders are well catered for with clinics for all levels.

Founded by fur traders in 1811, Jasper has developed into a typical Canadian railroad town, with a wide choice of restaurants and bars. In spite of the long transfer time (Calgary International Airport is a five-hour drive to the south) visitors say that the resort is an exceptionally good place to unwind.

There is a choice of luxury accommodation, with the Jasper Park Lodge, a huge Canadian Pacific hotel at Lac Beauvert on the outskirts of the town, leading the field. It has 442 rooms spread out in bungalows and two-storey buildings in extensive grounds, plus four restaurants, a nightclub, shopping mall and an outdoor heated swimming-pool, and is a resort in its own right.

Its main rival, Chateau Jasper, is a quarter of the size and much closer to the action, with friendly staff and fine food. The Whistlers Inn, named after a local mountain, is smaller still and even more central, with its own Italian restaurant (the Mondis), pub (the Whistle Stop), and wildlife museum.

Alternative entertainment in the resort includes ice-climbing, sleigh rides, snowmobiling and skating on the lake. The ice-covered Maligne Canyon is unique, and heli-skiing is possible at Valemount, which is an hour's drive away.

TOURIST OFFICE
Tel 1 403 852 3816
Fax 1 403 852 3533
Email info@skimarmot.com
Web site www.skimarmot.com

BRITISH COLUMBIA

Big White
top 7,606ft (2318m) bottom 5,056ft (1541m)

The recipient of lavish funding that many resorts would envy, this Australian-owned mountain is in the process of transforming itself into a major player in the Okanagan Highlands, to the east of the huge Lake Okanagan. Local lore has it that Big White is named after the cloud that often conceals it. The resulting humidity creates a phantom forest of snow-ghosts: trees frozen into eerie formations reminiscent of the dinosaurs in *Jurassic Park*. The extensive, but predominantly gentle, ski area is better suited to families than radical adventurers but, given sunshine and powder, Big White is a magical place.

The upgraded lift system provides high-speed access to a wide variety of green and blue trails via the Ridge Rocket Express, the Bullet Express and the Black Forest Express, while the much shorter Plaza quad-chair gives access to a first-timer's area and children's park below the main village. Advanced skiers must head for less speedy lifts: the Alpine T-bar for steep, open slopes, or the Powder chair for glade skiing.

All the accommodation is ski-in ski-out, in a resort where the paint is hardly dry on the walls. Last season the smart and comfortable Coast Resort was added. The White Crystal Inn has rooms as big as football pitches and is just about as chilly, but its Grizzly Bear lounge is popular for après-ski. Snowshoe Sam's is a particularly good example of the one-stop nightlife that is typical of the British Columbian interior: rough-hewn and friendly, with pool tables, a dance area and a restaurant – it is all things to all visitors, which is fortunate because there are few alternatives.

TOURIST OFFICE
Tel 1 250 765 8888
Fax 1 250 765 1822
Email bigwhite@silk.net
Web site www.bigwhite.com

Panorama
top 8,100ft (2469m) bottom 3,800ft (1158m)

Panorama lies a two-hour drive to the south-west of Banff. It is best known as a heli-ski centre, but its lift system also gives it 4,300ft (1310m) of vertical, one of the longest in North America. It is a small family resort with a single ski-in ski-out hotel and 8 lifts serving 55 runs. More than half of the terrain is intermediate, with long, sweeping runs making the most of the impressive vertical, but there is some advanced glade skiing in what is fancifully called the Extreme Dream Zone. Beginners can gain confidence on easy and magnificently groomed runs. The heli-skiing operation, based in the village, involves an exhaustive instructional preamble in the earnest Canadian way, followed by three to four runs and a picnic lunch in an unheated mountain hut.

The Pine Inn is functional but comfortable, with breakfast included in the price. The Glacier is said to be the liveliest après-ski bar. The T-Bar and Grill Inn are recommended for pub-style food and music, and Toby's leads the way for fine dining.

TOURIST OFFICE
Tel 1 250 342 6941
Fax 1 250 342 3395
Email skiinginfo@panoramaresort.com
Web site www.panoramaresort.com

Red Mountain
top 6, 800ft (2072m) bottom 3,888ft (1185m)

Rossland, the distressed mining town that serves Red Mountain, had its heyday in the 1890s when the discovery of gold and copper attracted fortune hunters, among them immigrant Scandinavians, who established the first local ski club in 1896. Their rugged, macho view of skiing has been carefully conserved by Eric Skat Petersen, who has been running Red Mountain in his own ebullient image since 1989. By refusing to invest in state-of-the-art lifts, he has kept the pioneering spirit intact, and the terrain has done the rest. The resort has five lifts, and the longest run is 7.5km (4½ miles).

Located in the Kootenay Mountains very close to the US border, Rossland enjoys a microclimate that results in higher temperatures and clearer skies than elsewhere in the Canadian Rockies. It is most readily reached via Spokane in Washington State, a two- to three-hour drive away, although it is also possible to fly into Castelgar via Calgary. Red's hard core is made up of ski bums, many of whom have small incomes, enjoying the machismo that goes with the territory throughout the winter. Most of the passing strangers see their visit as a rites-of-passage pilgrimage to a resort with a reputation for testing the best.

Beginners and intermediates have limited prospects in Red Mountain. However, the old slow double chair-lift has been replaced by two triple chair-lifts which have greatly improved access to some of the less formidable runs. Because everyone who skis Red skis trees, all the pistes have sizable moguls to add to the general sense of hazard. Most of the runs have open bowls interspersed with gladed sections of varying degrees of difficulty. Beer Belly, Short Squaw and Powder fields are skiable one way or another, but the trees tighten up on Roots and Paleface, while Cambodia, with its 15-ft (4.5-m) drops over frozen waterfalls, is a stretch too far for most people.

The main hotel in Rossland is the Uplander, which has simple rooms but serves unexpectedly good meals in the Louis Blue Dining Room. The hotel also has the Powder Keg Pub, the town's hotspot, with pool tables and a video ski game. The Ram's Head Inn, a comfortable bed-and-breakfast establishment, is close enough to the slopes to ski back to, but the most convenient place to stay is the family-run Red Shutter, right next to the car park; it is so small that it is often booked by groups of up to 12. The Scotsman Motel has been renamed the Swiss Alps Inn and still serves the best rösti breakfast in town. The only on-mountain restaurant is at Paradise Lodge, but Rafters, on the third floor of the base lodge, has a simple but substantial lunch menu, a well-stocked bar and a cheerful ambiance.

TOURIST OFFICE
Tel 1 250 362 7700
Fax 1 250 362 5833
Email redmtn@wkpowerlink.com
Web site www.ski-red.com

Silver Star
top 6,280ft (1915m) bottom 3,780ft (1152m)

The design of Silver Star is a law unto itself – a colourful ski-in ski-out village, which is said to be modelled on a typical British Columbian mining town of the 1890s and painted in unexpectedly bright colours. However, the cheerful paint is welcome in a place where the wind-chill factor can be fearsome – even though it is said to have the best weather of any Canadian ski resort. The most challenging skiing is to be found on the north-facing Putnam Creek side of the mountain, reached by a long high-speed quad-chair. This newly developed area has a network of black trails cut through the forest and a very welcome warming hut at Paradise Camp mid-station. The south-facing Vance Creek area overlooking the village is recommended for intermediates who will enjoy the long cruisers: Sundance, Whiskey Jack and Interloper. The Yellow Chair serves a snowboard park, and the Silver Queen Chair a beginners' area. In all, Silver Star has five chair-lifts (including two detachable quads) and two T-bars.

The heart of the village resembles a pedestrianised film set, with horse-drawn sleighs adding a further touch of theatricality. The Delta Silver Star Club Resort is the most prominent hotel. The recently-modernised Vance Creek has two acceptable restaurants – Lucciano's Trattoria and Clementine's Dining Room. Even better is the Silver Lode Restaurant, a genuine Swiss outpost serving *Apfelstrudel* and *Bratwurst*. The kindergarten takes children from 18 months of age.

TOURIST OFFICE
Tel 1 250 542 0224
Fax 1 250 542 1236
Email star@silverstarmtn.com
Web site www.silverstarmtn.com

Sun Peaks
top 6,814ft (2077m) bottom 3,970ft (1210m)

Nancy Greene, the *grande dame* of Canadian ski-racing after winning Olympic gold at Grenoble in 1968, came to Sun Peaks via Red Mountain, where she was born and raised, and Whistler, where she played a key role in developing the resort. Now she and her husband, Al Raine, are aiding the transformation of Tod Mountain, the local hill for the logging town of Kamloops for the past 30 years, into Sun Peaks, a state-of-the-art resort for the millennium funded with $150 million of Japanese money. Sun Peaks lies deep in the British Columbian heartland, a four-hour drive east of Whistler. Alternatively, it can be reached by plane to Kamloops, via Vancouver or Calgary.

The change of name was prompted by the need for an international image – Tod means 'death' in German – but the best skiing is still on Mount Tod. The Top of the World area is a steep-sided dome above the tree-line, with advanced skiing in chutes and bowls. The toughest terrain is on the lower half of the Burfield quad chair-lift. Challenger is one of the steepest marked trails in Canada. Other demanding runs are on the Headwalls, a wide face of short, double-black-diamond shots above the main on-mountain pit stop, the Sunburst Lodge. However, a 5-mile (8-km) green trail leads from the top of the skiing back to the resort, making it user-friendly for all standards. Below the treeline, the mountain flattens out progressively, with the easiest slopes just above the resort. This is an excellent arrangement for beginners and lower intermediates, who have their own zone served by the Sundance Express quad. The snowpark and the Cowabunga area are served by a platter-lift.

The Village Day Lodge, a study in elegant design in local timber and glass, has a gastronomic restaurant and an excellent ski rental shop. Nancy Greene's Cahilty Lodge, in a sheltered position overlooking the valley, offers four-star comfort. Sun Peaks Village now has six slopeside hotels.

TOURIST OFFICE
Tel 1 250 578 7842
Fax 1 250 578 7843
Email info@sunpeaksresort.com
Web site www.sunpeaksresort.com

COLORADO

Arapahoe Basin
top 13,011ft (3967m) bottom 10,768ft (3283m)

Arapahoe Basin (A-Basin) is a small, steep ski area five miles from **Keystone**. Its altitude means that skiing is assured here in the late spring after neighbouring resorts have closed. From the top of Lenawee and and Norway lifts, almost every run down the middle is intermediate or beginner terrain, and Dercum's Gulch gives access to the long easy runs of Wrangler, Sundance and Chisholm. At the top of the ski area, Palivacinni is one of the longest bump runs in North America, and the Alleys and East Wall provide some exciting off-piste.

TOURIST OFFICE
Tel 1 970 0718

Fax 1 970 496 4546
Email abasin@colorado.net
Web site www.@arapahoebasin.com

Copper Mountain
top 12,313ft (3767m) bottom 9,712ft (2926m)

Copper Mountain, situated on the Denver side of the Vail Pass, was not included in the deal when **Vail** bought its two 'Ski The Summit' partners, **Breckenridge** and Keystone, in 1997, but it has now been snapped up by arch-rival Intrawest. Some $66 million was invested last summer in improvements including the six-person detachable Super Bee chairlift, which should cut the 'ride' time to the summit from 30 minutes to eight minutes. A new day lodge at the base of the Super Bee is also under construction.

Copper likes to describe its ski area as one of the best-designed in North America. There is a natural tendency for the tree-lined trails to become more difficult as you move east (left on the piste map). Thus, advanced snow-users tend to stick to the main face of Copper Peak, and beginners will find little beyond their capabilities on the west side of the resort. In between, the terrain is mainly intermediate. The addition of Copper Bowl and Spaulding Bowl has provided some of the best off-piste skiing in Colorado. Copper has a total of 21 lifts serving 118 groomed trails.

Copper Mountain Ski School offers group and private lessons, as well as bumps and powder workshops and beginner packages. The resort itself is architecturally no great charmer, constructed in a concrete style reminiscent of a French purpose-built resort – which may explain the presence of Club Med.

Most of the accommodation at Copper Mountain is in apartments. O'Shea's, at the base of the American Eagle chair-lift, is a popular restaurant and meeting place. Pesce Fresco in the Mountain Plaza Building has 'excellent fresh fish and home-made pasta'. The Double Diamond Grill, Farley's Prime Chop House and Racket's are three recommended eating places. Imperial Palace is an oriental restaurant which 'does a first-class takeaway'. The Corner Grocery provides a reasonable choice for shoppers.

The Copper Mountain Racquet and Athletic Club has excellent facilities, including a swimming-pool, indoor tennis and racquet-ball courts. Belly Button Babies kindergarten accepts children from two months to two years old, and its stable-mate, the Belly Button Bakery, caters for children over two and skiers over three years of age. Copper Mountain has Junior and Senior Ranch ski programmes for children.

TOURIST OFFICE
Tel 1 970 968 2882
Fax 1 970 968 6227
Email cmr-res@ski-copper.com
Web site www.ski-copper.com

Crested Butte
top 11,875ft (3620m) bottom 9,100ft (2774m)

This small, historic town is one of the most attractive ski resorts in Colorado. In the old town's Main Street, 40 of the original nineteenth-century buildings, with their colourful wooden façades, have been converted into shops and restaurants, giving the place a Wild West atmosphere. The town is overlooked by the Butte (pronounced as in 'beaut-iful'), which is a mountain that stands alone. Hotels and guesthouses scattered around the town include the Nordic Inn, a family-run ski lodge that is firmly recommended. The other option is to stay at either the Marriot or the new Sheraton Resort three miles away at the base of the ski slopes.

Crested Butte is renowned for its steep skiing and each year hosts ski-extreme championships. At the opposite end of the scale, it also has some of the easiest skiing in Colorado. The resort's 13 lifts serve 85 trails spread over 1,150 acres (460 hectares) of ski terrain. A high 58 per cent of the runs are classed as difficult, 29 per cent intermediate and 13 per cent easy. The Extreme Limits area comprises some 550 acres (223 hectares) of ungroomed extreme skiing, which locals claim is some of the most challenging in Colorado.

TOURIST OFFICE
Tel *freephone* (0800) 894085
Fax 1 719 349 2250
Email info@rmi.net
Web site www.crestedbutteresort.com

Telluride
top 12,247ft (3734m) bottom 8,725ft (2660m)

A colourful history surrounds Telluride, an old mining town in a beautiful box-canyon in the San Juan Mountains. At the height of the gold rush, 5,000 prospectors crowded into the town, the name of which derives either from tellurium, a non metallic element in gold and silver ore, or less probably from 'to hell you ride' – a sobriquet that could apply to Butch Cassidy, who robbed his first bank on Main Street in 1889 before escaping on horseback. In keeping with the rollicking climate of those times, Main Street divided the town, with a residential district on one side and a flourishing red light district on the other.

The wide street, dominated by the New Sheridan Hotel, is little changed today, but over the last decade the nature of the resort has been radically altered by the construction of the Mountain Village Resort. Four miles away by road, it is connected to the town between 7.30am and 7.30pm by gondola. The development of condominiums, shops and a golf course triggered a real-estate boom, which has attracted a number of Hollywood investors. The new ranching classes include Tom Cruise and Nicole Kidman, Sylvester Stallone and Oprah Winfrey.

Both town and mountain village are equally convenient for the skiing, though the descents to the Oak Street and Coonskin base-stations via

black runs such as Plunge and Jaws are too steep for cautious intermediates. The backbone of the area is the appropriately named See Forever,
a long, rolling blue (intermediate) run from the top of the skiing to the
mountain village; it provides encouragement or speed, according to
ability and taste. The Galloping Goose area, isolated to one side of the
mountain village, is perfect for beginners.

Aggressive skiers head for the double-black-diamond Spiral Stairs or
hike up the ridge towards Gold Hill to the short, off-piste glades. Last
season a giant funpark was opened with a half-pipe built to the same
specifications as the one used in the Nagano Winter Olympics.

The choice of where to stay is dictated by the nightlife, which is much
better in the downtown area. The New Sheridan is central and traditional, with a handsome mahogany bar, while the restaurant serves fashionable dishes of alligator, ostrich and kangaroo. The Ice House is
modern, central, smart and convenient for the Oak Street base-station.
The Skyline Guest Ranch on the outskirts of town is run as a home from
home by the hospitable Farny family.

TOURIST OFFICE
Tel 1 970 728 6900
Fax 1 970 728 6475
Email jackiek@telski.com
Web site www.telski.com

Winter Park
top 12,057ft (3676m) bottom 8,973ft (2735m)

As it is the closest resort to Denver, only 67 miles (108km) away,
Winter Park has a high number of weekend skiers, and with its limited slopeside accommodation and nightlife will probably disappoint
those used to international resorts. However, in summer 1998 work
started on a new village at the base which will be open for the
1999/2000 season.

The skiing here is excellent, with long, wide runs, challenging mogul
fields, few midweek queues, efficient lifts and perfectly manicured
slopes. The skiing is divided into two main areas – Winter Park and
Vasquez Ridge, which is mostly intermediate, and Mary Jane, which has
hard bump-skiing as well as tree-level runs and long blues from the
Parsenn Bowl. At present there are 20 chairs including seven detachable
quads which serve 1,414 acres (572 hectares).

Last winter the resort opened the Vasquez Cirque, a further 1,200
acres (486 hectares) of extreme off-piste skiing. There is a funpark and
a half-pipe for snowboarders. The children's area has a 'magic carpet' lift
and a good ski school.

Mountain restaurants include the Dining Room at the Lodge at
Sunspot, which is on the summit of Winter Park Mountain, as well as
several cafeterias and a pizza parlour mid-mountain. For the present, the
town of Winter Park, two miles from the ski area, has the main accommodation.

TOURIST OFFICE
Tel 1 970 726 5587
Fax 1 970 892 5993
Email mwoolwine@mail.winterpark.com
Web site www.skiwinterpark.com

IDAHO

Sun Valley
top 9,150ft (2789m) bottom 5,750ft (1753m)

America's oldest ski resort has been a magnet for the Hollywood élite since it opened in 1936. As with so much of the USA, Sun Valley's rise to prominence was railroad-led. Averell Harriman, then the chairman of the Union Pacific Railway, commissioned Count Felix Schaffgotsch to find a place to build a ski resort near a Union Pacific railhead. His choice, Proctor Mountain and Dollar Mountain, near the dilapidated mining town of Ketchum, was inspired – both for its terrain and its sunshine records. In August 1936, the world's first chair-lift, adapted from a system for moving stems of bananas in Panama, was installed on Dollar. However, no allowance was made for the snowfall – by the winter, it was completely stuck.

Today, Dollar is Sun Valley's second mountain, used mainly by beginners, both on- and off-piste. The prime terrain is on Bald Mountain, served by seven high-speed quads. Sun Valley hit the doldrums in the 1970s and 1980s, but during the 1990s there has been a dramatic revival, with investment in upgraded lifts and three handsome day lodges – one on Seattle Ridge, the other at the Warm Springs base-station, and the newest at the base of River Run.

The skiing is predominantly intermediate, with a choice of inviting cruisers, but advanced skiers face a serious challenge on runs such as Inhibition and Exhibition.

The resort is a chic complex of low-rise buildings clustered round the Sun Valley Lodge, the original hotel. In its heyday it numbered Clark Gable, Claudette Colbert and Gary Cooper among its regulars, as well as Ernest Hemingway who wrote *For Whom The Bell Tolls* in room 206. Today's stars, among them Clint Eastwood, Arnold Schwarzenegger, Richard Dreyfuss and Brooke Shields, have their own mansions. Demi Moore and Bruce Willis have invested heavily in the neighbourhood, restoring a cinema and opening a restaurant and night club.

Sun Valley is staid, but Ketchum has some surprisingly lively nightlife in bars like the Casino Club, the Roosevelt Tavern and Whiskey Jacques. The upmarket clientèle has encouraged the establishment of some excellent restaurants, on and off the mountain. Gourmet dining is to be had at the Soupçon and the Evergreen Bistro. The Pioneer Steakhouse, Clint Eastwood's favourite, is cheerful and much cheaper.

TOURIST OFFICE
Tel 1 208 726 3423
Fax 1 208 726 4533
Web site www.visitsunvalley.com

MONTANA

Big Sky
top 11,150ft (3399m) bottom 6,970ft (2125m)

In Montana, big is good but bigger is better, which provides the rationale behind the Lone Peak Tram – a tiny cable-car cabin that briefly and slightly dubiously gave Big Sky the right to claim the longest vertical drop in the USA – 4,180ft (1274m) – from previous holder Jackson Hole. Both resorts have now been upstaged by Snowmass. Nevertheless, Big Sky's skiing is worthwhile, largely because its extensive slopes are among the least crowded in the northern hemisphere. This is not surprising, as it is an hour's drive from Bozeman, the nearest airport, and seven hours from Salt Lake City, the nearest major city. However, the wide, open snowscape is attractive, especially to Europeans accustomed to crowds.

The runs are on two well-linked mountains: Lone Peak, which has the bulk of the serious skiing, and Andesite, where beginners and intermediates will find plenty to occupy them. The Lone Peak cable-car has opened up the A–Z chutes, but all except the most extreme skiers will prefer the bowl off the triple-chair and the glades off the slow 'experts only' Challenger chair.

Big Sky was created by the 1960s NBC newscaster Chet Huntley, a Montana man who wanted to give something back to the state in which he was born. The Huntley Lodge and the Shoshone Condominium Hotel provide comfortable ski-in ski-out accommodation, but the nightlife is limited to a poker game in Chet's Gaming Parlor and a small assortment of bars. These include Dante's Inferno, Scissorbills, Lolo's Saloon and the Black Bear Bar and Grill. At lunch-time, Mountain Top Pizza is the main source of sustenance.

The road from Bozeman winds along the River Gallatin, where Robert Redford directed *A River Runs Through It*, a taster for the magnificent scenery that makes Montana a favoured hideaway for contemporary Hollywood. Andie MacDowell rates the acreage of her ranch as 'too big to count'. Her not-very-near neighbours, Ted and Jane Fonda Turner (Big Sky regulars), are prepared to be more specific with '100,000 acres' (40,470 hectares). There is a sense of history too, with Little Bighorn, the location of Custer's last stand, a mere two-hour drive away. As Montana has abolished the speed limit, that may well be quite a distance.

TOURIST OFFICE
Tel 1 406 995 5000
Fax 1 406 995 5001

Email bigskymail@mcn.net
Web site www.bigskyresort.com

NEW MEXICO

Taos
top 11,819ft (3603m) bottom 9,207ft (2807m)

Even in the varied spectrum of American skiing, the Taos Valley has a charm that is all its own. Although it is at the same latitude as Rome, the snow in a north-facing bowl in the Carson National Forest is surprisingly good. A few miles down the road, the cacti and sagebushes that characterise the New Mexican desert stretch as far as the eye can see. The town of Taos, an art-led, cosmopolitan melting pot with a dominant Native American culture, is 20 miles (32km) away.

The Taos Ski Valley was created by the legendary Ernie Blake, a Swiss-born German who discovered what he recognised as perfect terrain while flying over the Rockies in the early 1950s. In 1956 Blake was joined by the French racer Jean Mayer in an enterprise that still combines Teutonic efficiency with Gallic flair. Blake was a firm believer in ski classes, even for cocky Americans who thought that they could ski, and he created the best ski school in the country in his own image. Mayer's interest was gastronomic, and he indulged it at the slopeside Hotel St Bernard, which is usually booked out for the next season by early June.

Blake died in 1989, but Taos continues in the same distinguished tradition under the stewardship of his son-in-law, Chris Stagg. The mountain is imposing, especially from the village perspective. Al's Run, the tough mogul field under the lift line, makes such an impression that a notice reassures visitors of easier skiing further up the hill. While this is true, there is also even more difficult skiing, especially off the high traverse, where runs like Oster, Blitz and Stauffenberg testify to the founder's anti-Nazi stance during the Second World War. Sir Arnold Lunn, the father of modern European skiing, is also commemorated on the piste map. The key run in the beginner's area is Honeysuckle, while intermediates should head for Porcupine and Powderhorn, both ego-boosting cruisers.

The town of Taos is extremely compact, and hotel accommodation is limited to the St Bernard, the Edelweiss, the Inn at Snakedance and the Hondo Lodge. The choice of condominiums is wider, with the Kandahar at the top of the list of recommendations. Four miles (6km) down the valley, the Quail Ridge Inn has a desert ambience, indoor and outdoor tennis and an outdoor swimming-pool.

TOURIST OFFICE
Tel 1 505 776 2291
Fax 1 505 776 8591
Email res@taoswebb
Web site taoswebb.com/skitaos

Andorra

Beginners ✳✳✳ Intermediates ✳✳ Snowboarders ✳✳

Good snow cover and a steady programme of lift system improvement has allowed Andorra to reinforce its position in recent seasons as the most popular ski destination for those on the tightest of budgets, despite rising prices and some stalwart competition from eastern Europe. We have occasionally been taken to task for our criticism of both the quality of skiing on offer in this tax-free principality sandwiched between France and Spain. We have suggested that better – and not necessarily more expensive – skiing and snowboarding can be found elsewhere on both faces of the Pyrenees.

✔ Low prices
✔ Facilities for children
✔ Excellent skiing tuition
✔ Lively après-ski
✘ Few mountain restaurants
✘ Lift queues
✘ Lack of resort ambiance
✘ Heavy traffic (Pas de la Casa)

If you are in your 20s, have never skied or snowboarded before and want to combine tumbling down the slopes with some equally exhausting and raucous nightlife, then Andorra could be for you. Similarly, families on a budget will find that the overall cost of a skiing holiday here is lower than in most Alpine destinations. The standard of tuition is high (although class sizes can be gargantuan at peak times) and much of it is provided by native English-speakers. The low cost and high quality of both new and rental equipment is remarkable. However, the scope of skiing is limited, and anyone above confident intermediate standard should look elsewhere. The scenery, architecture and ambience do not compare favourably with mainstream European resorts.

Andorra has a reputation for 'supermarket skiing', a low-cost, duty-free way for the rowdier end of the British market to don their anoraks, reverse their baseball caps, give the art of snowploughing a try and ''ere we go, 'ere we go' long into the night. As the Pas de la Casa tourist board is the first to acknowledge: 'Certainly from our point of view we watch the quality of our clients with increasing apprehension as the season unfolds'. Mass market tour operators sell holidays at rock-bottom prices and seek to recoup profit margins by pressurising their reps to achieve maximum in-resort commissions from pub crawls and other activities that often leads to rowdy behaviour.

Snow-users aged between 16 and 25 might find a holiday here off – and even on – the slopes an enjoyable experience. If you are older, you will need to choose your resort and both the location and quality of your accommodation with the greatest care.

Andorra is bordered by Catalonia in Spain and the Pyrénées Orientales in France. The closest airports are Barcelona, Lourdes, Perpignan and Toulouse. The country's population of 55,000 inhabitants lives within an area of just 464-square kilometres, and Catalan is the official language. Alcohol, perfume, electrical goods, ski equipment and clothing are all available at bargain prices. Unlike its counterparts in eastern Europe, the food in all resorts can be surprisingly good, with a choice of French or Catalan dishes.

Encamp, 20 minutes by road from Soldeu, is a cheap bed base with no skiing and few other attractions ('it would have been worth paying the extra £30 to £70 to stay in Soldeu simply to avoid the hassle of travelling').

Arcalis
top 2600m (8,530ft) bottom 1940m (6,363ft)

Arcalis is one of Andorra's higher resorts, with skiing on wide runs above the tree-line. The village of **Ordino** is 25 minutes by road from Arcalis and neighbouring **La Massana** and has more attractive scenery than other Andorran resorts. This season a new chair-lift opens. Thirteen lifts serve 30km of pistes, and Arcalis has the highest percentage of difficult skiing in Andorra. Reporters are lavish in their praise: 'The sheer variety of the skiing makes it a great place'.

TOURIST OFFICE
Tel 376 838 115
Fax 376 839 225
Email ito@andorra.ad
Web site www. andorra.ad/comuns.ordino

Arinsal
top 2573m (8,442ft) bottom 1550m (5,084ft)

At first sight, Arinsal fails to live up to anyone's expectation of a ski resort. A row of shops, bars and apartment buildings line the road above this small town, and the only visible clue to its winter raison d'être is an ancient double chair-lift, which follows the path of a bubbling stream. This takes you to the start of the main skiing at 1950m, in a bleak and treeless area enclosed between two ridges. However, this season a new six-person gondola from the town centre will transform access. The main ski area can also be reached by road. The resort now has a total of 18 lifts serving 28km of groomed runs, which collectively provide the least variety of all Andorra's skiing. The area has a half-pipe and a fun-park. The two main pistes – the black La Devesa and the blue Les Marrades 1 – drop from the top of the main Arinsal lift down to the resort and are sometimes closed due to lack of snow. This limits the remainder of the area to beginner and lower-intermediate terrain. As all the runs are channelled into a V shape that ends on the nursery slopes, even beginners will feel the pressure of the limited runs ('crowded nursery slopes with resultant long queues'). One reporter complained of 'hordes of uncontrolled Spanish youngsters whose behaviour appeared to be condoned by their instructors'.

With few exceptions, the mountain restaurants are criticised as 'shabby and overpriced'. Asteric's, at the bottom of the Arinsal chair-lift serves local dishes ('a warm and friendly place with delicious food, especially the Catalan sausages'), as does its sister establishment, Obelic's ('good, inexpensive food'). The pick of après-ski entertainment is the Red Rock bar, with a vibrant ambience, which is welcome after the bleakness of the skiing.

Much of the accommodation is basic and cheap. The Poblado apartments are recommended, and hotel Rossell has 'basic food'. Attitude and service at the Hotel Font came under fire. The Hotel Daina, 15 minutes' walk from the centre, is a newer addition, while Hotel Janet is a small, family-run place on the outskirts. The large, modern Hotel St Gothard also houses Skydance, one of the village's main nightspots. The Hotel Solana is said to have the resort's best facilities, with an indoor swimming-pool, steam room and sauna. Cisco's and the Red Rock bar are both noted for their food. The Solana and the Surf Bar are recommended for evening entertainment. Cisco's stays open until 5am, and Asteric's has live guitar music in the early evening. We have good reports of the children's ski school, and the resort also operates a crèche.

TOURIST OFFICE
Tel 376 835 822
Fax 376 836 242

Pal
top 2358m (7,736ft) bottom 1780m (5,840ft)
Pal is a small village down the road from Arinsal, with a separate ski area further up a winding road. It shares a lift pass with its neighbour, and the skiing has considerably greater variety. The 14 lifts and 30km of piste are accessed from four different points. Of its 24 runs, half are graded red, and 80 per cent of the skiing terrain is covered by artificial snow. From the top of the ski area at the Pic del Cubil you can either come straight down to Coll de la Botella via two red runs or ski over towards Refugi Pla de la Cot on a choice of four red runs. Off to one side is Edifici La Caubella, where most of the shorter and easier runs are situated.

TOURIST OFFICE
Tel 376 836 236
Fax 376 835 904

Pas de la Casa/Grau Roig
top 2580m (8,465ft) bottom 2095m (6,872ft)
This is the first resort you reach after crossing the French border. The fundamental impression is of a brash city of giant advertising hoardings, scores of tacky shops, crowds of shoppers and choking traffic fumes. The architecture is both higgledy-piggledy and ugly. The town feels like

a resort that owes its existence to dime stores rather than skiing. Supermarket shelves are piled high with cut-price alcohol, much of it produced locally.

The skiing in **Pas de la Casa** and linked **Grau Roig** is now connected to neighbouring Soldeu/El Tartar which together offer a respectable 150km of skiing served by 50 lifts. However, for the present, no joint lift pass is available, and skiers and snowboarders have to pay a daily supplement of 1,700 pesetas to stray from home territory. Pas de la Casa's own skiing takes place mainly in two bowls on either side of the 2600-m pass, making it the highest resort in Andorra. Its 29 lifts serve 85km of pistes, which are well covered by snow-cannon. The resort has a half-pipe, and the Font Negra piste above the village is floodlit for night-skiing.

Main access to the pass is via an efficient but usually oversubscribed quad chair-lift. From the top you can return to the resort via a choice of runs, which can be crowded and icy. Alternatively, you can ski on down the gentler but more rewarding pistes to Grau Roig, which is little more than a car park and a hotel on the floor of the adjoining valley.

The Del Cubil quad chair-lift, gives access to a handful of red (intermediate) and blue (easy) runs; all are fairly short, and the snow tends to disappear quickly here. The better alternative is to catch the drag up to Mont Malus, where two short but very enjoyable reds or, snow permitting, the black (difficult) Granota take you back to Grau Roig. Riders congregate at the half-pipe at La Coma III in the Grau Roig area. One major complaint is that beginners in Pas de la Casa are forced to buy a full area lift pass just to use the two short drag-lifts on the nursery slopes. One reporter griped: 'During February half-term the resort was overcrowded, the ski school overloaded and the lift queues enormous'. Here, as in other Andorran resorts, the standard of English spoken by instructors is high, and many have BASI or similar Australian or New Zealand qualifications.

The five mountain eating-places in the Pas de la Casa/Grau Roig ski area are little more than cheap and functional snack-bars. The Bar El Piolet at the bottom of the Del Clot drag-lift is said to have 'the best baguettes I have ever tasted – especially the hot bacon ones'. Refugi de Pessons has 'a log fire, pleasant food and service'.

While Pas de la Casa cannot in any way be called attractive, it does have a large variety of accommodation ranging from the comfortable to the very basic. Two of the more expensive hotels, which receive favourable comment from reporters, are the Sporting and the Central, both at the lower end of the resort. The budget hotel Llac Negre has a varied local menu and friendly staff. Much of the resort accommodation is in apartments. One reporter commented: 'Many of the younger people choose the apartments close to the slopes, while families and those seeking a quieter life choose the hotels'. Of the many self-catering apartments, neither Paradis Blanc nor Lake Placid seem to have many admirers; reporters complain about their small size and lack of sound-proofing.

The restaurants in Pas de la Casa are cheap and cheerful. The food is mainly Spanish, with fresh seafood and the ubiquitous paella, although some concessions have been made to the French. La Braza and La Gratinada in Pas de la Casa were recommended by reporters with small children for their friendly atmosphere. Most of the bars in Pas de la Casa are cheap, and even the ones with dancing seem to have resisted the urge to charge for entry. The Marseilles 'is the place for a quiet drink and has great lasagne'. The Discoteca Bilboard is popular and is split into two with 'general nightclub music played in one half and house/garage music in the other; there is no entry fee and you are able to roam between the two halves'. Other favourite nightspots include Milkaukee's, Crack, and KYU. Le Pub has a happy-hour each evening and holds weekly theme nights. Most of the British tour operators organise weekly pub crawls.

> **WHAT'S NEW**
>
> Pas de la Casa/Grau Roig linked with Soldeu
> 8-person gondola from Soldeu village to Pla dels Espiolets
> New 6-seater gondola at Arinsal
> Additional chair-lift at Arcalis

The fact that all the runs in Pas de la Casa end in one area is a big advantage for meeting children after lessons. There are two crèches, one in town and the other on the piste. The Jardi di Neu kindergarten is set in a small wooden hut with its own fenced-off ski and play area; it has a button-lift close to a smelly, diesel-driven drag-lift and the busy car park.

TOURIST OFFICE
Tel 376 801 060
Fax 376 801 070

Soldeu/El Tarter
top 2560m (8,399ft) bottom 1800m (5,904ft)

Soldeu and linked **El Tarter** together provide the best combination of skiing, accommodation, architecture, scenery and – above all – ambience of any resort in Andorra. Readers are unanimous in their praise: 'I would recommend Soldeu to anyone. It is especially great for beginners, and the ski school is excellent for all levels. The nightlife is cheap and suitable for anyone of any age'. The ski area is now linked to Pas de la Casa/Grau Roig although as yet they do not share a lift pass and you have to pay a daily supplement of 1,700 pesetas to cross the ridge between the two.

Soldeu and El Tarter provide a marked contrast to Pas de la Casa, consisting of little more than a ribbon of stone-and-wood buildings alongside the main road. Environmentally sympathetic regulations mean that even the recent constructions are much more attractive than those of their neighbour. The night life is considerably less raucous, and for families with small children this is the better of the two bases.

An eight-person gondola has at last been built from the village to provide direct mountain access to Pla dels Espiolets and the main skiing area. The alternative is a chair-lift from El Tarter, 2km down the road.

The ski area is made up of mainly long cruising runs, with open terrain going up to the top of the area and forest from the mid-mountain downwards. The 21 lifts serve some 60km of mainly intermediate skiing. At weekends a snowcat tow service gives advanced skiers the chance to explore off-piste terrain accessed from the 2491-m Pic de Encampanada. The area is otherwise highly suited to beginners and wobbly second-weekers, although one reporter commented 'some of the greens are like cross-country runs'. The ski school has an admirable reputation but finds it difficult to cope with the additional crowds during the two British half-term weeks in February. Soldeu has a snowpark and an ungroomed snowboard zone.

The Esqui Calbo restaurant is recommended for its service and value for money. Xalet Sol I Neu, at the bottom of the mountain at Soldeu, serves 'very tasty chicken curry made with better cuts of chicken breast than I have ever experienced in an English curry house'. Both mountain cafeterias are usually overcrowded between 11am and 4pm.

Hotels include El Duc, a comfortable chalet-style hotel in the village centre opposite the ski slopes. Beside it is the comfortable and traditional Sport Hotel with its own fitness centre incorporating a sauna, a gym and a physiotherapist. Aparthotel Edelweiss and the Cabo apartments both share the Sport Hotel's facilities. At the foot of the slopes in El Tarter is the conveniently placed Hotel Llop Gris, which has a swimming-pool, squash courts, and satellite television in every room. Further down the road is Parador Canaro, which offers an even higher standard of comfort.

The Deu Sol apartments are situated midway between Soldeu and El Tartar ('a 15-minute walk along a busy unlit road with no pavement'). Readers say they are 'poorly equipped and maintained' while inadequate cooking facilities and a lack of local food shops 'made a mockery of any notion of self-catering'.

The Esquirol and the Hard Rock Café are both recommended. El Pi is said to be good value for money. One reader warned that supermarkets are 'far more expensive here than anywhere else in Andorra. It pays to do your shopping in Pas de la Casa'. Soldeu's nightlife ('great for such a small resort') centres around the Pussycat, Aspen and El Duc discos. The Piccadilly Pub has 'something going on every night'. The Sport Hotel has a friendly bar. We have good reports of the nursery slopes in Soldeu, which are 'well prepared and fenced off from the rest of the pistes'. The ski school has a long tradition of teaching British children. Non-skiing children are cared for at two crèches.

TOURIST OFFICE
Tel 376 851 151
Fax 376 851 337

Eastern Europe

RESORTS COVERED Bulgaria: Bansko, Borovets, Pamporovo, Vitosha
Romania: Poiana Brasov, Sinaia. Serbia: Kapaonik
Slovenia: Bled, Bohinj, Kranjska Gora

Beginners ✱✱ Intermediates ✱

Something is stirring in the mountains of eastern Europe, and it is not just the customary brew of social and political unrest. Encouraged by the relative conversion to market economies, there are positive signs that the skiing countries of the former Warsaw Pact are beginning to get their act together – albeit not quite as quickly as some might have hoped. Admittedly **Bulgaria**, **Romania** and **Slovenia** have been attracting international skiers for more than 30 years, but it is only recently that foreign investors have turned their attention to the considerable potential offered by these countries' mountain resorts.

> ✔ Low prices
> ✔ Fascinating cultural experience
> ✘ Poor-quality food
> ✘ Lack of alpine charm
> ✘ Few consumer goods

In Bulgaria, **Serbia**, and Slovenia – but not Romania – transport and accommodation are slowly being improved and augmented, and standards of snow-grooming, rental equipment and the traditional bug bear of unappetising food and drink are changing for the better. But it is doubtful whether eastern Europe will ever offer realistic competition to the more sophisticated winter sports destinations of western Europe – not least because their areas are almost exclusively located in national parks, and are therefore restricted in terms of the expansion of marked ski terrain. But off-piste skiing, made all the more accessible by remarkably low-cost guiding (about £40 per day), offers extensive possibilities in many resorts, notably Bansko in Bulgaria. However, the most persuasive reason for choosing this part of the continent remains its unparalleled value for money. Although we have had reports that bars and restaurants in Pamporovo (Bulgaria) have been hiking up their prices from week to week, it is still true to say that eastern Europe represents excellent value for skiers on a budget.

Poland, **Slovakia** and the **Czech Republic** are poised to join the bigger players in the east; the latter has become particularly active in promoting itself as a skiing destination. Its three biggest resorts, all in northern Bohemia, have been attracting international skiers since the Second World War. Less surprisingly, the majority of them come from the former Soviet Union and East Germany.

We have not given the telephone numbers of the local tourist offices because we recommend that you travel through a bonded tour operator or via a country's own state travel agency (see *Skiing by numbers*).

BULGARIA

Bulgaria is the leading eastern European destination for British skiers, with **Borovets** and **Pamporovo** the most popular. **Vitosha**, a short hop from the capital, Sofia, can be recommended only for a short break, while the remote mountain town of **Bansko**, the most recent addition to the country's skiing portfolio, has much to recommend it.

Reports of Bulgarian hospitality are mixed, with opinion split fairly evenly between those who found their hosts brusque and unhelpful, and more positive assessments of an affable people who are keen to please. A turbulent history of occupation by neighbouring powers has left the Bulgarian people unsure of how to deal with foreigners. The political changes of the early 1990s may have led to a progressive thaw in attitudes towards visitors, but there is still some way to go before the country will be fully geared to a tourist industry. Visitors will find badly maintained roads, indifferent accommodation, expensive entry visas for independent travellers and inadequate facilities for transacting currency. Credit cards are rarely accepted except in the major hotels, and worn foreign banknotes are often refused, even by banks. Journeys by taxi can be unnerving, and public transport is unpredictable. One irate skier complained that she was charged £1 for a square of loo paper in a mountain restaurant in Borovets.

On the positive side, Bulgaria is a country with a fascinating cultural heritage. The ski resorts are located in areas of considerable natural beauty, close to places of great historical significance. The Rila Monastery, midway between Borovets and Bansko, is one of the most perfectly preserved medieval structures of its type in the world. Equally, the ancient town of Plovdiv and the old quarter of Sofia have much to recommend them. Shoppers will find a range of unusual goods, from hand-carved music-boxes to pirate CDs on street-corner stalls and even at the base of the Borovets ski lifts.

Bulgarian skiing is, by Alpine standards, limited. The largest ski area is not much bigger than a relatively unknown resort in the French Jura. Lift transport is variable, with ancient one-seaters and rudimentary drags much in evidence. However, lengthy queues are the exception rather than the rule. Mountain restaurants tend to be temporary-looking: indeed, some are just caravans on the hill. Few serve more than toasted cheese, chicken and chips, and soup, and even fewer have WCs ('when I asked for directions to the lav, I was pointed to a little hut amongst the trees with no door'). But something that Bulgarian ski resorts do better than anywhere else in Europe is to offer irresistibly low prices.

Bansko

top 2000m (8,202ft) bottom 936m (3,079ft)

A little over 160km south from Sofia and about an hour's drive beyond Borovets, Bansko is a largely unspoilt resort now emerging into the late twentieth century. The town lies in the shadow of the 2915-m peak of Vihren, the highest mountain in the spectacularly beautiful Pirin range close to the borders with Macedonia and Greece. There are few shops and no supermarkets, but what the town lacks in retail facilities it more than compensates for in its surprisingly extensive cultural diversions: three museums, and a magnificent old church that is unlikely to have altered much in 500 years.

The main focus of the skiing is located out of town at Shiligarnika, the largest of three ski areas at the foot of the 2746-m peak of Todorin. This is reached by a free, half-hour ski-bus ride along a narrow, picturesque mountain road through dense forest. The base-station at Shiligarnika is little more than a couple of new hotels in the midst of a forest clearing. The area offers about 20km of mainly wide, tree-lined slopes reached by a fast, modern three-seater chair-lift and two drags. The Chalin Valog area, a little further down the mountain, offers the most difficult piste skiing.

Although the region's pisted ski area is small, Bansko offers upper intermediate skiers something that no resorts in the Alps could begin to compete with. An estimated 750km of skiing through areas of remarkable natural beauty is accessible to those who want to venture off-piste, courtesy of arguably the best-value ski guides in Europe.

The Dado Pene, a converted eighteenth-century town house, and the equally atmospheric Mexana Rumen Baryakov are highly recommended restaurants. The Torino cabaret bar is unexpectedly upmarket, and popular with prosperous-looking Sofians. The Pension Sema, and the central Hotel Alpin, are both recommended as places to stay in town. Up the mountain, the new Hotel Todorka is impressive if somewhat isolated. However, it does offer free transfers to the town centre three nights a week.

Borovets
top 2540m (8,333ft) bottom 1323m (4,339ft)

Bulgaria's oldest and most sophisticated ski resort is attractively located amidst a dense pine forest in the southern Rila Mountains, but like much of eastern Europe it has squandered the natural beauty of its setting by erecting buildings of dubious architectural merit. However, the quality and extent of the skiing surpasses anything found elsewhere in the country, with the added attraction of lifts sited a short walk from the resort centre. These comprise the six-person Yastrebets gondola ('extremely unpleasant queues'), which services one of the area's three ski sectors, and two chairs – one of which is a four-seater accessing the predominantly intermediate Martinovi Baraki runs. Yastrebets and the Markoudjik sector above it offer arguably the best of the resort's 40km of marked skiing, which is mainly above the tree-line with a highest ski point of 2540m. Baraki is appreciably lower, and therefore less snow-sure, but offers some interesting glade runs from the top of the Sitnyakovska chair. All the nursery slopes are located amidst the six lifts at the base of this area.

The ski school is well regarded, with English widely spoken. The ski kindergarten is praised, and additional daycare is available for three – to seven-year-olds in the Rila Hotel. Accommodation is almost exclusively hotel-based, with the conveniently located Samokov standing out as by far the best example, offering a range of modern facilities, which include a swimming-pool, sauna, bowling alley and fitness room. It also has a nightclub and 'American' bar, both of which appear to be magnets for what one reporter described as 'young single women of entrepreneurial disposition'. Hotel Breza is 'quiet, comfortable, and rooms have adequate showers and WCs'. The Hotel Mura has also earned good reports.

A wide choice of bars and discos is located around the resort centre, including an establishment that the locals suppose to be a faithful replica of a traditional English pub.

Pamporovo
top 1925m (6,316ft) bottom 1450m (4,757ft)

Pamporovo is a small resort; the majority of its accommodation is in hotels strung out between the centre and the lift station, about a ten-minute journey by free ski bus. Most of the hotels face the area's only ski mountain, Snezhanka, whose summit is crowned by the Bulgarian equivalent of the Post Office Tower. This affords spectacular views of the rolling Rhodope Mountains from its restaurant and viewing platform.

There is one semi-precipitous black (difficult) run – optimistically called 'The Wall' – immediately beneath the summit and a couple of good-quality red (intermediate) runs on either flank. One of these provides the resort's longest run of 4km. Otherwise, the whole resort is mostly geared to novices and lower intermediates and could easily be skied in a morning. But the 25km of marked skiing, the majority of which is on tree-lined runs, is undeniably pretty.

Runs and lifts are well-linked, but the actual standard of uphill transport is a mixed bag. One modern three-seater chair links base and summit, but the remaining lifts comprise a couple of old-fashioned single-seaters and an assortment of buttons and T-bars. Lift queues are rare, except for a 15-minute spell in the morning when all the ski school classes set off simultaneously.

The locals claim that the Pamporovo Ski School is internationally renowned, although one reporter queried whether this might be for 'the grumpiness of its instructors'. Another reader, an experienced skier who chose the resort for a week's snowboarding course, reported that her instructor was 'charming, helpful, could board like a dream but, alas, wasn't all that gifted at passing on his undoubted talent'.

Of the resort's hotels, the Perelik was described as 'basic but comfortable – unless your room is above the disco that closes at 3am'. The hotel also houses Pamporovo's only swimming-pool and the main shopping centre. Among the opposition, the Chevermeto restaurant is recommended for its 'folk' nights when whole sheep are roasted over open fires, and dancers in traditional dress provide a colourful floor show; the £11 per head entrance fee includes a bottle of local wine.

Vitosha
top 2295m (7,530ft) bottom 1650m (5,413ft)

Bulgaria's highest resort is on Mount Vitosha, overlooking Sofia, which is 20km away and can be reached by a cheap bus service. The resort consists of a couple of comfortable hotels, old hunting lodges, a hire shop and lift station. A total of 22km of north-facing slopes above the tree-line are served by a small network of lifts. Vitosha is an ideal resort for beginners and early intermediates. The ski school is said to be excellent. Vitosha's proximity to the capital means that it is inundated with week-enders, and lift queues can be a problem.

Hotels include the Hunting Lodge, a unique residence set in its own grounds, 700m from the nearest ski lift. The Proster is the largest hotel, with facilities including a swimming-pool and the resort's only disco. One reporter commented: 'the view was fabulous, but the maintenance appalling; it was very noisy, and the food was poor'. Hotel Moreni is 'basic, with no frills'.

ROMANIA

Prices in Romania are even lower than in Bulgaria, but this is its only appeal as a ski destination. Bus and taxi fares can be measured in pence rather than pounds. As little as £5 will buy dinner for two with wine. While other former eastern-bloc countries have embraced a market economy and seriously improved facilities for tourists, Romania seems stuck in a time warp from which it shows no signs of freeing itself. Consumer goods are scarce. Ski lifts are dilapidated, prone to lengthy delays, and the safety of some of them must be seriously questioned. However, rental equipment has improved, and English is spoken everywhere. The standard of ski tuition is generally high, although classes can be oversized.

Poiana Brasov
top 1775m (5,823ft) bottom 1021m (3,350ft)

This is the best-known resort in Romania, located three hours' drive north of Bucharest in the attractive Carpathian Mountains. It is a purpose-built resort, founded by the Ceauşescu administration in the 1950s to promote tourism, and resembles an enormous holiday camp rather than a village. A few hotels, restaurants and a large sports centre are set back from the base of the ski area; the furthest hotels are about 2km away. The 14-km ski area is reached either by gondola, an antiquated open-air affair 'like a series of mop buckets on a string', or by two cable-cars ('do not expect them both to be running at the same time') to the summit. Piste-marking, grooming and artificial snow are non-existent. The nursery slopes are at the bottom of the mountain, but when there is a lack of snow, beginners are taken to a gentle slope at the top of the gondola. Most of the skiing is intermediate, with runs roughly following the line of the lifts. There are two black runs, one of which circumnavigates the mountain and ends at the base.

The ski school is unanimously recommended: 'Exceptionally good value'. There is no shortage of ski-school instructors who speak fluent English and are keen to show you a good time. One reporter warned that medical facilities are poor, and Brasov hospital 'is a sight to behold'. Of the two simple mountain restaurants, the best is a wooden chalet at the top of the gondola. The food is cheap and basic: 'Expect to pay less than £2 for lunch with a couple of beers'. One reporter found the resort 'full of British yobbos on cheap drunken sprees', but at the same time described his holiday as 'a culturally fascinating experience'. The Sport is the best-situated hotel. The Bradul has a faded air. The Alpin is of a slightly higher standard, but one reporter complained that 'the public rooms were full of surprisingly pretty prostitutes haggling with fat old Turks'.

Non-skiing activities are limited; other sports include skating, bowling and swimming. The après-ski takes place in the hotels, nearly all of which have discos or floor shows. The centre of activity is Vicky's Bar. Dinner at The Outlaws Hut is lively, starting with musicians playing around a log fire ('it is OK if you can cope with eating roast bear'). Alternatively, you can take part in a wine tasting and folklore dinner at the Carpathian Stag in Brasov. The Dacia restaurant specialises in wild boar. You can take an excursion to Dracula's Castle, and cheap buses and taxis can take you into the town of Brasov for limited shopping. It is worth spending a day in Bucharest.

Sinaia
top 2219m (7,280ft) bottom 855m (2,805ft)

Sinaia is where the Romanian Royal Family used to spend their summers. Each monarch built a summer residence and, while some of these are now run-down, the beautiful Peles Palace should not be missed. The old Royal Palace is now a hotel and is a short walk from the cable-car.

A two-stage cable-car from the town, its top section duplicated by a chair-lift, serves long intermediate runs down the front of the mountain. These runs are poorly marked and are consequently challenging in poor visibility. The main area is on exposed, treeless slopes behind the mountain and on subsidiary peaks beyond. It consists of short intermediate runs with some variety and plenty of scope for off-piste. Snowboarding is not encouraged. Hotel Palace is a traditional place overlooking a park and is a short walk from the lifts. The town is quiet and has just a few bars and restaurants.

SERBIA

This corner of former Yugoslavia was attracting novice skiers in increasing numbers from Britain and other countries in western Europe until hostilities started in 1992. Last season, Thomson. brought British tourists back again, but the honeymoon was brief as 'ethnic cleansing' of Albanians in the province of Kosovo once again thwarted attempts to kick-start international tourism. Prices are reasonable but not as low as you might expect.

Kapaonik
top 2027m (6,650ft) bottom 1666m (5,466ft)

Kapaonik has been a popular Balkan ski resort since it was developed in the 1980s. The 50-mile massif of the same name lies four hours along deserted roads from Belgrade. Throughout the long years of civil war Serbians continued to ski at Kapaonik, which despite housing the largest radar station in the Balkans remained unscathed. An assortment of 20 chair- and drag-lifts takes you up through a landscape of frozen, stunted pine trees to the twin 2000-m peaks of Pancicev Vrh and Suvo Rudiste. From here a network of 57km of well-maintained pistes meanders back down the mountain to provide excellent beginner slopes. Second- and third-week snow-users will also find sufficient terrain for improvement, but experts are limited to a couple of short sharp blacks that are not always open early in the season because of insufficient snow. The resort is particularly popular with Russians and Greeks.

The four-star Grand Hotel is 'large, clean, and comfortable – even if the food leaves much to be desired'. One reporter complained that food elsewhere was made up of 'turgid, greasy stews which the Serbs love, but it is not what we are used to. Part of the problem is that no menus are translated, and you can only imagine what you might be eating'. Welcoming mountain huts serve snacks and a bewildering assortment of alcoholic drinks. Visitors should beware of Bear's Blood, an innocuous-looking fruit brandy with the 120-proof kick of a grizzly.

Rental ski and snowboard equipment is of a surprisingly high standard. The ski school is run by a former trainer of the Serbian ski team ('the instructors spoke fluent English and exhibited a level of enthusiasm for teaching beginners that is markedly absent in major Alpine resorts'). One slope is floodlit at night. Day- and night-time snowmobile tours of the mountain are a popular diversion. Warmer and less energetic après-ski centres on a huddle of bars beneath the Konaci apartments, which range from a facsimile of an English pub to Royal Caffé, a sophisticated jazz bar with quality live music. Most hotels have discos but, with 'Living Doll' and 'Downtown' forever frozen in their joint Number One spot, pop lacks the progression Serbs have made in other spheres.

SLOVENIA

'A poor man's Austria with less skiing and less alpine charm,' is how one reporter described it. Like other eastern European countries, Slovenia is reasonably priced. Food, drink and internal travel are about one-third of British prices. Reports of the ski schools are generally favourable, with English widely spoken and the video analysis helpful.

Bled
top 1275m (4,183ft) bottom 880m (2,657ft)

The attractive old spa town of Bled looks on to a seventeenth-century church on an island in the middle of a lake. Its main, simple ski area is 8km away at Zatrnik, where a total of five lifts serve 18km of easy wooded slopes in a bowl; these are ideal for beginners in good snow conditions but provide little challenge for intermediates. Another even smaller area is Straza, which has just two lifts; both areas have artificial snowmaking. The Golf, a quiet hotel set slightly away from the main centre, is recommended, while the Lovec is an older, wood-panelled hotel.

Bohinj
top 1800m (5,906ft) bottom 569m (1,867ft)

Bohinj is a lakeside village in the Triglav Alpine National Park. The skiing takes place above it on Mount Vogel. A cable-car takes you to a plateau where nine lifts conveniently connect a handful of easy and intermediate runs among the trees and a small nursery area. When conditions are fine you can ski the 8.5-km run all the way down to the lake.

The accommodation at the base of Mount Vogel in the Zlatorog Hotel near the Vogel cable-car station is recommended for skiing convenience but is rather isolated in the evenings. The Ski Hotel Vogel, at the top of the cable-car, is an ideal place to stay, as are the hotels Jezero and Kompass, both situated above beautiful Lake Bohinj. The other skiing area is Mount Kobla, 5km away, which consists of a mixture of easy and intermediate runs below the tree-line and is served by six lifts. Together the two ski areas give a total of 48km of piste. Bohinj has a few pizzerias and discos with reasonable prices, and other activities include skating and curling on the frozen lake.

Kranjska Gora
top 1630m (5,348ft) bottom 810m (2,667ft)

This is one of the best-known resorts in the region. It is close to the Italian and Austrian borders and is Austrian in ambience, even down to its domed church. Hotels are improving although they are not comparable in standard to cosy Austrian gasthofs. The setting, in a flat-bottomed valley between craggy wooded mountains, is a pretty one. The four nursery runs are fairly short, wide and gentle and set right on the edge of the village; the transition to real pistes is rather abrupt, with the mountains rising steeply from the valley floor. A total of 30km of pistes, the majority of which are blue, is covered by the lift pass. The longest run, Vitranc, is reached by chair-lift to the top of the ski area and is graded red. The other lifts go only halfway up the small mountain, which means limited skiing and the danger of poor snow cover.

The Alpine Ski Club offers both group and private lessons, with only private snowboarding and cross-country lessons available. Children are catered for in the ski school but there is no kindergarten. Several of the slightly institutional hotels have swimming-pools and saunas, as well as some discos and bars. The Kompass is one of the resort's best hotels, with a swimming-pool and disco. The modern Hotel Larix is recommended for its location and facilities, and Hotel Prisank has a friendly atmosphere.

Scandinavia

RESORTS COVERED Norway: Geilo, Hemsedal, Lillehammer, Oppdal, Trysil, Voss.
Sweden: Åre, Sälen

Beginners **✱✱✱** Intermediates **✱✱** Snowboarders **✱✱**

English is widely spoken in all the Scandinavian resorts, and both Norway and Sweden are particularly keen on the British. Traditionally, skiers travelling to Norway tend to be beginners, intermediates and cross-country enthusiasts. It is fair to say that Norway is not the best destination for advanced skiers. Although the country has almost 200 locations where skiing is possible, including scores of langlauf centres and some very small ski hills, Norway's mountains have vertical drops of only 300 to 750m, and less than a dozen ski areas can truly be called downhill resorts. It must be stated that downhill skiing in Norway bears no comparison to that in the Alps or the Rockies. It is more like the alpine skiing of the 1960s, in that there is no pressure to ski serious vertical or lots of hours – skiing here is treated as part of an all-round winter holiday. The T-bar is still prominent, although the high-speed quad-chair has found its way to a few resorts, notably Hemsedal.

✔ Ideal for small children
✔ Extensive cross-country skiing
✔ Few lift queues
✔ Relaxed atmosphere
✔ Reliable snow cover
✔ Good-value lift passes
✔ English widely spoken
✘ Low altitude
✘ Few long runs
✘ High-priced alcohol
✘ Extremely cold temperatures

The ski schools are well-organised with English-speaking instructors who are described as 'friendly and helpful'. Telemarking is making a big comeback to this, its country of origin. Norway is highly recommended for families, and there is a keen emphasis on safety. Hemsedal and Geilo even provide free lift passes along with free helmets for children of up to seven years of age, provided that the helmets are worn. Children's ski areas are often roped off with netting to stop fast adult snow-users hurtling into them at the end of a downhill run. For children of three months and over, the resorts have Trollia (Troll Club) kindergarten for skiing and playing, which are usually open seven days a week.

The Norwegians on holiday are late risers, and the slopes here are almost deserted until midday. This means that morning lift queues do not exist even in high season, although the slopes are busier in the afternoon. Travelling by train in Norway is particularly comfortable – with exemplary restaurant cars and wonderful facilities for small children including a 'crèche-carriage' on inter-city trains, containing baby-changing and feeding rooms and an indoor play area complete with climbing frame and Wendy house. Some of the Norwegian resorts offer a Winterlandet card, which allows you to ski more than one area. For example Geilo, Hallingskarvet, Hemsedal, Gol and Al are on the same lift pass, offering a total of 74 runs and 45 lifts at 910Kr for six days.

Skiing in **Sweden** is an altogether more serious affair and is much more comparable to that in mainstream Europe. Daylight hours are limited in mid-winter, and temperatures can be extreme. The skiing season is a long one in Scandinavia, but nowhere more so than in the resort of Riksgransen in Swedish Lapland in the Arctic Circle. Here the pistes stay open for night-skiing in the light of the 'midnight sun'.

Throughout Scandinavia alcohol remains expensive – even more so in Sweden than in Norway. Expect to pay about £3.50 for a bottle of beer and a minimum of £22 for a bottle of imported wine, whether from Bulgaria or Bordeaux. Spirit prices are off the scale. However, ski rental and lift passes are now about one-third of the price of their alpine counterparts. Most important of all is that Scandinavia's snow record is not subject to the peaks and troughs experienced in more southerly latitudes. The Scandinavian buffet with a predominance of fresh, smoked and marinated fish is the staple dinner diet and is eaten uncomfortably early. Reindeer features strongly in the meat section of any menu.

Other activities in Norway include dog-sledding, snowmobiling, snowshoeing, snow rafting, squash, sleigh rides, swimming and water-fall-climbing. In Sweden there is dog-sledding, go-karting on ice, hang-gliding, heli-skiing, ice-climbing, ice-fishing, parapente, snowmobiling, sleigh rides, telemark and tyre-racing.

NORWAY

Geilo
top 1178m (3,864ft) bottom 800m (2,624ft)

This is a traditional resort mid-way between Bergen and Oslo and only 30 minutes' drive from Dagali Airport. It is especially recommended for cross-country skiers as one of the centres on the famous Hardangevidda Plateau. The downhill skiing, which comprises 32 pistes served by 18 lifts, is relaxed and uncomplicated, with several reporters describing the terrain as 'perfect for novice and intermediate skiers'. Although there are seven notional black (difficult) runs, advanced skiers will quickly run out of steam here.

The skiing is made up of two areas inconveniently situated on either side of a wide valley, with the resort beside the lake in the middle. The only way to get from one side to the other is by snow-taxi, which costs 15Kr per adult and is free for children: 'A useless arrangement, which involves much waiting in the cold and seriously detracts from enjoyment,' said one reporter. What the resort desperately needs is a free ski-bus service.

The Vestlia area, with a vertical drop of about 244m, has the easiest skiing and is where the excellent ski- and non-ski kindergarten, the Troll Club, is based. The highlight is Bjornloypa, a popular long green (beginner) run. The main area has a much wider selection of pistes than Vestlia, including some steeper terrain and a vertical drop of 378m. Apart from its three ski schools, Geilo also has Aktivitets Guiding for off-piste skiing; snowboarding lessons are available, and there is a snowpark. Norway is famous as the home of cross-country skiing and nowhere more so than Geilo, which is a traditional cross-country resort with 175km of loipe both on the valley floor and on the Hardangevidda Plateau at 1312m.

Six restaurants are scattered around the two ski areas: most of them are rather soulless cafeterias. The fast-food restaurant at the top of the main area at Geilohovda is popular. Apart from hotels, Norwegian resorts have an abundance of usually expensive cabins and apartments. Geilo has the stately Dr Holms Hotel, one the most famous in Norway, 'stylishly furnished and patronised by sleek Scandinavian families exuding wealth and health'. You can ski to the three-star Solli Sportell Hotel, and the Highland Hotel is also recommended. The Vestlia Hotel is said to be 'warm and comfortable, the food was excellent and we were two minutes' walk from the lifts'. Reporters praised the Usterdalen Hotel, which has 'friendly owners, an excellent buffet, a crafts club for children, and after-dinner live entertainment with free coffee'. The Ski Bar at the Dr Holms Hotel is popular for early evening drinks.

Geilo's Troll Inn, where children under three can take part in indoor and outdoor activities, is warmly praised. The downside is that lunch is not provided, which means that because of the inconvenience of having to take snow-taxis to and fro it is almost impossible for parents to leave the small Vestlia ski area during the day. Geilo children's ski school receives much acclaim: 'the children were very well looked after', and 'the lessons were fun and my son couldn't wait to go back the next day'.

TOURIST OFFICE
Tel 47 32 09 59 00
Fax 47 32 09 59 01
Email geilo@skiinfo.no
Web site www.geilo.no

Hemsedal
top 1497m (4,911ft) bottom 675m (2,214ft)
Although only an hour's drive from Geilo, in the heart of Norway's Winterland region between Oslo and Bergen, Hemsedal's peaks look a lot more mountainous than Geilo's rounded ski hills; psychologically, this helps you feel that you are in a serious ski resort. In addition, despite the fact that Hemsedal has fewer runs than Geilo, and Oppdal has a larger ski area and more off-piste, Hemsedal has some of the best skiing in Norway, with a vertical drop of 800m and a long season stretching from mid-November to May.

In a country where ski resorts are dominated by the T-bar, Hemsedal also has the most modern lift system, with one quad chair-lift and five triple chairs among its 16 lifts serving 30 runs.

The resort has a couple of genuinely steep black runs and some entertaining tree-line skiing. One snag is that the village is about 3km from the ski area, and the free ski-bus service is infrequent (two go from the village in the morning and two return in the afternoon). One of the planned new lifts will go straight from the village to the ski area. Hemsedal has some good tree-level skiing, which is known as 'taxi skiing' because you will need to organise transport to get you back to the slopes or to your base. It also has a severe off-piste run called Reidarskaret, which starts with a steep, narrow couloir that is usually too dangerous to attempt unless snow conditions are perfect. Snowboarding is popular in Norway, particularly in Hemsedal where there is a funpark with floodlit boarding and a self-timing course.

In Hemsedal the excellent – and free – slope-side babysitting service operates a simple but effective way of telling anxious parents that their toddlers are sleeping soundly in their cots at afternoon nap time: if the curtain closest to their infant is closed, all is well – if drawn open, the child would appreciate prompt return of parents.

Two mountain restaurants are near the top of the Hollvinheisen triple-chair. A third, Skistua, is at the base area and has the option of self- or waiter-service. Hotels include the Fossheim ('small, family-run, and very comfortable'). If you like packed, noisy bars, try some of Hemsedal's in-places during a busy weekend. You will be lucky if you can get near the Garasjen (the old bus garage), as it can become so crowded that skiers overflow on to the street and those left inside have to come to a tacit agreement as to the moment when snatching a quick sip of beer in unison is possible. You may have more room to breathe at the Kro Bar in the Fanitullen apartment block.

TOURIST OFFICE
Tel 47 32 06 01 56
Fax 47 32 06 06 37
Email hemsedal@skiinfo.no
Web site www.skiinfo.no/hemsedal/

Lillehammer
top 1050m (3,444ft) bottom 200m (656ft)
Lillehammer resembles an American frontier town with its clapboard houses and single main street. The nearest skiing is based 15km away at **Hafjell**, which has 23km of prepared pistes, 7 lifts and 9 runs. The best pistes are from Hafjelltoppen (1050m) down either the Kringelas or Hafjell runs. Both are graded black and formed part of the 1994 Winter Olympic slalom courses. Night-skiing is also available once a week.

Kvitfjell, 50km from Lillehammer, was created specifically for the Olympics and is effectively a downhill course and nothing else; its 4km of pistes are closed to everyone but competitors and officials on race days.

TOURIST OFFICE
Tel 47 61 26 64 43
Fax 47 61 25 65 85

Oppdal
top 1300m (4,265ft) bottom 545m (1,788ft)

Oppdal lies 120km south of Trondheim and is one of Norway's most northerly downhill resorts. It is also technically its biggest. Although it has only 28 runs (fewer than Hemsedal and Geilo) and a vertical drop a little lower than Hemsedal, it has extensive areas of off-piste terrain spread between its four ski areas. It offers 78km of pistes served by 16 lifts. The most challenging marked trails, Bjorndalsloypa, Hovdenloypa and Bjerkeloypa, were enjoyed by Italian gold medalist Alberto Tomba when he was here for a World Cup race and are on the front face of Hovden, the central ski area.

The Vangslia area also offers a mixture of terrain, while Stolen at the other end of the resort is made up entirely of beginner and intermediate terrain. The fourth area, Adalen, is set in a huge bowl behind Hovden and is dominated by long, mainly blue (easy) cruising runs. At 1pm in Oppdal, for a fee, snowcats will take up to 50 skiers at a time to the top of the mountain at Blaoret for sightseeing and an additional 240 vertical metres of off-piste skiing.

Oppdal has a specialist guiding service called Opplev Oppdal; guides escort skiers around the area and carry a full kit of safety equipment, including avalanche transceivers (rarely used in Norway), shovels and avalanche probes. The resort offers 'night-snowboarding' with special floodlit courses – complete with rental equipment and a buffet – on Wednesday evenings at the Sletvold Park slope. Oppdal also has 150km of cross-country trails; five of its tracks are floodlit.

The resort has six mountain restaurants: one at the bottom of each base area, and two more at the top of the Hovden and Stolen lift complexes. Only the Vangslia lifts are without a mid-mountain restaurant. The semi-circular restaurant at the top of Hovden was originally part of a water-storage structure. The restaurant at the bottom of Stolen, where most of the easiest family skiing takes place, is usually the busiest on the mountain.

The recently refurbished Hotel Nor is a sound choice, and guests at the 75-room Hotel Oppdal, right by the (not busy) railway station describe it as cosy and quaint, in spite of its size. It is worth trying the so-called 'Viking evening' (a misnomer) at a timbered roundhouse in the woods, where local stews, patés and sausage are served in front of a roaring fire with accordion accompaniment. Although Oppdal is a fair-sized town, nightlife – apart from a few bars and restaurants – is limited.

TOURIST OFFICE
Tel 47 72 42 17 60
Fax 47 72 42 08 88
Email post@oppdal-turist.st.no
Web site www.oppdal.com

Trysil
top 1132m (3,714ft) bottom 600m (1,969ft)

This is an expanding resort three hours' drive from Oslo. Its 85km of piste served by 23 lifts are spread across the wooded slopes of Trysilfjellet at 1132m. It is said to have the most reliable snow cover anywhere in the country. In common with many Norwegian resorts, the lifts are several kilometres from the resort centre. The skiing varies from easy beginner trails to some more challenging red (intermediate) runs but is often criticised for having too many green runs ('cross-country tracks in disguise'). Accommodation in Trysil is mainly hotel- and apartment-based, although mountain cabins, notably the Trysilfjellet, make a pleasant change for hardy self-caterers.

TOURIST OFFICE
Tel 47 62 45 05 11
Fax 47 62 45 11 65
Email info@trysil.com
Web site www.skiinfo.no/trysil

Voss
top 945m (3,100ft) bottom 91m (300ft)

In spite of its low altitude, Voss has a reasonable ski area for beginners and lower intermediates. The 40km of prepared pistes includes three black runs, two of which are reasonably challenging, and some off-piste. The nine lifts (almost one for each run) include a cable-car, and the longest descent is 3km. Enthusiasts of cross-country skiing will certainly not be disappointed with Voss and its 63km of prepared trails. Snowboarding classes are available.

TOURIST OFFICE
Tel 47 56 52 08 00
Fax 47 56 52 08 01
Email vossn@online.no

SWEDEN

Åre
top 1274m (4,180ft) bottom 380m (1,312ft)

Åre, or Arefjallen Resort, in the North of Sweden, provides some of the most challenging skiing in Scandinavia – 90km of piste served by 44 lifts stretched across four ski areas beside a scenic fjord. The skiing here is certainly comparable to a medium-sized Alpine resort, with enough challenging runs including the Salombacken and the World Cup downhill to keep accomplished skiers happy. The transfer time is about 90 minutes from Östersund Airport.

English is spoken to a high standard in Sweden, and the head of the ski school at Åre is British-born. Cross-country is also popular here, with the Södra Arefjallen area on the south side of the lake at Åre offering extensive trails. Children are well catered for, with a free lift pass and free – compulsory – helmets offered to children up to the age of 11.

We have positive reports of both the four-star Åregarden and Renen hotels. The Backpackers' Inn ('cheerful') is the budget option. Restaurants include Down Under, hybrid Mexican/Australian establishment, Grill Hörnan, and Tännsforsen which welcomes children. The Skier's Bar at the Diplomat Ski Lodge, Sunwing, and Broken Dreams are all lively bars which are busy when the lifts close. Lively night spots include the Bygget and the Country Club.

TOURIST OFFICE
Tel 46 64 71 77 20
Fax 46 64 717712
Email info@arefjall.se
Web site www.arefjall.se

Sälen
top 950m (3,135ft) bottom 550m (1,815ft)

Sälen is Scandinavia's largest ski area. It is made up of four resort bases and two separate ski areas, Lindvallen-Högfjället and Tandådalens-Hundfjället, which are linked by ski bus. Together they offer a total of over 100 pistes covering 85km with a maximum vertical drop of 303m. The skiing is best suited to beginners and intermediates, although there are also a few testing black runs. The Wall area at Hundfjället is used for speed skiing.

Ski school instructors in Sälen are fluent English-speakers, and snowboarders are also catered for, with snowparks at both Lindvallen and Hundfjället and a half-pipe at Högfjället. Skiing is free for children under seven years old, and there is a children's ski school as well as ski- and non-ski kindergarten. A total of 20 mountain restaurants are divided between Sälen's two ski areas. You can ski to and from the Högfjalls Hotel in the resort.

Sälen buzzes after skiing with live music in a whole range of bars, including Grandfather's Corner and the Piano Bar at the Högfjället hotel. Recommended hotels include the Tandådalens and the Högfjället. Restaurant Onkel Jean is praised for its 'delicious elk steaks'. McSki is the world's first and only ski-thru McDonalds. Late night action centres on the HC night club at the Högfjällshotellet and Fjällis in the Tandådalens.

TOURIST OFFICE
Tel 46 280 20250
Fax 46 280 20590
Email turist.saelen@malung.se
Web site www.malung.se

Scotland

Beginners ✳✳✳ Intermediates ✳✳ Advanced ✳ Snowboarders ✳✳

The success of Scotland's ski areas is entirely reliant on the weather and on the type of snow that falls. On the one hand, a sudden temperature rise can bring a rapid thaw, or rain and gale-force winds can make life on the mountain extremely unpleasant as well as closing vital access lifts. On the other hand, you can experience beautiful sunshine and no wind, with temperatures low enough to keep the snow crisp. When this happens swarms of enthusiastic Scottish skiers clog up the car parks, rental shops and ticket counters as foreplay to creating horrific lift queues and overcrowded slopes. Scottish skiing is keen to update its old image of wind-blown slopes, obsolete lifts, nasty cafeterias and even nastier WCs. Much has been done to improve facilities, but the unkind winter climate remains unchanged.

✔ Friendly atmosphere
✔ Wide range of non-ski activities
✔ Late-season skiing
✔ BASI tuition
✘ Unpredictable weather conditions
✘ Lift queues at peak periods
✘ Limited skiing

Because of the weather, it is a constant battle for the resort operators to groom the slopes effectively, and they have to erect chestnut paling fences everywhere in an attempt to catch and contain drifting snow. Rapid temperature fluctuations make the manufacture of artificial snow difficult. The positive side of all this is summed up in one reader's comments on Cairngorm: 'Although the weather and snow conditions can be disappointing, to me they just make an otherwise limited mountain more challenging'.

The five ski centres in the Scottish Highlands are often marketed together. **Nevis Range** is on the west coast, 33 miles (55km) from **Glencoe**. **Cairngorm (Aviemore)** is in Strathspey, in the Central Highlands, and **The Lecht** and **Glenshee** lie to the east.

The achievements of the resort operators and their staff cannot be overstated. Managing to build and maintain their operations against this background of meteorological unpredictability, while persuading public and private institutions to invest the capital needed to expand and improve the centres, shows a dedication that is the reality of Scottish skiing. While many moan about Britain's standing in competitive world skiing, it is Scotland that provides most of the national team members.

Scotland boasts an exceptional number of ski schools, many of them based at or near Cairngorm. Most offer a high standard of tuition under the auspices of the British Association of Ski Instructors (BASI), the teaching methods of which are internationally accepted. The Nevis Range Ski School runs various courses, including 'over the back' guided trips, clinics for steep skiing and bumps, over-50s and women's workshops.

British interest in snowboarding was pioneered in Scotland in the late 1980s, and riders are now a common sight at all the centres. Most of the local ski schools offer tuition, and the rental shops have boards for hire. Cairngorm has a funpark and an on-slope shop where you can hire equipment and book tuition. A Ride Guide, a map written in snowboarding lingo, is available in addition to the ordinary piste map. Nevis Range has several specialist snowboard shops including Mach, where lessons can also be booked.

Scotland offers plenty of opportunities for cross-country skiing. However, due to the cold winds, clothing needs to be extra-protective. Most of Scotland's cross-country skiing is along forest trails, which hold the snow better than the more open terrain. The season runs from early January to mid-March on the lower, wooded trails and until early May higher up the mountain. The most challenging routes are on the rounded mountains of the Central and Eastern Highlands.

The changeable snow and weather conditions mean that a Scottish skiing holiday is not suitable for those who have to plan ahead. It also makes sense to be based where you have access to more than one centre, and not invest in a week's lift ticket for just one resort.

It is unrealistic to expect to enjoy the same sort of skiing holiday here as you would in the Alps, but it is possible to have an excellent time simply by keeping an open mind and being flexible. The Highlands are so used to uncertain weather that the range of alternative outdoor pursuits available puts even the world's top ski resorts to shame: they include canoeing, climbing, gliding, gorge walking, hang-gliding, skating, off-road vehicles, shooting, squash, swimming and tennis.

Cairngorm (Aviemore)
top 3,608ft (1100m) bottom 1,804ft (550m)

Aviemore is located about 120 miles (192km) north of Edinburgh and Glasgow on the A9 and is the nearest town to the Cairngorm ski area, which lies 10 miles (16km) to the east. It is served by rail direct from Inverness and the south. Daily flights operate from Heathrow, Stansted and Luton. In the 1980s Aviemore suffered from having its facilities based around the Aviemore Centre, a hideous 20-year-old concrete development, which has been in a serious state of decay for the last ten years. Planners have optimistically renamed the area Aviemore Mountain Resort and hope to invest £15 million in it over the next few years. The Centre itself has been left behind by developments on Aviemore's main street and on the outskirts of the town ('a modern sprawl with large hotels'), where high-quality accommodation and leisure attractions have emerged, helping to make the region more of an appealing outdoor holiday destination.

At present, parts of the medium-sized ski area are often shut because of poor weather or snow shortage: 'When the top chair-lifts are closed due to high winds, it can be infuriating if the snow conditions are good on the runs that are affected'. This will change if plans for the long-promised funicular finally materialise. Funds and planning permission are in place, but at the time of writing the scheme was still subject to the findings of judicial review brought out by conservationist pressure groups. If permission is granted, work on the funicular will start in May 1999 and it will open in time for the winter of 2000. The 17 lifts serve two distinct sectors, which are accessed from separate bases at Coire Na Ciste and Coire Cas, meeting below the 4,084-ft (1245-m) Cairngorm peak. Head Wall offers challenging skiing, and White Lady has some excellent moguls. West Wall and Ciste Gully are recommended 'first thing in the morning before most skiers are on the hill'. The Cairngorm Snowboard School has an excellent reputation, and the area also boasts a funpark.

Trail-marking is not one of the region's strong points, and you need to keep an eye out for half-buried snow fences. Off-piste routes include the East Wall gullies and Coire Laogh Mor; these are reached by a long traverse, which often has wind-broken snow, and a guide is necessary for both. The Mercury Hotel in the Aviemore Centre has a crèche for children aged two to eight years, and the ski schools arrange children's tuition on demand ('in good weather' according to the local tourist board).

Cairngorm has four snack bars: two at the base lodges, Shieling at the mid-station, and the fourth at the panoramic Ptarmigan, which is popular for drinks and short breaks. The Shieling is one of the only restaurants in Scotland that allows skiers to eat packed lunches at the table. The funicular scheme will allow for a new 250-seat restaurant at Ptarmigan.

Between Aviemore and the Cairngorm slopes is the Stakis Coylumbridge Resort, which has plenty of facilities, including a swimming-pool, and a wide range of children's activities. In nearby Carrbridge, the An Airidh Ski Lodge recreates the cosy 'open-house' atmosphere of an alpine ski chalet, and in Aviemore itself the Mercury offers good-value accommodation.

Scotland is still saddled with an unfair reputation for a limited choice of eating places. Littlejohns restaurant in Aviemore has a friendly atmosphere, with 1930s paraphernalia and copious quantities of American and Mexican food. The Gallery is at Inverdruie, a mile outside Aviemore; readers praise its food and recommend booking in advance as it has few tables. The Taverna Bistro has reasonable prices.

Aviemore used to be known for its rowdy and sleazy nightlife, but most of the bars have been refurbished, and there is now less of the tough, hard-drinking Scottish pub atmosphere. Crofters is one of the most popular of Aviemore's clubs, and the bar at the Highland Hotel is also recommended. Non-ski activities include a theatre, cinema, swimming and skating. Reporters generally found the nightlife 'disappointing', with the disco stopping at 11pm. Prices for drinks are 'at the usual pub rates but somewhat inflated in the more expensive hotels'.

TOURIST OFFICE
Tel (01479) 810363/Ski Centre (01479) 861261
Fax (01479) 811063/Ski Centre (01479) 861207
Email cairn@sol.co.uk
Web site (all resorts) www.ski.scotland.net

Glencoe
top 3,637ft (1109m) bottom 2,001ft (610m)

Glencoe Ski Centre, 74 miles (118km) north of Glasgow, has attracted a dedicated following for four decades (Britain's first chair-lift opened here in 1961), and during the past few seasons there has been considerable investment in infrastructure at the Centre. It has 6 miles (10km) of piste and 15 runs. A museum of Scottish skiing and mountaineering contains mementos from home and abroad, including Chris Bonnington's ice axe from the 1985 Everest expedition. The Centre is open seven days a week (snow permitting) and has a ski and snowboard school as well as a rental shop. Glencoe has no childminding facilities, but the ski school can arrange lessons. The resort shares a Monday-to-Friday lift pass with Nevis Range. Recommended accommodation nearby includes Kingshouse Hotel and the Clachaig Inn. The Isles of Glencoe Hotel has a swimming-pool, sauna and whirlpool.

TOURIST OFFICE
Tel (01397) 703781/Ski Centre (01855) 851226
Fax (01397) 705184/Ski Centre (01855) 851233

Glenshee
top 3,504ft (1068m) bottom 2,000ft (610m)

Glenshee operates 'Britain's largest network of ski lifts and tows, covering four mountains and three valleys'. Its 26 lifts give access to 25 miles (40km) of piste. The centre is on a rather desolate pass on the A93, with the lifts located on both sides of the road. The skiing has considerable variety and in fine weather it offers plenty of scope for strong intermediate and advanced skiers. A number of reporters rate Glenshee as having the best skiing in Scotland. There is a modest café at the base and a better high-altitude restaurant, the Cairnwell. A crèche operates in high season for children aged three to seven years. The Invercauld Arms Thistle Hotel, 7 miles (11km) away in Braemar is warmly recommended. Alternatively, staying near Balmoral places you within 30 minutes' drive of Glenshee.

TOURIST OFFICE
Tel (013397) 41600/Ski Centre (013397) 41320
Fax (013397) 41643/Ski Centre (013397) 41665
Email glenshee@sol.co.uk

The Lecht
top 2,600ft (793m) bottom 2,109ft (643m)

The Lecht is Scotland's smallest ski area, a network of a dozen short button-lifts on both sides of the A939 Cockbridge to Tomintoul, 56 miles (89km) west of Aberdeen and about 45 miles (72km) from both Glenshee and Cairngorm. One reader said 'it is hardly mountainous and you could mistake it for a winter scene at various locations in England, but it is friendly and unpretentious'. The area is best suited to beginners and intermediates living within reasonable driving distance – The Lecht could not be described as a destination resort. The longest run is 800m. Snowmaking and a 200-m artificial slope are a precaution against the vagaries of Scottish weather, which last season only allowed the ski area to open fully for less than two-and-a-half months. The nearest accommodation is 3 miles (5km) away at Corgarff; a choice of hotels and bed-and-breakfast options 6 miles (10km) away at Tomintoul includes the 'comfortable and welcoming' Gordon Hotel.

TOURIST OFFICE
Tel (01330) 825917/Ski Centre (019756) 51440
Fax (01330) 825126 /Ski Centre (019756) 51426

Nevis Range
top 4,006ft (1221m) bottom 2,148ft (655m)

Nevis Range, formerly known as Aonach Mor, is Scotland's nearest equivalent to an alpine resort. It is located just north of Fort William and close to Ben Nevis, Britain's highest mountain. Its 11 lifts and 35 runs are reached from the car park by a modern six-seater gondola, which takes you up to the Snowgoose Restaurant; from here a quad-chair and a series of tow lifts fan out ('the views are stunning, with mouth-watering scenery in every direction'). The Braveheart chair-lift gives easy access to the back bowls of the Coire Dubh. This provides excellent off-piste terrain after a fresh snowfall for skiers and snowboarders alike. Queues for the return gondola journey back down the mountain can be huge when the weather is good. These develop at about 4pm when the Snowgoose Restaurant has standing-room only. The crèche accepts children from three years old.

The delightful nearby hamlet of Torlundy offers bed-and-breakfast, but most of the accommodation is in Fort William, an old lochside town with strong tourist appeal. It has a wide choice of hotels and restaurants, and a leisure centre with 10-pin bowling and a swimming-pool. Nearby hotels include Inverlochy Castle, which is frequented by Hollywood stars and the occasional US president. The Crannog restaurant has a good reputation for its seafood.

TOURIST OFFICE
Tel (01397) 703781/Ski Centre (01397) 705825
Fax (01397) 705184/Ski Centre (01397) 705854
Email nevisrange@sol.co.uk

Spain

RESORTS COVERED Baqueira-Beret, Sierra Nevada

Beginners ✱✱   Intermediates ✱✱   Snowboarders ✱

Spain does not have a historical connection with skiing and, indeed, it seems surprising that a country associated with beaches and summer sunshine should have any skiing at all. However, in recent years the popularity of skiing, and particularly snowboarding, within Spain has greatly increased. As a consequence, its main resorts have undergone considerable improvements.

Spain has two quite separate mountain ranges, the Pyrenees and the Sierra Nevada, which both normally receive adequate winter snowfalls, regardless of what is happening in the main Alpine countries. Avid Spanish snow-users forsake the cities for both areas at weekends and holiday times – led by the sport's prominent champion, King Juan Carlos, and other members of the royal family.

- ✔ Efficient lift systems
- ✔ Typically Spanish après-ski
- ✔ Reasonable prices
- ✗ Lack of resort charm
- ✗ Short runs

The rate of exchange of the peseta against the pound makes Spanish skiing some of the more affordable in Europe. Foreigners on the slopes are few, and the Spanish vociferously enjoy their skiing – and après-skiing – with the same passion they dedicate to other sports. We have generally poor reports of the Spanish ski schools, largely because a proportionately low number of instructors speak English in comparison with those at Alpine schools – and few British speak Spanish.

In Spain partying is an even more serious business than skiing. Anglo-Saxons who stray into this completely alien ski-resort environment either adopt local hours or suffer from what quickly develops into a severe Latin mutation of jet-lag. Local skiers hit the slopes at a leisurely 10am and ski furiously until lunch at 2pm. They grab a final hour on the piste before the lifts close at 5pm and then head for the tapas bars before an evening snooze. The length of the 7pm ski siesta is largely dependent on ski energy expended, the size of the paella you ate for lunch and your intake of *calamares* and Rioja at tea-time. Nobody (not even families with young children) sits down to dinner before 9pm, and restaurants begin to get busy at 11pm. Dancing does not begin before 1am and can carry on into daylight hours. As one reporter put it: 'If your aim here is to après-ski enthusiastically, then it would be a good idea to book an additional week's holiday on return to recover'.

The high and usually snow-sure resort of **Sierra Nevada** lies in the far south of the country in the mountains of the same name. However, most of the skiing takes place hundreds of kilometres to the north-east in the Pyrenees, which also usually provide reliable snow cover between Christmas and March – and sometimes into April. **Baqueira-Beret** remains the most important of the Pyrenean resorts – a small but smart development much loved by King Juan Carlos – and attracts wealthy skiers from Madrid and Barcelona.

Baqueira-Beret
top 2510m (8,235ft) bottom 1500m (4,920ft)

Baqueira-Beret is Spain's answer to Megève, a smart and fashionable resort where not all the designer ski suits you see parading down the main street ever make it on to the snow. It lies at the head of the beautiful Val d'Aran, near **Viella** on the northern side of the Pyrenees; access from France is easy, and the drive from Toulouse Airport takes less than two hours. In keeping with its chic status, prices are higher than you might otherwise expect in Spain.

The skiing takes place on four wide, well-linked mountains with a vertical drop of about 1000m over varied, often exciting terrain; most of it is suited to intermediates, but one icy couloir, evocatively called 'Where Goats Tumble', is a real challenge. The opening up of the Bonaigua area has greatly enhanced its appeal to good skiers. Reporters widely praise the standard of piste grooming and the amount of snow-making.

Plans to expand the already extensive skiing into the next valley and increase this impressive area by 40 per cent have still not been realised. At present it has 24 lifts covering 77km, with the main mountain access by quad-chair from the top of the village ('it goes up the mountain like the proverbial scalded cat'). The lower slopes are well covered by snow-cannon. Reporters in Baqueira complained that the instruction was mainly of the 'follow-my-leader' type.

Baqueira's mountain eating-places serve good food at reasonable prices but lack atmosphere. However, one exception is Restaurant 1800 ('wonderful paella for eight, but you must order a day in advance'). The restaurant at Bonaigua 'resembles a Gothic castle and is cheaper and better than anywhere else'. Baqueira is still largely unknown outside Spain, mainly because of the small number of rental beds available. However, it is no newcomer to winter sports – it is now 34 years old – and at a time when even big-name resorts are struggling financially, Baqueira as a ski resort is operating efficiently at a handsome profit.

The terrain, right down to the scrubby Engelmann spruce which grows here at the lower altitudes, is strongly reminiscent of Squaw Valley in California. But here the resemblance ends. Baqueira is purpose-built in an aesthetically adequate style. The village lies beside the road that leads up to the very high Bonaigua Pass, which is often closed in winter. Recent sympathetic development has increased its appeal as a base, with some good shops, hotels, restaurants and a leisure centre. The atmosphere is relaxed and friendly. Beret is the second base-area rather than a separate resort and consists of little more than a car park and a cafeteria. The veteran Olympic skier José Moga, who taught Juan Carlos to ski and

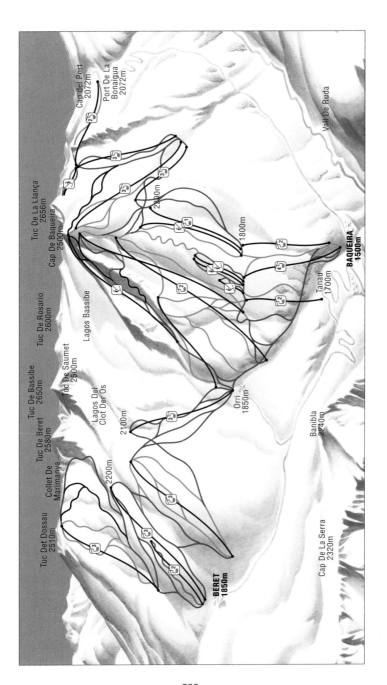

who also runs the main ski shop in town, described it as 'the best-value skiing in a less pretentious atmosphere than you can find anywhere in Europe'.

Baqueira has 12,000 beds, many of which are owned or rented for the season by Spaniards, who make the journey here every weekend from Barcelona and other cities. The four-star Hotel Montarto is widely praised, although one reporter commented: 'the décor is in need of being revitalised'. The less expensive Hotel Tuc Blanc has a strong following. Many regular visitors prefer to stay in the more traditional hotels further down the valley. There are good *paradors* (inns) in nearby Viella.

The menus in Baqueira are truly international and they come in three versions: Spanish, Catalan and Aranes (a language peculiar to this corner of the Pyrenees). Fortunately, the resort's proximity to the border means that French is also widely understood, if not spoken. This is not a place for vegetarians or the culinary squeamish; Borda Lobato is a lavishly converted cow shed which is considered to be the best restaurant in town ('barbecued rabbit was followed on my second evening by a choice of roast suckling pig or whole baby lamb carved with garden shears'). Other recommended restaurants include La Perdiu Blanca, La Ticolet for pierrade and Tamarro's for tapas. Tiffany's is the busiest nightclub.

Baqueira has three good ski- and non-ski kindergarten, which cater for children from three months to eight years old.

TOURIST OFFICE
Tel 34 73 64 44 55
Fax 34 73 64 44 88

Sierra Nevada
top 3470m (11,385ft) bottom 2100m (6,888ft)

Sierra Nevada lies in Andalucia, 32km from the ancient Moorish city of Granada, and offers mainland Europe's most southerly skiing. The existence of a ski resort here seems at total odds with the nearby resorts of Marbella and Malaga, with their yacht clubs and golf courses. The resort used to be marketed under the name of Sol y Nieve (Sun and Snow), and the purpose-built village in which most skiers stay (at 2100m) is known as Pradollano.

The village is short on alpine charm but has a new square, Plaza Andalucia, which gives it the focal point it previously lacked ('it is certainly nowhere near as ugly as the Andorran resorts'). The ski area is extremely vulnerable to bad weather, and the mountain range as a whole is exposed to high winds. One reporter commented: 'too much snow and too wintry conditions are almost as likely to stop you skiing as too little snow'. When the weather here is bad everything stops, but when conditions are good the skiing can be excellent and the views striking; on a clear day you can even see Morocco. However, because of its proximity to Granada and the Costa del Sol, the resort suffers from extreme crowds at weekends and on public holidays ('on a high-season Monday we queued 50 minutes for the main gondola, but once you know the lift system, you can avoid this').

About £60 million was invested in the resort in preparation for the Alpine World Championships, which were to be held here in 1995, but which had to be postponed for a year because of a lack of snow. The resort now has 19 lifts serving 34 mainly intermediate pistes totalling 61km. Access to the main skiing area is by a choice of three lifts, including a gondola, from the edge of the village. Sierra Nevada has a choice of three ski schools. The Spanish enjoy their lunch, and the main bowl houses a wide choice of mountain eateries.

The accommodation is mainly in hotels. The Melia Sol y Nieve and the four-star Melia Sierra Nevada, both near the main square, are convenient and pleasant. The Melia Sol y Nieve has a mini-club for children between 5 and 11 years of age. Melia Sierra Nevada has a swimming-pool, disco, its own shops and was described by one reporter as 'the best hotel we have been to in 28 years of skiing'. The Kenia Nevada is quiet: 'Most guests were Spanish, the service was generally friendly and attentive and the bedrooms comfortable and clean'. The chalet-style Parador, set on its own above Pradollano (accessible by chair-lift and piste), is fairly functional but has exceptional views. The Albergue Universitani is said to be excellent value and clean. A small range of restaurants serve local, French, Turkish and Italian cuisine. The Borreguiles is one of the most popular eating-places.

Most of Pradollano's buildings date from the 1960s and 1970s. It is not an attractive place ('just like Torremolinos with snow and litter'), but the atmosphere is 'quiet, with quite a Spanish feel to the resort'. The late-nightspot is Sierra Nevada 53. Early action is centred on the Crescendo bar. Others recommended include Chimay, Sticky Fingers, Soho and Golbe. One reporter warned: 'Nightlife only begins after 1am and carries on until 6am. The taxi service doesn't run at night and so you are in for a long walk home unless you are staying in the village centre'. Excursions can be made to Granada, famous for the spectacular Alhambra Palace, as well as for its beautiful Renaissance and Baroque buildings. A kindergarten operates for children aged three months to four years.

TOURIST OFFICE
Tel 34 58 24 91 00
Fax 34 58 24 91 31
Email cetursa@globalnet.es
Web site www.cetursa.es

Offbeat resorts

If **Australia's** mountains were transported without their flora and fauna to Europe, they would probably attract fewer skiers than France's Jura range. However, in their rightful place in New South Wales and Victoria, with the ubiquitous eucalyptus trees and abundant semi-tropical bird life, they have a charm of their own. If the snow is reasonably good, skiing in Australia is not to be sneered at.

Skiers in Australia should note that regardless of conditions – even on a hot day with no snow on the approach roads – the authorities here insist that you carry chains. Chain rental stores are en route to the slopes.

The skiing in **New Zealand** is of a higher quality than that in Australia, with some moderately impressive resorts in the southern Alps, together with numerous 'club fields' (these are less sophisticated than ski resorts, with rope-tows, no grooming, but cheap lift-tickets) and some formidable slopes at Whakapapa on the North Island. Prepare yourself for some hair-raising mountain roads, which, in the absence of on-mountain accommodation must be negotiated twice a day. It is important to realise that weather conditions in the southern Alps can be even more changeable than in other mountain ranges, and that conditions here at up to 2400m can be as severe as they sometimes are at much higher altitudes in the European Alps, the Rockies and the Andes. As often as not, a blue-sky day will be followed by a day of unsettled weather, and vice versa.

The South American Andes are more easily accessible than the New Zealand and Australian mountain ranges are from Europe, with excellent skiing to be found in both **Chile** and **Argentina.** The mountains are mystically beautiful, and the skiing unusually varied. Unfortunately, the most breathtaking scenery and the best slopes do not always go together; the further south down the Cordillera you travel, the more intriguing the scenery is, but the less challenging and extensive the skiing tends to be.

The ski season in **Japan** corresponds to those in the Alps and North America. Although there are hundreds of ski areas here, they are mainly of insignificant size. Among the notable exceptions are the resorts in the Hakuba Valley, where the 1998 Nagano Winter Olympics downhill took place at Happo'one.

ARGENTINA

Gran Catedral (Bariloche)
top 2050m (6,725ft) bottom 1050m (3,445ft)

Gran Catedral is the newer name given to the ski resort on Catedral Mountain, which used to be called Bariloche. Confusingly, like many resorts that change their name, it is still also known as Bariloche. This is Argentina's most celebrated ski area and was the first in the country to install mechanised lifts during the late 1930s. It is a large, attractive and vigorous area in the south-west of this vast country, near the Chilean border, on the northern end of a range that extends from Lake Nahuel Huapi to Lake Mascardi in the south.

However, it has two serious flaws: its snow record is unpredictable and, because of its history of fragmented ownership, it lacks organisation and direction. One typical shortcoming is inadequate trail-marking – often it is difficult to tell whether the sticks at the side of a slope are to give warning of rocks or to mark the piste. The resort is perched above beautiful Lake Nahuel Huapi and attracts considerable precipitation, much of it falling as rain. Fortunately, Bariloche has good beginner slopes at the top of the mountain as well as the bottom, so in the event of heavy rain at the base, beginners can be taken higher. Only when the rain is accompanied by strong winds do the vital lifts to the higher nursery slopes close. But with 32 lifts and 50 runs, Bariloche can still justify its claim to be South America's biggest single resort.

Las Leñas
top 3340m (11,243ft) bottom 2240m (7,349ft)

Ski purists would almost certainly place the terrain at Argentina's most recently built resort above that of its oldest, Bariloche. Las Leñas, constructed almost entirely from a brick-red, wood-lookalike material, was built in 1983 with the tourist board of Les Arcs in France acting as consultant. Hotels and lifts are named after signs of the zodiac. Although it is not the easiest of resorts to get to (1127km from Buenos Aires) the powder is some of the best on the entire continent. The Marte chair-lift feeds what amounts to a separate ski area, with 40 challenging chutes, but when the lift is closed by the frequent high winds, only the more mundane main ski area of 10 lifts is accessible.

AUSTRALIA

Falls Creek / Mount Hotham
Falls Creek: top 1842m (6,043ft) bottom 1500m (4,921ft)
Mount Hotham: top 1845m (6,053ft) bottom 1750m (5,741ft)

While Thredbo was recovering from its mud-slide disaster in 1997, the main focus of Australian skiing fell on the state of Victoria, where the two major resorts, Falls Creek and Mount Hotham, are now owned by the same company as each other and linked by a helicopter service. The six-minute flight – almost two-and-a-half hours quicker than by road – and a shared lift ticket provide skiers at each resort with much wider options. Future plans include a major hotel in each resort and an airport at Horsehair Plain, 20km from both.

Falls Creek, which is 30km from Mount Beauty on the edge of the Bogong High Plains, is Victoria's attempt at bringing a flavour of the Alps to Australia. It has a European-style ski-in ski-out village atmosphere with a difference – the accommodation is among the gum trees. Parking is at the base of the village, and luggage is transported to your lodge by snow-cat. You can ski directly to eight different lifts from every lodge.

Altogether there are more than 20 lifts spread across four distinct areas: Village Bowl (with the principal slopes), Sun Valley, the Black Diamond Maze Area and the Terrain Park. Falls Creek is famous for its bumps under the Summit quad-chair, particularly on Exhibition run, and provides the venue for many of Australia's mogul competitions. Development plans include the construction of three quad chair-lifts on nearby Mount McKay. The terrain in Falls Creek is also ideally suited to snowboarders. The resort is four hours' drive from Melbourne, the state capital.

Mount Hotham is the highest alpine resort in Victoria, and it really does have a down-under flavour. It is divided by a road that effectively separates the beginner slopes at the top of the area from the intermediate and more advanced slopes lower down, although the areas are now linked by a bridge. A special tunnel was built under the road to allow the pygmy possum, a threatened species, to reach its feeding and breeding grounds.

Runs such as Mary's Slide, the Chute and Gotcha are quite challenging. The three recently constructed lifts at Mary's Slide above Swindler Valley have doubled its lift-served ski area and opened up new off-piste opportunities. The best pistes are in the Heavenly Valley region. Good nursery slopes are served by the Summit quad-chair and T-bar, and the Big D quad at Mount Higginbotham. The 13 lifts include the recently installed Drift T-bar.

Mount Buller
top 1804m (5,917ft) bottom 1390m (4,559ft)
The principal area for Melbourne-based skiers has the largest lift capacity in Australia. The 25 lifts include 8 quads, one of which is the recently installed Wombat. The resort is a three-and-a-half hour (320-km) drive from Melbourne through Ned Kelly country and has some of the most impressive scenery in the Victorian Alps, with extensive views across the gum forests. There is substantial snowmaking and 80km of trails, including one that is 2.5km long.

Perisher Blue
top 2034m (6,672ft) bottom 1605m (5,264ft)
What were originally the three separate resorts of **Perisher/Smiggins, Blue Cow** and **Guthega** in New South Wales have combined to form the largest ski area in Australia. Perisher alone has 20 lifts, and altogether the

area has more than 50. The only way to reach the main complex is by train; the modern Ski Tube takes skiers through 10km of tunnels on a 20-minute journey to Perisher and Blue Cow from Bullocks Flat. The name Smiggins refers to the 'smiggin holes' formed by cattle gouging the soil for salt licks. Blue Cow prides itself on its testing terrain and the high proportion of black-diamond (difficult) runs, including one named Kamikaze. However, 60 per cent of the terrain is graded intermediate.

Thredbo
top 2037m (6,683ft) bottom 1365m (4,478ft)
This New South Wales resort 450km from Sydney has arguably the best skiing in the country, plus extensive and sophisticated snowmaking and an attractive alpine-style village. Thredbo was the scene of a tragic mud slide in July 1997 in which 18 people died. A significant number of Austrians came here to work on the Snowy Mountain hydro-electric scheme in the 1950s and stayed on to take an active part in the skiing business. The 40 runs are served by 13 lifts.

CHILE

El Colorado/La Parva/Valle Nevado
El Colorado: top 3333m (10,935ft) bottom 2430m (7,972ft)
La Parva: top 3630m (11,909ft) bottom 2670m (8,760ft)
Valle Nevado: top 3670m (12,040ft) bottom 2880m (9,450ft)
These three resorts, which are more-or-less linked, comprise the best conventional skiing in Chile and are the closest major slopes to any capital city in the world, less than 64km north of Santiago: it is so close that Santiago's pollution causes magnificent sunsets on the slopes. The ski areas offer excellent off-piste as well as some 37 lifts. **El Colorado** tends to serve skiers from Santiago and is therefore busy at weekends but quiet during the week. **La Parva**, which has the most varied skiing, has no real hotels at present and remains a second- or third-home resort for affluent Chileans.

Valle Nevado, purpose-built by the French a decade ago, looks like a smaller version of Les Arcs in France. It is the only true destination resort of the three and attracts an international clientèle.

Portillo
top 3348m (10,984ft) bottom 2512m (8,241ft)
This picturesque but slightly quirky ski area is situated in a steep-sided valley next to the breathtakingly beautiful Laguna (lake) del Inca. It is in the heart of the Southern Andes close to the Argentine border and just under 160km north of Santiago. Access is via the awe-inspiring Uspallata Pass, one of only two passes between Chile and Argentina accessible during the winter. Engineers on the old Trans-Andean railway were the first to ski here. Most visitors to Portillo stay at the bright yellow Hotel Portillo, which dominates the resort. A delightful 1950s

atmosphere still pervades, with the red-and-white jacketed waiters scurrying around the vast lakeside dining-room.

The resort is run by a venerable American, Henry Purcell, and therefore the grooming and signposting on the 23 runs, served by 11 lifts, is as efficient as you would expect to find in any North American resort. Portillo also has the only serious snowmaking programme in Chile. The strong North American influence is reinforced by a large number of US ski instructors and a resort manager from Heavenly in California.

Portillo has two bizarre but exhilarating *va et vient* lifts specially designed for accessing the steep chutes in avalanche-prone areas. The largest, Roca Jack, hauls five skiers at a time on linked platters at considerable speed to the top of the chute before suddenly coming to a halt; skiers must disengage backwards. These lifts are unique to Portillo and were designed by the Pomagalski lift company, which was also responsible for the invention of the 'Poma' lift. *Va et vient* lifts are a combination of a conventional cableway and a towerless cable tow. Should an avalanche hit the lift, the cable drops and is buried until it can be located again. It can then be repaired or replaced, and reinstalled.

Termas de Chillán
top 2500m (8,200ft) bottom 1800m (5,900ft)

For skiers in search of the more offbeat face of the Chilean Andes without sacrificing quality skiing, this is the resort that best combines the two. But beware, the more exotic the location, the more treacherous the access road is likely to be. Do not attempt to reach Termas de Chillán without a four-wheel drive vehicle or at least chains; the final 29km of the journey is on an icy, rocky and potholed road. The resort itself is 407km south of Santiago. The Don Otto chair-lift is reputedly the longest on the continent, and the excellent off-piste includes the 14-km Shangri-La run, with its volcanic scenery, and Pirigallo, one of the resort's most celebrated itineraries, which comes complete with fumaroles belching sulphur fumes. There is also good cross-country touring to the west of the ski area and below the tree-line.

JAPAN

Happo'one/Hakuba Valley
top 1831m (6,007ft) bottom 760m (2,493ft)

Happo'one was the site for the men's downhill and Super G at the Nagano Winter Olympics in 1998. Nagano is 200km from Tokyo. As well as offering splendid mountain scenery, some challenging terrain and longer-than-average runs for Japan, Happo'one is one of the prettiest ski villages in the country. Another advantage is the quick access to other ski areas in the same valley, including **Hakuba 47**, **Iwatake**, **Goryu-Toomi** and **Sunalpina Sanosaka**. All are about four hours' drive from Tokyo's Ueno railway station. Among the endless Tannoy announcements and musical refrains broadcast over the resort are quaint messages in

English, such as: 'Please avoid paging your friends very often over the public address system'.

Naeba
top 1800m (5,905ft) bottom 900m (2,953ft)

This bustling ski area in Niigata Prefecture is one of the most frenetic resorts in the Northern Japan Alps. It is dominated by the Naeba Prince, said to be the largest ski hotel in the world with more than 40 restaurants, including one that stays open all night. This enables skiers who are anxious to pack in as many hours on the slopes as possible to take breakfast at 3.30am and ski under floodlights at 4am. There is no need to stop skiing until 11pm, which means that die-hard skiers can keep going for 19 hours. At weekends, when packed bullet trains and buses bring their human cargo, an almost absurd number of skiers floods the slopes – the record stands at 40,000 skiers in one weekend – so at least at 4.30am there is some chance of finding a little space.

Shiga Kogen
top 2305m (7,562ft) bottom 1228m (4,028ft)

Nagano's largest resort, Shiga Kogen, was the venue for the bulk of the 1998 Winter Olympic events. It is an extraordinary patchwork of 21 different 'resorts' served by more than 80 lifts dotting six interlinked mountains. None is big or particularly difficult; in alpine terms the whole area would make up just two or three linked resorts of reasonable size. A competent skier could cover all the terrain in a couple of days. Apart from skiing, another major tourist attraction is the hot sulphur baths into which monkeys sometimes leap from the surrounding trees.

NEW ZEALAND

Craigieburn
top 1811m (5,942ft) bottom 1570m (5,151ft)

New Zealand's club fields offer cheap, but not necessarily cheerful, skiing. Try battling to get up the slopes on a primitive 'nutcracker' ropetow, then battling to get down them in crusty, ungroomed snow. Unlike almost all commercial resorts, club fields usually have on-mountain accommodation, albeit fairly basic hostels with bunk-beds. Craigieburn deserves special mention because of its unusually challenging and spectacular terrain and, by hiking up its 725-m vertical drop, one of the longest in Australasia. However, because of its primitive facilities it attracts only hard-core skiers.

Mount Hutt
top 2075m (6,808ft) bottom 1585m (5,200ft)

The most famous of New Zealand's resorts is often patronised by Northern Hemisphere race teams for training out of season. Mount Hutt is on the South Island and has magnificent views across the Canterbury

Plains. It is a 35-minute drive from Methven and 70 minutes from Christchurch. It is also renowned for its access route: 12km of unsurfaced road at the mercy of strong winds, with somewhat alarming drops. The skiing can be excellent, although unpredictable weather has given the resort the rather unfair sobriquet 'Mount Shut'; a more flattering one is 'Ski field in the sky'. However, it does have one of the most extensive snowmaking systems in the Southern Hemisphere. The 672-m vertical drop is helped by the South Face runs that end up below the base area.

Porter Heights
top 1980m (6,495ft) bottom 1280m (4,200ft)

The closest commercial ski field to Christchurch, this is a rather underrated resort which has evolved from club-field status. Apart from a couple of beginner 'platter' lifts at the base area, it has just three T-bars, but these serve a significant amount of interesting and quite steep terrain. Much depends on whether high winds and/or avalanche danger close the all-important No.3 T-bar, which gives skiers access to the ridge above the headwall. From here you can reach one of the country's greatest off-piste runs, Big Mama, which is a steep descent with a vertical drop of 720m. There is further fine off-piste skiing and snowboarding on the other flank of this fairly steep valley, down McNulty's basin and Stellar Bowl. No.1 T-bar provides some good mid-valley intermediate terrain.

Queenstown (Coronet Peak/The Remarkables)
Coronet Peak: top 1620m (5,315ft) bottom 1200m (3,937ft)
The Remarkables: top 1957m (6,421ft) bottom 1600m (5,315ft)

New Zealand's best known ski centre – an effervescent and picturesque lakeside town – offers two separate resorts, the old and the new, with interchangeable lift passes. Situated in the south-west of the South Island, the traditional resort at **Coronet Peak**, with a vertical drop of 420m, has been modernised and enlarged and now provides a wide variety of good all-round skiing and a much improved lift system. **The Remarkables**, which opened for skiing in 1985, is visually exciting but has fewer options than Coronet Peak. From Queenstown the range seems impossibly steep, with the peaks resembling a range of sharp, pearly-white teeth, which dominate the shoreline of Lake Wakatipu. Fortunately the ski area is on the other side, where gentle bowls belie the severity of the mountains. Although The Remarkables provides predominantly intermediate terrain, some short, sharp couloirs, including Escalator and Elevator, add challenge. Among the steep off-piste sections for those who are prepared to walk up, are the Homeward Runs, which emerge at the road below the resort from where a truck takes skiers back up to the base area.

Treble Cone
top 1860m (6,102ft) bottom 1200m (3,936ft)

Lake Wanaka is as tranquil as Lake Wakatipu is vibrant, and is the idyllic gateway to Treble Cone. Although it ranks as one of the country's top three resorts, Treble Cone is not well known outside New Zealand. It once had a reputation for favouring advanced snow-users, but in recent years some good beginner terrain has been developed. Advanced skiers can hike for 20 minutes to the 2100-m summit to enjoy some of the best off-piste in the area. Challenging heli-skiing can be found nearby.

Turoa
top 2322m (7,618ft) bottom 1600m (5,249ft)

Turoa, on the south-western face of Mount Ruapehu, offers the biggest vertical drop in Australasia, even exceeding that of Whakapapa, its better-known neighbour. The upper slopes, like Whakapapa's, include some of the exotic qualities associated with volcanic terrain. Because Mount Ruapehu and other nearby volcanoes attract sudden storms and high winds, conditions in the off-piste areas above the lifts can be extreme. A climb to the summit affords breathtaking views of the Tasman Sea. It is possible to ski down, but check with the ski patrol first as the top of the mountain can be dangerous. Apart from an unusual and exhilarating terraced effect – steep little sections followed by long, flatter sections – the lift-served slopes provide rolling, wide-open and generally uneventful cruising, with a few runs of up to almost 4km.

Whakapapa
top 2300m (7,546ft) bottom 1625m (5,331ft)

The country's largest resort, Whakapapa, has a vertical drop of 675m, a wide selection of cruising runs, exciting off-piste in its Black Magic area and some severe terrain below the magnificent, snow-encrusted Pinnacles, which resemble a scaled-down version of the jagged Teton Mountains of Jackson Hole in Wyoming. The area is wonderful but frustrating due to unpredictable weather. However, in good conditions it has some of the best skiing in the Southern Hemisphere.

The resort is built on the flanks of the Mount Ruapehu volcano, which attracts some of the more inclement weather on the North Island, with storms moving in fast and furiously. Until 1995, when a series of spectacular volcanic eruptions brought the ski season to a premature close, it was possible to make the three-hour climb to the Ruapehu crater lake and then ski down. One reporter who skied here on his final afternoon commented: 'We spent most of the time looking over our shoulders at the fireworks, rather than concentrating on the slopes in front of us'.

Heli-skiing (New Zealand)

New Zealand claims to have more helicopter skiing than anywhere apart from Canada, and South Island has a bewildering number of options. Most companies offer one-day packages, with between three and five drops a day, although seven or more are possible. The biggest and best known is Harris Mountains Heliski (HMH), based in two of the principal resort towns, Queenstown and Wanaka. The company, which has been running for almost 20 years, has a fleet of Aerospatiale Squirrel helicopters, which access six different mountain ranges as well as the Harris Mountains themselves. HMH skis and snowboards behind the local resorts of The Remarkables, Coronet Peak, Treble Cone and **Cardrona**, as well as **The Doolans**, **Tyndall Glaciers** and **The Buchanans**. It also offers five-day heli-ski 'intro' weeks, and 7- and 12-day 'Odyssey' packages.

Methven Heliskiing covers some of the best terrain in the country, with 100 named runs in the **Arrowsmith** and **Ragged Ranges**.

Southern Lakes Heliski operates in the **Hector Mountains**, The Remarkables, the **Thomson Range**, the **Richardson Mountains** and the **Harris Range**.

Heliski Mount Cook is based around the Main Divide in the centre of the Southern Alps. The **Mount Cook** region features some of the country's highest mountains and most dramatic glaciers. There is skiing on the Ben Ohaus, and the Richardson Glacier in the **Neumann Range.** In good conditions, some runs provide as much as 1500 vertical metres. The Mount Cook Airline has recently introduced heli-skiing, but also flies its clients by ski-plane to the **Tasman Glacier**. The skiing is easy and might be boring if it were not for the striking scenery, which is somewhat akin to the Vallée Blanche in Chamonix. But snow and weather conditions are unpredictable. Your guide will almost certainly let you explore one or two cavernous crevasses with domed ceilings of ice, which are known to be completely safe – not something you can do on many glaciers. Mount Hutt's heli-skiing includes the North Peak run – an ungroomed basin with a 700-m vertical drop. A helicopter collects skiers from the bottom for around NZ$50.

Cyberskiing

Booking a holiday or buying equipment on the Internet can take skiing and snowboarding beyond the boundaries of the brochures and far from the confines of the glossy catalogues. You may start out snow-ploughing feebly, mouse in hand, but soon you will be taking the Net equivalent of 'big air', clicking hyperlink icons to surf across the Web with ease.

The pros and cons of virtual skiing

For someone who wants to be a little adventurous and surf off-piste, the advantages of the Internet are immense. Products unavailable in Britain and details of little-known resorts are just a click away, often at a discount. For example, some resorts in the Alps offer 'white week' packages on their web sites, which usually beat anything in the brochures. Some American resorts have central reservations offices on-line, which offer far more flexible deals than those available from the UK.

Developments in 'Push' technology on the newest-generation browsers mean that the information now comes looking for you. Many resorts will email you free daily snow reports. Electronic magazines (e-zines) like *The Buzz* (www.iski.com) and special offers on ski gear (www.rei.com) also appear free in your mailbox along with day-by-day news.

But the Internet is also pitted with crevasses: time-wasting in bloated, poorly designed, slow-loading pages is inevitable. Information is only as good as the most recent update. Resort information can often be blatant propaganda on pages that purport to be impartial. Email avalanches await the unwitting, with junk mail arriving from everywhere.

Getting started

If you type the word 'skiing' into one of the powerful web search engines such as AltaVista (www.altavista.digital.com) you can get over a million worldwide entries. Yahoo UK, another search engine but limited to the UK (www.yahoo.co.uk) has a more manageable 22 sites for skiing and 14 for snowboarding. But for starters it is advisable to go to one of the umbrella sites featuring resort profiles, clothing, equipment and snow reports. Take note, however, that the primary focus of these is America.

SkiCentral (www.skicentral.com) is the biggest gateway to snowsports topics, with links to more than 6,000 other sites. Iski (www.iski.com) is a lively site, with news of ski races and directories of snowboard camps and helicopter operations. Fronting for the major American ski magazines, Skinet (www.skinet.com) has news, snow reports and video clips. Resorts Sports Network (www.rsn.com) is the headquarters for resort cameras, allowing you to see snow reports and slope-side pictures from 30 different American resorts on one screen. These snow reports are in conjunction with SnoCountry (www.snocountry.com) in New England, a site with no news or gear links but with weather information delivered in both audio and video formats.

For equipment and industry statistics, the Snowsports Industries of America (www.snowlink.com) pages are to be recommended. GoSki (www.goski.com) presents unedited comments from visitors to resorts in the Alps and North America. Ski In (www.skiin.com) has blander reporting on its 2,200 resorts but a good link to Michelin's route-planning software. Hyperski (www.hyperski.com) is an on-line magazine that accepts articles from anyone.

Snow reports and weather

Watching the flurries fly on resort cams and the fronts heading in on satellite can be a pleasant alternative to waiting for tomorrow's newspaper. Most of the North American umbrella sites above have comprehensive links to weather, cams and snow data. For resort cams in the Alps, Top In (www.topin.ch) is best. In Britain, an excellent – if optimistic – snow-reporting service is provided by the Ski Club of Great Britain (www.skiclub.co.uk), most notable for its on-line database of snow depths going back four years. Ski Hotline in Glasgow (www.skihotline.com) features even more detail and has a faster interface.

Resorts not covered by the two UK sites above can be found in France (www.skifrance.fr), in Switzerland (www.rsag.ch/snow/e/overski), and in Austria (www.austria-info.at/winter/index.html). No such service exists for Italy, although details of the Dolomite resorts can be found (www.dolomitisuperski.com).

The Weather Channel (www.weather.com/ski) provides exhaustive coverage of America and has a colour satellite image of Europe with a time-lapse loop for watching the weather move. But for the Alps Météo France (www.meteo.fr) provides more detail. See, too, the fast-loading black-and-white satellite image covering an even larger area of the Alps (www.ccc.nottingham.ac.uk/pub/sat-images/e2.jpg).

Snowboarding

As dedicated and slick as ever, the site of the International Snowboarding Federation (www.isf.ch) is home to everything a boarder could desire from party calendars to race results. Key in the name of any one of 4,000 riders and the ISF will treat you to action photos and personal details. Snowboarding Online (www.solsnowboarding.com) is a huge umbrella site, with links to gear, profiles of the big boys of boarding (it also features a section on women) and even the company reports of Quicksilver clothing. A derivative of this, (www.solsnowboarding.com/school/lexicon.htm) provides a useful dictionary of snowboarding terms, which is regularly updated as the language evolves.

Resorts

Today scarcely a major winter sports resort in the world is without a web site. Vail Resorts has details of its four resorts at an incredibly hot site, (www.snow.com). By filling in a questionnaire on-screen (a 'wizard') you can find out which of the Vail resorts is best-suited to your requirements. But, particularly cool is the video virtual tour: from any spot in any resort you can zoom in and move left or right, just as if you were using your own eyes. Zermatt's panorama video (www.zermatt.ch) uses a similar free plug-in (software you can download from the site) to Vail's, but Zermatt's webmaster (the person responsible for maintaining the web site) has failed to provide any sort of conventional piste map at all. Sunshine Village in Canada (www.skibanff.com/shock.html) also needs a plug-in, and has the most entertaining resort site by far – zippy zither music and pop-up figures with sound effects. It has to be seen.

Useful round-ups of their regional resorts are featured at Colorado Ski Country (www.skicolorado.org) and Ski Utah (www.skiutah.com). For European round-ups you can access Switzerland (www.switzerlandtourism.ch), France (www.skifrance.fr) and Austria (www.austria-info.at).

Tour operators

Some day, maybe in the not-too-distant future, we will be able to take virtual tours through chalet accommodation, opening bathroom doors and listening to hear how loud the fridge hums, before booking it. In 1997 fewer than ten per cent of British tour operators had web sites; in 1998 the percentage has trebled. Despite this impressive rise, British tour operators remain mired in the bottom league of commerce (Internet business). Companies such as Thomson (web site still under development) and Crystal (www.crystalholidays.co.uk) have not progressed to the immediate interactive interfaces common on American pages. Inghams' pages (www.inghams.co.uk) are slow to load and uninteresting. First Choice (www.first-choice.com) has a limited and unappealing web site. Even the best of British sites such as Ski Esprit (www.ski-esprit.co.uk), Meriski (www.meriski.co.uk) and Ski the American Dream (www.skidream.com) do no more than replicate their printed brochures on screen. On the bright side, Powder Byrne (www.powder-byrne.co.uk) entices custom with special offers available only over the Internet. Snow Line (www.snow-line.co.uk) offers a chalet search engine and a brochure bank service, which will post free your selection of tour operator brochures. Alas, the former requires you to wait for a reply after you go off-line. But Snow Line's list of late offers on-screen is bang up-to-date, even if you cannot book them on-line.

Gear

Two of Britain's biggest retailers, Ellis Brigham (www.ellis-brigham.com) and Snow and Rock (www.snowandrock.com) have their catalogues on the Web, with links to major manufacturers of both ski and snowboard gear.However, across the Atlantic on-line shopping has really taken off. REI (www.rei.com) has one of the fastest shopping sites on the Web; you can pick sizes and colours on screen and purchases can be mailed to Britain. Volant are the makers of one of the best off-piste skis on the market, not currently available in Britain; find out about stainless steel, titanium-tipped PowerKarve at (www.volantski.com). Awards for lush graphics and plush fabrics go to Helly Hansen (www.hellyhansen.com) and Patagonia (www.patagonia.com), the latter with a cool short-cut ordering system for clients who already have a catalogue.

Weird and wonderful

Hard-core skiing and snowboarding screen-savers can be downloaded for free: (www.webshots.com). Check out the future of skiing, at Freeze (www.skinet.com/freeze), the brashest snow magazine yet. Ride the world's weirdest taxi, with live on-line up-links from the cab as it roams the streets of Aspen with its sometimes celebrity passengers (www.ulti-mataxi.com). And finally, proof that the Internet can mean business is a small site hosted by the Parkway Inn (www.sisna.com/jackson/park-wayinn) at Jackson Hole, Wyoming. Encouraged by four Internet book-ings per day from Britain, the Parkway is dispensing with tour operators and is passing on savings directly to the public.

Listed below are a selection of other web sites which readers have noted as being of interest to skiers and snowboarders. Take note, how-ever, that sites are constantly changing and some only operate during the winter months. While daily additions to the Web are numbered in tens of thousands, old information is rarely removed. We therefore apol-ogise for any inaccuracies in this roll call of snow-related web addresses.

```
www.mountainzone.com/postcards/
www.awe.co.nz/skiland.html#skiland
www.csac.org/Bulletins/
www.csac.org/Incidents/
www.rnrsports.com/bca/
www.couloir-mag.com/links/links.html#Avalanche
www.geocities.com/Colosseum/Loge/1805/
www.dynastar.com/
www.skishoot.net
www.couloir-mag.com/
www.csac.org/Other/links/
www.csac.org/
www.mountainzone.com/ski/features/coombs/
www.xtremescene.com/ski.htm
www.greatoutdoors.com/gearorama/
www.greatoutdoors.com/gear/geartop.htm
www.headusa.com/skiresort.htm
www.ncl.ac.uk/~n6004176/snow.htm
www.marmot.com/
www.netica.net/skinetica.html
www.offpiste.com/
www.thex.it/top/meteo/welcome.html?lan=eng
www.alaska.net/~wesc/pastwinners.html#biotop
www.iski.com/people/profiles/meganh.htm
```

www.iski.com/search/
www.skinet.com/gear/skis.html
www.skinet.com/news/
www.skinet.com/netguide/coolsites/coollinks.html
www.slf.ch/slf/slf.html
www.snowcountry.com/
www.skisocal.org/other.html
www.skisocal.org/manufact.html
www.mountainzone.com/zoners/thanks.as;p
www.mountainzone.com/toc.html
www.wzone.com/snozone/
www.volkl.com/skis.html
www.k2sports.com/
www.eng.utah.edu/~ldl/extremeski/welcome.html
www.couloir-mag.com/sponsors/lou_dawson/wild_snow.htm
www.meteo.fr/tpsreel/images/wnalp.gif
www.val-disere.com/fr-meteo.htm
www.intellicast.com/weather/gva/
www.goski.com/rfr/valdiser.htm
www.nottingham.ac.uk/pub/sat-images/d2.jpg
www.intellicast.com/ski/
www.intellicast.com/weather/lys/
www.rsn.com/cams/val/?cx=rsn&rsn_ref=sn
www.rsn.com/cgi-bin/wt.cgi/cams/val/welcome.html

Snowboarding

Snowboarding is the world's fastest-growing winter sport. Despite predictions within the snowboard industry, it is not going to overtake or come close to equalling the popularity of skiing by the millennium. However, in time – in reality that may be a decade – it will surely do so. What was dismissed initially as a fad is now an integral part of the scene in the ski resorts of the world. From Courchevel to Copper Mountain, resort managers and owners no longer tolerate the presence of riders on their mountains as they did just five years ago, they actively encourage them. The most recent French ski industry statistics show that about nine per cent of the snow-users riding lifts in major resorts were snowboarders (in Avoriaz, the European capital of the board, this rose to 23 per cent).

The idea of snowboarding is credited to an American Tom Sims who designed the first 'ski board' for a school carpentry project in New Jersey in 1963. Three years later, fellow American Sherman Poppen patented the 'Snurfer' – two skis he had bolted together for his children's amusement. In 1969, Jake Burton Carpenter received a Snurfer as a Christmas present and went on to become one of the biggest names in board design. However, it has taken these past 35 years – nearly twice the age of the sport's main caucus of exponents – for snowboarding to be accepted fully into the predominantly conservative world of skiing. While it remains youth-oriented, it is slowly losing its image as an icon of rebellion. Skiers of all ages are being drawn to the raw excitement of the sport, joining others who come from a background not of snow, but of surfing and skateboarding.

The learning curve

The essential attraction of snowboarding to newcomers is the brevity of the learning curve and the unrivalled sense of freedom – particularly off-piste – that can be attained in a remarkably short time. The first few days must be spent with a qualified instructor, who ideally should be a dedicated snowboarder and not a ski teacher who does a bit of riding on the side. Much of that first week will be spent on your (very bruised) bottom because, while the learning curve is short, it is painfully sharp. But if you persevere the rewards follow quickly. Progression from the tremendous feeling of making your first few turns to enjoying deep powder comes to most within only two weeks. For comparable progress in skiing you can multiply that by at least ten. The high percentage of skiers who fail to return to the snow after their initial week of lessons is not mirrored in snowboarding.

As with skiing, you can start snowboarding at any age between 4 and 80. The majority of small children who holiday with their parents are, for the foreseeable future, more likely to take ski lessons before they try riding a board. A certain amount of body weight is required to assume full manoeuvrability, and most children aged under seven years will find it hard to progress beyond the basics. At the other end of the age spectrum, it should be noted that snowboarding requires greater physical mobility than skiing; when not riding you sit – not stand – on the snow and it can be hard to pull yourself up again.

Peer pressure

Even the most passionate skiing parents soon discover that snowboarding's image as the 'cool' sport means that children aged ten and over experience considerable peer pressure – a force which is directly transferred to parents, who will be obliged to dig deep into their pockets to pay for lessons, clothing and equipment. Teenagers on their first winter-sports holiday are much more likely to opt for snowboarding than skiing. Adult skiers making the switch have the advantage of snow awareness but quickly discover that here the similarity stops. The two sports demand wholly different techniques, and even advanced skiers will find the early stages tricky.

Borrow or rent a board for your first lesson. The first decision is one of stance: regular or goofy. In a regular stance the left foot is forward, and in a goofy one the right boot leads. About 70 per cent of riders opt for the regular position. Your preference is not necessarily related to whether you are left- or right-handed, or even with which foot you prefer to kick a ball. To find out which you are, imagine you are running and then sliding on a polished or icy surface, and you will naturally put one foot forward.

Riding styles

Snowboarding divides into three distinct disciplines – freestyle, alpine and freeriding – although this matters little during the first few days as you grapple with the basics. Once these have been mastered you need to make your choice of style before acquiring your own equipment.

Freestyle snowboarding is like skateboarding on snow and is the most popular discipline. The boards are short, wide and flexible. Alpine snowboarding is at the other end of the spectrum; hard boots and relatively stiff and narrow boards with much longer edge contact lengths (the amount of edge in contact with the snow when laid flat) are necessary. This style of snowboarding is the closest to skiing and is often the skier's first choice when switching camps. Pursuit of the graceful carved turn rather than 'big air' is the prime objective in this discipline. Freeriding is a combination of both freestyle and alpine and will no doubt become the most important style of riding in the future. Soft boots are preferable for this style, but hard boots remain an option. Boards are of a similar overall length to alpine ones but have a raised tail and nose to allow both carving and freestyle performance; they are the true all-round boards and are the eventual choice of all off-piste fanatics.

Try before you buy

It is sensible to test both board and boots before you buy them. The multitude of board types available makes it difficult to choose the one that will be right for you, and at about £400 each a mistake is expensive. Many snowboard and ski shops in Britain offer reasonably priced hire packages with up-to-date equipment. If you like the board you try, the hire cost can often be deducted should you decide to buy it upon your return. The obvious disadvantage of hiring at home is that if you don't like the board or experience problems with it during your holiday, you may have to hire a second board in the resort. If you are certain of finding the equipment you need in the resort, then it may be better to hire when you get there.

If you are a complete beginner, consult the expert in the shop. Your main decision will then be whether to use soft or hard boots. Both are equally good for learning, with hard boots slightly superior on hard snow and soft boots better in soft and fresh conditions. In general, experienced 'crossover' skiers will be used to hard boots, whereas young newcomers to snow sports will feel more comfortable with soft ones. In Britain soft boots account for about 90 per cent of the market.

What to wear

You can snowboard in your existing ski gear. However, specific snowboard clothing is a prudent investment. Snowboard clothes are currently worn much looser than skiwear to allow for the greater physical mobility required, as well as for reasons of fashion. For its longevity and your comfort, clothing should incorporate waterproof reinforcement at the knees, bottom and elbows. These are the impact areas, and also the ones that come into contact with the snow when you are resting in the sitting or kneeling positions common to all snowboarders. Snowboarding gloves are probably the wisest investment of all. Snow is extremely abrasive, and even the most expensive ski gloves will wear out very quickly if used for snowboarding. Look for waterproof, seam-free gloves with reinforced palms; your hands are now your ski poles and outriggers.

Choosing a resort

Each chapter in the guide gives details of snowboarding facilities in every resort, including funparks and dedicated snowboard schools, but of course most of the information in the book applies equally to snowboarders and skiers. However, unlike for skiing, if you do not know which resort to choose, then big is often best. In general, larger resorts generally have more riders so there is more chance of finding specific snowboard areas, instruction, shops and 'snowboard friendliness'. Nevertheless, you need to be aware that the pisted areas of larger resorts are generally closely geared to the requirements of the skiers they have grown up with, and not the quite different needs of snowboarders. Any information you can get from other snowboarders, rather than skiers, on the resort you are considering will be invaluable.

The ideal terrain for snowboarding is quite specific and different from that for skiing. Also, the number of runs is of much less importance to snowboarders than to the majority of skiers. Once snowboarders have found a couple of good runs they tend to stick to them.

Reasonably wide, easy and intermediate runs are the snowboarding favourites, especially those with varied terrain and a few potential jumps to the sides. Not at all popular with snowboarders are narrow runs, runs with long flat sections and runs that traverse around the mountain. When snowboarding you do not have the snow-plough option on narrow paths, nor do you have ski poles to push you along the flat. Long traverses are simply very uncomfortable.

However, for beginners a large and flat nursery slope at the bottom of the resort is as ideal for snowboarding as it is for skiing. For advanced boarders, steeper resorts with good off-piste areas and a small number of lifts in relation to the size of the ski area, as well as pistes that closely follow the fall-line, are best.

Special pistes

An increasing number of resorts have dedicated pistes for snowboarders. Most popular with the younger freestyle-oriented rider is the snowboard park or 'funpark'. These usually come with their own lifts and contain such delights as fun-boxes, table-top and gap jumps, a bordercross (obstacle) course, a quarter-pipe and half-pipe. In some of the larger resorts, the funpark may also cater for the hard-booted alpine rider, with a parallel slalom or banked slalom course to test racing technique.

Types of lift

Drag-lifts (button and T-bar) are never an enjoyable exercise on a snowboard, so look for plenty of chair-lifts and cable-cars, particularly on the red and blue runs within a given resort.

Finding instruction

Instruction is now easy to find, and most countries have their own national snowboard associations that train snowboard instructors. As well as learning on snow, it is also possible to employ the services of a British Snowboard Association (BSA) instructor at all good dry ski slopes in the UK. Although the 'plastic snow' is less forgiving than the real thing, a short lesson before you go on holiday will certainly help. This can be followed up later with more advanced tuition on your return.

If you would like further information on snowboarding and where to find instruction in the UK, contact: The British Snowboarding Association, 1st floor, 4 Trinity Square, Llandudno LL30 2PY. Tel 01492 872 540.

Ski-touring

Ski-touring stinks. Alas, this is the view most recreational skiers share of a sport where Mr Hand-knit, with his pipe and straggly beard, has for so long typified those who forge far away from resort lifts under their own steam – and sweat. This perception is changing now that off-piste snow-users· are crossing over, encouraged by safer and more user-friendly gear, to the only skiing discipline which swings both ways – up the hill and down. The arguments that have won over downhill-only devotees are manifold. No ski lift in the Alps rises as high as 4000m. The highest summits, the best-quality powder snow and the most thrilling, long-range descents all demand some uphill climbing.

Ski-touring extends the dedicated skier's season for a month or more after the last resort lift has shut down. In the Alps, touring is the entrée to the world's top hotel chain, a network of some 2,000 mountain inns and refuges with views to die for. Touring is the final frontier, with escape and evasion the order of the day. But touring is also skiing at the extreme, should you choose that route. Tours court, or skirt (according to desire), couloirs and untracked bowls. Glaciers with their seracs and crevasses are everywhere to see, and ski.

Safety

Ski-touring is by definition off-piste skiing. All the warnings detailed under the section *Safety on the slopes* apply. Minimal technique requirements are: a strong wedge in all snow conditions; and the ability to stop on command. Essential requirements include: a mountain guide and an avalanche transceiver such as Pieps. The classic touring season, from March to June, is when the snow is most stable at altitude, but crevasses and slides are hazards at any time.

Equipment

If you can ski to intermediate standard, you can ski-tour. Touring below 3000m involves minimal levels of fitness, skiing ability and experience. You can begin near a piste any day of the winter using recreational skis and boots; you will also require climbing skins and touring adaptor bindings. SecuraFix is the best-known manufacturer of the latter. These bindings fit over the top your regular downhill bindings and are for hire at most resort ski shops.

Skins define touring. Originally they were the pelts of seals, chosen for their ability to glide freely in one direction (uphill) while resisting backsliding. Today's synthetic skins come with a permanent glue, for easy application to the bottoms of any skis. New skin sizes are now available for wide-body powder skis, semi-fat skis, and for parabolic carving skis.

Long tours above 3000m and glacier tours should not be attempted without more specialised equipment and experience. Dedicated touring skis are lighter, shorter and have a fatter, softer tip than recreational skis. Touring boots have corrugated Vibram soles for rock climbing and are also softer and lighter than recreational ski boots.

Dedicated touring bindings, to which ski crampons can be attached, are vital for steep traverses and comfortable and secure uphill work. A Swiss firm, Fritschi, recently introduced the Diamir, the first-ever touring binding with full safety-release features, which enable it to double as an everyday downhill binding. A strong rucksack, specifically designed for skiing and for carrying loads of up to 15kg, is important. Adjustable-length poles make climbing easier.

For glacier tours, mountain guides usually insist on crampons for ski boots, glacier sunglasses and a full-body skiing harness. An ice axe is a useful accessory, and tourers will need maps, compass, altimeter and perhaps a GPS navigation device (hand-held Global Positioning Satellite). Your guide should carry ropes for crevasse rescue, a radio and a first-aid kit. You will need a metal water bottle and food for lunch, as well as sun cream, aspirin for minor altitude sickness, and blister remedies. Special skin wax to prevent snow balling up underfoot is also useful, as is a head-torch for pre-dawn ascents and unlit huts.

At home in the huts

Alpine club refuges generally provide hot meals and dormitory sleeping accommodation but seldom running water. Lavatory facilities in glacier huts are usually primitive – and outdoors. Etiquette demands that rucksacks and ski boots are left in an antechamber. One heated common-room serves for dining and day use. Dormitories are equipped with army blankets and large, communal bunk beds, but are not normally heated. However, below 2500m, especially in Italy and Austria, mountain inns may have all the comforts of a small hotel.

Touring routes

The joy of ski-touring is that you can make it as long and far or short and as sweet as you want. The most famous tour is the Haute Route, from Saas-Fee in Switzerland to Chamonix in France, passing through Italy. This was first negotiated in the summer of 1861 by members of the British Alpine Club, although it was not skied in winter until 1903. The classic line of the Haute Route takes in 23 glaciers and about 10,000 vertical metres of uphill and downhill work.

Austria's Stubai and Ötztal regions, Switzerland's Bernese Oberland and Italy's Gran Paradiso National Park and the Dolomites are renowned touring areas, as is the Mont Blanc massif in France. The Corsican High Route, the Caucasus Mountains in Georgia and the High Atlas itineraries in Morocco are just a few of the worldwide trails open to adventurous tourers. For details on ski-touring organisations, see *Skiing by numbers*.

Safety on the slopes

The mountains are like the sea: they give enormous pleasure but they can also be dangerous and should be treated with the utmost respect at all times. Only when you find yourself in a potentially dangerous situation, or witness an accident at first hand, do you fully appreciate what the risks can be. All the information below applies to both skiers and snowboarders.

Weather and exposure

Mountain weather can change at a moment's notice and varies dramatically at different altitudes. Always dress with this in mind and be prepared for all conditions. Several layers of clothing are best and it is always preferable to be too hot, rather than too cold. More heat escapes through the head than any other part of the body, and you should never set off without a hat as well as sunglasses or goggles. In the event of an accident a 'space blanket' (these fold to handkerchief-size and can be bought from any reputable ski or mountaineering shop) can save a life.

All young children should wear safety helmets, preferably with chin guards. These can be worn on their own, or over a thin balaclava or hat on extremely cold days. Unfortunately, apart from in a few Scandinavian resorts, helmets are not yet compulsory. In the USA, more adults now wear helmets for recreational skiing, and we applaud this trend.

Never ski with a baby or small child in a backpack; anyone, however competent, can catch an edge and fall, or someone could crash into you.

Exposure to bad weather can result in frostbite or hypothermia. Frostbite is the excessive cooling of small areas of the body, usually the fingers, toes, nose, cheeks or ears. The affected tissue turns white and numb. This is called first-degree frostbite and can be dealt with by immediate, gentle re-warming. In cold conditions, watch out for signs of frostbite in your companions. Hypothermia results from a drop in the body's temperature. It is difficult to diagnose; some of the more obvious symptoms are physical or mental lethargy, sluggishness, slurring of speech, spurts of energy and abnormal vision.

Rules of the slopes

The FIS (International Ski Federation) has established rules of conduct for skiers and snowboarders. This is a summary:

Respect Do not endanger others.
Control Adapt the manner and speed of your skiing to your ability and to the general conditions on the mountain.
Choice of route The skier in front has priority – leave enough space.
Overtaking Leave plenty of space when overtaking a slower skier.
Entering and starting Look up and down the mountain each time before starting or entering a marked run.

Stopping Only stop at the edge of a piste or where you can be seen easily.
Climbing When climbing up or down, always keep to the side of the piste.
Signs Obey all signs and markings – they are there for your safety.
Assistance In case of accidents, provide help if you can or alert the rescue service.
Identification All those involved in an accident, including witnesses, should exchange names and addresses.

All the above rules are legally binding and apply to both skiers and snowboarders. You could be in serious trouble if you are to blame for an accident while in breach of these rules.

Important guidelines for skiers and snowboarders
- You ski at your own risk.
- Pay attention to all signs and markers.
- Ski on marked runs – these are protected from unexpected mountain dangers.
- Watch out for piste machines.
- Respect nature – take care not to ski in areas where young trees or wildlife will be disturbed and do not drop litter.
- Consider fitness sessions and taking lessons on a dry slope before going on holiday.

Special rules for snowboarders
- Your front foot must be firmly tethered to the board by a safety strap.
- It is essential to look carefully to the right and left when changing direction, especially when starting a turn heelside – look backwards.
- The ability to ski does not automatically mean you have the ability to snowboard.
- Do not attempt the sport without instruction.

Off-piste
Outside the marked pistes and itineraries are areas that are NOT protected from mountain dangers.

Signs and flags around the ski area may warn you when avalanche danger is present, but do not rely on these alone. Take local professional advice. Even when there is no warning of avalanches there could be localised snow slides.

Only venture off-piste with a fully qualified guide. This rule applies particularly to glacial terrain, where the risk of crevasse is added to that of avalanches. Always wear a recognised avalanche bleeper and take the time to learn how to use it by carrying out a practice grid search before you set off. Carry a map and a compass and learn how to use both. The chances of survival after an avalanche deteriorate rapidly after the first five minutes beneath the surface of the snow.

Listen to your guide, learn basic snowcraft and how to read a slope. However, it is important to remember that guides can be fallible and that you alone must take overall responsibility for decisions concerning your safety. In the event of an avalanche, try to ski to the side. If you fall, try to get rid of your skis, poles and backpack. Make swimming motions with your arms and legs and fight to stay on the surface.

Tips to remember when skiing or snowboarding off-piste
- Always ski in a group, never alone.
- Always ski in control behind the guide.
- Always stop behind the guide (there may be cliffs or other hazards ahead).
- Carry a map of the area and a compass. Know how to use both.
- Be wary of slopes where the run-out is not clearly obvious from the start. Following other skiers' tracks does not necessarily mean the route is safe.

Accident procedure
Speed is essential when an accident has occurred:
- Secure the accident area – protect the casualty by planting crossed skis in the snow a little way above the accident. If necessary post someone above the accident site to give warning to other skiers.
- First aid – Assess the general condition of the casualty:

Airway – check it is clear. Make sure nothing is obstructing the mouth or throat.

Breathing – if the casualty is not breathing, administer artificial respiration (mouth-to-mouth resuscitation). If the casualty is breathing but unconscious, turn him/her on to his/her side to minimise the risk of choking.

Limbs – protect any fractured limb from movement. Do not remove the ski boot if there is injury to the lower leg as it acts as a splint.

Circulation – check for pulse. Cover any wound using a clean handkerchief or scarf and **Provide warmth** – keep the casualty warm. Give nothing to eat or drink, especially alcohol. If the accident victim appears to be in shock, e.g. is going pale, cold and faint, he/she should be encouraged to lie with his/her head lower than his/her feet.
- Alert the rescue service – Contact ski patroller, ski teacher or lift attendant. Give the place of accident (piste name and nearest piste-marker), the number of people injured and the types of injury.
- Establish the facts of the accident – take names and addresses of people involved and of witnesses. Note place, time and circumstances of the accident, terrain, snow conditions, visibility, markings and signs.
- Report to the police as soon as possible.

Which tour operator?

Below is a list of ski and snowboard operators which offer inclusive holiday packages and fully satisfy government requirements for bonding. A large number of other companies and individuals offer accommodation-only holidays or have limited bonding (often through 'borrowed' ATOL licences), which we feel is insufficient. However, many of these firms are well-established and have sound reputations. Our decision to exclude them does not necessarily mean they should be avoided, but before parting with any money, it is wise to satisfy yourself what would happen in the event of sudden company closure. Payment by major credit card may act as a secure secondary insurance on your investment. Web sites and email addresses are included where available.

AA SKI-DRIVEAWAY
AA Motoring Holidays, Fanum House,
Basingstoke RG21 4EA
Tel (0990) 655555
Fax (01256) 493875
Web site www.theaa.co.uk
Ski-drive holidays

ABT SKI
Shepperton Marina, Felix Lane,
Shepperton TW17 8NJ
Tel (01932) 252025
Fax (01932) 246140
Email brewski's@abtski.demon.co.uk
Chalets in St-Martin-de-Belleville

AIRTOURS SKI
Wavell House, Holcombe Road,
Helmshore, Rossendale BB4 4NB
Tel (0541) 504001
Fax 0161-819 2044
Major operator to 51 resorts

ALL CANADA SKI
Sunway House, Raglan Road, Lowestoft
NR32 2LW
Tel (01502) 565176
Fax (01502) 500681
Email mail@all-canada.com
Web site www.all-canada.com
Ski holidays to Canada

ALPINE ACTION
3 Old Salts Farm Road, Lancing BN15 8JE
Tel (01903) 761986
Fax (01903) 766007
Small operator to the Trois Vallées

ALPINE TOURS
54 Northgate, Canterbury CT1 1BE
Tel (01227) 454777

Fax (01227) 451177
Schools and groups

ALTOURS
31 Princess Road, Dronfield S18 2LX
Tel (01246) 292010
Fax (01246) 290520
Web site www.sheffield.co.uk/altours
Groups operator

BALKAN HOLIDAYS
Sofia House, 19 Conduit Street, London
W1R 9TD
Tel 0171-543 5555
Fax 0171-543 5577
Holidays to Bulgaria

BALKAN TOURS
61 Ann Street, Belfast BT1 4EE
Tel (01232) 246795
Fax (01232) 234581
Email mail@balkan.co.uk
Holidays to Bulgaria and Romania

BIGFOOT TRAVEL
186 Greys Road, Henley on Thames
RG9 1QU
Tel (01491) 579601
Fax (01491)576568
Email ann@bigfoot-travel.co.uk
Web site www.bigfoot-travel.co.uk
Holidays in Chamonix Valley

BRITISH AIRWAYS HOLIDAYS
Astral Towers, Betts Way,
London Road,
Crawley RH10 2XA
Tel (01293) 722020
Fax (01293) 722703
Web site www.baholidays.co.uk
Scheduled operator to five countries

BORDERLINE
Les Sorbiers, F-65120 Barèges, France
Tel (01963) 250117
Fax 33 5 62 92 83 43
Email sorbiers@aol.com
Holidays to French Pyrenees

CHALET SNOWBOARD
31 Aldworth Avenue, Wantage OX12 7EJ
Tel (01235) 767575
Fax (01235) 767576
Email info@chalet-snowboard.co.uk
Web site www.chalet-snowboard.co.uk
France and California

CHALET WORLD
PO Box 260, Shrewsbury SY1 1WX
Tel (01952) 840462
Fax (01952) 840463
Alpine chalet holidays

CHINOOK-IT
30 Sansom Street, London SE5 7RE
Tel/Fax 0171-252 5438
North America and Chamonix

CLASSIC SKI
College Keep, 4–12 Terminus Terrace,
Southampton SO14 3QJ
Tel (01703) 212144
Fax (01703) 638220
All-inclusive holidays to France

CLUB EUROPE
Fairway House, 53 Dartmouth Road,
London SE23 3HN
Tel (0500) 026 366 FreeCall
Fax 0181-699 7770
Email ski@club-europe.co.uk
Web site www.club-europe.co.uk
Schools and groups

CLUB MED
106 Brompton Road, London SW3 1JJ
Tel (0700) 258 2633
Fax 0171-581 4769
Email clubmed@compuserve.com
Web site www.clubmed.com
All-inclusive holiday villages

COLLINEIGE SKI
30–32 High Street, Frimley GU16 5JD
Tel (01276) 24262
Fax (01276) 27282
Email info@collineige.com
Specialist chalet operator to Chamonix Valley

CONTIKI
Wells House, 15 Elmfield Road,
Bromley BR1 1LS
Tel 0181-290 6422
Fax 0181-290 6569
Web site www.contiki.com
18–35s holidays in Hopfgarten

THE CORPORATE SKI COMPANY
12 Franconia Road, London SW4 9ND
Tel 0171-622 6700
Fax 0171-622 6701
Email Jane.A@vantagepoint.co.uk
Corporate ski events

CRYSTAL
Crystal House, The Courtyard,
Arlington Road, Surbiton KT6 6BW
Tel 0181-399 5144
Fax 0181-390 6378
Email travel@crystalholidays.co.uk
Web site www.crystalholidays.co.uk
Holidays to over 100 resorts

ELEGANT RESORTS
The Old Palace, Chester CH1 1RB
Tel (01244) 897333
Fax (01244) 897770
Luxury hotels in major resorts

EQUITY TOTAL SKI
Dukes Lane House, 47 Middle Street,
Brighton BN1 1AL
Tel (01273) 298298
Fax (01273) 203212
Email travel@equity.co.uk
Web site www.equity.co.uk
All-inclusive holidays to Italy

ERNA LOW
9 Reece Mews, London SW7 3HE
Tel 0171-584 2841
Fax 0171-589 9531
Email ernalow@easynet.co.uk
Web site www.ernalow.co.uk
Apartments and hotels in France and USA

FAIRHAND HOLIDAYS
Suite 5, 216–218 Main Road,
Biggin Hill TN16 3BD
Tel (01959) 540796
Fax (01959) 540797§
France, Switzerland and Austria

FANTISKI
The Oast, Warmlake Estate, Maidstone
Road, Sutton Valence ME17 3LR

Tel (01622) 842555
Fax (01622) 842458
Email fcti@dircon.dir.co.uk
Small operator to France and the USA

FINLAYS SKIING
The Barn, The Square, Ancrum TD8 6XH
Tel (01835) 830562
Fax (01835) 830550
Email finlayski@aol.com
Specialist operator to French Alps

FIRST CHOICE SKI
Olivier House,18 Marine Parade,
Brighton BN2 1TL
Tel (0870) 7542754
Fax (01273) 675747
Email msheil@fchmailmhs.compuserve.com
Web site www.first-choice.com
Holidays to over 60 resorts

FLEXISKI
Crogen Stables, Corwen LL21 0SY
Tel 0171-352 0044
Fax (01490) 440446
Web site www.flexiski.co.uk
*Specialist operator with weekend and
ten-day breaks*

FREEDOM HOLIDAYS
Solar House, Market Square,
Petworth GU28 0AS
Tel (01798) 342034
Fax (01798) 343320
Weekends and flexible holidays to the Alps

FRONTIER SKI
Winge Travel Ltd, Broadmead House, 21
Panton Street, London SW1Y 4DR
Tel 0181-776 8709
Fax 0181-778 0149
Email sandra@whistler.demon.co.uk
Web site www.frontier-ski.co.uk
Holidays to Canada

FUNWAY SKI
1 Elmfield Park, Bromley BR1 1LU
Tel 0181-466 0222
Fax 0181-313 3547
Email funwayUK@msn.com
Flexible holidays to North America

HANDMADE HOLIDAYS
Queen Anne House, 66 Cricklade Street,
Cirencester GL7 1JN
Tel (01285) 658989
Fax (01285) 658990

Specialist to Serre Chevalier

HANNIBALS
Farriers, Little Olantigh Road, Wye,
Ashford TN25 5DQ
Tel (01233) 813105
Fax (01233) 813432
Email sales@hannibals.u-net.com
Web site www.hannibals.u-net.com
Specialist operator to French Alps

HEADWATER HOLIDAYS
146 London Road, Northwich CW9 5HH
Tel (01606) 813333
Fax (01606) 813334
Email info@headwater.com
Ski and cross-country holidays

HUSKI CHALET HOLIDAYS
63a Kensington Church Street, London
W8 4BA
Tel 0171-938 4844
Fax 0171-938 2312
Email huski@compuserve.com
Web site www.huski.com
Specialist chalet operator to Chamonix

INDEPENDENT SKI LINKS
Little Arram Farm, Bewholme Lane,
Seaton, Hull HU11 5SX
Tel (01964) 533905
Fax (01964) 536006
Web site www.meribel.com/independent
Holidays to Alps and North America

INGHAMS
10–18 Putney Hill, London SW15 6AX
Tel 0181-780 4444
Fax 0181-780 4405
Email travel@inghams.co.uk
Web site www.inghams.co.uk
Holidays to over 80 resorts

INNTRAVEL
Hovingham, York YO6 4JZ
Tel (01653) 628811
Fax (01653) 628741
Email inntravel@inntravel.co.uk
Specialist cross-country operator

INTERHOME
383 Richmond Road,
Twickenham TW1 2EF
Tel 0181-891 1294
Fax 0181-891 5331
Email interhome.uk@ibm.net
Chalets and apartments in the Alps

INTERSKI
Acorn Park, St Peter's Way,
Mansfield NG18 1EX
Tel (01623) 456333
Fax (01623) 456353
Italy specialist with own ski school

KUONI
Kuoni House, Dorking RH5 4AZ
Tel (01306) 740888
Fax (01306) 740328
Email sdd@kuoni.co.uk
Operator to 20 Swiss resorts

LAGRANGE HOLIDAYS
168 Shepherds Bush Road,
London W6 7PB
Tel 0171-371 6111
Fax 0171-371 6999
Web site www.lagrangeholidays.com
Self-catering to 118 resorts

LEISURE DIRECTION SKI
Image House, Station Road,
London N17 9LR
Tel 0181-324 4042
Fax 0181-324 4030
Email richard@ldl.u-net.com
Web site www.leisuredirection.co.uk
Ski-drive to 24 French resorts

LE SKI
25 Holly Terrace, Huddersfield HD1 6JW
Tel (01484) 548996
Fax (01484) 451909
Web site www.leski.co.uk
Courchevel and Val d'Isère chalets

LOTUS SUPERTRAVEL
Sandpiper House, 39 Queen Elizabeth
Street, London SE1 2BT
Tel 0171-962 9933
Fax 0171-962 9965
Email joyce@lotusgroup.co.uk
Holidays to Alps and North America

MADE TO MEASURE HOLIDAYS
43 East Street, Chichester PO19 1HX
Tel (01243) 533333
Fax (01243) 778431
Email
madetomeasure.holidays@which.net
Tailor-made holidays to 118 resorts

MARK WARNER
10 Old Court Place, London W8 4PL
Tel 0171-761 7002

Fax 0171-761 7001
Chalet-hotels with crèches

MASTERSKI
Thames House, 63–67 Kingston Road,
New Malden KT3 3PB
Tel 0181-942 9442
Fax 0181-949 4396
Email mplan1uk@aol.com
Web site www.itsnet.co.uk/mastersun
Christian holidays to France

MERISKI
The Old School, Great Barrington,
Burford OX18 4UR
Tel (01451) 844788
Fax (01451) 844799
Email meriski@compuserve.com
Web site www.meriski.co.uk
Chalets in France, crèche in Méribel

MOMENTUM TRAVEL
4 Cortayne Road, London SW6 3QA
Tel 0171-371 9111
Fax 0171-610 6287
Email momentum@mailbox.co.uk
Web site www.mailbox.co.uk
Tailor-made holidays

MOSWIN TOURS
Moswin House, 21 Church Street, Oadby,
Leicester LE2 5DB
Tel (0116) 2719922
Fax (0116) 2716016
Ski holidays to Germany

MOTOURS
Buckingham House, Longfield Road,
Tunbridge Wells TN2 3DQ
Tel (01892) 518555
Fax (01892) 518666
Email sales@motours.co.uk
Web site www.motours.co.uk
Ski-drive to French Alps

**MOUNTAIN AND WILDLIFE
VENTURES**
Compston Road, Ambleside LA22 9DJ
Tel (01539) 433285
Fax (01539) 434065
Email skiing@mwventures.demon.co.uk
Nordic wilderness skiing holidays

NEILSON SKI
71 Houghside Road, Pudsey LS28 9BR
Tel (0990) 994444
Fax (01132) 393275

Email sales@neilson.co.uk
Web site www.neilson.co.uk
Holidays to 62 resorts

PANORAMA
28 Queens Road, Brighton BN1 3YN
Tel (01273) 220013
Fax (01273) 205338
Email panorama@pavilion.co.uk
Web site www.phg.co.uk
Budget holidays to Europe

PASSAGE TO SOUTH AMERICA
Fovant Mews, 12 Noyna Road,
London SW17 7PH
Tel 0181-767 8989
Fax 0181-767 2026
Email psa@scottdunn.com
Specialist to South America

PGL SKI EUROPE
Alton Court, Penyard Lane,
Ross-on-Wye
HR9 5GL
Tel (01989) 768168
Fax (01989) 768376
Email general-enquiries@pgl.co.uk
Web site www.pgl.co.uk
Schools and groups

PISTE ARTISTE
1874 Champéry, Switzerland
Tel 0171-436 0100
Fax 41 24 479 3344
Email ski@PisteArtiste.com
Web site www.PisteArtiste.com
Flexible holidays to Champéry

PLUS TRAVEL
9 Eccleston Street, London SW1W 9LX
Tel 0171-259 0199
Fax 0171-259 0190
Specialist to Switzerland

POWDER BYRNE
4 Alice Court,
116 Putney Bridge Road,
London SW15 2NQ
Tel 0181-871 3300
Fax 0181-871 3322
Email powder.byrne@dial.pipex.com
Web site www.powderbyrne.co.uk
Luxury holidays to Alps and Rockies

RAMBLERS
Box 43, Welwyn Garden City AL8 6PQ
Tel (01707) 331133

Fax (01707) 333276
Email ramhols@dial.pipex.com
Group cross-country holidays

SILVER SKI HOLIDAYS
Conifers House, Grove Green Lane,
Maidstone ME14 5JW
Tel (01622) 735544
Fax (01622) 738550
Email hazal@silverski.co.uk
Web site www.silverski.co.uk
Catered chalets in France

SIMON BUTLER SKIING
5 Woodbine Cottages, Shalford Common,
Guildford GU4 8JF
Tel (01483) 502897
Fax (01483) 452001
Holidays in Megève with tuition

SIMPLY SKI
Chiswick Gate,
598–608 Chiswick High Road,
London W4 5RT
Tel 0181-742 2541
Fax 0181-995 5346
Email ski@simply-travel.com
Web site www.simply-travel.com
Catered chalets with crèches

SKI ACTIVITY
Lawmuir House, Methven PH1 3SZ
Tel (01738) 840888
Fax (01738) 840079
Email brochure@skiactivity.com
Web site www.skiactivity.com
Operator to North America and France

SKI THE AMERICAN DREAM
1–7 Station Chambers, High Street North,
London E6 1JE
Tel 0181-548 2421
Fax 0181-552 7726
Email holidays@skidream.com
Web site www.skidream.com
Specialist operator to North America

SKI AMIS
Alanda, Hornash Lane, Shadoxhurst,
Ashford TN26 1HT
Tel (01233) 732187
Fax (01233) 732769
Email skiamis@msn.com
Holidays to France

SKI BEAT
Metro House, Northgate,

Chichester PO19 1BE
Tel (01243) 780405
Fax (01243) 533748
Email skibeat@compuserve.com
Web site www.skibeat.co.uk
Chalets in French Alps, crèche

SKIBOUND
Olivier House, 18 Marine Parade,
Brighton BN2 1TL
Tel (01273) 677777
Fax (01273) 604259
Specialist schools operator

SKI CHAMOIS
18 Lawn Road, Doncaster DN1 2JF
Tel (01302) 369006
Fax (01302) 326640
Chalets in Morzine

SKI CHOICE
27 High Street, Benson,
Wallingford OX10 6RP
Tel (01491) 837607
Fax (01491) 833836
Email travelchoice@btinternet.com
Web site www.wallingford.co.uk/travel
Tailor-made holidays to the Alps

SKI CLUB OF GREAT BRITAIN/FRESH TRACKS
The White House,
57–63 Church Road,
London SW19 5SB
Tel 0181-410 2000
Fax 0181-410 2001
Email hols@skiclub.co.uk
Web site www.skiclub.co.uk
Specialist holidays, guided courses

THE SKI COMPANY
The Old School, Great Barrington,
Burford OX18 4UR
Tel (01451) 844788
Fax (01451) 844799
Email meriski@compuserve.com
Web site www.meriski.co.uk
Luxury chalets in Alps and Rockies

SKI CONNECTIONS
10 York Way,
Lancaster Road,
High Wycombe HP12 3PY
Tel (01494) 473173
Fax (01494) 473588
Email amcon@httrav.co.uk
A la carte skiing in North America

SKI EQUIPE
27 Bramhall Lane South, Bramhall,
Stockport SK7 2DN
Tel 0161-440 0010
Fax 0161-440 0080
Chalets in Alps and Rockies

SKIERS WORLD
6 Cwrt-Y-Parc, Earlswood Road,
Llanishen, Cardiff CF4 5GH
Tel (01222) 764477
Fax (01222) 764455
Email info@skiersworld.com
Web site www.skiersworld.com
Schools skiing to Alps and Rockies

SKI ESPRIT
Oaklands, Reading Road North,
Fleet GU13 8AA
Tel (01252) 616789 618300
Fax (01252) 811243
Email travel@skiesprit.demon.co.uk
Web site www.ski-esprit.co.uk
Family chalet holidays to the Alps

SKI FAMILLE
Unit 9, Chesterton Mill, French's Road,
Cambridge CB4 3NP
Tel (01223) 363777
Fax (01223) 361508
Email ski.famille@dial.pipex.com
Web site www.fr-holidaystore.co.uk/ski-family/
Family holidays to France

SKI FRANCE
Interworld House,
60 Bromley Common,
Bromley BR2 9PF
Tel 0181-313 0690
Fax 0181-466 0653
Email interworld@cybernet.co.uk
Flexible travel to France

SKI FREEDOM
PO Box 377, Bromley BR1 1LY
Tel 0181-313 0999
Fax 0181-313 3547
Versatile holidays to the Rockies

SKI GOWER
2 High Street, Studley B80 7HJ
Tel (01527) 854822
Fax (01527) 857236
Email linda@gowstrav.demon.co.uk
Tailor-made holidays for schools and groups

SKI HILLWOOD
2 Field End Road, Pinner HA5 2QL
Tel 0181-866 9993
Fax 0181-868 0258
Family holidays with crèches

SKI INDEPENDENCE
Broughton Market,
Edinburgh EH3 6NU
Tel (0990) 550555
Fax (0990) 502020
Email ski@ski-independence.co.uk
Web site www.ski-independence.co.uk
Specialist operator to North America

SKI LES ALPES
20 Lansdowne Gardens,
London SW8 2EG
Tel 0171-720 7127
Fax 0171-720 7134
Weekends and ten-day holidays

SKI MIQUEL
33 High Street, Uppermill,
Oldham OL3 6HS
Tel (01457) 820200
Fax (01457) 872715
Operator to the Alps, Spain and Canada

SKI MORGINS HOLIDAYS
The Sett, Badger, Burnhill Green,
Wolverhampton WV6 7JS
Tel/Fax (01746) 783005
Small specialist operator to Morgins

SKI NORTH AMERICA DIRECT
Freepost LON 6861,
London E6 1BR
Tel (07000) 325325
Fax (07000) 710116
Email sales@skidirect.itsnet.co.uk
Direct-sell holidays to North America

SKI NORWEST
8 Foxholes Cottages, Foxholes Road,
Horwich, Bolton BL6 6AL
Tel (01204) 668468
Fax (01204) 668568
Email skinorwest@compuserve.com
Web site www.ourworld.compuserve.com
Ski weekends and coach trips to Scotland

SKI OLYMPIC
Yew Tree Lodge,
Hangmanstone Lane,
High Melton; Doncaster DN5 7TB
Tel (01709) 579999

Fax (01709) 579898
Chalets and hotels in France

SKI PARTNERS
Friary House, Colston Street,
Bristol BS1 5AP
Tel 0117-925 3545
Fax 0117-929 3697
Schools operator to Alps and North America

SKI PEAK
Campbell Park, Milland, Nr Liphook
GU30 7LU
Tel (01428) 741144
Fax (01428) 741155
Web site www.ski-peak.ltd.uk
Specialist operator to Vaujany with crèche

SKI SAFARI
13 Leinster Gardens, London W2 6DR
Tel 0171-262 5069
Fax 0171-262 1301
Email ski@safari.demon.co.uk
Specialist operator to Canada

SKISAFE TRAVEL
Unit 4, Braehead Estate,
Old Govan Road,
Renfrew PA4 8XJ
Tel 0141-812 0925
Fax 0141-812 1544
Operator to Scotland and Flaine

SKISARUS
Suite 5, 216–218 Main Road,
Biggin Hill TN16 3BD
Tel (01959) 540796
Fax (01959) 540797
Tailor-made holidays to North America

SKI SCOTT DUNN
Fovant Mews, 12 Noyna Road, London
SW17 7PH
Tel 0181-767 0202
Fax 0181-767 2026
Email ski@scottdunn.com
Luxury chalet operator with crèches

SKI SOLUTIONS A LA CARTE
84 Pembroke Road, London W8 6NX
Tel 0171-471 7777
Fax 0171-471 7701
Email alc@skisolutions.com
Hotels and luxury apartments

SKI TOTAL
3 The Square, Richmond TW9 1DY
Tel 0181-948 3535

Fax 0181-332 1268
Email ski@skitotal.com
Web site www.skitotal.com
Chalet operator to the Alps and Canada

SKITREK
Old Road, Braunston, Daventry NN11 7JB
Tel/fax (01788) 890049
Ski and board driving holidays to France

SKI VACATION CANADA
Cambridge House, 8 Cambridge Street,
Glasgow G2 3DZ
Tel 0141-332 1511/(0345) 090905
Fax 0141-353 0135
Canadian Rockies and Quebec

SKI VAL
41 North End Road, London W14 8SZ
Tel 0171-371 4900
Fax 0171-371 4904
Email sales@skiworld.ltd.uk
Chalets in the Alps and Rockies

SKI VERBIER
172 Eversleigh Road, London SW11 5XT
Tel 0171-738 0878
Fax 0171-924 2620
Chalet holidays to Verbier

SKI WEEKEND
2 The Old Barn, Wicklesham Lodge Farm,
Faringdon SN7 7PN
Tel (01367) 241636
Fax (01367) 243633
Email ski-weekend@msn.com
Web site www.skiweekend.com
Weekend breaks with specialist courses

SKI WORLD
41 North End Road, London W14 8SZ
Tel 0171-602 4826
Fax 0171-371 1463
Email sales@skiworld.ltd.uk
Holidays to the Alps and Rockies

SKI YOGI
Jasmine Cottage, Manor Lane, Great
Chesterford CB10 1PJ
Tel (01799) 531886
Fax (01799) 531887
Holidays to the Italian Dolomites

SLOPING OFF
31 High Street, Handley, Salisbury SP5
5NR
Tel (01725) 552247

Fax (01725) 552489
Email nickadams@dial.pipex.com
Coach holidays for schools and groups

SNOWBIZZ VACANCES
69 High Street, Maxey PE6 9EE
Tel (01778) 341455
Fax (01778) 347422
Family specialist to Puy-St-Vincent

SNOWCOACH/CLUB CANTABRICA
146–148 London Road,
St Albans AL1 1PQ
Tel (01727) 866177
Fax (01727) 843766
Email info@snowcoach.co.uk
Web site www.snowcoach.co.uk
Value holidays to Europe

SNOWLINE HOLIDAYS
Collingbourne House,
Spencer Court, 140–142 High Street,
London SW18 4JJ
Tel 0181-870 4807
Fax 0181-875 9236
Email ski@snowline.co.uk
Web site www.snowline.co.uk
Small operator to Alps with crèche

SOLO'S
54–58 High Street,
Edgware HA8 7ED
Tel 0181-951 2811
Fax 0181-951 1051
Email travel@solosholidays.co.uk
Web site www.solosholidays.co.uk
Singles holidays to the Alps and Rockies

STANFORD SKIING
The Old Bakery, South Road,
Reigate RH2 7LB
Tel (01737) 242074
Fax (01737) 242003
Specialist operator to Megève

STENA LINE HOLIDAYS
Charter House, Park Street,
Ashford TN24 8EX
Tel (0990) 707070
Fax (01233) 202371
Ski-drive holidays

STS
Miry Lane, Wigan WN3 4AG
Tel (01942) 823503
Fax (01942) 322749
Schools specialist to Europe

SUSIE WARD COMPANY
54 Vicarage Road, St Agnes TR5 0TQ
Tel (01872) 553055
Fax (01872) 553050
Chalet holidays to France and Switzerland

SWISS TRAVEL SERVICE
Bridge House, 55–59 High Road,
Broxbourne EN10 7DT
Tel (01922) 456123
Fax (01922) 448855
Email swiss@bridge-travel.co.uk
Quality holidays to 18 Swiss resorts

THOMSON BREAKAWAY
Centenary House, 3 Water Lane,
Richmond TW9 1TJ
Tel (0990) 329329
*Major operator to Europe and North
America*

TOP DECK SKI
131–135 Earls Court Road,
London SW5 9RH
Tel 0171-370 4555
Fax 0171-373 6201
Email res.topdeck@dial.pipex.com
Alps and Pyrenees

TRAIL ALPINE
40 High Street, Menai Bridge,
Anglesey LL59 5EF
Tel (01248) 716550
Fax (01248) 716616
Email trailalpine@compuserve.com
Ski holidays to Morzine

TRAVELSCENE SKI DRIVE
11–15 St Ann's Road, Harrow HA1 1AS
Tel 0181-427 8800
Fax 0181-861 3674
Ski-drive apartment holidays in France

TT SKI TANGNEY TOURS
Pilgrim House, Station Court,
Borough Green TN15 8AF
Tel (01732) 886666
Fax (01732) 886885
Email tangney@mail.compulink.co.uk
Specialist operator to Pyrenees

UCPA/ACTION VACANCES
30 Brackley Road, Stockport SK4 2RE
Tel/fax 0161-442 6130
Email av4ucpa@btinternet.com
Web site www.btinternet.com/~av4ucpa/
18–40s budget ski and snowboard

VIP
Collingbourne House, 140–142
Wandsworth High Street,
London SW18 4JJ
Tel 0181-875 1957
Fax 0181-875 9236
Email ski@valdisere.co.uk
Holidays to Val d'Isère

VIRGIN SKI
Galleria, Station Road,
Crawley RH10 1WW
Tel (01293) 617181
Fax (01293) 536957
Web site www.virginholidays.co.uk
Hotel holidays in North America

WAYMARK
44 Windsor Road, Slough SL1 2EJ
Tel (01753) 516477
Fax (01753) 517016
Cross-country specialist

WHITE ROC SKI
69 Westbourne Grove, London W2 4UJ
Tel 0171-792 1188
Fax 0171-792 1956
Email ski@whiteroc.co.uk
Web site www.whiteroc.co.uk
Weekend and tailor-made holidays

WINETRAILS
Greenways, Vann Lake, Ockley,
Dorking RH5 5NT
Tel (01306) 712111
Fax (01306) 713504
Email sales@winetrails.co.uk
Web site www.winetrails.co.uk
Gourmet catered chalet in Filzmoos

WINTERSKI
31 Old Steine, Brighton BN1 1EL
Tel (01273) 702222
Fax (01273) 620222
Email winterski@fastnet.co.uk
Schools and groups to Italy

YSE
The Business Village, Broomhill Road,
London SW18 4JQ
Tel 0181-871 5117
Fax 0181-871 5229
Email yseski@dircon.co.uk
Specialist chalet operator to Val d'Isère

Who goes where?

ANDORRA

Arcalis Panorama, Snowcoach
Arinsal Airtours, British Airways, Crystal, First Choice, Neilson, Panorama, Ski Partners, SkiSafe Travel, Snowcoach, Thomson
Encamp First Choice, Ski Partners, Thomson
Pal Crystal, Panorama, SkiSafe Travel, Snowcoach
Pas de la Casa Airtours, First Choice, Inghams, Lagrange, Neilson, Panorama, Ski Partners, Thomson, Top Deck
Soldeu-El Tarter Airtours, British Airways, Crystal, First Choice, Inghams, Lagrange, Neilson, Panorama, SCGB/Fresh Tracks, SkiSafe Travel, Thomson, Ski Partners, Top Deck

ARGENTINA

Gran Catedral (Bariloche) Passage to South America
Las Leñas Passage to South America

AUSTRALIA

No current tour operator

AUSTRIA

Alpbach First Choice, Inghams, Interhome, Sloping Off
Altenmarkt Alpine Tours, Interhome, Made to Measure, Sloping Off
Axamer Lizum Fairhand, Interhome, Lagrange, Ski Partners
Bad Gastein Club Europe, Crystal, First Choice, Inghams, Interhome, SkiBound, Ski Miquel, Ski Partners
Bad Hofgastein Crystal, Inghams, Interhome
Bad Kleinkirchheim Alpine Tours, Crystal, Interhome, Ski Partners, Skiers World, Sloping Off
Brixen Alpine Tours
Ellmau Airtours, Crystal, First Choice, Inghams, Neilson, SkiBound, Thomson
Fieberbrunn Ski Partners
Filzmoos Inghams, Made to Measure, Winetrails

Finkenberg Crystal
Flachau Club Europe, Interhome, Made to Measure
Fulpmes Alpine Tours, Crystal, Interhome
Galtür Crystal, Inghams, Thomson
Gargellen Alpine Tours, Interhome, Made to Measure
Haus im Ennstal Neilson
Hopfgarten Contiki, First Choice, Interhome
Igls Fairhand, Inghams, Interhome, Lagrange, Made to Measure
Innsbruck Interhome, Made to Measure
Ischgl Crystal, Inghams, Interhome, Thomson
Jenbach Sloping Off
Kaprun Airtours, Club Europe, Crystal, Inghams, Interhome, Neilson, PGL Ski Europe
Kirchberg Crystal, Fairhand, Interhome, Lagrange, Neilson, Ski Partners, Top Deck
Kirchdorf Crystal, Interhome, Snowcoach
Kitzbühel Airtours, British Airways, Crystal, Fairhand, First Choice, Independent Ski Links, Inghams, Interhome, Lagrange, Neilson, PGL Ski Europe, SCGB/Fresh Tracks, SkiBound, Skiers World, Ski Partners, Skisarus, STS, Thomson
Kleinarl Made to Measure
Kolsass Weer Airtours
Kühtai Alpine Tours, Inghams
Lech Elegant Resorts,Inghams, Ski Choice, Ski Les Alpes, Ski Scott Dunn, Ski Total, Trail Alpine, White Roc
Leogang Interhome
Lofer Interhome, Ski Partners
Maria Alm PGL Ski Europe, Ski Partners, STS
Mayrhofen Airtours, British Airways, Crystal, Equity Total Ski, Fairhand, First Choice, Inghams, Interhome, Lagrange, Motours, Neilson, Snowcoach, Thomson
Neustift Alpine Tours, Crystal, Inghams, Interhome
Niederau/Oberau Airtours, Alpine Tours, Club Europe, First Choice, Inghams, Neilson, PGL Ski Europe, Ski Partners, Sloping Off, Thomson

Obergurgl/Hochgurgl Airtours, Crystal, First Choice, Inghams, Neilson, Thomson
Obertauern Club Europe, Crystal, Inghams, Skiers World, Thomson
Pettneu Crystal
Saalbach-Hinterglemm Airtours, Club Europe, Crystal, First Choice, Inghams, Neilson, PGL Ski Europe, SkiBound, Skiers World, Ski Partners, Sloping Off, STS, Thomson
Scheffau Crystal, First Choice, Thomson
Schladming Crystal, Equity Total Ski, Made to Measure, Neilson, SkiBound, Skiers World, Ski Partners, STS
Schüttdorf Airtours
Seefeld Crystal, First Choice, Inghams, Interhome, Lagrange, Motours, Neilson, Thomson
Serfaus Alpine Tours, Interhome, Made to Measure
Sölden/Hochsölden Crystal, Interhome, Made to Measure
Söll Airtours, British Airways, Crystal, First Choice, Inghams, Interhome, Motours, Neilson, SkiBound, Skiers World, Ski Hillwood, STS, Thomson
St Anton Airtours, British Airways, Chalet World, Crystal, Elegant Resorts, First Choice, Inghams, Lotus Supertravel, Mark Warner, PGL Ski Europe, Powder Byrne, SCGB/Fresh Tracks, Simply Ski, Ski Equipe, Ski Les Alpes, Ski Total, Ski Val, Skiworld, Thomson, White Roc
St Johann in Tirol Crystal, Interhome, SkiBound, Skiers World, Ski Partners, Thomson
St Johann im Pongau Alpine Tours, Club Europe, Ski Partners
St Michael Alpine Tours, Club Europe, Ski Partners, Sloping Off
St Wolfgang Airtours, Crystal, Inghams, Interhome, Neilson, PGL, Ski Europe, Thomson
Tulfes Interhome, Ski Partners
Wagrain Club Europe, Interhome, PGL Ski Europe, STS, Thomson
Waidring Fairhand, Thomson
Westendorf Crystal, First Choice, Inghams, Neilson, SkiBound, Thomson
Zauchensee Made to Measure
Zell am See Airtours, Altours, Crystal, First Choice, Inghams, Lagrange, Neilson, PGL Ski Europe, Skiers World, Ski Partners, STS, Thomson

Zell am Ziller Club Europe, Equity Total, Inghams, Lagrange, PGL Ski Europe, SkiBound, Skiers World, Ski Partners, Sloping Off, STS
Zürs Made to Measure

BULGARIA
Borovets Balkan Holidays, Balkan Tours, Crystal, First Choice, Inghams, Neilson, Ski Partners, Solo's
Pamporovo Balkan Holidays, Balkan Tours, Crystal, First Choice, Neilson, Skiers World, Ski Partners

CHILE
La Parva/Valle Nevado/Portillo Passage to South America

FRANCE
Abondance Interhome
Alpe d'Huez AA Ski-Driveaway, Airtours, Altours, Club Med, Crystal, Erna Low, Fairhand, First Choice, Independent Ski Links, Inghams, Lagrange, Leisure Direction, **Motours,** Neilson, PGL Ski Europe, SCGB/Fresh Tracks, Ski Activity, Skiers World, Ski Miquel, Ski Partners, Ski Trek, Skisarus, Ski Val, Skiworld, Stena Line, Thomson, Travelscene
Les Arcs AA Ski-Driveaway, Airtours, Club Med, Crystal, Erna Low, Fairhand, Independent Ski Links, Inghams, Lagrange, Leisure Direction, Motours, PGL Ski Europe, SCGB/Fresh Tracks, Ski Activity, Ski Amis, SkiBound, Ski Trek, Ski Val, Skiers World, Ski Weekend, Skiworld, Thomson, Travelscene, UCPA, Virgin
Argentière Collineige, Crystal, Fairhand, Interhome, Lagrange, Motours, Ski Hillwood, Ski Trek, Ski Weekend, Snowline, Susie Ward, UCPA, White Roc
Auris-en-Oisans Fairhand, Lagrange
Avoriaz AA Ski-Driveaway, Airtours, British Airways, Chalet Snowboard, Club Med, Crystal, Erna Low, Fairhand, First Choice, Inghams, Lagrange, Leisure Direction, Motours, Neilson, SkiBound, Ski Trek, Ski Weekend, Stena Line, Thomson, Travelscene
Barèges Borderline, Lagrange, Thomson, TT Ski
Brides-les-Bains Erna Low, First Choice,

Interhome, Lagrange, Leisure Direction, Motours, Neilson, PGL Ski Europe, Ski Trek, Snowcoach, Stena Line

Les Carroz Erna Low, Interhome, Lagrange, Ski Choice

Cauterets Lagrange, TT Ski

Chamonix AA Ski-Driveaway, Airtours, Bigfoot, Chinook-It, Club Med, Collineige, Crystal, Erna Low, First Choice, Fresh Tracks, HuSki, Independent Ski Links, Inghams, Lagrange, Leisure Direction, Motours, Neilson, Powder Byrne, SCGB/Fresh Tracks, Simply Ski, Ski Choice, The Ski Company, Ski Esprit, Ski Les Alpes, Ski Scott Dunn, Ski Trek, Ski Weekend, Skiworld, Snowline, Solo's, Stena Line, Susie Ward, Thomson, Travelscene, UCPA, White Roc

Champagny-en-Vanoise Erna Low, First Choice, Lagrange, Leisure Direction, Motours, Skisarus, Stena Line

Chamrousse STS

Châtel Fairhand, First Choice, Freedom Holidays, Interhome, Lagrange, Leisure Direction, Made to Measure, SCGB/Fresh Tracks, Ski Partners, Ski Trek, Susie Ward, Travelscene

La Clusaz Classic Ski, Club Europe, Erna Low, Fairhand, First Choice, Lagrange, Leisure Direction, Motours, Silver Ski, Ski Amis, Ski Les Alpes, Ski Partners, Ski Trek, Ski Weekend, Stena Line

Les Coches AA Ski-Driveaway, Erna Low, Lagrange, Leisure Direction, Motours, Ski Olympic

Les Contamines-Montjoie Club Europe, Interhome, Lagrange, Leisure Direction, Ski Activity, Ski Total, Ski Val, Skiworld, UCPA

Le Corbier Lagrange, Motours

Courchevel AA Ski-Driveaway, Airtours, Alpine Action, British Airways, Chalet World, Crystal, Elegant Resorts, Erna Low, Finlays, First Choice, FlexiSki, Independent Ski Links, Inghams, Lagrange, Leisure Direction, Le Ski, Lotus Supertravel, Mark Warner, Masterski, Meriski, Motours, Neilson, PGL Ski Europe, Powder Byrne, Silver Ski, Simply Ski, Ski Activity, Ski Amis, Ski Esprit, Ski France, Ski Les Alpes, Ski Olympic, Ski Scott Dunn, Ski Total, Ski Trek, Ski Val, Ski Weekend, Skiworld, Stena Line, STS, Thomson, Travelscene, White Roc

Les Deux Alpes Airtours, Chalet Snowboard, Club Europe, Equity Total Ski, Crystal, Fairhand, First Choice, French Impressions, Independent Ski Links, Inghams, Lagrange, Leisure Direction, Motours, Neilson, PGL Ski Europe, SCGB/Fresh Tracks, Sloping Off, Ski Activity, SkiBound, Ski Trek, Ski Val, Skiers World, Ski Partners, Skiworld, Thomson, UCPA

Flaine Airtours, British Airways, Classic Ski, Crystal, Erna Low, Fairhand, First Choice, Fresh Tracks, Inghams, Lagrange, Leisure Direction, Motours, Neilson, SCGB/Fresh Tracks, Ski Choice, Ski Les Alpes, SkiSafe, Ski Trek, Solo's, Stena Line, Thomson, Travelscene, UCPA

Font-Romeu Lagrange

Jouvenceaux Equity Total Ski, Ski Partners

Les Gets Fairhand, Fantiski, Leisure Direction, Ski Famille, Ski Hillwood, Ski Les Alpes, Ski Total

Le Grand-Bornand Fairhand, Headwater, Lagrange, Motours, Skisarus, Stena Line

La Grave SCGB/Fresh Tracks, Ski Weekend

Les Houches Collineige, Interhome, Lagrange, Motours

Isola 2000 Made to Measure

Megève Fairhand, Lagrange, Motours, Simon Butler Skiing, Ski Barrett-Boyce, Ski Choice, Ski Les Alpes, Skisarus, Ski Scott Dunn, Ski Trek, Ski Weekend, Snowcoach, Stanford Skiing, Thomson, White Roc

Les Menuires AA Ski-Driveaway, Club Europe, Club Med, Crystal, Erna Low, Fairhand, First Choice, Inghams, Interhome, Lagrange, Leisure Direction, Motours, Skiers World, Ski Partners, Ski Trek, Ski Weekend, Travelscene, Virgin

Méribel AA Ski-Driveaway, Airtours, Altours, Alpine Action, Chalet World, Club Med, Equity Total Ski, Erna Low, First Choice, Independent Ski Links, Inghams, Lagrange, Leisure Direction, Lotus Supertravel, Mark Warner, Masterski, Meriski, Motours, Neilson, Powder Byrne, SCGB/Fresh Tracks, Silver Ski, Simply Ski, Ski Activity, Ski Amis, The Ski Company, Ski France, Ski Les Alpes, Ski Olympic, Ski Scott Dunn, Ski Total, Ski Trek, Ski Val, Skiworld, Snowcoach, Snowline, Solo's, Stena Line, Thomson,

Travelscene, White Roc
La Mongie Lagrange
Montalbert Erna Low, Interhome, Ski Amis
Montchavin Erna Low, Lagrange, Made to Measure
Montgenèvre Airtours, Crystal, Equity Total Ski, Fairhand, First Choice, Lagrange, Made to Measure, Motours, Neilson, Thomson
Morillon Erna Low, Lagrange, PGL Ski Europe, Ski Trek
Morzine Chalet Snowboard, Crystal, First Choice, Inghams, Lagrange, Leisure Direction, SkiBound, Ski Chamois, Ski Esprit, Ski Les Alpes, Ski Moose, Ski Partners, Ski Trek, Ski Weekend, Snowline, Thomson, Trail Alpine, White Roc
La Plagne AA Ski-Driveaway, Airtours, Altours, British Airways, Chalet World, Club Med, Crystal, Erna Low, First Choice, Independent Ski Links, Inghams, Lagrange, Leisure Direction, Mark Warner, Motours, Neilson, SCGB/Fresh Tracks, Silver Ski, Simply Ski, Ski Activity, Ski Amis, Ski Beat, Skiers World, Ski Esprit, Ski France, Ski Les Alpes, Ski Olympic, Ski Trek, Ski Val, Skiworld, Solo's, Thomson, Travelscene, UCPA, Virgin
Pra Loup Airtours, Club Europe, Lagrange, Snowcoach, Stena Line, STS, Thomson
Puy-St-Vincent Club Europe, Interhome, Lagrange, PGL Ski Europe, Ski Trek, Snowbizz, STS
Risoul/Vars Airtours, Altours, Club Europe, Crystal, Fairhand, First Choice, Inghams, Interhome, Lagrange, Motours, Neilson, Skiers World, Thomson, Travelscene
La Rosière Erna Low, Fairhand, Hannibals, Motours, Ski Esprit, Ski Olympic, Ski Trek
Samoëns Erna Low, Interhome, Lagrange, Ski Trek, Stena Line
Serre Chevalier/Briançon Airtours, Altours, Crystal, Equity Total Ski, Fairhand, First Choice, Handmade, Hannibals, Inghams, Lagrange, Motours, Neilson, SCGB/Fresh Tracks, Skiers World, Ski Les Alpes, Ski Miquel, Ski Trek, Skiworld, Sloping Off, Thomson,

Travelscene, UCPA
Sixt Erna Low
St-Gervais Lagrange, Masterski, PGL Ski Europe, Ski Barrett-Boyce, Snowcoach
St-Lary Lagrange
St-Martin-de-Belleville ABT Ski, Interhome, Virgin
Superbagnères Club Med
Ste-Foy The Ski Company
La Tania AA Ski-Driveaway, Crystal, Erna Low, Fairhand, Inghams, Lagrange, Leisure Direction, Motours, Neilson, Silver Ski, Ski Amis, Ski Beat, Ski France, Ski Trek, Snowline, Stena Line, Thomson
Tignes Altours, Club Med, Crystal, Erna Low, Fantiski, First Choice, Independent Ski Links, Inghams, Lagrange, Leisure Direction, Masterski, Motours, Neilson, Ski Activity, SCGB/Fresh Tracks, Ski Amis, Ski Beat, Ski Choice, Ski France, Ski Olympic, Ski Trek, Ski Val, Skiworld, Ski Weekend, Stena Line, Thomson, Travelscene, UCPA, Virgin
Val Cenis Equity Total Ski, Hannibals, Interhome, Lagrange, UCPA
Val d'Isère AA Ski-Driveaway, Airtours, Altours, British Airways, Chalet World, Club Med, Crystal, Elegant Resorts, Erna Low, Fantiski, Finlays, First Choice, Independent Ski Links, Inghams, Lagrange, Leisure Direction, Le Ski, Lotus Supertravel, Meriski, Mark Warner, Motours, Neilson, Powder Byrne, SCGB/Fresh Tracks, Silver Ski, Simply Ski, Ski Activity, Ski Amis, The Ski Company, Ski France, Ski Les Alpes, Ski Scott Dunn, Ski Total, Ski Trek, Ski Val, Ski Weekend, Skiworld, Sloping Off, Stena Line, Thomson, Travelscene, UCPA, VIP, Virgin, White Roc, YSE
Valfréjus Airtours, Lagrange, Made to Measure, Ski Trek
Valloire/Valmeinier Club Europe, First Choice, Lagrange, Motours, Snowcoach, UCPA
Valmorel/St-François-Longchamp AA Ski-Driveaway, Altours, Crystal, Equity Total Ski, Erna Low, Inghams, Lagrange, Leisure Direction, Motours, Neilson, Simply Ski, SkiBound, Skiers World, SkiSafe Travel, Ski Partners, Ski Trek, Stena Line, Thomson, Travelscene
Val Thorens AA Ski-Driveaway, Airtours, Altours, Crystal, Equity Total Ski, Erna

Low, Fairhand, First Choice, Inghams, Lagrange, Leisure Direction, Motours, Neilson, Ski Activity, Ski Amis, Ski Choice, Ski France, Ski Les Alpes, Ski Olympic, Ski Trek, Ski Val, Skiworld, Solo's, Stena Line, Thomson, Travelscene, UCPA, Virgin, White Roc
Vars Motours, Ski Trek
Vaujany Erna Low, Fairhand, Ski Peak

ITALY
Alagna Altours, SCGB/Fresh Tracks, Ski Weekend, Winterski
Andalo Airtours, Alpine Tours, Equity Total Ski, PGL Ski Europe, Skiers World, Ski Partners, STS, Winterski
Aprica Altours, Club Europe, Equity Total Ski, Interhome, PGL Ski Europe, Ski Partners, STS
Arabba Neilson, Ski Yogi
Bardonecchia Airtours, Crystal, Equity Total Ski, First Choice, Motours, Neilson, PGL Ski Europe, Sloping Off, Stena Line, STS
Bormio Airtours, Altours, Crystal, Equity Total Ski, First Choice, Inghams, Interhome, Neilson, Panorama, PGL Ski Europe, Skiers World, Thomson
Campitello Airtours, Crystal, First Choice, Inghams, Neilson, Thomson
Canazei Airtours, Crystal, First Choice, Inghams, Neilson, Ski Partners, Thomson
Cavalese Airtours, Alpine Tours, First Choice, Inghams
Cervinia Airtours, Crystal, First Choice, Inghams, Lagrange, Neilson, Thomson
Cesana Torinese First Choice, PGL Ski Europe
Champoluc Crystal
Clavière Crystal, Equity Total Ski, First Choice, Neilson, PGL Ski Europe
Cortina d'Ampezzo Crystal, Powder Byrne, SCGB/Fresh Tracks, Ski Equipe, White Roc
Courmayeur Airtours, Crystal, Equity Total Ski, First Choice, Independent Ski Links, Inghams, Interski, Interworld, Lagrange, Mark Warner, Motours, Neilson, Ski Activity, Ski Les Alpes, Ski Val, Ski Weekend, Skiworld, Stena Line, Thomson, White Roc
Folgarida Alpine Tours, Altours, Club Europe, Crystal, Equity Total Ski, PGL Skiers World, Ski Europe, STS, Winterski

Foppolo Altours, Crystal, Equity Total Ski, First Choice, PGL Ski Europe, Ski Partners, Winterski
Grangesises Motours, Stena Line
Gressoney Altours, Crystal, Inghams, Motours, Ski Weekend
Limone Altours, Neilson, Sloping Off
Livigno Airtours, Crystal, Equity Total Ski, First Choice, Inghams, Neilson, Panorama, SCGB/Fresh Tracks, Ski Partners, Thomson
Macugnaga First Choice, Interhome, Neilson, Solo's, Ski Partners, Thomson
Madesimo Airtours, Altours, Crystal, Inghams, Neilson, Thomson, Winterski
Madonna di Campiglio Alpine Tours, Altours, Crystal, Equity Total Ski, Inghams, Interhome, Skiers World, Solo's, Thomson, Winterski
Marilleva Alpine Tours, Club Europe, Equity Total Ski, Winterski
Ortisei Interhome
Passo Tonale Airtours, Altours, Club Europe, Crystal, Equity Total Ski, First Choice, Inghams, PGL Ski Europe, Skiers World, Ski Partners, STS, Thomson, Winterski
Pila Crystal, Interski
Pozza di Fassa Crystal
San Cassiano First Choice
Sansicario Equity Total Ski
Santa Caterina Airtours, Crystal, Equity Total Ski, First Choice, Skiers World, Thomson
Sauze d'Oulx Airtours, Crystal, Equity Total Ski, First Choice, Inghams, Neilson, Panorama, Ski Partners, Thomson
Selva Crystal, First Choice, Inghams, Thomson
Sestriere Airtours, Club Med, Crystal, Equity Total Ski, Interhome, Lagrange, Motours, Neilson, Stena Line, Thomson
La Thuile Crystal, First Choice, Inghams, Interski, Interworld , Motours, Neilson, Thomson
Vigo di Fassa Crystal
La Villa Neilson, Ski Beach Villas

JAPAN
Sahoro Club Med

NEW ZEALAND
No current tour operator

NORTH AMERICA

Aleyska Crystal

Aspen/Snowmass Airtours, Crystal, Fantiski, Funway, Independent Ski Links, Inghams, Lotus Supertravel, SCGB/Fresh Tracks, Ski Activity, Ski the American Dream, Ski Connections, Ski Freedom, Ski Independence, Skisarus, Ski Scott Dunn, Ski Val, Skiworld, Solo's, Thomson

Banff/Lake Louise Airtours, Accessible Isolation, All Canada Ski, British Airways, Chinook-It, Crystal, First Choice, Frontier Ski, Funway, Independent Ski Links, Inghams, Interworld, Lotus Supertravel, Neilson, Ramblers, Solo's, Ski Activity, Ski the American Dream, Ski Canada, Ski Connections, Ski Equipe, Ski Val, Skiers World, Ski Independence, Ski Partners, Ski Safari, Skisarus, Ski Scott Dunn, Ski Vacation Canada, Skiworld, Thomson

Big White All Canada Ski, Frontier Ski, Ski the American Dream, Skiers World, Ski Independence, Ski Safari, Skisarus, Ski Vacation Canada

Blue River SCGB/Fresh Tracks, Ski Scott Dunn

Breckenridge Airtours, British Airways, Crystal, Equity Total Ski, Inghams, Funway, Neilson, Ski Activity, Ski the American Dream, Ski Connections, Ski Freedom, Ski Independence, Skisarus, Ski Val, Skiworld, Thomson

Copper Mountain Club Med, Funway, Ski the American Dream, Ski Activity, Ski Independence

Crested Butte Altours, Fresh Tracks, Funway, Neilson, SCGB/Fresh Tracks, Ski Activity, Ski the American Dream, Ski Equipe, Skiers World, Ski Freedom, Ski Independence

Deer Valley Made to Measure, Ski the American Dream, Ski Freedom, Skisarus, Virgin

Fernie Frontier Ski, Ski Safari, Skisarus

Grand Targhee Lotus Supertravel

Jackson Hole Crystal, Funway, Inghams, Lotus Supertravel, Neilson, Ski Activity, Ski the American Dream, Ski Connections, Ski Freedom, Ski Independence, Skisarus, Ski Scott Dunn, Ski Val, Skiworld

Jasper All Canada Ski, Crystal, First Choice, Frontier Ski, Inghams, Neilson, Ramblers, Ski the American Dream, Ski Activity, Ski Canada, Ski Connections, Skiers World, Ski Safari, Ski Independence, Skisarus, Skiworld, Ski Vacation Canada, Thomson

June Mountain Virgin

Keystone Crystal, Funway, Ski the American Dream, Ski Connections, Ski Freedom, Ski Independence, Skisarus

Killington Crystal, Equity Total Ski, First Choice, Funway, Inghams, Neilson, Ski Activity, Ski the American Dream, Ski Connections, Ski Val, Skiers World, Ski Independence, Ski Partners, Skiworld, Solo's, Virgin

Lake Tahoe Altours, Chalet Snowboard, Crystal, Funway, Inghams, Ski Activity, Ski the American Dream, Ski Connections, Skiers World, Ski Freedom, Ski Independence, Ski Val, Skiworld, Virgin

Mammoth Mountain Airtours, Crystal, Funway, Inghams, Ski Activity, Ski the American Dream, Ski Connections, Skiers World, Ski Freedom, Ski Independence, Ski Val, Skiworld, Virgin

Mont Sainte-Anne All Canada Ski, Club Europe, First Choice, Ski the American Dream, Ski Connections, Skiers World, Ski Partners, Ski Vacation Canada

Mont Tremblant All Canada Ski, Crystal, First Choice, Frontier Ski, Inghams, Neilson, Ski the American Dream, Ski Canada, Ski Connections, Skiers World, Ski Independence, Ski Safari, Ski Vacation Canada, Thomson

Mount Norquay All Canada Ski, British Airways, Ski Safari

Panorama All Canada Ski, Frontier Ski, Inghams, Ski Safari

Park City Crystal, Funway, Neilson, Ski Activity, Ski the American Dream, Ski Connections, Ski Freedom, Ski Independence, Skisarus, Ski Val, Skiworld, Virgin

Pico Ski Independence, Virgin

Red Mountain All Canada Ski, Frontier Ski, Ski Safari

Silver Star All Canada Ski, Frontier Ski, Made to Measure, Ski the American Dream, Ski Safari, Skisarus, Ski Vacation Canada

Smuggler's Notch Club Europe, Ski the American Dream

Snowbird Crystal, Funway, Ski the American Dream, Ski Freedom, Ski Independence, Skisarus, Ski Scott Dunn,

Virgin
Solitude Ski the American Dream, Virgin
Squaw Valley Crystal, Ski the American Dream, Ski Independence, Virgin
Steamboat Airtours, British Airways, Crystal, Funway, Inghams, Lotus Supertravel, Neilson, Ski Activity, Ski the American Dream, Ski Connections, Skiers World, Ski Freedom, Ski Independence, Skisarus, Ski Val, Skiworld, Thomson
Stowe Club Europe, Crystal, Equity Total Ski, First Choice, Funway, Inghams, Neilson, Ski the American Dream, Ski Connections, Skiers World, Ski Independence, Ski Partners, Ski Val, Skiworld, Virgin
Sugarbush Crystal, First Choice, Funway, Inghams, Neilson, Ski the American Dream, Skiers World, Virgin
Sunday River Crystal, First Choice, Inghams, Neilson, Ski the American Dream, Skiers World, Ski Independence, Ski Partners
Sun Peaks All Canada Ski, Frontier Ski, Ski the American Dream, Ski Independence, Ski Safari, Skisarus
Sun Valley Lotus Supertravel, Ski Activity, Ski the American Dream, Ski Independence, Skisarus
Taos Ski the American Dream, Ski Connections, Ski Independence, Skisarus
Telluride Lotus Supertravel, Made to Measure, Ski the American Dream, Ski Freedom, Ski Independence, Skisarus
Vail/Beaver Creek Airtours, British Airways, Crystal, Funway, Inghams, Lotus Supertravel, Neilson, Ski Activity, Ski the American Dream, The Ski Company, Ski Connections, Ski Equipe, Ski Freedom, Ski Independence, Skisarus, Ski Scott Dunn, Ski Val, Skiworld, Thomson
Whistler/Blackcomb Airtours, All Canada Ski, Altours, American Connections, British Airways, Chinook-It, Crystal, First Choice, Frontier Ski, Funway, Inghams, Interworld, Lotus Supertravel, Neilson, Powder Byrne, SCGB/Fresh Tracks, Simply Ski, Ski Activity, Ski the American Dream, Ski Canada, Ski Equipe, Skiers World, Ski Independence, Ski Miquel, Ski Safari, Skisarus, Ski Scott Dunn, Ski Total, Ski Vacation Canada, Ski Val, Ski Weekend, Skiworld, Solo's, Thomson
Winter Park Crystal, First Choice, Neilson,

Ski the American Dream, Ski Connections, Ski Freedom, Ski Independence, Skisarus, Solo's, Thomson

NORWAY
Geilo Crystal, Inntravel, Neilson, Waymark
Hemsedal Crystal, Neilson
Voss Mountain & Wildlife Ventures

ROMANIA
Poiana Brasov Balkan Holidays, Balkan Tours, Crystal, First Choice, Inghams, Neilson
Sinaia Crystal

SCOTLAND
Aviemore Ski Norwest, SkiSafe
Glencoe SkiSafe
Glenshee Ski Norwest, SkiSafe
Nevis Range Ski Norwest, SkiSafe
The Lecht SkiSafe

SERBIA
Kapaonik Thomson

SLOVENIA
Bled Alpine Tours, Thomson
Bohinj Alpine Tours
Kranjska Gora Alpine Tours, Inghams, Thomson

SPAIN
Baqueira-Beret Ski Miquel
Formigal Inghams, Panorama, Thomson
Sierra Nevada Airtours, First Choice, Neilson, Thomson

SWEDEN
Åre Crystal
Sälen Crystal

SWITZERLAND
Adelboden Freedom Holidays, Inghams, Kuoni, Plus Travel, Swiss Travel Service
Andermatt Interhome, Made to Measure
Anzère Interhome, Lagrange, Made to Measure
Arosa Inghams, Kuoni, Plus Travel, Powder Byrne, Ski Choice, Ski Gower, Swiss Travel Service
Celerina Interhome, Made to Measure
Champéry Kuoni, Made to Measure,

Piste Artiste, Plus Travel, Ski Les Alpes, White Roc

Champoussin Interhome, Snowline

Château d'Oex First Choice, Interhome, Kuoni, Skiers World, Swiss Travel Service

Crans Montana Fairhand, Inghams, Kuoni, Lagrange, PGL Ski Europe, Plus Travel, SCGB/Fresh Tracks, Ski Les Alpes, Ski Weekend, Swiss Travel Service

Davos Freedom Holidays, Inghams, Kuoni, Plus Travel, Ski Choice, Ski Gower, Ski Les Alpes, Ski Weekend, Swiss Travel Service, White Roc

Les Diablerets Fairhand, First Choice, Kuoni, Lagrange, Plus Travel, Ski Gower, Ski Weekend, Sloping Off, Solo's

Engelberg Freedom Holidays, Kuoni, Made to Measure, Plus Travel, Ski Gower, Swiss Travel Service

Flims/Laax Freedom Holidays, Interhome, Kuoni, Plus Travel, Powder Byrne, Ski Choice, Ski Weekend, Swiss Travel Service, White Roc

Grindelwald Inghams, Interhome, Kuoni, Neilson, Plus Travel, Powder Byrne, Ski Gower, Swiss Travel Service, Thomson, White Roc

Gstaad Elegant Resorts, Interhome, Made to Measure, Ski Gower

Interlaken Interhome, Kuoni, Skiers World, Ski Gower, Swiss Travel Service

Kandersteg Headwater, Inntravel, Kuoni, Waymark

Klosters Kuoni, Inghams, Plus Travel, Powder Byrne, The Ski Company, SCGB/Fresh Tracks, Ski Gower, Ski Les Alpes, Ski Weekend, White Roc

Lauterbrunnen Ski Miquel, Top Deck Ski

Lenk Made to Measure, Swiss Travel Service

Lenzerheide/Valbella Club Med, Inghams, Interhome, Kuoni, Plus Travel, Ski Choice

Leysin Plus Travel, Skiers World

Morgins Ski Morgins

Mürren Inghams, Kuoni, Made to Measure, Plus Travel, Ski Gower, Ski Les Alpes, Swiss Travel Service, Thomson

Pontresina Club Med, Interhome, Made to Measure

Saas-Fee Crystal, Independent Ski Links, Inghams, Kuoni, Neilson, Plus Travel, SCGB/Fresh Tracks, Ski Choice, Ski Gower, Swiss Travel Service, Thomson

Saas-Grund Interhome, Ski Gower

Samedan Interhome, Kuoni

Surlej Made to Measure

St Moritz Club Med, Elegant Resorts, Inghams, Kuoni, Plus Travel, Powder Byrne, SCGB/Fresh Tracks, Ski Gower, Swiss Travel Service

Verbier Airtours, Chalet World, Crystal, FlexiSki, Freedom Holidays, Fresh Tracks, Inghams, Lagrange, Lotus Supertravel, Mark Warner, Neilson, Plus Travel, SCGB/Fresh Tracks, Simply Ski, Ski Activity, Ski Esprit, Ski Les Alpes, Ski Scott Dunn, Ski Verbier, Ski Weekend, Skiworld, Susie Ward, Swiss Travel Service, Thomson, White Roc

Veysonnaz Interhome

Villars Club Med, Fairhand, First Choice, Interhome, Kuoni, Made to Measure, Plus Travel, Ski Weekend, Swiss Travel Service

Wengen Club Med, Crystal, Inghams, Interhome, Kuoni, Neilson, Plus Travel, Ski Gower, SCGB/Fresh Tracks, Ski Les Alpes, Swiss Travel Service, Thomson, White Roc

Zermatt Elegant Resorts, Inghams, Kuoni, Lagrange, Lotus Supertravel, Neilson, Plus Travel, Powder Byrne, SCGB/Fresh Tracks, Ski Choice, Ski Gower, Ski Les Alpes, Ski Scott Dunn, Ski Total, Swiss Travel Service, Thomson, Trail Alpine, White Roc

Zinal Club Med, Interhome

Skiing by numbers

NATIONAL TOURIST OFFICES

Andorran Delegation
63 Westover Road, London SW18 2RF
Tel 0181-874 4806 (no fax)

Argentinian Embassy
27 Three Kings Yard, London W1Y 1FL
Tel 0171-318 1340 **Fax** 0171-318 1349

Australian Tourist Commission
Gemini House, 10–18 Putney Hill, London
SW15 6AA
Tel 0181-780 2229 **Fax** 0181-780 1496
Helpline 0990 022 000
Email london-helpline@atc.gov.au
Web site www.aussie.net.au

Austrian National Tourist Office
14 Cork Street, London W1X 1PF
Tel 0171-629 0461 Fax 0171-499 6038
Email oewlon@easynet.co.uk
Web site www.austria-tourism.at

Balkan Holidays (for Bulgaria)
Sofia House, 19 Conduit Street, London
W1R 9TD
Tel 0171-491 4499 **Fax** 0171-543 5577

Cedok Travel Ltd (Czech Republic and
Slovakia)
53–54 Haymarket, London SW1 4RP
Tel 0171-839 4414 **Fax** 0171-839 0204

Embassy of Chile
Commercial Department, 12 Devonshire
Street, London W1N 2DS
Tel 0171-580 6392 **Fax** 0171-436 5204
Email echileuk@echileuk.demon.co.uk

French Government Tourist Office
178 Piccadilly, London W1V 0AL
Tel (0891) 244123 **Fax** 0171-493 6594
Email piccadilly@mdlsdemon.co.uk
Web site www.franceguide.com

German National Tourist Office
PO Box 2695, London W1A 3TN
Tel (0891) 600100 **Fax** 0171-495 6129

Email german-national-tourist-
office@compuserve.com
Web site www.germany-tourism.de

Italian State Tourist Office
1 Princes Street, London W1R 8AY
Tel 0171-408 1254 **Fax** 0171-493 6695
Email enitlon@globalnet.co.uk

Japanese National Tourist Organisation
Heathcoat House, 20 Saville Row, London
W1X 1AE
Tel 0171-734 9638 **Fax** 0171-734 4290
Email jntolon@dircon.co.uk
Web site www.jnto.go.jp

New Zealand Tourism Board
New Zealand House, Haymarket, London
SW1Y 4TQ
Tel (0839) 300900 **Fax** 0171-839 8929
Web site www.nztb.govt.nz

Norwegian Tourist Board
Charles House, 5 Lower Regent Street,
London SW1Y 4LR
Tel 0171-839 6255 **Fax** 0171-839 6014
Email london@nortra.no
Web site www.tourist.no

Romanian National Tourist Office
83a Marylebone High Street, London
W1M 3DE
Tel/Fax 0171-224 3692

Scottish Tourist Board
23 Ravelston Terrace, Edinburgh EH4
3EU
Tel 0131-332 2433 **Fax** 0131-343 1513
Web site www.holiday.scotland.net

Slovenian Tourist Office
49 Conduit Street London W1 9FB
Tel 0171-287 7133 **Fax** 0171-287 5476

Spanish Tourist Office
57 St James's Street,
London SW1A 1LD
Tel 0171-486 8077 **Fax** 0171-629 4257

Swedish Travel & Tourism Council
11 Montague Place, London W1H 2AL
Tel 0171-724 5868 **Fax** 0171-724 5872
Email info@swetourism.org.uk
Web site www.visit-sweden.com

Switzerland Tourism
Swiss Centre, Swiss Court, London W1V 8EE
Tel 0171-734 1921 **Fax** 0171-437 4577
Email stc@stlondon.com

Tourism Canada
The Visit Canada Centre, 62–65 Trafalgar Square, London WC2N 5DY
Tel (0891) 715000 **Fax** 0171-389 1149
Email vcc@dial.pipex.com
Web site www.info.ic.gc.ca/tourism

Visit USA Association
Tel (0891) 600530 (recorded message)

SKI TRAVEL AGENTS AND CONSULTANTS
Alpine Answers
The Business Village, 3–9 Broomhill Road, London SW18 4JQ
Tel 0181-871 4656 **Fax** 0181-871 9676
Email alpineanswer@compuserve.com

Erna Low
9 Reece Mews, London SW7 3HE
Tel 0171-584 2841/7820 **Fax** 0171-589 9531
Email ernalow@easynet.co.uk
Web site www.ernalow.co.uk

Ski Solutions
84 Pembroke Road, London W8 6NX
Tel 0171-471 7700 **Fax** 0171-471 7701
Email skihols@skisolutions.com

Ski and Surf
37 Priory Field Drive, Edgware HA8 9PT
Tel 0181-958 2418 **Fax** 0181-905 4146
Email janm@skisurf.com

Ski Travel Centre
1100 Pollokshaws Road, Shawlands, Glasgow G41 3NJ
Tel 0141-649 9696 **Fax** 0141-649 2273
Web site www.ski-travel-centre.co.uk

Skiers Travel Bureau
79 Street Lane, Roundhay, Leeds LS8 1AP
Tel (0113) 266 6876 **Fax** (0113) 269 3305
Email skiers-travel.co.uk
Website www.skiers-travel.co.uk

Snowline
1 Angel Court, High Street, Market Harborough LE16 7NL
Tel (01858) 433633 **Fax** (01858) 433266
Email sales@snow-line.co.uk
Website www.snow-line.co.uk

Susie Ward Company
54 Vicarage Road, St Agnes TR5 0TQ
Tel (01872) 553055 **Fax** (01872) 553050

WEATHER AND SNOW
Snowline
Tel (0891) 700 333
Gives 24-hour up-to-date information direct from 200 resorts in 10 countries

Met-Ski Scotland
Tel (0336) 405 400
Information on the Scottish ski resorts

HELI-SKI COMPANIES
ITALY
ETI 2000
Quart, Aosta
Tel 39 165 765417 **Fax** 39 165 765418
Cervinia, Courmayeur, Valgrisenche

Lacadur Heli-Ski
38 Ch du Rocher Nay, Le Tour, F-74400 Chamonix, France
Tel 33 4 50 54 08 40 **Fax** 33 4 50 54 18 45
Email cybercopter@netsurf.it
Chamonix and Gressoney

SWITZERLAND
Bohag
3814 Gsteigwiler
Tel 41 33 828 9000 **Fax** 41 33 828 9010
Bernese Oberland

Trans-Heli SA – Air Glaciers SA
Box 236, CH-1868 Collombey
Tel 41 24 473 7070 **Fax** 41 24 473 7071

CANADA
Canadian Mountain Holidays (UK agent)
61 Doneraile Street, London SW6 6EW
Tel 0171-736 8191 **Fax** 0171-384 2592

Nine locations in British Columbia.
Packages include accommodation

Mike Wiegele Helicopter Skiing
Box 159, Blue River, British Columbia, BC
V0E 1J0
Tel 1 250 673 8381 **Fax** 1 250 673 8464
Email mail@wiegele.com
Web site www.wiegele.com
Blue River in British Columbia. Packages
include accommodation

Ski Club of Great Britain (UK agent for
Mike Wiegele)
The White House, 57–63 Church Road,
London SW19 5SB
Tel 0181-410 2000 **Fax** 0181-410 2001
Email hols@skiclub.co.uk
Web site www.skiclub.co.uk

Ski Scott Dunn (UK agent for Mike
Wiegele)
Fovant Mews, 12 Noyna Road, London
SW17 7PH
Tel 0181-767 0202 **Fax** 0181-767 2026
Email world@scottdunn.com

Whistler Heli-Skiing
Crystal Lodge, Village Stroll, Box 368,
Whistler BC V0N 1B0
Tel 1 604 932 4105 Fax 1 604 938 1225
Email heliski@direct.ca
Web site www.heliskiwhistler.com

SKI-TOURING

The Eagle Ski Club
Eastlea, Felix Lane, Shepperton TW17
8NN
Tel (01932) 248628 **Fax** (01932) 253558
Email mike.hendry@dial.pipex.co
Web site www.ds.dial.pipex.com/mike-
hendry/eagleskiclub
Europe's largest ski-touring club

Mountain Experience
Pike View Barn, Whitehough Head,
Chinley, High Peak SK23 6BX
Tel/Fax (01663) 750160
Email brianphall@msn.com
Guiding and ski-touring in France, Italy
and Switzerland

GUIDED SKI COURSES

The names listed below specialise in ski

clinic holidays and do not appear in the
tour operators list. Note, several of the
tour operators in the main list also offer
ski clinics

John Arnold Skiing
39 Manor Place, Edinburgh EH3 7EB
Tel/Fax 0141-943 1740
Ski clinics in Scotland, Europe and the USA

Lauralee Bowie Ski Adventures
Hongkong Bank Building, Suite 1500- 885
West Georgia St, Vancouver, Canada
Tel 1 604 689 7444 **Fax** 1 604 689 7489
Email llbski@canuck.com
Personalised ski instruction in Whistler and
Lake Louise

Ski Barrett-Boyce
Suite 29, Westmead House, 123 Westmead
Road, Sutton SM1 4JH
Tel 0181-288 0042 **Fax** 0181-288 0762
Email skibb@atlas.co.uk
Small operator to France with instruction

BEST
Tel (01803) 859075
British European Ski Teachers is a co-
operative of BASI-qualified instructors
licensed to teach worldwide

British Alpine Ski School
British instructors, licensed to teach skiing
and snowboarding in France

(Avoriaz)
7 Orleigh Court, Buckland Brewer,
Bideford EX39 5EH
Tel/Fax (01237) 451099
Email imckellar@compuserve.com
Web site www.ski-school.co.uk
Instruction for paraplegics also available

(Morzine/Les Gets, Les Arcs and La
Plagne)
4 Chilvers Place, Heacham PE31 7JT
Tel (01485) 572596

Fred Foxon
The Old Vicarage, Merton, Bicester OX6
0NF
Tel (01865) 884342 **Fax** (01865) 331621
Email fred.foxon@virgin.net
Personal performance weeks in Val d'Isère

International Masterclass
Adjewhella Cottage, Penponds, Camborne
TR14 0QW
Tel/Fax (01209) 718297/ 33 4 76 80 93 83
BASI instructors based in Alpe d'Huez

Made to Measure
43 East Street, Chichester PO19 1HX
Tel (01243) 533333 **Fax** (01243) 778431
Email madetomeasure.holidays@which.net
Personalised ski courses in Altenmarkt

McGarry The Ski System
5 Barnhill Road, Dalkey, Co Dublin,
Ireland
Tel (353) 1 285 9139 **Fax** (353) 1 284
9932
Email mcgarryski.ie
Web site www.mcgarryski.ie
Specialist clinics in Châtel, France

Mountain Experience
Pike View Barn, Whitehough Head,
Chinley, High Peak SK23 6BX
Tel/Fax (01663) 750160
Email brianphall@msn.com
*Guiding and ski-touring in France and
Switzerland*

Optimum Ski Courses
Chalet Tarentaise, Le Pré, Villaroger, F-
73640 Sainte-Foy, France
Tel (01992) 561085 **Fax** 33 4 79 06 93 56
Email optimumski@aol.com
*Ski clinics in Les Arcs and Tignes with
BASI trainer*

Ali Ross
Ski Solutions, 84 Pembroke Road, London
W8 6NX
Tel 0171-471 7777 **Fax** 0171-471 7701
Email sales@skisolutions.com
Specialist ski courses in Tignes

Ski Club of Great Britain
The White House, 57–63 Church Road,
London SW19 5SB
Tel 0181-410 2000 **Fax** 0181-410 2001
Email info@skiclub.co.uk
Web site www.skiclub.co.uk
Ski courses for all standards

Ski Principles
19 Church Street, Brixham TQ5 8HG

Tel (01803) 852185/ 33 4 79 00 52 71
Personal performance courses in Méribel

The Ski Company
13 Squires Close, Bishop's Park, Bishop's
Stortford CM23 4DB
Tel (01279) 653746 **Fax** (01279) 654705
Email theskicompany@compuserve.com
Year-round ski courses

Roland Stieger
Route de Taconnaz, F-74310 Les
Houches, France
Tel 33 4 50 54 43 53 **Fax** 33 4 50 54 46 26
Chamonix-based courses and guiding

Supreme Ski School
Birchview, Railway Terrace, Aviemore
PH22 1SA
Tel (01479) 810814 **Fax** (01479) 811659
Hotline (0845) 6062020
Email supremeski@compuserve
*English-speaking classes with BASI
instructors in Courchevel*

Top Ski
Galerie des Cimes, BP 41, F-73150 Val
d'Isère, France
Tel 33 4 79 06 14 80 **Fax** 33 4 79 06 28 42
Email top.ski.val.isere@wanadoo.fr
Leading alternative ski school

SKI INSURANCE COMPANIES
American Express
American Express Services Europe Ltd,
Freepost (RCC 1938), Department 870,
Burgess Hill RH15 9ZA
Tel (0800) 700737 **Fax** (01444) 235257
Web site www.americanexpress.com

Douglas Cox Tyrie Ltd
Central House, 32–66 High Street,
Stratford, London E15 2PF
Tel 0181-534 9595 **Fax** 0181-519 8780

Eagle Star Direct
Montpellier Drive, Cheltenham GL53 7LQ
Tel (0800) 333800 **Fax** (01489) 885978
Web site www.eaglestardirect.co.uk

Endsleigh Insurance Services Ltd
97–107 Southampton Row, London
WC1B 4AG
Tel 0171-436 4451 **Fax** 0171-637 3132

Europ Assistance
Sussex House, Perrymount Road,
Haywards Heath RH16 1DN
Tel (01444) 442211 **Fax** (01444) 459292

Fogg Travel Insurance Ltd
Fullerton Lodge, Crow Hill Drive,
Mansfield NG19 7AE
Tel (01623) 631331 **Fax** (01623) 420450
Email col@fogg.itsnet.co.uk

Hamilton Barr
Bridge Mews, Bridge Street, Godalming
GU7 1HZ
Tel (01483) 426600 **Fax** (01483) 426382

Snowcard Insurance Services Ltd
Lower Boddington,
Daventry NN11 6XZ
Tel (01327) 262805 **Fax** (01327) 263227
Email snowcard@dial.pipex.com
Web site www.ski.co.uk/snowcard

Touchline Insurance Company
1 Port Way, Port Solent,
Portsmouth PO6 4TY
Tel (0800) 777143 **Fax** (01705) 210176
Web site www.touchline.co.uk

SKIING AND SNOWBOARDING ORGANISATIONS
Artificial Ski Slope Instructors (ASSI)
The English Ski Council, The Area Library
Building, Queensway Mall, The Cornbow,
Halesowen B63 4AJ
Tel 0121-501 2314 **Fax** 0121-585 6448
Web site www.bluedome.co.uk

**Association of Independent Tour
Operators (AITO)**
133a St, Margaret's Road, Twickenham
TW1 1RG
Tel 0181-744 9280 **Fax** 0181-744 3187
Brochure line 0181-607 9080
Email aito@martex.co.uk
Web site www.aito.co.uk

**British Association of Ski
Instructors (BASI)**
Glenmore, Aviemore PH22 1QU
Tel (01479) 861717 **Fax** (01479) 861718
Email basi@basi.oug.uk
Web site www.basi.oug.uk

British Ski and Snowboard Federation
258 Main Street, East Calder, West
Lothian EH53 0EE
Tel (01506) 884343 **Fax** (01506) 882952
Email britski@easynet.co.uk

British Snowboarding Association
1st Floor, 4 Trinity Square, Llandudno
LL30 2PY
Tel/Fax (01492) 872540

SKI COUNCILS
These bodies govern the sport as a whole,
taking responsibility for promoting and
developing skiing and skiers' interests with
the aid of grants from the Sports Council.

English Ski Council
Area Library Building,
Queensway Mall, The Cornbow,
Halesowen B63 4AJ
Tel 0121-501 2314 **Fax** 0121-585 6448
Web site www.bluedome.co.uk

Scottish National Ski Council
Caledonia House, South Gyle,
Edinburgh EH12 9DQ
Tel 0131-317 7280 **Fax** 0131-339 8602
Email admin@snsc.demon.co.uk
Web site www.snsc.demon.co.uk

Ski Council of Wales
240 Whitchurch Road,
Cardiff CF4 3ND
Tel (01222) 619637 **Fax** (01222) 522178

SKI CLUBS
Alpbach Visitors Ski Club
c/o Dinny Patterson, Barhaus, A-6236
Alpbach, Austria
Tel 43 5336 5282 **Fax** 43 5336 5073
Individual and package holidays

Bearsden Ski Club
The Mound, Stockiemuir Road, Bearsden,
Glasgow G61 3RS
Tel (0141) 943 1500 **Fax** (0141) 4705
Ski club with artificial slope

British Ski Club for the Disabled
Springmount, Berwick St John,
Shaftesbury SP7 0HQ
Tel (01747) 828515

Helps would-be skiers with physical or mental disabilities

Downhill Only Club
c/o Jenny Alban Davies,
Troutbeck, Otford,
Sevenoaks TN14 5PH
Tel/Fax (01959) 525439
Ski club with junior racing, based in Wengen, Switzerland

Kandahar Ski Club
c/o Mrs J Holmes, Woodside, Benenden,
Cranbrook TN17 4EZ
Tel (01580) 240606 **Fax** (01580) 241684
Ski club with junior racing, based in Mürren, Switzerland

Ladies Ski Club
c/o J Glasson, 40 Aynhoe Road,
London W14 0QD
Tel 0171-603 7464 **Fax** 0171-602 4970
Supporters of women's ski racing

Marden's Club
c/o Mrs WA Sanders,
9 Chimney House, Balsham,
Cambridge CB1 6ES
Tel (01223) 893063 **Fax** (01223) 890846
Based in Klosters, Switzerland

Scottish Ski Club
11 Frogston Terrace, Edinburgh
EH10 7AE
Tel 0131-477 1055

The Uphill Ski Club of Great Britain
The Print House,
18 Ashwin Street, Dalston,
London E8 3DL
Tel/Fax 0171-254 1944
Email colin@baggend.demon.co.uk
Web site www.baggend.demon.co.uk
Organisation for disabled skiers

Ski Club of Great Britain
The White House,
57–63 Church Road,
London SW19 5SB
Tel 0181-410 2000 **Fax** 0181-410 2001
Email info@skiclub.co.uk
Web site www.skiclub.co.uk
The premier club for British skiers
(see p.11 for details)

GETTING THERE
GOING BY AIR
The main airlines listed below offer international scheduled flights to airports close to the ski areas.

Air Canada
Tel (0990) 247226
Air France
Tel 0181-742 6600
Air New Zealand
Tel 0181-741 2299
Alitalia
Tel 0171-602 7111
American Airlines
Tel 0181-572 5555
Austrian Airlines
Tel 0171-434 7300
British Airways
Tel (0345) 222111
Canadian Airlines
Tel (0345) 616767
Continental Airlines
Tel (01293) 776464
Crossair
Tel 0171-743 7300
Delta Airlines
Tel (0800) 414767
Lauda Air
Tel 0171-630 5924
Northwest Airlines
Tel (01293) 561000
Swissair
Tel 0171-434 7300
United Airlines
Tel (0845) 8444777
Virgin Atlantic Airways
Tel (01293) 747747

CAR AND TRAIN
See 'By car or train' on page 582

CAR RENTAL COMPANIES
Alamo Rent-A-Car
Tel (01895) 443355
Avis
Tel (0990) 900500
Budget Rent-a-Car
Tel (0800) 181181
Europcar Inter Rent
Tel (0113) 2422233
Hertz
Tel (0990) 996699
Holiday Autos
Tel (0990) 300400

By car or train

Anyone who has experienced Gatwick and Geneva Airport on a Saturday in February will understand why about 20 per cent of the estimated 800,000 British skiers will go by car to the Alps this winter. Apart from avoiding check-in chaos, the rigidity of charter travel and the weekend lottery of air-traffic control in the skies over Europe, driving to the snow offers greater flexibility of destination as well as the freedom to travel with as many pairs of skis and as much luggage as you choose.

Limited holiday time and the desire to spend as much of it on the snow as possible has largely refined ski-drive destinations to the French Alps as well as to a handful of Swiss and Italian resorts easily accessible from Lake Geneva or via the Mont Blanc Tunnel.

Given fair weather and a co-driver you can comfortably travel from Calais to Courchevel in under ten hours without breaking the speed limit.

Route planning

Finding your way to the French Alps is simple. Take the A26 autoroute from Calais and carry on past Reims and Dijon. At Mâcon, branch off on to the A40 towards Geneva, or carry on past Lyon for Albertville and Grenoble. Skiers travelling to the Tarentaise will find the autoroute ends at Albertville. However, the road from there to Moûtiers is, thanks to the 1992 Winter Olympics, a fast dual-carriageway. The final stretch to Val d'Isère/Tignes beyond Bourg-St-Maurice takes 40 minutes in good weather conditions.

The AA will prepare personalised routes to individual requirements at a cost of £14.95 for members or £17.95 for non-members. The RAC no longer offers a route-planning service. However, both motoring organisations supply reports on current road/weather conditions. For details of web sites which contain useful information on French weather conditions, see 'Cyberskiing' on page 545.

Be prepared

It is essential to have your car fully serviced before encountering what may be seriously cold conditions in the Alps. Check the battery and replace it if in any doubt as to its efficiency. The level of anti-freeze should be topped up to the manufacturer's handbook recommendation for temperatures as low as −30°C. Anti-freeze may not be effective if it is more than two years old. You will also need a stronger solution of winter screenwash. Carry a windscreen scraper and a can of de-icer.

It is a legal requirement to attach a GB sticker in a vertical or near vertical position at the rear of your car. You must also carry a warning triangle and attach headlamp beam converters to avoid dazzling other drivers. Take with you a torch, a shovel, an old pair of gloves and a tow-rope.

Motorway tolls

You can calculate in advance the exact cost of French motorway tolls to and from your destination by contacting the main motoring organisations or the French Government Tourist Office (see 'Skiing by numbers' page 576). Rather than carrying small change, it is easier (and surprisingly quicker) to pay by credit card.

Austria now charges ATS70 for ten days or ATS550 for one year for a windscreen sticker which allows usage of all Austrian motorways. It can be purchased at the border or from service stations close to the border. Switzerland has a similar system, which costs SF40 for one year. You can buy stickers from the Swiss Tourist Office (see 'Skiing by numbers') before you leave home, or at the frontier. In both countries, ignorance of the law is no excuse.

Breakdown insurance

The AA estimates that about half of those people who drive to ski resorts do not have vehicle breakdown cover, yet as many as one in five has some sort of car trouble.

The approximate cost of having a car recovered to Britain from France is £2,100. An out-of-hours local tow costs £30 to £40.

Green Cards

The international motor insurance card or Green Card is a standardised proof of insurance which is no longer compulsory. Some companies continue to issue Green Cards – either free of charge or for an administration fee. Others, including the AA, no longer do so. However, you must carry your insurance certificate, vehicle registration document and a current tax disc.

Before driving abroad you must inform your car insurance company of the dates of your departure and return. If you have a comprehensive policy it is important to confirm that your cover abroad is the same as at home.

Driving regulations

In France, the speed limit on non-motorways is 90kph (56mph), on urban motorways 110kph (68mph), on autoroutes 130kph (81mph). In built-up areas the limit is 50kph (31mph) or 70kph (44mph). You can be fined up to 2,500FF on the spot for speeding. You must carry with you at all times a full UK driving licence and your passport. If you have held a licence for less than two years you are subject to set speed limits: 80kph (50mph) on non-motorways, 100kph (62mph) on urban motorways, 110kph (68mph) on autoroutes. The drink/drive limit is 50mg in France as opposed to 80mg in Britain. This is rigidly enforced. However, you do not necessarily lose your licence for a first offence.

Snow tyres and chains

Most cars in Britain are fitted with standard summer tyres which provide insufficient grip in serious alpine conditions. The legal requirement is for the tread of all tyres to be over 2mm. If you travel regularly to the mountains or plan an extended stay, it is worth investing in a set of high-profile snow tyres which can also be used (with some increase in noise and wear) on motorways and other 'dry' roads. Studded tyres are for resort use only and are neither advisable nor necessary.

Even though you may not need to use snow chains during much of the winter, it is a legal requirement to carry them when driving on mountain roads in all European countries. Failure to do so can result in on-the-spot fines of up to £200 and there is evidence to suggest that police forces in France and in Switzerland in particular are increasingly enforcing the law.

Do not wait until you need them before buying snow chains The price at garages in the mountains is as extortionately high as their quality is low. Modern chains come in three basic types – the greater the traction and the easier they are to fit, the more expensive the chains. At the bottom end of the range is the Cable Grip, which is laced around the wheel. The more sophisticated Euromatic is mounted on a flexible steel hoop. The Centrax-Steg is the easiest of all and leaves you with clean hands. You attach an adaptor to one wheelnut, throw as much of the chain as you can over the tyre, and it fits and tightens automatically as you drive off.

Snow chains can be bought – but not hired – from the AA. They cost from £44.99 (£42.74 for members) at larger AA shops. They are also available from the AA by mail order. They can be bought from the RAC at between £44 and £99 or can be hired at £2.95 per day for a minimum of ten days. Postage and packing costs an extra £5, and there is a £45 deposit.

Rud Chains of Whitstable, Kent supplies the Ministry of Defence and claims to be the world's largest supplier of snow chains. Its chains cost between £46 and £250 depending on the type of chain and vehicle. The Centrax-Steg costs £176. The company will exchange chains – whether used or unused – if you change your car. Snowchains of Borough Green in Kent rent standard chains for £29.50 for ten days and sell three different types ranging in price from £50 to £250. Fitting for even the basic types should not take more than a minute per wheel, but both companies strongly recommend you practice before you leave home.

Cost of driving

The cost of driving the 2010km (1,400 miles) from London to Val d'Isère and back in an 1800cc family saloon works out at approximately £340. This price includes Euro Tunnel, petrol, tolls and chain hire. It does not include wear-and-tear, pre-trip servicing, refreshments or accommodation en route.

Trains

Eurostar, in partnership with French Railways (SNCF), operates a direct service from December to mid-April which has proved to be one of the most hassle-free methods of getting to the Alps. The train leaves Waterloo on a Saturday morning at 08.57 (or Ashford at 09.57) and arrives in Moûtiers rather less than eight hours later at 17.41 and arrives at Bourg-St-Maurice at 18.27. The return journey begins on Saturday at Bourg at 09.53, departs Moûtiers at 10.40, and reaches Waterloo at

16.43. Times may be subject to minor changes. Fully flexible return fares cost £299 for first class and £199 for standard class. Fixed date non-exchangeable fares are £229 and £149 respectively. Lower promotional fares of £199 first class and £129 standard class may also be available on certain low-season dates. The 770-seater trains have sufficient space for baggage and ski equipment.

Tour operators favour the cheaper but indirect Friday service. You take a Eurostar to Paris in the afternoon, change stations, and catch an SNCF sleeper, which gets you to Moûtiers at 06.44 on Saturday and to Bourg-St-Maurice at 07.25. The return service leaves Bourg on Saturday evening – allowing eight days' skiing rather than six within a one-week holiday. Similar day and overnight services runs via Lille but involve a change of train and station at Lille.

The weekly Snowtrain, chartered by a group of tour operators, continues to rattle slowly on in the face of all the hype surrounding Eurostar. Passengers leave Calais at 9.22pm on Friday and arrive in Moûtiers at 9.21am and Bourg-St-Maurice at 10.11am on Saturday. The return journey is on Saturday evening and again allows almost two extra days of skiing. The Snowtrain is inconvenient, uncomfortable, crowded and surprisingly praised by almost every reporter who has tried it.

USEFUL NUMBERS

GOING BY RAIL

British Rail International (for European rail bookings) **Tel** (0990) 848 848
Eurostar Tel (0345) 303030
Motorail Tel 0171-203 7000
Rail Europe Tel (0990) 300003
Swiss Rail Tel 0171-734 1921

GOING BY CAR

Brittany Ferries (Portsmouth–Caen) **Tel** (0990) 360360
Euro Tunnel (Folkestone–Calais) **Tel** (0990) 353535
Hoverspeed (Dover–Calais, Folkestone–Boulogne, Dover–Ostend) **Tel** (0990) 240241
P & O European Ferries (Portsmouth–Le Havre, Portsmouth–Cherbourg) **Tel** (0990) 980980
P & O North Sea Ferries (Hull–Zeebrugge, Hull–Rotterdam) **Tel** (01482) 377177
P & O Stena Line (Dover–Calais, Newhaven–Dieppe) **Tel** (0990) 980980
Sally Ferries (Ramsgate–Dunkerque,

Ramsgate–Ostend) **Tel** (0845) 6002626
Seafrance (Dover–Calais) **Tel** (0990) 711711
Stena Sealink Line (Harwich–Hook) **Tel** (01233) 647047

Breakdown insurance
AA Five Star Services Tel (0800) 444500
Autohome Ltd Tel (01604) 232334
Britannia Rescue Tel (01484) 514848
Europ Assistance Tel (01444) 442211
First Assist Tel 0181-763 1550
Green Flag National Breakdown Tel (0345)670345
Leisurecare Insurance Services Tel (01793) 514199
Mondial Assistance Tel 0181-681 2525
RAC Travel Services Tel (0800) 550055

Snow chains
AA (0800) 854641 mail order
RAC (0800) 550055
Rud Chains (01227) 276611
Snowchains (01732) 884408

Reporting on the resorts

Use the structure set out below and send your reports to: Dept CD, Consumers' Association, FREEPOST, 2 Marylebone Road, London NW1 1YN. No stamp is needed. Please write, or preferably type, your reports clearly. A separate sheet must be used for each resort, however short the report. You can also contact us via electronic mail. Email address: guide.reports@which.net

Please keep sending us your reports; they are an invaluable contribution to the essence of the book. **Writers of the most informative resort reports win a free copy of the next edition of the Guide.**

Resort report checklist:

BASICS
Your name and address
Your skiing background (experience, competence)
Resort name/country
Date of visit
Tour operator you went with
Hotel/chalet/apartment block stayed in

VERDICTS
Your reaction to our 'ticks' and 'crosses' verdicts on the resort

ACCESS
Remarks on airport transfer by coach or car to your resort, parking, rail connections if used

OPERATION OF LIFTS
New lifts, upgraded lifts, lift queues, lift passes (and where they cover) and other payment systems

OPERATION OF RUNS
Remarks on piste-marking, piste-grooming, piste closure, artificial snow, accuracy of resort piste-map. Name any favourite runs and interesting off-piste descents

MOUNTAIN RESTAURANTS
Specific named recommendations, comments on type and quality of food, prices and service

SKI SCHOOLS
Name the school on which you are commenting. Remarks on organisation, tuition, language, use of time, allocation of pupils to classes, group

size etc. Cover private lessons, guiding and special courses (including cost)

SNOWBOARDING

How user-friendly the resort is for snowboarders. Tuition, terrain, facilities, funparks

CHILDREN'S FACILITIES

Name the school, ski- and/or non-ski kindergarten on which you are commenting. Remarks on facilities, staff competence and attitude, language, approach to tuition, meals, hours and cost

LOCAL TRANSPORT

Transport within the resort: where you can and cannot get to, frequency, reliability, convenience, cost, crowding. Parking, value of having a car

SHOPPING

Food shops and supermarkets, including quality, service and prices. Range of other shops

NON-SKIING FACILITIES

Range, quality and convenience of non-skiing facilities; excursion possibilities

EATING OUT

Range and type of restaurant; specific recommendations with type of food, prices, atmosphere and service

APRES-SKI

Range, style and prices in bars, restaurants, discos; what happens in the resort after skiing until the small hours (recommendations essential)

ACCOMMODATION

Apartments, chalets or hotels (must be named), size of bedrooms. Advice on choice of location within the resort

PRICES

General observations on the cost of meals and drinks. Examples should include a beer, soft drink, house wine, cup of coffee, dish of the day

SUMMARY

What did you particularly like and dislike about the resort? What aspect of the resort came as a surprise (pleasant or otherwise)? Who does the resort suit? And who does it not suit? On the whole, do you regret choosing this resort, or would you go back there? If so, why?

WEB SITES

Please list any useful sites

Resort index